'Pure joy. All Christmas presents chosen, all "Book of the Year" dilemmas solved – this is the book of the year, the decade, the millennium. Forget all the cavils about whether these diaries are as good as the first volume, or whether they might have been improved by Alan Clark had he lived – we must simply thank our lucky stars that we have them. The only question now is whether Clark is the greatest English diarist of the 20th century or merely one of the top five'   Lynn Barber, *Daily Telegraph*

'As I read on, I came to cherish Clark. For while he was undoubt-edly a bounder and an idler, he emerges from this book as a classic minor character who would have been thoroughly at home among the dramatis personae of Restoration comedy, named, perhaps, Mr Sneerwell'   Gerald Kaufman, *The Times*

'In the end, Alan Clark and his diaries are engaging and tolerable because we will not, cannot, grant him the thing he most wants from his audience – we cannot take him seriously . . . The diaries of the high-minded and consistent cannot be nearly as amusing'
          Andrew Marr, *Observer*

'Those of us who knew and loved him immediately recognise an utter authentic portrait of the man. In his writings, no prisoners are taken, no fear is shown of causing offence. Presumably, given the first-class editing job, they were even ruder beforehand . . . You could not get away with inventing Alan Clark in a work of fiction'
          Simon Heffer, *Daily Mail*

'A great deal to enjoy . . . The principal target of Alan Clark's feline dissection – mesmerically untrustworthy, cackhandedly ambitious, by turns unctuously sycophantic and coldheartedly backstabbing – is, of course, Clark himself. How he relishes each description of his own perfidy! . . . when the earnest self serving memoirs of count-less Prime Ministers are gathe[   ] will still be read with glee . . . H[   ] . . .

like Jane Austen, he is able to perceive the large significance in apparently humdrum activities'   Craig Brown, *Mail on Sunday*

'A vastly entertaining writer. His diaries of his years as a junior minister have granted him a kind of immortality . . . All the familiar ingredients are here – disdain for his constituents and the lower orders generally; alternate cynicism about the House of Commons and ecstasy when he got to hear the sound of his own voice, which he did as a super-jingo during the Falklands War; together with yearnings, often frustrated at this period apparently, for more sex'   Max Hastings, *Evening Standard*

Alan Clark – Diaries: In Power 1983–1992

'The best diarists, from Pepys and Boswell to "Chips" Channon and Harold Nicolson, have been the souls of indiscretion. But none so indiscreet as Mr Clark. If he is made the scapegoat for the Matrix Churchill affair, he may be written down politically as Baroness Thatcher's little loose cannon. But literature and the great British game of gossip will judge him for his diary. For its Pooterish self-assessment, for Mr Toad's enthusiasm for new things, for Byron's caddishness, for its deadly candour, it is one of the great works in the genre'   *The Times*

'Frank and vivid diaries . . . Mr Clark performs the invaluable service of cheering us all up and giving us something to talk about'   *The Times*

'Unputdownable'   David Mellor, *Mail on Sunday*

'Diaries are the raw material of history and these are elegantly and pungently written'   Sir Charles Powell, *The Times*

'Absorbing . . . staggeringly, recklessly candid . . . tells the truth as he saw it without fear or favour'
Anthony Howard, *Sunday Times*

'A wonderful book . . . these diaries combine the naïve candour of an Adrian Mole with the imagination of a devil and an angel'
Matthew Parris, *Sunday Telegraph*

'The best political book for at least a decade. It is unlikely that Thatcher, when her autobiography is published, will provide such an entertaining and incisive account of the personalities, scandals and conflicts of her years in office'
Scotsman

'The sheer fun of politics shines through . . . this wonderful book'
Robert Rhodes James, *Guardian*

Alan Clark – The Last Diaries: In and Out of the Wilderness

'This book is as necessary to read and absorb as the two that preceded it, not for a better understanding of the milieu in which Clark was writing, but for a better understanding of the human condition . . . the last pages are incredibly moving and compound the sheer, Technicolor humanity of what we have read before'
Simon Heffer, *Literary Review*

'The skill in the diaries and memoirs of most politicians lies in the delicate airbrushing out of their faults and weaknesses. Alan Clark's self-portrait, on the other hand, is defiantly warts-and-all . . . His three volumes of diaries will ensure his immortality'
Craig Brown, *Mail on Sunday*

'Ever present in this volume is his preoccupation with the illness that finally claimed him. It is more sombre, infinitely more foreboding than his other work . . . The last entries, by Jane recording Alan's final days, are hugely moving . . . This is simply the best book I have read since – well, since the last Clark oeuvre'
Steven Norris, *The Times*

'A rare record of what it is like to be dying by a master of the English language'   Bevis Hillier, *Spectator* (Books of the Year)

'This volume of Clark is better on small details of an indulged life, of Eccles cakes and stilton, the vanity of his timed runs up flights of stairs, his befriending of jackdaws whose pellets he takes abroad for good luck'   Quentin Letts, *Daily Mail*

'The last diaries are a muted version of the others, full of Sten gun judgements, scorn, candour and opinion – also ambition recollected in imperfect tranquillity'   Edward Pearce, *Tribune Magazine*

'Alan Clark's relationship with God in these diaries is both funny and moving . . . These diaries do not stalk the corridors of power. There is very little high-level gossip, but some of our favourite characters from the early diaries make appearances . . . As his hypochondria gives way to real sickness, his moral gambling to terror, his selfish and equivocal attitude towards his wife to absolute love and gratitude, the diaries assume an immense sadness and profundity . . . Alan Clark was not a good man, but he was a dazzling diarist. He writes, self-pityingly: "I suppose I will be remembered for the Diaries." He will, and for this one most of all. A grand love story eclipses a political career'
                                              Sarah Sands, *Daily Telegraph*

'A long way from the acerbic knockabout looked for by Clark's admirers . . . The latter part of the book is darkened by the diarist's recognition that [those] frissons of demise are no illusion: he has brain cancer . . . the journal of a disappointed man becomes that of a mind at the end of its tether. At the same time the heartless, even caddish, candour gives way to impassioned avowals of devotion to a sorely tried wife. When he finally abandons his pen, Jane Clark adds her own brief log, in which reciprocated devotion sits uneasily with sick-room grue. "I love God," she writes, "but this is such a cruel way to demolish such a brilliant brain"'
                                              E.S. Turner, *TLS*

'Pure pleasure . . . there ought to be a constant supply of Alan Clarks'   Sue Townsend, *Mail on Sunday* (Books of the Year)

Alan Clark, MP for Plymouth (Sutton) 1974–1992 and Kensington and Chelsea, (1997–1999), was Minister of Trade, 1986–1989, and Minister of State, Ministry of Defence, 1989–1992. He was married with two sons and lived at Saltwood Castle, Kent. He died in 1999.

Ion Trewin is a London publisher. Originally a journalist and Literary Editor of *The Times* (1972–79), he changed gear and entered into publishing in 1980. He was Alan Clark's editor and publisher from 1992 until his death, and has edited three volumes of Alan Clark's diaries, and written an acclaimed biography of the MP. Married with a son and daughter, he has since 2006 been literary director of the Man Booker Prize. He was chairman of the Cheltenham Literature Festival 1996–2007.

By Alan Clark

FICTION
Bargains at Special Prices
Summer Season
The Lion Heart: a tale of the war in Vietnam

NON-FICTION
The Donkeys: A History of the BEF in 1915
The Fall of Crete
Barbarossa: The Russian-German Conflict,
1941–1945

Aces High: The War in the Air
over the Western Front 1914–1918

A Good Innings: the private papers
of Viscount Lee of Fareham (*edited*)

Suicide of the Empires:
The Eastern Front, 1914–1918

Diaries: In Power, 1983–1992

The Tories: Conservatives and the
Nation State, 1922–1997

Diaries: Into Politics, 1972–1982 (*edited by Ion Trewin*)

Back Fire: A Passion for Cars and Motoring
(*edited by Robert Coucher*)

The Last Diaries: In and Out of the
Wilderness (*edited by Ion Trewin*)

By Ion Trewin

Alan Clark: The Biography

ALAN CLARK:
A Life in His Own Words

The Edited Diaries
1972–1999

Selected and Edited,
with an Introduction and Notes
by Ion Trewin

PHOENIX

A PHOENIX PAPERBACK

First published in Great Britain in 2010
by Phoenix
an imprint of Orion Books Ltd,
Carmelite House
50 Victoria Embankment
London EC4Y 0DZ
An Hachette UK company

Originally published as three volumes

Diaries
First published in Great Britain in 1993 by Weidenfeld & Nicolson

Diaries: Into Politics
First published in Great Britain in 2000 by Weidenfeld & Nicolson

The Last Diaries: In and Out of the Wilderness
First published in Great Britain in 2002 by Weidenfeld & Nicolson

7 9 10 8 6

A CIP catalogue record for this book
is available from the British Library.

ISBN 978-0-7538-2673-7

Typeset at The Spartan Press Ltd,
Lymington, Hants

Printed and bound by CPI Group (UK) Ltd, Croydon, CR0 4YY

The Orion Publishing Group's policy is to use papers that are natural,
renewable and recyclable products and made from wood grown in
sustainable forests. The logging and manufacturing processes are expected
to conform to the environmental regulations of the country of origin.

www.orionbooks.co.uk

For my beloved Jane,
around whose cool and affectionate personality
there raged this maelstrom of egocentricity
and self-indulgence.

CONTENTS

GLOSSARY

covering the period of the diaries

FAMILY

AC – Alan Clark
Jane – sometimes Janey, BLJ
James – AC's elder son (aka 'Boy', 'Jamie')
Julie – married to James
Angus – James and Julie's son
Andrew – AC's younger son (aka 'Tip', 'Tip-book', 'Tup', 'Cin', 'Lilian')
Sarah – married to Andrew (together aka 'The Amazings')
Albert, Archie – Andrew and Sarah's children
Lord Clark (aka Bonny papa) – AC's father, Kenneth Clark
B'Mama (aka Bonny mama) – AC's mother, Jane Clark
Colette – AC's sister (aka 'Celly')
Colin – AC's brother (aka 'Col', 'Pin')
Nolwen, Comtesse de Janzé – AC's stepmother
Pam (Ma) – Jane's mother, living in Benalmadena in Spain
Nick – Nick Beuttler, Jane's brother, living in France

STAFF AND ESTATE

Lynn Webb – housekeeper, and her husband Ken
Edwin ('Eddie') Wilson – retired groundsman, and his wife Peggy
Cradduck – gardener at Saltwood
Leonard (Len) Lindley – Lord Clark's butler at the Garden House
Nanny (aka 'Greenwood') – nanny to James and Andrew, and
   living in a grace and favour cottage on the Saltwood estate

ANIMALIA

Tom ('T.O.') – Jack Russell terrier
Eva ('E') – Rottweiler
Hannah and Lëhni – Rottweiler sisters
Gangster and Grandee – beagles
Jason – Labrador at Seend
Marshal – Great Dane, also known as Plato or Big Dog
Eva – Jane's Rottweiler
Angus – black Labrador
KK – James's Labrador
Bok – Bokassa, Labrador, successor to KK
Max, George, 2Boy, Bromley – jackdaws

WESTMINSTER

OFFICE

Jenny Easterbrook – head of AC's private office at DE
Judith Rutherford – her successor
Matthew Cocks, Marjorie and Glyn Williams – successive heads of
    AC's private office at DTI
Steve (Stephen) – assistant private secretary at DTI
Julian Scopes – head of AC's private office at MoD
Doug Widener – number two in AC's private office at DTI
Simon Webb – head of Tom King's private office
Jane Binstead – number two in Tom King's private office

SECRETARIES AT HOUSE OF COMMONS

Sue Line
Alison Bacon
Veronica
Peta Ewing
Alison Young
Trisha Cill-Johnson

The Bailey (inner and outer) – the two courtyards
Courtneys (aka the Secret Garden)
The 'Black Route' – a walk along the sixty-foot-high wall of the
  ruined chapel in the Inner Bailey
Quince – the grandest cottage on the Saltwood estate, occupied by
  Nanny (qv) until her death

ALBANY

B5 Lower/Upper – Piccadilly chambers which AC inherited from
  his mother. The Upper, more an attic, had once been servants'
  quarters

ERIBOLL

The Lodge – principal house on the estate
Shore Cottage – Jane's croft at Eriboll, where Jane and AC always
  stay
The Creaggan Road – connects Loch Eriboll to Loch Hope by way
  of the Creaggan Ridge, some seven miles in length and climb-
  ing from sea level to 600 feet at the ridge
Foulain – a shepherd's cottage at the foot of the loch
Strathbeg (sometimes *Stra'beg*) – a remote croft at the head of the
  Polla Valley
Arnaboll and *Cashel Dhu* – crofts on the Loch Hope side of the
  estate
Ardneackie – the peninsula that juts out into Loch Eriboll
Birkett Foster – rocks that reminded AC of a seascape by the
  Victorian painter Myles Birkett Foster

ZERMATT

Châlet Caroline – the Clarks' house in the village, which they built
  in the early 1960s
The Kiosk – built by the Clarks in 1985, adjoining the chalet
Trift – an inn at an early stage in the ascent to the Rothornhutte
Othmars – an inn on the Blauherd

BRATTON-CLOVELLY

Town Farm – an early home; in west Devon, near Okehampton
and about three-quarters of an hour's drive north of Plymouth

SEEND MANOR

Broomhayes (aka *Cherry Cottage*) – near Devizes in Wiltshire;
retained by the Clarks when they moved to Saltwood. Latterly
the home of Andrew and Sarah Clark

RYE

Watchbell Street – including No. 11, where the Clarks first lived
after they married, and No. 31

MISCELLANEOUS

Portland Place, W1; Upton House, Tetbury; Capo di Monte and *Upper
Terrace House, NW3* – Clark homes before, during and after the
Second World War

HOUSE OF COMMONS

House Library – House of Commons, a favourite spot for writing
Dean's Yard – an office, mainly for secretaries, by Westminster
Abbey
1 Parliament Street – where AC had an office after his return to the
Commons in 1997
White Office – ministerial office in the Commons during AC's time
at the Ministry of Defence

SOME CARS AND RELATED MATTERS

(Where cars mentioned in this volume are transitory purchases, they are sometimes identified within the text)

The Mews – composite name for various vintage car dealers' establishments in Queen's Gate, London

Coys – dealers in classic cars

Macrae & Dick – Land Rover dealers at Inverness

P. & A. Wood (Andy Wood) – specialists in Rolls-Royce and Bentley

Scott Moncrieff – purveyors and restorers of classic cars

SS 100 – owned by AC since his undergraduate days

Rolls-Royce Silver Ghost – the nicest to drive on a fine day if you are not in a hurry

The Porsche (aka *The Little Silver*)

The 2CV – Citroën used when in de-escalation mode

The 'Bustard' – a very old 4½-litre Bentley

The Loco – a chain-drive racing car of 1908

Big Red – Bentley Continental, number plate AC1800

XK 120 – owned by AC since his undergraduate days

Chapron – the Citroën, the *decapotable*, the very last of the DS cabriolets, built in 1978 to special order, belonging to Jane

The Bus – Transit van, at Eriboll

Winifred – Austin 7

The Mehari – a little plastic truck with an air-cooled engine and a very light footprint used for clearing grass clippings and prunings from the garden because it does not mark the lawn. A kind of self-propelled wheelbarrow

Argocat – at Eriboll, performs the same function as the Mehari, but will also go through peat bogs, and swim

Hymet – mechanical digger at Eriboll

Countax – successor to the Westwood ride-on mower

Atco – cylinder mower for the Inner Bailey

SLANG

ACHAB – 'anything can happen at backgammon', a saying
   originally from 'the Room' at Brooks's where games can swing
   at a late stage on an unpredictable run of the dice, used often as a
   consolation in times of depression. Adaptable in other circumstances, substituting 'politics' for 'backgammon', for instance

AF – what AC called aortic fibrillations – not literally, but
   circumstances that set the heart racing

BHLH – a description of perfect male dress sense, right for the
   specific occasion. The initials were those of Basil Liddell-Hart,
   one of AC's heroes, who also invariably dressed immaculately

The bike rule – introduced after James had a serious accident on a
   motorbike at the age of fifteen. Children out at night always had
   to check in no matter how late they returned (guaranteed to
   stop parents sleeping until this happened)

Cutting peat/burning heather – sometimes literally at Eriboll, but also
   getting away from it all

Dave at eight – getting up in time for the arrival of the official car,
   driven by Dave (or whoever the driver was)

Dutch – blusteringly confident though tainted with insecurity
   (variant of Dutch courage, though without inference of alcohol)

Grey water – diarrhoea

Grunge – country clothes

Lala – self-regardingly overdressed or noisy (females only)

Longies – long johns

M. Goisot – white burgundy (the proprietor of the small vineyard
   at St Brie from which the Clarks import their house wine)

Men's tea – elevenses in the Saltwood kitchen where all employees
   assemble (if they wish)

Naylor-Leylandish – named after the aquiline features of Sir Vivian
   Naylor-Leyland

Nonnoish – buffer-like

Norwegian Embassy – weak at the knees (AC had many variants of
   this, especially Lenin Stadium – extreme nervous tension)

Piccolo – minor, but telling, as in 'piccolo triumph'

Rest the eyeballs – sleep

Sadismoid – virtually the same as sadistically, though less *transitive* in meaning; the suffix -moid, or -moidly, is often attached to adjectives

Samuel French-thingy – dramatic, acting a part

Satisly – arousing satisfaction, inducing complacency

Softies – recreational clothes

Straight to the Lords – another consolation phrase (see ACHAB)

Thompson/plopson – defecation

Too-hot-Henry – a phrase much used by a film crew on location at Saltwood during a heatwave

Tinky – diminutive, insignificant

Two second rule – a parable recounted in a graveyard illustrating finality: 'You can't put the clock back – not even by two seconds'

Venice train – completely asleep on a journey

'w' – walk, as in going for a walk

white screen – computer

ABBREVIATIONS AND ACRONYMS

NAMES

AC – Alan Clark

Aspers – John Aspinall

BLJ – Beloved little Jane

CH – Charles Howard

CP – Charles Powell

CS – Christopher (aka 'Daisy') Selmes

DD – David Davis, MP

EG/EDG – Euan Graham

IG – Ian Gow, MP

Franko – Frank Johnson

JM – John Major, MP

GJ – Tristan Garel-Jones, MP

LPF – L. P. Fassbender, accountant

MH – Michael Howard, MP

MRDH – Michael Heseltine, MP

TK – Tom King, MP

OTHERS

AF – Armed forces

BAe – British Aerospace

BB – Big Book, otherwise *The Tories: Conservatives and the Nation State 1922–1997* (published 1998)

CCO – Conservative Central Office

CDS – Chief of the Defence Staff

CFE – Conventional Forces Europe
CGT – Capital Gains Tax
DoE – Department of Environment
DE – Department of Employment
DTI – Department of Trade and Industry
EDM – Early Day Motion
EMT – early morning tea
K&C – Kensington and Chelsea constituency; Kent and Canterbury hospital
KTH – Kensington Town Hall
LCA – Love, care and attention
LLG – loch like glass
MFA – Multi-fibre Agreement
MFT – Minister for Trade
MoD – Ministry of Defence
M o S – *Mail on Sunday*

MSC – Manpower Services Commission
N o W – *News of the World*
o/d – overdraft
OECD – Organisation for European Cooperation and Development
PC – Privy Councillor
PQ – Parliamentary Question
RCB – Regular Commission Board
RREC – Rolls-Royce Enthusiasts' Club
SE – Stock Exchange
SEDOC – out-of-hours doctor service in Kent
SoS – Secretary of State
UBS – Union Bank Suisse
UCH – University College Hospital, London
VCC – Vintage Car Club
VGL – very good looking
WD – 'wet' dream

INTRODUCTION TO THIS EDITION

Until now the three volumes of Alan Clark's magnificent diaries have been viewed as separate entities. Alan himself saw the original *Diaries* (1993) as 'Memoirs of a Junior Minister', covering essentially his service under Margaret Thatcher. Such was its success – both critically and commercially – that his publishers quickly urged him to contemplate a sequel. He was, though, uncertain. Might it prove a 'Titanic II'? he wondered at one point. But in 1998 he finally agreed, signing two £250,000 contracts for further volumes. One, a prequel, he decided, would begin in 1972, an *annus mirabilis* as his selection for the first time as a Conservative candidate coincided with his and his family's move to Saltwood Castle in Kent. The second, which he called 'The Wilderness Years', was to start with his retirement from politics in 1992 and end . . . well, that depended. At one point it was to be his return to Westminster in 1997 as MP for the deluxe constituency of Kensington and Chelsea, but ultimately the decision was beyond his control as he died from cancer in 1999.

Having been his editor at Weidenfeld & Nicolson for *Diaries* and subsequently for *The Tories*, his history of the modern party, I was asked by his widow Jane (and his long-standing agent Michael Sissons) whether I would transcribe and edit what became *Diaries: Into Politics* (2000) and two years later what we called *The Last Diaries: In and Out of the Wilderness*. Between them these three volumes have sold more than half a million copies, testifying to their quality and their wide appeal. Not for nothing was Alan's journal-keeping likened to that of Samuel Pepys.

This one-volume edition of the diaries follows *Alan Clark: The*

Biography,[1] which tells the full story of his life and career and which should be consulted for further information, not least for major events in which he was involved, such as the Matrix-Churchill trial (and the Scott inquiry which followed) and his legal action against the London *Evening Standard*, about which, to my surprise, he wrote so little. In editing the diaries as a single narrative I am conscious how Alan's writing style changed over the years from 1972 to 1999. Partly this was to do with increasing confidence as a politician following the Falklands War, during which he first gained media prominence. Even though he had previously had enormous success as a historian (*The Donkeys* and *Barbarossa* in particular), he was also maturing as a writer and enjoying the opportunity to write what he saw as 'set pieces' of particular events or experiences.

If the period after 1992, when he made 'the biggest mistake' of his life by retiring as MP for Plymouth Sutton, often has a maudlin feel, this reflects the wilderness he was now experiencing, and not enjoying.

I have included Alan's original Preface; also a selection from the glossary of family names, of Clark argot, of his own personal abbreviations. In cutting for a single volume I have tried to keep as many threads as space allows. I could have added further glosses on existing entries that were unearthed and appear in *Alan Clark: The Biography*, but this might have destroyed the rhythm that Alan was so keen to preserve. There is one exception: an account of the fortieth birthday of his friend, the journalist Frank Johnson, which turned up as a self-contained item that had been separately typed and misfiled among some insurance policies at Saltwood. For good measure Alan even added many of the footnotes.

Ion Trewin
January 2010

---

[1] By Ion Trewin. First published 2009 by Weidenfeld & Nicolson, and now available in Phoenix paperback.

PREFACE TO THE ORIGINAL DIARIES

Diaries are so intensely personal – to publish them is a baring, if not a flaunting, of the ego. And for the author also to write a preface could be thought excessive.

Let me explain. These are not 'Memoirs'. They are not written to throw light on events in the past, or retrospectively to justify the actions of the author. They are *exactly* as they were recorded on the day; sometimes even the hour, or the minute, of a particular episode or sensation.

I wrote, in longhand, in a variety of locations; principally at Saltwood, or in my room at the House of Commons, or at my desk in the Department(s). Also in trains, embassies, hotels abroad, at the Cabinet table in Number 10 and at international conferences. When I had completed an entry I closed the notebook and seldom turned to that page again.

During the whole of this period, nearly eight years, I was a Minister in three successive Tory administrations. Politics – Party, Governmental and Constituency – dominated my life and energies. But on re-reading the entries I am struck by how small a proportion – less than half – is actually devoted to the various themes that dominated political life over the period.

Expurgation, from considerations of taste or cruelty, I have tried to keep to a minimum. My friends know me, and know that I love them, and that my private explosions of irritation or bad temper are of no import. And as for taste, it, too, is subjective. There are passages that will offend some, just as there are excerpts that I myself found embarrassing to read when I returned to them.

Much of course has been excised. But of what remains nothing has been altered since the day it was written. Is this conceit – or laziness? A bit of both, I suppose. But I found that when I attempted to alter, or moderate, or explain, the structure and rhythm of the whole entry would be disturbed.

There remain certain passages that vex me considerably. Mainly they refer to friends and colleagues with whom I have worked – or who have worked for me with loyalty and dedication: for example, Dave, my competent driver for many years; Rose, my sweet diary secretary at DTI who coped with 'harassment' with dignity and decorum; Bruce Anderson[1], one of my closest confidants; Tom King, Secretary of State above me in two departments, whom I still regard with affection in spite of the way in which we treated each other in the heat of our political careers. And there are many others to whom references coloured by the irritation of the moment are ill-suited.

There are also passages that, to some readers, will be unintelligible. Family joke-words, Eton slang, arcane references to events in the past, crude expletives, all these are present but I have done my best to illuminate the unfamiliar in a glossary that covers events, locations, individuals and so forth.

Sometimes lacking in charity; often trivial; occasionally lewd; cloyingly sentimental, repetitious, whingeing and imperfectly formed. For some readers the entries may seem to be all of these things.

But they are real diaries.

AC
March 1993

---

[1] A political commentator with Conservative leanings.

EDITOR'S NOTE

Footnotes give the present and past – but rarely future – positions of individuals, usually at their first appearance. Nor is an MP's political allegiance listed except where this may be unclear from the text.

AC's occasional inconsistencies in style, dates, capitalisation and even English grammar have sometimes been left as written. I have followed his own practice and where appropriate silently edited passages.

IT

THE DIARIES

1972

Centre of gravity moving incxorably to Saltwood. Only pause
for thought – where the hell do the years go? Cradduck[1] (naturally) can't get possession of his cottage – and there is nowhere
else – *quelle est la solution? . . . averne?* (Gamelin with Churchill
May 1940 . . . *'ou est la masse de manoeuvre?'*) Very heavy expenditure looking at interior. Hence dilemma. How far to go?
What degree of compromise, or not, between having it as a sort
of show-place for summer and occasional smart weekends and
living at Broomhayes?[2] Or living there with the whole caboosh,
cars, trading, dogs, peacocks. And then, even while we are there
I think it might be more 'sensible' in the Victorian part, keeping the medieval part as a show area. Real thing is, it's lovely
with the boys, but when they are away, then I rather dread the
existence solitaire (just) the two of us. If only we could have
another baby!

On the financial front, still trading like crazy, though taking
profits too soon I don't doubt. Periodic waves of 'panic' at my
gearing cause me to shorten the line. 'Garaging' (huh!) a lot of
the profits by putting them in cars, but could well have a car sale
in October. The objective must be ELIMINATION OF ALL
DEBTS.

    'Daisy'[3] on the phone, ill, in Paris. 'I'm terribly worried that
you're going to waste all that money (from the field), Alan . . .' So

---

[1] Cradduck, head gardener at Saltwood 1951–80.

[2] The house at Seend where the Clarks were living before the move to Saltwood.

[3] Christopher (aka 'Daisy') Selmes, a friend of many years' standing, who had
made a fortune in the City.

am I.[1] I am resorting to the primitive technique, *caching* it in different hollow trees like a squirrel and his nuts; the other school is concentrate, Rommel, turn it into 500[2] this year.

Politics too, that spurious sense of activity (without achievement). Plymouth Sutton – sounds promising and a spy in the camp who told me already more than I ever got out of that shower at Ashchurch. As for Langstone, incredibly the tables have *again* turned; poor old Lloyd really looks done for now, having lost all his 'list' at the AGM and slightly gone off his rocker, discussing the agent, stopping surgeries etc.[3] But will they wear me?

Saltwood   *Saturday, 6 May*

Still not properly unpacked here, many things not 'come to hand' as yet, packing cases in the upper hall etc. *Absolutely* no decoration at all (to my parents' puzzlement . . . 'is Al just going to sell the whole thing to an institution? etc).

Plymouth Sutton is a situation of considerable promise. My spy (Graham Butland[4]) has leaked all the questions so I am dutifully preparing fluent, moving answers. He has given me the names of the others short-listed and will meet me on Saturday morning to disclose how Friday's interviewees fared and see if there are any questions I want posed!

Went to Bratton on Wednesday of last week prior to going on to Plymouth. How lovely and soft and restful the West Country is! And how evocative of those early distant happy days with Jane and

---

[1] AC was selling the cricket field to the south of Saltwood, and houses were planned on part of it, but the builders went bankrupt. The cricket club bought its corner. A quarter of a century later, in 1998, AC was able to buy back the field as a wedding anniversary present for Jane.

[2] An example of how, when referring to financial sums, AC often leaves off the final '000'. In this case he means £500,000.

[3] AC was being intemperate. Sir Ian Lloyd (Kt 1986) may have had problems with the Portsmouth Langstone constituency association, but it wasn't long before he was selected by nearby Havant in 1974, which he represented until 1992.

[4] Graham Butland, a member of the Plymouth Sutton Conservative Association committee.

the babies and the blue Oldsmobile. Now we hardly have time to breathe, but I can still get a great draught of peace when I am at Bratton-Clovelly. Whether it would still be the same if I was an MP down there, I don't know.

Duke of Cornwall Hotel, Plymouth   *Friday, 12 May*

I sit at a table in the bay window of a comfortable room in this old-fashioned hotel. Tomorrow I have a preliminary interview for the 'safest' of the three Plymouth seats. This afternoon I have been in reconnaissance.

I first visited Plymouth ten years ago, when I collected Jane and new-born Andrew from the maternity ward at Freedom Fields hospital whither she had been rushed by ambulance from Bratton in the bitter winter of 1962. There are some fine buildings in a hard grey stone, almost granite; especially along the Hoe where Nancy Astor[1] had a grand house. Also tracts of rubble-covered wasteland where the planners have not yet built over the bomb damage.

There are now three parliamentary divisions. I have been advised by the Central Office list of 'Drake', a marginal, and applied. A short while afterward I was gratified to receive a telephone call from two complete strangers, who were on the Executive Council of the third seat, entitled 'Sutton' by the Boundaries Commission, out of homage to Nancy, but in fact taking in a large swathe of Heseltine's former Tavistock constituency[2] and thus, putatively, very Conservative. 'Forget Drake' they said, 'it's marginal. Go for Sutton.'

As the preliminary interviews, which started at 4pm, are taking

---

[1] Nancy Astor (wife of the 2nd Viscount Astor) and her husband had a lengthy association with the city. She became the first woman to take her seat in the House of Commons when she was elected MP for the Sutton division in 1919 (a seat her husband had previously held). She retired in 1945.

[2] Michael Heseltine, MP for Tavistock since 1966. Rather than fight one of the reorganised seats in west or south-west Devon, he found a seat nearer London. At the February 1974 election he was elected MP for Henley.

place in this actual building there is much to observe. I have been sitting with a tea tray in front of me since half past three. I am clean-shirted and in a light tweed suit. My features are composed, set you could say, into an expression at the same time fresh and obliging.

A big chap, fifty-ish, balding, spectacles, sat about three tables away. He too appeared to be waiting. Was he the Chairman? Practically anybody could be the chairman at this stage, it seemed. Or at least the Treasurer, or the Vice-chairman. Silently ingratiating, I endeavoured to radiate good will.

Several times I caught him looking at me. Curiously, but *cholerically*. Finally he lumbered over – 'Mr Fowler?'

'No.' Some sixth sense told me not to identify myself.

Scattered about the room sat other candidates. Two of them greeted each other with braying declarations, plainly false, of affection and respect. Standard Party Conference templates; i.e. not very big, not very masculine. Spectacles, new-looking suits, tightly-knotted ties. For much of the time I looked at the ceiling – but *intelligently*, like Richthofen's dog, Moritz.

Only one of these characters was actually seen back down stairs by an escorting bigwig. I recognised Michael Howard, much plugged in the broadsheet press as *thrusting*, a barrister, a high-flyer certain to enter the new Parliament, etc.[1]

The bigwig held him in 'politician's grip'; one hand holding his, the other on Howard's elbow. Not necessarily a good sign, more usually an indicator of impending betrayal of some kind.

However – 'Well done', I overheard. 'You'll be hearing from us very shortly . . .'

That's that, then. All sewn up. Except, who the hell is 'Mr Fowler'[2]?

---

[1] Michael Howard had unsuccessfully fought Liverpool Edgehill in 1966 and 1970. In fact AC was wrong in his forecast. Howard did not finally enter the Commons until 1983, when he won the Folkestone and Hythe seat, thereby becoming the Clarks' Member of Parliament, as Saltwood is in the constituency.

[2] Norman Fowler, MP for Nottingham South since 1970, but his seat would be disappearing at the next general election as a result of the boundary revisions.

Saltwood   *Saturday, 27 May*

The Plymouth interview was a great success.

Graham Butland and David Holmes[1] brought the crib of the set
questions to my germ –, as opposed to smoke-filled room. Euphoria and might even have carried the whole thing on the spot –
but (according to Graham) a serious decline set in over the
weekend. Apparently 'nigger in the woodpile' was Betty Easton[2]
– curious as I should have thought she would be a push-over; I
answered her question (about tactics) at greater length than any
other. Next step is a 'cocktail party' for wives, the speech and Q&A
session – the very idea makes my stomach turn over. My chances
rated low. But anything-can-happen-in-backgammon/politics.

Saltwood   *Wednesday, 14 June*

Went to Plymouth for the 'lives' after some shrewd publicity in *The
Times* and a huddled but productive conference in mid-week in
Horrabridge with my contacts. That evening I was dead flat. The
speech a flop, response tepid. We went to bed early, in daylight,
and slept 'more tired than I have been before or since . . .'

But next day, the good news. Voting was 10. 11. 9 for Fowler,
Hunt, Clark. Final stage now scheduled for Friday, 30 June at
Duke of Cornwall Hotel.

Saltwood   *Thursday, 22 June*

'Mounting' opposition to development of the cricket field, a
likelihood of council throwing it out; sale of Woodfall Street[3]
fallen through; heavily overbought in SE with 'climate' moving

---

[1] David Holmes, like Butland a leading light in the Sutton Conservative
Association.
[2] Mrs R. M. Easton, a pillar in Plymouth Conservative circles, who later became
the city's Lord Mayor, married to Rodney Easton.
[3] London property in SW3, held in Jane Clark's name; its sale is a running saga
through these pages.

against me. Obviously heading for a bad trough – hold tight, stay calm and systematic and try to see it through.

Saltwood   *Saturday, 1 July*

Yesterday was the most memorable of my life with the exception of James being born on 13 II 60.

Of course it is easy enough now to look back and say that I knew I'd get it – all the Bratton magic, the fore-ordained aspect of it all. I can only say that the moment when Tom Bridges[1] gestured to Doc Mac and Howard Davies to console the other two – well! Like a Miss World contestant for a few minutes I couldn't believe it was actually happening to me, and didn't what you might call 'come to' until the Press were taking pictures and data. At last up to darling Jane who received one in triumph, a *nuit guise* from *sheer elation*.

Saltwood   *Thursday, 3 August*

Somewhat depressed – what's it all in aid of? Just want to be civilised and scholarly and mean in these surroundings, 'working' the place for cash, a little lechery, keeping fit, some b'gammon in London, a little trading in the Mews. Key thing to protect the boys (Tip worryingly asthmatic lately, in spite of visit to quiet-spoken homeopathic doctor). In fact now faced with massive prospects of 'commitment' building up to crazy level after election.

Saltwood   *Sunday, 17 September*

A note of my adoption meeting at the Duke on Friday (15th):

We had spent the previous two days at Carlyon Bay, delightful, evocative, appropriate. I had done the traditional clamber along the rocks to my old sunbathing place of 1947, and walked down

---

[1] Tom Bridges, the Sutton association chairman.

the road to the 'Riviera Club' which I so well remember when I used to go up and down in the black SS100 and that woman, greyish, semi-crazy in her big Buick cabriolet. At high tide I rolled up my trousers and walked about that hard, granulated sand. I stood first on the long rock at the western end that one never notices at low tide and watched the waves come streaming in, and felt Carlyon Bay's momentous evocation. Nearly thirty years ago – but it could have been five – the burgeoning sexual desire, the endless hot days, the happy certainty that the future could only hold excellence and pleasure.

Left the speech-making/learning a little late and had a demi-panic at lunch in the hot enclosed front lawn at Bratton. However recovered, washed my hair and did my stuff in the Duke ball-room. First mike since Havant dinner way back – and I got a hang-up half way through. Lesson, don't get slack about prepositions. Link passages *must* be learned by heart.

Speech centred on violence, but all the publicity went to my answers on the Asians afterwards.[1] Gloom by many on the platform, Latimer, Easton, Bridges among them, but *response* from the hall; stayed till the bitter end drinking. A good feeling. Afterwards Peter Latimer[2] reproached me for a 'Monday Club speech' instead of a political generality.

Zermatt   *Tuesday, 3 October*

My peace of mind somewhat spoiled by the sad death on Saturday evening walk with Col,[3] of dear Grandee.[4] Evidently he had a stroke (similar to that attack of paralysis which he suffered about three weeks ago in the kitchen) and drowned in the stream in the far valley.

---

[1] 'The Tory Party should capitalise on the public outcry against the coming influx of Ugandan Asians and ban all further colonial immigration' was how the *Western Morning News* reported AC's remarks next morning.

[2] The Sutton association agent.

[3] AC's brother, Colin.

[4] Grandee and Gangster, the beagles.

I didn't give it a thought at first when they started a slight hue and cry, he has so often been lost before and the last I had seen of him, quite close to home, with his nose to the ground picking up a scent. But when dinner-time came and he still hadn't turned up I knew, secretly, the worst. We had walked the full round of the Wakefield Trust that evening, and at the top of the crest I had lifted the fence for the beagles to go underneath. Gangster went straight through, but Grandee stopped and thanked me – he *always* thanked one, but this was something special, quite soppy, he put both his paws up and almost looked unhappy (as I now realise looking back). He had been saying good-bye.

Jane looked for him by the lights of the Mehari, while I was watching *The Two Ronnies* (mediocre), then after a silent supper we went out again and I found him in the stream, very near where I had last seen him with his fine glossy coat quite dry, rigid in the 'show' position, but his poor little muzzle choked and jammed with mud and grass. I do hope he didn't struggle for too long, didn't feel abandoned. We brought him back, and dug the grave straight away, by the Barbican where he can keep an eye on the comings and goings.

How I hate that moment when the earth goes down on the body (he was shrouded in his red blanket with his steel dish and dinner buried beside him). One must have faith, but haunting me is the endless journey, faster than the speed of light, of the soul into infinity.

Anyhow the death of the beagle reminded me very forcibly (and Heaven knows, it is never very far below the surface) of how very vulnerable we all are; those lovely boys and, just lately, the old-head-of-the-house has been somewhat breathless and suffering from back pain and potential dizziness.

Saltwood   *Saturday, 21 October*

A very wearing week. Friday down to Plymouth for Girls School speech in afternoon. They universally hostile and brainwashed into a whole series of 'progressive' clichés.

A girl, a slim dedicated Marxist, asked me why I was like I was, what motivated me. 'Because I am British,' I said, 'because I want to advance and protect the British people.' 'So what's special about the British?' she answered, 'what makes them so different from everybody else?' Well I could have answered that what makes them different from anyone else is the capacity they seem to have for producing at every level of society people like yourself who ask a question like that. But I get a dark foreboding, sometimes; I feel it at Saltwood as people encroach more and more, with higher sense of justification, on the boundaries and fences – 'it's not right that something so important/beautiful/interesting/historic should belong to one man . . .' There are the boys with their patriotic instincts quite natural, also the sense of privilege and assurance – but will they be able to hold it or will they be crushed before they get an innate strength and cunning such as I have? And what does the future hold for me? How far will I go? Will I be assassinated, or die venerated and venerable, or crabbed and embittered? I don't want to die anyway, at all, and hope it's a long way off.

Must not neglect the physical by the way. This bloody back of mine always lurking inhibiting me from doing all the exercises I need. Stomach at last weakening, ravaged lines (in some lights) on face. On Thursday last week went for a run along the front in my new track suit, did 3km+ by the 2CV speedo and plunged in the sea – felt marvellous. Now the week has changed course. High winds and drizzle, pool temperature 52°.

All Souls, Oxford   *[no date] November*

John's[1] Scout has brought me tea and digestive biscuits. The room is comfortable, but now warm.

Yesterday I was in confident form. I had been invited to address a Bow Group dinner, black tie, good claret (or so I would assume), F.E. Smith in his early days. My apotheosis. But the Bow Group are

---

[1] John Sparrow, Warden of All Souls College, Oxford, whom AC had known since his childhood.

just a bunch of arse-lickers really. Creepy little aspirant candidates who tremble at the thought, still less the sound of someone Right Wing. And they have one other thing in common, namely that they all want to enter Parliament. In the past they used to shun me, probably on instruction from Central Office, but now here I am with, having been adopted for Plymouth Sutton, something of an *edge*. Plus the delight of being based in the Warden's lodging. Plus with a black Bentley convertible parked in the quad.

Dear John. I remember walking with his affectionate arm draped around me in Brewer Street on a summer evening in 1948, when I was a clever but *extremely* feckless undergraduate, and his saying that perhaps I really 'ought' to have a shot at becoming a Fellow. It was rather lovely, this diffident homosexual advance, and I was complimented, like I used to be at Eton; though not, of course, in the slightest bit 'aroused'. At the time I didn't like the sound of All Souls. No girls and no racy company. But quite soon afterwards I regretted having done nothing. I'm sure John could have fixed, or demi-fixed, it for me. Although his advice on preparing for the exam – 'Re-(sic)-read Ranke's *History of the Popes*' – was a little daunting.

John had always, though, a certain private sense of mischief for which he was notorious and of which his guests expected at least one ritual demo. This time it took me completely by surprise. Freshly bathed and in a black tie I had meandered into the Warden's drawing room, hoping for a *firm* gin and tonic before going down to Hall and meeting the (presumably mixed) Bow Groupers. There, standing by the piano looking quite beautifully bouffed and powdered, was Harold Macmillan,[1] an old friend of John (John had worked for him against Rab[2] when the question

---

[1] Harold Macmillan, now aged seventy-eight, had been Chancellor of Oxford University since 1960. He was prime minister for six years from 1957 and retired from active politics at the 1964 general election.

[2] R.A. ('Rab') Butler had twice hoped to become leader of the Conservative Party: in 1956 when Anthony Eden resigned from ill-health in the aftermath of Suez; and in 1963, when Macmillan resigned (ill-health again, but prematurely as it turned out) and Lord Home was chosen. Home renounced his peerage and as Sir Alec Douglas-Home became prime minister. Butler was now Master of Trinity College, Cambridge.

of succession had arisen in 1956) and clearly the guest of honour that evening at high table (a grander dinner than the one I was to attend).

'Ah,' said John. 'Here's Alan Clark. He is proposing to stand for Parliament . . .'

I simpered, deferentially offered my hand.

'. . . on a platform that advocates denying the franchise of persons of the Jewish persuasion.'

Macmillan neither smiled nor frowned. Very, very briefly he looked at me. Pale hooded eyes. No point, I judged, in saying anything, although it was so monstrous that I got a short *fou-rire*. 'I'm talking to the Bow Group,' I offered weakly.

Saltwood   *Sunday, 3 December*

Now the 'prophet's' visit. Powell[1] down for the day to chat, advise and hold forth! He was benevolent, articulate, by no means cagey, but somehow impenetrable. I *really* don't know what he thought of me – though clearly 'raw', naïve, inexperienced etc were among them. He cautioned me against too high a degree of personal commitment to the Conservatives in Sutton; also against saying things outside the Party line prior to the election . . . 'as a candidate you have no constitutional position'. Would not say how he hoped to attain power, '. . . the Lord will provide.' Right, he often is, clever he undoubtedly is, but whether he has that sheer finishing touch which Conservatives have to have to get to the top I don't know.

At least I started his car for him, forcing him (to everyone's amazement) to give up the driving seat after many ineffectual yur-yurrings (vet with *chien méchant*) and it fired second time.

---

[1] Enoch Powell, MP for Wolverhampton SW since 1950. AC shared many of his views, particularly on immigration.

Zermatt   *Thursday, 14 December*

Poor James *again* broke his leg today – allegedly green stick, but
low down in the ankle and causing him a lot of pain. His fault – he
had been skiing *beautifully* on the Rothorn and Tuftern, then full of
confidence on his new Atomics, but led, far too fast, on the road
and fell just before Patrilav. I came round the corner and he was
howling. When I noticed, I broke down, and cried, screamed,
blamed poor Tip, who, it turned out wasn't really (much) to blame
as James was miles ahead.

1973

A month gone by. Christmas itself quite good. Got Jane a gold-bar in her stocking. Then two set-backs. My back briefly popped when bending down to undo my shoes leaving me crazily twisted and immobilised. I caught a short, sharp cold from the silly, titty little masseuse.

We decided to go home early, and the day before our departure James went to have his confirmatory x-ray which revealed that the bone had slipped a bit and should be reset under a general anaesthetic. We returned to the surgery later that night (he had to wait some hours for the food, water to be digested). Naturally he was apprehensive. The hall of Gentinetta's[1] was dimly lit, no one was about. Slowly the personnel gathered, junior actors first, and a nurse gave him an Atropine injection in the behind – unheralded and unwelcome. Then it deteriorated fast: the two specialists wrenched the plaster off, muttering imprecations at their predecessor who had put it on so tightly. James – horrified – gasped and groaned with pain and simulated pain. Madame Gentinetta played her part in the 'you-must-be-brave' role as she prepared the gas. When they finally put James under we retired, Jane broke down in the waiting-room and I couldn't stand it, but took our things back to the chalet where Tip had already retired (he was incubating flu).

The next day we travelled.

Tip was drowsy and flushed. Boy drawn and apprehensive.

Tip ran a high temperature and deteriorated at nightmare speed so that one had to give penicillin from the emergency pack. Once arrived, he made an amazing recovery – but what a reversal! Jane got flu, then I got it; or was/is it flu? A highly violent upper respiratory infection, leading to at least one day of feverish coma,

---

[1] The Zermatt doctors.

but had it to shake-off. Got horribly depressed, achingly so, as I contemplated the scene. Rung up by Graham Butland this evening with news that 'some disgust' in the constituency at my non-publicity/attendances. All bound up with life pattern for this year.

Saltwood   *Wednesday, 14 February*

Fairly heavy political activity (not before time). Fortunately had a piccolo success at the Bickleigh Down meeting on the eve of the Western Area Conference. The food, though, was terrible. Feminine company negligible except for the young daughter of that ridiculous ego-woman from Tavistock who boldly hung about – were we establishing a rapport? In the lift she said (2nd day) 'This can't hold eight people, surely?' 'Bags I stand next to you if it does,' I said. From that time on our relations improved.

Saltwood   *Saturday, 31 March*

Spanish trip itself desperately close in the is-it-quite-reliable '600' following an incomplete rushed job at Mercedes, a mad drive to Plymouth and back for Papa's Romney lecture and canvassing. Am going through disappointing phase at Plymouth, not seen enough, enough publicity etc; people openly saying they will vote Liberal. Finally broken with Valeri/Ali.[1]

Benalmadena   *Sunday, 8 April*

Arrived last night after wearing drive – hands blistered from holding the big white plastic wheel (of the '600') for hour after hour. Beuttler[2] villa very nice, marvellous growth – wisteria etc. Interior improved by decent English furniture. Spain revolting,

---

[1] Variously described as 'the coven', the 'blondes' and the 'i's – a mother (Valeri) and her daughters (Ali and Joei) whom AC knew for many years.
[2] The home in Spain of Jane Clark's parents.

though individual Spaniards reasonably anxious to please. Architecture, pollution, simply awful.

Journey out was plagued by blocked fuel filters. Changed at Paris, inspected at Bordeaux, packed up in Madrid rush-hour. Total nightmare sequences supervened (memorable land-mark in horror experience) no tools, no language, no *garages*, 7.30pm and sweating, *no map* (so no idea where we were etc etc). Pleasant shop-owner, obliging taximan etc brought apparent relief in due time, though further intervening horrors (mechanic trying to butcher the '600', me wondering where Jane and the children had got to – after blithely packing them into taxi and saying 'Excelsior', calling on totally strange man's flat and asking for telephone directory etc) before at last oasis of Ifa Hotel.

Here money insulation worked. Food, service (Mercedes mechanic came out next day, changed filter etc). Back on the road at 11am and great heat drive.

Talking about air-travel (I had postulated different planes for the return journey) James said touchingly but alarmingly that he rather we all die together; he was near to tears. The next morning I tried to explain that the line must go on, that one day one of us must do something for his country that merited a column as high as Nelson's.

Grey-watered twice, feeling sickish. Lost God-knows-how-much weight, sunken cheeks, match-stick forearms. Query cancer? How are we going to get home?[1]

Saltwood   *Wednesday, 16 May*

Nothing done, everything growing like crazy, tho' Cradduck still keeping garden looking fabulous. No drive, car parks, toilets, signs,

---

[1] AC provided the answer (written in December from memory) in what he called 'The Sequel': 'In fact we devised a route using entirely trains and sleepers; spending a day (again) at the Ifa – already forgotten by the staff in spite of being tipped massively. Memorable was the old-fashioned dining-car out of Madrid to Paris via Bordeaux. The great brown mountainsides in the failing light and the small station halts with their oil-lamp interiors and Goya-like attendants in upturned coat collars. How wonderful travel must have been when restricted to the few – the Grand Tour!'

garages *or any decoration at all* – visits start on May 28. American party on June 11. Headache.

I am concerned that relations with my parents may be deteriorating.

The were standing on the lower terrace. My mama *exceedingly* dreamy, of both tone and deportment. She swayed at a lavender bush. Then, turning to Jane, 'I never told Cradduck to cut that back'.

'But I employ Cradduck now, Mama.' I spoke very gently. In fact the shrub had barely been cut back at all.

'It's all wrong; all wrong.' Pulling at my father's cardigan (it was a very hot afternoon but he was wearing a cardigan) she set off back towards the bridge. He, sensing this was something not to be drawn into, smiled and mumbled.

That was yesterday. This morning we were in Canterbury. When we returned Mrs Yeo[1] said that they had both been over and 'gone upstairs'.

This has happened a great many times since my parents moved out. They lie awake in the Garden House and brood on the various items of 'contents' that they left behind. I think, but cannot be sure, that there was even a sort of verbal protocol agreed at the time of the conveyance that they should reserve a right of selection for items for which a 'need' became apparent. At the time it would have been graceless, as well as ill-judged, for me to turn this down. Already quite a few things, mainly books, they have retrieved.

Sometimes Lindley[2] (who fancies himself as an *antiquaire manqué*) is sent over in the car to collect objects, which, whenever practicable, he does without referring to us.

Anyway, this morning my father apparently made off with a very nice early XIXc whalebone box about a foot in diameter which carried charming ink-engraved Eskimo drawings of seals and hunters. Jane loved this box, and was very upset. I found myself getting cross. I telephoned to the Garden House. My mother answered.

'So sorry we missed you this morning.'

---

[1] Mrs Yeo, housekeeper, who came with the Clarks from Seend.
[2] Lindley, the butler at the Garden House.

'Papa had to come over and find a book.'

'He appears also to have taken the whalebone box which was in the dressing room.'

'Papa has always *loved* that box.'

'In that case why did he leave it behind when you made over the contents?'

My father took over. 'Oh God, God, don't say you are really making a fuss about the box?'

'No of course I'm not making a fuss. If you want the box, you must have the box. Jane is in tears, that doesn't matter at all. But . . .' (I must *not* be so icy in tone, it's only one stage off bellowing in rage.) '. . . mightn't it be a good idea if we worked out exactly what is left her which still belongs to you . . . ?'

'I'll bring it straight back; I'll bring it back over now, immediately. Take, take, take . . .'

Then Mama came on. 'How can you do this to Papa? All he wanted was that box . . .'

'Keep the bloody box. I just would like to know what else he must have . . .'

I went for a walk around the garden. An exquisitely beautiful evening, and all the birds singing goodnight.

Bratton   *Friday, 1 June*

'Prowling' about, came across the blue and white push-chair, Jolly's, and almost wept as I recalled 'More Run' and the oggley-oggley noise 'Boy' made going round past Dick's hens. What did I feel so sad about? Would I was back then, I suppose, to play it again – yet I have been incredibly lucky, the inability to have more children the only blight.

Broomhayes   *Sunday, 5 August*

Here on the way back from Bratton/Plymouth. First, reasons for being low. Back, after apparently slightly improving, very painful

as both 'low back pain' *and* no deviation of tightening down R.
side and buttocks which makes it agony in bed by about 5am.
Apparently this is an osteo-arthritic symptom and (I suspect)
irreversible. My father in his memoirs says that growing old (like
growing up) is the progress from one *shelf* to another, not a gradual
ascent or descent, and with this new variant of my back 'trouble' I
have now descended another shelf. Another reason, worried, in a
kind of hopeless way, about the boys – particularly James – being
so sort of rotten and anarchic, languidly lacking in initiative and yet
very ready to take offence. In fact, noticeably poorer in quality
than one or even two years ago. James 'gets away with things'
(being quick and fly in retort) too easily and that coupled with
natural laziness leads him to dodge anything in the slightest bit
arduous. Yet without nourishment his intelligence, initiative,
eagerness will all wither. He's such a dear, I do hope it 'turns out
all right'. I don't quite know what I ought to do.

Third reason: the 'Liberal revival'. They are simply picking off
the safe seats in the by-elections. Ludicrous. May be different in a
General Election,[1] although at present so much momentum that
looks bad – certainly Sutton no longer a cake-walk, a three-corner
marginal that needs a lot of work. Very fortunately Banks[2] a little
pimple of a candidate really, chosen when the whole thing was
just a joke, and now they are lumbered with him, hair-lip and
all – 'sympathy vote' John Miller[3] quickly asserted during dinner.
I've lost quite a bit of money playing b'gammon lately. Suppose
I'm all-square, having been nearly £1,500 up at one stage this
year.

---

[1] The previous Thursday the Liberals won by-elections in two hitherto safe
Conservative seats: Isle of Ely (Clement Freud overturned a Conservative
majority of 9,606 to win by 1,470) and Ripon (where the Conservative majority
of 12,064 became a Liberal majority of 690 for David Austick). At the February
1974 general election Freud retained his seat; Austick lost his.
[2] Simon Banks, Liberal candidate, who fought the seat in two elections.
[3] John Miller, a member of the St James' Club.

Saltwood   *Sunday, 26 August*

The fine weather proceeds, endlessly. Lounging (discontentedly) by the pool this afternoon I started grousing to Jane about my plight and, with her usual combination of wit and good sense, she tried to sort me out. First rightly pointing to how much I already had, that to most men was just greedy. Quite right. I must connect within my own parameters. Then said – think how much 'time' spend sunbathing, no wonder you're short of it.

Rightly pointed out that 1 am: (a) Relaxed millionaire and superimposing on that; (b) Gov. St Thomas' Hospital;[1] (c) Parliamentary candidate for distant seat; (d) stately-home-owner; (e) car-dealer; (f) fighting single-handed battles with Council, developing property etc.

And yet if I was your (c) and (d), with just a little of (e) thrown in, there would be nothing creative going back; nothing in value for all that God has given one. I still think I should go flat out, go for the Monday Club choice, take in the whole lot, National Front and all.

I suppose it is this that really fills me with gloom – the prospect of sacrificing probably for ever, certainly until I am too old to enjoy it, the happy celebration of a secure and lazy family life for the unrelenting grind of a mission. Yet, I suppose I must do it. I checked on 'Boy', wanting to help him, but only realising too late that he was now ready to board and to stand on his own.

Great Library, Saltwood   *Saturday, 13 October*

In my father's study and maudlin on an empty stomach with suspected latent salmonella – result of one mouthful of an appalling 'steak sandwich' at a road-side pub in Preston on the way back from the Blackpool conference.

---

[1] AC had been a governor of London's St Thomas's Hospital since 1969, thanks to the chairman, Hiram Winterbotham, a friend of Kenneth Clark's since the 1930s.

Isn't Blackpool appalling, loathsome . . . ? Impossible to get even a piece of bread and cheese, or a decent cup of tea; dirt, squalor, shanty-town broken pavements with pools of water lying in them – on the Promenade – vulgar common 'primitives' drifting about in groups or standing, loitering, prominently. The conference, not a specially happy one. Bullying of the Right by the Heathites (self again not called; fifth conference in a row). Heseltine, Peter Walker[1] wouldn't speak to me; Sara Morrison[2] and Richard Webster[3] chilly; even Ian Gilmour[4] amusingly changing the subject. I *suppose* it will be all right on the night.

Went on television for *Points West* BBC and hope did some good, though not plugging the Party line. Valeri there plus usual accoutrements of regularised intimacy which make me so jealous (in this case a geriatric Great-Uncle in Holy Orders who is presumably being cultivated for a hand-out). Really, too much. If one could paraphrase Haig's epigram on Derby – the only good thing, incidentally, that the F-M ever did – 'she is like a feather cushion, carrying the imprint of the last person to roll on her'.[5]

Various other matters conspire to prevent me looking as smooth and relaxed as, say, Heseltine: Tip still gets a lot of ashtma, inc. *every* Sunday without fail; crazy expenditure with three different contractors now going full blast on the interior. We can *just* carry

---

[1] Peter Walker, MP for Worcester since 1961, now Secretary for Trade and Industry.

[2] The Morrisons were at this time a powerhouse within the Conservative Party. The Hon. Sara Morrison, whose husband Charles had been MP for Devizes since 1964, was in her second year as chairman of the party organisation; her father-in-law, Lord Margadale, was, before being elevated to the Lords as a baron, MP for Salisbury 1942–64; she herself was the daughter of Viscount Long and Laura, Duchess of Marlborough; and her brother-in-law, Peter Morrison, had been personal assistant to Peter Walker and had just been selected as candidate for Chester.

[3] Sir Richard Webster, Director of Organisation, Conservative Central Office.

[4] Ian Gilmour, MP for Norfolk Central since 1962, had been rising fast through the junior ministerial ranks at Defence since 1970. Edited *The Spectator* (1954–59).

[5] Haig wrote to his wife in January 1918 that Derby bore 'the marks of the last person who sat on him'.

it, but long-term prosperity heavily dependent on sale at a profit of Newton Farm.[1]

Saltwood   *Sunday, 11 November*

On top of all the crazy expenditure, just bought a beautiful Alma–Tadema at Sotheby's for £9,000 – suddenly got a demand for £28,000 to pay my father's Capital Gains Tax on the transfer of Saltwood.

Saltwood   *Wednesday, 14 November*

I have now been the prospective Parliamentary candidate in Plymouth for more than a year. I suppose it's all going to be ok. People, not just in Plymouth but at various kinds of political function keep saying 'You'll be all right'; by which, I suppose, they mean 'you will win the seat'. But I don't like the word 'safe'. Perhaps because I am superstitious, or just wary of hubris. When Brian Somebody, a tiresome left-wing Fellow at All Souls, told [John Sparrow] that he wanted a 'long sabbatical' to go into Parliament and John inquired as to the putative constituency . . . said . . . 'It's a safe seat, of course.'

To which John retorted, 'Safe? Safe . . . ? Oh, you mean *unopposed?*'

But I've got this feeling I'm not absolutely a billion percent welcome in this outfit; not, at least, in its present 'configuration'.

Heigh ho. More fool them, I say.

Zermatt   *Wednesday, 19 December*

Lower than ever, after quite a good day yesterday. Had taken pain-killing drug (Distalgesic – sinisterly indicated for 'malignant

---

[1] A farm in north Cornwall bought for £105,000 in 1973.

conditions . . . allowing the administration of morphine to be postponed') the previous night.

On my walk this morning looked with real longing at the perfect snow and piste of the little 'Home National'. It is a real deprivation for me not to be able to ski. All my fitness 'program' jeopardised. I must be in shape when I return at Easter – for the Election tone-up.

Zermatt   *Wednesday, Boxing Day*

I thought maybe I was going to be struck down with paralysis – like my poor mother, post-stroke in UCH with her left side paralysed and hopelessly depressed. She returns tomorrow by ambulance to the Hythe nursing home and then (putatively) to the Garden House and a regime with special beds, chairs and apparatus that can only end when she dies, but may project into the future for a very long time. My feeling – what a loss, ie 'loss' = 'nuisance' to us. But Jane, with her real *goodness* of nature, said quite naturally and spontaneously that we must all look after her as well as we can and hope that she never feels discarded or neglected before she dies.

1974

Saltwood   *Tuesday, 1 January*

Low and grumpy and self-pitying after a late night, punishment at
Aspinalls[1] losing £460 and bringing up my total losses to £820
certain. So now have 'given up b'gammon' following a self-denial
chucking (or being chucked) by the 'i's and superimposing a
certain amount of pure masochism – 'not drinking again until I
have paid off all the money I owe . . .' etc.

Prospect is gloomy, and not enhanced by my poor back: skiing
being so handicapped; also the prospect of my poor Mama fading
away in the nursing home though with her mind still beautifully
clear and wittily cynical in the best style. What an irony that she so
often feigned, for reasons of convenience, slurred speech and
detachment – should now be quite literally stricken with it. What
a cautionary tale for us all!

1974 is not going to be good – though how bad remains to be
seen.

Saltwood   *Friday, 18 January*

In tremendous form yesterday morning at prospect of election(!)
on anti-union platform – v. good for Sutton prospects. Now total
reversal; Heath lost his nerve at the last moment that afternoon,
morale shattered,[2] John Miller took £96 off me at tea, I got drunk

---

[1] John Aspinall founded a series of London clubs beginning with the Clermont in
Berkeley Square. AC and Aspinall had first met at Oxford. In these diaries he is
usually referred to as 'Aspers'.

[2] The prime minister threatened to call a general election if the miners' union, the
NUM, failed to settle their pay claim.

– boringly sitting between Harold Lever[1] and John Miller at Jimmy's[2] dinner.

Jane tested me when I got back – 'you're never here' etc. We were walking along the old railway line. Vowed to give up b'gammon.

B5 Albany   *Friday, 25 January*

I was in Lister's[3] waiting room. One of my teeth aches periodically, and when I bend over I can feel a pulse in it. This must be bad. I have a feeling that you can get absolutely fearful, *terminal* blood poisoning from a bad tooth. Even if this is unlikely I do not want 'trouble' over this Election.

At the far end of the room an old gentleman wearing a mac was stooped over a *Times* which he rustled and page-turned in a rather ego, demonstrative, manner. Silvery hair, pebble-lens specs. Suddenly I realised who it was – *Uncle Harold*! – and walked across. I thought it more prudent not to remind him of our last meeting [see page 12] thinking in any case that mutual embarrassment and (in his case) very poor vision would occlude the recollection. 'Sir, can I introduce myself? Alan Clark, I am the prospective parliamentary candidate for Plymouth Sutton.'

'My dear boy! Well done, well done. Nancy Astor's old seat, well I never, sit down . . .' etc. He was incredible. Lucid, compos, clear and incisive of speech. Said the election would be a disaster – 'The working class will see it as a loyalty vote . . .'; that there should be an Energy ministry with sweeping powers; that the miners had to be bought off until North Sea oil came on stream; that it should not be difficult to outmanoeuvre Len Murray;[4] that

---

[1] Harold Lever, Labour MP for Manchester Cheetham since 1950 (Manchester Exchange, 1945–50). Originally a barrister, he was a minister under Harold Wilson and chairman of the Public Accounts Committee in 1970.

[2] James (Jimmy) Goldsmith, a successful businessman, of Anglo-French parentage, chairman of Générale Occidentale SA Paris, and a friend of AC's since Oxford.

[3] AC's dentist.

[4] Len Murray, General Secretary of the TUC since 1973 (he had been with the TUC since 1947).

McGahey[1] wasn't popular in the TUC; that the real agitator was (*Scrimgeour* was it? — the words came thick and fast and I was transfixed[2]); that it was urgent to find some way of reassuring the middle classes who were puzzled and that we ought to be talking now to the Liberal Party. Thorpe[3] was a 'show-off' and unreliable, but could probably be enlisted from flattery . . .

On and on did Macmillan speak. I have never listened to anyone so compelling, and with such sense of history. Lister's nurse appeared at the door and said he was ready, but I sent her away. What has happened to the Conservatives? How could they possibly ignore this man, so sage and so authoritative? I have already received ten tons of bumf from Central Office, most of it useless and unreadable. I don't see how we can actually *lose* this Election, or at least how I can lose it, but the whole encounter was rather unsettling. I wish I had not wasted so long before going into politics, and could ingratiate myself with Uncle Harold, and defend him from ambitious and scheming mediocrities. Is it really too late? I suppose so.

I had quite forgotten about my tooth, which anyway took hardly a minute.

Bratton   *Thursday, 14 February*

The Campaign is On! With Jane to Guildhall to hand in nomination papers; went to wrong door so kept everyone waiting, the ludicrous stilted formality with Labour Mayor. Pouring rain. Went out to Plympton Police to show documents. Canvassed a little in Embankment Road on way back (not bad). Some sour looks en route as we sped by in Land-Rover, self repeating inanely — or so it seemed — 'Hello, everybody, this is your Conservative candidate. Please vote for me on Feb 28, vote AC, vote Conservative.'

---

[1] Mick McGahey, Scottish miners' leader.
[2] Presumably Arthur Scargill, although, as president of the Yorkshire NUM, he was only just coming to prominence.
[3] Jeremy Thorpe, MP for Devon North since 1959, succeeded Jo Grimond as leader of the Liberal Party, 1967.

Thankfully back to Bratton for pasty supper (wrong sort of pastry).

Bratton   *Friday, 22 February*

Graham seemed reasonably calm about result, but I don't like talking about 'when you're in the House etc.' Shattering of the make-believe too close.

It was agreed how much of a threat the Liberals are. Actually I think they are a threat, but don't want confirmation of this opinion.

This evening for the first time really thought perhaps am going to lose this seat after all – total disaster, struck off by Sir Richard Webster[1] instantly etc etc. The whole of that period since May 71 wasted, all that hubris.

Bratton   *Tuesday, 26 February*

Morale improved by Graham late last night. '. . . when you wake up on Friday morning you'll be a Member of Parliament.' L.K. Way[2] poo-poohed idea of Liberal victory – 'see you in London, 6 March'. Confidence returned. Took many plaudits and then on to an excellent curry restaurant with Jane. Nothing to drink so lit a small Rössli cigar.

11pm. Back in bed with a piece of fruit-cake and the latest *Motor Sport*. One of the best days so far.

The general election on 28 February
Conservative: 296; Labour: 301; Liberal: 14; Others: Ulster Unionists: 11; Scottish Nationalists: 7; Plaid Cymru: 2; others: 4.

---

[1] Sir Richard Webster, Director of Organisation, Conservative Central Office since 1966.
[2] L.K. Way, lobby correspondent of Plymouth's daily paper, the *Western Morning News*.

Bratton   *Friday, 1 March*

Toured (very cold) in the Land-Rover, thanking people. A delicious moment, when testing my speaker, said: 'This is your Conservative *candidate* speaking . . .' 'Member of Parliament, you
twit,' said Graham.[1]

Train to Plymouth   *Thursday, 7 March*

Fabulous day of lingering euphoria and luxuriation in being MP.
    Started with climb of Summerhouse Hill in glorious spring
morning. Then *just* caught 11.18 from Ashford (driving there in
little borrowed Triumph 1500 of my parents) still wearing anorak
and check trousers/pink shirt.
    Changed and showered and to House. Collected huge bundles
of (miscellaneous) mail and through to Euan's office[2] where he got
me *monstrously* drunk; then drifted around the Palace of Westminster peeping and pottering, and observing massive available
perks; drink in Strangers Bar and to (quite good) lunch. Hailed in
Strangers dining room with incredible hurrahs by Jeremy Thorpe,
more guardedly by David Steel. Then spent rest of afternoon
'walking off' drink going round various Sergeant-at-Arms type
offices drawing vouchers etc.

Saltwood   *Sunday, 10 March*

After the euphoria the depression. Jane found the invitation from
Ali (though fortunately not her letter) and she took it out on James
– I didn't realise this at the time – and then had a very late night.

---

[1] Sutton result: AC, 21,649 votes; Fletcher (Labour), 13,545; Banks (Liberal),
    12,683.
[2] Euan Graham, AC's friend from Oxford days, had been Principal Clerk of
    Private Bills, House of Lords, since 1961.

Probably saved from row then by presence of Celly and, to a lesser extent, Nick.[1]

To Jane at breakfast I said 'your only real motivation, whether subconscious or conscious, the only yardstick by which you judge things, is whether I am more or less likely to get people to go to bed with me . . .' and developed the theme. She cried when I tried to console her. We were interrupted by the back door bell, it was Tim, calling for James. Went and tidied around in the dressing room, with Andrew soft-spokenly helping me with my ties, then over to the Garden House, to find my mother in tears, my father his usual crotchety self.

Also aware on this lovely fine spring morning of the great weight of undone duties. Financial stringency looms with disallowing of loan interest (probably), plus inevitability of Labour victory in next election.[2]

Plymouth train   *Friday, 15 March*

Down on the 1.30, suspect slightly flu-bound and picked up Johnny Hannam.[3] (For a few minutes he didn't know who I was.) We sat at lunch together. Self-medicating generously, talked of politics throughout the meal to the grumpy consternation of a *New Statesman*-reading geriatric opposite. Quite a nice chap, interesting and helpful. Concepted Margaret Thatcher as possible successor to Heath.

---

[1] Nick Beuttler, Jane's brother.

[2] AC found himself at Westminster as a backbench MP for a party in opposition, with Conservatives nor Labour having an overall majority. Edward Heath, as 'the Prime Minister in possession' (related AC in *The Tories*) and leading a party boasting 1,200,000 more votes than Labour (but five fewer seats), had spent 'five painful days' attempting to 'form' an administration. Jeremy Thorpe, leader of the Liberals (6,000,000 votes, but only 14 seats), demanded nothing less than proportional representation to turn their future voting strength into seats; Heath offered no more than a Speaker's Conference to examine the question of electoral reform. The coalition did not happen, Heath resigned and Harold Wilson became prime minister, leading a minority Labour government.

[3] John Hannam, MP for Exeter since 1970.

Saltwood   *Monday, 25 March*

Been going great guns in politics: on ITN, BBC West, *This Week*, Radio 4, all arising, more or less, from the article in the *Sunday Times*.[1] Sometimes, I think, fabulous; a new face, just the right combination of attitudes, appeal etc. Rommel. Press on and on. At others I feel so far to go, such parlous resources, what a waste of the lovely weather and possessions and XVIIIc freedom. My morale suffered from mutterings at Plymouth (reported to me); Dunstone,[2] needless to say, plus letter from Sir Henry Studholme[3] in *Western Morning News*. Bloody fools had none of them read the *ST* itself, only L.K. Way's extracts.

Albany   *Tuesday, 30 April*

Put in to do my 'maiden' today.[4] Sat in Chamber for quite a time, with 'everybody on board most helpful'.[5] Rose to my feet and

---

[1] Under the heading 'Tory Party needs a rethink, but where are the thinkers?', AC was highly critical of the party machine, its reliance on the findings of opinion pollsters in formulating an image and packaging policy; he also attacked Tory Central Office for its condemnation 'amounting in the later years almost to a witch-hunt' of all expressions of dissent, particularly those who supported Enoch Powell's views. It was widely seen as a brave, if foolhardy, view to voice, not least by a new MP.

[2] A Sutton constituency ward chaired by Mrs H.O'N. (Nan) Howard.

[3] Sir Henry Studholme, 1st Bt, MP for Tavistock, 1942–66, part of whose constituency had been redistributed into Sutton.

[4] AC chose the debate on the Channel Tunnel, that project being so close to Saltwood (as he declared to the House), if not his constituency, but in his speech he gave a foretaste of his views from Defence through patriotism to continental Europe, when he reminded the House that the country had always been protected from invasion by the English Channel. An attack would be by 'blitzkrieg, a lightning strike', and its most likely form would now be a parachute landing 'to seize the tunnel head and defend it for a short enough period for the invader to pass through the tunnel and completely bypass our natural protection'. And, he added, that if the tunnel went ahead a fail-safe system should be installed allowing for its instant demolition.

[5] From one of AC's favourite books, Evelyn Waugh's *The Ordeal of Gilbert Pinfold*, a copy of which he kept by his bedside in Zermatt.

spoke clearly and, I believe, it was appreciated once the House realised what I was doing – quite wittily.

Saltwood   *Friday, 7 June*

A very low day. Extremely tired (did late night at Aspinalls) and awoke as unpleasant thoughts slotted into place (i) b'gammon losses last night £470; (ii) Valeri out of my life; (iii) Jimmy Goldsmith warnings about world slump.[1] My mind was racing as to how reduce o/d and then came crashing in on top of this the recollection that CGT also (of minimum 30) is needed shortly.

My parents low; my mother now deteriorated again, although still beautifully poised and witty; talk of wealth tax, obliteration of the 'gentry', look round at the unbelievable driving up of protest sympathies by the press for the IRA and hunger strikers etc.

Given up b'gammon . . . statistical analysis shows it just is too expensive.

H of C Library   *Wednesday, 12 June*

Yesterday (instead of the House), when I was lying up on the castle's terrace/battlement walk (new spot, just this side of Thorpe's), did absolutely no good tan-wise, but suddenly realised the enormity of the interest charges running against me – 87 + 63 = 150 or £20,000 a year, or £500 a week. Must stop the drain and can only do so by selling cars.

Is it going to be easy to sell cars? CH[2] very gloomy. Money drying up fast. From time to time, as I drive about in my blue Bentley – to which I am very attached, 'MP's car' – I think what a personification of Privilege I am. Silk shirts, beautiful suits, write a cheque or sign an Amex for anything you want; chambers in

---

[1] Sir James Goldsmith, founder and proprietor of a number of commercial enterprises.

[2] Charles Howard, a motoring friend, who also regularly played backgammon with AC.

Albany, castle in Kent, châlet in Zermatt, credit accounts everywhere, the Parliamentary pass to flash. Press the button, the
machine will respond. Total confidence. How easy to be pleasant
– that calm inner assurance of superiority (like I have sometimes
noticed with people who are very good at Judo, the way they move
quietly and confidently in crowds). Well, could it be in jeopardy? I
got the aerial photos of Saltwood today, thought God what a
wonderful place, worth hanging on to, and preserving for the boys.

Dean's Yard   *Wednesday, 17 July*

Reflecting on most unwelcome position, the evidence of (sic)
which has been building up for some time, that not only am I in a
very uncomfortable financial situation – but that I totally mismanaged (from optimism, *folie de grandeur*, total lack of Scotch
canniness, gross miscalculations of economic symptoms and also
sheer inability, or at least unwillingness to *count*) the one last great
get-out deal, namely the sale of the cricket field.

     This could have got me permanently out of debt and allowed
consolidation with a lot of excess assets on a well diversified
earnings basis – rents, royalties, salaries, public visits. Really, after
earlier reverses one would think that lesson had been learned. It *has*
been learned now. Just pray I can impart it to James and Tip – one
can never entirely, of course, but even *some* of it would help. Also
means giving up some things I like, eg Lago-Talbot and D-type. (If
– and it is a bit of an 'if' because these are days of great panic and
depression – I sell them, should get my o/d down below 20.) The
days of limitless cash flow are over.

Saltwood   *Sunday, 21 July*

For the first time, coming back in sleeper from Plymouth, did not
feel that delicious sense of relief and anticipation – the mirror-
image of the towers reflected in the water as you come through
the Barbican, generated anxiety instead of calming. The whole

structure unchanged with absurd signs of wealth and stability but as
the hot summer days (now shortening) slip by the bills accumulate,
so far without *any* sales to relieve them. This had the effect of
reducing, at last, adrenalin flow (contentment must be an ingredient to get a proper flow, I think). And last night I went down with
a summer cold, first cold for eighteen months. During the night an
enormous chunk of the north curtain wall slid down, and will cost
£12–14,000 to repair. I remember talking to my old pal Euan
Graham in a bar in the House of Lords last week, and he told me
how as well as being by-passed for the long-awaited promotion he
had been cut out of his mother's will – 'when one thing hits you,
they all do.'

Saltwood   *Monday, 5 August*

Conceivably, the last day of the old regime.[1] Not impossible that
by the winter I should be (a) wiped out and (b) have lost my seat. I
sometimes seriously think of how much I could get out to Zermatt
(Bavarian Redoubt) before actually going under. A few objects and
pictures out – Degas, Bull, snuff-boxes, some Moores and Suther-
lands etc. But how would one live in the long term? On reflection,
must preserve Saltwood, so it can be run 'as a business'.

Later
Am I a Renaissance Prince, a philosopher, or a big ageing dud?
Looking back at all those lost opportunities of money-making,
starting with the waste of the first £15,000 my father gave me in
1948, like properties in Rye (going for nothing), the Torridon
Estate (£40,000 in 1964, now ½ million I suppose).
    Fortified by two things – first how all that really matters is the
boys' health and survival and how lucky we are, second how God
did work his miracle for Plymouth Sutton. *That* was the real

---

[1] The House of Commons had risen for the summer recess; everyone expected
that Harold Wilson, the prime minister, would call an election in the autumn in
an endeavour to get an overall working majority.

achievement, *that* is what must be built on. Easy to recharge the batteries with Zermatt and Bratton . . . and exercise. I've learnt my lesson about financial speculation at last having been through fire – forget it. Security you can (still) attain. So, thank-you-God-for-any-good-luck and hold on to what you've got, a happy family and fulfilment of your secret – and apparently impossible – ambition.

Charing Cross   *Thursday, 19 September*

Confident (Sutton *not* on the *Guardian* list of marginals).[1]

I went off to face Hoare's, going through the Temple. Seen in a top front room. First dear old Q. Hoare to soften me up, then 'Dick' Hoare – the head man. That was clearly his designed role, but it so happens we took an intense dislike to one another. He's determined to 'get' me. I can feel that; enjoyed bullying me to sell assets – regardless of right price or no. Made some acid quips while Q. Hoare muddled the figures from time to time. At the end (circa 5.30) dear old Q. Hoare asked me if I would like a whisky (!) Have got till 1 April next year (due to Q. Hoare's shuffling – originally in two stages with Christmas the first).[2]

Everything happening at once, ie financial collapse *and* having to fight an election. Waking early with all these worries. Fool, Clark, to have repeated your errors on such a huge scale.

Duke of Cornwall Hotel, Plymouth[3]   *Saturday, 28 September*

It was icy in (or rather on) the Land-Rover this evening.

'*Firm Government – but Fair Government*'.

Umpteen times have I called this out. A simple enough phrase. So simple, indeed, as to be devoid of meaning or even inference.

---

[1] The general election had been called for 11 October.

[2] Despite the severity of Hoare's stipulations, the Clarks retained accounts with the bank.

[3] As in February, AC was to use 'The Duke' as his base for the October campaign.

Yet all too easy to get, in some perverse way, tied around one's tongue. We were driving in those streets that lead uphill from Plymstock to Hooe, there was practically no one about and Jane accelerated. The wind made my eyes water uncontrollably, and for some reason I started a longer discourse and *affected a Devonian accent.*

She jammed on the brakes. 'What *are* you doing? You just make yourself utterly ridiculous.'

Back here I ordered and consumed a lot of tea and buttered toast (both arrived tepid) in the lounge. I am depressed, irritated, suffering from exhaustion. Even in the 'good' areas the electorate are flinty-faced. What's going on?

Bratton   *Thursday, 3 October*

The dear old boy conducting me round Mt Gould – very effi-ciently – won my heart by suddenly saying: 'Of course you're the one, the one with fire in you.'

Later Jack Weatherill[1] came on the phone: 'How's it going?'

'So, so, only.'

'No I mean this Coalition idea.[2] Are you getting it across?'

'They won't understand. It's far too late to start trying to sell that . . .'

'Well, that's the line. Do your best.'

'Look, Jack, we're not going to get anywhere while Ted is leading us. He's had it.'

'Later. That comes later. Leave it for the moment.'

Odd. Particularly that last sentence. Actually, I think we are

---

[1] Bernard (Jack) Weatherill, MP for Croydon NE since 1964. A whip in govern-ment and opposition (he had been opposition deputy chief whip since February 1974). Such were his skills with the more independent-minded Conservative members that he was known, not always affectionately, at 'the shits' whip'.

[2] At mid-point, Tory strategists, at the behest of Edward Heath, came up with the notion that to appeal 'over the heads' of the Labour Party to 'people of good will' might save a number of seats.

going to lose, again. And that will be one of the exciting things about the new House. Getting a real change.

Saltwood   *Saturday, 12 October*

Back last night after a (foreshortened) tour of Sutton with the loudspeaker (just did a 'blast' outside the Eastons' house so that they would hear me – for alibi reasons). A glance at the *Evening Standard* was enough to show that Plymouth results were *exceptionally* bad[1] – many safe seats had *increased* their majorities. Only consolation was that of course, most of Liberals had also been slashed.

Concocted a formula to get one to sleep, of selling the plot adjacent in Zermatt for 90,000 (!). I passed out in bed at 10.30 and woke at 11.20. This gave me back a bit of confidence again, a determination to concentrate on exercises, library, eschew late nights, b'gammon, the Mews etc. Clearheadedly see this through. 'No relaxation without implementation.'

Saltwood   *Thursday, 31 October*

Been in a state of considerable 'nervosity' all day. Waves of angst wash over me at the Hoare's indebtedness (wake every morning at 4am for about ¾ hr of panic). Also Lenin-stadium type cramp-angst at so much to resolve

(1) ked-up at b'gammon (which I love, and am addicted to)
(2) Virtually ignored in the House this time – in spite of our quite jolly and successful performances
(3) Rows – sic – with parents being against my advantage over possible – indeed vital – money-raising sales

---

[1] Sutton result: AC, 20,457 votes; Priestley (Labour), 15,269; Banks (Liberal), 10,131. AC's majority, 5,188 (February, 8,104).

(4) Feeling tired cold and looking strangely pressured with hair now degenerating in quality as well as colour and density
(5) Sick of Plymouth – will quit journeys and the sleeper etc – and their introspective minuscule horizons
(6) Badly need energy and will-power to concentrate on problems this winter

Saltwood   *Saturday, 16 November*

Filled with gloom and foreboding as market continues to slide (Coats at <u>26</u>[1]), probability of yet another Arab/Israeli war with total collapse of industry, currency etc (not to mention 'Nuclear Exchange'). November is a terrible month, the equivalent of 3.10am during the night.

Desmond Corcoran[2] coming down this morning. Have prayed to God I make the right decisions.[3]

---

[1] A stock long held by AC and in considerable quantities. It had been at a year high of 74. Coats had amalgamated with the Clark cotton thread business J & J Clark in 1896.

[2] Desmond Corcoran – from the Lefevre Gallery in Mayfair.

[3] AC's comment at foot of entry: 'I was very trembly to start with, but got 31,000 for nine pictures'.

Saltwood   *Sunday, 12 January*

Got back today [from Zermatt]. Nanny had cleaned the place fantastically, throughout, and our fears that various vandalisms would occur proved unfounded. Even the 'No Parking' notice sensibly erect outside the Barbican, and Cradduck's stripping of the ivy from the walls over the Bailey gate most successful. Of the various anticipated disasters only one – the euthanasia of Gangster – took place as predicted. I'm sorry that I couldn't be there to bid him goodbye. But he's buried next to Grandee. And I will always remember the Beagles and their period of great physical prowess, particularly Dartmoor (that time I lost them on the twin boggy ridges that stretched out towards Meldon) and Salisbury Plain (chasing the prototype Chieftain[2]) because it coincided with the longer period of contentment and tranquillity (at Seend) in my own life.

Reasonable (and unexpected) aura of contentment in spite of letter from the Tate semi-reneging on Saltonstall.[3] Beautifully insulated here in panelled library with log fire.

But much will be decided this year. 'Survival' yes, but there must also be a platform built, because if I don't get established in '76 there can be no further attainment of my goals without a miracle. My age does seem to have jumped one this last year.

Dean's Yard   *Friday, 17 January*

'Punishment' phase. Lost £1320 to Goldsmith/Slater/Zilkhan at a £40 chou[4] at Lyall Street after Aspers' (only moderate) 'talk' to

---

[1] AC heads the entry: START OF 'SURVIVAL YEAR'.

[2] The Chieftain was to become the British army's principal tank of the Cold War era.

[3] *The Saltonstall Family*, c1636–7, by David Des Granges.

[4] Chou is the abbreviation for Chouette, a backgammon game in which more than two players participate.

Bow Group last night. Jane rightly tested me for no constituency visits, no publicity, far too much old cars. *Absolutely nothing* in the papers about me for nearly six weeks, don't open constituency letters any more, no questions tabled, no intervention, no time to work up speeches, complaints about showing my face in Plymouth – haven't even signed all the election thankyou letters yet! Now very tired indeed (7.30 train tomorrow) with cold symptoms.[1]

Saltwood   *Monday, 24 March*

Threatening position welling up in Plymouth. As I somehow suspected Larry Speare[2] undergone total personality change as chairman – head cropped, unsmilingly and *folie de grandeur*. He'd already shown incipient signs of this at the AGM with his *very* reserved compliments and injunctions to 'help the name of Sutton forward'. Then last Thursday, totally dry-minded and fatigued (I had driven down flat out that morning in the 230 SL, spurting out oil through a misplaced filler cap) he told/warned me of possibility of not being readopted due to having been anti-Heath, anti Referendum. That evening, at the F&GP, he, fortunately, clashed with Rodney Easton; but if he, Easton, and Speare started ganging up (Nazi-Soviet non-aggression pact) then one would be in trouble.

Saltwood   *Thursday, 10 April*

A note of the last day of the Common Market (approval) – or whatever it should be called – debates.

---

[1] AC is silent on the change in party leadership, which was about to take place. In the first ballot of Conservative MPs on 4 February, Margaret Thatcher gained 130 votes to Edward Heath's 119, with 16 for the backbencher Hugh Fraser. Heath resigned as leader. A week later Thatcher, with 146 votes, gained an overall majority over four Shadow Cabinet colleagues: William Whitelaw (79 votes), Geoffrey Howe and James Prior (19 each) and John Peyton (11).

[2] Lawrence Speare, a significant member of the Sutton Conservative Association and sometime chairman.

Entertainment, indeed History, promised with Heath, Powell *and* Heffer[1] all hoping-to-catch-the-eye. Walked up the aisle and turned right past Heath, occupying the prime position in corner seat. He bronzé in grey suit, check shirt (semi-Heseltine outfit) but rather more pinched, less ripplingly. Ugh! What a purse-mouth ('*Bonjours* . . .') he made as I momentarily swished him. Humphrey Atkins[2] smiled in friendly fashion, though. Had John Stradling Thomas[3] already told him that I was going to vote anti? John himself uneasily asked me if I had 'read Margaret's speech'. Oh yes, I said, splendid stuff (I hadn't); of course if she told me to vote 'for' I would. But I welcomed the 'free' vote in order to make my little personal statement. Gloomily he accepted this.

Front bench jammed solid. 'Throng' at the Bar. Heath spoke, reasonably competent and without notes, in the 'Coningsby position' (or hand in d/b jacket pocket). For a second, when he was speaking about sovereignty, I could have interrupted him, but it passed.

'Where's Margaret?' asked nasty little Tony Nelson of Chichester.[4] 'He listened to *her* speech.'

'But wasn't very polite about it,' I said. He looked cross at this.

The Heath 5th column cheered loudly when he sat down. He was followed, immediately by Enoch! Tortured, baleful, intense, he stood only a few feet away from me, on the same row the other side of the gangway. Spoke well, gestured pointedly. Heath interrupted him three times, having to unfortunately twist his neck and his eyes round and was slightly worsted. Enoch very good and moving and made one feel *all right* about voting anti. 'That's one of the good ones', came from one of Dennis's group as I walked through afterwards and sexy little Miss Horseface (I don't recall her

[1] Eric Heffer, MP for Liverpool Walton since 1964, and a leading left-winger. Died from cancer in 1991.

[2] Humphrey Atkins, MP for Spelthorne since 1970 (Merton and Morden, 1955–70) and opposition chief whip. Earlier he had a spell as secretary to the Conservative Parliamentary Defence Committee. Deputy and ultimately government chief whip, 1973–74.

[3] John Stradling Thomas, MP for Monmouth since 1970 and an opposition whip.

[4] Tony Nelson, elected MP for Chichester in October 1974, previously with N.M. Rothschild.

name, but took Dick's place at Lincoln)[1] seductively said 'I didn't know you were an anti.'[2]

Went back to St J and got into b'gammon game, and ended losing <u>again</u> – £226. When I collected my mail Dennis Skinner[3] was standing near. I had to give my name to an unknown PO official. 'Alan Clark' . . . 'The goal scorer,' said D. 'You scored one last night.' 'Not enough of us,' I answered. In the tea-room queue I said, 'I'd rather live in a socialist Britain than one ruled by a lot of fucking foreigners.' He seemed surprised as well as pleased.

Saltwood   *Sunday, 11 May*

An evocative date. The great German offensive across the Low Countries in 1940. Churchill gets the premiership, the die is cast in the country's fight to the death. And, five years later, VE Day, with its illusions that took so long to disperse.

And here is my own life, its 'serious', ambitious, political and however-you-like-to-call-it side so emphatically biased by those experiences, well over half-way through, even deducting the childhood years. I've got ten – *tennish* – more years active, eight as an 'active buffer', the remainder as a sage. That's always assuming freedom/deliverance from the screech of brakes, sickening thud and rending of metal from the head-on crash over the brow of the hill. Now that the 550A Spyder is roadable I often take it out on fine evenings. So intoxicatingly fast and agile – but so vulnerable. Going onto the slightly blind hump-back of the A20 Sandling Bridge I visualised (as so often) that horrid impact.

---

[1] Margaret Jackson (later better known by her married name Beckett) had regained the Lincoln seat for Labour in October 1974 after the sitting MP, Dick Taverne, defected to the SDP.

[2] AC was one of a small number of Tories to vote against, but their stance was overshadowed by Eric Heffer, who was dismissed as Minister of State, Department of Industry, for not supporting the government.

[3] Dennis Skinner, MP for Bolsover since 1970 ('good working-class mining stock', *Who's Who* entry) and already a left-winger with a reputation for parliamentary repartee.

Have I recorded that nightmare spin in the 230 SL that night when I was unscathed? Let us hope it means that 'what is written, is written'.

Dean's Yard   *Tuesday, 27 May*

A certain delicious calmness – one of the first really tranquil entries for nearly a year – since the enormity of the financial crisis and the threat to Saltwood came home. Working up in my (new) 'collegiate' quarters on the quad – Abbey Gardens – on a long summer evening. Sent £18,000 odd to Hoare's today, now bringing o/d to agreed April 1st limit and reductions. The magic moment when the deeds are returned to me not so far away.

What is to be the outcome of the terrible decline of the country – the total absence of leadership and inspiration in the Conservative Party? In 1939 at least we had Fighter Command and the Navy, and Winston around. Now we have nothing. My windows here are filthy, dirtier even than at Saltwood. *US News and World Report[1] quite right – whole thing tatty, bad-tempered, lazy, in collapse. Yet of course there is no crisis; everyone flush with money. When will the recovery come? And how?*

Yet even as I write this, I feel – too slack, too easygoing. In the train the other evening I thought perhaps I should go the whole way, stand as a National Front candidate, a *switch* if the Plymouth Association kicks me out. Or is the very thought that I am 'waiting for the call' a concealment of my natural laziness?

After two days very successful openings, fired by the cash flow, the possibilities. One of the few 'enterprises' unlikely to be troubled even by the envy, the jealousies all around us. I also have these romantic fantasies of the besieged aristocracy. 1791. I do hope the boys will catch on in the end. James in particular is unbelievably idle about it at the moment. He has passed through girls (for the moment) and drink (largely speaking) and now is

---

[1] The American news magazine had compared the Britain of the 1970s – unfavourably – with the 'swinging sixties' period.

obsessed by driving. He had cleaned the Bang Bang[1] meticulously during garage invigilation on the public days. Last night Tuppy suddenly cocked an ear and said, 'that's the Bang Bang engine . . .' I looked out of the door and saw it going down the drive – James was turning it prior to putting it in the garage. I waited in the shadow of the Barbican. The car came back, turned in the car park gate and then out back down the drive! I knew what would follow an engine opened up (so like an aero-engine it sounds) and the lights clearly shone charging up Sandy Lane! I got the Land-Rover, but by then he was already returning. Oh dear, I do love 'Boy' so much, in spite of all his bolshiness of growing up. I do dread his having a motor accident. I must train and nurture him on the road. He wants to go to Lydden[2] and one might do that.

Saltwood   *Saturday, 13 September*

More or less decided and broke the news to Jane – who took it very philosophically – to 'stand down in Sutton'. At this range, it simply isn't possible to satisfy the (insatiable) demands of the Conservative 'workers'.

Draft press release
SUTTON MP STANDS DOWN

'Mr Alan Clark, Member of Parliament for the Sutton division of Plymouth, said in a statement: It is with great regret that . . . for family reasons . . . I shall not be standing for re-election for the Sutton division . . . I will of course continue to represent and defend the rights of my constituents who have so loyally supported me in two elections . . .'

---

[1] R Type Bentley Continental, the only Continental to be recorded stolen in the 1950s. Written off, it was rebodied by Bradley Brothers into a cut-down two-seater.

[2] Motor-racing track off the A2 north-west of Dover.

Albany, B5 Lower   *Tuesday, 23 December*

Really flying at tree-top height with only one engine at *top of the valley*(!) Bought a beautiful SI Hooper from Charles and had to cheque-write today (another 3+). Also ought really to get Valeri her coat (2), plus inspected latest tax liabilities from Meeson to cripple the New Year. Went round to the House to make a couple of free calls.

Zermatt   *Wednesday, 31 December*

Year end, and gathering strength. *Very* slight improvement in health and morale. But my personal resolution for the next Christmas: I just bloody well won't have any debts at all – but of course if intention hangs fire that won't be possible. This is the one difference from last year – Newton *is* saleable.

Sitting at my desk with a heavy heart. On top: the ineradicable, obsessional worry about money. Just what am I going to do when we get back, faced with instant outgoings like mortgage on Silks cottages, school fees, stock exchange, *plus* balance to be paid Zermatt for the delightful 2-door Shadow. Immediate decision on 'culling' rest of collection to bare minimum – but will these be dissipated, when I meant to concentrate them in the Classic car a/c? One side effect of this obsession is growing identity of salvation with Hitler in 1943, that carries with it unhappy overtones of inevitability.

Central Fact finally agreed today: Hoare's insisting on a reduction [of o/d] to 100 by 1 April – ie less than two months, effectively, from 100 + 35 + 26. Reduced me to a *total* tension blubber, with slight headache, waves of fatigue and then sudden, crazy snapping-out of it, back into realisation of possible total collapse. God knows what kind of a night I'm going to have. At least I don't drink or take pills to combat this.

Need all my energy and testosterone to cope with the Central Fact. Second occurrence, which also seemed to have a kind of predestinational quality in forcing me to determine life pattern was the strange accidental delivery by postman of Mama's draft will (!), 1976 model, which one opened, read, took to H of C library and photocopied and then reposted in a WC2 pillar-box (!). It was a nasty, cold document; no bequests – other than to the British Museum and to servants; Celly got the old clothes and Col and I (it said me, but clearly a mis-print for Col) got the residue after everything (including B5) to Papa. Dealt with Col at 25% of what the other gets, but as he points out, it is an ominous indication and fact is one will get *nothing* over and above what one can steal – odd bits of silver and objects . . .

Must record the visit to the Tate last Monday. Parked 'the little white', and the Indian lady at reception made me wait, before a youngish assistant appeared and took me up a spiral staircase to the Director's landing. She studied me intently at one point and I thought, somehow, like a nurse looking at a patient going to theatre or surgeon for examination. In the curious white ultra-modernism reception room we sat down, and in a very short time I realised that Reid[1] was expecting me to ask more money for the Saltonstall (while I was apprehensive that he might be going to renege). So, lying, that I had been offered £100,000, ie £50,000, we went through the pretence of working out what I would save in CGT by selling to the Tate and settled at £48,000. On air I descended the spiral staircase and had a wonderful dinner at Brooks's,[2] lost £170 to Kennedy and then collapsed in bed.

Since then some misgivings and still has to go to Trustees for confirmation.

Saltwood   *Thursday, 19 February*

Delicious spring day, first hint of warmth in the sun after fog, and absolutely still. Dread the Tate trustees procrastinating. Walked round and round the battlements in an inner panic, thinking of this beautiful place, the sale, the whole collapse. Joined by Jane; didn't communicate it to her of course, but we continued to drift about absorbing the beauty of the place. This is real torture, let us hope it is the aversion therapy. Please God see me through this.

Dean's Yard   *Tuesday, 24 February*

Cleared to the extent of the Trustees confirming Saltonstall – so that will eliminate number 2 loan with Hoare's.

Albany, B5 Lower, 6am   *Friday, 5 March*

Woke early – as one does post Zurich and listened to the delight of blackbird singing. Terribly sad that with all my pressure and odious responsibilities I am cutting myself off even from nature. Got

---

[1] Sir Norman Reid, director of the Tate Gallery since 1964.

[2] The St James' Club had the previous year merged with Brooks's in St James's Street. Where the St James was 'cosmopolitan, artistic, boisterous', Brooks's was 'old-fashioned, almost Whiggish', according to the Brooks's historian.

cheque for Saltonstall, but felt sick opening envelope in the Commons' phone box. Kept thinking of the quality of the painting, the shock of the blank wall – I went into the Music Room on my return.

Albany, B5   *Friday, 19 March*

This morning woke absolutely *frantic* about being wiped out. Balance of Saltonstall consumed in serving interest charges of £8,750. Hoare's letter yesterday morning with firm refusal to release Castle deeds. Went to bed v. tired and woke with the knowledge that unless I can get the Saltwood deeds away from them *somehow* have got exactly six months left until next demand.

H of C Library   *Tuesday, 13 April*

Birthday boy. Woke several times in the night and with the glorious Albany blackbird looked from the mattress on the floor (my father has taken all the furniture) and this reinforced the dream of being wiped out. The bailiffs had been in and taken everything.

Fact is cash run out – nothing left to live on. Also 24 light to Hoare's limit, 44 light for release of Saltwood deeds. Get intermittent waves of panic – all my means of relieving indebtedness are in goods – supposing corporate collapse and nobody will *buy* goods?

Strange morning – picked up by Winston[1] in the lobby and asked to a lunch with him 'for' Averell Harriman; I think he said 'my stepfather' so may see Pam[2] again.

---

[1] Winston Churchill, MP for Stretford since 1970, married Caroline d'Erlanger in 1964; the marriage was dissolved in 1997.

[2] Pamela Harriman (née Digby) married first Randolph Churchill, by whom she had a son, Winston, MP for Stretford since 1970. She later married the American theatrical and film producer, Leland Hayward, and, following his death in 1971, the American statesman, Averell Harriman. She became a leading light in the Democratic Party, a legendary Washington hostess and US ambassador in Paris.

These ironies please me. But God please don't let me go right
under. How my health and appearance stood up to these stresses I
don't know.

Saltwood   *Tuesday, 20 April*

What could have been a grotesque weekend was lightened by
Desmond [Corcoran] agreeing to take another 34 of pictures and
then, on Thursday eve, came a call to say Newton had sold for 40!

Saltwood   *Saturday, 24 April*

'On the mend' physically, after really awful nights of muck-sweat,
minute tortured dribblings, and fear of galloping prostate cancer.

Albany, B5   *Tuesday, 4 May*

Another glorious morning. Does London have the finest weather
in England? Always look out of that little lavatory window behind
the Corinthian columns of the R.A.[1]
    I had walked into Chamber last night for a minute and stood by
Chair as Joel Barnett[2] was saying that 'Heritage Houses' can now
also have a fund to protect them, ie if only I can do my bit,
Saltwood Estate can be a candidate and passed on in perpetuity.
Rushed out and phoned Jane who said '. . . it makes it all seem
worthwhile'.

H of C Library   *Monday, 10 May*

Incredibly hot and stuffy, though sitting by open window. Today
(actually took place on Saturday) one of those lucky breaks –

---

[1] The Clark apartment at Albany backed on to the Royal Academy.
[2] Joel Barnett, MP for Heywood and Royton since 1964, Chief Secretary to the
Treasury since 1974.

tipped by George Hutchinson[1] for instant inclusion in 'shadow cabinet'. Suddenly felt fine, burgeoning.

Port Lympne   *Thursday, 3 June*

Drove over here to my favourite spot in the whole of E Kent – one of the most evocative in the world – and shortly to vanish for ever. I sit on the terrace where one would occasionally get tea <u>limone</u>, and indescribably thin cucumber sandwiches before being sent back up to 'Bellers'.[2] Can still look through the glass doors at that marbled, Moorish interior, black and white floors and arched ceilings. Totally still outside, but trees now grown enormously, hemming it in, better even than in Philip's heyday. The place has *slept* for 30 years, no one lived in it since Philip died, nothing disturbed. At any moment Philip could come out and call – to this day I can hear his drawl. And in time it will be over-run, damaged irretrievably by the tramping public with their toffee papers and the Kleenexes.[3]

As I pottered about at Saltwood this morning, realised hadn't been up to London for a week – so hadn't needed any cash. Yet cash dribbling in from public – if only 'indebtedness eliminated', could submit very happily. Will I ever emerge? I remember calmly going to Hoare's when it was 190 and trying to borrow *another* 20 to buy Selmes' car and business! Have got until October – or

---

[1] George Hutchinson, political columnist in *The Times*.

[2] Bellevue, known by the Clarks as 'Bellers', was close to Port Lympne, the magnificent country home of Sir Philip Sassoon, MP for Hythe and for much of the 1930s the highly influential Under-Secretary of State for Air and chairman of the board of the National Gallery (hence his original links with the Clark family). His mother was a Rothschild. To the designs of Sir Herbert Baker, he started building Port Lympne just before the First World War, lavishing upon it his enormous knowledge of art, furniture, china and old silver. He died in 1939 after a short illness and not yet sixty. Port Lympne was commandeered by the RAF during the Second World War.

[3] AC, happily, was proved wrong. He recommended Port Lympne to John Aspinall, who bought it and its 275 acres for £360,000. Aspinall restored the house and used the grounds for a zoo park to complement his original zoo near Canterbury.

possibly till next April (2nd half year interest) then – explosion. Unless 'House in order' first.

H of C   *Tuesday, 22 June*

Another glorious evening – every day has been fine, Friesian weather, except needless to say the two days of the weekend.

Sitting in a new perch I've discovered, theoretically allocated to a member of the staff and (tidily) congested with his gear, it is pleasingly situated in a corner, the last one before the non-smoking room, beside no fewer than three open windows, so that the lazy fresh river smells of wet varnish and tidal aromas come in together with the sounds of the chuggy engines of tugs and pleasure craft and the occasional guffaw from the terrace below.

Just a note from dinner at Saltwood for Norman Tebbit:[1] 'Many would like you as Folkestone's next MP . . .', one woman said. Jane, with her usual good sense just replied flatly: '. . . many wouldn't.' And certainly balance of that number hasn't necessarily shifted in my favour since being in 'Parly'.

Zermatt   *Saturday, 4 September*

Out here in poor shape. Really *alarmed* at appearance last night. Yet again trying the Zapata moustache, which adds to haggardness. What's the point? On arrival got letter from UBS in the C. Hoare and Co style wanting Sw FR 17,000 immediately, and this morning opened (quite by chance) something from La Suisse apparently noticing that house had not been insured since April and premium of 1,200 Sw overdue.

Also a little depressed about leaving James at home – as he is himself. Going through one of those phases – only gets excited when talking about aeroplanes – of which he is incredibly knowledgeable, better even than I was in 1939. Mercedes 300 car ran

---

[1] Norman Tebbit, MP for Chingford since 1974.

badly, roughly at best (though no Mercedes is ever completely perfect to drive). Sad? Next year will probably be in Citroen convertible. James rather gloomily said 'our cars get shabbier and shabbier'.

Zermatt   *Monday, 6 September*

Politically an autumn of application. Allotted three committees: finance, home affairs, defence.

Genuinely excited and keen to get back to the House. Ladbroke apparently giving *evens* on a coalition by 1st Jan. I *must* lay against that. Tories all chattering and yearning about an early election. Personally I don't see it. Why? How can it come about? PMs call elections when they think they are going to win, not in order to commit hari kari. But the gossip and *jockeying* will be fun.

Saltwood   *Sunday, 14 November*

Very nice last night and woken this morning about 8am by banging noises at main door. 'Lady Clark died last night'. Jane and I dressed quickly, hoping to beat Col. Found my father 'in tremendous form' wiping mouth with back of hand, having just eaten brown egg and grapefruit, little tray in library.

Spoke briefly and inconclusively, then next went in to see Mama, signalling to Jane *not* to come. Apprehensive about pulling back the sheet, but found her face composed, determined, rather beautiful, not in any way distorted (my father had quite unnecessarily, and alarmingly, said, '. . . the body does undergo certain changes by now . . . etc'). Jane came in, and as we agreed about her expression – Jane said 'she hasn't given up' – I started briefly crying and she also.

Went back to breakfast. Rang Celly and put her mind at rest about Mama's appearance. Then Col – he wouldn't come over. Changed into black and went up to Cenotaph on green where Jane meant to be laying wreath. Small crowd expected. Jane did her stuff quite well and I spoke to a few (prospective) constituents. Back, briefly to GH, where Father turned up, looking like death warmed up.

After spaghetti lunch snoozed on upright sofa in green room while Jane went over to GH to keep Celly company and (apparently) go through the jewellery. She ran back after an hour – I had woken, washed my face – with a very few insignificant items. We took a walk, much plagued as usual on Sundays by ogling, loutish public who won't say 'Good afternoon' even. After a good tea, Col arrived. We chatted a bit and I walked him up and down, explaining that he won't get anything, as my Father will block my mother's estate and leave his own to his new wife.[1] This made Col very gloomy (later that evening he rang and said he had spoken to Celly about the will and it was a c1971 model!).[2]

My father came over for dinner, shuffling but compos. Only drank 'a little claret', talked, but without much warmth. Wonder how long he will last? Rang Jamie late. He was a bit low, and made lower by news of Granny. Dear Boy, how I love him. God please protect us.

---

[1] AC was in no doubt that his father would remarry and soon.

[2] In a later note he added that he had just read his mother's last will (sent by the Clydesdale): 'She did leave everything to me . . . the fact that she did so is a tremendous liberation for me . . . the way in which she died fills us with grief and affection.'

1977

A YEAR OF TRAVAIL

Indebtedness:	Saltwood to Trust for Jane etc
	Pension Fund
Politics:	Pamphlet on law and order as CPC booklet
B'Gammon:	REDUCED RATION (£64 a week)
Girls:	Mens (presumably) – in cupo sano. Yoga
	[mens sana in corpore sana]

Zermatt   *Saturday, 1 January*

Sometimes gloomily see myself as Hemingway, 'Ernst' in Hochner book.[1] Best years gone by etc. But at least I don't drink. Seem, in fact, strangely, suspiciously fit and non-tired compared with dragged out days at the House.

What can I do about the House? This year I must have a go. It is impossible to get called. [Speaker] Thomas simply will *not* notice me.

I must –
(a) plan questions seriously. Defence. Home. Foreign. Europe. Chancellor. PM – all got edges. Now I have no excuse for lack of confidence, or fucking sarcasm for that matter.
(b) Sit in for every Question Time until Easter Recess.

This is last chance for 'impact'. It is 1977. Pretty bullish year, three books to write, and Saltwood to improve. Something's got to give and I suppose it will be b'gammon and sex – with the blondes away.

---

[1] A.E. Hotchner's *Papa Hemingway*, an account of the author's friendship with the American writer, had been widely acclaimed.

Saltwood Library   *Sunday, 16 January*

Eight days back and peculiar 'improvements'. Are they attributable
to that head or helmet that I bought at Christie's? Decided last
night that it was bringing me luck following Jane recounting to me
(on the phone on Tuesday night) her curious experience of hearing the Yellow Room door opening in the middle of the night and
lying frozen in terror. The next day she moved the head *into* the
Yellow Room thinking (quite rightly) that it might have been
trying to communicate. We both agreed how 'powerful' it is. And
who knows it might – there is no reason why not that I know –
have been here in the past.

What an incredible, marvellous, romantic place Saltwood is, and
how I am wedded to it. I must have a little *cache* at Zermatt just in
case, a few period things, a kind of mothball fleet in Northern
California or Canada, but my roots are here in this glorious piece
of English medieval history.

Albany, B5   *Thursday, 27 January*

There are few nicer things than sitting in bed, drinking up strong
Indian tea, and reading Chips' diaries – which loosen the mind,
and cause reflection. Just reached (or rather re-reached for the
umpteenth time) that passage when he has been caught out, and
Rab gone to Education, '. . . a bad mistake',[1] Chips thought,
wrongly, and how the Commons seemed to have changed focus.
But concerned to see that Chips of 44 felt himself alone and still
more by his reference to Richard Wood as Halifax's 'immense
auburn young subaltern'.[2]

---

[1] 18 July 1941: 'Winston offered him the Board of Education which he accepted
willingly. A mistake, I think, as he is now in a back-water' (*Chips: The Diaries of
Henry Channon*, edited by Robert Rhodes James).

[2] 14 September 1943. Wood, MP for Bridlington since 1950, was the second son
of Chamberlain's foreign secretary, Lord Halifax. He was wounded in action
later in 1943 and retired aged twenty-three.

Saltwood   *Sunday, 6 February*

Watched Enoch on TV – quite by chance. Jane spotted that he had already been on for fifteen minutes. Quite wonderful. His clarity of speech and thought, his administrative experience, his living and incomparable patriotism and they ignore him.

Billy Wallace died of cancer . . . aah.[1]

H of C   *Tuesday, 29 March*

Spoke in the House last night about Air Raid Shelters (there aren't any) and frightened myself. Sat down to deafening silence. Plymouth crumbling. Will I get Folkestone? Old and grey-looking.

To add to the burden – Stradling Thomas suggested I maintained an anti P-R group in the parliamentary party. Must start catching the eye. Breathe deeply.

Saltwood   *Monday, 4 April*

My father over last night and grumpily teasing about his will – left James 'the clock' which is in Great Hall study and belongs to me anyway!

Albany   *Thursday, 28 April*

Had interview yesterday with Margaret Thatcher for first time. She sat, china-blue. Almost *too* text-book sincere. No intimacy. The half-finished sentences, the implied assumption, that mixture of Don, Colonel-of-the-Regiment, 'Library', which one gets from almost every other member of the Shadow – Pym, Willie,[2]

---

[1] Billy Wallace, the millionaire son of Euan Wallace, a former MP and wartime adviser to George VI, and part of Princess Margaret's circle from the 1950s. He and AC had known each other since Eton.

[2] William (Willie) Whitelaw, MP for Penrith since 1955.

Gilmour – even the lower rank like Paul Channon[1] and William Clark[2] – totally absent.

Actually the *point* of my call, which at one time had looked so promising, was to explain that the anti-PR strength would *not* be adequate as the Labourites would not join us in the lobby. 'Only 130, Alan, what worries me . . .' 'Another 80 with you, of course,' I said and mumbled.

I also slightly fluffed it when she was talking about Callaghan's soft-centre – good for publicity, but inadequate underneath. Instead of saying 'like Heseltine', I mumbled something about 'I could mention a few like that in our party'. She looked startled. There were silences and she mentioned Defence – I half got going when we were interrupted.

H of C   *Tuesday, 21 June*

Summertime in the Library of the House; could go to bed early after some sherrys and white wine and sleep 14 hours – but instead, faced with 'until this business is concluded, which could be at a very late hour . . .' so further harrowing of the body.

Still shampoo'd my hair at Albany after an All-bran box there on return from a day out to Seend. Oh how Cherry Cottage has been exposed, its character altered, by the loss of the Great Elms in the clump. I pottered about in the orchard, *recherché du temps perdu* as always at Seend, thinking of the high spots – my happiest period.

Had my triumph in the House last week – getting both sides to laugh at my 'quip' as the *Telegraph* called it about 'anyone who has been to Eton . . . has already served the equivalent of five years in gaol.'[3] A piccolo triumph, *prolonged* laughter with people leaning

---

[1] Paul Channon, son of 'Chips', succeeded his father as MP for Southend West in 1959; deputy leader of the Conservative delegation to the Western European Union and the Council of Europe since 1976.

[2] William Clark, MP for Croydon South since February 1964 (E. Surrey, 1970–74), joint deputy chairman, Conservative Party Organisation since 1975.

[3] To which Merlyn Rees, the home secretary, replied: 'There is one difference – in prison they learn to read and write.'

down the benches to congratulate me, and so on. A little H of C
moment.

Albany, B5   *Tuesday, 12 July*

Ex-morning tea and reasonably euphoric – though *mouvementé*.

Must record the drive back in THEBUS, splendid on Auto-
route and Alp alike, even though grossly loaded with dear 'Boy's'
kit, stereo etc. The great, unusual heat of the Le Rosey[1] garden
party (certain shades of Verdon Hill in *Hemlock and After*[2]) with
Boy going round getting his book signed by his chums . . . 'See
you . . . keep in touch . . . etc etc . . .' The dress standard bum-
boys. David Niven[3] *very* well preserved. Certain beautifully-
dressed beauties.

Back at Saltwood, Le Rosey inflections already fading, though
having given him, as he rightly said after going into Blades on his
own, total confidence.

The week was, of course, the week of the heatwave. I say 'of
course' because I was locked into the standing committee on Bill
Benyon's Abortion Bill. Curtains drawn to shield us from the
sun, endlessly Zombie-like, eating the occasional rock-cake in the
corridor or muck-sweating making phone calls from the little, very
open phone there.

At night sleeping, perhaps too much absentee sleeping, in
committee room 7 where I had found a tiny curved leather
armchair, and putting two others in a row could make a sort of
couch. Woken in the night by muffled bangings and clatterings
and at dawn found that Dr Jeremy Bray, of wealth tax fame (he
appeared to be suffering from hay fever)[4] had built up a camp bed

---

[1] Le Rosey, the oldest private school in Switzerland with pupils from all over the
 world, and, uniquely, two campuses, at Le Rolle for spring and autumn, and at
 Gstaad for winter.

[2] Angus Wilson's 1952 novel.

[3] David Niven, the actor, lived in Switzerland and had daughters at the school.

[4] Jeremy Bray, MP for Motherwell since October 1974 (Middlesbrough West,
 1962–70).

in the corner. Every two hours or so we were roused by the amiable but somewhat limited poison-dwarf Ian Campbell (Lab)[1] 'on whip' who kept going on whisky.

Saltwood   *Saturday, 27 August*

C. Hoare & Co letter this morning – always sent to spoil one's weekend. Debts now total £80,000 AGAIN.

Reading David Irving's brilliant, stylish but scholarly biography of Hitler.[2] I remember in that curious white living room of his flat with all its files and things the only time we met when he told me – 'there won't be a dry eye at the end of my next book'. Certainly I find it very unsettling.

Albany   *Saturday, 12 November*

Saturday morning, a pre-breakfast, post 'Chips', waiting to catch the 11.30 – is there one on a Saturday morning in winter? *Oh* how these fucking Plymouth things drain one (as Heseltine warned me they would). As I sit here now, decided finally to make the announcement almost immediately after the next election that will not stand again there. This should give me three minimum more years without these pressures. Catch is, what if Albert [Costain] makes last-minute announcement *this* time. Personally I don't think he will, is chattily delivered to become deputy speaker or something.[3]

On Sunday we were committed, somewhat reluctantly, to go to the Dedication of Standards service and general ceremonies in Hythe (British Legion). Actually it was lovely. Uplifting service – brilliant address by new vicar of St Leonards: 'Old men dream

---

[1] Ian Campbell, MP for Dunbartonshire West since 1970.

[2] *Hitler's War* had just been published.

[3] Albert Costain, MP for Folkestone since 1959. In fact Costain fought another election (1979) and only retired from Folkestone in 1983. His successor was none other than Michael Howard (see entry 12 May 1972).

dreams; young men see visions', and he recited the names off the monuments and then the battle honours. Afterwards to the new BL hall – a piece of cake, as I said to Jane. The sort of thing one would have sat eight hours in the Plymouth train to do and all one had to do is to climb back into the Land-Rover and drive for five minutes!

Saltwood   *Sunday, 4 December*

I took the train down to Plymouth, where it was mildly cold and was glad of the Winter Car, MoT'd by Mumford. I was late getting to the Duke – no time for a bath – for the CPC dinner.

I wasn't absolutely happy about it from the start. A little red wine (I drank as much as I could of this). Of course I spotted immediately the shit one – something about each ward electing a representative to liaise between the Member and his constituents. I 'good-naturedly' suggested that it should be discussed at the F&GP or the Executive. The session rumbled on, after a bit getting somewhat perilously philosophical with my talking about the Conservative being the party of appeasement, and 'declaring' for the National Front – I got *so* irritated by Kay Mansfield trying to say we were going to lose votes to the NF – 'there won't be a candidate against me,' I said. She still didn't get the point. '. . . because they know I'm the nearest thing they're ever likely to get to an MP.'

Will I just be able to hold out through till the election? Yes, probably, because I have (a) recourse to a special meeting (b) threat of standing against as anti-common market/NF.

Albany   *Friday, 9 December*

Been v depressed these last few days. So much to do. My briefcase goes back and forth on the train, stuffed and gasping with endless little folded bits of paper many of them, I don't doubt, dealing with engagements and grievances that I am missing and ducking.

Real sadness is that some of the *taste* is going from things I like. This is a sign of age. Saltwood itself, early morning tea, the cars. Only the House retains its unique appeal, the Chamber, the tea-room, good company at dinner (as last night with Gow and Straubenzee[1]).

Duke of Cornwall Hotel, Plymouth   *Saturday, 10 December*

John Dobell[2] calling for special meeting of Executive Council to 'question me about my attitude to the National Front.' Gach!

---

[1] Ian Gow, MP for Eastbourne since February 1974. William van Straubenzee, MP for Wokingham since 1959.
[2] John Dobell, sometime chairman of the Sutton Conservative Association and chief whip of the Conservative group on Plymouth City Council.

Frightful pain in arm and wrist – those evening attacks are now the norm though, touch wood, nights are not so bad.

Rang 'Boy' and not too happy about him. In fact, there's a good 'Boy' scare building up: he was talking 'yeh man' to such an extent that I had to reprimand him – 'don't use that "y'know" interjection . . .' etc. He was cross at the prospect of coming back to go to the Rolls-Royce school (I thought I was so clever in getting him into an early vacancy there after their putting one off until July) – but for the first time, particularly when signing off, his voice lacked that special spontaneous affection – 'God bless you too', which I can still hear him say when he was at Rosey even, and in other places.

Rang Jane immediately, and of course she remembered it too from *her* conversation with him last Sunday. The gulf had opened. 'We've become parents,' I said, instead of family, elder bro or sister. I might be wrong. He might recover, snap out of it. Oh dear I said (speaking to Jane), 'much love to Tip.' Good old Tip . . . 'I know what you *mean*,' she said. 'Oh dear, let's hear no more.' God, how I wish that we could.

Perhaps I'm being punished for my total indifference to my poor father's plight (into Sister Agnes today for a prostatectomy, and still under the anaesthetic).

Just back from Oxford after talked to small – later grew larger – audience of Monday Club in upstairs room at Union. Kept thinking of Saltwood, Jane and all's well and almost immediately the sudden pain of the realising Jane in Spain (Bertie[1] died last night), and Tip

---

[1] Jane's father.

quite alone with Nanny. No warmth, no decent food then. Got to
see my father tomorrow. Apparently he is 'somewhat muddled', and
already overshadowed by Nolwen, who has grey water.[1]

Saltwood   *Sunday, 29 January*

General condition no better. Concentration and creative ability
much inhibited, also my *cold hand*. I love this damp new weather,
don't object to it at all, but no strength to do anything.

Did at least get over the hurdle of the Executive Council
meeting where Radford Ward (who else?) were to raise the question of my attitude to the National Front. It was one of those
evenings that might have gone nasty if I had played along with
their rules, ie let myself get into a flap and on the defensive. There
was a slight – no, more than slight – atmosphere of lion-taming, if
not witch-hunt. Fortunately I had got there in time to get my
'pulls' of the 'report-back' leaflet from the printer and these
distributed on people's chairs so could first 'defuse' the situation
by referring to these.

Earlier, at my surgery, two real NF members had come in, for a
chat. And I thought how good they were, and how brave is the
minority, in a once great country, who still keep alive the tribal
essence.

Met Boy at the station last night, and quite marvellous he
looked in his belted Kardigan bought that morning at 'Drakes'
and having globally travelled back by Swissair, bronzed and strong.
But the fact is, he's 'gone'. This year he's suddenly discovered his
independence, all in a total rush, far more than at Rosey, or more
than the time we left him behind at Zermatt. He wants to go back
there and then to South Africa where he thinks he will make his
fortune (I have to keep stopping to hold my hand to warm it up –
shades of Gavin Maxwell)[2] and so one has accepted this – I don't,

---

[1] Nolwen, Countess de Janzé, who had married Lord Clark the previous year.
[2] The author Gavin Maxwell (*Ring of Bright Water*) suffered endless symptoms of
ill-health, including circulatory problems.

can't, any longer allow myself to fuss all the time that he's out and away and so on. I mean at this moment he's driving up to London in the Datsun, and formerly I'd have been scared stiff; now I'm just numb.

Saltwood   *Sunday, 12 February*

I just said to Jane – 'will there ever be a moment, a long lazy tranquil moment when lying in a chaise-longue (by a slip of the tongue I said wheel-chair) I can laughingly read through these terrible gloomy winter entries?'

'Not till you retire from Parliament,' she said.

'But what if I have to retire from ill-health?'

Saltwood   *Thursday, 23 February*

Had a bad night and rang Jane for Peter Morrison's 'new' osteopath – 'Johnnie Johnson' – thought, give him a try. Fighting a latent cold with Redoxon. Tracked him down at his block of flats at Peckham. He's an American (baldish) and in one of those Dr Kildare half white jackets. A very long session in which he produced every magical 'click' and a great deal of flannel. One very effective double-click of the neck side-ways. Lizard-eyes, wouldn't look one in the face.

Had a bath after the 11 o'clock vote and an intermittent night – fraught with anxiety at total seizing up again. Johnson had diffused the pain, but not reduced its intensity potential. Felt really awful this morning. Twice (once at Albany, once after getting to House) seriously thought of ringing Jane, getting her to come up to drive me down.

Later

I see my father and Nolwen taking a walk, and see myself in the main – 'waxen-facedly lying and inoperable.'

Please please God make me better soon.

Bratton   *Saturday, 18 March*

A sad melancholy – accentuated by accumulated fatigue.

I went to see Rowntree [London doctor] on Tuesday. 'You're playing your last card' said Jane, smiling; saw him at 6pm after a *very* bad day, stab pains, longish bouts of 'nerves' 99° temperature etc. He very splendid and calming, confirmed Beth's[1] diagnosis of 'bronchial nevritis' and prescribed heavily, saying if not better in 10 days – take a month off(!).

Felt better at once, of course, and went and bombed at Brooks's; two v. good days. Yesterday had to drive down from London via Plymouth on constituency matters and today very sleepy and aching and *looking awful* with the vile and ludicrous Primrose Ball hanging over us. Had felt so good that seriously contemplated Zermatt for Easter – but today not so sure, as deep, though remote, shoulder ache and cold had shown that all was not well. For the first time in the mirror, *qualitative* changes – most notably shape of body and shoulders (positively remedial) and hair at side – frizzled and sprouting, not sleek.

Depressed too, by something Rowntree said about Mama's 'awful last illness' – and suddenly realised she had committed suicide – hence all the notes and the tidy way it was done. Presumably got the medicine to do it via Kathy or what, I don't know. So even that last sneer was unjustified.

On the Thursday in the Commons realised that I was being virtually ignored. 'Messed alone' at dinner and watched Marcus Kimball[2] being dined at Humphrey Atkins' table. That serene corporate instinct which the House unfailingly exercises acknowledged fact that since return (ie Christmas) I have done NOTHING.

---

[1] Beth Evans-Smith, friend and physiotherapist.
[2] Marcus Kimball, MP for Gainsborough since 1956.

Saltwood   *Saturday, 25 March*

This evening feeling not too bad 'in myself', took 2CV down to St
Leonards to see when Easter Services and if possibility of a really
early communion. Church empty, though warm and light. Walked about, read prayers, said a brief contemplative prayer. Realised
that at 50 *must* have 'affairs in order', a conference at which I can
explain whole thing to Jane and James and Andrew. Especially <u>no</u>
<u>o/d</u>. Why do I still shrink from this?

Saltwood   *Friday, 7 April*

'Supervising' darling Jane clearing out the pool today. Will I ever
again bronzedly be leaping in and out?

H of C Library   *Tuesday, 2 May*

Jane at Saltwood, nursing Angus's wound.[1] He had his tumour
removed today poor darling. Why does a tumour form? And he
was so well and fine. Why have the operation? Will we be faced
with this dilemma? So many decisions and commitments. And
time, it seems, so terribly constrained.

Saltwood   *Sunday, 7 May*

Last night 'Boy' stayed in and played the piano and the organ.
Remembered his playing the organ in the pink room at Seend. At
one point woke in the night with a start and noted it was his last
night and full day at home before going to South Africa.[2] Monday
is a hellish day for me – when do I say goodbye to Jamie?

---

[1] Angus, the Clarks' black labrador.
[2] James was to dive on the wreck of the *Sacramento*.

East Cloisters   *Wednesday, 17 May*

'Painkilling drugs' a thing of the past. Can slump in chairs, as normal; can double-click fingers of right hand; today for the first time not cold hand first thing this morning.

House Library   *Wednesday, 14 June*

Wonderfully well-feeling; colonial appearance (weight to new 'high' of 11.6½).

Albany   *Thursday, 22 June*

At PM's Q's John Wells,[1] unexpectedly sitting on the 'Baronets' Bench', asked me bluntly if I wanted Maidstone after he'd gone. Said yes and he replied he could fix it. Would have been on air in previous times, but now . . . Especially after seeing what happened to Robin Cooke.[2] Still it allows one a little more peace of mind.

Plymouth train [start of recess]   *Friday, 4 August*

Really loathe Plymouth now, but can't chuck as less likely to get Folkestone due to age, passage of time.

Trouble is I just adore the House of Commons. I am seduced by its gossipy, club-like regimental atmosphere and love also the delicious karate-type confidence that being an MP gives me. Last night, called in to collect my razor and already the whole place in sepulchral hibernating gloom – just a few dim chandeliers and 'revealed' lights. Everything locked. Did a quick phone-call to Jane from the cheekie-chappie phone in the twilit Members' Lobby and thought how no life will be throbbing here until 24 October and

---

1 Wells, MP for Maidstone since 1959. AC was right to take the offer ...ically as Wells did not finally resign until 1987.

2 Cooke, MP for Bristol West, 1957–79, but his plan to move to Dorset was shattered when the constituency selected Lord Cranborne.

how much I shall miss it. Two attendants (dim flat-capped sort) emerged from the gloom and flashed their backs on me.

Saltwood   *Sunday, 27 August*

Only four more days of the season left. Saltwood looking incredible, practically never better with the new Atco [mower] definitely on top of the lawn. Still not really *relaxing*.

Politics dead – tho' election coming in time to save my bacon. Will probably not get a job with MT if the Tories win at all, still doubtful.

Zermatt   *Sunday, 3 September*

Early part of journey blighted by darling Jane very peaky and low about George[1] – who, I was privately convinced, must be dead – missing since breakfast the day before we left, and reported that evening down at the garage by the Military Canal! However, on arrival rang Mrs C, who said he had been brought back by 'Monty' (small world) who had a little boy called 'George' and had called for him that evening, and George had appeared!

Saltwood   *Sunday, 10 September*

Back last night after two very pleasant days driving across France. Delicious dinner in clip joint ** restaurant at Arbois. The Chapron went beautifully – being pressed in the last stage at continuous 160–170kph and running out of petrol, legally, in the customs shed at Calais.

Then, deterioration: missed 7 o'clock boat. Customs kept us waiting an hour and was foiled of a row by being let straight

---

[1] George was a tame jackdaw, not the first, or the last, to adopt Saltwood. were usually reared by the Clarks after falling from their nests as chicks.

through. Arrived extremely shocked to find George [the jackdaw] had 'gone on Friday'.

Morning wet and windy. No sign of George.

Albany   *Wednesday, 20 September*

Walked through St James' Park to the House of Commons to pick up the Chev and make some phone calls I did reflect how very lucky I am to be a member of the Privileged Classes, and how *filthily* (in Michael's[1] phrase) 90% of the rest of the population still live.

Plymouth train   *Tuesday, 3 October*

Letter from some member of the Conservative Assoc asking if Margaret T could come down and do a walkabout in Plympton St Mary's to put it on the map!

Saltwood 'winter office'   *Saturday, 14 October*

A certain delicious freedom about having forsaken b'gammon (presently owe Brooks's £888) and been chucked by the blondes.

Saltwood   *Monday, 23 October*

Last night George came back via a call from the train-driver's house after he had been trying to get into their children's window (his wife, as I always suspected, being extremely pretty). Althou' sleek he is very subdued and today was hardly off his 'perch' on top of the open kitchen door all day. Incredible, though, that he is still

---

[1] Michael Briggs – old friend from Oxford days.

alive and that, however torpid, he did make a bid for freedom, do hope one can rehabilitate him.

Saltwood   *Friday, 24 November*

Some shoulder pain and *cold hand*, but this morning a fabulous experience. Flew again with James, in the little '150' as one climbed high over Rye I could see Rye Harbour, the little boats, and the garage that used to be the 'Big' garden, and then we climbed high – into the clouds, a range of strato-cumulus like 'over Italy' from Trockener Steg. Fantastic beautiful moving experience as great cloud valleys rushed past and towering cliffs loomed over us . . . To think that my son, whom I used to kiss goodnight in his cot in that little room, was now piloting me in this fairyland.

On the way back, my mind miles away on 'George', James suddenly said/shouted, 'Daddy, what are you doing!' and I rammed some cheeky red-coloured, but new Peugeot 104 from behind, seconds later a Yank in a blue Ford ran into us! And what's more I'm in the Chapron!!! Set-back. It must go back to Chapron that's all. Darling Jane took it very calmly, but I was shattered – old person accident – also wondered about whether I might have aggravated my 'whiplash' injury.

Saltwood   *Sunday, 10 December*

I still haven't honoured my part of the bargain with God – to acknowledge and research defence book if George came back. Only God could have sent him back in that curious indirect way that didn't quite betoken a miracle, and yet, the more one thinks of it . . .

Saltwood   *Wednesday, 27 December*

Saying goodbye to James, off to California – mislaid his passport!

Saltwood   *Saturday, 24 February*

Back from Plymouth. More or less decided to 'go quickly'. But at breakfast when I told Jane she didn't reply – ominous. When I tackled her with this she said: 'I thought you always said "Never resign".' Yes, quite right, I did.

All the same, as the prospect of losing the House re-appears I am shocked and appalled by how little I have done, how much opportunity I have wasted these last four years.

Albany   *Friday, 9 March*

I've got £83,000 in my bag! Quite literally draft for 65 on Cézanne deal and 18 from Paymaster for NPG portraits.[1] Now we never thought we'd get here again. I'm also aware that it is net figure only. Must add up liabilities/debts and reduce all. Then work things out to see how to distribute assets.

Albany   *Wednesday, 14 March*

Savoured today the first pleasure of writing a 'surprised-not-to-have-heard-from-you' note to C. Hoare & Co who I had written to a week ago asking for exact figures with which to pay off my overdraft. Dropped it in by hand on way back from cigar-plus lunch.

---

[1] Portraits and sketches of AC's father by Graham Sutherland.

Saltwood   *Monday, 26 March*

Getting deeds back from Hoare's *is* within my grasp now.

Plymouth train   *Friday, 30 March*

Loathe election prospect [3 May]. Slight doubt about adoption meeting, even, but presumably will be ok. Filthy to be away from the estate and dear George also will pine and whose features I want to get shining and give some fresh air to. I think a lot about George, and love the way he taps on his box when I am on the phone; he even hears my voice right down the passage and into the Green Room.

'Boy' going to Pirbright[1] on 17 April, the day the campaign starts in earnest. This preferable, I think, to Army Air Corps, but involves US trip in summer (expensive and dangerous). Dear 'Boy' is so ravishing looking and maddening and engaging. Jane and I agreed on the phone that all we can do is grin-and-bear-it. Become dear old ga-gas.

Key factor, though, is elimination of dandruff.

Saltwood   *Friday, 6 April*

Tory lead now down to 6%. Realise it will be gradually whittled away and will lose my seat or the majority halved.

Bratton   *Friday, 13 April (Birthday boy)*

Calmer than might be expected at this 'break' in the campaign, but out here, almost resigned to humiliation at polls (must admit not relishing the re-count!). Wouldn't mind all *that* much just being a stately-home owner.

Being 51 makes me feel quite lecherous.

---

[1] Headquarters of the army training regiment of the Brigade of Guards.

That evening: a lovely relaxed day at Bratton – cleaning windows and paint and planning to revive it substantially, possibly to 'full Bloomsbury'.[1] Only relief in current gloom, Jack the baker, saying sing-song, 'all grown up, all grown up, gone away' about the boys.

Saltwood   *Easter Sunday, 15 April*

Saltwood 'smiling'. Tortoises all woke up, tipped their box over and were released in Courtenays. My 'eye' (left-side) a little suspect. Irritated and slightly stye-borne, but otherwise fine and randy. Gloom about beloved 'Boy'. On the phone last night he recounted how his Zermatt friend in the Scots Guards had just come out of Pirbright and told him how hateful it was; '4 hours sleep, and people paid to be nasty to you . . .'

This gave me a bad night. Cheered up a bit in the morning and thought 'what is written is written.' In the sunlight evening gloom of the 'formal' part of the Castle, I still get these terrible forebodings: Kipling and his son at Loos, Weld-Smith, even, of Seend Manor and his son on Blenheims.

Also filled with loathing of the Electorate. Those filthy carriages on the trip down yesterday which annoyed Jane so much, is the nation completely rotten? Yes, and has been since 1916. In the war we were saved by the middle classes who flew the Spitfires and manned the cruisers and frigates.

Saltwood   *Easter Monday, 16 April*

In a state of *désoeuvré* apprehension. My R eye now irritating definitely; would worry over this, but must get election out of the way (very depressed about this, Labour bound to win – at least in Plymouth, it seems). Still foremost worry is darling 'Boy' going in

---

[1] The Clarks did in fact turn Bratton into a miniature Charleston. After the house was sold in 1998 the Bloomsbury doors were returned to Saltwood.

tomorrow to the Pirbright crusher. A little soft-spoken about his coming ordeal. He may be going deliberately to 'flunk'. I don't know. It would be fabulous if he can get through and the world would be his oyster; but in a way thank God for the election to take my mind off it, otherwise I would be worrying non-stop.

This really will be the last entry until after the (re) count. Yeh yeh!

The general election on 3 May
Conservative: 339; Labour: 269; Liberal: 11; Others: 16

Saltwood   *Monday, 7 May*

Mrs Thatcher (or Mrs Carrington, as Papa amusingly – muddledly – called her) has announced her Cabinet, and I'm not in, any-where. Don't specially mind, though resentful of Pattie being in so high up and Hayhoe[1] (of all people) getting the Army. Wouldn't take a PPS or couldn't take 'disabled' or 'energy'. Lovely to have freedom of the Commons, consolidated at Plymouth,[2] and the summer before us.

But particularly bad-tempered and martyred, so in essence a little schizophrenic, I suppose. No one has been in touch. Where are the blondes? Did they send the 'AC rules OK' telegram, must have? But where are they? Sod them too.

Saltwood   *Saturday, 9 June*

One more little notch on James' separation – last night was the first ever that he has been in England and we didn't know where he was.

---

[1] Geoffrey Pattie, Parliamentary Under-Secretary of State, RAF; Barney Hayhoe, MP for Brentford and Isleworth since February 1974 (Heston and Isleworth, 1970–74) the same but for the army.
[2] Sutton result: AC, 28,892 votes; Priestley (Labour), 17,605; Scannell (Liberal), 6,225; AC majority: 11,287.

Folkestone Station   *Tuesday, 26 June*

Late for case (when it was expected I would lose my licence) as went to old court, and back to new one. In the little interview room I suddenly realised that I might lose it for a little while. However when I entered the court the Clerk of the Court said: one of the magistrates is known to you, have you any objection? . . . eh! 'None whatever,' I replied delightedly. And in due time, *very* narrowly, she declared that there were *special circumstances* which allowed them not to disqualify.

Albany   *Friday, 20 July*

Headache on side of head – right. Is it John Davies[1] or toothache?

House of Commons   *Thursday, 15 November*

The House got stuck into one of those days which follow long periods of torpor and ennui that conform to Fred Hoyle's theory of the concatenation of the Universe. We had, more or less simultaneously, the Chancellor's announcement of a 17 per cent bank rate i.e. 21 per cent overdrafts and a clutch of publicity-seeking Labour MPs each trying to beat the other to the draw (Dennis Skinner, I am glad to say, just beat Christopher Price.[2] The two were standing together and Skinner made it on a 'Point of Order') raising the matter of Anthony Blunt's treachery.[3] This was a lucky break for Geoffrey [Howe][4] because the whole Blunt affair

---

[1] John Davies, MP, former Conservative minister who suffered a brain tumour and died on 4th July 1979.

[2] Christopher Price, MP for Lewisham West since February 1974 (Birmingham Perry Bar, 1966–70).

[3] Anthony Blunt, former Surveyor of Pictures to George VI and Queen Elizabeth II, had been unmasked as the 'Fourth Man' in the group of Cambridge spies (Maclean, Burgess, Philby, etc.) who betrayed Britain to the Soviet Union.

[4] Geoffrey Howe, MP for Surrey East since 1974 (Bebington, 1964–66; Reigate, 1970–74), Chancellor of the Exchequer since the general election after four years as opposition Treasury spokesman.

diverted attention from the really alarming manner in which our economy seems to be conducted. He came to the '22' committee and the atmosphere was mildly critical. I asked the question which, perhaps fortunately, the Speaker had not called me to ask at the time of the statement – namely if we had really cut public expenditure then we would not need such devastatingly high interest rates.

House of Commons   *Wednesday, 21 November*

Ian Gow[1] is a very assiduous attender of Committees. In the last two days I have noticed him at the special meeting of the Finance Committee when the Chancellor came to explain the MLR increase, at the Legal Committee when the Attorney General was defending the Protection of Information Act, at the Home Affairs Committee immediately afterwards when the Blunt affair was being discussed and tonight he was at the regular meeting of the Finance Committee when Gordon Pepper[2] addressed them.

By chance I had taken tea alone in one of the armchairs at the far end of the Members' Tea Room instead of convivially at the table. This was because I was exhausted having spent the latter part of the afternoon tramping the streets of Battersea looking for a garage 'with flat over' for the coven. I was reading the financial columns of the *Guardian*, which contained a critique of a speech made by Pepper the previous day to the Society of Investment Analysts.

It is always nice to have a crib and I decided, unusually for me, to attend the Finance Committee that evening. Forearmed (the piece was by Hamish McRae[3]) I was able to ask him a penetrating question about the way in which the recent gilt sales by the Bank had been bungled. So penetrating was it that he became flustered, asked several times if we were off-the-cuff, looked around the room in an exaggeratedly conspiratorial way etc. I noticed Ian rise

---

[1] Ian Gow, MP for Eastbourne since February 1974, and parliamentary private secretary to Margaret Thatcher since May 1979.

[2] Gordon Pepper, noted member of the monetarist priesthood. Senior partner in Greenwells and gilt-edge expert.

[3] Hamish McRae, financial editor of the *Guardian* since 1975.

from this seat and pad silently around the outer perimeter of the crowded Committee table . . . I did not look round although everybody watches Ian wherever he goes because it is thought (rightly or wrongly – I suspect wrongly) that the Prime Minister confides in him and values his opinion.

He stopped behind my chair and tapped me very lightly on the shoulder bending forward and, speaking almost inaudibly, asked if I would come and have dinner. We left immediately, and as everybody watched us go out I was reminded of Oliver Lyttelton's[1] story about the French broker who had done one of the Rothschilds a good turn and asked him for a tip on the Bourse. Rothschild said, 'I never give tips, but what I will do is walk across the floor in your company.' This experience was repeated when we went briefly to the Smoking Room. At the corner table by the bar sat Ted Heath, bolt upright in a dinner jacket and having (apparently) had a special snow rinse on his hair which he now wears *en brosse*.

We drove to the Cavalry Club in the green Bentley and Ian ordered copious quantities of Tio Pepe, white Burgundy, Claret etc. I was soon surrounded by a number of half full glasses which I had no intention of emptying. He told me how the Prime Minister and the Treasury team were anxious that no real cuts in public spending had yet been made. He said she was out-numbered three to one in the cabinet. Eighteen were mutely or vociferously hostile.

Later

Sat through the Blunt debate (why in hell was Rhodes James[2] called *first* from the back benches to propound his mouldy clichés). At 9.03pm – with everybody comfortably settled down for the wind-ups I rose – alone – and was called.

A crowded House, a *full* House! And the PM leaning forward in what Ian [Gow] calls the 'Blue Peter' position. I put my questions – none of them particularly welcome – and, regrettably, applauded more from the Labour benches. But without an exception (the –

---

[1] Oliver Lyttelton (created 1st Viscount Chandos, 1954), member of Churchill's war cabinet, industrialist and first chairman of the National Theatre Board.

[2] Robert Rhodes James, historian and biographer, MP for Cambridge since 1976.

unsolicited – joke that anyone who knows anything about the KGB will verify that the Russian controllers in Kensington change every two years) I got a good feeling. The first time that Margaret T has heard me speak since she turned round and looked at me during my 'maiden'. Technique improved since then.

House of Commons   *Tuesday, 27 November*

I was talking to Tony Royle, eminently sensible, never seen him in a flap (ex SAS, I think).[1] But he can be very forthright, no words minced. 'Look at the people round here,' he said. 'Carrington[2] – hates her; Prior[3] – hates her; Gilmour – hates her; Heseltine[4] – hates her; Walker – loathes her, makes no secret of it; Willie – completely even-handed, would never support her against the old gang; Geoffrey Howe – no personal loyalties – durable politburo man, will serve under anyone. The only people committed to Margaret are Angus Maude, John Biffen and Keith Joseph[5] and the last two are so tortured intellectually as to cast doubt on their stability in a crisis.'

I paraphrase his analysis, but it brought home to one how precarious her position is and what a disaster was the assassination of Airey Neave[6] whose subtlety and insight would have helped to out-manoeuvre these quislings. Royle pointed out that the real danger would be that a mass sacking or resignation of the old guard

---

[1] Anthony Royle, MP for Richmond since 1959. He had served in the Life Guards at the very end of the war, ending up in the 21st Special Air Service regiment (TA), 1948–51.

[2] Lord Carrington, Tory grandee. Foreign Secretary since the general election.

[3] James Prior, MP for Lowestoft since 1959, now Secretary of State for Employment.

[4] Michael Heseltine had been Secretary of State for the Environment since the general election.

[5] Angus Maude, Paymaster-General; John Biffen, MP for Oswestry since 1961, and now Chief Secretary to the Treasury under Howe; Sir Keith Joseph, MP for Leeds North-East since 1956 and now Secretary of State for Industry.

[6] On 30 March 1979, the day after the announcement of the general election that would bring the Conservatives back to power, the party's Northern Ireland spokesman, and a close confidant of Margaret Thatcher, was murdered in the Palace of Westminster by a car bomb; the INLA, a republican splinter group, claimed responsibility.

heavies (nominally arising out of 'attitudes' to incomes policy or enforcement of measures disciplining a recalcitrant union) would create an alternative Cabinet and one which would naturally be expected to open its doors to the ageing, sulky, shapeless but still expectant Edward Heath. And that with such weight and so many 'names' it was a danger that more than half the Parliamentary Party might be drawn off to fill their wagons. Margaret would be left with a few young (and presumably discredited) monetarists such as Nott and Lawson[1] and a rabble of African Rightists, Hastings, Winterton[2] and the '92'.[3]

House of Commons   *Thursday, 6 December*

Last night I spoke, again, on the protectionist theme. And intervened to make my point. Again 'exposed' before Mrs T! These days I interrupt with total confidence. But must be careful not to become an Adley[4] (ie discounted before he even opens his mouth).

---

[1] John Nott, MP for St Ives (Cornwall) since 1966 and now Secretary of State for Trade; Nigel Lawson, MP for Blaby since February 1974, and now Financial Secretary to the Treasury under Geoffrey Howe.

[2] Stephen Hastings, MP for Mid-Bedfordshire since 1960; Nicholas Winterton, MP for Macclesfield since 1971.

[3] The '92' took its name from the London home (92 Cheyne Walk) of its first chairman, Sir Patrick Wall, MP for Haltemprice since 1954, with the main aim of keeping the Conservative Party conservative. Margaret Thatcher dined with the committee in 1978 and in her first government she appointed six of its members, most notably Norman Tebbit.

[4] Robert Adley had been MP for Bristol North-East since 1970. He went on to hold the seat for Christchurch and Lymington from 1974.

Saltwood   *Sunday, 27 January*

Back a fortnight – it seems like three months!

Saltwood   *Sunday, 3 February*

Anthony Buck[1] and John Wells down for the weekend with their wives. Hospitality was lavish – too lavish in the event – as all the guests drank too much and Aspinall, who came over for dinner, became extremely combative and made a great deal of noise. No scope for statesmanlike discussion.

Buck refused to go to bed at 2am when everyone else had dispersed and steered me back to the study 'for a last whisky'. He repeated several times the concept of an ideal arrangement whereby he was Secretary of State for Defence and I was Minister, '. . . or perhaps the other way round'.

'No, no,' I said, 'don't be ridiculous.'

Actually, there is not the slightest chance of his being promoted. I drank ginger ale (which, in the glass, looks like a medium strength whisky). Buck said 'goodnight' from time to time and made one or two efforts to rise to his feet, but slumped back (he was sitting in the corner of Bonny mama's red sofa). Finally he made it and *reeled* off upstairs.

The long-term purpose of the weekend was to create a 'good impression' to John Wells of the set-up; of my suitability to

---

[1] Anthony Buck, MP for Colchester since 1961, chairman of the Conservative Defence Committee since 1979 and thus AC's 'boss', AC being co-secretary with Robert Atkins, MP for Preston North since 1979. AC was convinced that he specialised in defence as the British Aerospace factory manufacturing the Panavia Tornado was situated in his constituency (his majority of 27 was the smallest in the House).

succeed him when he retires etc, probably less certain. JW did not
drink as much as the others and was somewhat inscrutable.

Cloisters   *Tuesday, 5 February*

I took ten minutes off and strolled out into the Members' Lobby
where Ian Gow was prowling. He asked me if I had a question in
mind (the Prime Minister was due to start answering in ten
minutes time).

'Nothing special,' I said. 'Anything I can do for you?'

Out of the corner of his mouth he said, 'Ask when they are
going to put some teeth into the Employment Act.'

I know that Ian loathes Prior and never ceases to complain
about him, but what I found worrying was that the Prime Minister
is so isolated in Cabinet that she has to send her PPS out into the
Lobby to try and raise support at random from backbenchers at
Question Time.

Albany   *Tuesday, 26 February*

Not having any appetite I decided to go and listen to the Prime
Minister being interviewed by Robin Day. She was wonderful and
very glamorous looking, though slightly spoilt the effect with
over-much ocular grimacing.

To such an extent that I worried that she might have got a blob
of mascara into her eye and was alarmed, at some camera angles,
to see a tell-tale red glow therein. As always she let out a few
impromptus, notably the revelation that Jim Prior was 'very, very
sorry' for his indiscretion.[1]

There was still three-quarters of an hour left before the vote and
I thought I ought to eat something. I couldn't face the dining
room, so went down to the cafeteria. I was chatting to Tony Buck

---

[1] Some days before, Prior, Employment Secretary, had 'leaked' to the lobby that
the chairman of British Steel 'would have to be replaced . . . as soon as the strike
was over'.

and David Madel[1] at their table when I saw Ian Gow come in, almost immediately followed by the Prime Minister who stood alone at the counter waiting to be served. I rushed up and congratulated her on the programme and Ian invited me to join them. I told the Prime Minister that a guffaw had gone round the television room when she said that she had found Ian Gilmour's speeches 'scintillating'.

Almost coquettishly she reminded me of her other comment . . . 'something in there for everyone.' Peter Hordern[2] joined us during the meal and was grave, thoughtful and 'correct' about financial matters. But I could see the Prime Minister preferred gossip. Ian grinned benignly as I joked about Prior's reproof and her breaching for the first time the notion that she might 'think about considering whether to withhold our EEC budget contributions'.

But goodness, she is *so* beautiful; made up to the nines of course, for the television programme, but still quite bewitching, as Eva Peron must have been. I could not take my eyes off her and after a bit she, quite properly, would not look me in the face and I detached myself from the group with the excuse that I was going up to heckle Michael Foot[3] who was doing the winding-up for Labour.

After the 10 o'clock vote I walked back to Albany and at the lower crossing place in St James's Street I saw two shadowy forms, elderly, decrepit even; but with a strange Episcopal authority, in their great black cloaks. The traffic – as always at that hour – made up of drunks and car thieves, was travelling at a colossal speed, so I helped them make it to the first island. I saw to my delight that one of them was Harold Macmillan, wearing his long-range multi-focals that look like sections of a glass rolling pin.[4]

---

[1] David Madel, MP for South Bedfordshire since 1970.

[2] Peter Hordern, MP for Horsham and Crawley since 1974 (Horsham, 1964–74), a member of the Public Accounts Committee and the Executive of the 1922 Committee, and before entering politics a member of the Stock Exchange.

[3] Michael Foot, MP for Ebbw Vale since 1960 (Devonport, 1945–55); the successor to James Callaghan as leader of the Labour Party later in the year.

[4] Macmillan had celebrated his eighty-sixth birthday a fortnight before.

'Are you going, sir, to Pratt's or Brooks's,' I asked him. 'The Carlton,' he replied tersely and shuffled off. But then paused, turned and called after me, 'It's too late for Pratt's anyway,' and waved an enormous half-hunter watch. 'They will be shut.'

A pleasant evening. Two Prime Ministers in the space of an hour and a half. Odd, how I keep meeting Uncle Harold when I least expect it.

Albany   *Thursday, 20 March*

Joei now gone mad; rings only making threats – it's a highly innocuous, run-of-the-mill heterosexual tale, but I suppose it could 'sell' – eg scandal about MPs is news and would certainly screw any career prospects. Just think of formula: 'I do not under any circumstances discuss my relations with the ladies. I am a gentleman, not a hairdresser.'

Cloisters   *Friday, 18 April*

On Wednesday night I was feeling ghastly and was dropping a 1 mg tablet of Redoxon into a glass of mineral water at the Smoking Room bar when Peter Morrison *volunteered* that he could 'help' with a pair the following day, Thursday. An unprecedented suggestion – was I really looking that ill? But on Friday morning I realised why: there had been a revolt of 37 back-benchers against a provision of the Employment Bill and he had wanted to get me out of the way, or save me embarrassment? Nothing in this place is what it seems. The Machiavellian undercurrents, the need to be permanently on one's guard, to know how to read the codes and smoke signals; how to assess people's real motives, and discount their superficial courtesies and protestations – is what makes the game here so fascinating.

Headland Park, Plymouth   *Saturday, 19 April*

Now time for a last *reflectif* to close the 'black book'. I don't want to make it sound too melodramatic, God is so good to me in waves. But it must be sadder, this note, than the close of earlier volumes.

Financially these have been appalling times. I don't really miss the Moore bust, only a showing-off colour, but haven't yet told Jane who didn't want it to be sold (not realising the extent to which one was still in hock on Zermatt). The half-Cézanne deal is a mystery – where the hell did it all go? On doing the rooms (although the Great Hall still leaks and drips ominously) and the kitchen and wood system, school fees and heavy expenditure on 'Boy'. Had to sell the Bira – and this with the windfall of Dennis Wright's[1] could get us nominally 'straight'. Even so, as darling Jane who so nobly struggles now with the VAT books laments, output still rages ahead of input, or 'coin'. We can only last a certain amount of time longer and I would say my father is good for at least another four years.

Politically, one might say I have advanced, or at least consolidated. I would have said that I have made *considerable* progress in this new parliament – with my confident interventions, better relationship with the whips, distinct and lucid and insistent advocacy of protectionism – being 'noted' by even John Biffen and 'The Lady' – but all of a sudden 'The Lady' has gone cold, freezing cold on me. Ian Gow, too, seems to be avoiding me in the lobby.

I've catalogued these random impressions, not all by any means. But it's maudlin really, isn't it? The full, full life. One is never content, but think of poor Nanny, nothing to do but walk slowly in Hythe and listen to what people say. I thank God for the incredible variety and privilege he has bestowed on me, also for strength to take advantage of it. God? I hardly ever speak to him now, except for the ritual 'touch wood' of thanks on my knees before getting into bed.

---

[1] Cottage in Saltwood village.

Cloisters   *Monday, 21 April*

At a loose end I went to the European Affairs Committee. I am due on Welsh Radio the following morning to talk about Carter and United States 'sanctions' against Iran and as Europe is plainly feeble and divided on this subject I thought I might pick up some tips. Ian Gow came in and sat at the far side of the room. On impulse I went over to him and asked him if he was free for dinner.

'Sadly not,' he replied. 'What are you doing after this?'

This was good, but unfortunately I had the Home Affairs Committee at 6pm and as we were due to discuss the Bristol riots I could hardly shirk it.

'Come to my room at 5.30,' he said.

We sat in the leather chairs of the PPS's room. As always he was serious, attentive and conveyed that special sense of urgency and concern of which he is a master. I plunged straight in.

'I say, am I in the Prime Minister's bad books at the moment?'

'No, no, not at all . . .'

'I just seem to detect a certain *frisson* . . .'

'Oh no, she has a very high opinion of you, you are one of her . . .'

'Say no more, no, no, please say no more', I held up my hand in the time-honoured Trevor-Roper gesture.[1]

I went straight into the topic of the 'rebel' votes against various aspects of the Employment Bill. It was immediately plain that Gow was anxious to encourage them, 'I can assure you that if you should vote in that lobby it would not make the slightest difference to your standing or reputation' (he only just stopped himself from saying 'career prospects'). He speaks quite openly about hostility between Prior and the Prime Minister. Gow said that if he were to be sacked he would be more dangerous as a focus of old Heathites and progressives on the backbenches. I said that I hoped the Prime Minister realised the full extent of the armoury of weapons at her

---

[1] Hugh Trevor-Roper, now Lord Dacre, had been AC's tutor at Christ Church and had a special characteristic wave of the hand which he used indiscriminately to halt praise or criticism, or to dismiss argument.

disposal and how she had nothing to fear provided she realised that whatever happened – short of a defeat on a vote of confidence – she was in power, personally, for another 3½ years. 'It is very difficult to promulgate any policy without the agreement of the Cabinet,' said Gow. 'Well the obvious answer to that is to change the Cabinet,' I replied, 'but I agree there are strategic considerations.'

'We have never had this conversation,' said Ian. 'Of course not,' I said. Somebody tried the door, we both looked round guilty and I got up to go. Ian unlocked the door and Tony Royle walked in.

'Six of the best,' I said, 'I hope you have got your telephone directory in place.'

The door closed behind him with the key turned.

House of Commons   *Monday/Tuesday, 28/29 April*

Horrible 'austerity' book[1] opens with gloom.

Woken last night by the Albany blackbird, so glad he is still around, he went off quite quietly, almost as soon as the chorus started.

I thought through the various 'last times'. This thing I have. There is, is bound logically to be, a 'last time' you do everything before you die. The first times you know about; they may be good or they may be bad. Sometimes they mirror first times, sometimes they overlap. I mean the first time you are impotent does not immediately follow the last time you have sexual intercourse (in my own case 1955 and . . . open). But the last time you don't know, not really know because there is always hope, until much later.

When the boys were tiny I used to go up to their room and kiss them goodnight, always with Jane, and this was lovely, the very best part of the whole day. Then Jane dropped out and I used to tell a story (the 'Badgers', the 'Tidy Pig' etc), and this was even better. Then that stopped (to much protestation, some of it slightly

---

[1] New journal, government-issue A4 hardback.

formalised) as a punishment for 'tinkling' behind the cupboard on the top floor at the Manor. I think I still did occasionally tell a story, as a treat only for a bit, although often urged to I never wrote them down and can remember very few, only the theft of the cartridges for Guy Fawkes day in full – but a little, dimly, of the kidnapping on the *Hesperides*. Anyway, the next stage was just saying 'goodnight' and perhaps a little chat with them in bed; then with them standing, and dressed in their room; then often downstairs or in the corridor; finally (in James's case) *they* had to check in with *us*.

I composed the letter, which I still have to put on paper, to Tip, both explaining how much I love him and how I agonised when he was tiny. James always outshone him. He wants a black GTI. I can't refuse, because he never asks (until now) for anything. But of course it's even more like OLA – much more – and much faster (because OLA, being as it were 'vintage' imposes its own discipline). I hope to pose certain restrictions – no dicing? – not over 70 etc.

Saltwood   *Monday, 5 May*

Jane stays lovely, always bright, happy and has lovely grey eyes and magic powers of observation. She 'found' a Miro in the drawer in the library table yesterday looking through old Christmas cards.

Albany   *Monday, 19 May*

I awoke this morning and decided to pick a fight with Willie Whitelaw. I am sick of him. I am pretty sure he does not like me and I suspect that he has a big influence in the higher counsels of the Party. I have long admired his intuition and political skills, but I read over the weekend that the Home Office was actually increasing the grant to the Voluntary Services Unit, an outfit devoted exclusively, it seems, to funding subversive activities and concerning which I had asked a number of pretty taut questions when we were in Opposition. I thought this was really too much.

However, in politics we are all in the kaleidoscope; give the thing a kick, or even a light tap and it may change out of all recognition. And later that day when I was in the Tea Room eating a rock bun and preparing myself to raise the VSU question aggressively at the Home Affairs Committee in five minutes time, up came Ted Gardner[1] and asked if I would chair the new sub-committee which Willie had asked to be set up to look at the question of Civil Defence. I realised at once that this could be a very useful rung on the ladder. In Committee Ted approaches these things in a very circumlocutory way. I do know whether he had second thoughts or doubts of any kind, but he almost failed to manage to announce it to the Committee, who nonetheless applauded loudly, led by Hugh Fraser[2].

Albany   *Tuesday, 17 June*

Was feeling randily expectant as Nanny had told me the previous day that someone 'well-spoken and cheeky' had rung and said that (as it were) 'Mimi Schluckleberger will dine with you on Wednesday night.'

The phone rang as I was making cocoa; Ali; I knew Valeri was there. Suddenly *she* snatched the phone and said, all Lausanne-station-voice, 'you stupid little bastard' twice and rang off. I was scared and thought of bolting; went down and told 'Shea'[3] not to let anyone in. Was somehow randily expectant, in spite of it. However, Ali rang and said (late, about 10.30) that 'she' was livid, got it in for me, was going to get Bodoni to work me over etc.

Ugh. Totally dry mouthed.

I rang Janey. She had had *two* tours, bless her. And that morning

---

[1] Edward (Ted) Gardner, MP for South Fylde since 1970.
[2] Hugh Fraser, MP for Stone and Staffordshire since 1950 (Stone, 1945–50), had married Lady Antonia Pakenham (better known by her married name), the daughter of Lord and Lady Longford (as they would become).
[3] A porter at Albany.

had mowed the Bailey herself, because if Cradduck had seen Eddie on the new (sit-down) Atco he'd have been hysterical with rage. But what's the point of employing two gardeners if the *chatelaine* has to do the work herself? I wish I was at Saltwood.

Saltwood   *Tuesday, 24 June*

First day of a lovely long weekend, full of promise. I was on Gossie[1] most of the morning. Burning hot sunshine, and chasing Tom[2] almost as hard work as beagling. The soil on the bank is very sandy. Not pure sand, which would be dangerous of course, and put the Jack Russell in peril when, as he does most often, he goes underground. He was out of sight for almost an hour, although occasionally I could hear him barking. Tom 'makes free' with the warrens, going in at one hole and coming out at another. Which must be a bore for any resident rabbits. Watership Down with a difference.

When I got back there was no sign of Jane. Nanny was disapproving. Apparently a young, unidentified, female had been on the telephone. 'Is Al there?' Nanny doesn't think people outside the family should call me 'Al'. When offered Jane instead the caller hung up.

Nanny drawing on fifty years of experience both Up-, and Down-, stairs, said that she was '*well-spoken, but cheeky*'.

'Was she in a call-box?' Didn't know.

Could something tiresome be about to happen? Damn, damn, blast, etc.

Saltwood   *Wednesday, 9 July*

More girl trouble.

Someone rang at the House and asked for an appointment. Alison told me that she was calling back which she did on the dot

---

[1] A steep cliff of downland at Saltwood.
[2] The family Jack Russell terrier.

of 4.15. Clearly going to put the bite on. I icily shook. Went and
dug out a senior police officer – useless. Gave mouldy advice,
wouldn't get me bugging kit; said Yard 'would only supply if I
preferred charges . . .' etc. Dived about the place in a state of high
anxiety and found myself sitting next to Nick Budgen[1] and confided in him. He wasn't much use, but did give me one name –
Jonathan Aitken.[2] Caught Jonathan in the lobby at the 10 o'clock
vote. He said he was at a dinner, but pressed me to come along; I
demurred; it turned out he was with a bird at some flat . . . He was
calming, gave good advice. Trysted me for next morning at his
(incredibly) sumptuous Saudi Arabian offices. We discussed tactics,
then round to 'counter-spy' shop for a 'recorder brief-case'. Tried
to settle for smaller (lapel-type) recorder, but trial showed defective
workmanship. Walked out as couldn't get discount, then, with just
20 minutes to spare back and bought it. (Amexing it.)

Briefly experimented, centred it on my desk and up to lobby
(no sign of the police, I may say). She was waiting, *very* pale . . .
out to the Harcourt Room. Oh she was so silly, wasn't she . . .
eased gently into the subject – no hint of pressure, almost as if she
had been warned against being recorded. Strictly according to
schedule good old Jonathan A turned up to testify that he had
seen us together. Finally she came out with it – wanted £5,000.
'Certainly,' I said – 'you can have £5,000.' I don't think she
thought her victory would be so easy; she mellowed and allowed
the occasional sparkle to shine through – so much so that at the
end, and feeling generous . . . I invited her to 'come round the
block' in the Cadillac. This, however, she declined. I was greatly
relieved. Put me in the clear, a 'good omen', acted as a signing off
gesture.

Later that afternoon, in the lobby, I told Jonathan I had agreed
to pay her £5,000. Amusingly he said, 'I should have offered her
£4,000 and the briefcase.'

---

[1] Nicholas Budgen, MP for Wolverhampton South-West since February 1974.
[2] Jonathan Aitken, MP for Thanet East since February 1974.

Cloisters   *Thursday, 10 July*

Met her (less good mood this time) and 'handed over'. She a bit
waspish – 'it's only gnat's piss to you' etc.

Bratton-Clovelly   *Saturday, 12 July*

Out here very late after a 'meet-the-Member' party. Dear Jane
came down and I met her train in the hired, colourless, Vauxhall
Cavalier. I said, 'we'll have to stay till ten.' She said, 'nine.' I didn't
make my piccolo speech until 9.20. Left as soon as one decently
could after that. Eileen clearly disappointed. This morning I said,
'perhaps we should have stayed for the washing up.' 'No, the
Heseltines always left after half an hour,' she replied.
    Meeting of the Executive on 25 July – 'West MP on the
carpet . . .' Have rehearsed my little 'I have nothing to say' speech
in which I end by saying '. . . and I bid you goodnight', and pick
up the Aitken briefcase and walk out.

Saltwood   *Thursday, 14 August*

Broke off to help Jane move the new broody, then, impromptu, to
clear out the 'junior' hen house; then spray Winifred's radiator
grille (very effective); then go back to clean out 'senior' or matrix
hen house. Very hot and muggy. Decided, while struggling on
major sell-off, for a 'tight ship' plan from now on.

Saltwood   *Tuesday, 14 October*

We did two days at conference – struck standard Brighton typhoon
weather, wind sucking with extractor force down those little side
streets that lead off at right angles on to 'Royal Parade' (or whatever it's called). Was being 'done' by Thames TV as one of the

subjects in *Westminster Man* and so followed around by cameramen. Invited on to platform for Civil Defence debate and 'mentioned' by Leon Brittan[1] (unusual). *Naturally* no Plymouthonians in the hall at the time. Still, this gave me enough confidence to ride through them at the dreaded 'W. Area cocktail party' that evening.

Cloisters   *Monday, 27 October*

For some reason Ted was in the Chamber, sitting in his usual place, which is three away from me, but with no one between us. To my amazement, as I sat down he swivelled massively in his seat (though retaining two fingers in the famous 'V' position against his right cheek) and said, 'At last you're beginning to learn something', then swivelled ponderously back and stared ahead. I simpered acknowledgement (a mistake) but said nothing. What on earth can he have meant? At first sight it seemed to be a compliment, but on reflection I suppose it wasn't. What I suppose he meant was 'all of you idiots who voted for The Lady are now beginning to realise the mess you are getting yourselves into.'

Cloisters   *Tuesday, 28 October*

There was an urgent message this morning to meet in Francis Pym's[2] room at 2pm (ie before Questions). But the discussion was very light, being confined simply to tactics.

That evening at 6pm we again met, this time at Francis' room in the Ministry of Defence. It did not take long for me to realise that the substance of *this* meeting was in fact very significant. What in effect Francis was saying was that he was going to resign if any further cuts were forced on him. In his declamation he managed to include a number of coded asides about his doubts on existing Government or, as he called it, 'Treasury' policy. As I listened to

---

[1] Leon Brittan, MP for Cleveland and Whitby, 1974–83.
[2] Francis Pym had been Secretary of State for Defence since 1979.

this I realised exactly how significant Francis' resignation could be, as he is the only person who can take such a step without splitting the Party.

Cloisters   *Wednesday, 29 October*

Just before the ten o'clock vote Hal Miller[1] caught me in the Members' Lobby and said that Francis would, after all, be able to see me for a couple of minutes afterwards if I waited outside the 'Aye' lobby. I duly hung around until it was almost empty. Still no Francis. The trouble when one is waiting to catch a colleague is that others — most people are a bit tight by that time of the evening — try and get into conversation, tell one scraps of gossip, etc. I was simultaneously fending off dear John Wells who wanted to invite Andrew to go shooting with him on Saturday, and I was conscious of Ian Gow hovering (I did not want him to see me in conclave with Francis). Then the Secretary of State, round-shouldered as ever and wearing a dinner jacket, finally emerged through the division doors. Better leave it, I thought. I was getting cold feet. But Hal spotted me and waved at me to come over.

'Can I see you quite privately?' I asked. We turned right into the long corridor that cuts down towards the Speaker's Room. Even there it seemed a seething mass of people bellowing and eavesdropping. I made some variant of Oliver Lyttelton's joke about the trenches, '. . . too many people', with which he agreed. He seemed quite benevolent so, encouraged, I told him that speaking as a historian I felt obliged to put a case to him, but that I would neither invite nor even expect him to comment. He looked a little wary of this, but I pressed on.

'If you should finally get pushed into the position where you have to resign . . .'

'Which I certainly hope I do not have to,' he interjected.

'. . . you must realise that you are the only person who can take

<hr />

[1] Hilary (Hal) Miller, MP for Bromsgrove and Redditch since February 1974, PPS to the defence secretary since 1979.

such a step without splitting the Party and that you would, in fact, have a broad franchise, spreading right across from those who are opposed to public spending to include those who, like myself, are sometimes depicted as being on the right. And the likelihood is that you would be Prime Minister in two years time.'

As I finished the concluding sentence the effect was electric. A huge slug of adrenalin visibly shot through his system. Far from dismissing me (as, eg, Willie might have done) his manner became very intense. 'Come upstairs to my room,' he said, and we turned round and went to the stairs, pushing past three people who were all waiting to see him, including Hal and Keith Speed.[1] Once we got into his room I could see he was highly excited about what I had to say. I developed the theme; explaining that if The Lady were to crash within the next 18 months, there was no need to have a general election, but obviously the Party would have to find a new Leader and were he to resign now and on this issue he would be incomparably better placed than anyone else to unite it. I also pointed out that in the last 18 months of a Parliament it was far easier to alter course and frame election-winning policies if the personalities identified with the old and unpopular ones had disappeared. Francis was very attentive, claimed that his only feelings were for the Party and the Country, etc, etc. But plainly he was greatly encouraged, indeed fortified by the concept which I had put to him. I cannot believe it had not occurred to him; but he is so cautious he probably had not taken any *soundings* and was cheered to get some back-bench encouragement from a (probably) unexpected source. Hal is amiable but too bluff and 'straight' to see things long.

What a rich, endlessly varied and exciting world politics is for those who are addicted to it. And how inextricably woven are the different strands of greed, ambition, cowardice and idealism. No one's motives are pure; certainly not mine.

---

[1] Keith Speed, MP for Ashford since October 1974, and Minister for the Navy since 1979.

Saltwood   *Sunday, 16 November*

John Erickson[1] says Russians are going into Yugoslavia soon, and identified 'hit' units in SW order of battle, so that requires major strategic think-out. I drove Jane back up to London in Winter Car and asked her where she would like the shelter, Bratton or Saltwood. She prefers Saltwood, I think rightly, although am apprehensive of Dungeness explosion.[2]

Cloisters   *Tuesday, 25 November*

Yesterday the Chancellor made a 'statement on economic policy' (generally hailed by the press as a 'package', with all the uncomfortable evocation of that word). Very unsatisfactory. He gabbled through an unintelligible Treasury brief, couched in their most obscure jargon, then came to the point. Only £1 billion further cuts in public expenditure – of which £200 million were to come from Defence – in other words £800 million was coming from all other sectors combined. So the shortfall had to come from revenue, in the form of increased 'contributions' under National Insurance. The net effect is that the workers are going to get less in the righthand column of their payslips, while the so-called Social Wage remains intact. This is precisely contrary to the theme in which our campaign was presented and a rejection of the endorsement we received from the electorate last year.

At the very end of his statement the Chancellor announced, with what for him was presumably meant to be a flourish, but which came out in Evelyn Waugh's phrase '. . . more in the tones of a nanny than a Master-at-Arms',[3] that interest rates would be reduced by 2 per cent. The cut in interest rates is totally

---

[1] John Erickson, historian at the University of Edinburgh, specialising on the Soviet military.

[2] Dungeness nuclear power station being south-west and across the bay from Saltwood.

[3] Evelyn Waugh's *The Ordeal of Gilbert Pinfold*.

unjustified by the present state of the money supply or public
sector borrowing and the measures that the Chancellor had
described would not be becoming operative until next year anyway. It is perfectly plain that Government policy is now seriously
off course – with consequences that can only be bad both for the
Party and the country.

Cloisters   *Wednesday, 26 November*

The *Daily Mail* ran a huge front page editorial about the manner
in which the Government is falling down on all its policies and
pledges and urged the Prime Minister, though not, in my view,
strongly or prominently enough, to purge her Cabinet and return
to the straight and narrow. At breakfast Jane reinforced this with
her own pure common sense views laced with wisdom from
working-class people like Eddie and Peggy. What the hell *is*
going on? I have had no fewer than five telephone messages
from Plymouth Sound asking me to call them back. But I won't
do so as there simply is not a comment that I can make on the
present state of affairs that would not sound subversive or
demoralised.

Later, walking across the Members' Lobby I saw Ian Gow, and
asked him if I could have a moment. As always he was delightfully
attentive and we went down to the Terrace, which was deserted.
Up and down we paced in the biting East wind. What was
dangerous, and almost unprecedented, I told him (as if he needed
telling), was that the Prime Minister and the Treasury team in
combination had been defeated in Cabinet. We all knew that she
had made an error of judgement in weighting her Cabinet so
heavily with passé Heathites. But was not the theory that by
retaining all the Treasury posts for her own supporters she would
in the last resort be able to get her own way on economic policy?
In fact, this did not last and she is now being defeated even on this
selected battlefield. No wonder she looks so wan (though still
beautiful) and sits with her head bowed at Question Time.

I urged Ian to press her to stand alone, appeal to the country, stage a night of the long knives,[1] stressed that there was still time left for a ruthless policy to pay off. What I cannot make out is to what extent Ian's expressed views reflected his own prejudices, and what he believes to be mine; and to what extent they present a true picture of The Lady's own misgivings and anxieties. One must always remember that she is, must be, a more adroit politician than sometimes appears. Perhaps she, being plagued by inner feelings of insecurity, and being determined to hold on to her position, is consciously trimming now.

Saltwood   *Tuesday, 2 December*

And *still* we are ground down (though not yet, fortunately, in the lower millstones of God's foundry). Yesterday Barclays produced a most insulting letter giving (effectively) three weeks notice to put account in credit. Signed cheque on C. Hoare & Co. and sent down by hand. This means CH is 25+ and then the loan (now down to 20) and also the Clydesdale at 20. *But* Westminster is out of the way and now Barclays. How the hell do I raise the 65 to get completely clear? Had a bad night, early waking etc. Fictionalised with collapse of Italian front.

Cloisters   *Wednesday, 10 December*

I caught sight of Adam Raphael[2] in the lobby and taxed him with his extraordinary theory that the likeliest 'candidates' in a reshuffle were Francis, Ian Gilmour and Norman St John-Stevas.[3] But no, this was his assessment on the basis of a hard tip. He told me that all three, who were used to talking to him freely, had been bitterly

---

[1] As Harold Macmillan had done on 13 July 1963, when he dismissed six cabinet ministers. AC observed, 'butchery on this scale unprecedented in the annals of the party' (*The Tories*).

[2] Adam Raphael, political correspondent of the *Observer* since 1976.

[3] Norman St John-Stevas, MP for Chelmsford since 1964. Leader of the Commons 1979–81.

offended. Raphael's theory is that Francis will be moved to Leader of the House, Norman dropped or, more likely, sent to Education in place of Mark Carlisle[1] who will *definitely* be going (everyone seems agreed on that). But anyway what about this dam' reshuffle? The Lady appears to have got into a face-loss situation here, ie whatever she does will be an I-told-you-so, so she is just holding on. When there was an official briefing, printed in the *Sunday Telegraph* about three weeks ago that '. . . there will be no Ministerial changes for at least six (or was it twelve?) months . . .' I got a few laughs in the tea-room by saying that this meant they were imminent. Now I'm not so sure. Raphael thinks that it may be the Treasury team that goes, and not of their own volition.

Cloisters   *Thursday, 11 December*

At the start of Business Questions there was a scuffling noise and a massive thump at the bar of the House. The Chief Whip,[2] carrying papers, had fallen flat on his face. 'A slip', presumably (to quote one of Harry Carpenter's over-used phrases) as he doesn't drink. He was livid.

A little later, who should be called but 'Sir Harold Wilson'.[3] Amazing. He stood erect and slim (cancer-slim one could say) in a beautifully pressed blue suit, in contrast to his usual rumpled and hunted demeanour, and asked a question about his Report on the City's institutions. Down memory lane, with that curious flat nasal twang, that I used to hear so often and so maddeningly at PM's questions when we were in opposition. A certain sadismoid pleasure as I reflected on how the roles were reversed in more than one sense.

---

[1] Mark Carlisle, MP for Runcorn 1964–83. Education Secretary 1979–81. Made Life Peer, 1987.

[2] Michael Jopling, MP for Westmorland since 1964, Chief Whip since 1979.

[3] Harold Wilson, MP for Huyton since 1950 (Ormskirk, 1945–50), prime minister 1964–70, 1974–76, Knight of the Garter 1976.

Saltwood   *Saturday, 13 December*

Saltwood just not a haven at the moment. Untidyness as piled papers seems even worse (like indebtedness) than when one began.

My father *distrait* on the phone (this is tricky as he is going to get my Cézanne letter this week – ugh![1]) Also have a loose front tooth, obviously going to pack up over Christmas or in Zermatt.

Saltwood   *Sunday, 21 December*

Walked out on the steps and looked at the full moon behind the trees. Very cold, but clear. Had spoken to C, who had agreed to meet me at Albany tomorrow to discuss Cézanne still-life. Looked around, and up at the towers. Am I, at last, some £500,000 later, really going to own it all, unencumbered? Will have to do a *really* careful think through at the turn of the year.

---

[1] The incomplete draft of AC's letter begins: 'Dearest Papa, this is bad, I'm afraid . . .'

Zermatt   *Monday, 5 January*

Apprehensive as freedom from worry poor – only really brighten up when talking about my o/d being paid off – appearance *not* improving, and then this evening blow fell: RESHUFFLE.

And, monstrously, not announced what it was in detail, just that it will be announced later this evening! Took one totally by surprise. A sad blow for me. I had never really expected to get into government at formation, but hoped and felt that I had made enough general ground in the interim; friendship with Ian Gow, giving notice of questions etc. Perhaps I had, then blew it just recently.

Recalled how I had prayed for George to come back and promised that if he did I would do my Defence Study. He did come, and I didn't. One's relationship with God shouldn't be like that. I should be grateful for everything that he has given me, accept that what-is-written-is-written. But I still have this residual hope, belief, that I can do something for my country. What must I do to deserve it and pave the way? Perhaps this year should be much more political.

Zermatt   *Tuesday, 6 January*

I still feel *very* uneasy about 1981. 'Flagellation Year' its provisional title.[1]

---

[1] In Mrs Thatcher's first reshuffle, appointments included Francis Pym as Leader of the House (succeeding Norman St John-Stevas), thereby proving Adam Raphael's tip (see 10 December) correct. John Patten moved to the Northern Ireland Office as Parliamentary Under-Secretary of State.

Saltwood   *Saturday, 10 January*

Got back today. Looked through the mail, incredibly dull, only pleasurable indication of new regime, just fucking boring all round. Last a/c of Hoare's still being kept in credit by income. Looked at the Whip, and got really quite angry as I think of these bloody people just bossing us around. *Waddington*[1] a minister; that self-same little tick who blocked me from going to Europe or whatever it was. Goodlad a whip, Goodlad of all people![2] The stock example of an MP who looks like a pig and did NOTHING. Much of the flavour will be diminished from the House I suspect.

Cloisters   *Tuesday, 13 January*

I had been dictating letters until ten past three, but had foresight to put in a Prayer Card as I knew my place would be kept free for Prime Minister's PQs.

Just before going I had soaked myself with Vetiver, even so this did not attract the attention of the former Leader of the House who I noticed was standing at the bar when I entered. (Nick Winterton was putting a long rambling question and because of his position at the end of the front bench it would have been out of order to have walked past him to our places.) When Nick sat down Norman 'made his entry' with that curious mincing step of his. I was glad to see that he got massive applause – not all of it ironic by any means – from the Opposition.

Later, in the course of Questions he was sorely tried by the Prime Minister who said how glad she was that the Arts were no longer an independent ministry, etc. But he did not rise.

I returned to the House and went into the Smoking Room. Julian Amery was holding court in the corner table between the

---

[1] David Waddington, MP for Clitheroe since 1979; now a Parliamentary Under-Secretary of State, Department of Employment.
[2] Alastair Goodlad, MP for Northwich since February 1974.

bar and the fireplace. He was in good form. I noticed George Brown[1] and one or two Labour MPs in the outer circle.

'Now Alan, we are just agreeing that we are all hand-to-heart behind the Prime Minister in her economic policies, but the trouble is we don't know what these are, can you tell us?'

This is not a good sign, this kind of irreverence from senior and respected Privy Councillors on the Right of the Party.

When I got back to the Library I saw bright, intelligent, able little Robin Cook[2] from Edinburgh North, who was always a very keen and very well informed interrogator of Ministers in the defence field, but has been promoted by Mr Foot to a shadow Treasury job. I congratulated him. I remarked ruefully that talent was being better used in the Labour Party than in our own. He said that this was due to Michael's innovation. He cited the example of Tam Dalyell,[3] saying that he was absolutely brilliant, then adding somewhat to my surprise, '. . . but he is unreliable'.

'Unreliable? What do you mean?'

'Well, he sometimes goes his own way, you cannot rely on him always to speak to the ministerial brief. Which is a good thing of course,' he said hurriedly, but unconvincingly.

Cloisters   *Monday, 19 January*

I received a very friendly reply from Ian Gow, totally disclaiming any disapproval of my celebrated article in the *Daily Telegraph*[4] before Christmas.

This evening, just as I was dictating letters at my desk the telephone rang and it was IG's secretary suggesting dinner.

I found Ian in the Smoking Room and he took me to the Savoy.

---

[1] George Brown, former Labour MP and minister in Harold Wilson's 1964–70 government, took the title Lord George-Brown on being made a life peer in 1970.

[2] Robin Cook, Labour MP for Livingstone since 1983, Foreign Secretary since 1997.

[3] Tam Dalyell, opposition spokesman on science since 1980.

[4] On defence policy.

Really, his driving in his little blue Mini is now completely berserk. He delights in it, and it makes one's hair stand on end – particularly as he is not a specially skilful driver. At one point as we screamed along the Embankment (it was pouring with rain) I envisaged a terrible accident with the tiny Mini somersaulting across the dual carriageway, an incandescent fireball. He told me that he sometimes drove the Prime Minister in the car with a detective sitting in the back.

Over the food he said, 'Who do you think should succeed me as the Prime Minister's secretary?'

'Very difficult,' I replied 'I very much hope that you are not going to stand down.' (On looking back I see that this was rather tactless as he would not stand down but be promoted and given a department of his own.)

'Would you do it?'

'Nothing I would like more outside the Cabinet itself.'

'But how would Jane take it?' he said.

We talked a bit about wives living in the country etc. I tried hard to steer the subject away from this as (perhaps wrongly) I did not want to appear to be too keen. I do not know how much power he has to recommend his successor or – same thing – how much attention the Leader would pay to what he says. But of course the more I thought about it the more excited I became. So there it is, one is quickly forced back by a combination of bribes and compulsion into towing the line, being a good boy, etc. I do not quite know what I should do to make myself, or perhaps confirm myself, as being the most suitable over the next six months. One lives in hope, but this one seems almost too good to be true.

Cloisters   *Thursday, 22 January*

To Brooks's, where I was going to meet Euan, and driving somewhat *Frenchly* I just failed to slip inside a red Hillman as he accelerated away from a pedestrian crossing. The occupants immediately put on police caps and flagged me down. They insisted I take a breath test. 'If this bag changes colour one iota I will give you £100,' I said. Of course, looking back I now see that might have been constituted as an overture for a bribe. However, fortunately the celebrated 'crystals' did not alter colour at all. It is somewhat alarming though as one puffs down the plastic tube to see them darkening. This is simply the moisture in one's breath and not the alcohol content, which in my case was nil. All the same, I noted that the division of the colour beyond which a positive reading is indicated and a blood or urine test follows seemed very high up the tube; I got the impression that not much of a drink would get one into trouble.

A little later that evening I went downstairs into Pratt's, which was empty except for, sitting heavily and gloomily in one of those upright circular leather chairs, holding a whisky and soda dark as a mahogany veneer, the Home Secretary.

'Ah, Alan,' he said, not greeting me with any great warmth.

'I have just been breathalysed,' I said mischievously (breathalysed invariably means '. . . and produced a positive reading').

But the Home Secretary was very splendid, thundered and spluttered, said it was monstrous, where did it happen, on what grounds did they stop me . . . To my delight I realised that he was angry with the police at breathalysing me, not the other way round. I told him that the test had been completely negative and he was almost disappointed. I think that he might well have done something about it if it had been positive. The Drinker's Union.

Saltwood   *Saturday, 24 January*

Things *consistently calmer* with 'indebtedness eliminated'. But real thriller at the moment is IG's mention of the possibility of my taking his place (!!!). Jane and I think of nothing, talk of nothing else. Of course it must, I suppose, still be reckoned an ambition.

What a coup to overtake, with the most sensational of all ladders, everyone else! The third or fourth most powerful person in the parliamentary party! How they will all cringe and creep! And how well will I do it. A 'posting' – darling little Jane said.

I think of my clothes – a series of dark grey suits and waistcoats with the gold watch chain, grandpapa's, in morning, and BHLH in evening with dark blue. Blue shirts in morning, white in evening. Always Eau de Cologne and Turkish cigarettes in the offices. Also a terrace party in May, constituents from Plymouth and Folkestone (!), colleagues and carefully chosen people. Oh, bliss! But also has more serious possibilities. It would still leave all doors open. On to the FO (with a knighthood), then back to Lord Privy Seal (general duties), then Defence, the Home Office and the leadership elec- tion. Truly in politics, as in backgammon, anything is possible.

After some torment I decided to write to Ian, affirming both my total readiness to serve and making a general request of advice on how to conduct myself. Jane agreed with this course of action. Then I changed my mind and decided to write a formal letter expressing my readiness to serve and an informal letter with a request for advice and enclose the two in the same envelope. However, partly because time was pressing (due to the last col- lection from Saltwood Post Office), I decided to confine myself to the formal letter of readiness to serve. I wrote it on Saltwood writing paper, did not use a House of Commons envelope, but paid for the stamp (!), marked it 'strictly private' and sealed it using the big James II silver seal of the lion on to which my grandfather had grafted the family crest. I sent the letter to Downing Street as I know that is his first port of call in the mornings.

Cloisters   *Tuesday, 27 January*

To my gratification I find that my criticism of Keith Joseph[1] got very wide coverage – twice on the radio and reported in full in every paper.[2] Far from diminishing its effectiveness the use of the word insouciance seems to have pleased people. These tiny trivial- ities which seem to determine whether something is effective or not are very hard to predict.

There was a strange messenger on the Letter Board who did not recognise me and so the internal mail may have been accumulating

---

[1] Keith Joseph, Education secretary.
[2] Over the payment of another £1 billion to prop up British Leyland.

there for some time. Just after tea I saw my light was on and with considerable alarm noticed that one of the letters on the Board was marked 'First Lord of the Treasury' in the top right-hand corner, which always means Downing Street. I took it away to a quiet corner of the passage which leads down to the Telephone Lobby and, conscious of an accelerating heart rate, tore it open. Inside was *another* envelope, also marked '10 Downing Street' and endorsed 'Private and Confidential' (shades of Ruth Lee and Arthur's communication with Ll G!).[1] I opened the second envelope and inside was a very short note:

'My dear Alan, Thank you so much for your letter of 24 January. You were not dreaming and I am glad to have your note for my file. We will have a further word. Yours ever.'

Cloisters   *Tuesday, 3 March*

I sat throughout the Trident Debate today and made my long deferred speech recommending the withdrawal of the Rhine Army. The House was thinly attended, but not as empty as it usually is at that hour (7.50pm) and I was gratified to note that quite a few people from both sides came in and stood at the bar while I was talking. Enoch 'hear-hear'ed' energetically throughout, which is always encouraging and it was extremely 'well received' by everybody present. Unless one disposes of power (which I do not) congratulations from colleagues are rare and so all the more welcome. I even got a note from the Chair, delivered immediately by one of the badge messengers, expressing appreciation and ending 'well done indeed.'

Cloisters   *Monday, 16 March*

Brocklebank-Fowler staged his defection today.[2] The air was already heavy with rumour about the number of colleagues who

---

[1] AC had edited the memoirs of Arthur Lee, *A Good Innings* (Murray, 1975).
[2] Christopher Brocklebank-Fowler, MP for Norfolk NW since 1974 (King's Lynn, 1970–74), crossed the floor and joined the Social Democrats.

were going to abstain or vote against the petrol tax. Michael Spicer[1] told me before lunch that it was going to be a 'surprisingly close thing'. I thought, but kept it to myself, that the only time I had ever known it a surprisingly close thing was the celebrated no-confidence vote that brought down Callaghan's Government in 1979. Usually when it comes to the point the Government of the day always wins more comfortably than people in their excitement estimate for

J. Prior opened the debate adopting that well-known technique of the moderates of bellowing any point concerning which his conscience makes him uneasy. We had Norman St John-Stevas, mellifluous, reasonable and without any bitterness. Then Enoch, who was perfectly brilliant – what a superb Chancellor he would make – totally demolishing Peter Shore's[2] speech the previous day when he had argued for reflation. A large number came in while he was speaking and by the end the Chamber was almost completely full.

Then up spoke Brocklebank, pretty objectionable stuff it was, much laced with reference to electoral reform, third world and so on, then in a rather stilted little display he walked down the gangway from his own place and over to the front bench right opposite me, where, mysteriously, all the Tribunites had disappeared except Russell Kerr,[3] who was still asleep, and the Social Democrats were sitting on one another's laps. Poor nice Roddy Maclennan[4] got up to make way for Brocklebank. The whole House roared with laughter, which was not the reaction intended by the Social Democrats. Various members leant across to try and shake his hand, one of them, John Roper, actually missed three times.

---

[1] Michael Spicer, MP for South Worcestershire since February 1974.

[2] Peter Shore, MP for Stepney and Poplar since 1974. Opposition spokesperson on Treasury matters.

[3] Russell Kerr, MP for Feltham and Heston since 1974 (Feltham, 1966–74).

[4] Robert (Roddy) Maclennan (Caithness and Sutherland since 1966) and John Roper (Farnworth since 1970) had both crossed the floor from the Labour benches to join the SDP.

Afterwards, Jim Prior came into the Tea Room and said that he thought Brocklebank had made a 'very good speech'. I have reported this to Ian Gow.

Cloisters   *Thursday, 19 March*

Just as I was going into Prime Minister's Questions Jonathan Aitken caught me in the Lobby and told me that he had been talking to Chapman Pincher, who was now going to 'blow' the whole story of Roger Hollis[1] and the penetration of MI5 by the KGB. As I sat in my place waiting for the Prime Minister I chatted intermittently about it to Peter Hordern, who confirmed my view that it could have the most damaging effect on the Government.

At 3.14pm on the digital clock (ie with less than a minute to go) I scuttled up the aisle in the stooping position, turned left up the gangway and push-stumbled my way along the bench behind Ian's place. I whispered to him that the whole Hollis affair was going to blow at the weekend and did he know, should I have a quiet word with him afterwards? He indicated assent and I went back to my place.

When we met in his room it was clear that he did not have any idea of who Hollis was. ('Where is Hollis at the moment . . .' etc.) I sketched in the background briefly, said that I felt the Prime Minister ought to be forewarned in case she did not know. Security scandals always seem to bounce up and hit governments when they start to get a little shaky. Although, of course, I did not say this.

On my way back from the Prime Minister's room I was caught by Adam Raphael in the Members' Lobby. He told me that he felt conspiracies to displace the Prime Minister were now becoming quite flagrant; that she had made so many powerful enemies (the Governor of the Bank of England, Chairman of the CBI, etc) and that he regarded her as being highly vulnerable if the policies did not start to show results during the summer. But we both agreed

---

[1] Sir Roger Hollis, Director-General of MI5, 1956–65, was alleged to be the 'Fifth Man' among the Cambridge spies. Subsequent historians disagreed.

that the 'wets' were useless – not called 'wet' for nothing. Raphael said that the unanimity of speeches last weekend arose simply because each in turn had been 'screamed' at by the Prime Minister and told to go out and do something.

AR went on to say that this was going to be the theme of his article this Sunday, coupled with the implication that Francis Pym was the obvious choice of successor. I suggested that he kept Francis Pym's name out of the article as it would be dangerous to draw attention to him at this stage, his own reputation being so high, that people would pay special credence to what he was saying and so on. AR mumbled something about flattery did not make any difference, he must stick to his theme, but he would do it very carefully.

So, I had to go back to IG and warn him of this also. I felt that the Prime Minister should be forewarned of a text which might come as a disagreeable shock to her. Ian nodded gloomily, but made no comment.

Later, when I got home, I thought it would also be appropriate to telephone Francis and let him know as he, too, might appreciate a word of warning, as there was always the risk that The Lady might read the piece first, ring him up and scream at him without his knowing what it was all about. 'But what can I do,' he said plaintively. Nothing, I agreed, but it was just as well to be forewarned.

Saltwood   *Monday, 23 March*

A rejuvenating experience today. Sitting in my place for (boring) Employment questions, I allowed my eye to range along the gallery opposite. Lots of birds and birdettes. On the far edge of the front bench, where it joins the Members' Gallery, sat a blonde. I looked up at her, wearing my glasses, she briefly returned my gaze; haughty, composed. I took off my glasses, chatted on with the boys (JB-D[1] and Tony Fell[2]). My thoughts became obsessive. I

[1] John Biggs-Davison, MP for Epping Forest since 1974 (Chigwell, 1955–74).
[2] Anthony Fell, MP for Yarmouth (Norfolk) since 1970 (also 1951–66)

contemplated going upstairs and sitting beside her – clearly impossible and ludicrous. Well, anyway, let's have a good old stare . . . put on my glasses again and stared. Same routine. She *was* strangely attractive in the true sense. Went back to talking and joking with the lads. Then thought, well, sod it, let's go up to the gallery, 'have a look round'.

To reach it you have to go through various colleagues' offices, the door opening *in* towards you as you step out (to an incredible view and acoustics, incidentally). I went over and sat beside her noticing with a faint pang of anxiety that she seemed rather young, not to say child-like, and under-nourished. And yet in that subtle, secret way that one's animal senses tell one, not *rebarbatif.*

After a few seconds in which I gained my confidence by waving and grimacing at B–D and Fell below, I said 'How're you enjoying it? Is it frightfully boring?'

'Oh . . . not yet' she answered (!). With each step surmounted, as in all seductions, retreat by either party becomes more difficult than advance. We chatted, I joked. To my delight I noticed she was very, very pretty. Mouth and eyes terrific; skin a little puppy-spotted. She did not mind, indeed *initiated* remarks and questions. Also she leaned towards me at intervals when not quite 'catching' what I had said. Finally emboldened, I said, 'Come and have some tea'. (Willie had been taking PM's questions and Heseltine had got up. She said she was quite keen on him, but having seen him close to was disappointed.)

'Yes, I'd love to' (with some disclaimer about having to be back). A marvellous, ecstatic moment, comparable almost to getting into bed for the first time – indeed more perfect as less fraught – as I unhooked the ropes and she skipped through into our gallery and off we went!

Tea in the members' cafeteria. Gosh she was pretty! On the way back she said, 'I like this place'.

'I hope you'll come again', I said.

We exchanged phone numbers in the gallery (as Division Bell was ringing) and I kissed her hand. Super.

Cloisters   *Wednesday, 1 April*

I did not make an entry for the Monday, when I rang the bird from the gallery, Jessica by name, and she gave 'blanket' refusal – '. . . I'm terribly busy' etc, and how low this made me.

Went to Sotheby's this morning to tie up the deal for my introductory commission on the Clark Collection Sale. There was David Westmorland[1] looking a little less confidently polished than in former years; I noticed that his hand shook when he was folding the documents. But of course the great advantage of Sotheby's is that they have discarded all pretence – unlike Christie's – of being *gentlemanly*. We construct a deal and do not waste time on the veneers. Col pronounced a sound dictum about the upper classes in such circs: 'When you do a deal with a New York Jew, or even an Italian, there is a kind of residual acceptance that although they are trying to get the better of you, they hope to leave you with just enough satisfaction and self-esteem to come back for a bit more of the same later on. But with the English aristocracy they simply want to take you for as much as they possibly can and hope you drop dead the next day.' However, in our case it was Greek meets Greek. I am getting £12,500 down on an introductory commission for the whole sale of £180,000. To avoid tricky questions about special interest, breach of equity etc, it is being presented (quite legitimately) on a purchase of the copyright to the tapes which I am cutting with my father in which he describes the items in the collection and how he acquired them.

Cloisters   *Monday, 13 April*

Dined at Downing Street after a really frightful day of trivial but insistent pressures – compounded by that special sense of angst and frailty that affects one's birthday. No cards or tributes (fortunately I

---

[1] The Earl of Westmorland, chairman of Sotheby's since 1980.

am not on *The Times* list. I say 'fortunately' because I do not like people knowing how old I am).

I was exhausted, as there was a tube strike and no cabs so earlier I had to *walk*, carrying a full two gallon can of petrol, from the House of Commons to Albemarle Street where I finally got a taxi by *force majeure* and then on to Sussex Gardens where the faithful Citroen had puttered to a halt on Friday while I rushed to catch the Plymouth train. The only bonus was that she had stood unharmed and unticketed on a resident's parking space throughout the weekend. She started instantly, as always, and I drove back to the Albany so that Jane could use her to pick me up at the Commons.

We arrived at Number 10 a little late, after the Rumanians had made their entry. Filing up the stairs I noticed a few stars, like Michael Foot, Keith Joseph, John Biffen, Michael Havers[1] etc, so was glad to realise that it was not a 2nd or 3rd XI affair. Not having done this before I did not know how good the drink would be at dinner, so hastily and greedily downed three dry sherries off the itinerant salvers while talking and joking with Biffen. His wife, Sarah, is surprisingly young and pretty to wed someone so staid and avuncular.

Julian Amery, now the complete senior statesman, heavy in girth and ludicrously empurpled, introduced me to the Rumanian Ambassador as (his excellency spoke only the language of the Corps Diplomatic) 'Un de que brillants de nos jeunes députés'. The Ambassador was tall, handsome and corrupt looking, very much the old, Mdme Lupescu[2] school. No ascetic nonsense about people's courts etc.

On the way into dinner each person was handed a map of the *placement* with a little red hand indicating their own name. The table was an inverted 'U' and I sat down at the end between a blonde in a red dress and a rather matronly lady in a

---

[1] Michael Havers, MP for Wimbledon since 1970, Attorney-General since 1979.

[2] Madame Lupescu, mistress of King Carol of Romania in the 1940s, was always a favourite character of AC and in *Barbarossa* he told how, in 1945, a convoy of fourteen motor cars was needed to move her luggage out of Bucharest when the Russians invaded.

blue chiffon blouse who turned out to be Jane Parsons, one of the original Number 10 boiler-room girls (to use Harold Evans' expression).[1] She told me that she had been there for 35 years and had served under nine Prime Ministers, starting with Attlee. Naturally, Macmillan was easily her favourite and as he is also mine we got on top hole. This was just as well, as at the halfway stage I had foolishly and mischievously 'got on the wrong side of' the blonde in the red dress.

It happened like this. She turned out to be a German and I, having reluctantly and timorously consumed the sea-food cocktail, had turned away the second course which was a minute and delicious looking poussin stuffed with grapes. (After all 85 per cent of all chicken is supposed to contain salmonella bacteria isn't it?) I told the waitress I would just have vegetables. The waitress was sympathetic, but the blonde said rather haughtily,

'Are you a vegetarian?'

'Yes, like the Führer.'

She affected not to know that Hitler had been a vegetarian and I elaborated on Frau Maziali and the delightful vegetarian dishes she would prepare for him. I could see that this was not going down very well and so, partly to provoke, I said, 'He was ahead of his time in that as in so many other things.'

'What other things?'

Well here I am afraid my precise memory fades, but I did construct some sentence, clear in syntax but ambivalent in meaning, about the genetic need for racial purity. Then, seeing how shocked she was, developed it. I had not anticipated the intensity of her reaction. Her eyes filled with tears, she kept looking at me in horror and saying, 'You are appalling, I think you are appalling, how can you represent people and say these things,' etc.

I gave as good as I got, said that she was really condemning me for my opinions – because she certainly could not condemn me for

---

[1] At the time AC was reading *Downing Street Diary*, Sir Harold Evans' book on life at Number 10 under Harold Macmillan, 1957–63, when he was the prime minister's official spokesman.

my actions. Was it not as wrong to condemn people for their opinions as it was for their race or the colour of their skin?

I turned my attention to Jane Parsons and kept it there for the rest of the meal. Actually, it may have been an ill-wind as the following day Jane suggested that I might have been put next to Jane Parsons as part of a scrutiny process for Ian's succession. However, this has faded so dim that I hardly think about it any longer, although as he is still there the vacancy presumably remains.

Ian and I, and Michael Havers left together for the vote. After the Division we went to Ian's room and watched The Lady do a TV interview with Alastair Burnet. Ian had been apprehensive about this, but I did not think it such a disaster, although she was very strained and intense in her expression – quite different from her demeanour at the dinner.

Afterwards we returned to Downing Street. Ian had told me to wait behind until the other guests had left, but I did not do so and we took our leave at the same time as our own Ambassador in Bucharest who wanted a lift to Grosvenor House. I swished him round there in the S2 (always be nice to Ambassadors as they can be so helpful when one is travelling), but the effect may have been somewhat spoiled if the trade plates, that were lying on the back seat, were noticed.

Cloisters   *Monday, 11 May*

Willie is quite changed. He has lost over two stone. But it is not a cancer loss, it arises out of a regime, a purging. His skin is clear where formerly it was blotchy and his eyes water less. Ostentatiously he refuses drink. Like the Reichs Marshall (though of course not on that scale), he has made a tremendous effort of will and kicked the habit.

But why? He should be amiably, but sozzledly tottering towards an Indian summer in the Lords. Instead he is slim, vigorous, attentive and, most unexpected of all, amiable.

Saltwood   *Thursday, 14 May*

I am drinking *far too much*.

    Yesterday   1 bloody mary ⎫
                         1 glass wine   ⎭

                         2 glasses red wine   ⎫
                         2 glasses white wine ⎬
                         1 vintage port   ⎭

Day before   3 glasses wine   dinner

Before that   wine and port

Cloisters   *Monday, 18 May*

The *Daily Telegraph* carried the most appalling scare headlines about 'slashing' the Navy, getting rid of the three-deck cruisers and the marines etc Jane quite rightly worked me up into a rage about this and I left early for the Commons where I suspected that there would be plenty of action.

The phone had been ringing all weekend with journalists asking for my comments on Keith Speed's speech to his 'constituents' about running down the Navy.[1] To my mingled gratification and alarm, I saw myself described in two of the Sunday newspapers as *Chairman* of the Defence Committee. I suppose it is a tribute to my personality that most people in and out of the Party think I am the Chairman, but this annoys Tony [Buck].

As soon as I got to the Commons it was clear that Keith's number was up. The whips were spreading it around that he had been 'disloyal' and senior backbenchers were echoing this with the

---

[1] Keith Speed had served in the Royal Navy and was appointed Minister for the Navy in 1979.

view that he had 'mismanaged' things – should have resigned simultaneously etc.

Almost immediately after I got in I had to do a broadcast on the *World at One* programme and that evening I went on television twice. It is so easy, even for someone relatively experienced like myself, to allow the journalists to lead one into rather extreme, or at least excessive, comments. As the whole thing was rumour anyway, I suppose I may have overdone it, but colleagues who had heard the broadcast were enthusiastic. Although, in some cases, of course, this could have been tinged with satisfaction at my so obviously putting the kyebosh on my own chances.

In the evening we had the celebrated and long-postponed dinner for Francis Pym and the old officers of the Defence Committee. The postponement had been due to my own spasticity in not getting the original invitations confirmed. But as it happened, it was almost theatrically timely. Someone, presumably Buck himself, had told the press, and the *Evening Standard* featured it as a major item, putting the word 'coincidence' in double quotes.

I made sure that the food would be good and the wine excellent (on the previous Thursday I had won £70 playing backgammon with Lord Armstrong[1] and this led to my credit in the restaurant). We had two bottles of white burgundy and three of excellent claret and Francis became mellow and benevolent – except towards little Winston, with whom he was sharp; 'you are obsessed by your grandfather and comparisons with his period' etc. I would not say that anything very spectacular came out of the meeting except 'goodwill' and we all know what a soft currency that is.

I had kept a place at the table for Hal Miller[2] but he did not turn up as he was making his resignation speech on the floor of the House at that time. Just in case Francis asked me to take Hal's place I rang Jane to clear it with her that I would, as tactfully as I could, say no. It is the second or third most important PPS in the House, but although I like Francis and hold him in high regard, the

---

[1] William Henry Cecil John Robin Watson-Armstrong, 3rd Baron, an underwriting member of Lloyd's.

[2] Hal Miller resigned from his position as PPS to the Chancellor of the Duchy of Lancaster in protest at the government's attitude to the private steel sector.

drudgery of mucking around with the business of the House does not appeal to me. The right answer, but I am not sure if I would have the courage to give it, is 'ask me again when you are Prime Minister'.

Cloisters   *Wednesday, 20 May*

I have lost count of the number of people who have come up to me and asked me if I am going to be the next Navy Minister.

There are cruel disappointments in the House of Commons at every turn and their piquancy is aggravated by the hot-house atmosphere in which one's hopes can soar.

Cloisters   *Thursday, 21 May*

At Brooks's Norman St John-Stevas told me how terrifying The Lady could be, and of one spectacular row that they had had, with her pacing up and down the room screaming at him. Were they alone? I asked. Only Willie, he had replied, but he was slumped in a sofa and said nothing from start to finish.

Later, we moved on to Pratt's and Norman continued to confide in me out of the corner of his mouth. He said he was determined to remain in politics; that the Queen had been perfectly charming to him when he surrendered the seals of office and said what a horrific business politics was; that the Queen Mother had made a point of inviting him to dinner a few days later and then not letting him leave after the meal and so on.

I was impressed by him. He is delightful company. But I am afraid the Tory Party will only tolerate someone as eccentric and witty as he is if they (a) dispose of real personal power and (b) offer the prospect of patronage. And I fear that in his heart Norman realises that this is true.

Saltwood   *Wednesday, 27 May*

At this moment I have got what darling Jane called 'reshuffle
chumblies'. Still no Navy Minister appointed . . . Buck still
tipped. Wouldn't mind this as the Party wouldn't specially like it
and I should then be able to be Chairman [of the Defence Com-
mittee]. A flat election, anyway. But of course even better if I
could get the Ministry myself. Really impose reform, impress the
House and The Lady and be moved to Secretary of State when
Nott becomes Chancellor.

The great thing about politics is that at any time one can throw
double 4's. I am unlucky at backgammon and psychic. I have this
capacity to psyche my opponent into throwing the shots I've
thought of. Alas, it has got to stop. I've said this a great many
times. Now I have decided on it.

Finally there is the 'question' of *The Gems of Brazil*. It started
a year ago when I saw a Mallets ad – presumably for the 'Two
Humming Birds' – identified the artist and forget his name . . .
'An American'. Then last year, after his good job on the Fantin
[Latour] I got Valentine[1] to get them cleaned. He brought them
back – very satisfactory; they really looked nice, rich, decorators'
items and with a certain 'something'. I was glad to have them.
Then on his second visit, at the end of the evening, he produced a
colour ad from (as it were) the *American Connoisseur* showing the
'Two Humming Birds' – possibly the same picture that I had seen
earlier at Mallets – and identifying the artist as Martin Johnson
Heade. I lost the reference and Valentine left the next day.

Then, coming back on the train from Paris, after changing out
of the sleeper, with *The Times* bought at the Gare du Nord, I saw
Geraldine Norman quip that 'American artists of the XIXc are
now worth more per square inch of canvas than any other except
Cézanne and Rembrandt'; she gave a few artists and prices, among
them 'Martin Johnson Heade'. I still didn't twig. Not for some
days until I rang Valentine and asked for a copy of the ad. Yes it

---

[1] Valentine Gould, conservation adviser and old friend of the Clarks.

was. Then it moved quite fast. I contacted the shop by phone, and they told me . . . sold at $40,000, would now ask 50 or even 75. Contacted West Central reference library and looked up Theodore Stebbings Junior's book and found out that there were the 16 missing paintings done in Brazil for the 'Chrome Lithographs' and later sold to Sir Morton Peto (Valentine had told me that on the back, when cleaning them, he had discerned the word 'Peto').

Took them round to Desmond – exaggerating the story of Martin Johnson Heade and a provisional 'price' was 'agreed' of $1.2m.

I could hardly, can hardly, don't really believe that this is actually happening. And now Desmond seems to have gone cold (total radio silence). Am so tired, depressed and martyred, but hourly remind oneself that one has got 16 highly important and interesting missing items by a very valuable XIXc American artist. In the slides they look incredible, so skilful and touching, the 'Luminist' school. Jane rightly said they were a present from George and the birds, and that we ought to keep two.[1]

Continued Saturday

We go to bed *so* late, and Angus got us up so early that I am *averaging* 6–6¾ hrs sleep a night! The Estate endlessly demanding. It is only because it is steadily, insistently summer raining that I have been able to spare the evening in the Gt Hall writing this text. So, am ash eating. The motto is 'can't afford it'. Not drinking (!) now 2½ days. No b'gammon. Sod the cars '. . . not interested, old boy.' The Philosopher Prince – *reflectif*. But thanking God, none-the-less. I said on the 'w': 'I'm certainly not going to Zermatt this September.'

'At the present rate,' said Jane, 'one probably won't be alive by September.'

'Probably alive, but in hospital and on drip-feed.'

She rebuked me, and rightly. We are enormously, colossally

---

[1] Heade (1819–1904) visited South America in the early 1860s to paint the humming birds for *The Gems of Brazil*. It is thought that he did twenty paintings in all. In the end the Clarks sold their sixteen.

lucky. Such a glorious place, such possessions, fulfilment and security. I am enjoying my martyrdom – St Gregory; and may God continue to protect us in the future.

Cloisters   *Friday, 12 June*

I believe that these last few days have been the ones when I finally (or is it first?) realised that I was not going to get any office or preferment whatever.

Spurred on by Jane, I had felt it my duty to caution the Prime Minister against putting in Heseltine as Chairman of the Party. This is a perennial threat, much bandied about by the media from time to time and had been trailed on the front page of the *Sunday Telegraph* last weekend. Also, interestingly, with Norman Tebbit's name. T, too, is completely ruthless and ambitious, but in some way not quite so odious as Heseltine, not so totally synthetic and opportunist. I remember first warning dear Airey about Heseltine and explaining that once installed as Chairman he would try and change, or covertly encourage the changing, of the rules governing election of the Party leader. Because of course the Parliamentary Party would never give him a majority. But if we widened our franchise as have the Labour Party and the Liberals, he would have a chance.

Cloisters   *Monday, 15 June*

The weekend papers are full of forecasts that the Government are contemplating major 'strategic' changes in policy. But what did it all boil down to? Building the Channel Tunnel. I ask you. One is moved to despair. They have cocked the thing up solidly for two years and are now proposing to win the election on an inflationary programme of public works. Depression both personal and general drags at one.

JULY 1981   121

Saltwood   *Saturday, 4 July*

Sitting in the Great Hall – always lovely here on summer evenings. The only remaining place in the estate where one can reach a truly contemplative state. I prefer it to my father's study. I love the high, high hammerbeam roof, the swallows darting excitedly in and out, the looming presence of so many books that I will never, could never, read.

Cloisters   *Tuesday, 7 July*

Today is the debate on the Defence White Paper. I would quite like to speak, but I gather the list is enormous. However, I will sit it out and, hopefully, get on the record with a few interventions

Later, as I was walking back from the Tea Room, I thought I should just check with the Speaker if I had any chance, and my steps took me through the deserted 'Aye' lobby. I heard my name called and IG sidled up beside me. 'Ted is going to speak,' he said.

'Oh really, is he going to be objectionable?'

'I should think inevitably,' he said. 'Can you do anything about it?'

'Yes,' I answered. 'He only sits a couple of places from me. I will find a good time to interrupt him, leave it to me.'

Having an official assignment and sense of importance I went back to my seat.

In the fullness of time Ted got up and started off. When he came to the bit about renewing our presence East of Suez I forced him to give way. Everyone listens to Ted's speeches in the expectation of, and more or less exclusively for, some critical reference veiled or otherwise to The Lady and her Government. But this speech seemed to be perfectly clean.

'I have been listening with great attention to my Honourable Friend,' I said, 'and most of us would agree that what he has said *so far . . .*' (lip curling); I went on to point out that the withdrawal East of Suez had been carried out by his Government. It was a carelessly-phrased intervention and it allowed him to slap me down, as in fact it was *implemented* by the Labour Government. I should have said, 'was *decided* upon by . . .' etc.

Anyway, I sat down, conscious of the fact that I had not covered myself with glory, and listened to the rest of his speech. It was extremely good, slightly isolationist and with a number of ingenious suggestions for arms control negotiations. Sometimes I think that Ted is really rather marvellous. After he had finished, I popped out and wrote a little handwritten note of appreciation. In it I more or less admitted that I had been put up to it, 'you know how these things are arranged'. At the time some great grey cloud exuded warning as it hung over the desk. This was pure sneaking and trouble-making. I lightened it with a benign reference to that charming little piece that he wrote about his childhood at Bexhill and popped it straight on to the Board.

Much later I was still in my place when Ted, still in his pale, pale grey suit, returned for the winding up. With a thrill of horror I saw that he was holding my note in his hand. He opened it, read it and very slowly and deliberately put it back into the envelope. As usual his face was totally expressionless. Was he offended? I had a sudden nightmare that he would take it straight to the Chief Whip and complain.[1]

Saltwood   *Saturday, 11 July*

We gave a good dinner party for Aspinall's Ball at Port Lympne. Edward and Fiona Montagu, Jonathan Aitken and his wife, Lolicia (or Lutz as, disconcertingly, appears to be her nickname),[2] also Jonathan Guinness[3] with his wife and two of his sons, Valentine

---

[1] In fact some days later AC received a very polite and appreciative note from Edward Heath, thanking him for his letter and saying that he 'quite understood'. Sequels with a wider impact were to follow later, however.

[2] 'Lutz' was the name of the SS commandant at the Colditz camp where AC's son James had worked the previous summer.

[3] Lord Montagu of Beaulieu and his second wife; Jonathan Guinness, former chairman of the Monday Club, and his second wife.

and Sebastian. One of these latter never combed his hair or took off his overcoat, as far as I could see, throughout the weekend, but was quite sympathetic nevertheless.

The food was delicious and the table almost overloaded with Meissen, solid silver, Venetian glass, etc. I gave them two magnums of Batailley '61, as well as much other good stuff. They polished off a full bottle of Cockburn '55.

Aspinall promised that his Ball would be the most expensive since Charlie Bestigui in Venice in 1951. He had boy scouts holding torches of pitch the whole way down the drive and girl guides doing the same thing on the walk up from the car park. The floodlighting was spectacular and the flower arrangements quite incredible. Everything had been done on a kind of nothing-but-the-best principle, and there were literally vats of caviare, surrounding polar bears carved out of ice etc. I noticed faces from the past: Vivian Naylor-Leyland, still consorting with the young, I saw. His face seemed curiously swollen and stricken and his speech impaired. Surely, he is still too young to have had a tiny occlusion?

Jane and I spent most of the time sitting on stone seats in the garden or walking in the more secluded regions (naturally most of the guests simply turned left and went straight down to the marquee where they stuffed themselves with as much free food and drink as they could for four hours).

We wondered how Port Lympne was taking it. I know, because I went there as a child and because Sybil[1] showed me the visitors book, just how much of a centre it was on every summer weekend for twenty years, and of course tonight's party was not really grand in the full sense. The boys, who stayed until the bitter end, told me that there was one person there being referred to as 'Your Royal Highness', who was 'covered in rocks' and Jane told me that she spotted quite a lot of good jewellery. But au fond it was an unselective 20 per cent of café society, a leavening of aristocratic gamblers, from whom Aspinall had won large sums twenty years earlier, and an unfortunately high number of more shadowy

---

[1] Marchioness of Cholmondeley, sister of Philip Sassoon, who built Port Lympne.

figures, presumably Mafia, or 'multinational', who have access to enormous bank accounts.

Yet the presentation was tasteful, no vulgarity whatever, except in the sheer abundance. It was sad too, Gatsby-like in its transience, because poor old Aspers has no money at all, not in the real sense; he could go broke overnight. The great house with all its memories and evocations, that had slept for so long, then drowsed uncomfortably in the last two years while the public trampled about its gardens and ground floor, had been put into a time machine – but a synthetic one: it had not really been awakened, simply put on a life support system that was turned off again at 5am.

Cloisters   *Thursday, 16 July*

I suppose today was the high point of my social life to date – in so far as that depends upon my status as a politician. As I boasted to Charles Howard, 'I have got the Queen at four, the Prime Minister at six, and a private dinner with the American Ambassador at eight . . .' 'Watch out it is not God at midnight,' he answered, quite wittily.

It was my first time in the Buck House garden, although to get to it we walked through that courtyard where I remember dismounting for the great Armstrong-Jones wedding ball in 1959, when Dukey [Prince Philip] tried to pick up Jane.

We joined the line to catch a glimpse of the Royals and seeing Tony Buck I mischievously asked him if he was going to dinner with the Americans that night (they had marked the invitation 'in honour of Mr and Mrs John Nott'). He was startled and angry to hear about it, almost more so than I had anticipated. Said he would complain etc.

We sheered off to another part of the line. The Queen slowly made her way along, preceded by a posse of buffers in slightly better-fitting morning dress than the majority of the guests, and made conversation with certain selected invitees – the statutory person in a wheel chair with bearded mentor etc. When you see the Queen in the flesh she is always smaller and more beautifully made up than one remembers. She was wearing a white silk coat (like Jane) and a navy blue straw hat.

The Lady, although as always enthusiastic in her greeting, struck me as being a little bit triste and blotchy, which I recognise as being one of her stress symptoms. Notters was already in his black tie and so we shot back to Albany in order to dress up for the Americans.

It always takes longer to get to Regents Park than one anticipates. I was using the old green Bentley as my faithful 2CV is presently immobilised with a puncture. The custodian at the gate said, 'The name must be Clark', from which we inferred (rightly) that we were the last to arrive.

A number of speeches were exchanged and I was delighted to hear the Ambassador say that 'We have the whole defence department here this evening . . .' (!) How *did* I get on to that invitation list? All the Ministers were there and the PPS, but I was the only officer of the Committee.

Saltwood   *Saturday, 18 July*

A lovely family day. Both boys around, and divine.

The [*Gems of Brazil*] cash – 950 US is already on deposit in UBS Brig. Due to emerge at 960 (or 910 ex Desmond) on 3 August. It is agonising to dispense any of it, as it edges its way up so close to the big 'M' – I mean this in *cash*, that's really quite good at any time, and particularly now.

Cloisters   *Tuesday, 21 July*

Very surprisingly, England won the test match [against Australia] by 18 runs when Willis took 8 wickets for 43 in just over the hour. Charlie Morrison, deaf and gangling and ill-disposed, got up at PM's Questions and made a characteristically awful intervention. As he can neither compose nor articulate a perfectly normal English sentence, he was unable to get through even his opening words of congratulations to the English Test side without furtively glancing down at his notes. 'Reading,' everybody bellowed with ritual glee. Then he came to the tricky bit. 'Was this not a good example of change of tactics,' he asked, 'which we might emulate?' In fact it was very much less clear than this and brought in some muddled reference to change of *captains* also. So the lobby went abuzz with the news that he had recommended – as may well have been his intention – a change of captain.

In the evening I had my end of term dinner with Ian Gow. I got to Pratt's early and ordered half a bottle of champagne, which I thought we could split. However, 'George' poured the whole bottle into a large silver tankard and set it in front of me; very healthy and reviving.

Ian arrived a little late, having walked across the Park. I noticed that he had lost weight and he seemed nervous. He is smoking a great deal. He reproached Benyon,[1] or 'Buckingham', as he calls him, for advocating selective reflation. Jonathan and I also argued for this, although I was more candid. 'You have got to bribe the electorate, buy the votes,' I said, 'in order to get you through the next election. It is far too early to start now, but it is something that you must carry in your mind when you plan the '83 Budget.' IG was shocked by this, genuinely shocked I think. 'You are an innocent', I told him, 'a complete babe in arms.' How can someone who is so good at his job and so very alert to political undercurrents and attitudes in the Parliamentary Party have standards of integrity that make him so dangerously vulnerable in policy matters? Fortunately, I think that The Lady is more realistic.

We moved on from Pratt's and had a tête-à-tête meal at Brooks's. IG mellowed with a good bottle of claret. He told me that The Lady was completely unperturbed (personally I doubt this) and determined to press on. He asked me who should be Chairman of the Party. I simply could not make a convincing suggestion. He mentioned the two leading contenders, Heseltine and Tebbit, and added a third, Tom King. A bit light on charisma and bell-ringing I told him. He looked gloomy. Was there anyone in the Lords? he asked. 'Here we are, knowing the Party as we do,'

---

[1] William Benyon, MP for Buckingham since 1970.

he said, 'and we cannot think of a single candidate of whom we could wholeheartedly approve.' I did not answer.

Cloisters   *Wednesday, 22 July*

The Lady came to the 1922 Committee and to suit her convenience we sat one hour earlier than usual, at 5pm. It was not a happy occasion. The mood of the Commons was gloomy, sepulchral almost. The Lady was 'lackluster' (as the *Wall Street Journal* describes, every day, the bond market).

Edward du Cann[1], that master of the coded message, who conceals the dagger in his toga until the very last moment, ended by saying that '. . . although a week is a long time in politics, two years is a very short time until a general election . . .'. And everyone got the message – although of course du Cann is nothing like as powerful or as influential as he was in 1974–75 when he was manoeuvring the '22 to overturn Ted.

Saltwood   *Thursday, 23 July*

July fatigue/gloom. Everything should be lovely, but there is, in some sense, too much of it. If I were to write down the *good* things they would be:

Total solvency for the first time ever, nil indebtedness and ¾ m in
    US, giving 100 US per annum.
Both boys lovely and settled in what they want to do.
Reasonably high status in H of C.
Hobbies – cars, writing, restoring – all give pleasure.
'Active' and in good health.

---

[1] Edward du Cann, MP for Taunton since 1956. Long-term Chairman of the Conservative 1922 Committee.

Cloisters   *Friday, 24 July*

The House sat all night and those who were not on their feet had been told to return by 8am for a 'closure'. Needless to say, there was no vote, but I had a cup of coffee while waiting with Jim Lester[1], who told me that he thought the Prime Minister would announce her reshuffle immediately we rose as a tactical device to muffle the sounds of protest – many people being away on holiday, lobby correspondents in the South of France, etc. I do not believe it. I do not think there will be a radical reshuffle and such as there is will, I think, take place in September and be conformist in the extreme.

This view was confirmed to me by Michael McNair-W[2]., who also said that Peter Walker had told him that Quintin[3] (whom I have always suspected of being disloyal) said that The Lady was like Herbert Hoover and would lead us to such a defeat that we would be out of office for thirty years.

Saltwood   *Friday, 31 July*

The weather this summer has been appalling. Usually I swim every day once the pool has been filled – this year less than six times I should think. As I swam 'powerful strokes' the other day I said to Jane: 'The truth is I'm not a Renaissance Prince any longer.' I have a little spare tyre, which flaps over my belt when I'm sitting down. My canine tooth is very short and discoloured and can give the impression of a gap.

---

[1] James (Jim) Lester, MP for Beeston since February 1974.
[2] Michael McNair-Wilson, MP for Newbury since February 1974.
[3] Quintin Hogg, Lord Hailsham of St Marylebone. A minister in the Eden, Macmillan, Douglas-Home and Heath cabinets. Lord Chancellor 1970–74.

Saltwood   *Monday, 14 September*

The sun has shone every day since the wedding of the Prince of Wales on the 29 July, and the pool temperature is still over 70°, but the last fortnight I don't seem to have had nearly as much time to myself, and 'on the land' as I would have wished. On the day after Bank Holiday I had to be in Plymouth at 10am for a day's voyage on *Valiant*.

My God, it's nasty on a submarine. They submerge as soon as they leave port and may stay at sea for *months*, not surfacing again until they return to their home port. The viruses and bacteria go round and round in the ventilation (sic) system which recycles the stale air through some acidifier that 'purifies' it. The heat in the engine room (115°), the lurking menace of the reactor, which needs four people constantly monitoring its evil dials, the claustrophobia, not just of being submerged in the deep, but of sheer confinement, of having nowhere to which one could retreat for any level of privacy at all. The only area, curiously, with any sense of space is the torpedo room in the bows, and firing the torpedoes or 'fish' as they call them (we staged a mock attack) is exhilarating.

Most of the time it was painfully boring – like going round the laundry at St Thomas's[1] (which is, of course, in the basement), and it was all I could do to stop myself nodding off everywhere that our stooping, shuffling tour came to a halt. Once we had surfaced again for our return into the Sound, I insisted on going up into the 'Fin', as the Conning Tower is now called. And that was marvellous. One climbed up this narrow, wet – the whole fin is flooded while the boat is submerged – iron ladder, some 30 feet up and there one is, in this iron balcony, with the black hull below, foam pouring off her as she cleaves the waters at seventeen knots.

The only other MPs on board were David Hunt[2]: still putting on weight, but reasonably amiable; and poor Neville Trotter[3] who works so hard and has so much defence expertise and is always

---

[1] AC was a governor of St Thomas's Hospital, 1969–74.

[2] David Hunt, MP for Wirral since 1976.

[3] Neville Trotter, MP for Tynemouth since February 1974.

being passed over. On the platform of Plymouth Station I said something about the reshuffle. I can't remember his exact reply, but it was very much to the effect that all junior appointments were made by the Chief Whip and so (implied) I didn't have a chance, a view which had been most unwelcomely also propagated by Peter Hennessy,[1] one of my August visitors who had let it go almost as an aside.

I reflected on this gloomily last night and throughout this morning as the reshuffle, or reconstruction as it has been in some quarters predicted, gets (apparently) under way. Long-heralded, like some ponderous offensive by the Russian Army, and preceded by much leaking and counter-leaking chiefly by the protagonists of Prior and Tebbit, it has of recent days appeared that The Lady is going to get her way, and purge the wets, as Ian promised me she would when we dined at Brooks's just before the House rose. But I am afraid, I kind of *know* that I am going to be left out. As Jane percipiently observed, the Whips would have rung by now '. . . to check on your whereabouts'.

I had been looking forward to today as little Graham Turner, mole-like journalist famous for his in-depth articles for the *Sunday Telegraph*, was due to pay me a special visit to collect material for an article he is doing for pre-Conference Sunday on the state of the Party. I waited around all morning and the phone rang less and less frequently.

We sat in the red library. The Yquem smoothly did its work on an empty stomach and I sparkled. (I am often, but on each occasion too late, reminded of Tim Rathbone's[2] comment, 'Al should realise that there is more to politics than being amusing'). All the time I was unhappily aware that the phone was silent. Completely silent.

I took Graham Turner to Sandling at 4.30 and from the platform he telephoned, with much clicking and crashing of 10p pieces, to Ian Gilmour of all people! Confirmation that he (Ian),

---

[1] Peter Hennessy, Whitehall correspondent of *The Times* since 1976.
[2] Tim Rathbone, MP for Lewes since Februray 1974.

Soames and Carlisle had all been sacked.[1] Other changes '. . . still going on'.

With a heavy heart I drove back to Saltwood. By now I must have had it. We listened to the hourly bulletin on the news, but little else came across. That evening I re-watched *Cabaret*,[2] which kept me diverted. After that wonderful, uplifting scene in the beer garden, when the young SA boy leads the singing of 'Tomorrow Belongs to Me' I switched off and went to bed.

Blackpool   *Tuesday, 13 October*

Ted Heath has been making a number of fierce attacks on The Lady and her Government, clearly timed to provoke a crisis at the Conference which opens at Blackpool today. Last night he was appearing on *Panorama* with David Dimbleby. To my great alarm – though a sixth sense warned me of this – Ted, when questioned about the Dirty Tricks, concerning which he had mentioned a number, cited a distinguished journalist, who admitted to having been fed misinformation, and a Member of Parliament, who quite recently had been put up to interrupt one of his speeches but later retracted and apologised [see entry for 7 July 1981].

Cloisters   *Monday, 19 October*

I was crossing the Members' Lobby, George Gardiner[3] asked me if I was thinking of standing against Tony Buck for the Defence Chair. I hummed and hahed. It is always tricky opposing a friend – especially if you are not certain of the outcome. Then I had a brainwave. Why not ask David Hunt, that way I could both gauge

---

[1] Ian Gilmour, Lord Privy Seal since 1979; Lord Soames, Leader of the House of Lords since 1979; Mark Carlisle, education secretary since 1979.

[2] *Cabaret*, film with Liza Minnelli, of the Kander and Ebb 1966 musical based on Christopher Isherwood's *Goodbye to Berlin* stories.

[3] Sir George Gardiner, MP for Reigate since 1974. Secretary of '92.

the mood of the Whips Office and of the Secretary of State, whose PPS he was until recently.

Somewhat to my surprise Hunt said that the move would be very welcome, gave me the impression that the Whips Office would support it. 'It will be interesting to see how effective this support is,' I said. 'One reason I was asking you was that I had wanted Phil Goodhart's job and had been told by three people, including one in the Whips Office [Nick Budgen], that John Nott had opposed the appointment as he thought that I would obstruct the renewed cuts that he is going to have to impose on the Services.'

Hunt denied this with real vigour, said that Nott did not know anything about the change until the last moment and was very upset to have lost Philip. He more or less said that the Whips had chopped Philip because he was inarticulate at Question Time.

I was uplifted by this, even though, as Jane astutely observed when I told her the following morning (I left early and went down to Saltwood for the day): 'You cannot trust any of them. It is just their little way of consoling for not getting a job.'

Saltwood   *Sunday, 25 October*

It was a week ago yesterday that Albert Costain publicly announced that he was not going to stand again for Folkestone. I do not know why, but I get the impression that my position is very much weaker than it was two years ago. I do not seem to know anyone in the Association, and it seems ages since I had a speaking engagement down there. In the past I could never go anywhere without somebody asking why I wasn't the MP yet.

Yesterday we saw Beth[1] in the street. 'Are you putting up?' she said. I said I was and asked her round for drinks today to talk about it.

However, when she arrived she avoided the subject until the

---

[1] Mrs Evans-Smith, the physiotherapist who treated AC for his back trouble, was an officer of the Saltwood and Newington Ward of the Folkestone Conservative Association.

very last minute. Then, more or less said that I was too much disliked locally by people I had been rude to, thrown off the grounds, etc. I am not sure if I think this is all that important, or indeed incorrectable by personal contact, but it was all lowering nevertheless. It must be said, too, that Beth is nowhere near the centre of the Association (not, for example, the way Graham Butland was in the Plymouth Association in 1972).

I had already decided to give a posh weekend, have Anthony Royle down and precede the dinner the previous evening with a drinks party for all the local big wigs. Beth agreed that this would be a good idea. A bit obvious I feel. But there is no harm in that.[1]

Cloisters   *Monday, 26 October*

At the seven o'clock division John Nott came up to me in the Lobby and said: 'I hear you are putting up.'[2]

'Yes, I am,' I said. 'Can I see you privately about it for a minute?'

I told him that Tony was very upset, put me in a difficult position, what did he think?

'I could not possibly comment, you must understand I could not, it would be quite wrong for me to say anything.'

'In that case, why did you raise the subject?' I said.

'Well, if you will not repeat this to anyone, I must not really, should not say anything . . .'

'No, of course I won't.'

'Well, I think you should put up.'

'Thanks. In that case I will.'

An encouraging little exchange, I suppose.

Plymouth train   *Friday, 30 October*

I must admit I like the Plymouth express. The 3 hour journey is almost too short as one comfortably rolls along suspended from

---

[1] Royle declined.
[2] As chair of the Defence Committee.

communication or pressure, travelling *free* and closeted with one's papers. I must look at my career prospects. How bad will they be when the dream goes – for good I mean, and people push past?

Incidentally, what is perfectly clear is that my 'intimate' with IG and The Lady has blown. They know the truth about the Dirty Tricks letter!

Trouble is, have lost zing and no adrenalin. A back number. The lobby correspondents no longer approach me as I walk across the lobby.

Bratton   *Saturday, 7 November*

Beleaguered at Bratton, I watched the birds, tits and blackbirds from the first floor window. A blackbird worked his way right along the path, getting at the leaves and poking at wormholes.

'En Garçon' as Jane has to lay the wreath at Saltwood tomorrow, while I had constituency engagements on Friday, Saturday, Sunday and Monday. Armistice weekend (as I call it) is always loaded.

On the Friday I had undertaken to 'talk to' the F&GP of the Association about 'my intentions' regarding Folkestone and Hythe, and they were summoned to Headland Park, the dingy, peeling, and dry-and-wet-rot smelling, terrace headquarters off North Hill, at 6pm.

My problem was, how to finesse the hand. Of course I would prefer to sit for Folkestone. Bigger majority (even), less travelling, easier to socialise, new faces, honeymoon period, etc. The night before I had come across Tony Royle and Albert Costain talking in the Lobby – 'We were just speaking about you.' Ugh. Tony and I went to a private corner and he gave me a 'fatherly' talking to. Albert had said I hadn't a chance, they would never choose the laird, wanted someone he just stopped himself saying 'younger', substituted 'more in touch with ordinary people'. Utter balls of course. Why should it be legitimate to 'discriminate' against the rich and well-educated, when heavy penalties are attached to doing so against the black, the fat, the homosexual, the handicapped, the female, etc, etc?

I was quite prepared, I said, to answer the charge of carpet bagging. Wasn't I deliberately making the sacrifice of throwing up a safe seat, putting everything at risk, simply for the honour of representing my home division, the place where I had spent my childhood, my own children had been brought up? He mellowed slightly. Perhaps if I did it *cleanly*, notified my own people of my intention not to stand . . . As he said this I thought of that draft letter of resignation, first written in 1976, and a great weight seemed to lift. How wonderful, and yet how sad! But how tempting!

But then Tony's brow furrowed again. What if I *was* adopted in spite of everything, and then Albert died suddenly and there had to be a by-election? 'Two by-elections', I said. He looked unhappy. 'Your name will be mud in the Party.' But still he is a friend. The bond of the upper classes, pretty thin on the ground, even on the back benches of the Tory Party. He said he would have a word with the agent on Monday, make some enquiries. 'The Agent hates me.' Worse and worse. He'd speak to the chairman, ring him up.

But all this, and the fact that no one in Folkestone *has* been beating a path to my door, has lowered my estimate of my chances. And so, at the meeting of the Plymouth F&GP, I funked it. When Mr Boyette asked me which I would prefer, '. . . if both were in the hand', I paused reflectively for a long time (knowing full well which was my *real* preference) then said emphatically 'Plymouth'.

Several of them, real dears, clapped. John Arnaud led the testimonials, very splendidly saying that it didn't matter that I wasn't living there. Mike Gregory also came down on my side though with a few qualifications, and Wally Rowland, a well-known Vicar of Bray, also came out pro, though with the coded disclaimer that it might be better *for me* to change. Only that little gnomeprick Jack Courtney said that the matter ought to be 'referred back to the wards.' So we ended friends, with my position here greatly consolidated. Any sign of trouble in the future and I can always refer to that meeting as justifying (a) my fighting all the way, and (b) threatening to stand in any case as Independent-Conservative – against-the-Common-Market or whatever.

All the same I felt a somewhat heavy heart after they had all dispersed. *It might have been.* I am not really *of* Plymouth, and I don't know how much longer I can keep up the pretence.

Cloisters   *Wednesday, 11 November*

In the Members' Lobby, where I was hailed by Tony Royle. He told me that, as he had promised, he had spoken to the Chairman at Folkestone and that, in fact, he (the Chairman) was not ill-disposed to my candidature and that although no guarantees could be made, I would certainly have a 'good run' if I put in. This is too vexing. Particularly as Tony said that both he and the Chairman and Albert all agreed that it was essential that I should write to my own constituency and 'completely clear the decks' with them.

Now what the hell am I going to do? I suppose that I must proceed with Folkestone. But of course it is more difficult in one sense because of last week's 'statement' in Plymouth. Fortunately though they are not selecting until January. This means that the 'statement' will have bought a little time, quietened the thing down and allow me to write the letter of resignation over the Christmas holiday.

In the meantime I have got to look more closely at the situation in Folkestone and revert to the plan of having a great baronial party before Christmas, somewhat on Astor lines, more official, that is to say, than social. I telephone Jane to ask her to book the bell ringers for the first Saturday evening in December.[1] Jane, bless her, gave a kind of spluttering giggle at this volte-face. She asked me very pertinently whether I was not making the same mistake, in political terms, that I had already made in the bond market. Namely of switching out of one great lump into another, just as the first one was about to fructify. I am afraid there may be something in this.

---

[1] A group of locals in the Saltwood area who play a (limited) repertoire of musical tunes on handbells.

Cloisters   *Tuesday, 17 November*

We assembled in Room 10. Little David Trippier[1] started to say something in his flat northern tones about how he thought I was probably doing the right thing . . . etc. Knowing that he would vote against me I said, 'No, no, no, all the officers must vote for Tony (grand seigneur!).' As I looked round the room I noted complacently that my supporters predominated. A whip (I cannot remember which one) handed me a pile of ballot papers. I marked one and distributed a few others while holding on to the pile. Unfortunately, Tony was sitting next to me, otherwise I might have succumbed to a reckless impulse to 'vote often.' As it was when I went up with my ballot paper to the return pile I did manage, surreptitiously, to vote once more. I am sure Buck didn't see, but little Neil Thorne was watching me closely.[2]

The committee elections are a shambles. Perhaps just as well, I thought, although I was rather alarmed when Buck said: 'You have voted three times.' Supposing Neil Thorne had seen me cheat? Was Buck going to make a scene? He seemed good natured, though on edge. I thought my majority would be so huge that I could, if he insisted, readily submit to a recount, excluding my own ballot paper. But the thing died down. Bob Boscawen[3] handed over the ballot papers to Tony Berry[4] who took them outside. Then Boscawen came back. He had the result. I didn't catch his eye, although he was only a few feet away from me. Relaxedly I stretched my legs out below the desk; a sidelong glance at Buck showed that he was both sweating *and* smoking.

Boscawen announced, in an extremely flat tone, the result – Anthony Buck has been elected.

I felt like one of those characters in melodrama who scream

---

[1] David Trippier, MP for Rosendale since 1979.
[2] Neil Thorne, MP for Ilford South since 1979.
[3] Bob Boscawen, MP for Wells since 1970.
[4] Anthony Berry, MP for Southgate since 1964. Younger son of Lord Kemsley, who had owned the *Sunday Times*, and nephew of the proprietors of the *Daily* (and *Sunday*) *Telegraph*.

'No, No!' or 'I can't *believe* it.' I had, of course, made instant and ritual obeisance to Tony and congratulated him. What the hell had happened? Perhaps Berry, who loathes me and had, I believe, blackmailed me for the Whips Office, had subtracted the necessary number of ballot papers on the way back to the Chief's office where the count took place? This would have been divine punishment for my shiftily voting twice, just as God always punishes one, instantly, for cheating in a backgammon game.

Dear old 'Tone' has, of course, no enemies. He is the personification of '. . . always has a cheery word for everyone around him'.

Oh dear, though, how very flat making. I slipped away and telephoned Jane who, as always, was sweet, loyal and indignant.

Cloisters   *Thursday, 26 November*

Everything is dreadfully depressing. Clearly the SDP are going to win Crosby.[1] How fickle and spastic the electorate are. How gullible, to be duped by someone as scatty and shallow as Shirley Williams.

Plymouth train   *Friday, 27 November*

Filled with 'set-backs' – devastatingly dear, beloved Tip-book's rejection by RCB.[2]

I just don't understand this; like Jane I am *shitted* by it, shitted *for him*, who so genuinely and unbelievably against all the odds triumphed at Pirbright and 'swotted up' for his lecturette. I was so proud, with all his new friends, and circle and prospects. What a blow it must be for him. What now? I somehow feel that whatever job he gets he will always think wistfully of the Guards. As will I. I will hardly be able to look at a Guards detachment, just as soon, it

---

[1] Crosby by-election, caused by the death of Sir Graham Page, where one of the SDP's 'Gang of Four', Shirley Williams, was standing.

[2] Andrew retook his RCB (Regular Commissions Board) the following year and passed. He would join the Life Guards, rise to the rank of major and retire in 1994.

seems, I will never be able to cross Westminster Bridge again or drive round Parliament Square.

Saltwood   *Sunday, 29 November*

Still very depressed. The Winter Office is so nice, but like everything and everywhere, it needs tidying, attention, TIME. A fine day, but cold, cold, and with a keen wind. Before breakfast darling Jane had 'hysterics' because the kitchen fire wouldn't light. I wish, I really do wish, I could find some way of saving her some of the drudgery. A minute ago I went into the kitchen and she was brillo-scrubbing the bottom of a saucepan.

At breakfast I grumbled something about the Deeds not being in the Deed-box.[1] She pointed out that she had not got the time to clear out the safe – with VAT two weeks behind, Christmas shopping to do, all the food for the party *and* the dinner to prepare, plus Christmas in prospect – and anyway from the bedroom window she could see ten vehicles 'standing out'. Perfectly true.

Cloisters   *Thursday, 3 December*

In some strange way I continue to warm to Ted Heath, who these days sits only one place away from me. David Howell[2] had made a singularly inept and colourless presentation of the case for allowing heavy, or heav*ier*, juggernauts to free range over the roads of the Kingdom and the House was restive. Criticisms came from every side, although after about a half hour they had retained a respective quality. In an effort to produce something new Richard Mitchell,[3]

---

[1] Although, surprisingly, AC makes no mention in his journal, all indebtedness to C. Hoare & Co. had finally been cleared a year before. The deeds arrived back at Saltwood on 23 December 1980.

[2] David Howell MP, Energy and Transport Secretary from 1979.

[3] Richard Mitchell, Labour MP for Southampton, Itchen from 1971 (Southampton Test, 1966–71) until joining the SDP earlier in the year.

now of the SDP, raised the question of the dangers presented by static juggernauts at night – 'particularly as they are usually parked outside houses belonging to persons other than the driver.'

It was a case of the big-man-move-with-surprising-speed. Although he inclined his head very slightly, and his smile was arched and lethargic, Ted's reaction was instantaneous, faster than anyone else on our bench. 'That is a very insulting thing to say about lorry drivers,' he said to us, 'that they are always parked outside other people's houses at night.' Genuinely funny and unexpected.

Cloisters   *Tuesday, 8 December*

Lunched with Frank Johnson.[1] He is so quick and alert and youthfully intelligent; delightful company.

'There is an incredibly beautiful waitress who sometimes serves this table,' he said, nervously apprehensive. And our luck was in and she materialised, an absolutely devastating honey-blonde of about twenty-two; incredible, faultless in appearance, but when she spoke, utterly anaphrodisiac, ridiculous hockey-girl voice, 'Righty-ho,' Betjemanesque.

Frank pretended he wanted to talk about the Tory Party, but he really prefers to talk about the Nazis, concerning whom he is curious, but not, of course, sympathetic. Yes, I told him, I was a Nazi, I really believed it to be the ideal system, and that it was a disaster for the Anglo-Saxon races and for the world that it was extinguished. He both gulped and grinned, 'But surely, er, you mean . . . (behaving like an unhappy interviewer in *Not the Nine O'Clock News* after, eg, Pamela Stephenson had said something frightfully shocking) . . . ideally in terms of administrative and economic policy . . . you cannot really, er . . .' Oh yes, I told him, I was completely committed to the whole philosophy. The blood and the violence was an essential ingredient of its strength, the heroic tradition of cruelty every bit as powerful and a thousand times more ancient than the Judaeo-Christian ethic.

---

[1] Frank Johnson, parliamentary sketch writer on *The Times*.

Even he, I think, was slightly shocked. How can you say such a thing? he kept repeating. Meaning, not how can you say such a thing, but how do you dare put it into words. 'You might be quoted in Atticus.' I said I didn't care and, anyway, I had already been quoted as saying this very thing in Atticus.[1] He agreed, he and Hitchens had talked about it at the time and just like everyone here they took refuge in the convention that Alan-doesn't-really-mean-it. He-only-says-it-to-shock, etc. Frank said that people simply will not allow the reality that a 'toff' could be serious about these views, whereas if they were being expressed by someone like Tony Marlow[2] or Nicholas Winterton, he would be ostracised.

The only time we talked about the Tory Party was when we both spontaneously at the same moment expressed our growing admiration for Ted. I said that it was not necessarily his policies – although these were being expressed in a much more sensible and original style than of old – but his whole personal demeanour was creditable. He had been through the furnace, of rejection and contempt, and emerged unalloyed. Frank agreed. As ardent Heath-haters of old we felt that such a change was a credit to our objectivity.

Later that afternoon in the Economics Debate Ted spoke very brilliantly, ranging far and wide, a relaxed demolition job. He even managed to turn Enoch on the ropes when The Prophet, his own features contorted with fury, told Ted to 'take that grin off your face.' 'The Rt Hon. gentleman can ask me to do many things, but that is not one of them,' said Ted, and the House roared with laughter in support.

Cloisters   *Wednesday, 9 December*

The Chef had sent a message, as I require him to do, that there was fresh lobster and so I left Brooks's early and went back to the

---

[1] AC was profiled in the *Sunday Times* Atticus column by Christopher Hitchens in February 1980.

[2] Anthony (Tony) Marlow, MP for Northampton North since 1979.

House Dining Room at 9pm. Ian Gow was at the other end of the table I joined at which were also seated two Whips (John Stradling Thomas and John Cope[1]), and two Ministers (Lynda Chalker[2] and Tom King[3]). When he got up I followed him and gave him the amusing news, which I had discovered when I took Andrew to Pratt's, that both Peter Walker and Michael Heseltine had been black-balled. As Jane had said, this was practically the only encouraging bit of news in the last six months. What a splendid bastion of ancient squirearchical values that place is, that it should even these days feel strong enough to black-ball two up-and-coming Privy Councillors and members of the Cabinet!

However, things then turned nasty for, as we paced along the corridor, Ian told me that little Albert Costain had been making trouble about my intentions regarding Folkestone. Ian said it would be a 'snub' to people who 'had worked so long and loyally for me at election time, also the fact that I had abandoned them would "weigh very heavily" with the Selection Committee.' Sod, sod, sod, sod. Not only was this a tiresome thing to hear from such a source, but it also illuminated Ian's deviousness. Quite feline he is, or rather like some Russian Grandmaster, seeing always many moves ahead. Just as the reason he had taken me out to dinner the night after my defeat for the Defence Chair was not primarily to console me, but just as much (I suspect) because he already perceived my somewhat tetchy manner when I had questioned the Prime Minister about referenda the previous week and, knowing that I was number two on her list the following week, felt obliged to ensure that I didn't use that position to make trouble. And similarly his open impression of friendship and trust at the dinner table was designed to put me in a good mood before he warned off my overtures to the Folkestone constituency.

---

[1] John Cope, MP for South Gloucestershire since February 1974.

[2] Lynda Chalker, MP for Wallasey since February 1974, a junior minister at Health and Social Security since 1979.

[3] Tom King, MP for Bridgwater since 1970, local government minister since 1979.

Cloisters   *Thursday, 10 December*

I had a mini-triumph today, and quite unexpected. The fascination of the House of Commons is that one can never be certain in one's prediction of the outcome of events, even from hour to hour.

I had been placed at very short notice on the Committee of the Local Government (Miscellaneous Provisions) Bill and went in neither having read the Bill, nor attended any stage of the debates on the floor. To my alarm and amazement I noticed that the very first amendment was being put by the likeable, but low-key, Shirley Summerskill,[1] requiring the Government to license pop festivals – and Raison[2], dutifully reading his Home Office brief, was actually resisting this! I rose in my seat and made a totally impromptu speech, referring to the closet trendiness in the Conservative Party and the absurdity of resisting such a reasonable amendment. Colleagues pricked up their ears, abandoned their correspondence and it soon became plain to the Front Bench and the Whip that there was not the slightest chance of saving the clause after it was put to a vote. So now pop festivals will have to be licensed. One of those tiny little episodes for which one can claim credit – like me blocking the Local Government (again!) Ethnic Groups Grants Bill in 1979.

Saltwood   *Saturday, 12 December*

London has been snowbound all week. Lovely by the logfire – but not as relaxed as could be, hidden stress. I've really lost interest in Plymouth, that's the fact. Don't bother with press release any more, or any kind of self-promotion. I don't know anyone in Plymouth other than a few narrow Conservatives. I suppose it might be recoverable with 18 months dedication in the run-up, but can I afford the time? Have I the inclination? I must leave some

---

[1] Dr Shirley Summerskill, MP for Halifax since 1964, and opposition front bench shadow spokesman on home affairs.

[2] Timothy Raison, MP for Aylesbury since 1970. Junior Home Office minister since 1979.

record, and it should really be my big philosophico-historical treatise – can only do this with the Commons research facilities available. But everyone warns me against trying for Folkestone.

Drawing directly on from that there is our party next Saturday – the celebrated local benefit, now coming off in a rather different atmosphere to that which one had planned; people definitely wary, more suspicious. So much so that I said to Jane, only half in jest, that one should not put in for Folkestone at all, *but* announce an (sic) intention not to stand again in Plymouth. This would leave one free to apply for some of the other local seats (Rye, Maidstone etc). I would, though, be very sorry to miss the wheeling-and-dealing of the opening days of the new Parliament.

Saltwood   *Saturday, 19 December*

Our party for the local nobs. Much anxiety about who would or would not come, how the hell we identify them anyway, etc. Masses of flowers and greenery everywhere, log fires blazing in every fireplace and – for the first time in fifty years – upper and lower halls properly *lit*, as I had raided the Great Library and brought back a number of lamp standards. Jane valiantly changed plugs throughout the morning from three-pin to two-pin so that we could use all Mr Paine's old sockets put in in the early '50s. No fuses blew and the place looked wonderful.

First to arrive (and, incidentally, the last to leave) was the editor of the *Folkestone Herald* and his *very* young and pretty wife. He, a little Welshman with dark curly hair, not as unfriendly as I had feared. Soon they were pouring in. To get over the identification problem we had posted William[1] at the door in order to take guests' names and announce them. Jane and I stood in the lower hall and directed guests to the upper hall where Sarah and James handed them champagne. Thereafter they drifted about, most of them finding their way into the Library where soon a comforting roaring noise built up.

---

[1] 'William' had served Mrs Brown, a neighbour of the Clarks, as butler for many years and after her death he used to help at Saltwood on social occasions.

We had two set-pieces. First was the arrival of my father and Nolwen. He, very ga-ga and tottery (deliberately so, I suspect, like Harold Macmillan often is), was kind of wheeled across the Library by William who kept saying: 'Make way for his Lordship; his Lordship here wants to go to his chair,' etc. This went well and my father's eccentricities were much appreciated. Examples, when Sarah, who looked very glamorous, came near them with a plate of canapés, Nolwen introduced her, 'This is James' girlfriend . . .' A look of great pain spread over my father's features. All he said was, 'Oh dear.' I singled out and introduced a number of big-wigs. As each one approached, my father writhed and groaned. Sometimes he seemed almost to be holding up his hands with an expression of defensive panic, like those celebrated pictures of the Hungarian secret policemen being ushered out of their barracks before being mown down in the uprising of 1956. Curiously, though, this went quite well.

Everybody seemed contented and appreciative and, at just the right moment, the ringers of hand bells arrived (one of them, I noticed, being that attractive blonde from whom I had bought crab apple jelly at the St John's fête the previous Saturday). They rang their bells, to the the tune of a number of familiar Christmas carols, very prettily. It was a happy and nostalgic sound as it echoed off the gothic tracery of the lower hall and I saw poor Peggy,[1] looking drawn and beautiful in a black dress, put her hand round the pillar of the top corridor leading from the dining room. Was she thinking of her dear dead Robert? I fear she must have been.

The chairman of the Association arrived very late. He drank a great deal and gabbled. He is a shameless 'wet' . . . Why didn't MPs speak out? It was time to turn the tide, etc. I have seldom heard these arguments put so badly. He stayed until the very end, leaving simultaneously with the editor of the local paper. Indeed, in all but the narrowly medical sense, he was a complete spastic. I cannot make out whether this is a good or bad thing from the point of view of my own interests.

---

[1] Peggy Wilson, wife of the head gardener at Saltwood, who worked for the Clarks. Her younger son, Robert, worked as a keeper at John Aspinall's zoo at Canterbury and had been killed by a rogue tiger the previous year.

Saltwood   *Wednesday, 23 December*

Today we went to Jock Massereene's party (black tie) for not local
– as ours – but county nobs.[1] Icy cold, the Hall of Chilham,
standard medieval conditions as Jock had broken the central heat-
ing that morning and a huge oak tree blazed in the eight-foot
fireplace, scorching those who stood near it, while those guests
who stood at receding radii from twenty to sixty feet shivered and
could see the steam from their breath as they spoke.

Guests, mainly worthy and rich rather than smart in the Chips
sense. I saw Etonian chums like Robin Leigh-Pemberton[2] and
Adrian Swire.[3] But Billy Rees-Davies[4] struck a raffish note and in
some manner admirably contrived to have the three prettiest
women in the room around him and hanging on his words.
Perhaps he enjoys that mysterious gift of being able to compel
female attendance which William Orpen described so vividly in
Onlooker in France.

We carried plates of food, which was delicious, '. . . all come in
from mee estates in Scotland,' said Jock, into one of the ante-
chambers and I found myself in conversation with a well-ish
preserved blonde lady in her 50s who (something-something)
living at Leeds.

'Did you know Olive Bailey?' I said to her.

'I am her daughter.'

Unabashed I immediately asked her about David Margesson,[5]
who is the subject of fascination by me as he was Chief Whip at the
time that the Tory Party had all the right decisions available to it as

---

[1] Viscount Massereene and Ferrard, a friend of AC's with whom he shared an
interest in animal welfare.

[2] Robin Leigh-Pemberton, chairman of the National Westminster Bank and Lord
Lieutenant-elect of Kent. Friend of AC since they were at Eton.

[3] Adrian Swire, chairman of John Swire & Son since 1966.

[4] William Rees-Davies, MP for Thanet West since 1974 (Isle of Thanet, 1953–
74).

[5] David Margesson (1st Viscount). Legendary Tory chief whip from 1931; appointed Secretary of State for War by Churchill in December 1940, but made
the scapegoat after the fall of Singapore in 1942.

options and made all the wrong ones. But she clammed up and wouldn't say anything wider than that 'David-was-so-sweet-to-everyone . . .' etc.

Bill Deedes[1] and I had a long chat. We agreed that the miners strike was the key battle ground on which a spectacular victory could turn the tide of public opinion in favour of the Government. The Lady must *not* give in on this. Unpopular though she is at the moment, she could not be loathed as much as Arthur Scargill. All at once we could redeem our pledges 'to do something' about the unions.

Saltwood   *Boxing Sunday*

Lowered by the decline in the quality of my looks. My face now fat – I can feel it in the neck and cheeks when I wash in cold water, and all those double chins and neck creases. On Christmas Eve I went down and tried to contact the Rev Woods about times of services.[2] Just as I arrived an enormous congregation of worthies started leaving, filed out and down the steps of St Leonards Church, not *one*, or rather only one, a foxy-faced blonde, looked at one, even out of curiosity.

God, yes. How moving the *Brideshead* film was, because of course Lady Marchmain won, in the end. And the drama of that moment when 'C' went in to talk to him and tried to persuade him to see the priest! I would convert, I would love to convert, if there was someone sympathetic I could talk to.

I wondered what's happened to 'Desmond'?[3]

---

[1] William Deedes, editor of the *Daily Telegraph* since 1974. MP for Ashford, 1950–74, and minister without portfolio, 1962–64. Allegedly the 'Dear Bill' to whom *Private Eye*'s Denis Thatcher letters were addressed (Thatcher and Deedes had long been golfing partners).

[2] The Reverend Canon Norman Woods officiated at AC's funeral, with the Reverend Canon Reg Humphriss of Saltwood.

[3] Desmond Hazelhurst, friend of the Beuttlers, who left the army to become a priest.

Saltwood   *Friday, 1 January*

First day of the New Year – ORDER AND SECURITY. Not especially inspiring objectives but if we set certain relatively moderate resolutions, to be adhered to, improvements may occur within the frame (sic).

A little more care of fitness, figure and appearance. New Lesley & Roberts suits and San Marco shirting shall help here, plus shampooing, brilliantine, 'smell' etc. (I wonder if the Shadow will materialise from Michael Walker.)[1]

A general 'watching brief' in politics. The die is not yet cast with Folkestone, but looking unlikely. This will impose extra loading in Plymouth for a 'resurgence', but not impossible.

Total financial security now, but must hope in the finish to throw 4x4.

Cloisters   *Monday, 22 February*

The night of our [Home Affairs Committee] annual dinner with the Home Secretary in a private room at the Garrick. Things a little stilted to begin with; we drank champagne out of silver mugs. Mellowing set in. Willie is just a tiny bit uncomfortable with his officers, particularly as Michael Mates,[2] who will always do as Willie tells him, had not turned up. John Wheeler[3] has moved away from him a little, conscious, I suspect, the Willie Whitelaw's reign is to be of finite duration and he should start a little 'distancing'. Ivor Stanbrook[4] he loathes – and I must say, both to

---

[1] AC had fantasised over Christmas about buying this Rolls-Royce 'just to keep in London for suits, scents and cigars'.
[2] Michael Mates, MP for Petersfield since October 1978.
[3] John Wheeler, MP for Paddington since 1979.
[4] Ivor Stanbrook, MP for Orpington since 1970.

Stanbrook's credit and in justification of Willie's feelings, Ivor never stops attacking him at every opportunity, both public and private. Ted Gardner he is suspicious of, told John Major[1] that he was '. . . too much under Alan Clark's influence.' And Alan Clark, well there *is* a very tricky relationship. I think he is a little frightened of me; he seldom catches my eye, but when he does there is sometimes a watery, pleading look in his expression. The trouble is, each regards the other as a traitor to his class.

The Home Secretary soon became jolly. He told, with much bellowing and groaning, of his experiences last week at St Aldate's Church in Oxford where, booked over a year in advance, he turned up for one of those lay preaching, question-and-answer sessions in the pulpit. To his great alarm he found that the Church was filled to bursting and the atmosphere evangelical in the highest degree. He described how the entire congregation *mimed* the words of each hymn, raising both hands to heaven at such words as 'arise', etc. A man in the congregation had turned to him and said: 'I found God here on Wednesday of last week, do you think you will, today?' 'I, er, don't know,' bellowed Willie, miserably looking round.

He went on to recount how half way through they had a break and he and other distinguished visitors, clerics, etc went up to a room above the vestry with the preacher. They knelt and various dignitaries started to recite prayers in turn. 'I suddenly realised with horror that it was moving round the circle and *I* was going to have to say a prayer.' Very splendidly, when it came to him, Willie simply mumbled, 'For what we are about to receive may the Lord make us truly thankful.'

Cloisters   *Tuesday, 23 February*

At breakfast today Tristan Garel-Jones[2] surprised me by saying that he thought Willie should be 'moved'. I think he may even have

[1] John Major, MP for Huntingdon since 1979.
[2] Tristan Garel-Jones, MP for Watford since 1979.

used the word 'sacked'. As a card-carrying wet and general softy on immigration etc I would have thought he would be one of Willie's rearguard. These tides of opinion in the Party are mysterious. There is no doubt that uneasiness about Willie has spread right across all shades of opinion. I told him to speak to his Whip.

He then told me that the real dynamo of opposition to the present Government on the backbenches was not Ian Gilmour, still less Geoffrey Rippon[1], etc, but . . .

'Chris,' I said.

He was rather crestfallen at my having spotted this. Apparently everyone shows Chris Patten[2] their speeches, asks him what they ought to be doing at any given moment etc. Garel-Jones had the brilliant idea that Neil Marten[3] should be sacked and Chris Patten put in his place. He could not afford to refuse; he would be out of the country for half the year; and he would be saddled with a reputable 'wet' job, but in a sector where, officially, he has reservations. G-J told me that he would ask for a meeting with Jopling[4] at which he would argue this. It is a very tidy solution and I will mention it to IG. I told G-J that as he was meeting Jopling privately he might just as well state his reservations about Willie at the same time.

House of Commons Library   *Monday, 22 March*

A bunch of Argentinians are horsing around in South Georgia. The thing started as an operation to retrieve 'scrap' (by what right do they go in there and remove 'scrap' anyway?) but they have now apparently hoisted the Argentine flag. I don't like this. If we don't throw them out, prefereably shedding blood at the same time, they will try their hand in the Falklands.

Before dinner we had a kind of *ad hoc* meeting of the '92' at the

---

[1] Geoffrey Rippon, MP for Hexham since 1966.

[2] Chris Patten, MP for Bath since 1974.

[3] Neil Marten, MP for Banbury since 1959; Minister for Overseas Development since 1979.

[4] Michael Jopling, a farmer, MP for Westmorland and Lonsdale since 1964.

far end of the Smoking Room. John Farr[1] has got a Question tomorrow, which is a Defence day. Quite narrowly drawn, on maritime air surveillance in the South Atlantic, but many of the boys are lining up to get in behind him. It's all down to that fucking idiot Nott, and his spastic 'Command Paper', which is effectively running down the entire Royal Navy so as to keep the soldiers in Rhine Army happy.

We are all of the same mind. We are the Henty boys – 'Deeds that Built the Empire', all that. But I am not sure how much support we can mobilise in the Party. 'Defence' to most colleagues only means The Cold War. They no longer think Imperially. I was saying, surely Margaret must sympathise? Nick Budgen sliced in – 'Don't bet on that, Alan. She is governed only by what the Americans want. At heart she is just a vulgar, middle-class Reaganite.'

We broke up ahead of the ten o'clock vote, but not before it was agreed that the strength of our feeling should be conveyed to the Chief [Michael Jopling]. Patrick Wall[2] and Julian Amery are to press for a statement tomorrow afternoon, from Atkins,[3] but the betting is that, remembering what we did to Nicky he will get one of his juniors to 'field' it.

Saltwood   *Wednesday, 24 March*

Yesterday went well. Notters funked the Question on air surveillance in the South Atlantic and delegated it to Jerry Wiggin, his most junior junior.[4] And a little later we got our FCO Statement and, sure enough, Atkins dodged it and put up languid, amiable, and faintly Godwatch Richard Luce.[5] The annunciator screen

---

[1] John Farr, MP for Harborough since 1959.

[2] Sir Patrick Wall, member of the Commons Select Committee on Defence since 1980.

[3] Humphrey Atkins, Lord Privy Seal since 1981.

[4] Jerry Wiggin, MP for Weston-super-Mare since 1969. Parliamentary under-secretary at the Ministry of Defence, 1981–83.

[5] Richard Luce, MP for Shoreham since 1974 (Arundel and Shoreham, 1971–74), Minister of State at the Foreign and Commonwealth Office since 1981.

conformed to the requisite minimalist note by signalling the Statement as *South Georgia (Incident)*.

Perhaps this wasn't as clever as they thought. When a Cabinet
Minister is answering there are many who, conscious of the whip-
on-the-bench taking notes, will not want to seem too 'unhelpful'.
With a Junior, though, such deference is not expected. Indeed
many of those questioning him will probably want (or may even
have been ejected from) his job.

Both Jerry and Richard are Etonians. Jerry is piggy-eyed, a
typical Library[1] bully; Richard is handsome and courteous. Typical
Pop. Jerry gave the show away immediately, 'The South Atlantic is
outside the NATO area'. In other words we (or at least the MoD)
don't give a toss.

Half an hour later Richard was almost swamped. At least thirty
people on their feet, bobbing up and down, including Jim Callaghan – a rare intruder – and Denis Healey. Richard stuck to his
brief. A few slices of pure FCO-speak – 'I much regret that some
of the action which has been taken has not created a helpful
atmosphere . . .', and he repeated the Argentine claim that the
whole operation was 'commercial', although having to admit that
the ship which carried the 'scrap-dealers' was a naval one!

I could see the whips fussing, leaning down to the bench and
whispering to Ministers. John Farr raised the usual Point of Order
after an unsatisfactory answer and signalled his intention to raise the
subject in an Adjournment Debate. We've got the whole thing
opened now. Clearly the Labour Party are also indignant, and if
she [Mrs Thatcher] doesn't get the Argentines out by next week
there will be a major disturbance.

But no sign of Ian Gow. He should be trawling the corridors,
'taking the temperature'.

On this topic I am disillusioned, as I believe are many, with The
Lady.

---

[1] 'Library' is Etonian parlance for prefect.

Saltwood   *Saturday, 27 March*

It's blissful. Next week we have the Easter Adjournment Debates. Vote free, and the House is winding down for the short recess. I have been cutting the Bailey lawn and the greens are so yellowy-fresh. When the air is still, as all day it has been, every scent of spring claims ascendancy. The birds are busy, and fly low as they pop to their nest with building materials, or food for the sitting mate.

Cloisters   *Wednesday, 31 March*

Roy Jenkins made his debut.[1] He speaks from the second row back and, of course, the moment he rose to his feet Dennis Skinner started firing abuse with the intention of disrupting him in the same way as he does with David Steel, as they share the same microphone. There was also a great deal of booing from our side, although quite a few toads were shusshing because they wanted to listen to him.

'ORDER,' bellowed the Speaker. He then delivered a personal warning to the Member for Bolsover [Dennis Skinner], saying that he would not tolerate interruptions from his position.

Thereafter, Jenkins, with excessive and almost unbearable gravitas, asked three heavy statesman-like non-party-political questions of the PM. I suppose he is very formidable, but he was so portentous and long-winded that he started to lose the sympathy of the House about half way through and the barracking resumed. The Lady replied quite brightly and freshly, as if she did not particularly know who he was, or care.

---

[1] Roy Jenkins, as leader of the Social Democratic Party; he had just won the Glasgow Hillshead by-election, to return to the Commons after a break of six years.

Saltwood   *Friday, 2 April*

I was due to go down to Plymouth this morning. But when I looked in at Dean's Yard to collect correspondence for signing in the train the whole room seemed to know that the Falkland Islands had been invaded.

No point in hanging about. I got back to Sandling at six o'clock. 'We've lost the Falklands,' I told Jane. 'It's all over. We're a Third World country, no good for anything.'

She is used to my suddenly taking the *apocalyptic* view. Didn't say much. I ate some brown toast and crab apple jelly and, it being such a lovely evening, went for a meander down the valley. I am so depressed by what I heard today – the shuffling and fudging, the overpowering impression of timidity and incompetence. Can it have felt like this in the Thirties, from time to time, when the dictators, Hitler and Musso, decided to help themselves to something – Durazzo, Memel, Prague – and all we could do was wring our hands and talk about 'bad faith'? I have a terrible feeling that this is a step change, down, for England. Humiliation for sure and, not impossible, military defeat. An apparition that must have been stalking us, since we were so dreadfully weakened at Passchendaele I suppose, for the last sixty-five years.

Cloisters   *Saturday, 3 April*

I had hardly got home last night when I realised that the House would be so crowded that I would have to be there to book my place before 8am. So I rose early – it was another glorious day with a thick heat haze – and took the 6.17am train. By 8.30am the Chamber was a snow storm of cards, like Budget Day.

I had spent the previous evening trying to convene a joint meeting of the Defence and Foreign Affairs Committees to discuss the question. For reasons of protocol I had advised Bob Boscawen[1]

---

[1] Robert (Bob) Boscawen, MP for Wells.

and he, predictably, tried to talk me out of it, said it would be better to have a meeting 'after Margaret had sat down.' I knew very well what this meant. It was an attempt to shift all the most pugnacious Tory MPs out of the Chamber up into Room 10.

I would have none of it. Buck was unobtainable, presumably out drinking somewhere. Little Winston, following his new appointment of what must be the tinkiest job in the whole Government – that of 'presenting' Government defence policy under the aegis of Central Office – was somewhat spaced out in his response. However, I managed to get hold of a few like-minded colleagues and we had agreed to assemble in Committee Room 10 at 10.15am.

Later, Bob Boscawen had rung back and said that he had arranged for Victor Goodhew (an old whip and very 'reliable' in crises) to chair the meeting. In fact when I got up to Committee Room 10 this morning I was gratified to find it extremely full and the panic that my moves had set in train was reflected in the fact that no lesser than the Chief Whip had been brought in to 'listen'.

Jopling led off by making a soft-sell appeal for (need one say) loyalty, absence of recrimination and so forth. This did not go down very well. Speaker after speaker expressed their indignation at the way the Foreign Office had handled things. Many were critical of John Nott. Much the best speech, and the only one that elicited the banging of desks, was by Robert Cranborne.[1] Expressionless, Michael Jopling took notes. Then, fortified by our mutual expressions of empathy, we trooped down to the Chamber for Prayers.

The place was absolutely packed. Julian Amery, who very seldom puts a card in, had to sit on the stairs in the gangway between the Government bench and the lower block.

First, Humphrey Atkins made a clear, short, but unsatisfactory statement explaining why he had misled (unintentionally, of course) the House about the timing of various announcements yesterday. This certainly did not make The Lady's task any easier as

---

[1] Robert Cranborne, MP for Dorset South since 1979. Heir to the Marquess of Salisbury.

it set the tone, giving further corroboration, as it were, to the general impression of almost total Government incompetence which was to pervade the debate.

The Lady led off. At first she spoke very slowly but didactically, not really saying much. But then, when she got to a passage, 'we sent a telegram . . .', the whole Opposition started laughing and sneering. She changed gear and gabbled. Far too fast she rattled off what was clearly a Foreign Office brief, without any reclamatory, or even punitive action.

This was depressing for the Conservative benches who were already in a grumpy and apprehensive mood. Michael Foot followed with an excellent performance. Fortunately, for those of us who wished to thump the Argentine, the fact that they are a fascist Junta makes it very much easier to get Labour support – and my God we are going to need this over the ensuing weeks as, apparently, it will take twenty-one days for the flotilla to arrive on station.

I was tense and had written an excellent speech, provocative and moving. But as the debate wore on I realised that it might, curiously, have been inappropriate and was glad not to have been called. Although I did intervene when provoked beyond endurance by Ray Whitney's[1] toadying defence of the Foreign Office, the weasel words in which he still and most ill-judgedly plugged the sell-out argument which we used to hear all the time from Ridley.[2]

The debate wore on with Bernard Braine[3] turning in a robustious performance. One of his great ham displays of indignation. So splutteringly bombastic that in a curious kind of way he makes the House, that most cynical of audiences, pay attention.

Poor old Notters on the other hand was a disaster. He stammered and stuttered and gabbled. He faltered and fluttered and fumbled. He refused to give way; he gave way; he changed his mind; he stood up again; he sat down again. All this against a

[1] Raymond (Ray) Whitney, MP for Wycombe since 1978.
[2] Nicholas Ridley, MP for Cirencester and Tewkesbury since 1959.
[3] Sir Bernard Braine, MP for SE Essex since 1955 (Billericay, 1950–55).

constant roaring of disapproval and contempt. I have seen the
House do this so often in the past. Like the pack that they are they
always smell the blood of a wounded animal and turn on it. The
coup de grâce was delivered by David Owen,[1] who had spoken
earlier. He forced Nott to give way and he told him that if he
could not appreciate the need to back negotiations with force he
did not deserve to remain one minute as Secretary of State.

After the debate we all trailed, yet again, up to Committee
Room 10. This time Carrington and Nott were both present.
Thirty-three Members asked questions and, with the exception of
three heavy-weight duds (Patten, Kershaw[2] and van Straubenzee),
every single person was critical. I asked a long, sneering question
about the failure of our intelligence.[3] I made a point of addressing
it to Peter Carrington whom, with my very long memory, I had
not forgiven for snubbing me at a meeting on Afghanistan in
December 1980, in the Grand Committee Room. As my irony
developed, people in the Committee Room started sniggering, but
poor Notters was still so rattled and blubbery that he leant across
and answered it, while Carrington sat staring at me in haughty
silence

This meeting finally broke up just before 4pm. I still had had no
early morning tea, no breakfast, no coffee and no lunch, but felt
wonderful, full of adrenalin. What an exciting and historic day. I
could not go home as I was booked to appear on Newsnight at
10pm. Ravenously hungry I went to the curry restaurant, but it

---

[1] David Owen, Leader of the Social Democrat Party, MP for AC's neighbouring
   constituency of Plymouth Devonport since 1974 (as Labour until 1981, then
   SDP). From 1966 to 1974 he represented AC's Plymouth Sutton seat.

[2] Sir Anthony Kershaw, MP for Stroud since 1955.

[3] After saying that he was not alone in the committee in feeling deep dissatisfaction
   with the answer given about our intelligence reports, AC went on: 'The
   questions I would like to put to the Foreign Secretary are three: First, do we
   maintain a diplomatic mission in Buenos Aires? Secondly, if we do maintain such
   a mission, is there anyone charged with collating and verifying intelligence
   material? Third, if there is such a person does he not have a duty to transmit this
   material to London? Finally, if he could find no material that was, in his
   judgement, worth repeating, could he not at least operate a press clipping service
   and send us extracts from the Argentine newspapers?'

was closed. I was lucky to find a plastic carton on the back seat of the Chevrolet in which there were some old sandwiches and an orange which Jane had given me for a train journey to Plymouth. I drove into St James's Park and ate them and fell asleep.

Cloisters   *Monday, 5 April*

I am certain that there has been collusion between the Foreign Office and the Argentine over this whole affair. Why were there no casualties among the Royal Marines? Seventy-five determined men, as the battle of Arnhem demonstrated (to take but one example), can hold off greatly superior numbers just using small arms and bazookas from drains and cellars in territory that they know. I have started the rumour that last night I rang Enoch, Julian Amery, and the *Guardian* – that there were sealed orders to the Governor to be opened when the invasion started, and that these orders were for him to declare an immediate cease fire. I believe this to be true. I also believe that unofficial representations were made by the Foreign Office to the Argentine indicating that all would be well provided no British blood were shed. And what is more, I believe that these unofficial contacts may still be taking place.

Accordingly, when I arrived in the House this morning at 9.30am I tabled three priority written questions on these three issues and sent copies to *The Times*, the *Telegraph* and the P.A. I then went along to James Callaghan, who had asked to see me privately in his room. I have a rapport with Jim. Nick Budgen says that he is an intellectual admirer of mine and, quite by chance, he has been in the Chamber when I have made three of my best speeches – on Blunt, on Bobby Sands and on the NATO commitment. I also sent him a copy of my Fortress Britain lecture, to which he replied at length. He was, as always, compos, amiable and clear-headed (it is in one's 60s, isn't it, that one starts to draw dividends from not consuming alcohol in middle age). But there is a certain detachment, impersonality, behind those powerful spectacles. I suppose this may be something that comes with the recollection of absolute authority – although of course little Wislon does not possess this at all.

Callaghan talked interestingly about the Falklands. He said it was the most frightful situation and fraught with danger, that it was important to find a way out, short of a full scale amphibious assault with all the casualties that might accompany it. He was gloomy about the long-term prospects about defending the Islands.

I tried to correct him about this and said that the Labour Party would rapidly back away totally from its position of support on Saturday. But he did agree that it was essential to punish the Argentines, and to sink some of their ships before negotiations restarted. He was very critical of the way the Foreign Office had handled the whole affair, said the whole administration was riddled with incompetence; the MoD was a mess, nobody there could think creatively.

He said that when he was Prime Minister, every week he had a briefing at which, on a Mercator projection, every major ship in the Royal Navy was shown, and every tanker. Apparently, this was an old practice dating back from Victorian times so that the Government would know at any moment the level of naval flexibility that they commanded. But the Civil Service finally got rid of it with the 'European commitment'.

After a bit Callaghan asked me to advise him on what he should say in his speech in the debate on Wednesday. This could be very important as he will be making a speech on a subject of which he has clear knowledge and a proven record of success, but from a position of objectivity as a senior statesman. Plainly he has to counsel against too bellicose an attitude, but I have got to make sure that his nerve holds and he includes a strong recommendation for a punitive strike to establish a grounding of strength on which to base negotiations. I will give this some thought and draft a memorandum for him. I will see him on Wednesday.

When I got down to the Members' Lobby from Callaghan's room there was a rumour running wild that Carrington had been sacked and sure enough it was confirmed a couple of minutes later. Carrington *and* Atkins and Richard Luce! A clean sweep. God knows what the consequences of this will be, but they cannot be all

bad as Carrington's influence was grossly appeasing and the col-
lusive element in the Foreign Office (see above) has now been
decapitated. Party feeling seems to indicate that Francis Pym will
become Foreign Secretary, but there are thrills – and spills – in
store.

The wets, of course, are livid and discomforted, they are taking
it out on poor old Notters, saying he should be sacked, that it was
intolerable that he should have survived, etc, etc. But Notters, I
fear, comes later. His turn will be after the failure, or abortion, of
the naval strike.

After lunch I went to 'Rab's' memorial service. Stuffed with
politicians. Guess who was down to read the lesson – Peter
Carrington. Listed, of course, as Her Majesty's most honourable
Secretary of State . . . etc. To do him credit he read the text with
great aplomb. He, too, has large and impenetrable spectacles that
conceal the emotions of the soul.

Very much less sleek was poor Richard Luce, who sat immediately in front of me in the stalls, grey and dishevelled, with a
glazed look and deep eye ditches. Cancroid, indeed, like the
wretched Notters on television yesterday and, as Jane rightly
spotted, as having auto-activated an instantaneous malignant
condition.

After Questions there was a Statement about commandeering
vessels and the trade embargo. Already the first odours of appeasement began to waft round the Chamber. Members on both
sides were muttering and shuffling about commercial contracts,
deliveries, banks, etc, etc.

On the way up to the Committee Corridor I was caught by
Norman St John-Stevas, who could hardly contain himself with
glee. 'Have you ever seen such a Government? So many
nonentities. It is really pathetic, it would be farcical if it were not
tragic . . .'

He, too, was heavily anti-Nott, said it was extremely dangerous
to have a Secretary of State for Defence, someone whose whole
career depended on a successful assertion of martial vigour. I said it
was not only the Secretary of State whose career depended on such

a showing, but the whole existence of the Government, and indeed of the Party. St J-S said not necessarily so.

Well, he would say that wouldn't he?

Cloisters   *Wednesday, 7 April*

People who should know better are striding up and down the Smoking Room Corridor telling anyone they can apprehend that the *Invincible* is sailing without her radar operative; that many of her weapons systems have already been moved; that the Sea Harrier cannot land on deck in a rough sea; that many of the ships in the Task Force have defective power trains, etc, etc.

It is monstrous that senior Tories should be behaving in this way. It is only on occasions such as this that the implacable hatred in which certain established figures hold the Prime Minister can be detected. They oppose Government policy whatever it is – they would oppose free campari-sodas for the middle classes if they thought The Lady was in favour. They are within an ace, they think, of bringing her Government down. If by some miracle the expedition succeeds they know, and dread, that she will be established for ever as national hero.

So, regardless of the country's interest they are determined that the expedition will not succeed. The greater the humiliation of its failure, the more certain will be the downfall of The Lady's Government, the greater the likelihood of a lash-up coalition, *without* a general election, to fudge things through for the last eighteen months of this Parliament.

At the moment the House of Commons is very determined. One angle from which that determination can be attacked is via the so-called 'expert' opinion, which is that we just do not have the equipment to launch and sustain an expedition of this magnitude.

Some others are openly going round making the comparison with the Sicilian Expedition that led to the downfall of the Athenian City State. Sometimes, I must admit, this analogy occurs to me also, although I keep my thoughts to myself. If we are going to go, I feel, let us go out in a blaze – then we can all sit back and

comfortably become a nation of pimps and ponces, a sort of Macao
to the European continent.

Saltwood   *Good Friday, 9 April*

Pleasantly tired after mowing the *whole* Inner Bailey in one swoop
– four hours dead. Daffodils out, but cold – though Saltwood just
starting to 'smile'.

As I said on the walks to Jane: 'It's even a fudge; two to one a
disaster and The Lady resigning from the despatch box; three to
one a naval victory and the bunting round Nelson column.'

Cloisters   *Wednesday, 14 April*

Yet another Falklands Debate today.

I took the 07.19 train from Sandling – how lovely it is in the
early morning. *Why* don't we, in the spring and summer, follow
the birds turning in at dusk and rise with the ever-recurring beauty
of the dawn? Train late, taxi to House, and wrote out note of
encouragement to The Lady (Jane's idea, and a very good one). I
had to do a second draft as I spelt Britannia with two t's, spastically.
I walked with the envelope up to Downing Street and handed it to
the policeman outside Number 10. A few mangy photographers
with heavy beards and leather bum-freezer jackets hung around the
other side of the barriers, but very few members of the public.

Anglia Television want me to do an hour long debate with Tam
Dalyell on Friday night. Every single day has been busted to pieces
by 'appearances' on the media. But I have to do it. I feel passion-
ately, really deeply, about this issue. And I am fortunate indeed that
I am getting so much opportunity to express my feelings instead of
just grinding my teeth in the dark.

In the Members' Cafeteria and there was Tam, gabbling and
dribbling and in the most frightful state. He has actually gone
slightly round the bend about the whole thing, most extraordinary.

He said that the *Hermes* was suffering from mechanical trouble and her propellers were seizing. Wishful thinking, I suspect.

I could not stay very long as I had a Prayer Card in. Once again the place was a snow storm of Prayer Cards, worse than the Budget. The debate was a fairly placid business. The Lady had recovered her composure and there was a level of unanimity on all sides. This is a relief as I had feared from trends that I had perceived in last Wednesday's debate that the House might be weakening; good-boys all trying to get in on the act with their disparate compromise solutions. But, other than a dotty plea for passive resistance by poor old Anthony Meyer,[1] and a ritual vote loser by Judith Hart,[2] the House remained firm.

Cloisters   *Thursday, 22 April*

Having boasted a great deal to people, including Plymouth Sound, that I am off to Washington today, '. . . with Francis Pym,' I cannot get out of it, however much I dread the journey. It is the usual story. If anyone can guarantee safe arrival and return one would spend all one's money on air fares. But I don't just hate taking off and landing; I loathe *going along*. And 'going along' at twice the speed of sound must be more hazardous than 'going along' sub-sonically.

Just as I was getting into my car outside Brooks's I saw Algy Cluff,[3] still very foppish, with a *very* thin golden and platinum watch chain, although having seen his net worth reduced by about £18 million in the last year. I told him I was off to Washington. He said that there was plenty of oil around the Falklands and he had the technology to extract it, '. . . if other disputes could be settled.' Good may yet come out of this dispute, because if we can really assert our strength there we should be able to participate in the exploitation of resources without being threatened or disturbed.

---

[1] Anthony Meyer, MP for West Flint since 1970.
[2] Judith Hart, MP for Lanark since 1959.
[3] Algy Cluff, founder of Cluff Oil, proprietor of *The Spectator* since 1981.

I did a couple of radio shows. Unusually Robin Day appeared to be hosting *World at One*, and then hitched a ride in a taxi to Heathrow. The Concorde lounge carried an agreeable aroma of riches, whether personal or corporate.

Concorde on take-off is everything that has been claimed for it. The feeling of superabundant power is absolutely overwhelming, fields and houses became minuscule dots and patches in the space of a few minutes. The aircraft was full of pressmen and commentators.

Right up in the front, head bowed over his papers so that no one should try and 'lobby' him, sat John Louis.[1] He now looks really alarmingly like the hit-man in *Bullitt*, who furtively prowled through the hospital in his raincoat in search of a badly injured witness who had to be eliminated.

I chatted with Simon Glenarthur.[2] Although rather chinless and stereotyped in appearance, he must be quite tough as he flew in the Army Air Corps and is a helicopter pilot with British Airways. He sometimes comes to the Defence Committee and is very hard line. Due to a muddle by the PA some people, including Robin Day, had thought he was Lord Glen*amara* (poor, nasty old Ted Short, of my opposition days) and the Concorde lounge had been plastered with urgent messages asking him to get in touch with correspondents who did not bother to conceal their disappointment when they found they were talking to a Scottish aristocrat instead of a Labour life peer.

About half way through the flight I strolled down towards the tail and had a quick word with Francis. As I parted the curtains to go into his cabin I felt like Ernst Strobe, when, as Goldfinger, he bobbed out and surprised James Bond and his girl when they thought they had escaped in the last reels of the film. The Foreign Secretary must have thought that it was really *too* much that I, who had been endlessly plugging the hard line on this dispute since the day it started, should now be pursuing him across the Atlantic.

---

[1] John J. Louis, United States ambassador at the Court of St James since 1981, previously a leading American businessman (director, Johnson Wax, etc.).

[2] Lord Glenarthur, Government Whip, House of Lords.

Simon Glenarthur had arranged with the captain that I should go through and sit on the Concorde jump seat for our landing at Dulles Airport. It was with some relief that I saw that Dulles lies in flat scrubland. No special problems on over-run or, indeed, even on engine failure at take-off. Surprisingly rapidly the white runway changed in size from a laundry name tape, to a ruler, to a roller towel, to the cloth at a long banqueting table; all the time holding steady and dead centre in the 'V' shaped windscreen of the great airliner – the supersonic nose had been 'drooped' at 18,000' as we started our approach.

The captain, Massie by name, was incredibly bland and unflappable. I suspect also highly competent, as he had been given the wrong glide angle to lock into his computer and we came in 350' too high. But he overrode it manually and still managed, by using one 'g' or better on both brakes and reverse thrust, to turn the aircraft at the first runway exit. The pasty and rather common co-pilot, on the other hand, was demonstrably nervous and lip-licking throughout descent.

We had been told to look out for a 'young man' who would be holding up a notice for us. When we arrived at the Dirksen building, a sort of American Norman Shaw, full of Senators' offices, where the Conference was being held, it was twenty-past four London time and some strong Indian tea and buttered toast would have been welcome. But in Washington it was only twenty-past ten and a bright sun blazed down on the blossoms. What did we do with our cases? We humped them up the great sham marble steps and through the double portals of the Dirksen. An armed security man examined them. 'Who do you work for?' he asked suspiciously. 'The British Government,' I answered. Unexpectedly this induced respect rather than hostility.

Saltwood   *Monday, 17 May*

This is *the* crisis. I am lucky to be in the House for it. Lucky, too, to be 'recognised' and allowed to 'achieve'. When one has seen this through, *then* one will have discharged one's duty.

Saltwood   *Tuesday, 1 June*

Back in the Great Hall. How lovely, its appeal this time of year hasn't altered for me in the slightest. Today spent lounging, sploshing, swimming – pool 72°.

Last night I left Saltwood at 2 in the morning to be driven up to the ABC studios for a night chat show, coast-to-coast on the Falklands (the drive back leaving London at 4.40, getting back to Saltwood after 6am). I have long since lost count of the number of appearances I have made on the Falklands – three times on Brian Walden alone, since the 'crisis' started.

And *what* a crisis! When I think back to the state of utter depression when I got out of the train at Sandling on 2 April – on trial, complete and utter humiliation; I even contemplated emigrating. Now not only have we redeemed everything that was at stake then, but one has advanced immeasurably in self-esteem and in the status accorded to us by the whole world.

And I *did* play my part in this – whether greater or lesser than if I had been a junior minister I don't know – I suspect the former. I was almost immediately recognised by the media – the 'leader of the war party' (Alan Watkins).

Saltwood   *Saturday, 5 June*

Financial dream blighted by discovery that £1 is worth about 5d (or say 2d) on 1936 figures.

Saltwood   *Monday, 7 June*

I sat 'within the walls'. Tremendous burgeoning greenery, baby birds everywhere: we just failed (by what chance I don't know) to revive two baby thrushes from the nest in the crab apple tree by the openings desk – having got them through to the fifth day; there is a rather sulky successor to George (named 'Max') in a box in the kitchen, and a few minutes ago I hooked a young sparrow out of the pool.

Cloisters   *Thursday, 10 June*

I telephoned Edward Adeane[1] at Buckingham Palace and told him that there was some concern that the Recognition Committee at the MoD might be parsimonious with their awards. I urged that these be distributed in the most profligate manner – and particularly in the Parachute Regiment which has performed such prodigies. He reminded me that the Prince of Wales was Colonel-in-Chief, and I hope he took my points to heart.

Saltwood   *Friday, 11 June*

Oh! How loathsome and draining it is to turn my footsteps westward instead of to the south on a Friday. I work very hard at Westminster and I am always *en poste* there, unlike other colleagues who scrabble around the boardrooms and come in late (if at all) for Questions, with expense-account fumes on their breath. And so, when the week is over I like best to go home and 'unwind' with the cars and the animals. And it is ghastly having to go to Plymouth and, racked with fatigue, keep silently mouthing 'brush'[2] as one moves round the faithful, and not-so-faithful.

Actually my status in Plymouth is quite high at the moment, due to all the 'exposure' that I have been getting over the Falklands. Enemies, like Speare and other malcontents, have gone quiet, they never turn up at meetings.

---

[1] Edward Adeane, Extra Equerry to the queen since 1972.
[2] The Clarks had, early in their political life, discovered that the word 'brush', in the act of expression, draws the features into a pleasing smile; neither chilly nor leering, but authoritative and benevolent – one degree less effusive than the word 'cheese'.

Cloisters   *Monday, 14 June*

I dined with Norman St John-Stevas, and, as always, he was
delightful company, talked obsessively about politics and what a
'dreadful' Cabinet we have at the moment.

'There cannot ever have been a Cabinet with such a dearth of
talent,' he kept saying. He recounted how Norman Tebbit –
whom he described in a number of scatological terms – had come
down to a Conservative Club in his constituency, 'not at *my*
invitation I hasten to say,' wearing a coloured evening shirt and
how, '. . . my dear, they were all over him.'

I said that The Lady's autocracy was complete. She could make
any policy or break any individual. At the moment, I said, she is
completely fire-proof. 'Yes,' he replied, 'and will be completely
combustible shortly thereafter.'

Cloisters   *Tuesday, 15 June*

I was woken at 4.15am by a beautiful song-thrush; she rivalled,
surpassed indeed, the famous Albany blackbird, to whom I used to
listen in the spring of '76 when I would wake early in torment with
the figures going round and round in my head of accelerating
interest charges on my different overdrafts, and how was I to get
the deeds of Saltwood back out of Hoare's clutches. But this thrush
sang incredibly, never once repeating herself and with variations of
infinite quality and delight.

I could not go back to sleep, still over-excited by the events of
last night. I had got back to the House about 9.30pm, after dining
at Brooks's with Edward Adeane, and was reading the tape over
Phil Goodhart's shoulder when I saw something about, '. . . individual British commanders at all levels have been authorised to
negotiate ceasefires'. 'It means they have surrendered,' he said.

The cloakroom attendant told me that there was to be a Statement
at 10pm, after the vote, and when I got up to the lobbies I found
the whole House, policemen, badge messengers, etc, everybody

bubbling with excitement. I rushed up to catch the news headlines before the Division Bell rang, but for once we seemed to know more than they did; the BBC was behind the times and fumbling.

Foolishly I lingered so, after going past the division clerk, I found that 'my' bench was completely crowded. However, among its magic powers, as is well known, is that of infinite expandability, and they allowed me in lowish down – next to Alan Glyn[1] – Peter Emery[2] very nobly making that ritual pivoting of the lap which actually permits the small statutory triangle of green leather.

Hastily I scribbled some notes on the back of a card in case there were questions – but the rumour was that it was to be on a Point of Order. (How? Monstrous collusion by the Speaker?) And then The Lady entered, radiant, and there was cheering – bellowing, indeed. She made a very brief statement, but it was important in that she used the phrase, '. . . negotiate a *surrender*' (not a ceasefire). Trust her. She had led from the front all the way.

Again we bellowed. Order Papers were waved and, not having one, I fluttered my little white postcard. Michael Foot fumbled gingerly round the subject, to some heckling, but finally and generously managed to get out his congratulations, '. . . in spite of our arguments in the past.' Little Steel was short, and inaudible. And even David [Owen], who has behaved so well and so enhanced his reputation, could not be heard properly and aroused grumpy heckling, I noticed, from the Opposition bench when he congratulated the Government.

For a few seconds we were stuck in our places by some procedural back-and-forth; Leader of the House accepting an Adjournment of Business, etc. I rose rapidly, pushed my way through the crowd at the bar of the House and shot round through the 'Aye' Lobby to catch the Prime Minister as she emerged at the back of the Speaker's Chair to get to her room. No one else had the idea and I had a completely clear run. Not even Ian was leading her, although Willie was shuffling benignly three paces behind. (What must he have been thinking?) Ignoring Willie I rushed up

---

[1] Alan Glyn, MP for Windsor since 1970.
[2] Peter Emery, MP for Homiton since 1967.

and said to her: 'Prime Minister, only you could have done this; you did it alone, and your place in history is assured.' She looked a little startled. Had she heard properly? She was still a little bemused by the triumph. Willie looked grumpy (maddeningly, he is not at all deaf); an unseemly display of emotion. We do not do things like that in the Tory Party.

So ends the Falklands Affair – which began in such despair and humiliation. How well I remember that first emergency debate and looking down the bench at The Lady when Enoch was speaking, at how low she held her head, how *knotted* with pain and apprehension she seemed as he pronounced his famous judgement, '. . . in the next few weeks the world, the country and she, herself, will discover of what metal she is made.'

I only hope he is generous enough to recall that moment when he speaks today.

Cloisters   *Wednesday, 16 June*

In the House I met Adam Raphael and we chatted about the political consequences of the Falklands. He told me that 'favourable mentions' about me had been coming out of Downing Street; this corroborates what Frank Johnson told me on the weekend – but what is the point? I went on up to the Defence Committee where there was much discussion about the advisability of postponing the White Paper.

After dinner Bob Boscawen said that John Nott wanted to see me in his room about the White Paper. Victor Goodhew and Winston Churchill had also been invited to go along, but I am glad to say that little Winston did not turn up.

While we were waiting for Victor I said to John that I was very worried about all the rumours that were circulating about his impending departure. JN said that there was a conspiracy against him. About half-a-dozen Admirals, many of the naval correspondents – Desmond Wetter[1] etc – and a coterie of disaffected

---

[1] Actually Desmond Wettern, a long-serving *Telegraph* reporter.

colleagues, notably Keith Speed, Michael Brotherton[1] and Freddie Burden[2]. JN said he had no intention of resigning.

We discussed the question of the White Paper. He wants to publish it as it is, but with a loose-leaf disclaimer of intent. Crazy, I said. Far better to issue a single-side Statement reaffirming our commitment to Trident, to NATO etc and asserting that the complex and deep-seated lessons of the Falklands Campaign will take some months to be digested.

John thrashed about on his seat, crossing and uncrossing his legs, taking his glasses on and off. Rattled, but attentive. He had started off asserting his intention to publish even though not to publish the obvious conclusion, and I had said that if he insisted I would not oppose the idea publicly, but I still thought it terribly risky. Victor Goodhew supported me and was sensible and wise. We left things that John would continue to think the matter over.

Later in the evening I saw Ian Gow, who walks about the place looking like the cat that has swallowed all the cream. But I had one quick word with him – 'the Prime Minister has complete freedom of action now,' I said, 'no other Leader has enjoyed such freedom since Churchill, and even with him it did not last very long.' I suppose he may have thought I was referring to freedom of choice in making appointments, but I was not, really, I meant freedom in imposing domestic, foreign and defence policies.

Cloisters   *Thursday, 17 June*

I was delighted to see that Julia Langdon had singled me out for mention in today's *Guardian* in an analysis of politicians who have emerged with credit from the Falklands affair. All the sweeter as Churchill and I were the only Tory backbenchers to be mentioned, and I was compared favourably to him. I wonder who she got this from? Perhaps Jim Lester, although I know she also talks to Norman StJS. It is useful as 'plugs' from that quarter are far

---

[1] Michael Brotherton, MP for Louth since October 1974.
[2] Frederick Burden, MP for Gillingham since 1950.

more valuable than, say, the *Telegraph* (not that I have ever had one there).

Cloisters   *Monday, 21 June*

This evening I dined with the Commandant General of the Royal Marines. A number of other officers were present at the banquet, which took place in the Stationers Hall – very collegiate, with polished oak tables on stone flags. They are all delighted about the Falklands – of course – and lobbied us (several MPs were present) for replacements to be ordered immediately, both for the Round Table class and for *Intrepid* and *Fearless*.

The officer next to me, a Major Hooper, was highly intelligent and soon showed himself to be a closet nationalist. We were in absolute sympathy over the direction of British defence policy in the '80s. He told me that the Russian attaché in Germany had said to him after the Crusader Exercise how glad he was that the British Army was so small. Hooper said the only other decent army was the German one. The US Marine Corps? The 82nd Airborne? He said they were useless. On exercise in Corsica last year, the US Marines were stoned so far that the officers in the Fire Control Unit were actually falling about and giggling for hours on end.

Cloisters   *Tuesday, 13 July*

Yesterday, a typically filthy Monday morning. A dentist appointment; and correspondence scattered and not to hand; many small things (in addition to massive ones) left undone. Little Jackie Felce, who is very amiable and pleasant, came up and wanted a mine detector to look for her watch; which she had mislaid in the straw. Where the hell was the mine detector? I looked in the garden entrance (where it is always kept, but needless to say was not), the garages, the outhouses, Andrew's bedroom, Andrew's old bedroom, James's bedroom, James's darkroom, sundry other rooms and localities. Time, time slipping past. The sand *rushing* through the hour glass. Jane found it in Winifred.[1]

Later, when I got up to the House of Commons, Frank Haynes[2], twinkingly, congratulated me on being the next Secretary of State for Defence. Being very vain and having a high opinion of myself I only dissimulated slightly, thinking he was referring to recent exchanges in the Commons (he kept talking about Jim Callaghan). But it turned out that Callaghan had written an article in the previous day's *Sunday Pictorial* entitled, *Why I Won't Rest Until John Nott Goes*, and had recommended me as his successor! It would not make the slightest difference in the Party. It may even be adverse. Perhaps fortunately, no Conservative ever reads the *Sunday Pictorial*.

I had a message from Mark Schreiber[3] to ring him. I thought he was going to talk to me about the revisionist defence school and my article in *The Times*. But he asked me about what I thought of Willie's Statement. Well, I know that Mark is congenitally pro-Willie as we talked before about the sort of pressures he has to endure from the Right, so I opened a little guardedly.

'Well I really did think it was a little inadequate . . .'

Finding that he agreed and was extremely indignant, I developed the theme, told him about the noisy meeting of the Home Affairs Committee last night, Jack Page[4] being literally apoplectic.

Mark described to me in detail the police arrangements for protecting the Palace, which are a complete shambles.[5] [He] continued to develop the theme of Willie's culpability. He pointed out that Peter Carrington had honourably tendered his resignation following what he judged to be a 'national humiliation'. Was this not a humiliation of an even higher order? I agreed, egged him on, I said I was keen on rehabilitating Peter Carrington (a total lie) and

---

[1] Winifred was the Clarks' name for a little Morris 8 two-seater which, owing to its extremely short wheelbase, fitted snugly into a far corner of the long garage.

[2] Frank Haynes, MP for Ashfield since 1979. A Labour Whip.

[3] Mark Schreiber, journalist from the *Economist*.

[4] Jack Page, MP for Harrow West since 1960.

[5] An intruder had got into the Queen's bedroom.

that it would do no harm as part of this process to draw the contrast between their two ways of behaving. I even suggested that they put it on the cover of the *Economist*, out tomorrow night. I doubt if he will manage this, but Mark is definitely indignant. It is very satisfactory when one can get the Left to bite each other.

I put a call through to Ian at Downing Street. He was in with the Prime Minister. I explained the 'delicacy' of the subject matter to his secretary and she took a note in to him and put it under his nose.

A few minutes later he rang me back. I told him that some on our side, possibly even myself, might call this afternoon for Willie's resignation and contrast his behaviour with that of Peter Carrington. 'Don't do it,' he said. 'Whatever you do *you* must not do this.'

'Well some people may do it,' I said.

'Let them, but whatever you do don't do it yourself.'

He was very intense about this. It really was a very direct message. So (needless to say) I won't do it. But I feel we are probably very near a now-or-never situation. Although whether he said don't do it because the Prime Minister has already decided to promote me (as Adam Raphael said she had), and if I had attacked the Home Secretary it would make it very difficult for her, or whether it is that Ian is hoping that it may happen, but still anticipates difficulty with Willie's veto, I really do not know. One is a strong position, the other a weak one.

My own natural inclination for cavalry tactics made me want to charge Willie head-on and hopefully get rid of him completely so the question of veto would not arise. But even if he did go, it might still be difficult for her to promote the first person on our side to call for it. Jopling would probably stop her. Ah well, we shall see.

Saltwood Great Library   *Tuesday, 20 July*

My father has had a *coup-de-vieux* and is now in unhappy decline. There is scarcely any longer a point in going over [to the Garden House] to call on him. He just sits, on his low green velvet chair by the big window. Col was very aggrieved the other day because as he approached my father smiled simperingly and said 'Ah, now, who's this?'

'It's your younger son, Colin, Papa.'

'Aha.' (Of course my father knew perfectly well who it was. He just gets irritated with Col blatantly sucking up to him and talking a lot of recycled balls about art.) Aha.

Of course my father would never have spoken like that to Celly. She would just have cackled, said 'You're completely ga-ga' or something equally brutal. He is frightened of her, as he is of most women. But, as far as I can make out, is still resisting pressure to set up a Trust Fund for Sammy.[1]

Most of the time my father does not speak, or read, or really show any vitality whatever, although at intervals his face may indicate a cross expression. What is he actually thinking?

Disappointment, I would surmise, more than apprehension. And principally with his marriage. At first he started off jolly. But Nolwen is so odious, and *false*. 'Sweetie' this and 'Sweetie' that (this is, I suppose, a literal translation of *Cherie*), but he is her third husband, after all. And Papa has twice suffered 'intrusive' surgery since their wedding five years ago, once on his gall bladder, once his prostate. 'No surprises,' as Nolwen over-brightly told everyone – by which I assumed her to mean no indication of malignancy. But the operation 'took it out of' him. He is going to die. It could happen at any moment; but equally he could last for another three years.

I hardly notice. Will Andrew and Jamie, if God spares them, feel like this about me? I suppose that is inevitable. The five stages of fatherhood. First, protective. Then, love. Then, an idolised elder brother, racing at Silverstone, 'parping' blondes. Then, an old friend, giving counsel and the occasional 'treat' (or cheque). Finally the *nonno*, selfishly in the way; holding on for far too long, obstructing the natural course of inheritance.

When I said all this to Jane she said yes, but his face still lights up when you come into the room. And at once I felt terrible. If my

---

[1] Celly's son.

father goes back to France this week (which I think improbable) I will write to him affectionately and just hope that Nolwen does not intercept it. She, of course, dreads him dying at the *Vieux Manoir*, knowing full well that I would seize the Garden House immediately and forbid her on her return.

Cloisters   *Monday, 26 July*

The day of the Falkland Islands Service at St Paul's. I only just made the 7.19am from Sandling as the horrible little Renault, which has already broken its reverse gear, stuck in bottom and I had to transfer to the Trelawneys' car at the village green.

I walked from the Commons to Horseguards where the coaches were waiting. We surged to St Paul's, crossing red lights with the assistance of police motorcyclists, and arrived an hour before the Queen was due. So I slyly dodged round the barriers and found a coffee shop, entirely staffed by black people, where I had coffee and a sticky bun.

In spite of this I was in my seat three-quarters-of-an-hour early. Every minute was interesting as the congregation assembled. I had an excellent place, under the dome, and there in front of me, still hunched and grey, just as had been on that Monday, 5th April, at 'Rab's' memorial service, was Richard Luce.

'What's going through your mind?' I asked him. He answered candidly: 'I am shattered, absolutely shattered.'

And sure enough, a little later, up came Peter Carrington, relegated to a row behind me with some very dud peers. Lady Carrington was *bright*, but Peter still looked a bit sulky I thought – and who can blame him, having to sit between Lord Peart and Lord De L'Isle. The first member of the Cabinet to arrive was Norman Fowler[1]; how common he always looks. A little later up came Heseltine and I was glad to see he had been (obviously

---

[1] Norman Fowler, MP for Sutton Coldfield since February 1974. Transport Secretary since 1982.

deliberately) put at the very end of the Government row so that he was blocked by pillars.

I squirmed and turned in my seat, staring shamelessly. Soon I realised that the block behind me was filling up with next of kin. Many of them were Para families and, very touchingly, they all wore something red – the red of the Red Beret – about their clothing. The girls wore ribbons or cardigans, the fathers hand-kerchiefs, and so on. Only two rows behind me sat three adorable winklers, two little boys and a girl, who were dressed in red jerseys with metal parachute badges, looking enormous, pinned on their chest. With the exception of the very young children, who were excited and jolly, most of the relatives looked deeply unhappy. Some of the wives, or Mums, were old NAAFI comforts and painted up to the nines, but the majority were beauties, many of them raging beauties, and none of the young ones wearing any make-up, which was probably just as well as most of them cried all the way through the service.

Willie arrived, stooping and flushed and wearing some heavy red ribbon round his neck. It looked like the Bath, what was it? He is absolutely imperméable. He now says that not only is he not going to resign, but he is going to fight the next general election.

The Royal Family arrived two by two, all in uniform I am glad to say, although the Duchess of Kent now looks very spaced-out indeed. Princess Diana looked thin as a rake and out-paced her consort with her special lanky stride. The Queen, as always, surprised one with how tiny she is; Philip consistent and splendid towers above her.

The service itself could have been worse. The most objectionable of the peaceniks' plans having been thwarted largely, I believe, following my question to the Prime Minister on 13th July. The second lesson was read by David Cooper, chaplain of 2 Para, and it was most fitting to hear that flat northern accent reading out the verses of St Mark, having last heard it coming directly from the tin church in Port Stanley on the day of the victory. Little Dr Greet,[1] with whom I have had several clashes in the last ten days,

---

[1] The Reverend Dr Kenneth Greet, Moderator, Free Church Federal Council.

turned out to have quite a good microphone voice and his prayers were not as awful as one might have expected. And we ended with Psalm 23, but sung to Irvine's music, and there cannot have been many dry eyes in the Cathedral.

Afterwards the crocodile moved its way out very slowly down the aisle, starting from the top. I was on the civilian side, passing row after row of next of kin. Anxiously I scanned their faces, but the only emotion I could see was anguish, sheer anguish.

Cloisters   *Tuesday, 27 July*

Lunched today with Norman St John-Stevas at 34 Montpelier Square, an expensive address. It is always a good (or is it bad?) sign when you see a house some distance away, obviously the chic-est and most painted-up in the street and, as you close the range, this turns out to be your destination. Lightheartedly, as we ascended the steps, I said, '. . . something-something fucking', to Jane and Margaret Argyll materialised at the same moment. But she is used to that kind of thing and did not object. She is *unbelievably* preserved – 'preserved' being the word; but gave the show away a bit by moving very stiffly and hesitantly, being uncertain about steps, etc.[1]

Cloisters   *Thursday, 29 July*

Peter Hordern had asked me to lunch. A rather boring terraced house in Cadogan Street, burgled four times in the last two years he told me. The other guests were Julian Amery and Nicholas Baker.[2] Hordern, who is very senior in the Public Accounts Committee, was trying to pick our brains about defence costings, concerning which he is quite rightly apprehensive. A very nice

[1] Margaret Argyll, around whom sexual gossip had been rampant; the third wife of the 11th Duke of Argyll, divorced amid much acrimony in 1963. At the time of this entry she was seventy.

[2] Nicholas Baker, MP for North Devon since 1979, parliamentary private secretary to the armed forces minister since 1981.

man, highly intelligent, but almost too fastidious for politics. It has always mystified me why he has not been made a Minister as he is extremely able.

Over the first course, and I cannot remember how the subject originated, I said what a dreadful and dangerous fellow Robert Armstrong[1] was. To my great surprise and delight, Carol Mather [a whip, also present] chimed in with support, said he too thought Armstrong was 'creepy'.

'It is my personal belief,' I said, 'that he is a full Colonel in the KGB.'

Nobody demurred.

Saltwood   *Wednesday, 8 September*

Telephoned to Jonathan Aitken today, to see if he could help over Andrew's expedition to the Yemen.[2] As always, he was pleasant and obliging; his wife has just given birth to a son so he was in a good mood. Just as I was ringing off he said, 'By the way I do hear, which is very good news, that there is a strong likelihood of your joining the Government . . .' I laughed, delighted. 'But,' (I can't remember exactly how he went on) '. . . Gow is arguing very strongly for your inclusion, and Madam is said not to be opposed, but apparently Jopling is against it . . .' My heart sank. Jopling and Willie combined would be unstoppable, or rather *insurmountable*, if they were to veto a junior appointment.

Jonathan had gone on to say that Jopling was trying to get rid of Gow himself – 'rid' of course meaning shifted to some dud ministry outside the Cabinet. J said that Jopling felt himself to have been worsted by Gow on a number of occasions – the Employment Bill, the N. Ireland Bill and was even elevating this into a test case. If that is so I *have* had it. Also I get the faintest

---

[1] Sir Robert Armstrong, secretary to the cabinet since 1976, joint head of the civil service since 1981.

[2] AC's younger son was going to North Yemen to work with the Catholic Church at Raymah, as part of a stint of Voluntary Service Overseas, before attending the Regular Commissions Board.

suspicion (not that I have not had it, wrongly, in the past) that IG's influence is waning. The new accent is on the managerial – hence the ghastly, planted rumour that Heseltine is to be the new S of S at Defence. Well, what is written is written. I know I am incredibly well off and blessed, and worry far too much – about Andrew in the Yemen, about James in helicopters, about falling interest rates,[1] about my crowded desk and my (non-existent) sex-life, even about Tom crossing the road[2] – but I have got a tension-headache. Monstrous, as I said to Jane, in the middle of the recess. Also a strange weakness, muscular dystrophy in the arms, particularly the left arm. Anxiety induces hypochondria, but I have had problems with my left arm for some months. Strange.

Bratton   *Friday, 10 September*

I arrived on the Hoe slightly late. Lots of smart Marines standing about, and the public arranged in a quadrangle with the nobs on tiered seats around a stand on which the clergy and senior commanders were located.

I had been put next to David Owen. We were surrounded by Conservative Councillors and dignitaries who greeted me. No sign of Janet Fookes. The service itself was acceptable, heavily slanted towards 'triumphalism' with a quite flagrantly political harangue by John Watson, the Vicar of St Andrew's Church, at the end. The Royal Marines Band played a number of patriotic tunes as a mist closed in and beside me David Owen bellowed out the words, '. . . God who made thee mighty, make thee mightier yet,' etc. When the music stopped there was a moment's hesitation before the crowds dispersed and we could see the navigation lights of a Nimrod coming towards us through the sea mist at a very low altitude. Just over the stands he lit all four after-burners and went

---

[1] AC now eschewed the stock market and kept his wealth in cash, on twenty-eight-day deposits.

[2] Tom, the Clarks' Jack Russell terrier, had no road sense, and had the habit of wandering off to the farm – which meant traversing Sandy Lane, a route frequented by heavy lorries and vans.

into a steep bank. The noise was absolutely deafening, twice as loud as the fiercest peal of thunder you could hear and very dramatic. How they got the timing so split second, I don't know, but it was a fitting end to an appropriately militaristic service.

Saltwood   *Monday, 13 September*

Our last day before we set off on a very short motor tour, which, hopefully, will end in Zermatt. Still no news or mention of the reshuffle and I could not resist telephoning Jonathan Aitken again, bearing in mind that Michael Jopling was presently trying to get me to do something. JA now admitted that his source was Ian Gow himself, claimed that they had both got extremely inebriated at Jonathan's house in early August. But, and this *was* significant, JA said that he had recently run into Norman Lamont[1] and asked him in jocular terms about his (NL's) prospects in the middle rank reshuffle. Alarmingly Norman Lamont had said, 'Apparently the whole thing is being held up because of Alan,' ie that some wanted me, others did not. It is really too vexing. I told Jonathan about Michael Jopling's request[2] and he brilliantly advised me not just to carry out the instructions, but to copy my speech both to Jopling and Willie.

After putting the phone down I decided to go one better – for all I know this blasted reshuffle is being argued about at this very minute, before The Lady leaves for China – and send them both *advance* copies of what I was going to say, 'in case you want anything altered.' Oh to be in the Citroen, wafting across France from one rosette to the next!

Cloisters   *Wednesday, 29 September*

I went today to Terry Lewin's[3] farewell party at the Admiralty building. I assumed that there would be a lot of politicians and a

---

[1] Norman Lamont, MP for Kingston-on-Thames since 1972.

[2] AC had been asked to make a law-and-order speech to support a colleague in difficulties with her constituency over capital punishment.

[3] Admiral of the Fleet Sir Terence Lewin, Chief of the Defence Staff, 1979–82.

large crowd, but in fact there were few people in the room and practically no one I knew. Only four people spoke to me, but each in turn initiated the conversation and drew me aside for their predecessor. First, the Secretary of State, then the Chief of the General Staff (Bramall); the First Sea Lord (Leach); and finally the CDS.

It was a memorable little moment that, when the First Sea Lord, who had himself got rid of Bramall, and was complaining to me about the Secretary of State 'hanging on', was then himself similarly dismissed by the CDS, who came over, 'This looks a very naval corner . . .' and made plain his wish that Leach should leave us alone.

Terry Lewin was most interesting and indiscreet about future defence spending, the Falklands campaign, the National purpose and spoke frankly and genuinely. Not a bad bag for a backbencher, but what is the point?

Cloisters   *Wednesday, 20 October*

In the Lobby Garel-Jones beckoned to me. He said that he had a special message from Jopling. A special message in the sense that it was not meant to be transmitted, but yet at the same time it was intended that I should hear of it. G-J more or less said that Jopling had undertaken to get me a job in the next reshuffle, we must do something for Alan, etc. After the vote I rang Jane and told her, but I said that I was not in the slightest degree elated by this. It is a what-of-it episode really. These undertakings are practically valueless. And if it was their intention to keep me quiet until January – well, that suits me fine as it conforms exactly with my own intentions.

Cloisters   *Tuesday, 26 October*

I was still in my flat at 11 o'clock this morning, washing up and pecking in a desultory way at housework. This always fills me with gloom – the cold empty chambers, the peeling wallpaper, the layers of dust and grease. Beautiful possessions surround one, but there is no warmth or vitality; the place is a dormitory only.

Then the phone rang. I was in two minds about answering. The telephone at Albany is nearly always bores or ill-wishers. It was the Chief Whip (the Chief Whip seems to be phoning me an awful lot at the moment). He told me that there was now a place in the Falklands delegation and would I like to go.

I could not refuse. 'When is it?' 'Tomorrow.' Christ! Apart from anything else this meant I would miss Andrew to whose return we had both been looking forward for weeks. I said I would have to talk with Jane, which I did and she said I 'must' go. I confirmed with Jopling and went straight round to the MoD where there was a briefing.

They had already started when I entered the room. Buck, who has been doing his best from the outset to keep me off the delegation, gave me what is known as an 'old-fashioned' look when I came in. They are a curious selection. Two knights, Hector Monro and John Biggs-Davison, Buck (nominally leader), myself and little Peter Viggers travelling, presumably, on a good-boy pass, and Member for Gosport. The Labour lot were somewhat more grizzled, if not actually elderly. Roy Mason (as a former Secretary of State for Defence, and Privy Councillor, he is the senior member of the delegation, though not, for Party reasons, its leader), Kevin McNamara, a shadow defence spokesman, Bruce George, from the Select Committee, Dick Crawshaw from the Speaker's Panel, and a dear old boy whom I have noticed before, but to whom I have never spoken, David Young.[1]

There were three votes that evening, all quite unimportant, but the whips would not let me leave until they were over. I got away to Saltwood about 8.00pm and spent the rest of the evening collecting my kit, warm clothes, etc in a high state of excitement.

---

[1] David Young, Labour MP for Bolton E. since February 1974.

Ascension Island   *Thursday, 28 October*

We breakfasted at 7.30am and then spent about an hour looking at our beautiful eggshell white VC10 through the windows of the VIP lounge before being told that there would be another hour's delay as 'an oleo strut has collapsed' (!) I started spreading alarm and despondency, saying that it was at least a four-hour job to repair it, that there should then be proper taxi-ing trials and so on. The Air Commodore who was our temporary 'nanny' denied this.

Roy Mason and I had the two best seats, with room to stretch out our legs by the emergency door. I was benefiting, as I often do, from people muddling up my courtesy title as son of a peer of the realm with that of *Rt.* Hon. which of course denotes membership of the Privy Council and great seniority.

At intervals neat little WRAFs gave us delicious (by airline standards) meals.

It was dark when we got to Ascension, after crossing the equator at 6.32pm. A marvellous scent, heat, sea spray and *pineti* entered our nostrils. Temperatures in the day time are in the high 80s, but every evening without fail the South-East Trades cool the island and condense and deliver a little soft rain on the upper slopes of the Green Mountain, which dominates its centre.

An enormous airfield, and everywhere looming out of the darkness the shapes of resting aircraft — Vulcans, Victor tankers, Hercules upon Hercules, Phantoms, American C141s, that are still bringing in stores and ammunition direct from Florida. Lit from below from the orange strobe lights, the aura was one of menace and great power. Already we felt ourselves to be on the fringes of the War Zone.

Port Stanley   *Friday, 29 October*

We were woken at ten past three by an apologetic Air Marshal. Breakfast was delicious, beaming chefs on duty, splatting eggs into huge dishes of exploding fat. Sizzling bacon, bubbling baked beans

– 'Open twenty-four hours a day,' it said. 'Last hot food for 4,000 miles.'

Then we were driving out to the Hercules, absolutely jammed with cargo up the centre of the fuselage with four ranks of side-facing seats on either side. The seats were webbing and the back bolt upright against a variety of spikes, taps, nuts and other protrusions. There was very little space, indeed, and those already established seemed not to welcome our arrival particularly, nor to be in any hurry to make room for us.

Just as we arrived on the outskirts of Port Stanley, I saw the doors of the nursery school open and out tumbled a lot of jolly fair-haired children in their anoraks, to be collected by their Mums. A completely English scene. We could not possibly have abandoned these people and packaged them up in some diplomatic deal. This has been a real war of liberation, not some dreary 'peace-keeping' effort on behalf of the UN, but a battle fought in obedience to a blood tie.

Our driver parked outside the Upland Goose and we trailed inside. The MPs, shabbily coughing and cigaretting, formed a queue outside the Reception hatch. I will never, under any circumstances, stand in a queue, so I chatted up some girls who were having tea at a table at the far end of the covered patio.

When the queue had dispersed I went to the Reception desk to claim my room. (Plainly if the reservations had been made there was no need to fuss or queue barge.) However, when I got to the desk it seemed that all the places had been allocated. Impossible, I remained calm.

I had noticed that the MPs were 'pairing off' and having to share rooms and thought perhaps that if I was the odd man I might get a room to myself. No, it was 104 I had to go to. Noises from within, spluttering and shufflings. We opened the door – and who should be my room mate, but Buck! Awkward, but not socially insurmountable.

Ascension Island   *Wednesday, 3 November*

From 22,000 feet the surface of the South Atlantic was rippled like the sand of a shallow tidal beach. But if I held an individual ripple in my gaze, I could watch it slowly alter shape and disintegrate into a thin white border that disappeared and blended into new patterns. With awe I realised that these were enormous waves, a giant swell that was rolling up the whole depth of the South Atlantic without interruption, the whole way from Diego Garcia, the Cape, or South Georgia itself. To have been visible to the naked eye from our altitude these rollers must have been seventy or eighty feet high. To our right were the great African cloud banks (I have never known good weather over Central Africa, invariably giant thunder heads), but Ascension Island was clear and blue.

Bleary and stubble-chinned we lurched out of the Hercules with our hand luggage. Senior RAF officers were ultra-creased and starched. Shorts, bleached stockings, chiselled tans, *they* had shaved twenty minutes earlier. In daylight I could see that the aerodrome consisted of two enormous runways in inverted 'V' formation pointing south into the alternative prevailing Trades. The centre of the 'V' was occupied by a knoll some 400 feet high of red volcanic strata – just as well that visibility was always perfect day and night – and our hosts immediately conducted us to the top of this knoll in a series of mini-buses to watch the scramble of another flight of Phantoms and their attendant tankers.

One by one the Victors lumbered down the runway. No fewer than seven were required to escort the two Phantoms to Port Stanley; three of the Victors would only be going half-way before topping up their colleagues who would give the last draft of 'motion lotion' in the latitude of the Argentine coast.

The Air Commodore then suggested that we should go on a tour of the Island and there followed one of the most memorable experiences of the whole trip.

The mini-buses climbed away from the airfield into the foothills of the Green Mountain and the beginnings of vegetation could be detected. As we climbed, the vegetation became greener and thicker, brilliant and towering banks of hibiscus and bougainvillea crowded up to the edge of the roadside; dense greenery with fleshy leaves, nameless white and yellow blooms and petals and voluptuous curving ferns. In the undergrowth one caught glimpses of Martin Johnson Heade[1] plumage. The gradient was very steep and often the mini-bus drivers had to reverse on the hairpins and hold bottom gear between swerves.

Then, quite suddenly, in this equatorial jungle, we drew up beside a perfect English vicarage of the Regency period. Everything was flawless, from the Georgian window panes, to the guttering, to the broken pediment over the arch that led into the separate kitchen garden. The lay-out of lodges and stables was precisely the same as the architect would have arranged on a hillside in Dorset in 1820. But when I walked into the yard at the back to say hello to the pigs in their teak and granite sties, clouds of tropical birds flew up from the troughs.

This was the dwelling built for the Commander of the Marine Garrison that had been stationed on Ascension to help defend St Helena after Napoleon had been exiled there. All the materials and craftsmen had been brought out from Britain and the result was the most perfect country house south of the Tropic of Capricorn.

But our hosts would not allow us to linger and led us on foot through the kitchen gardens and on up the Green Mountain. Now, as in *Erewhon*, the vegetation started to change back, not to the red volcanic dust of the lower altitudes, but to a rough springy turf, gorse bushes and stunted blackthorn, a cold and penetrating mist, moisture running in rivulets everywhere. In the space of an hour we had moved through 45° of Mercator from the tropics, the jungles to the vegetation and temperatures of the Moor around Tavistock.

The drive down the Green Mountain was a nightmare. Corporal Duffy, bandbox smart and sitting at attention, drove 'on his brakes' – and I mean *on* them. He was actually changing up to a higher gear whenever he had the space. It was a matter of minutes before we all went over the edge. 'Don't change up,' I hissed, and

---

[1] AC knew his work well from *The Gems of Brazil* (see p. 118).

actually put out my hand to hold the gear lever in second. Startled, he obeyed.

It had been suggested, and naturally welcomed by most of the delegation, that we should hang about on the balcony of the Exiles Club for the hour-and-a-half or so before take-off. But I preferred to explore Georgetown.

Just as I was about to turn down the hill into Georgetown quay I saw a white beach some half-mile away. I took a short cut and as I drew nearer could hear the thunder slap of those same giant rollers that I had watched from the Hercules crashing on to the sand.

'Do not whatever you do bathe,' had said the Air Marshal. 'The undertow is very dangerous and we lost quite a lot of personnel before we made it a Court Martial offence.' Court Martial offence! That made it even more irresistible.

The beach was deserted and I took off my clothes and went into the water. Perfectly incredible, the best bathe I have ever had, although the undertow *was* very very strong. It was dangerous to swim other than parallel with the beach, which meant one was rolled about and buffeted by the breakers.

I dried on my shirt and, towelled and full of white gritty sand, feeling marvellous, started back to the Exiles Club. On the way back I ran into two RAF erks who were goggle-faced. They said bathing was very dangerous and that sharks and Portuguese men-of-war came right up to the shore.

Letter to Michael Jopling   *4 November*

My dear Michael

Just a line to say how tremendously grateful I was for your including me on the Falklands visit.

It was without doubt the most memorable and invigorating experience of my entire Parliamentary career. Within half an hour of arriving, as we came into Port Stanley, the Infants School was letting its pupils out to be collected by their Mums, and seeing all those dear little fair-haired children in their anoraks – exactly like any village in one's constituency – brought home more effectively than anything else could have done what exactly we were fighting for, and how impossible it would have been to have abandoned them to a foreign power. There is absolutely no question in my mind that this realisation is present in the minds of all personnel out there. Service morale is extremely high and practically everyone we spoke to remarked (a) on the distinction between saving our own people and 'mucking about in the Third World', and (b) on how the excitement of being in a War Zone made up for all the discomfort.

We visited and had time with RAF – flying personnel and Rapier crews – Infantry, Sappers, Artillerymen, Pioneers – and had one hectic day being transferred by Lynx from various Royal Navy ships on station, and found everyone working flat out and proud of the job they were doing (though this did not restrain their very understandable impulse to scare the shit out of us with low-flying practice firing!).

Yours etc
Alan Clark

B5, Albany   *Thursday, 20 January*

Today we gave our Party for Frank Johnson's fortieth birthday.
Albany, so long a shrine of shabbiness and bachelor deprivation,
with its peeling wall paper, multiculture funguses in milk bottles,
its stacks of rumpled copies of *The Times*, had been transformed by
the simple act of throwing out a defunct night storage heater,
opening the fireplace in the hall and installing one of those *ultra
verité* log fires that burn gas with 'real' flames. Bridget[1] and Jane had
bought a mass of flowers and earlier in the week Jane had driven
the Morris Woody up with fabrics, cushions, lights and silver. It is
remarkable how I have tolerated, indeed almost enjoyed the
seediness of that place for nearly ten years, and it was quite simply
corrected in the space of three days (including reconnecting the
gas, which had been, needless to say, cut off for non-payment in
1979. I posed and blustered as 'Lord Clark' and reopened the
account in my father's name). Now the décor is perfectly acceptable with all those heavy gilt frames from Sudbourne and Shielbridge[2] – something of a rich, though mean, Edwardian don.

    First to arrive was Julian Critchley;[3] thoroughly cross and pouty
he was, and stayed that way throughout, leaving, as Jane also
remarked, in if anything, an even worse temper than when he
arrived. Admittedly he only drank orange juice. There were two
mini-scares. One when it was discovered that the champagne,
though iced and icy, could not be opened. However, Bridget's
cook had the brilliant idea of scalding the necks of the bottles
under a kettle. I was quite prepared to smash them against the side
of the bath. There was also a bad moment when Frank failed to

---

[1] Bridget Heathcoat Amory, daughter of Viscount Amory, Chancellor of the
Exchequer, 1958–60.
[2] Houses in Suffolk and Wester Ross belonging to AC's grandfather.
[3] Julian Critchley, MP for Aldershot since 1970.

turn up and it was feared that his acute shyness might at the last moment prevent him from coming at all.

As it was the entire British media were there, with the exception of Robin Day. Also a wide variety of politicians. Parviz Radji[1] hung back and was *not* lionised, although it was publication day of his memoirs. He is handsome with twinkling observant eyes. Is he colossally rich? Most expatriate Iranians are. He was beautifully dressed it is true, but perhaps he's 'what's the point?' Nico Henderson[2] seemed to be enjoying himself and drank copiously, 'I see every shade of political opinion here, Alan, except the Tory wets'. 'Here's one who got through the net', I said, indicating the (literally) pink and complacent Ferdinand Mount[3]. There is no love lost between FM and myself.

Bridget A. is a big and bossy girl, though very nice and almost attractive (if she wasn't *quite* so big and bossy). She spent a lot of dinner saying how plain she thought Carol Thatcher[4] was. As a matter of fact Carol Thatcher is not plain in the least, although on that particular evening she was rather oddly made up; too much eye pencil, which is pointless in her case as she has got a lovely pale skin.

At the small dinner which Franko gave afterwards I sat next to Anne Parkinson[5]. She is very ambitious for Cecil in an engaging affectionate way. I said that we have got to arrange things so that he becomes Prime Minister after The Lady. The alternatives – Heseltine and Tebbit are each in their different way unacceptable. When Cecil and I drove in his car to the division he waxed contemptuous of Heseltine – spoke gibberish, never read a book, etc, etc. Everyone loathes him and he is not really even a specially good Minister. How does he manage to get on all the time?

---

[1] Parviz Radji, ambassador of Iran, 1976–79.

[2] Sir Nicholas Henderson, former British ambassador in Warsaw, Bonn, Peru and Washington.

[3] Ferdinand Mount, head of the Prime Minister's Policy Unit since 1982. Previously and subsequently a journalist.

[4] Carol Thatcher, daughter of the prime minister.

[5] Anne Parkinson, wife of Cecil Parkinson, MP and chairman of the Conservative Party since 1981.

Saltwood   *Sunday, 15 May*

A fine evening at last, with delightful and abundant birdsong. It has been so wet that the ground squelches under foot and even the Mehari[1] marks the lawn. The greenery is lush, bursting on every side; so many vistas of tone across the arboretum. We visited the young trees this afternoon and were pleased by a copper beech that Jane had planted down in the spinney to carry the eye along from the Park. On the way back I had a confrontation with the 'country bumpkin' man, an inveterate trespasser. I cursed him, and he crumpled disarmingly.

Andrew is back from Sandhurst, and looking wonderful. But my poor father lies adying in the Hythe nursing home where, unhappily, he receives visitors. Together we went to see him, and found him weak and quavery. He went in for colonic lavage, to 'clear up' his diverticulitis (which he hasn't got, of course; but the fool of a doctor can't see, or won't accept that Nolwen is poisoning him).

Then he broke a hip trying to get out of the impossibly high hospital bed; then an operation to cure this led to (how?) a blocked urinary tract. Now he's on a catheter as well as heavily in plaster, and mildly doped. Before the operation he said to me, 'I am perfectly clear, and I say this with all deliberation, that I will not be alive in a week's time.'

I am sad, though not as sad as I used to be, that I never really made contact with him. And, as I think about it, I suppose I'm sorry that I reacted away from the world of 'Art', because that shut off a whole primary subject that we could discuss together. The world of 'Civilisation'. I must have been very crude and rough in my teens and early twenties (still am, some would say).

I am interested in Clare, the au pair whom Nolwen has just installed at Garden House. I strolled over this evening, deliberately entered by the back door and chatted her up. She's not pretty, but is sexual. Dairymaid.

---

[1] The little Citroën truck used for clearing the lawns at Saltwood.

Tomorrow we are off to Bratton for a three-week Election campaign.

Charing Cross train   *Friday, 20 May*

The Election campaign is less than halfway through, but I am returning, somewhat reluctantly and uncertainly, on account of my father's imminent (or so we are told) death.

Last night, as Jane and I approached the Hoe Conservative Club, following a successful Adoption meeting at which I spoke from the heart about the Falklands and got a standing ovation, we were accosted. In the twilight – it must have been about nine o'clock – a man in 'beadle's' regalia peered at me. 'I know you', he said, breathing pungent whisky fumes.

It turned out he was the Town Crier of London, *really* was, although at first I thought he was mobbing.[1] We had a light-hearted conversation. Then, unexpectedly, he said, 'I'm sorry to have to tell you that the police have been round. There is an urgent message for you to telephone Hythe in Kent.'

How good of him. None of the others had thought to let me know. Well-meaning and muddled, they groped their way through to an inner office (the 'Steward' had long since gone and no one could find the light switches) and showed me a telephone. I suffered a momentary *frisson* during the ringing tone in case it was something to do with the boys, and got through to Lindley[2] who was calming, though shifty.

I could just have made the sleeper that night but decided against. At lunchtime I rang the nursing home and spoke to the floor sister. I didn't like it. She was evasive. On being pressed she admitted that there were certain 'irreversible' signs. Like what? Well, reduction, or disappearance, of a pulse at the extremities, ankle, etc. ('The King's life is drawing peacefully to a close', all that.' But that

---

[1] Etonian parlance for 'making fun'.
[2] Len Lindley, Lord Clark's butler at the Garden House.

announcement was signed by Dawson[1] after he had poisoned George V, wasn't it, so he really knew.)

I went straight to the station and took the 125 to Paddington, taxiing across London to Charing Cross. Eddie met me at Sandling, and I dropped him at the bottom of the drive and drove directly to the nursing home.

Lindley was in the car park. 'He's not too good.' (If my father were going to survive he'd have said 'his Lordship'.)

My father's door was open (a bad sign). He was sitting up, breathing rapidly but shallowly, with his eyes closed. Nolwen was bending over him, mare-eyed; Catholic peasant at a deathbed. Guillaume[2] (what the hell was *he* doing there?) stood looking out of the window.

Nolwen immediately detached herself, came up to me and started talking about arrangements for the funeral! After a bit this got too much for my father and he became agitated, groaning and coughing. Nolwen was completely incapable of dealing with this. I strode over to the bed and said, 'Papa, it's Al.'

'Ah, Al. That's good, very good.' He seemed greatly relieved.

'Will you all please leave,' I said loudly. They shuffled out. Then I got hold of his wrist, very cold and clammy it was, and said, 'Papa, I think you're going to die very soon. I've come back to tell you how much I love you, and to thank you for all you did for me, and to say goodbye.' He mumbled, but his breathing calmed right down. Quite remarkable and fulfilling. I held on to his wrist for a good while, then left, kissing him on the brow.

The following morning Nolwen phoned to say that he had died at one in the morning.

Bratton   *Sunday, 5 June*

It looks as if we are heading for a substantial victory. A new Conservative Government. Will I be in it? We have spent the day

---

[1] Lord Dawson of Penn, physician to King George V, and generally reported to have 'eased' the monarch's passing in its closing stages.
[2] Guillaume de Rougemont, nephew of the Comtesse de Janzé.

lying on the front lawn, newspapers scattered around, just as we used to do twenty or more years ago, though now fully clothed and *white*-footed. I look at pictures of southern seas and bathing beauties. I have an awful feeling that this is my very last 'free' Sunday.

I just can't make up my mind if I want a job or not. Fool, Clark, of course you do. The House won't be much fun with nigh on 400 estate agents, merchant bankers and briefless barristers all OBN-ing[1]. Do I provide the opposition, with a few chums? We are having a private lunch at Brooks's for the 'Shadow Cabinet'. Should be pleasing. Then I want to go to the Chalet and walk out on to the verandah and touch the silver birch leaves and smell the clarity and ozone of the Alps.

I'm madly in love with Frances Holland.[2] I suspect she's not as thin and gawky as she seems. Her hair is always lovely and shiny. Perhaps I can distract her at the count on Thursday and kiss her in one of those big janitors' cupboards off the Lower Guildhall.

The general election on 9 June
Conservative: 397; Labour: 209; Alliance: 23.

Saltwood   *Monday, 13 June*

It was Ian Gow who telephoned. I had been getting more and more irritable all day as the 'junior' appointments were leaking out on to the TV screens, and had taken refuge on the big Atco. I was practically on the last stripe when I saw Jane coming across the lawn with a grin on her face. But when she said it was Ian I thought he must be ringing to console me. Surely it's the Chief Whip who gives you the news? And even then a slight sinking feeling at this words, 'The Prime Minister wants you to join the Government.' – 'Go on.' 'It's not what you wanted.' But still a certain delight when he actually enunciated the title, 'Parliamentary Under-Secretary of State at the Department of Employment'.

---

[1] A *Private Eye* expression – Order of the Brown Nose!
[2] Frances Holland was AC's twenty-two-year-old Labour opponent in the 1983 campaign. They had established a rapport during a hospital radio show together.

I had to ring Norman Tebbit.[1] (I don't really get on with Tebbit, he always seems slightly suspicious of me. I don't net into his style of humour.) 'Hur hur, you've drawn the short straw,' then a lot of balls about 'the rations are good . . .' but to come in the following morning at nine am!

Almost immediately afterwards Jenny Easterbrook (of whom, I don't doubt, much, much more) rang and said that she was my personal private secretary and what time would I like my car?

No point in hanging about. I dressed up, grabbed a briefcase, straight to Sandling. In London I collected the coven and off we went to Brooks's for dinner. At intervals Joei said, 'Gosh, Al, are you really a Minister, zowee.' Valerie was less forthcoming. Ali sulked and sneered. Endless well-wishers telephoned. I went in and out of the dining room like someone with prostate trouble. The only amusing call was from Morrison and Goodlad who were dining opposite at Whites. Peter said, 'Look, Alan, your secretary Jenny Easterbrook is very pretty. Whatever you do, don't lay a finger on her.'

Goodlad grabbed the phone, 'Especially in the lift.'

'Drunken youths,' I told them.

Driving away, we went past the Ritz and Joei said, 'Gosh, is that the Ritz? I wish we could go in there.'

'Why?'

'To go to bed, of course.'

I was thoughtful.

I have always been culpably weak in such matters

And when I got home I thought to myself – a new life, a new leaf.

Department of Employment   *Wednesday, 15 June*

Jenny Easterbrook has a very pale skin and large violet eyes. Her blonde hair is *gamine* short, her sexuality tightly controlled. She makes plain her feelings on several counts (without expressing

---

[1] Norman Tebbit had been Secretary of State for Employment since 1981. Created life peer, 1992.

them): one, that I am an uncouth chauvinist lout; two, that it is a complete mystery why I have been made a Minister; three, that my tenure in this post is likely to be a matter of weeks rather than months.

I did, though, get a reaction when I asked, in all innocence, if she would take dictation. She had, after all, described herself to me only yesterday as a 'secretary'. And I wanted to clear my head by writing my own summary memo. 'Can't you do shorthand?'

'I'm an official, not a typist.'

Faster than I can digest them great wadges of documentation are whumped into my 'In' tray. The subject matter is turgid: a mass of 'schemes' whose purpose, plainly, is not so much to bring relief to those out of work as to devise excuses for removing them from the Register. Among my other responsibilities are 'statistics', so it will be me who has to tell the House each month what is the 'jobless' total

Department of Employment   *Thursday, 16 June*

This morning I woke up with a jolt at 4.10am – the first anxiety-waking since the mid 1970s when Hoare's were holding the deeds of Saltwood and I used to worry about repaying the overdraft. Interestingly, my anxiety translated itself into a financial dream. I had asked the Manager of the UBS in Brig the state of my account and he told me that I was SwFrs. 250,000 overdrawn – but of course it is quite all right, Mr Clark, we have the security of the Chalet. In fact I'm not overdrawn at all in Brig. But the anxiety syndrome had surfaced in its old form – although in the days when I was short of money I never used to *dream* about it. I lay awake for some hour and a half, thinking how in the hell am I going to cope with this; how long is it going to take me to comprehend, to dominate this completely new field of expertise.

I made tea at about six am, got to the office at seven thirty am, unlocked the Red Box and started reading. Normally I am a slow reader, but in the last forty-eight hours I must have read more than in the previous two months.

Saltwood   *Sunday, 19 June*

Ever since I was elected, no, adopted for the Sutton Division there
has appeared annually, or more often, in the minutes of whichever
executive council meeting I have been unable to attend, devoted
to the topic of fund-raising and social events, the flat resolution
(passed unanimously), 'Alan Clark to invite a Personality'. Invariably it annoys me. I find it presumptuous and insulting as well as
being unclear. And so far – to their irritation – I have always been
able to dodge it. But this last weekend they had a Euro Party, to
raise money for the 'EuroConstituency' (a function always
enthusiastically attended, as it is known that I am filled with distaste
for all things 'Euro') and I had resolved, in celebration of our
famous victory, to produce a 'surprise' personality.

I am ill at ease with people in show business. I prefer the
company of journalists, or other politicians, or fellow Old Etonians, or classic car dealers, or dons. But Jane and I agreed that there
was one person who was sympathetic, and whom it would be fun
to have down – Reggie.[1]

It was soon apparent, though, that he had suffered a *coup de*
something-or-other.[2] He said nothing in the car, nothing in the
train, nothing in the Mayflower Post – whither I took him to show
his rooms and ply him with drink before we went over to the
Guildhall.

In some gloom Jane and I went off to change. 'A man of few
words,' I said.

'*Few*? He's *totally* dumb.'

But once the evening got under way Reggie performed professionally. He grinned his way through the lionising, made a 'funny'
speech ending with a joke (was it blue? I didn't get it, anyway)
about Anna Ford and 'Alan Clark's hammer'. Yet the moment we
were out of the building, he reverted. Hardly said another word.
Strange. I hope he's all right.

---

[1] Reggie Bosanquet, an old friend, who was newscaster at ITN for many years.
[2] At that time (and quite unknown to the Clarks) Bosanquet was tragically
suffering from cancer of the liver from which he was to die later in the year.

Department of Employment   *Monday, 20 June*

At 8.56am I heard Jenny's phone ring in the outer office. 'Yes, he's here,' I heard her say (so Yah Boo to whoever is asking, I thought). It was Donald Derx.[1]

Jenny padded in with that special sly gait when she thinks she has caught me out with something.

'Have you read the brief on the revised conditions for Job Splitting Scheme?'

'Yes.' (Lie.)

'Good,' she said (meaning, good I have caught you out), 'because Donald Derx would like to come round and discuss it with you.'

'When does he want to come?'

'Well, in about five minutes.'

'All right,' I said gritly. 'Have him round in five minutes.'

I calculated that I could just about read it well enough diagonally to be able to bat the ball back at least, in about five minutes. But some eighty seconds later the door opened, and Jenny showed in Donald Derx. He must have left his office immediately after he had put the phone down, as it takes roughly one minute to get from his office to mine.

He talked quite interestingly, and sagely, about certain changes that had to be made. I had *just* absorbed enough, using my Stabilo Boss illuminator, to be able to keep a discussion going, periodically taking a sly glance at the briefs which lay open in front of me.

The whole thing was a complete ambush. First, he wanted to see what time I came into my office, second, he wanted to see the extent to which I was reading the contents of the boxes. Jenny knows perfectly well that the earliest train I can get from Saltwood is the 7.19am. This means that on a Monday I cannot get to the office before about 8.48am (as opposed to my usual time of eight o'clock). At best, ie if it had been the very first document I read on opening the box, I would have had seven minutes, maximum, in which to read it. In fact, of course, it had been hidden about a quarter of the way down the box. But I am already wise to this trick and don't take things out in the order in which they are arranged. I fillet them first, and extract those little photocopied flimsies marked 'PUSS to see' and Jenny's initials, which are the really tricky items.

Department of Employment   *Tuesday, 21 June*

I was lunching with Jerry Wiggin in the House and he told me the horror story of his sacking.

The phone rang at his home on Sunday night.

'Jerry, hello, it's Ian here . . .'

'Oh yes, hello.'

'Jerry, the Prime Minister would like to see you at Downing Street tomorrow.'

Jerry's spirits soared, but before he could even say Yes, Ian went on, 'I'm afraid it's not very good news . . .' and his spirits plummeted cruelly as Ian went on, '. . . so would you mind coming to the back door.'

Oh, what a chilling, ghastly experience. I am very good at detecting from people's voices whether what they have to say is good or bad and I don't think I would have been misled by Ian's presumably sepulchral tone as he invited Jerry's attendance. What I do think I would have said, however, is, 'Stuff your fucking door, I am not going to bother. She can just write to me.'

And yet, as poor Jerry admitted, although he had meant to be dignified, when he actually got into the room, he plucked and pleaded and blubbed.

What on earth did he expect – to go in and change her mind, to get her to go back to her desk and cross somebody else's name out? When I told this tale to another Minister he wisely and shrewdly observed that in the end we are all sacked and it's always awful. It is as inevitable as death following life. If you are elevated there comes a day when you are demoted. Even Prime Ministers.

Department of Employment   *Thursday, 23 June*

It's not yet eight o'clock and already I've been in my office half an hour. I like to get here early, before anyone else arrives, then I can scowl at them through the communicating doorway as they take their places around the outer office. I am still so ignorant of the basic material that this is one of the few ways I can start to assert an ascendancy.

It is (naturally and heartbreakingly) a glorious summer morning, and I have drawn back to their maximum extent the sliding windows, thus buggering or – I trust – partially buggering the air conditioning system. There is a tiny *balcony*, a gutter really, with a very low parapet, below knee height. Certain death on the Victoria Street pavement eight floors below. Sometimes I get a wild urge to relieve my bladder over it, splattingly on the ant-like crowds. Would this get one the sack? Probably not. It would *have* to be hushed up. Trivial, but at the same time bizarre. Certainly it would tax the powers of Mr Bernard Ingham.[1] I might do it on my last day.

Department of Employment   *Friday, 24 June*

Jenny continues to bait me with her indifferent stare, and flat northern vowels. Why is our relationship so difficult? If only we were lovers.

This morning she was agitated about Sir Robert Armstrong, when she could put him in the diary, etc. I was offhand. She had said something about this yesterday, that he 'wanted to see me'. I assumed that it was some kind of social call, new junior Minister, make him feel at ease, show him the ropes. I wasn't bothered.

'I don't think so.'

'He's a friend of my sister. They're both Trustees of Covent Garden. She's probably told him to be nice to me.'

---

[1] Bernard Ingham, chief press secretary at Number 10.

'I don't think so.'

'Oh well, do as you like, put him in then.'

'Mid-day.'

'But what about Donald Derx?'

'Sir Robert is head of the Civil Service. Derx is a Dep Sec.'

Joan[1] drove me round to the Cabinet Office. He kept me waiting in an ante-room. When he came out, didn't invite me into his office. Rudeish. A certain amount of rather wary small-talk, and I could feel our mutual dislike rising. He made tepid boasts about working for Ted, writing his speeches. (That's all the unfortunate Ted needed, I thought.)

'Who do you admire most in the Commons?'

'Dennis Skinner.'

A longish pause.

Then, like a conjuror, two files appeared in his hand, one red, the other orange.

'There are certain matters that the Prime Minister has asked me to raise with you . . .'

'Really? Go ahead.'

'You have been spoken of with approval . . .' he paused, and I got ready to preen myself. Then he opened the red file. '. . . by the National Front.'

'Not at my solicitation.'

'If any of them should at any time try and make contact with you, I must ask that you inform my office immediately.'

Better not make an issue of this, I thought. 'Of course. It's most unlikely, but of course.'

He put down the red file on the table between us then, seeing my hand move, pushed it out of reach.

'There are also certain matters of personal conduct . . .'

I glared at him. We were on the orange file now.

'. . . which could quite possibly leave you open to blackmail.'

Shit!!

'No, no. Perfectly all right. They've all married into grand Scottish families by now.'

---

[1] AC's driver.

To do him justice, a very, very faint smile – what novelists call *wintry* – crossed his features. 'How's Celly?' he asked, and a few seconds later saw me out.

'How did that go?' asked Jenny when I got back to the office.

I suppose it was my imagination, but her eyes seemed slightly slit, malevolently gleeful.

'Perfectly all right. He's a dreary old thing, isn't he?'

She flounced out and back into her own room.

I thought about it for a little while. They *must* have been bugging my phone. There was no other explanation. And for ages.

Saltwood   *Sunday, 26 June*

Not for the first time I let my thoughts ramble around the many different ways that one could 'improve' the place – all, needless to say, involving vast expenditure and thus impossible. The great unexploited resource is the old lake, drained by the breach which the Parliamentarians opened in the dam in 1648 and now a lush meadow, rich in mushrooms. To close this up, contain the stream, produce a beautiful reflecting surface carrying water lilies, where one could drift in a punt and think great thoughts, with a weir and a series of waterfalls cascading through the arboretum – *Grandes Eaux* – that would be spectacular. But to what end? A beautiful private sanctuary, or a 'Stately Home' with the public trampling and soiling and scattering crisp packets?

Anyway, I can't contemplate such a scheme until I recover my liberty I told Jane. I'm imprisoned for eighteen months, then moved to another prison – perhaps an 'open' one – or discharged. What I can't allow is for them to keep me at DE for the whole four years just so as to be 'out of the way'.

Albany   *Tuesday, 28 June*

Today is the sixty-ninth anniversary of the assassination of the Archduke Franz Ferdinand at Sarajevo, the date from which the world changed. At the time no one realised what it meant, though I often think of that prize-winning spoof headline in the *New York Daily News* in 1920: 'Archduke found alive, World War a Mistake'. Surely the two best repositories of black humour are the Bronx and the Household Division.

I am a privileged prisoner. I sit in my little cell room off the top, white, ministerial corridor, listlessly opening a *mountain* of constituency mail, 'taken into solitary confinement for his own protection'. My mental process is already torpid with *ennui*. I wake up, get up, earlier and earlier. There is about an hour, from 5.45 to 6.45, when the mind is relaxed, its muscles deknotted by sleep. Then, once the clock hands are past seven, the pressure is on, the light tension headache starts behind the eyes.

Last night I drank with Franko in the Ritz. He is so clever, his wit and insight so engaging. And he is a scholar. I feel on my mettle. But he is a pessimist *au fond*. After a bit we both got depressed. Various lovelies, brown and rich, drifted about in their silk diaphanous dresses. We were gloomy voyeurs. The aura of power is an aphrodisiac, and all that. But I felt eunuch-like. It's all too bloody pasteurised. I'd like to revert to the old Ischian Al,[1] and get it raw.

Department of Employment   *Thursday, 30 June*

I still like to go to Prime Minister's Questions. I sit on the little cross bench below the bar on the Labour side, which allows me to hear a lot of what is said on their benches and also gives a good diagonal enfilade of our side.

Poor Bob Dunn,[2] one of the five back-bench promotions, made the most frightful hash of his Question Time, fumbling, stumbling and sitting down halfway through the answers until a Labour Member cruelly suggested that he may consider taking a course in

---

[1] AC often refers to his bachelor holidays in Ischia, where he would stay with John Pollock and Constance Mappin at Forio.

[2] Robert Dunn, MP for Dartford since 1979. He had just been appointed junior education minister.

articulacy. The Speaker, meaning kindly, attempted to defend him, but this only made matters worse. I dread my own Questions, set for 19 July; it must be absolutely terrifying. Once or twice in the last couple of weeks I have sidled into the Chamber in the mornings and held the Despatch Box and looked round. A very odd feeling.

Tony Kershaw asked the Prime Minister the very question that I had in mind and would have tried to get in with had I been in my usual place – something to the effect of how she had forced the resignation of the SDP Leader, of the Labour Party Leader, how the successor to the Labour Leader had already lost his voice, and the Leader of the Liberal Party had retired to the country with a nervous breakdown. She was delighted and led it on by saying, '. . . and I am happy to tell my Honourable Friend that pesonally I have never felt better.' For some reason this made me uneasy.

Plymouth train   *Friday, 1 July*

An absolutely glorious day; not a cloud, save the hanging vapour trails of aircraft in the Heathrow 'stack', gradually broadening into woofly white Christmas decorations. *Invariably* does it seem on such days that I am committed not to be heading south to Saltwood and sweet Jane and the gardens, but West, to the Constituency where, I am complacently told, no fewer than twenty-two people are booked for surgery. I won't even get a cup of tea there, and if there are too many life stories I won't even manage the 6.25, which is the last train that allows me to make the connection to Saltwood.

I have a stuffed box, mainly dreary PO cases[1] which will prevent me getting at this month's *Motor Sport* or, even better, resting the eyeballs. And when Joan meets me at Paddington (assuming I make it back to Paddington) there will be another box, possibly two, on the back seat.

---

[1] Private Office cases arise where an MP refers the problem of an individual constituent directly to the Minister for investigation.

And yet, I am enormously fortunate. I am not *compelled* to do any of these things, to endure any of these discomforts. And the boys are so lovely and strong and handsome. There was a fearful helicopter accident at Bristows yesterday.[1] No survivors. Always, unspoken in the background, Death lurks, carrying his scythe and lantern.

Department of Employment   *Tuesday, 5 July*

Norman Tebbit is truly formidable. He radiates menace, but without being overly aggressive. He seldom smiles, but goes straight to the heart of a subject, never gets diverted into detail, always sees the political implications.

I have just come from a meeting on 'Special Employment Measures' (these tacky schemes to get people off the Register). My own mind is a maelstrom of nit-picking detail, eligibility rules, small print of a kind that civil servants relish – not least because they can browbeat Ministers as a team, with one bespectacled *Guardian* reader in sole charge of each 'Scheme' and thus in complete command of its detailed provisions. The unfortunate Minister blunders about like a bull on sawdust with the picadors galloping around him sticking in their horrid barbed *banderillas* (if that's what they are).

'But no, Minister, ha-ha, in that case the eligibility entitlement would have lapsed . . .'

'Ah, yes, Minister, but there is no provision under the Order for . . .'

'Mmm, Minister, it would have to be discretionary and that could only be exercised in exceptional circumstance . . .'

This particular tautologous cliché always irritates me. 'I beg to enclose the enclosed enclosure,' I said.

The officials looked startled. Is the Minister going soft in the head?

But the moment Norman came in he took complete control.

---

[1] AC's elder son, James, was working as a helicopter captain, flying AeroSpatiale Super Pumas on the North Sea oil rigs for Bristow Aviation.

Admittedly, the Secretary of State is always right. Rule Number One of Whitehall. Even if he's as thick as a plank officials must rally round, and 'help' him. Norman's own position is particularly strong, as he is known to be a special favourite of The Lady, of whom they are all completely terrified. And with good reason. The wretched Donald Derx apparently became impatient with her thought processes some time ago – early in the '79 Parliament before the old *nostra* had been undermined, and these changes confirmed by the electorate; and at their first meeting was emboldened to be 'cutting' in response. She marked his card on the spot, and he is going to take early retirement, having 'had it conveyed to him' that he will never make Permanent Secretary.

So they arse-lick, massively, with Norman. Which he accepts, expressionlessly, but without letting it deflect him. At one point he turned to me. 'Well, what do you think, Alan?' I was tongue-tied. I couldn't speak the way he did, crudely but shrewdly; nor could I express myself in Whitehall, convoluted phrases, double negative conditionals. I was useless. Will I ever get any better? I've only been here three weeks, I suppose, although it feels like a lifetime. The trouble is, it's *so* boring, the material. I simply can't 'master' it. If only I was at the Foreign Office, or the MoD. Still, better get fit in the prison yard first.

Jenny is fussing about some Order I've got to put through the House on equal pay. Endless briefings she's arranging. What's the point? It's after hours, everyone will have gone home, all I have to do is stand at the Box and read a Civil Service briefing.

But I *am* a bit twitchy about 'First for Questions', now coming over the horizon. A couple of times I've been into the empty Chamber, and stood at the box on the government side, tried to get the feel of the geography. It doesn't help. I get butterflies in my stomach.

Department of Employment   *Wednesday, 6 July*

I sat drinking late last night, after the vote (Roman hot it was at eleven pm), with Jonathan Aitken in the garden of his house in

Lord North Street.[1] I remember thinking these houses were a bit poky, blackly crumbling, when I used to go to Sibyl's 'ordinaries'.[2] I now see, of course, that they are the choicest thing you can have if you are a Tory MP. Number 8 is bigger than the others; was Brendan Bracken's in the Thirties, and he built on a long drawing room at the back. Furniture not bad, but pictures ridiculous, art dealers' junk. Not even shiny decorative Mallet pieces, but smudgy gilt on cheap frames.

Jonathan was very complimentary about my prospects. He said it was no disadvantage getting in late; said I could go 'quite remarkably high'. I knew what he meant, and dissimulated delightedly. But everything depended on one's performance at the Despatch Box. I told him about my exchanges with Sir Robert Armstrong. He was sensible and wise and funny. We both agreed on how well Ian Gow was doing. His maiden speech demolishing Kaufman[3] was a classic. Ian is shaping up as a true heavyweight.

Public life now absorbs all my energies. I can't socialise. Politicians who try to do both can't be much good at either.

In the sleeper to Paddington   *Friday, 15 July*

What a day! On the go without let-up from the early hours. Jenny had put in place a murderous schedule, quite deliberately, and came along (v. rare) to make sure there was no malingering.

It came about like this. When my appointment was reported in the *Herald* I foolishly and fecklessly answered 'Yes' to the question (semi-spastic, like all the *Herald*'s questions), 'Now you'll be able to do something about Plymouth's unemployed, won't you. Will you

---

[1] At the election Jonathan Aitken had become the MP for Thanet South after nine years representing Thanet East.

[2] An 'ordinary' was a party given by Lady Colefax, who, unlike Lady Cunard, another political hostess of the period, was not well off. She discreetly billed her guests a few days after the event.

[3] Gow had become a junior minister at the Housing and Construction department. Gerald Kaufman, MP for Manchester, Gorton, after representing Manchester Ardwick from 1970; shadow home secretary.

be calling in on the Unemployment offices in the city? Da, da, etc.'
Result, banner headlines on the Friday after: ALAN CLARK TO
VISIT CITY UB OFFICES. Further result, according to the local DE
office (why is there such a thing? Waste of money and personnel)
who faxed through copies of the paper to Jenny, that all the staff
were keyed up for my visit and disappointed when I didn't show
up – 'Typical'.

Jenny snorted and stomped around saying 'visits' had to be
organised in advance, was I going there as an MP or as a Minister,
anyway I couldn't go there as an MP if I *was* a Minister, Ministers
couldn't make impromptu visits, had to be accompanied at all
times, the local office must be informed, we'd have to bring a press
officer 'in case there were questions . . .', *ad infinitum.*

Bleakly I heard her out. 'All right, then, lay it on.'

So there we were in the breakfast train to Exeter, the beautiful
Wiltshire countryside rolling past, the fields parched and yellowing
but the hedgerows and deciduous trees still heavy with foliage.
Drought in a temperate climate induces pleasing, unexpected
colours and vistas.

I am always nostalgic for Wiltshire, a delicious pain, where we
lived so happily when the boys were tiny, and every day seemed
free and golden. There is something about the train's wheel note,
something in the subconscious anyway, that I always wake up,
whatever I'm doing or reading when the train goes past the
Lavingtons.[1] There is a lovely rambling farm there, where Jane
went to a 'contents' sale; I should have bought the whole thing,
lock-stock-and, moved into it and lived happily ever after. But in
fact, at the time, I was restless. I wanted to get into politics, and the
years were going by. I could see my friends just beginning to get
old, and starting to repeat themselves.

Damnably, although I have a mountain of briefing on our
visit(s), Jenny has not packed in the box(es) the folder on First for
Questions, now ominously close at 2.30 on the afternoon of

---

[1] From the stretch of line between West Lavington and Market Lavington could
be seen the giant elms on the second escarpment where the Clarks inhabited the
manor house, 1964–72.

Tuesday of next week. Is this deliberate? Yes and no. She wants me to concentrate on it over the weekend. But that leaves hideously little time to clarify the errors and omissions in the crib. Never mind. Perhaps there'll be a *huge* IRA bomb in New Palace Yard and the whole thing will be cancelled. That's how I get to sleep at night, anyway.

All too soon Exeter came up. And there was a local big cheese, who'd come down from Bristol, to drive us about. Angela Croft, the press officer, is attractive. Smart summer suit, pretty legs. Jenny is Victorian, no, *sanatorium* pale, in her silk frock. I ought to be full of testosterone as I stride along the platform with these two cerebral cuties clip-tripping beside me. Quite the opposite. They've got me in a tungsten steel jock-strap. Within, there is nothing better than a champagne cork.

The big cheese had a new (red) Volvo. Thankfully, I made to slump in the back. But no, wouldn't you rather sit in front as it was 'easier to point things out'.

It was a relief to get to the UBOs. Some pretty operatives. One, who I know actually was called Sharon because I asked her, let me look into her computer screen. I moved closer, she moved closer, I moved closer, etc. Jenny scowled. No one else seemed to notice.

Then the Job Centres. Another conference, another tour. Here the buzz theme was 'the Disabled'. But why? It's the *able* I want to get back into work. If civil servants think their career prospects are centred round what they can do for the disabled, that is what they will focus on. But it all causes long-term dilution. Society will become an inverted pyramid with the whole load of pensions, benefits and hand-outs for minorities being carried by a few tough and house-proud workers. This is the kind of thing I went into politics to stop. And here I am going round saying yes, yes; well done, keep up the good work.

Gloom, frustration.

Finally, I got rid of Jenny and Angela. Surgery was almost a treat. Two hours, and at the end I had a mug (I *loathe* tea in a mug) of weak tea with powdered milk.

Two lunatics. Macrae, and little Mrs Thingummy with her thirty-nine murder attempts. Fourteen 'normal' cases. One must be polite. They are so sweet, most of them. They don't whinge, really. They're just bewildered, and put upon.

It must have been well over 80° all day, more than that in the poky little constituency office. Constantly, I perspired. In the gaps between interviews I thought of the gardens of Saltwood. How many perfect days like this am I going to jettison? Will I ever have anything to show for it? I can get very sentimental and long for darling little Jane who is left alone for so long, and always so game and jolly.

It wasn't until half past eight that I was free. But then I had a treat, supper (quite by chance) in Si Lam's[1] with David Owen. He's so engaging, such good company. Like me, he despises the Liberals. Like me, he admires The Lady. What is to become of him? I said, 'You must be Prime Minister' and later, 'You *will* be Prime Minister.' It's extraordinary how this extravagant compliment invariably gives pleasure, however ludicrously improbable, to whomsoever it is addressed. But in David's case it could happen. And we could do a lot worse.

Saltwood   *Sunday, 17 July*

By the pool, before breakfast. A warm breeze, a *Föhn* it is, blows yew needles into the water and the filter is choked. The water is 82°, its hottest ever, but dark yellowy green. When we returned from the Election campaign the pool was still blue, but now the algae are out of control. We have tried drenching it with chemicals, but this simply has the effect of making the water translucent; not transparent. You can't see the bottom. I go down with the mask, and the floor is covered with dark algae slime.

Yesterday, to much apprehension, we staged a musical evening for the Historic Houses Association. In fact, and to our surprise, it was

---

[1] Chinese restaurant in North Hill, Plymouth, where AC would often take late supper before catching the sleeper back to London.

quite delightful. Martin Muncaster recited and gave readings. The Dolmetsch twins played most pleasingly. Many excerpts which I didn't know, a contemporary pastiche. Moving and painful was the exchange of letters between Henry VIII and Ann Boleyn. His first avowing his love and torment; hers in dignity and solitude, three years later, before the scaffold. Oh, how the human predicament endures.

Saltwood was absolutely glorious, unique, the roses incredible. One of the loveliest places in the whole world. This coming week is my test and crisis. First for Questions on Tuesday; an Order to 'lay' before the Standing Committee and, after ten pm, before the whole House. I wax and wane between confidence and inspiration; and sheer terror and fatigue. I can only thank God that I have this lovely place to fall back on; and, please, to spare the boys.

Saltwood   *Friday, 22 July*

Fool, Clark. Fool, fool, fool. This week I went up a stubby ladder; then down a very long snake.

Questions were fine. The first one (my very first Question on the floor of the House of Commons; how many more will I answer before I am done?) came from Cyril Smith.[1] Naturally, the crib didn't cover it, but Norman told me the gist of an answer out of the corner of his mouth as I rose to my feet. Cyril whumped back in his seat with a sulky expression. Canavan[2] tried to give a bit of trouble but was maladroit, and I scored. Others were barely noticeable. To my great delight I read sideways in the Whip's book (it was Hamilton[3]), 'Clark dealt v. well with Canavan. He has a nice slow delivery which holds the attention of the House.' Could one ask for more? Afterwards Nigel Forman,[4] a good judge of most

---

[1] Cyril Smith, MP for Rochdale since 1972.

[2] Denis Canavan, recently elected as MP for Falkirk West, having represented West Stirlingshire from 1974.

[3] Archie Hamilton, MP for Epsom and Ewell since 1978, junior whip. Later PPS to the prime minister and Minister of State, Ministry of Defence.

[4] Nigel Forman, MP for Carshalton since 1976.

things, said, 'It's nice to hear a genuine toff's accent at the Box occasionally.' Many other compliments were paid.

Alas! An odious over-confidence burgeoned. Anyone can do this. Child's play. My friends encouraged me. In the dining room Tristan said, 'We're selling tickets for Al's performance tomorrow . . .' I resolved not to disappoint them. Looking back now, I realise I was amazingly, suicidally, over-confident.

I was booked to dine with Christopher Selmes, for a *wine-tasting*. I left the Department unusually early because I wanted to go to the Braque exhibition at the Tate. Tony Newton[1] (whom I like) was wandering round, and said something about it was nice to see Ministers broadening their minds even though they would be 'performing' in a few hours' time. Airily, I told him that I wouldn't be back in the House until ten; I was going on to a dinner.

That fucking text! I'd barely looked at it. Norman had sent for me at tea time, said good luck and all that, and 'just stick to the text'. In fairness, and presciently, he had also said, 'Don't try any jokes.' Situation not helped by the fact that officials had twice called in their original version and incorporated certain changes, Minister'. So I didn't really start to mark it up until I was in the back of the car going from the Tate to Christopher's house (not far). It seemed frightfully long. So long, indeed, that I would have to excise certain passages.

But which? And yet this didn't really seem very important as we 'tasted' first a bottle of '61 Palmer, then 'for comparison' a bottle of '75 Palmer then, switching back to '61, a really delicious Pichon Longueville. Geoffrey Roberts was the only other guest. By 9.40 I was muzzy. Joan had already been waiting ten minutes. I was meeting officials 'behind the Chair' before the ten o'clock vote. The text was still virtually unmarked and unexcised.

A huge Havana was produced, and I puffed it deeply while struggling with my speech under the tiny little reading light in the back of the Princess.

---

[1] Tony Newton, MP for Braintree since 1974, was whip to the Finance Committee; later Secretary of State for Social Security and Leader of the House of Commons.

There were the officials, all anxious but deferential. I exhaled smoke at them. Grand seigneur. I couldn't talk, I had to pee. In the lav, that nice clean one off the Aye lobby, was Barry Jones,[1] my 'shadow'.

'This shouldn't present any problems.'

'None whatever. They all want to get to bed.'

'That goes for me too.'

Nice chap. Good relations.

The Chamber was unusually full for an after-ten event. When I was called there was a ragged, undeferential cheer from the benches behind. But an awful lot of Labour people seemed to be in as well. Including, it seemed, every female in their parliamentary strength. I recognised many of the *tricoteuses* who kept us up night after night in the summer of 1976 filibustering (unsuccessfully) the committee stage of Bill Benyon's Bill to reduce the maximum age at which babies can legally be murdered from six months to three.

As I started, the sheer odiousness of the text sank in. The purpose of the Order, to make it more likely (I would put it no stronger than that) that women should be paid the same rate for the same task, as men, was unchallengeable. In my view, in most instances, women deserve not less but *more* than the loutish, leering, cigaretting males who control most organisations at most levels. But give a civil servant a good case and he'll wreck it with clichés, bad punctuation, double negatives and convoluted apology. Stir into this a directive from the European Community, some contrived legal precedent and a few caveats from the European Court of Justice and you have a text which is impossible to read – never mind read *out*.

I found myself dwelling on, implicitly it could be said, sneering at, the more cumbrous and unintelligible passages. Elaine Kellet-Bowman,[2] who has a very squeaky voice, kept squeaking, at me, 'Speed up.'

Some of the House got the point, enjoyed what I was doing, but I sensed also a certain restlessness starting to run round the

---

[1] Barry Jones, MP for Alyn and Deeside since the election (Flint East, 1970–83).

[2] Elaine Kellet-Bowman, MP for Lancaster since 1974.

Chamber. I did speed up. I gabbled. Helter-skelter I galloped through the text. Sometimes I turned over two pages at once, sometimes three. What did it matter? There was no shape to it. No linkage from one proposition to another. The very antithesis of an Aristotelian pattern.

Up bobbed a teeny little fellow, Janner[1] by name, a Labour lawyer who always wears a pink carnation in his buttonhole. He asked me what the last paragraph 'meant'.

How the hell did I know what it meant? I smoothed away. He started bobbing up and down as, it seemed, did about fifteen people on the other side, plus I couldn't see how many on my own, to my side and behind me. This had the makings of a disaster. Never mind. 'Heads down, bully, and shove.'[2]

Then, the inevitable. The one sure-fire way of breaking through a speaker who won't give way. 'Point of Order, Mr Deputy Speaker.' I sat down. A new Labour member whom I had never seen before, called Clare Short,[3] dark-haired and serious with a lovely Brummie accent, said something about she'd read that you couldn't accuse a fellow member of being drunk, but she really believed I was incapable. 'It is disrespectful to the House and to the office that he holds that he should come here in this condition.'

Screams, yells, shouts of 'Withdraw', counter-shouts. General uproar. On and on went the Points of Order. I sat, smiling weakly, my lips as dry as sandpaper. The Chamber began to fill up, and there were at least fifteen people standing at the bar of the House. (It is a golden rule: Points of Order on the annunciator screen for more than two minutes means a good row, so put your head round the door and enjoy it.)

On the whole, I'm pretty relaxed about rows and flare-ups. As far as Ministers go, provided they avoid taking money or money's worth from anyone except the Fees Office, even the most turbulent row will die down and soon be forgotten. But this had an

---

[1] Greville Janner, MP for Leicester since 1970.

[2] A slogan from the Field Game (played in the winter term at Eton).

[3] Clare Short, MP for Birmingham Ladywood since the election.

ominous feel to it. On and on went the shouting. 'ORDER,' kept
bellowing dear old Ernie Armstrong, the Deputy Speaker.[1] The
House was alight. Soon, wearing an uneasy half-smile, definitely
not catching my eye, appeared the figure of the Leader of the
House, John Biffen,[2] to sit in his appointed place.

Now this was a bad sign. The Leader only attends business after
ten o'clock when there is a *major row*. And a truly terrible threat
began to seep through to me. Perhaps we were going to 'lose the
business'. This is not the same thing as being defeated on a vote. It
simply means that the whole thing has to be brought back before
the House at a later date. The entire Government legislative
schedule is put out of kilter – and the Whips loathe it. Indeed, as
far as the Whips go, no other misdemeanour compares. I could see
anxious conferrals starting up with the Chair, and behind.

Bob Wareing[3] asked if it would be in order for an honourable or
right honourable Member to address the House if he were drunk.
Ernie said that this was a hypothetical question, 'and now we must
get on with the debate'.

Passions were (temporarily) spent and I rose to my feet. But the
atmosphere was different. I had lost confidence and in its special
extra-sensory way the House knew that something 'wasn't quite
right'. My supporters were silent. And others on our side were
emboldened to be portentous and, by implication, reproachful. I
forced my way through to the end, another fifteen minutes or so,
feeling like Lucky Jim at the award ceremony, before coming to
the magic signing-off phrase, 'I commend these regulations to the
House.'

Now if there's one vice in which the House really likes to
indulge, it is being sanctimonious. Each speaker took his cue from
the last: so sad, such an opportunity cast away, the great traditions
of the Department, Walter Monckton, Ernest Bevin, Macleod
(how the fuck did he come into it?), Harold Macmillan, Stockton,
breadth of understanding, unpardonable levity, offensive to both

---

[1] Ernie Armstrong, MP for NW Durham since 1964, Deputy Speaker since 1981.
[2] John Biffen, leader of the House since 1982.
[3] Bob Wareing, MP for Liverpool, West Derby since the election.

sides of the argument (what argument?), after-dinner speech. And, of course, incomparably menacing, that the House should have a full opportunity to debate the issue, send for more papers, data should be placed in the Library.

I assumed gravitas. Dear Peter Morrison was sitting beside me, his face pouring sweat. Periodically I said to him, 'We must *not* lose the business.' 'I think it'll be all right. I've had a word with Ernest.'

I held my breath. It was coming up to midnight and, thank God, it had been agreed that I was not expected to 'reply' to the debate. This in fact was a trap which Labour had laid, hoping that the Speaker would then rule that the matter should be heard another day. Sure enough, with only a few minutes left, Nigel Spearing,[1] one of their best barrack-room lawyers, rose and cited Standing Order No. 3 (1) (b), which gives the Speaker a discretion to decide that the matter be adjourned. Very splendidly, Ernie said that he 'had had this provision in mind throughout the Debate'

One more brief kerfuffle, and the Division was called. Nobody spoke to me much in the Aye lobby, although little garden gnome Peter Rost[2] sidled up and said, 'After a performance like that I almost considered voting against.'

Poxy little runt, what's he ever done?

In the car Joan asked, 'What was all that row about, Minister?' (Knowing full well, I don't doubt.)

'They were saying I was drunk. But I wasn't, was I?'

'No, Minister, of course you weren't. I've never seen you drunk.'

That's that, then.

Department of Employment   *Thursday, 28 July*

The House rises today, in effect. But we don't get our holiday until September. Other Ministers will take theirs in August, and come

---

[1] Nigel Spearing, MP for Newham South since 1974.
[2] Peter Rost, MP for Erewash since the election (Derbyshire South-East, 1970– 83).

back fresh. It'll be, 'Where's Alan?' and when my office say 'On holiday', it'll be, 'Clark's still on holiday'. *Les absents ont toujours tort.* Jenny is taking hers (thank God) in mid-August, but is busy filling up the rest of the month with dreadful draining visits to boring and inaccessible locations.

In the dining room conversation was mainly on this topic. Our table was joined by little Douglas Hogg, now a junior Whip.[1] I can't decide whether he is likeable or not. (But I should say that many do not have this difficulty.) I don't mind people being rude, provided that they are not uncouth with it. But he is colossally self-satisfied – or is it a chip? I suspect he has a tearful side. It is said that in the days of their courtship he used to follow the object of his desire and her paramour at a distance, and stalk them, peeping from shop doorways, like a bad secret agent.

'Well,' I said, 'how are you keeping all the new boys in order?'

Without a second's hesitation he got my middle stump. 'By offering them your job.'

Department of Employment   *Thursday, 4 August*

Last night I dined with Ian. I asked him if he was happy and he said he was not. To my horror he told me that he had not seen the Prime Minister since 14 June, which was the date that Michael Alison[2] took over. How ruthless women can be – far worse than men. Ian was completely in love with the Prime Minister and utterly devoted to her. He must have seen more of her in the last four years than anybody else except Denis, and possibly more even than him. He was enormously influential, too. And yet now the court has sealed over the vacuum created by his departure and I doubt if he will ever recover an equivalent position. Ian said that

---

[1] Douglas Hogg, Tory MP for Grantham since 1979. Elder son of Lord Hailsham and married to Sarah, daughter of former Tory minister John Boyd-Carpenter.

[2] Michael Alison, MP for Selby since the election (Barkston Ash, 1964–83) was appointed parliamentary private secretary to the prime minister in the new government and Ian Gow was transferred to the DoE, where he became housing minister.

he would gladly stop being a Minister at any moment and that he would gladly 'go back'. But you can never go back. It is the Two-second Rule. I said that he would be in the Cabinet in the next reshuffle and resume his old intimacy. But I am not so sure, and nor is he.

We both agreed that Michael Alison, although a pleasant and saintly man, could not possibly provide The Lady with the same alternating course of stimulus and relaxation. Of course MA sits in on Cabinet meetings, as a Privy Councillor, which Ian never did. But Ian told me how he used to wait in his little office at the bottom of the stairs at Number 10 and emerge to catch doubtful members of the Cabinet as they were coming in before an import-ant meeting, haul them into his room and explain to them that a particular decision was something to which the Prime Minister attached crucial importance. I can visualise the dedication, the *intensity* – with which he used to do this. It is something which Michael, with his diffident manner, simply could not manage.

Ian told me that even the present Cabinet could only guarantee her a majority of two when the chips were really down   'and supposing Geoffrey[1] is away?' Is that margin of one constituted by Willie?[2] I didn't ask, although his name has returned to the fore-front with this ludicrous assurance that he is '. . . standing by at his farm in Cumbria' in case The Lady goes blind and the ship of state becomes rudderless.[3]

It should have been a celebratory dinner, as last time we had dined the future was uncertain. Now we are both Ministers with a Government majority of 140 and no Opposition of any kind in sight. But there was a certain melancholy too. How often is it better to travel than to arrive.

---

[1] Sir Geoffrey Howe, Foreign Secretary since 1983.
[2] William Whitelaw, following the election created 1st Viscount and appointed Lord President of the Council and Leader of the Lords.
[3] Mrs Thatcher was having an operation on her eye.

Department of Employment   *Monday, 15 August*

An absolutely perfect morning of late summer, temperature already
66° and a light dew with mist in the valley. I walked the dogs at
seven am up past the dump and over the Seeds, and groaned aloud
at the sheer *crucifixion* of having to go to London and visit the
Brixton Remploy Office – of all places.

Ministers' Sundays are blighted by the prospect of Monday's
workload. By the evening I find myself short-tempered and
grimacing. Even the very minimum of correspondence and attention to pressing estate matters has been neglected. Saturday morning is wrecked by the box. Sunday morning is eyestrain headache
as one trawls one's way through the ten or twelve thousand words
of political commentary in the tabs and the broads. Yesterday
afternoon I broke the lanyard on the Osprey on the twenty-
seventh muck-sweat and cursing attempt to get it pull-started. I
had to mow the whole Bailey lawn with the faithful (but tiny)
Hayter as at this time of year the Atco won't cut the plantains. Up
and down I went, sweating and muttering, each length a strip no
wider than twelve inches

More depressing, because more relevant to today, and indeed to
the whole Whitehall purgatory, I had spent some time in the
muniment room. In a desk I had come across some of my father's
old engagement diaries of the Forties and Fifties. Endless 'meetings'
fill the day. Civil servants drift in and out. Lunches. Virtually
indistinguishable from my own. What's the point? Nothing to
show for it at all. He will be remembered only for his writings and
his contribution to scholarship. His public life was a complete
waste of time.

Department of Employment   *Thursday, 1 September*

I was working late at my desk, and Jenny had gone home, when
the phone rang. It was Norman Tebbit. He invited me round for a
'chat'.

Norman talked interestingly. He knows where in the Party his strengths lie, and he knows, too, which of the grandees want to do him down. St John-Stevas, of course; but then he's not a proper grandee, just popishly disapproving. And Willie. Sometimes Willie harrumphs menacingly about Norman, but is too shrewd not to recognise his qualities. There are others, who sneer and talk behind their hands to the pink press, but they are of little moment.

I fear Norman does have a chip, but it doesn't show – not all the time at least – and anyhow who could blame him?

We talked for a very long time. So long that the light started to fade, and as dusk entered the room so his style became more confessional.

What he really wants to do – curious how many serious politicians covet the post – is to be Chairman of the Party. Not just yet, I feel, but to keep it in his sights.

Now there was disconcerting news

'She wants to appoint a Parly Sec.'

'*What?*' (I did not say 'who?', judging that if he wanted to identify the person he would have named him.)

'She thinks we need someone young, to counter the Steel–Owen image.'

I said the image didn't matter. In the first two years after the Election the need was for organisational, not presentational skills.

Norman is of the same mind. But we agreed, The Lady does often want to 'bring forward' the very young. Reacting, I suppose, against Willie, Peter Thorneycroft, Humphrey Atkins – all these oldies who have been leaning on her since February 1975.

'It's a matter of having someone young and fresh to go on television the whole time and answer Owen and Steel.'

'At this stage it doesn't matter a damn. You must talk her out of it.'

He didn't answer, rose from his chair and switched on the light. I realised we had been talking for an hour or more, and went back to my own office.[1]

---

[1] Three days later John Selwyn Gummer, MP for Suffolk Coastal since the election (Lewisham West, 1970–74; Eye, 1979–83) and AC's co-parliamentary secretary in the Department of Employment, was appointed as chairman of the Conservative Party.

Saltwood   *Thursday, 8 September*

I am at my desk in the tower office, absolutely drowning in estate papers. Filing piles and Immediate piles and Pending piles are stacked haphazard on top of each other. I try to differentiate by stacking them criss-cross, like bricks, but I caught some that were sticking out with my sleeve and the whole Pisa-like tower collapsed, cascading the private and personal papers all over the floor.

So what? I haven't picked them up. I just walk on them. I will soon have plenty of time for the estate.

I am convinced that I have been allocated the black spot. To be dismissed at the earliest opportunity. Norman Tebbit doesn't address a word to me, of either welcome or farewell at the start, or finish, of meetings. Peter [Morrison] is more distant, it seems. The bloody Equal Ops Order still hangs round my neck. Albatross. Mill-stone.

Anything can happen. Norman had to 'go to the bathroom' twice during a meeting yesterday. Cecil looked *awful* on television, with sores showing on both upper and lower lips. The Lady's eye operation may go wrong.

Jenny came back from her holiday with a very very slight gold tan. Looks stunning in her oatmeal suit. At least now she allows me eye contact. I said, 'I don't expect I'll be here much longer.'

'Oh? We'll miss you.' Her stare is very direct, though limpid.

Department of Employment   *Friday, 9 September*

A lot of pointless activity in the Department, as officials start to drift back from their holidays. (We haven't had ours yet. Will we even get one, sometimes I ask myself?) Because the House isn't sitting Private Offices are having quite a little challenge to manage fulfilment of their Number One precept – *Ministers' diaries must be kept filled*. What they really like are full-scale meetings, preferably with so many in attendance that they have to be held in the small conference room. A far more economic solution would be just one intelligent civil servant guiding the Minister through the paper in his own office.

We had one of the PES [Public Expenditure Survey] preliminaries today. First time I've done one of these, and I was totally out of my depth. I'm responsible for all these spastic, money-consuming Employment 'measures', so the idea was that I should sparkle knowledgeably as a prelim to putting in higher 'bids', I heard them out in sulky silence. Was finally goaded by Fred Bayliss, the Under Secretary, who appears to be our resident Chief Accountant. He mumbled along, '. . . looks as if there is going to be a shortfall as our overall provision is £408 million and at present we are going to be pushed to get expenditure over £335–360 million'.

That's not a fucking 'shortfall' I thought, or at least not my idea of one. It slowly sank in that he was rambling round for suggested ways of getting last-minute expenditure authorised so as to 'approach more closely our provision'. 'Look, Fred, Ministers in this Department are members of a Government which is dedicated to – whose *raison d'être*, you could say – is the reduction of public expenditure. Surely it's a matter for congratulation?'

Ah no, don't you see – 'It's important to get as close as possible to last year's provision in order to have a firm base from which to argue for increases this year . . .'

This was crazy. Nightmare. Kafka.

Like other officials above the rank of Principal he won't call me 'Minister'; they try and avoid calling me anything.

Is it like this with all Parly Secs, or just me? Icily I asked in what other Departments of State 'is this kind of budgetary practice prevalent'?

'All of them,' they shouted triumphantly.

General laughter, of a *tee-hee* kind.

Afterwards Jenny said, 'It's not really a good idea to get the wrong side of Fred.'

'Yeah?' I was quite pleased with myself.

Saltwood   *Friday, 23 September*

I sit at the long table in the Great Library. The last entry of the year from this seat, because tomorrow we load up the Decapotable and set off on our holiday. We won't really be back here until after the Party Conference. By then the light will have gone, the place become too chilly for a *reflectif*. The deep autumn will be on us – mud and gumboots and log fires and early teas with brown toast and crab-apple jelly.

Yesterday we forecast as the last one of this lovely Indian summer and at lunchtime I went down to Hythe beach, being pleased to find it deserted. High tide and clear sunlight, with an onshore breeze that slapped the waves into friendly gusts of vertical spray. I lay on the breakwater, and thought of times past – the golden summer of 1955 when I was running Anne, Marye and Liz, all of them living within half a mile of each other. Another occasion, later on, when I had jogged the whole distance from the Imperial and back, and threw off my tracksuit, plunging naked into the November sea.

My total fitness held up for so long, with only tiny degradations, until *Parliament* took over. It's the late nights that are shredding it. I always hated late nights, and avoided them if ever I could, until well into my forties. And this allowed me to bank a lot of energy. My lymphatic system is still very low mileage.

I took off my clothes and swam for a long time. The murky salt-tasting water was a delicious contrast to the metallic chlorine tang of the swimming pool.

Zermatt   *Monday, 3 October*

We've been here a week, but I have neglected my diary. Glorious weather, navy-blue skies but Alpine cold in the early evening and on waking up I feel rested and randy, and reassured by my performance in the hills.

On Wednesday we went to the Schönbühlhütte, a hell of a

climb, where three years ago (was it?) I saw a wild cat just at the point where the rock track peters out and you have to rope up. Only a very few tourists. The season is over and many of the inns in the village are already closed. We took six and a half hours and by the time we got to the cable-car station at Furri the last one had left and they were closing for the night. Weary and footsore we stumbled down the hillside, the lights of Zermatt seeming to take an eternity to come within reach.

Yesterday we went across the Gornergletscher to the Monte Rosahutte. God, glaciers are frightening. A white maze, lifeless and implacable, so that the sight of a crushed plastic cup or, better, a fox's wispy business is reassuring beyond measure. The *patrouille* must have packed up some weeks back, because the skew poles and bright red and white tape that give early warning of the crevasses were in many places neglected or broken. Sinister and bluey-green, and *deadly* quiet (because at this season they remain frozen all day and there are no drips) these channels are interwoven for hundreds of yards, forcing detour after detour.

We must have been zig-zagging for more than an hour before we reached the moraine on the far side. I have never climbed Monte Rosa, always wanted to since, at Eton, reading Whymper's own account of the first climb which he accomplished, there and back *in a day*, alone and wearing little different than one would stalking hind in Argyll in October 1862.

Outside the hut a mound of fur moved sluggishly. 'Oh dear,' Jane said. 'It's a poor marmot who is too ill and decrepit to hibernate. He's stuck, and will die of cold.' Far from it. He was huge, massive, thrust and barged at us as we ate our sandwiches, rummaged in the rucksack, insisted on a 'tip' before we left. The 'Gondola Man',[1] we agreed.

Jane's stamina is incredible, and she is more supple than me. On the way back we both raced up the side of the Rotenboden cliff,

---

[1] Gondola man: a family saying denoting the man who always turns up out of nowhere just as you've found a gondola and demands 500 lire for standing beside it, like the commissionaire outside a hotel holding open the door of a taxi.

getting to the mountain railway station in forty-three minutes from the edge of the ice, and catching the train by a whisker. It was standing only. I was bathed in sweat and my pulse rate must still have been over 120. But I looked complacently at the other passengers. The gap between athletes and spectators.

Zermatt   *Tuesday, 4 October*

Our last day. We watched Sulag's men start opening the ground for the Kiosk foundation,[1] then climbed up to the Winkelmatten chapel, where I always find it easy to pray.

I was low at having so soon to return to the Department, its drudgery, sterile and repetitious. But as my head cleared I realised how absurd, and ungrateful it was to complain. What does it matter, the stuffed boxes, and the unwashed 7.19am train from Sandling? Tip is back safely from the Yemen, and through RCB. Jamie has got to nearly 2000 hours flying the oil rigs, and soon to be pulled out. What good fortune attends us. Yesterday Fons[2] was chatting, up by the Guides' Wall. He said to Jane, 'You haven't changed at all, not one little bit in twenty years,' and walked off shaking his head. We each lit a candle. I did Boy's, as he is a wee bit out of kilter at the moment, and Jane did Andrew's, which was easier.

I have had a Fernandez type haircut,[3] and am looking forward to Conference next week at Blackpool. My first as a Minister, to swagger and ponce.

---

[1] The Clarks had got permission from the Commune to build a new chalet at the bottom of their garden, which would harbour a 'kiosk' for the Sunnegga railway station. Sulag was the building contractor.

[2] Alfons Franzen, the guide who gave basic skiing tuition to the family, and looked after the Chalet Caroline for many years.

[3] A hairdresser in St Tropez favoured by AC on account of his gift for endowing a 'boyish' appearance to his customers.

Department of Employment   *Monday, 10 October*

In the first days back after a vigorous holiday one is always full of
zest. Spitefully, although other Ministers were meant to be covering my routine stuff, Jenny has kept a lot of it back and so there
were bursting boxes, sitting like red tombstones on my desk. But I
ripped through them, shouting queries and instructions through the
open door. I've got much more confidence with the Civil Service
now. Most of them are rather second-rate, with teeny vision scales.
They're really quite glad to submit to a forceful personality,
provided he knows what he wants.

Some of my colleagues are in trouble, and this always makes me
calm. Poor Cecil Parkinson looks like being in what Edwardians
called *hot water*, as the girl is making paternity claims.[1] But he can
ride that, surely? Perhaps not. It could be that the constituencies
turn nasty. They mirror, resolutely, the unhealthy combination of
prurience and hypocrisy to which editors competitively pander.
And Conference, where they all cluck and whisper, starts assembling today.

Then there's little Peter Rees.[2] For some reason all the commentators think he's going to be sacked. Malcolm Rutherford
(*Financial Times*) today: '. . . the most likely to become a casualty'.
(No mention of me anywhere in all this, I'm glad to note.) In
addition Nick Scott[3] is making a balls-up at the Northern Ireland
Office, and Julian Critchley[4] has suddenly written (anonymously,
this also incurring the stigma of cowardice) an offensive piece
about The Lady, referring to her as 'the great she-elephant', and in
other terms of disrespect.

---

[1] Sara Keays had had a long-term relationship with Cecil Parkinson, trade and
industry secretary, whose PA she had been 1971–79. She was now pregnant with
his child.

[2] Peter Rees, MP for Dover since 1970. Minister for Trade, 1981–83, when he
was moved to the Treasury as Chief Secretary.

[3] Nicholas Scott, MP for Chelsea since 1974. He survived a further four years at
the Northern Ireland Office.

[4] Julian Critchley was beginning to make a reputation as a writer.

Albany   *Thursday, 13 October*

We drove down from Blackpool this morning, as my father's memorial service is to be held in the church of St James's in Piccadilly in the afternoon.

Poor old Cecil had a bad time. The Lady is determined to save him, but Sara Keays is equally obsessed about getting her pound of flesh. The delegates are divided, and it is not easy to tell in what proportion. Those who support Cecil are vocal of course, and give little interviews to the camera. But I have a nasty feeling that there is a silent majority who are disapproving, and shocked.

Cecil himself is handsome and fresh-faced. Seems at times almost to be the injured party. But what an ordeal! His wife, his mistress and his boss, all throwing scenes, sometimes all within the same hour.

Apparently little Gummer,[1] who is demonstratively *churchy* and (unlike The Lady) moralistic, is making a lot of trouble.

My father's memorial service was strange. A motley collection of strays. Poetic justice, as he himself never went to anybody's.

Yehudi Menuhin played the violin, and I read the lesson in a very clear and sardonic voice, trying to convey that they were all a shower. Nolwen in particular. If you die in old age, of course, you get a completely different kind of attendance than if you are taken by the Gods.

Myself, I don't want one. Better just to disappear, like Zapata.

Plymouth train   *Thursday, 20 October*

In order to make time for a solid raft of engagements in the Constituency I crammed everything in yesterday. A really draining day.

---

[1] John Selwyn Gummer, MP for Suffolk Central since 1983 (Eye, 1979–83, Lewisham West 1970–February 1974).

Started at nine am with Wronski (dim German Senator). Wasn't a bad egg in one of the Bond films called Wronski? Boring. Stilted. I feel ashamed, when receiving visitors from abroad, of my poky little room. There are a few things, I suppose, that might make them prick up their eyes if they are 'connoisseurs', but they never are. And the rest of the stuff – cheap desk, stained carpet – says, unmistakably, junior Minister (very).[1]

Then straight through to the Home Office for the Race Relations Advisory Council. Leon Brittan[2] really *too* drawly, sneery-drawly almost. Why? Even Etonians don't drawl that much. But he does know his stuff. No stumbling around his notes, whispering to officials, puzzled pauses. I felt rather sorry for the Blacks, who declaimed their woes. But it is in the blood for thousand of years, atavistic. As was said (in another context) – you might as well try and limit sexual intercourse by decree.

I walked back slowly, past that pub in Caxton Street where they have tables out on the pavement. My footsteps did *not* want to turn into the Dept. What fun to cut and run – just disappear.

As I got out of the lift Les, Jenny's new Number Two, replacing Kate, was waiting in the corridor, holding the brief for the next meeting. (I selected Les at the interview stage because he was nice and keen and smartly turned out, though only just out of a Comprehensive. But at the moment he is over-conscientious, something of a fusspot.) Straight in to a roomful of officials to talk about the Enterprise Allowance Scheme. David Hodgkins was already there, 'sat in' at the back, not at the table, superciliously The whole encounter quite formless, without beginning, middle, or end.

I had hoped to pop across to the House, have baked beans and a nap in my office over there, with the phone pulled out. But the new S of S, Tom King[3] wanted me to sit in on his 'introductory'. He's going on TV tonight, and is clearly meant to be Mr Nice,

---

[1] AC embellished his office with an impressionist Victor Passmore, a painting by Graham Bell and two Roman porphyry urns as paperweights on his desk.

[2] Leon Brittan, now MP for Richmond, Yorks, and home secretary.

[3] Following the resignation of Cecil Parkinson, Norman Tebbit was transferred to the DTI, and Tom King took his place as Secretary of State for Employment.

after Tebbit's Mr Nasty. All I could get was eight minutes in the leather chair with my eyes closed.

First, he was going to meet some Union leaders. This was a bad augury. I thought we'd got rid of all that 'consultation' balls? There was much talk, comfortably in their old ways I thought, by civil servants, of 'Solomon Binding'. 'Bugger Solomon,' I said, 'it's "Binding" we want.' To Michael Quinlan[1] I quipped, 'Solomon Gomorrah.' He laughed uneasily, and inaudibly.

The assembled Barons were led by Bill Keys, who is rumoured to have bone cancer, and looked terrible. Len Murray, fidgety, sat beside him. Ken Gill, clearly the most formidable, on Keys' left. The rest of the company were under a vow of silence, stirring occasionally or, in the case of Clive Jenkins, tittering.[2]

Tom King was amiable, very different from the bleak and sardonic NT. I passed a note to Jim Galbraith.[3] 'The Czarina is dead'. I didn't put 'Carlyle', which I would have done for anyone else except Quinlan, as it might have offended him. He laughed, but not in a manner that made me think he understood.

Afterwards we repaired to Tom's room. 'Well, that went quite well.' Plainly he sees himself as a great arbitrator. But there's nothing to arbitrate *about*.

Suddenly Len Murray appeared in the doorway, breathless and furtive. Was there a basis for an intimate contact team, two on either side, to propose agenda, sort out loose points, etc? He pretended he was anxious not to be caught in there. But it looked to me like a put-up job. They were on the run. Now they want to put in place fresh 'machinery'. Yes, yes, yes, he was told, and sent on his way.

We went down to the press conference. 'Industrial' correspondents are a scruffy lot. There wasn't a member of the Lobby to be seen. Tom was amiable but not, in my view, assertive enough.

[1] Michael Quinlan, Permanent Secretary at the Department of Employment, 1983–85.

[2] Bill Keys (Society of Graphical and Allied Trades), Len Murray (TUC general secretary since 1973), Ken Gill (Amalgamated Union of Engineering Workers), Clive Jenkins (Association of Scientific, Technical and Managerial Staff).

[3] Jim Galbraith, under-secretary, Department of Employment Industrial Relations Division.

Now I am in this train with the lovely West Country fields going by, and I would rather be in the Bustard[1] thundering on 'B' roads and stopping too often for ale.

Tomorrow two boxes will meet my train at Paddington and, because it is Friday, Jenny will have arranged to keep me in the office until very late.

Department of Employment   *Thursday, 27 October*

I am in low water. A lot of little things are going wrong, and are irritating me.

First, I have got 'Willie's Eye'.[2] It makes me look awful. I was at a Number 10 reception with Jane last night, and The Lady said I looked 'tired'. Blast! I have to read so much, there's no reason why it shouldn't last for months.

Then, again, Max is missing. He's been gone for days, nearly two weeks. I know the 'daws all go off and scavenge the harvest fields', he's done it before. But he should easily be back by now. Max carries a lot of my good luck with him.

I'm apprehensive as my role in this sodding Committee Stage[3] approaches. I can handle it. But the sheer work*load* on top of all the other drudgery will be unbearable.

November is always a bad month for me. On Wednesday night I was playing backgammon late at Brooks's and Bartosik started to annoy me. I leaned across the table and thumped him. I must say he took it in the most gentlemanly way, even though bleeding quite badly. But Maurice Lancaster was outraged, has reported me to the Committee.

People are gloating.

---

[1] Family name for an old Bentley sometimes used in the summer months (also referred to in other entries as 'the 4½').

[2] A rheumy condition (named after William Whitelaw) that afflicts the whites and the iris of politicians' eyes.

[3] AC was lead minister in the Committee Stage of the Trade Union Bill.

Saltwood   *Saturday, 5 November*

Ghastly night. The young people are staying, guaranteed (bless them) to give bad nights. The old bike rule is still in place – rightly – which means one gets only fitful slumber until they have checked in.[1]

At dinner James had rung, soft-spoken, to say he would be 'about (sic) midnight'. At one-ish the dogs started barking and our bedroom door opened. Andrew. Looking beautiful, though with hair too long for a subaltern, even in the Cavalry. We chatted for a while. Just after two thirty James turned up – totally bland and matter of fact – said goodnight affectionately.

I had some difficulty falling asleep and woke with a start, convinced that lights had been left on. Stumbled out on to the landing, followed a trail of blazing light bulbs to – the Green Room, where James was calmly reading a book. It must have been nearly four o'clock. What can one do? I woke with the sparrows cheeping, but was still blearily in pyjamas when Matcham[2] arrived with the weekend box.

The box took nearly three hours, then Col turned up for a walk. The only way out of this sort of hell-sequence is to torture the body. I left him at the bottom of Gossie and turned in a record time of 2.50, helped by the hard ground.

Then one of The Four Worst Things happened – I LOST TOM. We flayed around on Gossie for about an hour, returned to the Castle – no sign; tried the farm – no sign; went back to Gossie with Jane. She is so observant, and I am always terrified that he might get caught in one of Felce's horrible fox snares – but no sign. At last, with the light failing, Anne phoned to say he had turned up and she had him in the kitchen at the farm.[3]

---

[1] From the days when James and Andrew rode motorbikes (James nearly lost his leg in an accident). Always check in on your return.

[2] Matcham, the postman.

[3] Felce and Anne: a local farmer and his mother.

Whole day gone, nothing since a boiled egg at eight thirty. Ravenously, I stuffed on carbohydrates, sloshed down Indian tea. Now I'm sitting in the tower office, contemplating a miserable and congested week. First for Questions on Tuesday, Second Reading of the TU Bill, Plymouth on Thursday, then *back* to Plymouth on Saturday for the wreath-laying at Remembrance, so no weekend at all. Another bad night in prospect, as the boys are going out to a firework party.

It all makes me feel so old. Reading last year's entries I realise how much I have aged just these last twelve months. I remember how quickly my father went off – although in his case there was no, as it were, environmental, reason. I saw Gunther Sachs on TV last night – totally unrecognisable from his old clips when he was courting Bardot. Men are OK from thirty to forty-five; if they're careful they can stay about the same. After that it's an increasing struggle because of jowl and neck lines, even if the waist can be restrained. And the bruising of repeated sexual rejection starts to show in the eyes.

Hotel Amigo, Brussels   *Tuesday, 22 November*

I'm here for some kind of Employment sub-committee of the Council of Ministers. Grandish hotel in the old part of the town, block booked by UKREP.[1] Jenny is with me, but I don't even know the number of her room. I share the facilities with other, nameless Europeans. Most of them, it seems, and doubtless for historic reasons, appear to be from the EFTA countries. Breakfast in sepulchral gloom, tiny pats of recycled butter in solid foil nodules.

Last night dreary sub-social dinner with a junior(ish) FCO official and his bright little Scottish wife who 'kept the meal going' à la Heddle.[2] When we got back here there was a convivial hubbub in the foyer, laughter from the bar.

---

[1] The permanent UK delegation at the EC in Brussels.
[2] Neighbours of the Clarks in Kent. Practitioners of the 'extended meal' theory.

'Come and have a drink,' I said to Jenny.

'Why?'

'Oh, all right, don't then.'

Earlier she had been made cross. At the airport there was one of those machines that measure your pulse through your handgrip. 'Go on, try it.' She scored 81. 'Watch this.' (I have always had a very slow pulse.) The band was graded – normal range, high normal, some hypertension, see your doctor, etc. I held on, far beyond the prescribed time. Obstinately, the needle wouldn't budge from the far green quadrant, under 55, the category – ATHLETE.

'Pah!' she said.

Department of Employment   *Tuesday, 29 November*

Stale air, bad diet. I have barely got the energy even to do yoga.

Anton Dolin is dead.[1] Another link with the carefree days of my flowering youth. Monte Carlo, the Beausoleil. If only one could return.

Dolin was the clipped, *un*-camp sort of homosexual. He out-lasted – just – John Gilpin,[2] his golden tart and great love, who died some weeks ago after his own brief marriage to a Grimaldi bad egg. I am always sad when I think of my days with the Festival Ballet. Pam[3] was such a dear girl, she is one of the very few I feel guilt about, along with that sweet child at the Gulf Breeze.[4] Because, in their own ways, most women are as lecherous and predatory as men, they just do it differently. It's the Thurber Sex War.

Later

Just back from a meeting with S of S, to discuss possible Govern-ment amendments to the Employment Bill at which I (a) dropped

---

[1] Anton Dolin, dancer and choreographer, who began with Diaghilev in 1923. Organised the London Festival Ballet, 1950. Knighted, 1981.

[2] John Gilpin, dancer. Originally with Ballet Rambert, Festival Ballet, 1950–60.

[3] Pam Hart, a dancer, AC's first great love.

[4] AC worked as a bell-hop at the Gulf Breeze Hotel, outside Sarasota, in 1950.

off, and (b) made one of those remarks which shows one understands nothing. Can't be good, as I am handling it 'upstairs'[1]
starting next week.

I feel weary. My dilemma is, if I stay on I waste the substance; if
I return to the estates can I even rebuild any longer? And even if I
do, what's it in aid of?

Department of Employment   *Thursday, 8 December*

I have only just found time to write up my ghastly experiences last
Tuesday.

Jenny had been going on and on about the day I started in
Committee, etc, was I fully prepared, did I want further briefing,
etc.

'No, no, I'll be quite all right, all I have to do is read out notes
which officials pass me, yes, yes.'

But, actually, I was a little uneasy because I remember that the
last time she had fussed like this was with very good reason –
before the Equal Ops order.

'You've never *dunn* anything in Committee have you?'

'Of course not, how could I have?'

'Have you ever attended a Committee?'

'Not really.'

'Have you ever read a Hansard of Committee proceedings?'

'No, have you?'

'Yes.'

'OK, then, what happens, what's it like?'

'Batty. Komm-pletely batty.'

In a way this cheered me up. But it was a bloody nuisance
because it was going to take the whole morning from ten o'clock
until one, and I had to start answering Questions in the Chamber
at two thirty. Also the sapping up time had been curtailed by Peter
Morrison calling a Ministers' meeting for 'nine-ish'. Les rang them
twice, but they were still 'getting ready'. When finally I got in they

---

[1] In Standing Committee.

were all sitting round, room full of cigarette smoke (ie Morrison must have smoked at least one) and *coffee cups empty*. Nobody said anything.

Afterwards I made a row with Barnaby[1] and that pasty round-shouldered maiden whom I discovered is called Di. 'Why wasn't I told in time? I'm not a dilettante. I get here before all the other Ministers.'

Naturally my colleagues, delighted, just thought I'd come in late.

Labour has a very tough team. Little John Smith, rotund, bespectacled, Edinburgh lawyer. Been around for ages. Their Whip is John Evans, AEU, tough, thick. Two from the far Left; a nasty young one called Fatchett, and a nasty (the *nastiest*) old one – Mikardo. And two bright boys called Brown and Blair. Also two chunks of old heavy metal, Frank Haynes and Mick Martin.[2]

I was on my own. Our team are under express instructions not to open their mouths. Tom King never comes in, although, crampingly, he had appeared in that morning to 'see me started'. Little Gummer isn't allowed to do anything affecting 'contributions' as he's the Party Chairman. (I don't follow this rule.) And of course it's nothing to do with Peter at all and he isn't even a member of the Committee.

Smith finished winding up, and I rose.

I had made some rough notes, intention being to be smooth, conciliatory, just 'get the Bill through'.

Huh! I got into difficulties immediately.They were bobbing up all over the place, asking impossible, spastic, questions of detail – most of them, as far as I could make out, to do with the fucking *Rule Book*. (I should have realised that this is a complete minefield.

---

[1] Barnaby, Head of the Secretary of State's private office.

[2] John Smith (MP for Lanarkshire North since 1970); John Evans (MP for St Helens since the 1983 election); Derek Fatchett (MP for Leeds Central since the 1983 election); Ian Mikardo (MP since 1945, currently for Tower Hamlets); Gordon Brown (MP for Dunfermline East since the 1983 election); Tony Blair (MP for Sedgefield since the 1983 election); Frank Haynes (MP for Ashfield since 1979); and Mick Martin (MP for Glasgow, Springburn since 1979).

That's all the Unions are really bothered by, lazy sods. Work-to-Rule, all that.)

The cribs were scrabblingly written out by officials, seated in an anxious row, at right angles to us, beside the 'Chair' (in this case that very splendid fellow John Wells, the MP for Maidstone). TK passed them up to me, thick and fast, with a resigned expression on his face. I couldn't read many, because they had been written out so urgently. Anyway, if you don't understand the question, how can you understand the answer? But when I could read something I recognised passages from the original brief that I had found so muddling or, in Jenny's phrase 'batty', that I had avoided them. Gah!

'We've got a right one 'ere,' Mikardo kept saying in his special plummy *artisan's* voice.

Gummer and TK whispered unhappily to each other. 'He's not up to it, what are we going to do?' – all that.

For two pins I'd have bolted from the room, driven down to Jane and the hens, never left the walls again.

Department of Employment   *Wednesday, 14 December*

Things were slowly improving in Committee. I am managing to impose acceptance of my own style, getting (both sides) to laugh occasionally. It is a totally different ambience, and requires an adapted technique, to the floor of the Chamber.

For a start (good) there are never any press there, so gaffes and cock-ups go unreported. The Official Report is printed late, and by the time it's out nobody bothers. But there is a kind of *tenu* to the whole thing, and if one ignores this one offends the Committee's corporate *amour propre*. There's always the risk, too, of an adverse report by the Whips, although in the main they're not concerned with 'performance', only with getting the business through smoothly. As for the esteem of colleagues, they're busy doing their constituency correspondence, and it needs a pretty monumental disturbance to attract their attention.

But (bad) there is this infuriating convention that Members can get up and down as often as they want. Unlike the Chamber, where you don't *have* to give way, in a Committee there has to be a very good reason – repetitious filibustering being really the only one which is acceptable – to refuse.

This afternoon I got completely tied up, with full brain seizure. Batty subclause (6) full of lawyers' gibberish. '*Nothing* which is done . . . shall affect *anything* . . ., etc.' I looked round early on for Leigh[1] to help me. He wasn't there! Total panic. An unknown civil servant standing in for him supplied illegible and inadequate notes.

I can't stand much more of this. And yet I've got to do the whole of Part III (Financial Contributions), on my own, because little Gummer is barred, and TK is too 'busy' (ie idle) to show up.

This morning I woke at three am and couldn't get back to sleep. Someone (I can't recall who) had mentioned John Davies.[2] Wasn't his brain tumour caused *entirely* by overwork? I am vulnerable. This *insupportable* load of absorption which presses. The other side now realise that any amendment can catch me out, have spotted me as the weak link in the array.

Thank God there are the Christmas hols coming up before it gets too frightful. But there are so many chores to do. I must stop now, to go over before the House 'Shop' shuts and buy ten tons of whisky, port, sherry and disgusting cigarettes for my own claimants. Outgoings, outgoings, all the time outgoings.

Later

I looked in on Jonathan Aitken's party. Didn't stay long. Too crowded. Tessa Kennedy[3] was there, totally unchanged in twenty-five years, ie good-looking, but clipped and guttural.

---

[1] Leigh Lewis, a principal at the Department of Employment, who greatly assisted AC with the bill.

[2] John Davies had been director-general, Confederation of British Industry, before becoming an MP in 1970. He served under both Heath (in government) and Thatcher (in opposition). He died in 1979.

[3] Mrs Kennedy had for a short while been married to Dominic Elwes, an old friend of AC and Jane Clark.

A Dudley woman said, 'Whatever you do, don't sell pictures.'[1]
Thanks.

Somewhat disconsolate, I strolled back to the House and ran
into Cecil on the Green. We had a long talk. I said it was a disaster,
the whole thing. He would have been Prime Minister. Yes, he
admitted, all this he knew privately. He was The Lady's own
choice, she had been grooming him, introducing him to the
Royals – especially the Prince of Wales. He was going to the
Foreign Office, would have really sorted it out, shifted it from
'diplomacy' to trade promotion. The switch could then have
happened when the time was ripe, certainly no later than her
tenth anniversary.

Was he, could he come back? Yes. Yes, if she wants me.

But he had to pine in the wilderness for some little time.
Colleagues were determined to keep him out. Of course they are,
I thought. 'Oh no, surely not. Who?'

Wakeham[2] was being unbelievable. The biggest leaker known
to man, 'he'd even brief journalists *in the street* on the way back
from Cabinet.' Cecil could never trust Gummer. Sanctimonious
little creep. And Cecil suspected that Willie was against him also.

'Plus all the mediocrities,' I said, 'like Fowler,[3] who are scared
you'll show them up. But Tebbit?'

Even Norman, he wasn't so sure. (Nor am I, because with Cecil
out of the way Norman *has* to be the candidate of the Right.) 'He
phoned me, said we were three; now we're down to two.'

Cecil said that the Prime Minister was much tougher than
anyone realised. She was getting stroppy letters from Colonel
Keays, all kinds of threat, never turned a hair. But once she decided
to chop him, that was it.

Cecil said he could never see the child. But what, I asked, if
it was a son? He didn't reply. You would have to embrace it.

---

[1] AC was at that time engaged in deep family consultations as to which pictures in
Lord Clark's collection should be sold to pay estate duty.

[2] John Wakeham, MP for Colchester South and Maldon since the election
(Maldon, 1974–83). Chief whip.

[3] Norman Fowler, MP for Sutton Colfield since 1974 and Secretary of State for
Social Services (AC had a low opinion of him).

You would have to go down on your knees to Ann, and ask for permission.

He drew the conversation to a close and we parted.

What a waste. He is a good man, Cecil. Underrated just because he is handsome. But he has come the whole way on his own. And once he had actually *got* there, no longer had to dissimulate, I think he would have been importantly good.

Saltwood   *Friday, 16 December*

I had a meeting with Ian. He tells me that he is working his way back in with the Prime Minister. She can't do without him, and he goes round to Number 10 very late, when all her engagements are over, sometimes even when she gets back from an official dinner, and they go upstairs to the flat and drink whisky.

She has no one to confide in. Not to confide in *personally* that is, although I think she is probably pretty candid on policy matters with Willie.

Alison is useless. Saintly, but useless. You need someone with guile, patience, an easy fluent manner of concealing the truth but drawing it out from others in that job. It is extraordinary how from time to time one does get people who have been through Brigade Squad, taken their commission and served, seen all human depravity as only one can at Eton and in the Household, and yet go all naive and Godwatch. The Runcible[1] is another – and he actually saw action.

Apparently (but some allowance must be made for Ian's jealousy and also for his own impossibly high standards of attendance) Alison is also a wee bit neglectful of his timing, comes in around nine am and tends to disappear in the evenings, only emerging for the ten o'clock vote. Does he attend the Party Committees? Apparently not regularly, except the '22.

How to correct this? Not simply by a change of incumbent. She

---

[1] Robert Runcie, Archbishop of Canterbury since 1980. Served in the Scots Guards in the Second World War and was awarded the MC.

needed something stronger, more permanent. Something on the lines of a Prime Minister's Department, with a Lord Privy Seal (or some such) sitting at Cabinet, and a couple of PPSs, the senior of whom would be a Minister of State. That's, Ian strongly implied, where I (whoopee) came into it.

The more I think this over, the more delicious it seems. Escape on magic wings, attached Mercury-like to my golden feet, from the hatefulness of Caxton House, the fire-and-water of Stage III of the Employment Bill, and to land with one bound into the very centrum, the vortex, of Power. And working closely with my oldest friend, someone who knows all my strengths (and weaknesses), who thinks alike on almost every issue.

He is seeing The Lady over Christmas at Chequers and will explore the idea further.

Saltwood   *Friday, 23 December*

Evening of the first day of the Christmas hols.

I don't seem to have done anything except get rid of a lot of cash filling all the cars with petrol. And cash is so scarce over Christmas. Again and again one goes down to the bank to draw, always the last cheque until the New Year.

At tea time I wanted pliers. I could not find pliers. Nowhere in this whole fucking place, with its seventeen outhouses, garages, sheds, eighteen vehicles. After stealing tool kits from every car I've sold on over the last twenty-five years – could I find pliers?

I was screaming frail. I ransacked the china room, where I kept my most precious things. My new red vintage tool locker was empty, except for a lot of useless stuff for an Austin Heavy Twenty. Why? I am surrounded by unreliables.

I've done practically no shopping. How could I? When? Yet tomorrow is Christmas Eve.

As for the Dept, I never want to go through its doors again. Total shit-heap, bored blue. Strained and befuddled by all the paper work. Fuck them.

Fortunately, I'm dining with Ian on Wednesday next. I hope he gives me a boost.

Letter to Ian Gow – Saltwood,   *27 December*

My Dear Ian
As always, a lovely evening. I can't tell you how much it lightens the cares, and the frustrations of our calling to be able to discuss everything so freely, and in such good humour and mutual accord.

I don't usually refer to the substance of what we talk about – but I must urge you to get the Prime Minister's dept promulgated as soon as possible, with yourself at its head and sitting at (preferably in) Cabinet. There is a long haul ahead, and these things are better done at moments of tranquillity rather than when the need urgently presses.

Complementary to this, I couldn't make out whether you were sounding me on taking MA's post. Of course I would jump at it, all the more so for having first experienced the privilege of a spell in Government. But who am I to say what I will, or will not do? To paraphrase a more sinister admonition:

La Signora comanda, il piccino va . . . e fa!

Both these changes shall take place as soon as possible – certainly before the House reassembles on 16 Jan.

Yours affectionately
Alan

Saltwood   *Saturday, 31 December*

New Year's Eve. I *always* go to bed early on New Year's Eve, and sleep the better for thinking of all those silly sods compulsorily 'seeing it in', drinking and driving.

Christmas was jolly. Jane and James had their ritual row, but got it over quite early on. Col was here, and there was much discussion of my father's estate, the snail's pace at which settlement with the Revenue proceeds, 'Mr Thom' as a Double Agent.[1]

At present he (Thom) is fussing about the Maillol bust of Renoir, why are there conflicting valuations, where is it, wouldn't it be better if the bank held it for 'safe-keeping', etc.

'It's broken.'

'Uh?'

'Smashed.'

'The Revenue will want to see the pieces.'

'I've thrown them away.'

No, Col suggested, show Thom a broken bit of flower-pot; the Revenue won't know the difference. Pleasing.

Last night I drank a lot of Sauvignon and had a strange dream. The Table Office had refused one of my Questions because 'by the time this comes up, you won't be an MP'. I realised that I had been concentrating on the 'new possibility' (Folkestone?) and had 'missed the nomination' for Plymouth. I was crying as I explained to Jane (in a hotel bedroom, was it Blackpool?) that I was now *out*. But twice I woke, and realised that it wasn't true, and was delighted. What does this portend? At dinner on Wednesday there was no doubt that Ian was sounding me on the possibility of taking Alison's place. But I got the impression that the 'large solution' had grown less likely.

---

[1] Mr B. D. Thom, manager of the Clydesdale Bank Trustee Department. Lord Clark's estate occupied the family attention for much of 1983/84.

Saltwood   *Tuesday, 10 January*

Two boxes arrived this morning, stuffed with PO cases and what officials call 'reading'. First thing, always, on top of all the folders are the grey sheets of diary pages. My heart sank as I looked at the stuffed days, the names of dreary and supercilious civil servants who will (never singly) be attending. I've got three months of this ahead of me, without a break.

At dinner the other night Peter [Morrison], who is a workaholic (not so difficult if you're an unhappy bachelor living on whisky) showed Ian and me, with great pride, his diary card for the day following. Every single minute, from 8.45 am onwards, was filled with 'engagements'.

'Look,' he said. 'How's that for a diary?'

Ian, unexpectedly and greatly to his credit, said, 'If my Private Office produced a schedule like that I'd sack the whole lot, immediately.'

After Peter had gone, Ian and I returned to the subject, which is occupying a lot of my thinking time at present, of how to reconstruct the Prime Minister's Office. He *must* push The Lady a bit on this. Her natural caution will cause her to delay otherwise, and the opportunity will recede. I must write to him on the weekend with my considered thoughts.[1] How delicious if I can bring this off!

Back in the House, the Club, but immensely strengthened by experience as a Minister, and yet commanding attention wherever I am seen – tea, smoking or committee room.

---

[1] Text of letter of 15 January below.

Letter to Ian Gow – Saltwood,   *15 January*

Dear Ian

I write with regard to the matters we have been discussing. I
believe them to be urgent and I want to commit some thoughts to
paper before our heads go back into the sand of our Departments
(there are three boxes in the house this weekend!).

I start with the premise that the Prime Minister is *everything*:
what diminishes or threatens her diminishes or threatens the
country – just as the country is itself enhanced by whatever does
so for her authority and freedom.

She must have a department of her own. Small – as it were a
floor of the Cabinet Office. The Paymaster General does not exist
at the moment: he should be re-born, and much departmental
paper 'copied' to him. (If necessary, some additional responsibility
should be attached to him for presentational reasons.)

It is an awkward thing to say, other than to those one can trust,
but policies are neither determined or evolved on a simple assessment of National, or even Party, interest. Personal motives –
ambition, mischief making, a view to possible obligations and
opportunities in the future, sometimes raw vindictiveness – all
come into it. The Prime Minister needs someone who can provide
early warning, counsel *and conduct lightning*.

One must never forget that the mob is always ready and its
leaders are in the Senate. I so well recall those early very anxious
days of the Falklands crisis when you could not attend a Party
committee without one or other of the predictable front-men
making their coded statements, whose real purpose was to prepare
the way for a coup if events should lead to humiliation or disaster.
To this day, I remember vividly the Chairman of the Select
Committee on Defence [Timothy Kitson] hanging about the Tea
Room Corridor, telling anyone he could waylay that *Hermes* had
propeller shaft trouble; that *Invincible* had sailed without her
electronics, etc, etc.

The question of the PPS is complementary to this. When you
held that job, your knowledge of the Parliamentary Party was such

that you could predict the reaction of practically every Member to any given aspect of policy. The collation of intelligence both through social contact, committees, and Prime Minister's Questions was more subtle than the Whips' Office and its reflexes faster. But now there are over a hundred new Members, the first glow of their new status has worn off. They want recognition (in every sense) and are a prey to blandishments from many different quarters.

I cite an example of how these two requirements might interact in the next 12 to 18 months. Michael [Heseltine] will have to cut defence spending by at least £2bn in the lifetime of the Parliament (as you know, I think it could be done by as much as £4bn quite safely). If he chooses to go to the stake on this and we have not made pre-emptive arrangements, he will greatly enlarge his own franchise. He picks up the Wet ticket at will. All of a sudden he will be able to bid for the Union Jack buffs also.

We can't tell what the future holds and it would be less than prudent not to do what one can to forearm against surprise.

Alan

House of Commons   *Wednesday, 18 January*

The office have found a new way of keeping me utterly exhausted. My time, already deeply curtailed by the demands of the Standing Committee, is being copiously allocated to an endless series of 'Fit for Work' presentations.

Like all Whitehall-speak, the term does not mean what first it would appear to. It is an 'Award' given, as far as I can see, to the (many) firms who 'imaginatively' overfill their statutory quota of disabled employees.

Joan drives me, accompanied by at least two officials, at break-neck speed to addresses in 'the Home Counties', or I take InterCity trains.

One mustn't be ungracious. It's a day off for many of the staff, who gather to peep and peer; there is a bad buffet, and someone who hopes that it may result at some future date in their 'recognition'. Etched with fatigue, compounded by boredom, I make the presentation, and off I go. Minimum three working hours poorer. Back at the Department in the late afternoon I read and sign till supper, then the ordeal of the Standing Committee until after midnight.

I must get out of this. I had a word with Ronnie Butt[1] about machinery-of-Govt difficulties, tried to coax him toward suggesting a 'Prime Minister's Office'. I think he took the bait. Of course I've got no control of the *form* in which he might put this in his article – even supposing he does – but the importance of 'constructive leaking' is to condition minds.

Plymouth–Paddington train   *Wednesday, 25 January*

On the way back from another of these sodding Award ceremonies.

Yesterday was one of *incredible* pressure; head-clutching. Standing Committee all morning, and boss-eyed with fatigue as we were kept up until well after midnight on Monday. (This is for no reason at all, pure Whips' incompetence; although just as likely it's deliberate, like a sadistic battalion CO periodically – when the weather is bad – ordering a compulsory five-mile run.)

I *loathe* Committee. I still get rattled even though, technically, I know the stuff. Yet little Gummer sails along by GABBLING. He gabbles away, and *they* don't understand *him*. While I speak slowly, and try and give rational answers, applying my mind to questions which are repetitious, badly constructed and ill-intentioned. It's like bad 'discussion-therapy' in a loony-bin.

Things were going quite well this morning until I had a slight skid, revealing that I didn't know what GMBATU[2] stood for.

---

[1] Ronald Butt, political columnist on *The Times*.
[2] GMBATU: General, Municipal, Boilermakers and Allied Trades Union.

Dennis Skinner (you've got to hand it to him, he's so quick on the ball) raised it at Questions on the floor, later. I affected blandness.

In the meantime, Ronnie Butt has run his article, almost going too far, running the whole concept of a Paymaster General, etc. Refers to the concept coming 'from impeccably loyal sources'. This might alarm IG. 'Al not reliable, not fully secure, better think again.' This close, one can't tell.

Saltwood   *Saturday, 18 February*

The daylight is already getting longer.

This evening I shut up the hens, meandered around the Outer Bailey and down to the Cloisters. I sat for some little while in the 2CV, which we use so seldom now, and my mind wandered back to when we bought it in Lyons in 1964. We whirred merrily down to the Bastide,[1] and on to St Tropez, Fernandez and Cannes.

Jane flew off to see her mother in Spain. I had the hots for the red-haired telephone girl, but was so nervous for Jane's safe arrival in Malaga that I was incapable. Nostalgic evocations.

Yesterday I travelled down by train, and a plump young lady came into my compartment at Waterloo. She was not wearing a bra, and her delightful globes bounced prominently, but happily, under a rope-knitted jersey, as the new coach/old chassis train joggled its way over the many points and junctions.

I gave her a huge grin, couldn't help it. After a bit I moved over and sat beside her. She was adorable. Am I crazy? Death wish? Above us in the luggage rack the Red Box gleamed like a beacon. She works as a shop assistant in Folkestone.

Department of Employment   *Thursday, 29 March*

I was in Peter Morrison's room early. Out of the blue he told me that my suggestions for reforming The Lady's Private Office would

---

[1] Home near Apt of Hiram Winterbotham, a friend of AC since his school days.

in all probability be put into effect over Easter. But who was going
to be put in charge? None other, or so he claimed, than David
Young.[1]

This is appalling. I hardly know the man. But from what I've
seen he's simply a rather grand H.R. Owen, the big Rolls-Royce
dealers' salesman. I got to know the type well when I was working
as a runner in Warren Street just after the war. Very much *not* one
of the 'Club'.

Worse was to come. Peter told me that he was going to have a
Red Box, Minister of State rank, and *'operate from the Lords'*. It is
virtually signed up, as Peter had to find a replacement as head of
MSC. The co-ordinating structure at Number 10 will be promulgated during the Easter recess. I said I was not too keen on the idea.
The Party never likes outsiders getting high ministerial rank without going through the mill.

This threatens to be the end of an era in more senses than one. It
finally writes off Ian's chances of getting back to the epicentre of
power, as well as any role for me in that scheme of things. I left
early for lunch and tipped him off using one of the lobby phones.
As I would have expected Ian was businesslike, showed no emotion. But he must have felt shattered. He said, as the appointment
was so imminent there was nothing that could be done to alter it.
That's right, I told him.

But I determine to have one try. There is only one journalist
influential enough to make an effective scene about this if he
minded to do so, and that is Peter Riddell of the *FT*.[2] He is well
informed about all three Parties and writes with great insight.

But he might approve. Supposing he likes DY? I contemplated
leaking the story to him, and made an assignment to speak to him
in the Lords' corridor. Then I got cold feet; too easily traced.

Almost immediately afterwards a brilliant idea, my old friend
and standby for many a dirty trick, Jonathan Aitken. I told him the

---

[1] David Young, property developer, director of the Centre for Policy Studies,
1979–82. Currently chairman of the Manpower Services Commission and a
special adviser to the prime minister.
[2] Peter Riddell, political editor of the *Financial Times*.

problem. He was very understanding, got the point at once, and promised that he would attend to it immediately.

House of Commons   *Friday, 30 March*

The fish has taken! A critical account, on the *front page* of the *FT*, setting out the Prime Minister's intentions, her decision to appoint David Young, the rank intended for him, etc, plus a beautifully restrained piece of comment about 'reservations' in the Party concerning DY's 'controversial past' in property development, etc.

It is very late, but might just do the trick,[1] partly because it is a leak of the intention, partly because it is couched in such distinguished, though disapproving language.

Department of Employment   *Tuesday, 3 April*

Last night, at last, the closing stages of the TU Bill, Report, on the floor of the House.

I had been nervous all day as we are resisting the Labour new Clause 4, on 'Political Objects', their *chef d'oeuvre*, and I expected trouble. But when it came, it was easy. The Whips wanted my speech foreshortened (for some obscure business reason of their own) and this gave me the excuse to avoid 'giving way'.

Even so, plenty of people tried to intervene, and the House almost got restive. I am still more constrained than I ought to be by the exposed *feel* of standing at the Box, being verbally jostled. I prefer to extemporise, but was forced into reading from the brief more than I like.

For TK's speech the PM came in. She sat next to me (first time ever) and, like Chips and 'Neville', I radiated protective feelings – and, indeed, feelings of another kind(s). She has very small feet and

---

[1] David Young's appointment was, in fact, deferred until the autumn. As subsequent diary entries show, AC's initial assessment of his qualities was entirely at fault and the two did become personal friends as well as allies in politics.

attractive – not bony – ankles in the 1949 style. (Julian Amery will nod his head sagely, and say in a gruff voice, 'There's blood there, you know, no doubt about it, there's blood.'[1] And I see what he means.)

The Prime Minister's foot twisted and turned *the entire time* although her eyes were closed, and her head nodded at intervals. The back of her hair is perfect, almost identical to previous days. It can't be a full wig, as the front is clearly her own. But I suspect it is a 'chignon'.

We engaged in desultory conversation, though without warmth on her side. At one point she rummaged in her bag and purse.

'Can I get you anything?'

'No,' she said, in tones of surprise. 'No.'

At the vote I walked with her into the lobby, and told her I was dining on Sunday with Jeane Kirkpatrick.[2] 'Oh are you? Where? She's coming to see me that evening.'

She's on the ball about everything, in spite of all her worries – the miners, the 'machinery of Govt', Carol (a sad, distant piece in today's papers), Mark (must be a source of anxiety).

Yet she is *not* forthcoming to me. Distantly abandoned me in the lobby on entering, and started talking to Dykes,[3] of all people. She used to be so friendly when we were in Opposition. Does she disapprove of my 'laid-back' style (today's *Telegraph*)? Or are people making trouble?

Alison never escorts her the way Ian used to. Ian did it so beautifully, just so that she never seemed alone, abandoned that is, but always accessible. She still needs him and, let us hope, me.

---

[1] 'Blood'/Breeding. The upper classes at one point (before the cause became hopeless) tried to appropriate Mrs Thatcher by spreading the rumour that her mother had dallied with Christopher Cust, a notorious *coureur* on the northern great house circuit, or more bizarrely, with the 10th Duke of Grafton.

[2] Jeane Kirkpatrick, academic, senior member of the State Department and US ambassador to the United Nations under Reagan since 1980.

[3] Hugh Dykes, stockbroker, MP for Harrow East since 1970.

House of Commons   *Monday, 9 April*

I drove up on Sunday evening in the SS 100. Should have been great fun, but the wrong side of Swanley the clutch went and I had to go the whole way through South London clutchless, which meant switching off the engine at red lights then doing Le Mans button starts in bottom gear when they changed to green. Tiring. And 'hairy'.

Joan picked me up at New Palace Yd, took me to Ed Streator's[1] for the Kirkpatrick dinner.

I was curious to meet this Anglophobe harridan. She, and a tall, albino official at the State Department called Enders (whom Willie used to call 'the White Rabbit') were adamantly, subversively pro-Galtieri during the Falklands crisis. Even up to the end she was urging Reagan to put pressure on the Prime Minister to allow the Argentine army to leave the Islands 'bearing arms' (thus allowing a kind of 'heroically these men fought the whole British Navy to a standstill' propaganda myth to arise), which might just, I suppose, have saved the General's bacon domestically. The line is, she's so clever, she's an academic really, all that shit. But where was she? At intervals Ed would withdraw, then return looking uneasy. 'She's so tired. She's desperately tired, you know . . .'

Finally she appeared, a mixture between Irene Worth and Eleanor Roosevelt. Immediately began 'putting it away'. Halfway through the meal, as is Ed's custom, general conversation ceased and the honoured guest delivered a monologue, invited (reluctantly) questions.

Odious, totally stalinist, humourless. Trotted out the Party line, consequential sentences, no rationale at all. Shades of 'Miss Newman',[2] loathsome.

---

[1] Ed Streator, American diplomat. Currently minister at the US embassy in London.

[2] Miss Elizabeth Newman, the Clarks' governess during the school holidays. Her sister 'Newie' was much loved.

Department of Employment   *Tuesday, 10 April*

I was in vile mood this morning, even on arrival. I had done a lot of washing-up, drying, wiping, etc, at Albany, and I always find this enervating. I do it so badly and so slowly. For someone as great and gifted as me it is the *most* uneconomic possible use of time.

Then, triumphantly 'marked up', a page of Mediascan[1] was pushed under my nose. *Impending sackings* (!!). Named were Arthur Cockfield,[2] David Mitchell,[3] Bob Dunn, John Butcher[4] and my self. Flushed and shocked I became.

Either way it's a bore
   (a) that anyone should believe that I'm a candidate
   (b) it becomes self-feeding (journalists draw from each other)
   (c) a plant from Ingham and Downing St

As long ago as 6 February I wrote in my Day Diary, on the space for 23 April (when we come back from the Easter break) 'Am I free today?' But now that I am actually faced with the prospect of being dropped as – allegedly – no good, I don't like it. All the gabblers are of course immune. As always, AS ALWAYS, Heseltine and that podgy life-insurance-risk Kenneth Clarke[5] are approvingly tipped. Apparently (this is what makes me think there is a bit of Ingham in it) the changes will not take place at Easter, but during the Whitsun break. Or (much worse) in September, after a summer of travail and misery.

I am going on *Question Time* in a couple of days. Might gallop.

---

[1] Mediascan: digest of that day's references to the department and its personnel.

[2] Arthur Cockfield (life peer, 1978), businessman (Boots), made chairman of the Price Commission (1973–77). Brought into government in 1979. Trade secretary, 1982–83. Currently Chancellor of the Duchy of Lancaster.

[3] David Mitchell, MP for Hampshire North-West since 1983 (Basingstoke, 1964–83). Currently Parliamentary under-secretary at the Ministry of Transport.

[4] John Butcher, MP for Coventry South-West since 1979. Currently Parliamentary under-secretary at Trade.

[5] Kenneth Clarke, MP for Rushcliffe since 1970. Currently Minister of State, Department of Health and Social Security.

Albany   *Wednesday, 11 April*

Today has been vilely full. Went early to Leicester after a late, late vote and impossible to drowse in the train as officials were watching me beadily in case (their excuse) anything in the brief 'needed explaining'. I dropped off, as good as, several times during monologues at the various offices. Heavy-lidded, I must have looked.

There was a demo by the unemployed. Uglyish mood, they created to 'rock the car' (the one thing of which civil servants are absolutely terrified). Police useless, as always, like Hindus defending a trainload of Muslims. One puzzled constable, a 'trainee' and a pi-faced young WPC.

'I must speak to them.'

'No, no, Minister, please don't try. Minister, you must not get out of the car. Please, Minister.'

Wretched people, they were angry, but taken aback by my actually dismounting to listen. Some SWP yobs tried to get a chant going, but the others really wanted to air their grievances. One man, quite articulate, looked dreadfully thin and ill. He had a nice brindle greyhound on a leash, but it looked miserable too.

Gravely I listened. At intervals I asked *them* questions. I told them that if there was no 'demand' no one could afford to pay them to make things. They quietened down. But that's a glib point really. It's foul, such a waste.

Uncomfortable, I thought what Soames[1] and I can spend between us on a single meal at Wiltons.

Later – House of Commons

I had intended to stay alcohol-free in the run-up to *Question Time* tomorrow evening. But my old friend[2] asked me along to his rooms in the House of Lords for white wine.

I partook of very little indeed, and our talk rambled. His room

---

[1] Nicholas Soames, MP for Crawley since 1983. He had been equerry to the Prince of Wales, 1970–72.

[2] A term used by AC to describe any single individual in his own close circle. In this case Euan Graham.

has been redecorated, *un*successfully. Bathroom Pugin instead of
the lovely heavy old red paper and curtains. (What happened to
them, I wonder?)

He told me he was thinking of retiring (he's sixty). He'd sat in
that chair for the last twenty-nine years, and was still slim and
'active', though hair thin wisps, and whitey-grey.

I had thought of bringing Soames round and looked for him in
the smoking room but – fortunately, as it turned out – without
success. The generations would not have mixed.

Yet I still think of myself as multi-generational. Today I saw
several pretty blondes, all clones with lovely grey eyes and clear
freckly skin – the BBC girl, the one on Nottingham station, the
new waitress in the dining room – they could all tell I was
'interested', but smiled nonetheless.

It seems only a few years ago, say three, that the Todd Buick[1]
was rumbling over the cobbles in Merton Street. Yet there are
other things that seem distant by an eternity.

Albany, 7.40 am   *Friday, 13 April*

A spot of turbulence.

Yesterday afternoon the car was waiting for me in New Palace
Yard, to put me on the train for Bristol and *Question Time*. I just
thought I'd pop up to the Chamber and listen to the Navy Missile
announcement, which came up on the annunciator as I was leaving
the Members' cloakroom.

The moment I saw it was being done by Geoffrey Pattie[2] I
knew we (the British kit) had lost.[3] If it had been good news with a
bit of Union Jack PR potential, Heseltine would have taken it.

---

[1] The Buick 'Roadmaster' owned by an American friend of AC, Burt Todd, who
was up at Oxford at the same time. AC and several others would borrow it for
'courting'.

[2] Geoffrey Pattie, MP, currently Minister for Defence Procurement.

[3] The Ministry of Defence had decided to purchase the American surface-to-
surface anti-submarine missile 'Harpoon' in preference to 'Sea Eagle', which had
been tendered by British Aerospace.

Geoffrey is good at the box. Knows his stuff and pretty unflappable. But it was bad news. One more domestic industrial capability diminished, still further reliance on the US inventory. I ran
downstairs without waiting for the Opposition response and just
caught the train.

Robin was *en retraite* for some reason and his place was filled by
Sue Lawley.[1]

Although (perhaps because) I get on well with Barbara and Liz[2]
we did not 'hit it off'. The worst possible basis for a relationship –
she, an 'attractive woman', spotted at once that I have lecherous
tendencies, but did not actually fancy her. She thought to put me
in my place in her introduction by saying, '*He* went into politics
because he thought it would make him more attractive.'

Ugh! She was paraphrasing some crack I'd made ages ago round
Malcolm Muggeridge's dissertation on the aphrodisiac effect of
money. 'Power is money in pasteurised form.' Embarrassment.

About halfway through came the question (must have been
planted as the news only broke after the audience had started
assembling) on the lines of 'does the Panel think it right that we
should always be preferring American weapon systems to British
ones'.

I didn't nibble at the bait. I swallowed, and most of the line, the
float, the rod, the fisherman's waders, the lot. Sod it, I knew as
much about this subject as anyone, a bad decision had been made –
say so. I expounded on the unwisdom of becoming more and
more dependent on the Americans, the shrinkage of our own
industrial capacity and (most recklessly and mischievously in
answer to a supplementary) that 'it takes a very strong Secretary of
State to resist recommendations from civil servants even though
these are often quite narrowly founded'.

Sue Lawley, still bitchlike, said, 'Well, since the Minister isn't
prepared to defend his own Government, is there anyone in the
room who is?'

---

[1] Sir Robin Day, renowned interviewer and chairman of BBC TV's *Question
Time*. Sue Lawley was currently a presenter of BBC TV's *Nine o'Clock News*.
[2] Barbara Maxwell and Liz Elton, producers of *Question Time*.

Afterwards, in the hospitality lounge, there was a slight kind of mouth-agape atmosphere. Barbara said something on the 'Gosh, that was a pretty racy answer' lines. But I thought little more of it on the return journey, being more apprehensive of the dear old boy charged with driving me back down the M4 in a hot, silent Granada. Terrible lurching swerves as, all too often, he 'nodded off'.

My first warning was from Tip who, night owl that she is, was hanging around the porter's lodge when I got back. He'd seen the programme. He's such a good mimic. But I became uneasy. 'Surely my answer on Sea Eagle was all right, wasn't it?'

He thought for a bit, then all he could manage was, 'Tricky subject, Officer.'

Oh dear.

Woken at seven thirty by the *Standard*, who read me the PA tape: 'Junior Minister disowns Govt. decision . . .' and plenty more. I just had the wits, through my sleep, to refer them to the DE Press Office. Poor dear Angela, what will she make of all this?

But FUCK, all the same.

Later – House of Commons

I got to the Dept as soon as I could. I was Dutch, blasé.

'Perfect timing,' I shouted to all and sundry. 'Sacked for Easter.'

Peter Morrison was waiting in my office (a bad sign). Mediascan was critical. 'The accident-prone Mr Clark . . .' In the *Telegraph* George Jones, who always articulates the mainstream (sic) Party viewpoint (ie talks to Mates, the Whips, and a couple of people on the '22 Executive) refers to 'another gaffe by Mr Clark'.

Dear Peter said gravely, 'You don't really want to be sacked, do you?' and advised writing to the Chief, which I did immediately.

Then, 'The Secretary of State wants to see you, Minister.'

TK was shaken, or pretended to be. Said the Chief Whip had been on to him at midnight. Of course, he's an old sidekick of Heseltine's, isn't he? I bet H. was 'on' to him as well. 'We'll do our best to hold the line . . .' said rather in tones of I-don't-think-I-can-stand-much-more.

What the hell? I was almost elated. At least I would be dismissed for something that related to my own subject, a hero in my own eyes.

On the bench I ran into George Young.[1] He was very support-ive, said I was quite right anyway.

By the time I got back to the Dept, the atmosphere had entirely changed. Angela reported on the Number 10 briefing: '. . . sees no reason why he should resign'. The latest PA tape is now headlined, 'No rebuke for Minister'.

Bernard's formula is bare-faced. He's simply issued a statement saying, 'What Mr Clark meant to say was . . .' and then something (*utterly* different from what in fact I said and is recorded on the video) about 'need to look carefully at all the options and give preference to British products wherever possible'.

Dear good kind sweet Lady.

Department of Employment   *Tuesday, 24 April*

The Easter recess is still on, but my 'In' tray groans and creaks. In New Palace Yard I ran into John Biffen. He told me that Heseltine had been determined that I should be sacked for 'undermining' him. Only he (Biffen) and Norman Tebbit had come out in support.

'And where it counts, of course,' he said, laughing.

House of Commons   *Wednesday, 25 April*

A glorious spring evening after a cloudless day. Starlings chatter in New Palace Yard as they jostle for their night-time perches. But in here the air is fetid. I am infinitely depressed. The passage of time, the prospect of another beautiful summer lost. I seem, rather pointlessly but quite pronouncedly, to have acquired a number of my father's mannerisms. This, too, is lowering.

---

[1] George Young (6th Bt), MP for Ealing since 1974. Parliamentary under-secretary at Environment since 1981.

This morning we had a meeting in the conference room; I've already forgotten what it was about, some MSC[1] balls. Somebody drew the attention of Peter, who is having a war with David Sheppard, to a quotation in this week's *Private Eye*. 'I remember dancing with him in 1952, and thought him rather gorgeous.'

'We were all "rather gorgeous" in 1952,' I said gloomily.

'I was eight,' he said.

'In your sailor suit,' I suggested.

I've been going such a long time. Yet sometimes it seems like yesterday.

House of Commons   *Thursday, 26 April*

One backbencher who is a great success is Nicholas Soames. In the old days I used to see him roaring in the Clermont, often with annoyingly pretty girls. I thought he was just a great chinless slob. Then he began to look for a seat. One Christmas Eve I saw him at Floris buying masses of presents. Afterwards, complaining to Jane, I was put in my place when she said, 'Don't be beastly. So few of the upper classes go into politics these days, you've all got to stick together.'

In fact, since getting in here he has been a great embellishment to the place. He is always in the Chamber and very often comes to lunch in the Members' dining room, just to keep in touch, even on days when the business is dreary. He has an endless fund of funny (genuinely funny) stories and his energy is inexhaustible.

Last night we had a very late vote at 3.15 am and Jill Knight[2] went through the lobby in her fur coat in order to be first in the taxi queue.

As they were waiting for the Whips to open the lobby doors I saw Nick put his arm on her shoulder and bellow, 'Now then,

---

[1] The Manpower Services Commission, for which Peter Morrison was responsible, were putting in place a scheme that involved the Diocese of Liverpool, where the Rt Rev. David Sheppard, former England cricketer, was bishop.

[2] Jill Knight, MP for Edgbaston since 1966.

you're not going to wander about on your own are you?' She flinched, but did not acknowledge.

A joke made purely for his own enjoyment, as we were all dead beat, and no one who could have appreciated it was within earshot.

Brussels Airport   *Thursday, 10 May*

Flying back to Gatwick after another Eurosession.

Forty-four years ago, to the hour, the Heinkels were returning from Rotterdam and Eben Emael, the great Belgian fortress on the Albert Canal, had fallen to the *Fallschirmjäger*. It was the opening day of the German attack in the West. The first Dorniers were flying tentatively down the Channel, as we were now, to probe the English air defence.

Now it's all conferences, and interpreter-speak and protocol and 'in the interests of achieving a harmonious solution' (preamble to statement conceding whatever it is you didn't want to give away). The Germans are correct and courteous, almost apologetic. Don't any of them think, 'Hey, just a minute. We had all this completely at our feet once. What the shit went wrong?'

This time I enjoyed the conference. Got the hang of things more. It's such an advantage to speak French impeccably, and really no one on our side does. Even the officials, whose grammar and syntax are OK, speak stiltedly, with Language-School accents. Robert Cotal, who is 'close' to Pierre Bérégovoy, who is 'close' to Mitterand said what a pleasure it was to converse with me.

I understand how one could easily become Euro-addicted. Everything done for one, so smooth and painless. Girls everywhere, cute little receptionists who chatter away to each other in *flamand*.

These visits make me realise how good I'd be at the Foreign Office. I startled an FCO official (all FCO personnel start with an ingrained suspicion and contempt for Ministers – I was going to say 'in other Departments', but of course it's true of their own as well) by interrupting a couple of Belgians who were talking to each other about a contentious passage in the communique, '*Mais les nuances sont très importantes.*' He was both awe-struck, and cross.

Saltwood   *Saturday, 12 May*

Yesterday, we went to Johnny Spencer's sixtieth birthday ball at Althorp.

Just after leaving the motorway at Thame I noticed a dark red DBS V8 Aston Martin on the slip road with the bonnet open, a man unhappily bending over it. I told Jane to pull in and walked back. A DBS V8 in trouble is always good for a gloat.

'Anything I can do to help?' He said something about a banging noise. I made him start the engine and, indeed, there was an absolutely *horrendous* noise, which could only come from a broken camshaft, or, at best, a timing chain. 'You mustn't drive this. Let me give you a lift.' He mumbled, got into the back of the Rolls.

There was something curiously sibilant and familiar about him. He was bending over the back seats collecting some hand luggage before locking and leaving the car, and as he turned round I couldn't resist pointing out to him that he looked very like 'an actor called Rowan Atkinson'.

Sure enough it *was* he. We drove him for some considerable distance, first to a phone box, and then to a friend's tea shop in Thame. I told him how much we enjoyed 'The Podule Sequence', a sketch in one of the *Not the Nine o'Clock News* series. But actors don't appreciate being paid compliments on anything that is past, they live entirely for the present. He didn't sparkle, was rather disappointing and *chétif*.

We were staying with Nick Bonsor.[1] A nice rambling house, mainly Jacobean, in red brick with a reasonable, slightly undulating home farm surrounding it. Pot-holed drive, bent, but not totally derelict, iron railings. He walked us round outside (before

---

[1] Sir Nicholas Bonsor (4th Bt), MP for Upminster since 1983 (Nantwich, 1979–83).

changing and bar); garden a bit of a mess and very few flowers in the house.

Nick pointed out a tumbledown black-and-white 'Tudor' shed that he claimed to have sold to America for a vast sum.

Dinner guests not especially memorable, except for a cheeky chappie in 'sharp' clothes with a Eurasian wife whom nobody knew (presumably parked on the Bonsors by Raine[1]). Apparently he was mega-rich and owned some shipping line. After a few drinks his accent 'went' completely and he communicated solely by nudge-and-wink.

Francis Dashwood[2] turned up and announced at dinner that he was worth £10 million. People often say they have 'got', or are 'worth', whatever it may be, but usually arrive at the figure by counting their assets and not subtracting from the total their liabilities. Whether he was doing this or not I don't know. In any case, it isn't much. Over the port there was much talk from him, Nick and myself about the impending collapse in the value of agricultural land. This aroused the indignation of some of the young farmers present. Jane was pleased by the behaviour of the second Lady Dashwood, of Mediterranean origin, who asked her how old her sons were, and on being told snapped acidly, 'step-sons then'.

At about ten pm the great cortège, led by a minion of Nick's driving a Volvo station wagon, departed. (Nick had promised Raine that we would arrive by nine-thirty pm and it was a forty-minute drive.) The order was Volvo wagon (Bonsor), Rolls Shadow (us), Rolls Spirit (the cheeky chappie), Range Rover (young farmers) and Mercedes 500 SEC (Dashwoods).

Fortunately the minion in the Volvo drove extremely slowly otherwise we would never have managed the cross country journey. I was already tight, so Jane took the wheel. Althorp itself was beautifully floodlit and looked perfect in scale, almost tiny. The arrangements for parking the cars – *endless* fleets of Shadows – were very efficient.

---

[1] Raine: Countess Spencer. Previously married to Gerald Legge, Earl of Dartmouth.

[2] Sir Francis Dashwood (11th Bt), owner of West Wycombe Park.

When we went into the Hall a magnificent sight presented itself: Barbara Cartland[1] wearing an electric pink chiffon dress, with false eyelashes, as thick as those black caterpillars that give you a rash if you handle them, was draped on the central staircase with her dress arranged like a caricature of the celebrated Cecil Beaton photograph of the Countess of Jersey, at Osterly. She and Mervyn Stockwood[2] were making stylised conversation, he complete with gaiters, waistcoat, much purple showing here and there, and various pendant charms and crucifixes.

All very gay and glittering. Even at dinner Jane ranked no more than equal third on the carat count, although she was wearing both the leaf diamonds and Aunt Di's necklace. Some of the more mature ladies at the ball itself could hardly move, so encrustulated were they. The Princess of Wales, on the other hand, looked absolutely radiantly beautiful and was wearing not one single piece of jewellery.

All the minor royals were there, but very few politicians. Besides us I only spotted George Thomas,[3] Norman St John-Stevas, the Heseltines and little Norman Lamont. NL is a social mystery, a complete *je-suis-partout*. Why? He is quite amusing, but I don't see the full cachet. Various other fashionable figures made their appearance, Rupert Lowenstein[4], *totally* unchanged and as he used to be when we all pennilessly frequented the Green Room in 1952. Having, as Oscar Wilde said of Max Beerbohm, been granted the gift of perpetual old age he now found that all his contemporaries had overtaken him, looked older than he, and was ebullient. A smattering, too, of fashionable dons, Tony Quinton, Isaiah and, grotesquely pedantic, Professor Asa Briggs.[5]

---

[1] Barbara Cartland, romantic novelist and Raine's mother.

[2] The Rt Rev. Mervyn Stockwood, retired as Bishop of Southwark, 1980.

[3] George Thomas, created Viscount Tonypandy, 1983, on retirement as Speaker. MP for Cardiff West, 1945–83.

[4] Rupert Lowenstein, lawyer, gained fame as a financial advisor to the Rolling Stones.

[5] Anthony Quinton (life peer, 1982). Philosopher. Currently president, Trinity College, Oxford. Sir Isaiah Berlin, Fellow of All Souls College, Oxford. The first president of Wolfson College and latterly president of the British Academy. Asa Briggs (life peer, 1976). Historian, vice-chancellor, University of Sussex, 1967–76. Currently provost, Worcester College, Oxford.

Jane and I detached ourselves from the throng and cased the pictures. Everything has been restored and the effect is pretty spiffing although, sadly, gold leaf has not been used where it should on the frames. I see that even if all the restorers in the world had been working simultaneously, they could not have done a proper job in that time on the eighteenth-century paintings. So many of these look rather hastily *scrubbed* and thin. As for the furniture, every single piece has been covered with new leather, or new veneers, or inlays, etc, etc, so that although there are some magnificent pieces, the overall effect is slightly that of the Schloss at Pontresina.[1]

Soon we had to leave, as I was due to make a speech to the Industrial Law Society's one-day conference at ten am the following morning and they could have got the wrong impression if I had addressed them in a dinner jacket. I drank nothing at the ball so could drive the whole way. At two thirty am the North Circular Road is deserted and sodium-lit yellow.

House of Commons   *Wednesday, 6 June*

This evening I dined with Charlie Douglas-Home.[2] *Very* ascetic. Cold salad, and a bought-out 'sweet' with a bottle of Perrier water to slake one's thirst. At intervals sub-editors brought in copy, which Charlie approved, or, in some cases, altered. The great paper was 'going to bed' round us. If you are Editor you can never get away for an evening. It's worse than a herd of dairy cows.

Charlie is very lame and gets about on two walking sticks with heavy-duty rubber grommets at their tips. He seems to have been lame for at least ten years.

I remember him calling on us at the châlet and he was in plaster for something or other then, sat in a deckchair which collapsed and he broke (another) bone in his wrist. This evening he told me he

[1] A beautifully furnished hotel reserved for grand German tourists.

[2] Charles Douglas-Home, nephew of the former prime minister. Editor of *The Times*. Died of cancer in 1985.

had been 'getting better', but a stool which he was using to mount a horse at the weekend had collapsed (again) and this had caused him a setback.

I have known Charlie for a very long time. He was teeny when we were children. My mother (with characteristic, but I now see hurtful, *insouciance*) used audibly to refer to him as a 'dwarf'. I remember one summer evening we, and his brother Robin, whom I preferred and who was brilliant on the accordion and later committed suicide, were having a bicycle race. I was in the lead and ran into a strand of barbed wire which had been stretched across the road, tearing the skin on my inner forearm, which caused blood and tears. I still carry the vestiges of the scar.

In 1960 he was sent out by Max Beaverbrook to interview me in Zermatt, just before *The Donkeys* was published. As a reporter he was (then) completely useless. We parted, but I had second thoughts and, stopping the car, dictated the whole article for him from a pay-phone in Martigny.

Charlie is well informed and thinks intelligently. He is a committed Conservative and a great supporter of The Lady, although he said she now drinks too much. He described an establishment dinner at Dorneywood.[1] She sat on the sofa with him and drank three Cointreaux and told him she would not bring Cecil back into the Government.

Charlie says the Prime Minister is extremely worried about the succession and that is why she intends to stay on for longer than she would have preferred. He says she is completely alone, no one to comfort her at all except Denis, and if anything happened to him she would pull out immediately.

I mumbled something about Ian. He said yes, but now she had discarded him. She never went backwards. No one was ever retrieved. We agreed that Cecil had ruled himself out now – not so much by the act of infidelity, but by the hesitations, blunderings and general aura of nerve-loss which had surrounded the episode.

---

[1] Dorneywood, near Burnham in Buckinghamshire, the mansion left by Lord Courtauld-Thomson for the use of a senior government minister, at the discretion of the PM, currently the official residence of Lord Whitelaw.

But who the hell was it to be? Between Tebbit and Heseltine – and of course one had to opt for Tebbit, although that was awkward and risky. Both aroused misgivings in the Party. But head to head H would probably shave it.

The subject of the Prime Minister's Inner Cabinet came up and I told Charlie of how I put the brakes on David Young.[1] That really took his breath away. He agreed it had been absolutely lethal, even though his own preference would have been for David Young to get the job.

He talked interestingly and constructively about defence. He has always been a maritimist and reminded me that he had written a paper about the ISS as long ago as 1968. I congratulated him on his leaders, which had been personally critical of Heseltine and of the [Defence] White Paper in general. He said that the answer was to put me there as Minister of State with a dry stick of an S of S, who would simply do what he was told and defend the more radical changes deadpan at the Box. Our first choice was Patrick Jenkin, but apparently he is already demoralised and wants to get out in the next couple of years, claim a peerage and pick up some compensation directorships.[2]

(How awful to be worried about one's pension! – That crumpled-faced man in the advertisements.)

Charlie finally came up with the best choice, namely, Peter Rees. Hard, beady, very good with figures and impervious to criticism from within the Party. We talked round the subject for a very long time.

When he saw me out I noticed that the ridges around the back of his jacket collar were absolutely filled with dandruff. Charlie is in bad shape. I hope he lasts out.

---

[1] See entry for 29 March 1984.

[2] Patrick Jenkin, MP for Wanstead and Woodford since 1964. Currently environment secretary. Created life peer in 1987. Became chairman of Friends Provident Life Office, 1988.

Department of Employment *Monday, 11 June*

Today's schedule was completely upset as a large twelve-volt battery which I had been carrying about in the Chevrolet had fallen over and spilled at some point – presumably when I lent it to Andrew at the weekend and he 'threw it (the car) about'. The whole of the boot was filled with dilute sulphuric acid, which hissed and fizzed ominously and ate through carpet, rubber and paint at nightmarish speed. Everything had to come out, hoses were played on the offending liquid and bags of bicarbonate of soda spread abundantly.

Tonight I am dining with Charles Moore.[1] A sort of cult figure with the Young Fogies. Simon Hoggart[2] told me that he canvassed them as to who they wanted to lead the Tory Party. Unanimous vote was, the late Sir Hugh Fraser; when told that that was not allowed, a majority vote for 'Dr Alan Clark'.

Saltwood *Sunday, 29 July*

Tipped for the sack in the *D. Tel* today (by, inevitably, George Jones).

This is always out-putting. Two days ago Euan [Graham] rang up, concealing (but only just) his satisfaction at having heard from Perry Worsthorne[3] that I was going to 'go'.

Now I come to think of it, Perry is himself something to do with the *Telegraph*, isn't he?

Presumably my name was the unanimous choice at some spastic 'Editorial Conference'.

I sometime think the only reason I want to stay on is to prove all those wankers wrong. Not that journalists ever notice – still less admit – when they've made a mistake.

---

[1] Charles Moore, editor of *The Spectator*.

[2] Simon Hoggart, former political correspondent on the *Guardian*, currently feature writer on the *Observer* and a political columnist for *Punch*.

[3] Peregrine Worsthorne, columnist and associate editor of the *Sunday Telegraph*.

They complain about this trait in politicians, but in fact they're far worse. Like share tipsters on the financial pages, they should be compelled to publish an annual audit.

Department of Employment   *Friday, 31 August*

I called in at Seend this morning, on my way back from the West Country, and said a prayer in the church – must be one of the few remaining where the vicar obligingly leaves the door open.

It's too frustrating. I can now only get this sense of peace, and of communication – something of the confessional, I suppose – in empty churches. There, in the silence, through which I can hear the whisperings of gossip and desire, the intoned devotions of two, three centuries, I feel tranquil. Strangely, I should think I have prayed here more often since we left, than in all the time that we lived in the village.

I was glad to see that the Guide, which I wrote, at Archie Kidd's insistence, with dear old 'Mr Wiltshire' (yes, I have to keep reminding myself, the sage of Wiltshire was actually *called* 'Wiltshire') is still on offer in the racks.[1]

But no proper Bible, or King James' Prayer Book. I am completely certain that this degradation of the ancient form and language is a calculated act, a deliberate subversion by a hard core whose secret purpose is to distort the beliefs and practices of the Church of England.

Every time – usually by accident – that I attend a service where 'Series III' is used, and suffer that special jarring pain when (most often in the Responses) a commonplace illiteracy, straight out of a local authority circular, supplants the beautiful, numinous phrases on which I was brought up and from which I drew comfort for thirty-five years, my heart sinks. All too well do I understand the rage of the *Inquisitadores*. I would gladly burn them, those trendy clerics, at the stake. What fun to hear them pinkly squealing. Or,

---

[1] AC had been persuaded to write a guide to Seend parish church.

perhaps, as the faggots kindled, they would 'come out' and call on the Devil to succour them.

The 'Secret Garden'[1] is now totally overgrown and the glasshouses lush and tropical with unpicked grapes and fireweed. The big green double gates still batteredly leaning, done up with baling twine, just as we left them when, two years ago, we called by to load the Range Rover with apples. The whole flavour of the place a little more remote, now twelve years or more away, and through a glass darkly. I climbed over the wall from the churchyard, trying not to put too much weight on the rickety corrugated iron roof of the Gravedigger's hut. A beautiful orange dogfox, as big as a setter, ran out of the potting shed and slithered away into the undergrowth, like Sredni Vashtar. A good sanctuary, the hounds will never find him there. The key for the Marley store was still under its usual stone and I let myself in, prowled about for a little while, collected some Bentley bits, yet still got to Chippenham in time to catch the 10.08 to Paddington and the Boxes.

Last night I stayed at Lygrove.[2] Atmosphere very subdued, conversation (in contrast to our last visit when it had been squawky), flat. At intervals Christopher had long telephone conversations with a man called Suter. They would start slowly and calmly, rise in pitch and go accusatory and loud. The only other topic was some new drug which is being 'tried out' in New York. AZ-something-or-other. It was working a dream, and would soon be readily available.

You can't get AIDS from bedlinen, can you? But plates and cutlery, I'm not so sure. I was trying to drink from the glasses like a fish, without actually letting my lips go round the rim. I'm not going there again for a bit.

---

[1] A piece of land, an old walled garden in the village, which the Clarks retained after selling the Manor House.

[2] Home of Christopher Selmes near Badminton.

Zermatt   *Saturday, 15 September*

I was determined to get away, out of reach, before the reshuffle got
started. We were a day late because Nanny had to be moved to
Quince[1] first. I would *not* pay a gang of piggy-eyed, nicotine-
smelling removal men £300 or thereabouts simply to carry her
furniture across Castle road from one cottage to another, and so did
the whole thing personally, most ably and heroically assisted by
Eddie. Now she can cluck away and polish things in her new nest
while we are absent.

We had two wonderful days crossing France in the Citroën,
meandering, almost, on the Routes Departmentales, crossing,
transversely, the principal Lemming routes and watching satisly
the belting straining jockeying holiday traffic and the massive
dicing juggernauts. We kept the hood down for almost the entire
journey. And for the first time we circled to the south of Lake
Geneva, staying the night at Evian, and not linking up with
familiar roads until we reached Aigle.

I fantasised, deluding myself that I might be going to go 'sideways' into Ray Whitney's job.[2] If I am going to have any future in
politics I've got to get to the Foreign Office or MoD. Now that I
know how to deal with officials, how the machine works, the time
is ripe. I quite see how it is better to learn these tricks in a
disagreeable dept, where you have to 'keep a proper lookout'[3] at
all times. But that's over now. I've served my apprenticeship, taken
a Bill through its Committee stage. I'm fully fledged. I didn't say
anything to Jane, fearing disappointment, but secretly hoping for
wonderful news.

But it was Renton who was chosen. Renton. I was very
dejected at first. Then cheered up a little, as I don't see that this

---

[1] A cottage on the Saltwood estate, preferred by staff as it is 'modern' (built in
1953).

[2] Ray Whitney had been sacked from his job as Parliamentary under-secretary at
the Foreign Office.

[3] A family phrase. (Barristers' standard 'pleading' in statements of claim in motoring litigation.)

necessarily rules me out in future. He was Geoffrey's PPS, had a cursory acquaintance with the FCO, was now due for a job.[1]

I am sitting at the desk in my study in the Chalet and the French windows are open on to the balcony. Fifty feet away the Wiesti foams and tumbles past, swollen by the melting glaciers. The Matterhorn is in full view, and the whole house carries that delicious aroma of high summer, pine needles and sweet geranium.

How distant, how very very distant and odious is the arid little left-right-left turn by the green fire escape sign, as I get out of the lift on the sixth floor. The messengers scuttling round with their sheaves of turgid paperwork. The unbelievable tedium of the subjects – Financial Management Initiative, Ombudsman cases (I no longer look even at the conclusions of these), anything-to-do-with-the-Disabled, the 'Measures'. This isn't politics, it's compulsory obsessional disorder.

The fact remains that there have been three vacancies now, at PUSS level, in Defence and Foreign Affairs, since I became a Minister. And I have missed out each time. Am I doomed to hang on at DE, suffering periodic humiliations, until summarily dismissed in September of next year?

I think hard of pre-empting, '. . . at his own request', getting free to argue for Toryism *à l'outrance*, to scorn the obligations of Party discipline (so often nothing more than the convenience of the Whips' Office) and become a true Maverick. Bang would go the 'K', of course, and any chance under the ACHAB rule. But one would gain a year. And I am uneasy that my reputation in the Commons may start to fade if I have to go through another year's drudgery. It really is impossible to dazzle the the box on the Job-splitting Scheme.

One's status is embellished by 'at his own request', diminished by being sacked.

---

[1] Tim Renton, MP for Mid-Sussex since 1974. PPS to John Biffen, then Geoffrey Howe, both as Chancellor of the Exchequer and as Foreign Secretary.

Saltwood   *Thursday, 20 September*

A gloomy blustery day. Low dark clouds. Saltwood is sleepy, almost as if we had been away a month instead of a week. Getting ready for its hibernation.

This afternoon, as I strolled round, I thought the one thing I am really loathing is the prospect of being back at the bloody House of C, being yerr'd at the Box by a lot of spiteful drunks, on subjects that bore and muddle me. I'd gladly chuck the whole thing in and become a Count[1] if it were not for the satisfaction this would give to others.

The nicest thing in the waiting postbag was a lovely letter from Julian Amery.

> I'm amazed you survived the Reshuffle. You stick out like a red poppy in the hayfield of mediocrities surrounding you. It is very offensive to them to be original, intelligent, courageous and rich.

What a marvellous compliment, from someone who has been in public life for almost forty years. Julian has known, closely known, Tito, Winston, Anthony [Eden] and Uncle Harold [Macmillan]. The *real* times. He's entirely right. What we could do, he and I. He so nearly made Foreign Secretary when Carrington legged it in '82. Loss of nerve by The Lady. She wasn't sure she was going to survive,[2] took the Whips' advice, chose Pym[3] – with whom she quarrelled incessantly thereafter.

Or was it? Perhaps she recognised something he and I won't accept. The climate has changed.

---

[1] Alternative family slang for retiring; cf. 'burning heather'.
[2] Lord Carrington served every Conservative prime minister since appointed as parliamentary secretary, Ministry of Agriculture, in Churchill's 1951 government. Foreign Secretary, 1979–82. Resigned following the Argentinian occupation of the Falkland Islands in April 1982.
[3] Francis Pym was Foreign Secretary 1982–83; subsequently returned to the back benches.

Saltwood   *Friday, 12 October*

'At any moment I could be killed by an assassin or a lunatic.' I often quote the Führer's reflective aside to Rauschning (and indeed he himself is recorded as reporting it to Goebbels and, by Halder, to Keitel). In my case, though, I am thinking more about Estate Duty and my luckless descendants – than of Posterity.

But today a vivid illustration, followed in the late evening by a curious, almost spooky episode of imagery *foretelling*.

Yesterday at Brighton (Party Conference) the DE debate was first off in the afternoon. TK bumbustioso'd, did a pretty smudgy job of introducing his 'team'; although pleasingly I got what, for a junior Minister, was quite a good cheer from the floor (due, I assume, to the coverage in Monday's *Mail*[1]). This disconcerted TK, who faltered momentarily.

I had a few meetings and oddments to attend to after the 'Debate', and Jane went off to go round an Art Nouveau exhibition with Charles Moore before we met up for tea. Later, the American Ambassador was having a small party (but wives, oddly, were excluded).

Tea at the Metropole is always fun. So much traffic of 'notables', so much peeping, prying and listening to do. The egos flare and fade and flare again like a stubble fire. The journalists dodge about excitedly, fearful of missing something. I prefer it to the hotel lobby later on, when everyone has 'had a few' and is slower (though louder). But when we had finished, and were standing on the steps wondering whether to take a walk along the front, it being such a beautiful afternoon of late autumn, a pleasing escapist impulse came to us both simultaneously. 'Bugger the American Ambassador. Let's just go home.'

We sometimes get these urges. Notably during Elections, when we have been sent off on our own with a lot of canvass cards.

---

[1] AC had been instrumental in closing off a particular kind of fraudulent claim by foreign students at benefit offices.

I cancelled the room, settled the account. We hopped straight into the car and were comfortably back here for supper.

But that evening an unsettling experience. The last episode of *Tripods*[1]. Little Charlotte wandered around Saltwood, everything so beautiful and timeless. Then she was claimed by the Tripods – remote, sinister, not of this world. She ascended, higher and higher (on that great lamp-engineers' lift, which made such a mess of the moat when they were shooting). Sadly she waved, and called her farewells. On its own the scene was curiously, unexpectedly moving. Now, with the knowledge that she had, at that time, been less than three weeks away from death, sliced in half on the M4 by some callous brute in a 30-ton artic, it was unbearable.

More was to come. Before breakfast, when I returned with the dogs, Jane told me that there had been a huge bomb at Brighton, the hotel had been all but demolished. They had 'got' Tebbit, Wakeham, Tony Berry, various dignitaries. Amazing TV coverage. The whole façade of the hotel blown away. Keith Joseph (indestructible), wandering about in a burgundy-coloured dressing gown, bleating. The scene was one of total confusion, people scurrying hither and thither, barely a police 'officer' to be seen.

Mrs T had been saved by good fortune (von Stauffenberg's briefcase!) as she was in the bathroom. Had she been in the bedroom she would be dead.

But what a coup for the Paddys. The whole thing has a smell of the Tet Offensive.[2] If they had just had the wit to press their advantage, a couple of chaps with guns in the crowd, they could have got the whole Government as they blearily emerged – and the assassin could in all probability have made their getaway unpunished.

---

[1] A BBC television series written by Alick Rowe and based on the novels by John Christopher.

[2] Tet Offensive: as part of the general offensive in South Vietnam in 1970, the Vietcong also made a brief foray into the US embassy.

Saltwood   *Wednesday, 7 November*

I am somewhat underemployed at the moment.

Before Questions I used always to repair to the drinks cabinet in my office in the Commons and down a teeny slug of neat vodka. No lunch, keep the stomach empty and then, in the very last seconds before going into the Chamber for Prayers – *Skol.*

I no longer need it. I had another good session last time knocked everyone around including poor old Eric Heffer. I used to be frightened of him but not any longer. He is suddenly ageing, quite fast. Afterwards John Stokes,[1] no mean judge, went out of his way to congratulate me, and the following day Godfrey Barker[2] gave me half his column, full of praise.

So what should I be doing? Slowly, too tentatively, I am working up a paper for The Lady. On the subject of defence, yes; but a strategic overview, a twenty-year projection. Does anyone else do this? Not as radically as I, that's for sure. And it needs to be done under a whole range of subject headings: overseas trade; industrial policy; diplomacy in the late Nineties, with whom we should be aligned, our relations with the new Pacific powers.

I am not sure, even so, how kindly The Lady will take to my reflections, which is probably why I only turn to them intermittently. Dear creature, she is somewhat *blinkered.* (But hastily I add, as is obligatory among believers when her faults are identified, 'this of course can also be a source of strength'.)

It's a gamble. Either she'll think 'he's wasted in that hole' or 'he's crazy. For God's sake keep him where he is, indefinitely.'

Saltwood   *Saturday, 10 November*

Tristan Garel-Jones asked himself down. Odd, you could say, for a Whip to take five hours off to see someone with whom he could converse for as long as he liked the following Monday.

---

[1] John Stokes, MP for Halesowen and Stourbridge since 1974 (Oldbury and Halesowen, 1970–74).

[2] Godfrey Barker, parliamentary sketch writer in the *Daily Telegraph.*

He is candid. At least he *seems very* candid. Slagged off most of
the '22 Executive. Said there was 'absolutely no point' in discussing the Under The Bus Syndrome (then devoted some fifty
minutes to doing so). 'If it happens, at any time, we – ie the Whips
– will cope.' Tristan said she would now lead us into the next
Election; then we'd have to choose someone 'from your generation'. This pleased me (presumably intended to).

He agreed that Ken Clarke was a 'butter ball' (my phrase), said
that Chris Patten said the same about him. Good. We gave Tristan
a lot of sticky cakes, and William served tea from the Fabergé
teapot, and off he went.

Saltwood   *Saturday, 29 December*

A very quiet Christmas. Poor Daisy [Selmes] came, bringing a few
cases of '61 (not, emphatically not, as a gift). He's gone to pieces
really. About six months ago he wanted to 'handle my invest-
ments', but without telling me what he was buying and selling. To
use my money, in other words, to prime his own dodgy little deals.

OK in 1972, not any longer. I have, in John Mendelson's
pleasing phrase, 'seen the movie'.[1] Get lost, I said.

Then, partly to placate him, I asked him to get some claret. He's
always going to the sales, makes out he's an expert. What did he
do? Go out and buy a lot of '61s. He knows I'm up to here in '61s,
all bought – yes, on his advice – fifteen years ago. Now they're far
too expensive. 'You're averaging,' he said. Bah.

James and Sarah turned up, full of the pleasures and plans for
Eriboll. As a Christmas present I'd bought a Dodge Command Car
– nominally for getting stalkers to the Hill, but actually as a big toy
– and we played with it.

---

[1] John Mendelson, at that time chief financial guru to Dean Whitter, the New
York broking house.

1985

I am not suffering quite the same degree of apprehension as I did this
time last year, with the Employment Bill and, in particular, the
dreaded Part III solo role overhanging. But the sheer dreariness and
drudgery of the Department; the cold and miserable squalor of
Albany, still (I assume) with its full sink of dirty china; the prospect
of long, pointless and disagreeable night votes – all this is lowering.
With something of a shock I realised that I will, this June, have been
in the same Dept, and at the same rank, for two years. Guy Sajer.[1] And
I have a nasty feeling that there won't be a reshuffle until September.

An article in *The Times* today by Selina Scott. She says that in
two years at Breakfast TV she aged ten. I have done exactly the
same in Parliament – a ratio of five to one. At this time of the year I
find myself pining for white sand and lapping waters. But that, too,
must be a sign of growing old. Because formerly I would want to
get to the slopes, and ski divinely.

Ponting, amid much turbulence, has been acquitted.[2] There are
accusations of 'lying' and insult. A set-piece Debate (inevitably it
will be disappointing) is imminent, probably for Monday.

You can find people – some of them quite influential and canny
people like Peter Morrison and G-J – who are saying that John
Stanley[3] will have to resign.

---

[1] Sajer, author of *The Forgotten Soldier*, a book to which AC often turned, served
on the Russian front for three years without relief.

[2] Clive Ponting, a civil servant in the Minstry of Defence, revealed details of the
sinking of the *Belgrano* during the Falklands War. He was tried for breaching the
Official Secrets Act and found not guilty by the jury.

[3] John Stanley, MP for Tonbridge and Malling since 1974. Minister for the Armed
Forces since 1983, which he remained until 1987.

Of course he *won't*. No one these days resigns for anything. (Perhaps, still, for direct proof of a huge bribe from a civil contractor?) But as I would greatly like his job, I am being extremely circumspect in my comments. 'No more than I myself would have done in the same circs.'

This *could* be the moment, though. For although I would have love to have gone to MoD immediately, if I do get there in the end I will be far stronger, because I have accumulated so much 'Whitehall' experience to back up my expert knowledge, hunches and prejudices. If John is sacked I must be among those with a claim to succeed him.

In the dining room last night John Wakeham shouted across from the Chief Whip's table to me that he had a special message – that I was 'loved'. And Tristan has a tale (one never quite knows with Tristan's tales, his motives are never singular) that Willie was defending me vigorously.[1]

Little Alfred Sherman[2] came to see me yesterday, at the Department, at his own request. He said that he 'wanted to discuss the Thatcherite Succession'.

Alfred said that he could 'steer me into it' using my wealth (!), that he had 'made' Keith, and then Margaret, and that he could do the same for me.

I could hardly not have been flattered, but I said little. He offered to write my speeches – but I don't like that. And anyway, time has moved on; we want not more, but less, of his medicine.

I can't decide whether Alfred would be a help or a hindrance. And anyway, have I got the oomph?

I'm not a 'hungry fighter', being too fond of my Baldwinesque leisure and hobbies.

Also, like many who have had an unhappy childhood, I am frightened of being laughed at.

Perhaps that is why I like making people laugh *with* me.

---

[1] AC was getting a bad press at this time because a senior civil servant had leaked his private (but 'politically incorrect') comment about Bongo-Bongo land.

[2] Sir Alfred Sherman, journalist on the *Daily Telegraph* since 1965. He co-founded the Centre for Policy Studies in 1974 and was its Director of Studies until 1984.

Saltwood   *Saturday, 16 February*

Before leaving London for the weekend I took time off to go to
the Westminster Hospital to see my old, almost old*est* friend, John
Pollock – 'Gianni' – who is dying there.
 'I've got this lump,' he said. 'Can you see this lump?' – and
indeed I could.
 Gianni needed funds, presumably for cigarettes and 'miniatures'.
I gave him all the cash I had in my pockets, some twenty-eight
pounds in notes, 'What about the silver?' he asked, 'Aren't you
carrying any silver?'
 He stuffed the notes into his pyjama jacket, and the change into
a box of 'Cook's Matches' on his bedside table.
 Apparently the other patients, no matter how ill, crawl over and
steal from those who are asleep.
 I used always to visit Gianni, and his elderly patronne, Constance Mappin, on the shores of the Mediterranean during long
vacation, and at other times.
 Sometimes Constance was broke ('waiting for War Loan') and
one evening, when 'the tables were unkind' – she was a raging
gambler – I bought from her the turquoise and diamond ring
which Jane still wears on occasion.
 Jane and I stayed with them at Positano on our honeymoon.
Christina[1] turned up, and a farcical triangular sub-plot developed
with Milo Cripps's[2] boy friend ('Barry') falling for her, and tears
shed all round.

Department of Employment   *Wednesday, 24 April*

I went on a ministerial visit to Wrexham. A pretty, peaceful town,
with the sun shining. How fortunate are the contented bourgeoisie
in such places – or are they too racked by pressures and frustrations? They certainly didn't look it.

---

[1] Christina was living in AC's house at Rye when he became engaged to Jane.
[2] Milo Cripps, now the 4th Baron Parmoor.

On the way up I saw Robert Atkins[1] in an adjoining carriage
and went and had a talk with him. He told me that David Young
had spoken to him for half an hour, asking RA what he should say
to the Prime Minister who was always asking him for advice about
personalities. I winced, as Atkins and I dislike each other quite
candidly. But he is a great show-off, besides having a keen political
sense of a below-stairs kind. It is not hard to extract intelligence
from him.

Poor Michael Jopling[2] is going to be sacked, and Peter Rees.
RA also thought Quintin[3] would go, although he recognised that
there was a shortage of candidates for law offices. I told him how
Paddy Mayhew[4] was desperate to get back into the main stream,
but RA said that although this was known, Paddy was being
considered as a possible Lord Chancellor (which of course he
could not refuse, even though he might not wish it). We agreed
that Adam Butler[5] was to go and RA said that John Stanley would
also be moved, though not, of course, dismissed, and that this
would mean two vacancies of Minister of State at Defence. He
paid lip service, though not very convincingly, that I should have
one of these. It is notorious that I do not get on with Michael
Heseltine but RA said that there was some talk of Peter Walker
going there as a reward for his performance at Energy. It might just
happen, as Defence is a poison chalice until the books have been
balanced, and The Lady might at present rate embarrassing Peter
Walker as a higher priority than humiliating Heseltine. But the
question would still remain, what then to do with MH?

All this, and more, was little more than the general semi-
informed small talk that one gets when gossiping with colleagues

---

[1] Robert Atkins, MP for South Ribble since 1983 (Preston North, 1979–83). PPS
to Lord Young when he was created a life peer in 1984 and joined the
government as Minister without Portfolio.

[2] Michael Jopling, Minister of Agriculture since 1983. In fact he survived until
1987.

[3] Quintin Hogg, now aged seventy-seven and serving his second term as Lord
Chancellor. He did not finally retire until 1987.

[4] Sir Patrick Mayhew, MP for Tunbridge Wells since 1974. Solicitor-General
since 1983.

[5] Adam Butler, MP for Bosworth since 1970. The son of R. A. Butler. Minister of
State, Defence Procurement, since 1984.

in the lower reaches of government about changes in the autumn. It was reassuring to hear that The Lady cannot stand Kenneth Clarke, and it is for that reason that he has been so long excluded from the Cabinet, which apparently (but not in my estimation), his merits demand.

RA did then produce a stick of dynamite. He told me that it was being actively considered that the whole Department of Employment be abolished! The payment of benefit would be delegated to the DHSS. The issue of work permits to the Home Office. Health and Safety matters to the DTI. Training and special measures to a new training division that would go into a revamped Department of Education. 'Science' would be shunted from Education to DTI. I could see only too well where this idea came from (although I had only been here a week to form the same opinion).

RA said that Tom King was a prat: 'a nice chap, but a prat'. This is not entirely fair as Tom King has got a shrewd Willie-ish side, but his balls are very weak. He always loses in Cabinet and will not hold out for anything. This, and his testy manner with officials, has eroded his support in Whitehall and the long, cumbersome and never finished sentences, of which my parodies are notorious across the Civil Service, have irritated many colleagues.

Anyhow, I did not waste any time on my return in repeating this communication to Tom personally. He took it very badly. He has felt somewhat threatened of late – indeed, since David Young's appointment was hailed with only the most perfunctory disclaimer by Bernard Ingham as 'Minister for Jobs' – and there have been many similar incidents that have led TK to believe that David Young was encroaching on him. He huffed and he puffed and got more and more agitated. Indeed, he exhibited under stress those same slightly uncoordinated and disparate reactions – lateral thinking, etc, that he so often shows in discussion. He said that David Young was not a member of the club, never fought an Election, always wheedling away, the only person who had time to make this sort of trouble, and so on. I tried to calm him by suggesting that presentationally it would be impossible to abolish the one Department identified in the public eye as being responsible for the country's principal social and economic problem, and he got well *lancé* into this theme, delivering a series of unfinished, and ungrammatical, monologues. His condition deteriorated further when I revealed that the machinery of government aspect had also been looked at, with Michael Quinlan going across to Defence and Robert Armstrong getting his cards a little ahead of time, and Clive Whitmore going across to be Cabinet Secretary.[1]

We ended with TK undertaking to go to the Chief Whip and 'tweak his nose', also to Willie. Willie is not the man he was, as in the old days he would certainly have resisted this. But John Wakeham – I am not so sure.

Duke of Cornwall Hotel, Plymouth   *Thursday, 9 May*

Wasting time, and substance. Yesterday I was in the Midlands, job centres and benefit offices. I tried to be polite as well as grave. I'm good at that. People expect something different and then they're pleased.

After the vote I boarded the sleeper, uncomfortable and smelly. Walked, a lovely clear morning, from North Road station, but no breakfast served here until 7.30. Then I will walk again, saying 'brush' and hoping to be widely seen and reported, from the hotel to the constituency office for my 'surgery'. There will be either twelve mendicants or three – it's impossible to predict. Let us hope three, as I have to take the 10.25 train *back* to London for an afternoon's work at the Dept. Then tomorrow back again, this time getting off the train at Exeter, motoring to Bratton where I will field a lot of phone calls from people complaining, or trying to make my flesh creep (usually both) about the SDP landslide which – by all accounts – is already under way.[2] The next day, Saturday,

---

[1] Michael Quinlan, CB, Permanent Secretary, Department of Employment; Sir Clive Whitmore, KCB, CVO, Permanent Under-Secretary, Ministry of Defence, since 1983. This last was the only prediction that was not, in fact, fulfilled: Sir Robin Butler succeeding Armstrong (and Armstrong did in fact survive until the civil service retirement age of sixty).

[2] The local government elections of 1985 marked the high point of SDP favour with the electorate.

it's the Dunstone Ward annual supper (Dunstone always choose a
Saturday because Nan Howard[1] knows I prefer Fridays, so as to
allow me to get back to Saltwood for the weekend) and more, this
time 'live', complaints.

'The sheer hell of being an MP.'[2]

Some wanker called 'Caserly' (that just has to be a false name,
probably someone on the editorial staff) has written an open letter
in the *Herald*, saying how arrogant and 'out of touch' (yeah) I am,
will lose my seat, SDP Wave of the Future, usual balls.

Financially everything is still a mess. For the first time I am
beginning to think that *I* may die before my father's estate is
settled, and that Jane and the boys will have to cope with two sets
of death duties simultaneously. I sometimes wonder whose side
Thom is on. He rolls his 'R's with relish when, as he always does,
calling them 'The Revenue'. This week he told me that they
would be 'looking for' another £150,000.

In the meantime I have half agreed to sell the mask to Jerdein
for $450,000, which is a whopping price really,[3] but after we had
packed it up its *eye* looked reproachfully at me from where it was
lying on the kitchen floor in Albany and I decided there and then
to 'withdraw' it. There is so much ju-ju in that object. God knows
what strange rituals it must have commanded, in steamy incense-
ridden pagan temples. Blood, fertility and revenge, it carries the
aura of all of these, and it is not seemly that it should be just
bartered around for money in dealers' 'galleries'.

I am apprehensive, too, that once it went I might desperately
want or need its return; some misfortune might be visited on me. I
took it straight back to Saltwood and hung it in the strongroom
where its mother-of-pearl eyes catch the light as the door opens. I
am mindful, too, of that account in Ruth's diary of how Arthur
[Viscount Lee] badgered and badgered an impoverished collector
to sell him a little Giorgione. The man kept refusing, said he feared
that once parted with it he might die. Arthur bullied and blustered,

---

[1] Mrs D. O'N. Howard, chairman of the ward.
[2] The title of a review of a TV series about an MP entitled *The Nearly Man*.
[3] The Torres Strait tortoiseshell mask which belonged to Picasso. Charles Jerdein,
    an art dealer and friend of AC.

said such thoughts were 'unchristian', that he must meet his maker 'with conscience clear', pushed and nagged. Eventually the man sold. Less than two months later he was dead.

Then, yesterday, came interesting news. The client on whose behalf Jerdein was bidding, a rich Frenchman, had just had his daughter kidnapped and was in a dreadful state. Very powerful ju-jus can operate at long range. We know that.

Bratton   *Saturday, 11 May*

It's so lovely here. Slow and peaceful, buds everywhere and bright greeny-yellow leaves bursting. Jane is so pretty, her hair always gets tawny streaks in the springtime. But my balls ache, and my lower back is stiff and creaky. I have been doing the weights, but not much, surely? I will *not* give in to middle, still less old, age. Maurice[1] always said that that was what did for poor old Ian Fleming, insisting on carrying Annie's bags up and down the stairs, even when gasping.[2] But he was on forty a day and I've never smoked one cigarette in my entire life.

Saltwood   *Sunday, 23 June*

A pleasing tale. Something of the Charley's Aunt donnée. William has always loved uniforms and panoply. For the last two years he has been 'due' a ticket to the Birthday Parade (or 'Trooping the Colour', as he calls it). Once again Lilian,[3] silly little fool, had left it too late. Or had he? At the last moment, and most covertly, he snatched or snitched one off the desk in the empty Adjutants'

---

[1] Sir Maurice Bowra, Warden of Wadham College, Oxford, from 1938 to 1979.

[2] Ian Fleming, creator of James Bond, married Ann Charteris as her third husband. Her first, Lord O'Neill, was killed in action in 1944; she married Lord Rothermere in 1945. They divorced in 1952 when she married Fleming, who died in 1964 aged fifty-six.

[3] 'Lilian': a family nickname for Andrew of ancient nursery standing, used when he is being unsatisfactory.

office at Knightsbridge. Didn't look at it too closely, stuffed it in his pocket.

I say 'ticket'. It was a beautiful embossed invitation, on stiff card.

William was delighted. Went up very splendidly in *full butler's regalia*, looking the picture of saturnine (though diminutive) elegance. Showed his ticket to a 'Greeter'.

'Aha, Excellency, how kind of you to come. Lovely. Good.'

William, who is nobody's fool, drew on his long years of experience in 'service'. Kept mum, grunted only.

'I hope you'll be comfortable here. Seats can get a bit hard after a while, ha-ha. But I can offer you a cushion.' (*I* never get a bloody cushion, I told him.) 'I do hope you enjoy the Parade . . .'

Better and better it got. After the Anthem the Greeter reappeared. 'This way Excellency, Excellencies . . .'

In company with other bemedalled and exotic-uniformed dignitaries William was gently shepherded across the gravel and through the wall gate into the garden at Number 10!

At one point Mrs T. made a brief appearance and dreamily mingled. The tiny pearl-handled assassin's pistol (could have) nestled in William's breast pocket.

I don't expect the Prime Minister was concentrating very much in the company of these Corps Diplomatique medium-fry. But she would surely have sharpened up if she'd been told that among them was Al's butler from Saltwood.

Bratton   *Thursday, 8 August*

Yesterday I did something for the last time.

When you do something for the first time, you always know. Gosh, I haven't done this before. That's what it's like, is it – nice, nasty, try it again sometime, or whatever.

But when you do something for the *last* time, you very seldom know. Until, months or years later you realise – 'That was the very last time . . . Never again.'

This is a phenomenon that induces melancholy. It is so closely

interleaved with the passage of time, the onset of infirmity. Death
at one's shoulder in the market square of Samarra.

Constituency rubbish all day yesterday, and I should have left for
Saltwood this morning. But at breakfast I saw in the *Western
Morning News* that Mrs Barnard, the fearsome matriarch of Penhalt
High Farm, had died, and the property was for sale. Something
made me drive over, if only to look at the beach hut which I had
coveted so long and so hard all the time we were living down here,
when the boys were tiny.

Out on the Bude road, through Stratton, where a lovely and
very young blonde used to stand at the crossroads in the summertime and wave. Past Widemouth sands where once Tip was
almost swept away, and had to be revived, soaked, in the back of
the car. And where when alone and driving the blue jeep I picked
up the girl from Bray Shop, and her Ma. Then over Millhook and
down to Crackington Haven, and the beach hut still stood, intact.

It was in the early Sixties that we used to come here most often.
And I remember one of the Barnard sons – strange and inbred they
seemed at our one and only meeting in that charcoal-smelling
kitchen with its long black range – baiting me by recounting how
special seasoned planking from (?) the *Mauretania* had been used to
build the hut.

Even in those days the paint had blistered and peeled, and the
Atlantic gales were lashing the bare wood for five months in the
year. But still it stood, the walls almost stripped, but without warp
or rot. Several panes of glass had been broken, and the door was off
its hinges. Someone had written 'Fuck Thatcher' with an aerosol
spray, and there was the detritus and excrement of 'Travellers', as
they style themselves. The stream was brackish, and the whole area
seemed smaller and more cramped, as do often the sites of golden
memories, when revisited.

I ground back up that very steep hill, with the 1 in 4 hairpin,
which so often I descended, having to use bottom gear, in the
[Citroën] ID 19 'Brake', loaded with children and picnic things.
And for some reason, I can't tell why, my mind strayed to the
possibility of 'starting again'.

I suppose it could still be done. But not while Jane is alive. I could not, would never wound her, the best human being in the entire world. And if she was taken from me I would be so shattered I couldn't do anything. All these thoughts were turning in my mind as I passed by the entrance to Penhalt High Farm and, out of curiosity, I turned in, walked some way along the track, then returned and got the car, undoing the baling twine on the gate.

It was completely deserted, not a soul. No livestock, no cat. Even the blue tits and house sparrows were in the fields.

They are handsome things, these walled Devon farmyards of the eighteenth century, with their low granite buildings, and the milking stalls floored and divided by Cyclopean fragments of slate. And there was a curious aura that hung over Penhalt, as it slept in the afternoon sun, with the seed grass everywhere overgrowing, knee-high.

I prowled about, scrambled over a wall into the little garden on the south side, terribly neglected but with two fig trees against the wall of the farmhouse, and some nice shrubs surviving. Intensely hot and still, a marvellous place for a pool.

Across the fields I could see one of those four-steepled Devon church towers, lying so perfectly in the trees in the hamlet of Trevinnick, and I entered the mind of others, the ghosts of former times, who must have looked upon this same view and, like me, felt wistful. Had someone, surely they must have done, served in the DCLI,[1] and looked on this for the last time on home leave from Flanders?

I was suspended, on but not of, this earth. I had detached myself from time, could move in any direction. Curious, but not in any way frightening, almost as if I had died not once but very many times.

I cannot tell how long my trance, or reverie, endured. But I became aware of a deep, heavy roaring sound, mingled with the fluttering noise of airscrews on coarse pitch. And very low, 200 feet at the most, a single Lancaster flew directly over the house, and on across towards Exmoor, being soon lost to sight.

---

[1] Duke of Cornwall's Light Infantry.

Afterwards, of course, on the journey home, I did my best to rationalise a supernatural experience. It is true that I often transpose the loss of young lives in the World War I no-man's-land, and the repetitive sorties by Bomber Command. And there is only one Lancaster left. And the 'Battle of Britain Flight' is stationed a very long way from Penhalt. And they are precluded from flying below 1000 feet, except at displays.

But the twenty-fifth anniversary comes up in a few weeks' time. He must have been practising.

Saltwood   *Tuesday, 13 August*

I am so *bored* by my work. It spreads right across and affects everything so that I am beginning to feel stale, and déjà vu, with all aspects of public life.

At the Cavalry Club last week Ian and I had our ritual summer 'round-up' lunch. But even that was not the same. We gossiped. But Ian's contributions did not have that electric quality which used to run through them in the days when he had come straight from The Lady's presence. He is peevish, and fussed about Ireland.

I said, don't. Ireland is a ghastly subject. Intractable. Insoluble. For centuries it has blighted English domestic politics, wrecked the careers of good men.

Ian said the pressure to concede everything to Dublin (and thus expose the decent Loyalists in Ulster to the full force of IRA terrorism) is coming from the Foreign Office, who are themselves reacting to pressure from Washington. One must never forget that the Irish vote in America is bigger than it is in Eire. We agreed that the Foreign Office now exists solely to buy off foreign disapproval by dipping into the till marked British Interests.

There will be a reshuffle next month. 'Quite a big one.' Norman Tebbit will be made Chairman.

'If you want a change, you should tell the Chief Whip.'

'Oh, come on, Ian, everyone knows what I want.'

Albany   *Tuesday, 3 September*

I went straight from Heathrow to the Dept. Officials are genuinely glad I am still there – which is nice, though of little value.[1] Peter Morrison rang from his new office at the DTI, too well-mannered to gloat[2] (not that he has much to gloat about, considering that for most of the spring and summer he was expecting to be made Chief Whip) and we went to the Ritz for lunch.

Peter was full of how, already, he was sorting out his civil servants. They were trying to put upon him 'a female' as head of his Private Office. 'I couldn't possibly have that.'

'Really? I've had nothing but women in charge of mine. I find it rather congenial.'

'Yes, but you see, she couldn't carry my guns.'

I grumbled away disconsolately. Peter tried to cheer me up by saying that there was 'bound' to be a 'really big' shuffle next Easter. Whatever for? I thought.

But of course Peter himself wants to get closer to the Cabinet soon. He is much younger than me, could indeed be my son, but I would guess our shelf life is about the same. After lunch, very sleepy and *désoeuvré*, I sat at my desk, riffled a few dreary PO cases.

Punctually (first difference from Tom) David Young had me in at the appointed time. He is pleasant, charming almost, and fresh (as distinct from stale). He talks at twice the speed of Tom King, but listens too, cracks jokes, is full of bright ideas. I quite see why The Lady fancies him. He is utterly different from the rest of the Cabinet – yet without being caddish.

---

[1] The postings in the autumn reshuffle were finally announced. AC was chiefly affected by Tom King's appointment to the Northern Ireland Office and the arrival of David Young as secretary of state at the department.

[2] Peter Morrison had been moved 'sideways' from the Department of Employment to become Minister of State for Industry.

Eriboll   *Wednesday, 4 September*

I caught the 8.50 flight, and sat next to a quite pretty blonde in a white jacket. Her husband, or consort, was miniature, bearded, scruffy – but had an upper-class voice. Who the hell was he? Normally one knows every one of any consequence on that aircraft.

I headed north, at a leisurely pace, and after Altnaharra took the Loch Hope road instead of going through Tongue. It was the first sunny day for two weeks, and there were climbers' cars parked in the layby where the start of the Hope ascent is marked. To my shame I have never climbed Hope, and suddenly, irresisitibly, I thought, why not?

There were some heavy shoes in the car, and in one of the door pockets I found a thermal belt. But I was suited, waistcoated, tie, collar stiffeners – Whymper.

At white TR 6 had parked close by, and a man was putting on a lot of gear; bright nylon windcheater, hood, gloves, special backpack. I set off immediately, nonchalant at his state of disapproval. I was carrying nothing, not even a thumbstick. I didn't have so much as a Mars Bar in my pocket.

The ascent became a duel. He must have left a minute or so later, and made two attempts to close the distance. But on each occasion I anticipated, knowing from experience on the Trift, and other frequented climbs, that there are few things so disheartening as to make a special effort and find your quarry, mysteriously, is still at the same distance. After about an hour I sensed he was content to pace me, but I still took care whenever I was in dead ground, to accelerate to my utmost, or even to run.

The last thirty minutes to the summit are steep and debilitating, a track through scree, easy to lose in the cloud which, from about 3800 feet, was persistent. I reached the second marker cairn – there was a double summit – in under two hours, without stopping once, and was pleased with myself. For the time being it quite compensated for Whitehall and its disappointments.

But this evening I am exhausted and must have been poor

company at dinner. When I recounted to Jane how relaxed and congenial David Young was she said of course – but he doesn't have to fill his mind with constituency detritus the whole time, suffer his weekends being ruined by mendicants, stay up until gone midnight voting on spastic and unnecessary measures.

Too right. The democratic overhead.

As I brood on all this, I find myself becoming crosser. I've had it. Chris Patten has been made a Minister of State; OK, he's brilliant. But so has Renton, and he isn't.[1] I can read the signs. At some point in this coming term I must seek out the Chief Whip, or possibly G-J. I want 'out' at Christmas.

House of Commons   *Tuesday, 26 November*

Today my old friend made his resignation speech.[2] The House was full. And by the time I arrived my usual place behind the Prime Minister had been taken and I sat at the far end, between Carol Mather and Peter Bottomley.[3] Kinnock was on his feet and, as it moved on to economic subjects, was making a hash of things and had 'lost the House'.[4] There was a general murmuration.

'When is Ian speaking?' I said to Carol.

He grunted non-committally. He is a Whip of the old school and they do not like resignations.

Last week a cruel piece by Peter Riddell in the *Financial Times* had treated Ian's resignation dismissively, for 'his career is already in decline', etc, etc, and other unwelcome truths.

Thinking it was a Whips' Office plant, I had complained to

---

[1] Christopher Patten had become Minister of State at Education and Science; Tim Renton, Minister of State at the Foreign Office.

[2] Ian Gow had resigned from the government in protest at the Anglo-Irish agreement (see also entry for 13 August 1985).

[3] Peter Bottomley, MP for Eltham since 1983 (Woolwich West, 1975–83). Parliamentary under-secretary, Employment, since 1984.

[4] Neil Kinnock, MP for Islwyn and Leader of the Opposition since 1983 (Bedwellty, 1970–83).

Garel-Jones, who affected horror and dismay. I remain suspicious.
I believe that it was a pre-emptive plant fed to Riddell on the day
of Gow's resignation in case he gave trouble. In fact, and as could
have been readily predicted by anyone who knows him, he gave
no trouble. But the piece was used nonetheless.

Ian was dejected and flat in tone. He spoke from the second row
from the back, which is *not* a commanding position, because you
fall between two banks of microphones, and this technical handicap aggravated the loss of confidence and authority in his voice.
Everything that Ian said about Ulster was painfully true and
although, perhaps, he over-quoted from humble correspondents
in the Province it was moving and, among nationalists like myself
at least, induced unease and guilt.

But the personal passage at the end was, frankly, embarrassing.
He described how disagreeable resignation was; how he spoke
from the bottom of his heart – 'and it is a very big heart' – (oh
dear). Ian went on to say the Prime Minister might welcome the
resignation of some of her colleagues more than others and he did
not know (sic) into which category he fell. How he had enjoyed –
exulted in? revelled in? – working for The Lady for four years; her
great and indeed paragonesque virtues, 'the finest Chief, the most
resolute Leader, the kindest friend that any Member of the House
could hope to serve'.

Cruel and sardonic, Peter Bottomley turned to me and said in
the middle of this eulogy, 'Give him a job.'

Will he ever get a job again? I doubt it. One more example of
Beaverbrook's dictum that politicians are irreparably flawed by
going up to Heaven in their early forties and coming back to earth
shortly thereafter. Originally said of Curzon, I can think of no one
to whom it doesn't apply, with the possible exception of David
Owen. But even he, although purged by passage through fire and
water, may never in fact have a 'job' again.

It is this *absolute* unpredictability that makes politics so irresistible. Who in 1982, when he was rightly described as the most
powerful man in the Government, could have predicted that IG
would be the first of her Ministers to resign?

I think it's probably true that she was getting irritated with him

in his closing months as her Secretary. Like many men who find
their love unrequited, he was becoming more and more sub-
servient and attentive. The stooping, obsequious family retainer,
speaking very often in a special high-pitched tone that was almost
tearful (my father, too, I have seen practising this technique).

I saw Nicholas Soames standing at the bar and afterwards he told
me that during the embarrassing passage The Lady closed her eyes
and went quite rigid in expression.

Much later, in the smoking room, Soames and Budgen plied me
with Black Velvet and spoke indiscreetly about Ian's speech. I say
indiscreetly because Ian himself was sitting only one table away
with Cecil and a couple of backbenchers. On the way out Ian
paused at our table and I said something gauche about not a dry eye
in the House. Worryingly, he took this badly and stomped off.
Poor monk![1] My only true friend in the Government. Who can I
talk to now? Peter Morrison is in another Department, and too
preoccupied these days. Garel-Jones is fun but unreliable, and
Celtic in his motivations.

The previous day the Chairman [of the party] had given a pep
talk to junior Ministers, telling us to be 'more political', to get
around the country making speeches and generally fluff up the
Associations.

I do not mind (much) fluffing up other Associations, and it
usually goes quite well. Although I grudge them the time, particularly at weekends. But my own is irreparably lost. I find most of
them boring, petty, malign, clumsily conspiratorial, and parochial
to a degree that cannot be surpassed in any part of the United
Kingdom. Once contempt and irritation passes a certain level, I am
not good at concealing my feelings and I fear that it has been
widely felt. My tactical energies are devoted simply to the narrow
goal of beating them to the draw with the announcement of my
'standing down'.

---

[1] Ian Gow was sometimes known as The Monk (as indeed, but for different
reasons, was Keith Joseph).

Letter to Ian Gow – House of Commons,   *27 November*

Ian

When we spoke briefly in the smoking room last night after your speech I fear that I may have seemed a little frivolous.

Alas, it is in the nature of my (– is 'background' the right word?) upbringing to affect casualness in the face of great and unwelcome events. You will understand this.

Yes, I was embarrassed as were others in the House by the personal note that you struck at the end.

But this embarrassment was founded not in the unease with which one attends on the ritualised and the synthetic, but in that deeper unhappiness of the soul which is restrained from its natural inclination to spring up and acclaim and say,

'Yes, you are right. Speak your message, speak it again. We are with you.'

Affectionately

Alan

Department of Employment   *Thursday, 28 November*

I suffer from some unease as I contemplate my time in Government, and in Parliament, drawing to a close. Because you are only a shadow, a wraith, a phantasm once you have announced your intention to 'stand down'.

I still do love the clubbable side. The swinging studded Pugin doors which exclude those unentitled; the abundance of facilities; the deeply comfortable leather chairs at the 'Silent' end of the library where one can have a sleep as deep and as refreshing as under the eaves of the Chalet Caroline. There is constant access to snacks, 'nips' and gossip. There are excellent and attentive library staff who will do all your work for you.

But all this is fully enjoyable only in winter time.

In summer and late spring it becomes oppressive and fetid. I get sudden, intermittent – like powerful twinges of pain – realisations of how *old* I am becoming. I spring in my step, look at girls, like laughs and fresh ideas. But when I was talking about this with Jane during one of those interminable telephone calls that we make most evenings, we agreed, what is my life expectancy? Fifteen years? If I spend two-thirds of that in London, or in the Constituency (actually it's more) what have I got left? Effectively – five.

At what stage does one's reserve of years change from being inexhaustible – of no concern or consequence – into a rapidly diminishing triangle of sand at the neck of the glass, which is scrutinised obsessively?

Yesterday, at lunch time, I drove the SS 100 still, forty years on, getting that wonderful evocative thrill as I settle into the driving seat and look down the long louvred bonnet.

At the Princes Gate traffic lights out of Hyde Park I drew up beside a black BMW, driven by a blonde, registered AMY 1. I looked sideways and saw browner, thinner in the face, but still with 'something', Andy Colquhoun.

As the lights went amber the faithful SS, always unbeatable for the first fifty feet of a standing BM was nowhere. She pursued me, *screeching* the revs to ignition cut-out, but locked brakes and overshot the right turn to the Albert Hall.

Had Andy recognised me? Or have I changed too much? Some disturbing photos have come up recently from the Press Office, showing a heavy jowl, but loose neck folds.

Department of Employment   *Tuesday, 17 December*

Today we had the DE carol service. As always, ego and 'rights' to an unbelievable degree. I only can properly enjoy carol services if I am having an illicit affair with someone in the congregation. Why is this?

Eriboll   *Sunday, 29 December*

My physique is improving. As I cut logs in the little woodshed I began to think that all this talk of retiring is balls. Stay on as Minister, and do the job. ACHAB, etc. Yet this view alternates with a kind of somnolent contentment. While I love to be out of doors all day long, I do start to feel tired and escapist if I have to consider any decision relating to Saltwood, the office, the Constituency, construction plans in Zermatt, husbandry at Broomhayes, or any one of a hundred things that I carry at the back of my mind.

It is not only Whitehall that is so far away. Everything going on in the world seems remote and unimportant. We have no television, hear no wireless save the shipping forecasts. We get one newspaper, the *Aberdeen Press and Journal*, which is resolute in its parochialism, and most soothing as a result.

I have to talk to the office occasionally, although I try to do it as little as possible. Judith[1] is telling me that the Westland row, which was smouldering when we broke up, is now ablaze. 'People are saying Mr Heseltine is going to resign.'[2]

I don't believe it. It's just the press stirring. Anyhow, no one resigns when the House is not sitting.

But Michael has always had this slightly scatty side. It is the only even half-endearing trait that he possesses. He is the man who pushed further out the definition of *folie de grandeur* than it has ever been hitherto.

Anyway, so what? If he does – good riddance.

---

[1] Judith Rutherford has taken charge of AC's private office in the department following the promotion of Jenny Easterbrook.

[2] The future of Westland Helicopters, which was undercapitalised, was the subject of two conflicting recommendations by the Ministry of Defence (under Michael Heseltine) and the Department of Trade and Industry (under Leon Brittan). Heseltine wanted 'a European solution' with joint venture arrangements with the European helicopter manufacturers. The DTI's preference was for an injection of capital from the US manufacturer Sikorsky, with whom Westland had often worked in the past.

Department of Employment   *Thursday, 9 January*

I was on the phone gossiping to Peter Morrison at his office in the DTI when Judith tiptoed in and put a piece of paper under my nose. 'Michael Heseltine has resigned.'

I whooped, and gave him the news, but at that very moment his own Private Office had done the same. I looked demi-stupid because until that point I had been saying how I didn't see how he could, it was not in his character, he was too ambitious.

Peter said, 'Well, this could mean some interesting changes,' and we both hung up in order to take more soundings.

Shortly afterwards the Sec of State rang. Would I come along for a chat?

David recounted to me the scene. Michael appears to have done it semi-spastically, *not* the *grand geste*. When he slammed his brief shut and walked out a lot of people just thought that he'd been a bit rude, and then gone out to the loo. But the photographers were all waiting in Downing Street, so he must have tipped them off in advance. Now he was holding a 'press conference' in the big lecture hall at the MoD. What was his authority for doing that, pray? I asked. He should be emptying his desk.

David referred *veiledly* to 'accompanying changes'. Said, reassuringly, 'I know what you want.'

Secretly cheered by this, I did not like to break the spell by telling Jane when we spoke on the telephone. Perhaps this was a mistake.

Saltwood   *Friday, 10 January*

Sensing 'developments' I cancelled a visit to Plymouth and came down here. At Men's Tea the Downing Street switchboard rang. 'Mr Alan Clark? The Chief Whip wants you.'

John Wakeham came on. Some pleasantries about being snow-
ed up, and then, 'The PM's contemplating a few changes and I
wanted to ask if you'd like to be asked (heart leaps) to dur-dur-dur,
move *sideways* (sic with a vengeance, heart sinks) and help Nick
Ridley[1] at Transport?'

I had taken the call under the stairs, and bought time by saying
that I was getting it transferred to the office. Foolishly, I think, I
didn't tell Jane all, only that the Chief Whip was on the phone, but
my heart was pounding. I had to refuse.

'John, I don't want to seem to be difficult about this, but I have
been a Parly Sec for over two and a half years. For the last eight
months I have really been doing a Min of State's work as I have
had to cover for Gummer since he was made Party Chairman. To
be perfectly honest, I was a bit miffed at not getting Peter
Morrison's rank last September when I took over all his duties.'

'Mmm. What would you like me to say to the Prime Minister?'

I put down smoke about the Channel 'Fixed Link',[2] how it was
a Department of Transport responsibility but I owned a lot of
the land at the mouth of the tunnel (if there was a tunnel). Could
look awkward if I was a Minister in that Department. John affected
to understand. He said he 'did not rule out' the possibility of an
upward move later. Said The Lady had a high opinion of me 'in
spite of all I tell her' (joke).

Saltwood   *Friday, 24 January*

And still the 'events' accumulate (though not yet any announcement about Lynda Chalker's job, now vacant a fortnight).[3] This
week it has been all leaks and statements and counter-leaks, and
fevered rumour.

On Wednesday the pressure mounted all day long for the Prime

---

[1] Nick Ridley, Secretary of State for Transport since 1983.
[2] As Eurotunnel was known at the time.
[3] Lynda Chalker, Minister of State, Transport, since the 1983 election, she had just
been appointed Minister of State, Foreign Office.

Minister to make a statement on the Purloined Letter,[1] accompanied by – source? – tales that LB[2] 'wouldn't go quietly'.

The story became current that she was tied until, in her statement, she could announce that she had accepted LB's resignation.
The unhappy fall guy.

But the House might not like that. Too obvious. In the evening
I called on John Biffen in his office behind the Speaker's Chair. I
said that it was better to defuse, or rather pre-empt, the row by her
coming to the House and making the statement *now*, ie after the
ten pm vote. Some of her tormentors would possibly be away and,
in any case, this would allow her to outwit the morning press and
to reduce the time available for them to organise. John completely
agreed. He was cagey, but I formed the impression that he already
recommended this very course.

However, the vote came and passed, and no sign.

We all drifted home eventually, but late and after much chattering in the smoking room and the corridors.

This morning the lobby was ablaze. Reporters everywhere, and
the atmosphere of a bazaar (as in the East, rather than the Constituency). Marcus Kimball had turned up and was standing about
– always a sign that something is afoot. He told of dining with
Willie the previous evening, and that there had been much talk of
'too many jewboys in the Cabinet'. It appeared that the Prime
Minister had decided against a statement last night and had opted
for the 'Resolute Defence' (as opposed to the 'Muzio Gambit'[3])
and would be making a statement at the usual time this afternoon.

I wandered along to the dining room and lunched with Julian
Amery and Robert Jackson,[4] whom I like for his dry, donnish
sense of humour. I say 'with' but there was much jocularity at our

---

[1] A letter from the Attorney General to Michael Heseltine rebuking him for
breaking the ministerial convention, which had been leaked to the press (as it
subsequently turned out) by the press office at the Department of Trade and
Industry.

[2] LB: Leon Brittan had been trade and industry secretary since 1985.

[3] Muzio Gambit: a reckless and now little-used opening gambit in chess.

[4] Robert Jackson, MP for Wantage since 1983, had been MEP for Upper Thames,
1980–84. At Oxford he was president of the Union and Prize Fellow of All
Souls.

end of the room, and shouting across from one table to another.
Julian had a good bottle of Burgundy in a basket, and let me have a
couple of glasses. He told various tales, and pronounced judgment
as an experienced statesman.

Then, unexpectedly, the Chief Whip came over and sat with us.
He showed me a copy of the statement. I read a few paragraphs,
started a *faux-rire*. I couldn't help it. 'I'm sorry, John. I simply can't
keep a straight face.' The paper passed from hand to hand. Others
agreed, but were too polite to say so.

How *can* she say these things without faltering?

But she did. Kept her nerve beautifully.

I was sitting close by, and could see her riffling her notes, and
turning the pages of the speech. Her hand did not shake *at all*. It
was almost as if the House, half horrified, half dumb with admiration, was cowed.

A few rats came out of the woodwork – mainly from the *Salon
des Refusés* – Fletcher,[1] Wiggin, a couple of others. Serene and
haughty, at its end she swept from the Chamber, and a little later
came to a meeting of the '22. The mood was wholly supportive of
her, and the Scapegoat was duly tarred.

This morning came the news. Leon Brittan has resigned.

But is that the end of it? Clearly it is intended to be; but I'm not
so sure.

Saltwood   *Sunday, 26 January*

A lovely still day, clear and crisp. As I set off with the dogs before
breakfast, Bob went past with a trailer of loose straw for the
shippon – the pleasures of husbandry and the land. I walked over
to the Machines, then round the Lake, along the valley and up to
Chittenden Stone.

At intervals I stole glances at *The Observer*. We are not out of the

---

[1] Alex Fletcher, MP for Edinburgh Central since 1983 (Edinburgh North, 1973–
83). Successively Parliamentary under-secretary to the Scottish Office and Trade
and Industry. Returned to the back benches in 1985.

wood, and The Lady is still terribly beleaguered. There is to be an emergency debate on Monday.

Is this the end of an era? Uneasily, I feel it may be. Perhaps they're actually going to get her, the same way the weevils got de Gaulle. Will I, alarmingly soon, be back with the books and the Heritage – but without the *cachet*?

Last night IG rang, full of gloom and portent. I discounted him, but that was before I had seen this morning's press. Ian's trouble, though, is that he is, *au fond*, a man of honour. Personally, I don't give a blow. Lie if necessary.

I have just put the phone down from Peter Morrison. Not much news, though he, too, is not optimistic. Peter said that F. Pym might vote against, with 'bad consequences' in the Lobby. Is the Conservative Party going through one of its recurrent bouts of militancy?

House of Commons   *Monday, 27 January*

Every seat in the House had been booked with a prayer card, and they were all up the gangways.

For a few seconds Kinnock had her cornered, and you could see fear in those blue eyes. But then he had an attack of wind, gave her time to recover.

A brilliant performance, shameless and brave. We are out of the wood.

Saltwood   *Friday, 31 January*

The last day of an absolutely incredible month.

Last evening Jane met me at Sandling. I could see she was excited. 'Do you want the good news or the bad?'

'Always the bad first.'

'You've got to go back up to London.'

I groaned.

'The PM wants to see you at Number 10 tomorrow morning at nine thirty.'

Wow! I rang Judith immediately. She had received a terse message from Wicks.[1] He wouldn't enlarge. But it was Trade, Paul Channon's old job.[2] David Young had confirmed it 'in the lift', talking to one of his own staff, and the news was all over the building.

Jane and I talked incessantly. We had a complete *nuit grise* with me turning on and off the light to make notes in my little green wallet. I rose before five, and paced about, my mind ranging.

Why on earth didn't I get an earlier train, the milk train, indeed? As it was, timing was tight. The 'usual' train was (inevitably) late, and instead of a leisurely grooming and preening at Albany I had to dress in a scrabble, plopped some toothpaste on my suit, spilt the aftershave, was my parting straight? etc.

I just got to Number 10 in time. Well, not really as I was *on* time and I should have been a deferential eight minutes early. No one seemed to know who I was or why I was there. I hung around in the little waiting room, repressing the urge to put my head round the door and see what now happened in Ian's old study, where he used to lie in wait and pull in Cabinet Ministers before a meeting and tell them 'what the Prime Minister was hoping to achieve'.

After a bit Wicks appeared.

'Right.'

'Eh?'

I followed him up the stairs.

'She's got a cold,' he said.

A man of few words. Five, to be precise.

But there was no sign of a cold at all. The Prime Minister looked wonderful, was effusive, genuinely friendly. Unusually, she saw me alone, not in the Cabinet Room, but the little 'parlour'. She told me how important the job was. I was to be Minister for Trade, *not* just a Min of S. It was the second most important

---

[1] Nigel Wicks. Since returning in 1985 from Washington as economic minister at the British embassy had been principal private secretary to the prime minister.

[2] Paul Channon, promoted to secretary of state following Leon Brittan's resignation.

Minister outside the Cabinet after the Financial Secretary – 'but don't shout that around'.

'Negotiation is the key. And I need someone with a *presence*, charm, someone *different* . . . and of course with a brilliant brain.' (No, really.)

She said someone (I wonder who[1]) had said that I would be unacceptable to, eg, the Nigerians because of (conveyed but not said) my remarks about Bongo-Bongo land. 'But of course you will be, *perfectly* acceptable, won't you?'

Then she praised me for my work in the Department, said I was the only person she could rely on there (uh?), how few of us there were. At the end, when she spoke of her determination to go on, and her blue eyes flashed, I got a full dose of personality compulsion, something of the *Führer Kontakt*.

An agreeable vignette occurred when 'Professor' Brian Griffiths, a courtier, came in.[2] After some small talk he said, 'No Minister for Trade has been appointed.'

The Prime Minister indicated me, and his demeanour altered quite markedly.

I returned to the Dept. Hugged the girls, and began to pack up my papers.

Department of Trade and Industry   *Monday, 3 February*

I am in my lovely new spacious office. I have rearranged the furniture so that my desk is up at the far end, with a 'conference' table three windows down towards the Private Office door – and this I insist is always kept open, being the best way of asserting discipline.

It means that visitors have to cover a good distance as they approach me. Mussolini-like. And is particularly welcome in the case of the diary secretary, who is called Rose. Rose (primly she

---

[1] On his own subsequent (that evening) admission, it was Douglas Hurd.

[2] Brian Griffiths, banking and economics academic, had been head of the prime minister's Policy Unit since 1985.

signs her notes, of which there have already been a good number, 'Rosemary') has hips, and a bust, which are almost too noticeable in someone of only (say) 5 foot 4½ inches. She looks very coolly and directly at me when she speaks. And when she comes into the room she holds her head up and does not shuffle or stoop.

The principal Secretary, Matthew Cocks, is very good news. High IQ, pleasant sense of humour, unshockable.

I had a good press – the *FT* was particularly complimentary – and this has cheered the outer office. But I lost no time in circulating my last 'Protectionist' article from the *Daily Telegraph*, and certain Hansard extracts from way back. Matthew told me that there are still believers in the various Desks, but of course they have to stay quiet at the present time, because the vogue has altered.

We'll see about that, I said. Matthew has an engaging way of biting his lip when suppressing a giggle.

Later

I went and had a chat with Paul Channon. He is quick, and funny. His rapid style of speech may make him seem more nervous than actually he is. At one time in the past he was very cross with me, did indeed upbraid me in the library, for saying unpleasant things about Chips, his snobbish, *arriviste*, but intensely observant father.

Paul has been in the Department for ages. And for long periods – the various interregna, particularly when Norman Tebbit was recovering from his wounds – acted virtually as Secretary of State. It is quite proper that he should have been promoted.

Paul was lively and amusing about my (until last week his) job. 'It's very much an independent command.'

He also told me, as indeed have many others already, that every Minister for Trade ends up in the Cabinet.

My head is swollen.

Albany   *Sunday, 2 March*

I loathe London on Sunday evenings, but today Jane and I were lunching with Willie at Dorneywood. She has gone on down to

Saltwood while I stay here to blitz the boxes, and tomorrow make
a dawn raid (which, as it will be a Monday, the office will not be
expecting).

I am really *in the Government* now. A completely different status
and experience from the days of 'Parly Sec' with the officials either
patronising or incredulous; journalists and colleagues alike regarding it as a fluke, liable to end with a bump, at any moment. Now
officials (and Ambassadors) are curious but, in their varying
degrees, deferential. All the accoutrements – attitude of the
Whips, of (with wide variations) ministerial colleagues, drivers,
policemen, journalists – are enhanced. I have a huge airy office,
and, at last, *interesting boxes*.

It is deliciously enjoyable, and I feel full of adrenalin most of the
time, although conscious that I am draining the substance. My hair
is, at last, thinning and beginning to show grey.

Dorneywood is a dreary red brick house in flat country much,
and I would guess expensively, built over. Inside, though, the
furniture is good. Pictures medium only, but some amusing
('amusing' means 'erotic' doesn't it, in an auctioneer's catalogue
description, and they are only mildly that) murals by Rex Whistler.
A lot of decent porcelain – mainly Wedgwood.

Lord Courtauld-Thomson looked down from the wall upon the
lunch guests. I told Cecilia Whitelaw that his father had perished in
the R 101 at Beauvais in 1932. (Or was I mistaken? Certainly a
Secretary of State for Air at this time carried the same name.)
Curiously, she didn't seem aware of this. And that his last radio
message had been on the 'just-opened-our-fourth-bottle-of-Kum-
mel' lines.

This made James Hanson, sitting on my right, splutter.[1] He and
I got on well, letting our hair down rapidly and using 'fuck',
'arsehole' and 'shit' all too freely, although Cecilia gamely pretended not to hear. Poor Swinton, opposite, who used to be fat
and objectionable is now diminished, having lost six stone (!) and is
quiet-spoken and polite.[2]

---

[1] James Hanson (life peer, 1983), chairman of Hanson plc since 1965.
[2] Earl of Swinton (2nd Earl), deputy government whip in the Lords.

After lunch the girls separated and Willie, pretty watery-eyed, boomed away about the Land-Rover balls-up.[1] Too extraordinary that no one told him about it until four days before the announcement. Yet I issued a warning minute to the whole of DE on 17 September last year. And I clearly remember thinking then that really I ought to slip a copy to Willie. I funked it as not having the rank or responsibility, and that he might think I was up to my sneaky ways.

But I always welcome confirmation of my infallible eye for what is or is not *political*.

Willie was very good about the need to *help* the PM see, in some situations, that there were other possibilities; excising her (erroneous) belief that if she threw her personal weight behind something it would always go through. Willie said that the PM's Private Office was greatly diminished by the loss of Robin Butler.[2]

Willie said that Nigel Wicks 'will be (sic) very good . . . is very good . . . BUT' – a marvellous Willyism. Everyone says Wicks is useless. The great man was also extremely funny, giving imitations of the juniors in the PM's outer Private Office. Little creeps and OBN-ers.

After Hanson had clattered off in his helicopter Willie took me on one side and said that I was *always* to contact him *immediately* if there was 'anything I wanted to talk about', which pleased me greatly. Also at the lunch was Woodrow Wyatt.[3] With the exception of Macmillan (and *he* does it on purpose) Woodrow is the only person I know who seems to be more ga-ga than he is.

---

[1] There was a tentative bid on the table for the former British Motor Corporation from Ford. AC had seen that one of the consequences would be that the ownership of Land-Rover would fall into US hands. When the bid became substantive this possibility gave rise to consternation among some members of the cabinet.

[2] Robin Butler, after three years as principal private secretary to the prime minister, had moved in 1985 to the Treasury as Second Permanent Secretary, Public Expenditure.

[3] Sir Woodrow Wyatt, journalist and businessman (printing) and for twenty years a Labour MP. Now a Conservative and chairman of the Horserace Totalisator Board. Elevated to the Lords as a life peer in 1987.

British embassy, Brussels   *Monday, 10 March*

Comfortable here; pleasant, ex-Rothschild town house. A long, curiously narrow entrance hall, then a wide staircase with important pictures of a Salvator Rosa-ish kind hanging sombrely.

Today I talked to other Ministers – my counterparts – and got my way with officials.

But in the long mirrors I see myself jowly and puffed. My shoulder muscles have almost gone.

How I pine for that long, long youth that I enjoyed! To leap and stride – with every new encounter a joy of *possibility*. The 'sluice of hearing and seeing'[1] that endured for so long.

Now, I suppose, in the timescale of my life, I am in the last week of a holiday – or however the analogy should be shaped – a Sunday afternoon. By Thursday, I will have to start 'packing'.

Boy has asked for a 'Mandat' to handle the Kiosk. I can hardly refuse. I go to Zermatt less and less now. But I have never been happier than I was at the Chalet.

British embassy, Belgrade   *Wednesday, 15 October*

We had a 'day off', although even here the schedule was drum taut. The 'Jugs' (a Thirties expression, I remember my parents using it, and think it came from Oliver Lyttelton) flew me to Sarajevo. A Lear – they are always fabulous on take-off, the Lears – flown by two uniformed and identical dwarves with a young and dissolute-looking navigator. We *just* got in through a gap in the early morning fog. The approach was frightening, with a few Bosnian 'Munro's' peeping up through a flat blanket of cotton wool.

Then, standard draining session with various local dignitaries before a very fattening lunch.

But I began to enjoy myself, having insisted (and being thought eccentric, even by my own Private Office, while the Embassy did

---
[1] Louis MacNeice.

their best to put me off) that we foregather in the very hotel where the Archduke Franz Ferdinand stayed his last night, and whence he journeyed into the city. Not only that. But after lunch we ourselves had to follow his *exact* route to the very point of his assassination.

It was quite short. We followed the tram lines, still there, having been laid, I suppose, at the turn of the century. And soon I was standing on the corner where Princip[1] had waited – totally unchanged in scale and dimension; pave, granite kerbstones.

That was where the 'old coachman', gaga Czech chauffeur, had taken a wrong turning (or did he do it on purpose? A line of enquiry that has been insufficiently purused) and gratingly engaged reverse gear. For more than a few seconds the car must have been stationary.

And then the shots, at point blank range.

I could still smell it, just as one can in a haunted room. A colossal, seismic charge of diabolic energy had been blown, released on that very spot some seventy-two years ago, and drawn its awful price.

> Not in the hands of boys, but in their eyes
> Shall shine the holy glimmer of goodbyes.[2]

Nearby was the little Princip museum, showing the youth to be exactly as I would expect. Tiresome, ego, mare-eyed, consumptive-looking. Something between Seventies CND and Baader-Meinhof.

Afterwards I was taken to the old Muslim Quartier. And I smelt here in the market for the first time that authentic Balkan tang – incense and bad fat. Sausages always frying. The women are hideous. Squat, moustachio'd and without shape.

---

[1] Gavrilo Princip, whose assassination in Sarajevo of Archduke Franz Ferdinand, heir to Emperor Franz Josef of Austria, and his morganatic wife, Countess Sofia Chotek, on 28 June 1914, precipitated the First World War.

[2] Wilfred Owen, 'Anthem for Doomed Youth'.

House of Commons   *Tuesday, 18 November*

I am over here, taking refuge. I did a quick trawl, to see if there was anyone sympathetic around, but it was a bad time of the afternoon. There are a multitude of telephones scattered around the Palace, in all the nooks and crannies adjoining the corridors. Every one of them, it seemed, had an MP crouched over it, pompously pontificating. It is the hour when one must catch the deadline for the local paper. Most of them are buffers, or demi-buffers, or *buffers-aspirant.* They amount to nothing.

  I couldn't go back to being a backbencher. It's so completely artificial. What democratic overheads we carry in our system of Government!

  Also, I am soft-spoken and apprehensive about going on *Question Time* this week. In addition to my inability, in practically every instance, to answer a direct question from Robin Day on 'But what is the Govt's postion on . . . ?' lines, I am on a hiding to nothing generally.

  Whatever I do they'll get me. If I am grave and responsible, they'll say, 'Hasn't he gone off?' If I'm jaunty and reckless, it'll be, 'There he goes again, another gaffe.'

  Interesting, that word 'gaffe'. Three-quarters of the journalists who use it don't, for a start, know what it means. It's monosyllabic, which is a help of course, to the Editor; and to them, it signifies 'soundbite', or 'unpalatable truth'. A true gaffe is accidental. Mine never are. I like to shock, and I do it (though not as often as I could) deliberately.

Saltwood   *Tuesday, 6 January*

The ground is dormant at present, with only a few snowdrops and
early crocuses showing. For most of the day we were along the
woodland walk, raking and pruning. The rake collects huge piles
of dead grass, twigs and brambles, and we had several fires going.

Just after tea Peter M. rang with the news that poor Robin
Cooke had died. Robin was two years younger than me, and on
occasion could look really quite youthful. He had been in the
House for an eternity, having come in on a by-election in the first
year of Macmillan's premiership. Robin overlapped even with
Chips – who was himself by then bright red in the face and (as he
candidly admits) feeling ghastly.

MPs die in batches. Just when one thinks that foul air, bad diet,
unlimited alcohol and late nights ought surely to be exacting a
higher toll, the Almighty springs a surprise. David Penhaligon was
killed in a car smash over Christmastide.[1] And Number 10 have
just been on the phone. Would I represent the Prime Minister at
his memorial service in Truro Cathedral on *Saturday* (ugh) of this
weekend.

What a bore. It's a long and tedious journey, that rail stretch
after Plymouth. I won't even have time to dismount and make a
splash on Plymouth Sound.

Still, always fun to represent the Prime Minister doing anything.

Truro–Paddington train   *Saturday, 10 January*

I have been talking with poor old Jeremy Thorpe. He was sitting
alone in the dining car, at one of the head-to-head double tables,

---

[1] David Penhaligon, Liberal MP for Truro since 1974.

being ostentatiously ignored by the Liberals who mill around, drab but noisy, and seem to have taken over the whole train. There is a hint of relief on this, the return journey, and drinks are being called for, and 'tossed off', as my mother used to say.

Jeremy has Parkinson's Disease, quite advanced, and looks gaunt, with staring eyes. He was pleased to have attention and, pathetically, tried to hold on to his right hand in order to prevent it trembling.

I tried to get him to reminisce a little, tell a few Macmillan stories. But he did not find it easy to speak. The listener must concentrate hard. I reminded Jeremy of his peak moment of glory and, had he played his cards differently, of power, when the 'hung' results of the Election of February '74 were in, and Ted tried to do a deal, offering him the Home Office. Jeremy was barely intelligible, but his eyes were full of pain.

Albany   *Tuesday, 27 January*

Sometimes there is just so much pressure at Saltwood that it is a relief to sink into the cushions, stale and dirty though they may be, of the Sandling train. For an hour and a half I am isolated, trundling along, and no one can get at me with a will-you, can-you, did-you, have-you, are-you, if-you, but-you? three bags full, query. But it's a kind of cop out, really, because I leave it all on Jane's lap, then ring in the evenings and bark at her.

I must be very near a nervous breakdown. The tower office is so bad that I dare not lift any stone there, for fear of what I may find underneath. And last night I dreamed – just before waking, almost the most vivid kind – that I had hailed a taxi, then could not remember my intended destination.

This evening the Prime Minister came to the '92 dinner at the St Stephen's Club. How déjà-vu it all seemed. Backbenchers bobbing up and down, trying to be goodboy. Same old subjects grinding round and round.

Even dear IG, next to whom I sat, was distrait and low. He

basted me for not having chosen a PPS. Ian said, with much truth, that no one in any Government Department knows, or cares (except when it causes them trouble) about the House of Commons, and a PPS would keep me in touch.

Possibly. But I prefer to get my gossip over a bottle of wine with Budgen, or others.

Department of Trade and Industry   *Tuesday, 10 February*

Just back from Harold Macmillan's memorial service in the Abbey.[1] I am filled with melancholy.

The Grenadiers' Return was played, and I thought of the fife music, and of the decimated battalion marching back in from Hulluch on 26 September 1915, past the wounded laid out in rows on either side of the street, groaning from their injuries. And the young classical scholar, less than a year out of Eton, pale and shaken but heroic, nonetheless. When Macmillan enlisted Britain was at the very height of her power and dominion. The habitual bearing, stoicism, self-sacrifice, sense of 'fair play'; the whole *tenu* of the English upper class was in place and unquestioned, looked up to and copied everywhere. Now look at us – and them!

Julian Amery read the second lesson. His voice, which still can command the attention even of a crowded House (for the very reason, I think, because it is so genuinely cast in the tones of the olden days, without self-parody and unlike, for example, the embarrassing plumminess of Derek Walker-Smith) has lost a little of its timbre. I nostalgicised for government by the upper class; which is what I thought it would be – the whole thing really run by the OE mafia – when first I wanted to get in in 1964, and Julian and I had a long conversation at the Chalet and he said I was too old. I did just, *just*, I suppose overlap. But by the time that Ted had got rid of Alec he was determined to keep all the others out if he could.

And who is to blame him? Profumo exposed their essential

---

[1] Harold Macmillan, 1st Earl of Stockton, had died aged ninety-two.

rottenness.[1] The few who remain – Gilmour, Whitelaw, Carrington – are impossibly defeatist. With the exception, I think the *sole*
exception, of Robert Cranborne the real toffs have opted out. I
looked up at the great circular window, to which I have raised my
eyes at so many services, and thought, I must – *when* will I – write
my great work, *Tories and the Nation State 1922–74*. Perhaps it is
for this that I will be remembered? If I am spared.

Department of Trade and Industry   *Tuesday, 31 March*

Last night Heseltine, a bit flushed-looking, came up to me when
we were going through the Aye lobby, and leered.
  'Have I lost you your seat?'[2]
  'Could be,' I shrugged. 'Could be.'
  'Never mind. I'll write you a letter of apology.'
  Odd. Unlike him. Many others would have found such behav-
iour disagreeable.

Saltwood   *Sunday, 5 April*

At mid-day the sun was high and we got the tortoises out of
hibernation. I lay on my back on the freshly cut grass in Courtenays, looking at the sky, hearing the slow deliberate rustle as they
emerged from their straw-lined boxes to a meal of tomato and
sliced banana. Fortunate creatures. If humans could do this at will
we, too, would live to be two hundred years old.

---

[1] In the closing phase of the 1959–63 Macmillan premiership, the war minister,
Jack Profumo, who was married to the actress Valerie Hobson, became involved
with a young lady who was also enjoying the attentions of the Soviet military
attaché.
[2] Michael Heseltine had just announced his plans to 'privatise' the Royal Navy
Dockyards in Plymouth.

Department of Trade and Industry   *Tuesday, 14 April*

I am feeling sickish and tired. Is my lymphatic system packing up?

I have just returned (on foot) from a thoroughly unsatisfactory meeting with Tim Renton at the Foreign Office. Henry Keswick[1] had asked me to put in a word for British contractors, who are being edged out of various important deals in Hong Kong disgracefully, in some cases where the Crown is itself the customer.

Downstairs the desk had made a balls-up of the times, and I hung around, getting cross. Senior Ministers shouldn't be kept waiting, except in the comfort of special rooms set aside for the purpose. Was it always like this in the entrance hall, with ugly common people cackling and shouting and banging things? Probably yes.

On the first floor the rooms have very high ceilings. They must be double cubes. And the furniture is still good and heavy. Tim explained to me, effectively, that Hong Kong had 'gone'. UK influence in matters of this kind was nil. One more piece of wealth and real estate that has been allowed just to run through our fingers.

'It's not 1935,' I said, thinking of all these white-painted ships on the China Station which I used to memorise from the *Jane's* of that year, the first in which I was given the book.

'No. Not even 1975.'

I lost interest in what he was saying.

I am blighted by the Foreign Office at present. Earlier today a creepy official, who is 'in charge' (heaven help us) of South America, came over to brief me ahead of my trip to Chile. All crap about Human Rights. Not one word about the UK interest; how we saw the balance, prospects, pitfalls, opportunities in the Hemisphere.

I'm Minister for Trade, for Christ's sake, what's the point of keeping an expensive mission in Santiago if they can't even tell me

---

[1] Henry Keswick, influential director of several Hong Kong businesses, not least Jardine, Matheson.

what to push? When I questioned him, he was evasive on all policy matters other than his own tenacious, *Guardian*esque obsession.

'Aha but,' soft-spokenly he gloated, 'Community policy is' we are but one in twelve, etc.

What *does* he mean? There is no exclusive 'Community Competence' in Foreign Affairs (yet!). I don't think that there is even a Foreign Affairs Commissioner, is there? This man is exactly the kind of mole who is working away, eighteen hours a day, to extinguish the British national identity.

I am depressed, and zestfree.

The general election on 11 June
Conservative: 375; Labour: 229; Alliance: 22.

Saltwood   *Wednesday, 17 June*

Tired and liverish with *reaction*. First day back at the House, and I was to rendez-vous with Soames in the smoking room for lunch.

Everyone very jolly – most had increased their majorities, although a few seemed to know I hadn't.[1] Jopling was in splendid form, grinning benevolently.[2] After being sacked, or 'dropped', that's really the only way – show your face in the smoking room at once – and mix it with the boys. (Whether I shall ever be able to do that is, I fear, extremely doubtful.) He'd always wanted Agriculture, and of course he was good with the farmers – the real ones anyway. But more and more the people who call the shots on the NFU are the nasty, computer-driven 'barons', who drench everything with nitrates and rip off the CAP. Thus, *mutatis mutandis*, Ministers don't spend their time any longer in tweed suits scratching pigs at county shows, but cooped up in the Charlemagne arguing with their 'counterparts' about the Green Pound. Hats off to him, though. Like most Chief Whips he knew who the

---

[1] AC's majority fell from 11,000 in 1983 to 4,000, owing to the threat of redundancies consequent on 'privatisation' of the dockyard (see entry for 24 March).

[2] Michael Jopling had been minister of agriculture for four years until the election.

shits were. Memorable remark about Heseltine: 'The trouble with Michael is that he had to buy all his furniture.' Snobby, but cutting. He and Gail (so pretty with her red hair and lovely skin) take their holidays in France, in leathers, on an old Honda. Now that *is* sporting.

As for myself – was I being unduly paranoiac in detecting a frisson of disapproval? Certainly Government colleagues – Renton, Baker, Mitchell, Patten J.[1] – all in their different ways radiated 'distancing' and John Wakeham, whose eye I had caught while we were listening to the Queen's Commission in the Lords, seemed to be saying, 'Phew, you really pushed it that time'.[2] That fat gossipy Critchley said something about 'rocking the boat' – rich coming from him. Sometimes he affects the mantle of Bufton Tufton.

Soames was twitchy concerning his 'last chance', as the junior Whips' appointments were being made at that moment.[3] And the meal wasn't a great success as the top end of the dining room was full and we had to sit among the Labour tables.

Department of Trade and Industry   *Friday, 26 June*

Rose wanted to go to *Les Misérables*. Naturally there were no tickets. However a quick call to James Osborne and a couple of good stalls were whistled up through the show business underground, and I collected them from the major domo at Aspers' – who wouldn't take a tip.[4] I'm out of touch with these things. I suppose my humble £20 note was beneath him, like Arthur Lee refusing the Star of India for his work on the Civil Service Commission.

---

[1] John Patten, MP for Oxford West and Abingdon since 1983 (City of Oxford, 1979–83).

[2] A reference to an interview which AC gave during the election campaign in which he had poured scorn on the Channel Tunnel project.

[3] In fact Nicholas Soames became PPS to the environment secretary.

[4] James Osborne, manager of the Curzon Club, at that time in the proprietorship of AC's old friend John Aspinall.

I haven't been inside a theatre for ages. How evocative is that smell – greasepaint, dust, scenery – that wafts out across the stalls when the curtain goes up. And how very tiresome and ego and generally oopsy-la are most of the audience (though not as bad, I must admit, at the Palace as at Covent Garden). On the way back, as we walked down Shaftesbury Avenue, everybody seemed to be staring. Women, in particular, were looking at Rose. Did they think they 'recognised' her? Or was it just prurient curiosity? Strange, and unusual.

We had a banquette at the Mirabelle. I kept looking sideways at Rose and thinking how remarkably pretty is her mouth; so cupidic, like those coquettish maidens hidden away in the upper corners of a Tintoretto ceiling. She wanted hock so I ordered a quite decent bottle of Gewürztraminer. But just after it had been poured she sliced through whatever inanity I was saying and asked the wine waiter to bring some soda water, which she made him pour *on to* the delicious white wine. He was equal to this and didn't bat an eyelid, although I doubt if it happens very often in the Mirabelle.

'Very Byronic,' I said.

Saltwood   *Sunday, 28 June*

The first day of summer (!). We swept the Bailey of grass clippings. Probably the most back-breaking of all gardening jobs is picking them up, moistly resisting and getting into one's nose and ears; throwing them into the back of the Mehari as little puffs of breeze coming from nowhere on a completely still day blow flakes and flickings back in one's face. Then I helped Jane get a buddleia down from where it had been growing in the wall below my father's study window. Then got the pool pump working which, amazingly, it did without too much demur.

We had planned our first outside lunch. M. Goisot[1] and a huge Brie, but forsook it to tend to a baby jackdaw who had got sump

---

[1] From whom AC bought wine in France.

oil on his wings and (how, for God's sake?) torn off one of his legs below the knee joint. I thought he was a goner – how *could* he survive? But he had so much fight in him, and his lovely pale blue eyes were so lively that we had to try. Jane washed his wings and tail feathers, rinsing and re-rinsing the Fairy Liquid. He didn't seem to mind; positively enjoyed the warm whirrings of a hair-drier. We stuffed a couple of worms down his throat and left him to gain strength in a basket with a heat bulb glowing over. In no time he appeared to make a full recovery and later that evening, after being returned to the wild, actually *flew* from the sleeper pile to the yew tree by the long garage. Cheered by this, I started the Silver Ghost and went for a drive.

On a fine evening there are very few pleasures comparable to driving a light, open Ghost on country roads. Some will get it from waiting for salmon to take, in dark peat pools, but I am too impatient, and can't stand the midges. In a Ghost you waft along, high enough to look over people's hedges, noiseless enough (as was the original intention) to leave horses unscared. It started at once, of course, although I hadn't been near it since last November. No (*no*) modern car would have done this. Because the Rolls Royce Silver Ghost has – except for the magneto which sparks on a turn – not one single piece of electrical equipment. No battery (flat) or pumps (stuck) or solenoid (up the creek, Squire) or 'black box' (I'm afraid we're talking about a factory replacement unit, Sir, at £873 plus VAT). There are twenty-one separate actions, all of them involving beautifully crafted mechanical linkages, from turning on the gravity petrol feed to actually cranking the starting handle. And after they have been completed in the correct sequence it will – infallibly – fire on the first compression.

My car was built in an epoch when the Grand Fleet dominated the world's oceans. And under the bonnet, in the brass and copper and the hugely overstrength componentry, there is much trace of marine influence. The factory record shows it going out to India, in Curzon's name (although I doubt he ever sat at the wheel).

Now the Grand Fleet is no more, and Lutyens's beautiful vistas in New Delhi have been overrun by shanty settlements. And yet, even when the Rolls was built brand new, 'there's something wrong with our bloody ships today'.[1]

It is the perennial problem, the need to arrest industrial decadence. At what point does the refusal of innovation overlap with the introduction of the 'black box'? – but not as an enhancement of quality, more a signpost to the soft life and 'shorter working hours'.

Department of Trade and Industry   *Monday, 29 June*

So hot and thundery. I am feeling exceedingly tired and old. My papers suddenly seem to have got into a total mess. Fatally, I started the practice of having *two* 'In' trays, a priority, or urgent tray and a more dreary waiting-for-attention tray. The dreary one now towers massively, sometimes sliding over on to the 'Out' side which means unsigned papers go back out into Private Office. I just don't have the energy to cope with it. I am flaccid.

At lunchtime I saw that randy little runt Ian Gladding trying to chat up Rose, and this made me cross.

Later I telephoned Jane and had a talk. She'd bathed.

'I'm so cross,' I said.

'You wouldn't be if you were down here.'

Too true. Ah well, only three weeks to go!

Saltwood   *Sunday, 19 July*

A social weekend at Saltwood. First to arrive (by train, naturally, I met him at Sandling Junction) was Peter Brooke,[2] in a lovely old tweed suit (ambient July temperature 70° plus) stooped and shuffling like a character from LP Hartley. He's so nice, gentle and

---

[1] Admiral Beatty at Jutland when he lost three battlecruisers, owing in part to the inferiority of their armour and the accuracy of the German fire-control systems.

[2] Peter Brooke, MP for City of London and Westminster South since 1977. Paymaster General since the election.

clever. But almost too Balliol. I know Chesterfield said that one
should never allow one's 'innate self' to show, but . . .

Then the Worsthornes.[1] Perry not in an especially good temper;
I had forgotten that David Young was originally meant to be
coming and that I had mentioned this to Perry and I suppose he
was disappointed. Andrew turned up with a couple of brother
officers. One of them, surprisingly young-looking, was in fact
Tara's[2] father. (She, very splendidly, on first catching sight of Jane
had said, 'For God's sake watch out for my father'.) Next was dear
Jonathan [Aitken] – *always* a delight in any gathering.

We were changed, drinking champagne in the music room
when a commotion was audible from the hall. Dogs barking. The
Parkinsons [Cecil and Ann] were trying to get in. But William,
now more and more a law unto himself, had been disconcerted by
Cecil's appearance, his (very loud) change jacket, and slammed the
door on him. 'Ooh, you can't come in like that, sir.' I mediated.
Cecil's Private Office had failed to tell him, although I had sent
many messages, that it was black tie. It's always black tie at
Saltwood on Saturday evenings. This is known.

Dinner was longish, before we got to the port and the ladies –
reluctantly in Ann's case – went away. Then serious conversation
began, punctuated at intervals by 'crude' laughs from the other end
of the table where Andrew and his Life Guard friends were
ensconced with their own decanter.

Perry flew his kite about where is the real opposition coming
from, what are the coming ideas, that kind of thing. Cecil
responded, but not really very effectively. Jonathan and I were
'ball-boys'. Peter Brooke was completely silent. Perhaps tired,
perhaps just faintly disapproving.

Later in the evening I had a chat with Cecil.

She *had* intended to put him in the Foreign Office, and how he
had a clear programme to 'sort it out'. He always said he wanted

---

[1] Peregrine and his first wife Claude. He had become editor of the *Sunday
Telegraph* in 1986.
[2] A girlfriend of Andrew.

me to go there with him as Min of State, although had it actually
come to the point, I'm not so sure. But it was not that that made
me feel a great opportunity had been lost. Because all that he said
rang so true; all his criticisms of their misplaced – but extravagant –
effort are so valid. Cecil also told me that she had clearly planned to
groom him as her successor, arranged little private meetings with
the Prince of Wales, that kind of thing. Will he ever be able to
build it back? I doubt it. She's in love with David Young at the
moment. But even there I get the feeling that it could already be
waning. *La Donna è mobile.*

After everyone had gone to bed Jonathan and I talked. I said that
I had finally blown it for the Cabinet. He, somewhat tenuously, I
thought, advanced the theory that I might be brought in as they
were all so *boring.* We both dread The Lady's health cracking up.
'No one can stand this pace,' he said.

Very late that night I tiptoed across the lawn to the Great
Library and turned off the tapestry lights. It's spooky over there
after midnight, and I was not strong enough to go through to the
little lobby where I have positioned that beautiful erotic marble,
Boucher's *Captive,* which I bought last week at Sotheby's for
double its estimate. (I wonder who the underbidder was?)

On Sunday everyone, thank God, left promptly. Perry had to go to
Chequers, and was not sure of the way.[1] We paced on the lawn for
a little while. He was disappointed in Cecil, 'He's not a philosopher king. I don't know who could play that role. Perhaps you
could?' I'm a sucker for any compliment, and this cheered me up.

There is no doubt that Cecil is better *à deux* than in a general,
High Table kind of conversation. He was quite funny about The
Lady's health and holidays. 'She *won't* relax, *won't* go to bed.' (I
have heard Willie say exactly the same thing.) 'That's why Ian
Gow was so bad for her. He *encouraged* her to stay up, later and
later. They would sit up in her flat above Number 10, and have

---

[1] In fact the Worsthornes, notwithstanding the clearest instructions from AC,
turned right instead of left at the M25, and were nearly two hours late at
Chequers.

just another "last" whisky.' Quite. I can see (but did not say) a number of reasons why Cecil might object to this.

They're expensive, these hospitalities. In drink alone I'm down three bottles of Dom Perignon, three Talbot blanc, four '78 Morgon, one Cockburn '60, and a lot of brandy.

Charing Cross   *Friday, 24 July*

A muggy, late July Friday, and I am sitting in a first-class compartment of the Sandling train, odorous and untidy, which, for reasons as yet undisclosed, and probably never to *be* disclosed, has not yet left Charing Cross. 'Operating Difficulties', I assume, which is BR-speak for some ASLEF slob, having drunk fourteen pints of beer the previous evening, now gone 'sick' and failed to turn up.

'Term' is over. I will not need to go to the Department more than three days a week – the rest can be done by phone, fax and Dave bringing down boxes. I must now make sure that the hols are not frittered away. Yoga, filing and paperwork backlog, *moderation in all things*.

I am not feeling particularly energetic or constructive. Last night we had the end-of-term binge, organised by Gow, and this year in the Macmillan Room of the Carlton Club. Not a wild success, as poor Ian had a setback at the outset. It came about like this. We had arranged to meet in my room, and go over to the Carlton together. But on the way, I wanted to drop in my little note to Charles about my conversation with the Governor.[1] Half mischievously I showed it to Ian.

He took a long time to read it, although it was only one side of one page. 'But this is addressed to a (sic) Mr Charles Powell.'

'That's right.'

---

[1] The governor of the Bank of England. On the Monday of that week AC had sat at dinner next to Robin Leigh-Pemberton. The governor had taken some time to enlarge on his views that the Community would in the end be moving towards a single currency (which was at the time anathema to the prime minister).

'But he's a civil servant, is he not?'

'Yes.'

'And you are a Minister in the Government, a Minister of State, indeed, the Minister for Trade?'

'Yes.'

'And you, a Minister of State, are communicating directly with a civil servant – and a very junior ranking civil servant – in another Department?'

'Oh come on, Ian, you know Charles's position . . .'

Ian sighed. I mean he Cone Ripman School of Acting sighed, and said no more. But as soon as we got to the Carlton and after sinking his first White Lady, he announced that he felt 'ill', and didn't (*most* unlike him) 'want to stay late'.

Poor fellow. He so misses Number 10. I don't really know how much she sees of him now. But those days when he controlled and monitored everything are gone. I suppose for ever. He was so good at it. But her problems are no longer (or not at present, anyway) political. Intelligence relating to the parliamentary Party, gentle massaging of their various egos, is less important. Her problems are machinery-of-government problems – both national, and international. And at coping with these Charles is brilliant. Workaholic, but cool.

Star turn at the dinner was (or was meant to be) Nicky Ridley.[1] But he was *desséché* and, as often these days, aggressive even to his friends. He said the 'Old Guard', by which (he made clear) he also included me, were finished. No new ideas. 'Where are the new, young radicals?' The same sort of crap I'd been getting from Perry last weekend.

'We don't want any fucking new ideas,' I said. 'We've got plenty of problems as it is.' I tried to play Baldwin. Consolidate. Stay calm. I told the story of my grandfather advising 'garaging' whenever one starts to get ahead. (Not everybody understood this, but Soames and Hesketh[2] did. Very much a café society litmus test.)

---

[1] Nicholas Ridley, now environment secretary.

[2] Lord Hesketh (3rd Baron). A government whip.

Richard Ryder[1] sparkled gravely and intelligently. I used to think he was a bit of a creep, confusing him – because he is one of that generation – with the Blue Chip[2] mutual admirationists. But he is far better than any of them. He knows his history, which is important. That's what makes Alastair Goodlad[3] (another example) so much more interesting than he first appears.

UK mission, Geneva   *Wednesday, 29 July*

I am out here for the UNCTAD meeting. It seemed safe enough, because of all the United Nations quangos this has to be the dreariest and least consequential. Nothing of substance is discussed, no decisions are ever reached, the political impact at home is nil.

My plan, to put in an appearance, shake a few hands, 'Excellency, how very agreeable to see you again; how well you are looking; I would so greatly value you opinion on . . . ; let us get our staff to arrange a short bilateral meeting; such pleasure, such pleasure.' And all that. A set speech to the assembly (not deviating by one iota from the turgid DTI text). And then, hand over to officials, take the train to Visp – one of my three favourite train journeys in the world – and up on the V-Z Bahn to Zermatt in time for a delicious meal in the station restaurant. And the following day a Whymper scramble. I gave them the Chalet phone number. 'I can be back in Geneva at two hours' notice' (lie).

I had reckoned without (how can I still be underestimating this?) the absolute determination of civil servants never to let a Minister out of their sight if they can possibly avoid it, and how they put this objective above all others.

Also, there is a heavy FCO input here, as indeed there is at every international gathering. The Ambassador fusses and clucks;

---

[1] Richard Ryder, MP for Mid-Norfolk since 1983. Mrs Thatcher's political secretary, 1975–81. At this time an assistant government whip.

[2] Blue Chip: a dining club, self-selected, of ambitious young fellows who entered Parliament in 1979. They met at 13 Catherine Place, the home of Tristan Garel-Jones. Their group portrait, in oils, hangs in the dining room.

[3] Alastair Goodlad, now parliamentary under-secretary, Energy.

actually offered his own brief of what I should say and do, on a
kind of spot-the-difference basis from the DTI brief. He appears to
be sending a totally separate set of the telegrams to the Foreign
Office while at the same time processing our set, which Tony
Hutton[1] is writing each evening, to the DTI. And for what?
Absolutely nothing.

What a bore for the desk clerk.

So it was no surprise to be woken by Marjorie this morning at
seven fifteen or thereabouts (the taxi to take me to Geneva Gare
was ordered for eight thirty) on my jangling bedside telephone and
be told, breathlessly – she always gets slight asthma when she
knows I'm going to be cross – that things had got rather 'difficult'.

'Meaning?'

'It looks, Minister, as if the UK is going to be *isolated*' (FCO
dread-word, she lowered her voice reverently, almost as if she was
saying *buggered*) 'on the Common Fund, both in the Community,
and in Group "B".'

'So?'

'Well, Minister, I've been talking to Christopher Roberts—'[2]

'Already?'

'Well no, Minister, I spoke to him last night' (once she
mentioned Christopher, I knew I'd had it as she's more frightened
of him than she is even of me) 'and he feels it would be unwise of
you to be away today, Minister.'

I thought it over. It was no good, I couldn't go. There would be
too much *angst*. I wouldn't really be able to enjoy the high Alps.
And it was the sort of tedious mini-dispute that might just get
referred across to Number 10 by the FCO – they certainly would
sneak if they could – and then there'd be a 'Where's Alan?' crisis.
Blast, though. I was thoroughly dejected.

Sadly I went for an early morning stroll along the corniche.
Very very faint evocations did I feel of earlier, unblighted strolls,
distant in time. Water slapping against the hulls of launches after a

---

[1] Anthony Hutton, civil servant in Trade and Industry, then dealing with external
European policy.

[2] Christopher Roberts, civil servant. Deputy secretary, Trade and Industry, since
1983.

speedboat had gone by. A man slaloming on water skis, and the burble of Riva exhausts; a girl getting out of her red swim suit and laughing. It was not yet eight o'clock and there was already the promise of great heat, with haze over to the Evian side of the lake.

Saltwood   *Sunday, 4 October*

Vilely depressed after a bad night. (Tom kept us awake fidgeting and flapping his ears and when finally I staggered down to the yard with him at two am he disappeared for three-quarters of an hour ratting, and at intervals barking shrilly, behind the log pile.) This morning a scotch mist, and everything soaked. You can hardly see across the Bailey.

The papers are full of Heseltine, 'to be the star of the Conference', etc. How can he be, if he hasn't got a perch? He'll have to speak from the rostrum, with a time limit – although even as I write I realise there isn't a Chairman of the National Union made who would cut off that man's sound. Four-fifths of Central Office are closet subversives anyway, always have been. He's got a word-of-mouth going, which is why Bruce,[1] who is a terrific Vicar of Bray, was all 'cor' at lunch yesterday. But *what a bore.*

Saltwood   *Saturday, 19 December*

On Thursday Ian and I had a very jolly dinner at the Savoy, indulged ourselves. Also present (at my suggestion) were Francis Maude,[2] and David Heathcoat-Amory.[3] Both the youngsters were good, and sparkled sensibly. Fine wines were ordered, and consumed. I really think that the Savoy River Room has the most

---

[1] Bruce Anderson, columnist on the *Sunday Telegraph*.

[2] Francis Maude, Parliamentary under-secretary at the DTI.

[3] David Heathcoat-Amory, MP for Wells since 1983.

reliably good food in London. Not the absolute best, perhaps, but I've never been disappointed there.

Ian talked about the next reshuffle, and we pricked up our ears. (But is he actually as close to things as he used to be? I would say not.) He started off circumlocutory, became more specific as Puligny-Montrachet gave way to Beaune. She intends to make Geoffrey leader in the Lords, and Nigel Foreign Secretary; John MacGregor[1] Chancellor.

This seems a pretty tall order to me. Maude, supported by David H-A, said Lawson couldn't be Foreign Sec as a Jew. This made Ian very indignant. 'Do you mean to tell me that today, this very day, in this the Conservative Party? – you are seriously suggesting, no asserting . . .' and so on.

Ian then switched to 'he's not a practising Jew, anyway'. But we couldn't quite swallow it. I said something – something Hurd, and Ian snapped. 'She can't bear him. Can't *bear* him.'

I thought, it's all very well for he and she to swop these sort of ideas over the third or fourth whisky after midnight but come the morning and she's usually more circumspect.

But it's nice to have the Christmas hols, which is always an agreeable time, spiced up by speculation about changes of this weight. I must ring Peter Riddell on Monday, although I expect his scepticism will match my own.

There were three late votes; then Francis and I went to the DTI basement, where the Christmas party was being staged. Matthew was there, having lost so much weight that he is now quite *markedly* handsome. As always full of sense, as well as fun. He told me that Lynda was going to take Arthur Cockfield's place on the Commission – or so the Brussels inner rumour mill claimed. If that happens it could mean Parkinson going to the FCO instead of Lawson (plus A. N. Other!). All greatly preferable to the version we had been getting from Ian at dinner.[2]

As I stood somewhat stiltedly making conversation with Matthew and Marjorie I could see Rose out of the corner of my eye.

---

[1] John MacGregor, MP for South Norfolk since 1974. Minister of agriculture.
[2] But equally ill founded in substance.

After a bit she braved their joint presence and came up to me: 'You're terribly late getting here.' I kissed the back of her hand and she stood in *very* close proximity. I could feel my veins raging. She pouted, and nobody pouts like Rose. Nobody has such (I suppose the Barbara Cartland word is *full*) lips. 'It's too hot.'

'Come for a drive,' I said.

Later, when I got home I thought – I've been behaving like this, absolutely unaltered, for forty years. Crazy. Scrawny old time-warp.

Saltwood   *Monday, 21 December*

It's too boring. This lovely holiday break is upon us, James and Sally[1] are coming down, and Jane always does Christmas so well, it's pure pleasure.

But I am now convinced I have got cancer of the jaw. Those symptoms that I have been carefully monitoring ever since that triple-view shaving mirror in my bathroom in the Embassy in Santiago, are gradually amplifying (is that the word?). Will I be able even to 'smile bravely' throughout the festivities?

I am going in shortly to drop in some of the local Christmas cards in Folkestone. Julian[2] is such a dear, I think I'll just ask him for a quick check-up.

Afternoon

Julian was marvellous; saw me immediately; didn't turn a hair when I told him. He said it was 'pretty rare', he'd only seen three cases in the teaching hospital. He made a thorough examination. Glands totally normal. No sign whatever of local swelling or ulceration. 'Pain?'

'Well, er, no.'

'Happy Christmas.'

Phew.

---

[1] Sally, James's second wife.
[2] Julian Smith, FRCDS, the Clark family dentist.

Saltwood   *Thursday, 24 December*

Christmas Eve. I've got £700,000 in my Abbey National Crazy-High-Interest account. But what's the use? Ash, ash, all is ash. Lay not up for thyself treasures on earth. The cars are all getting streaked and rust spotted, the books foxed, the furniture dusty. The window panes, all 52,000 of them are *revolting*, so greasily blotched. Translucent only. And there is moth everywhere. My grandfather's great Rothschild coat, bought in Wien in 1906, is terminally degraded . . . The whole thing is out of control.

And why? I know why. Because I'm not rich enough to have servants. We have to do everything ourselves, and we just haven't got the time, and things get neglected. This morning, rummaging up in the archive room I found the old Wages Book for 1960. That was the year James was born, and we bought our first new car, a dear little red Mini. It was the cheapo model with cloth seats, and we saved a further three pounds and ten shillings by hand painting the registration numbers ourselves. Total cost 'on the road' was £460.

The total wage bill, per week, for seven servants who worked at the Castle, was thirty-two pounds and five shillings. MacTaggart, a clumsy fellow who had such ugly hands that my mother always made him wear white gloves when he was waiting at table, and who crashed my father's Bentley in circs that will never wholly be explained, in Lee Green, got £12 per week and occupancy of the Lodge.

Everything has decimal points – to the right – or worse. I'm bust, virtually.

Saltwood   *Tuesday, 29 December*

Yesterday we went to lunch at Chequers. I was excited. Some of the lunches over Christmas are very *réclamé*. One is for 'family and close friends', one is for Cabinet intimates; one is for Court favourites and so on. I hoped, naturally, that it was the third category. But Jane, flier, said no such luck, it'll be Captains of Industry. All too true. They were amiable, quiet-spoken, on good behaviour. Except for her son Mark (is he a 'businessman'?) who kept muscling in on conversations, saying 'something-something *two million* dollars' in Cor! tones. After a bit I got sick of this and said, 'That's not much' (which it isn't) but people affected not to hear.

Sometimes on these occasions she draws me into another room for a little intimate chat. But not this time. Although I must still be in favour as she kept introducing me as 'My wonderful frightfully good Trade Minister', and she had read the book on the Japanese threat which I had sent her via Charles, and had marked passages.

As we left I caught Aunt Ruth's eye,[1] as I always do. 'See you again,' I said. 'Often.'

On the way back, on the last bit of the M25, Dave drove slower and slower, and slower. 'What's up?' He'd forgotten to check the petrol before leaving and was trying to 'conserve' what was left. After we'd filled up he felt 'kind of faint'. Usual story. None of the Government Car Service drivers is capable of driving outside the Metropolitan area. I took over and drove the rest of the way to Saltwood.

---

[1] Viscountess Lee of Fareham, the wife of Arthur Lee, whose papers AC edited. The Lees gave Chequers to the nation in order that the prime minister of the day should always have at his disposal a country house for entertaining. One of the provisions of the Chequers Trust is that Lady Lee's portrait by Sargent should always hang in the entrance hall over the visitors' book.

1988

The House has not yet returned but officials, who can't bear it when Ministers are out of the building, they don't quite know where, and they themselves are all in there, shuffling papers around, had arranged for me to meet the '2000 Group', some kind of conclave to assist Japanese 'Inward Investment'. Poor old Patrick Jenkin was 'leading' it. He who had once been Secretary of State, now soft-spokenly hanging about in the waiting area. The democratic cycle. David Young, on the other hand, into whose presence he was finally ushered, was bronzed and silvery-sleek.

Much time is wasted with these sorts of meetings. The delegation believe themselves (I suppose) to be getting 'access'; the 'leader' is earning his fee by 'delivering' access, and the civil servants, who fidget and fuss and make notes, justify themselves and, of course, find such occasions useful in attaining their principal objective, which is always to stuff a Minister's day diary so full that he can't breathe – still less think. I can't think of many occasions when a Minister's mind has actually been altered during a discussion – although it can happen, most notably with the Lynx delegation.[1]

As soon as I got back to my office I asked to see my own 'long term' diary. This threw them, and a long delay ensued. Through the open door I could hear mutterings, heavy rustling of paper, subdued internal phoning. 'Where is it?' I shouted at intervals. When, finally, it was produced I growled at every entry. I must admit, though, it was really quite light. Only two overseas trips, to the Balkans and, possibly, the Maghreb.

This, I suppose, is a bit of a swizz on the outer office. The great perk attaching to the Minister for Trade's staff is the ability to

---

[1] Lynx was a charity staffed by young volunteers who had visited AC on his appointment as minister for trade, and had found in him a kindred spirit.

accompany him abroad. As I can buy my own airticket anywhere, compulsory overseas trips aren't so much a privilege, more a bore. Paul went everywhere his officials pointed him at. I know better. *'Les absents ont toujours tort.'*

This is the last stretch, isn't it? Or is it? I *should* be made a PC in June, which will allow me to stagger on until the end of the summer hols, 'Government Changes' in September. And then what?

I never want to see Plymouth again. Sometimes I think that all I want is to stay in office here long enough to get my fur legislation on to the statute book. I was looking through some more papers which have come in this morning.

Horrific illustrations. Worst was a great circular crater, some 16-foot in diameter, dug out of the frozen earth (for all around was snow) by a poor badger, just using one hand, as he went round and round and round; caught by a steel jaw on the other leg, chained to a post in the centre, trying (for how long must it have taken him?) to escape, he dug that great pit. Until, finally, he just lay down and died.

There's stacks of stuff about the Inuits, who make their money out of these barbarities and among whom 'the incidence of alcoholism has risen sharply in recent years' (so what?), the likelihood of the fur trade applying for judicial review, the (inevitable) probability of the Foreign Office fussing. Ambassadors (lazy sods, nothing to do) filing whingeing telegrams and so on. Good. Makes me feel I'm doing something really worth while. Fuck them.

Department of Trade and Industry   *Monday, 11 January*

Back fully in harness this morning (fine and crisp – naturally – after a week of wet, moist oozing) and went first to Albany. I turned on fires and radiators, unpacked shirts and meagre provisions. As I rounded the corner into the 'B' staircase I was filled with gloom. Now for months of confinement. The Lent term (as it used to be at Eton) is always the longest of the House sessions. There are no

public holidays to break it up; and it gets dark so early that there is
no escape home at times of light whipping.

The Christmas break was lovely, but only in the last couple of
days did I start to 'feel a little better'. Recovery very limited. I still
get tired, overpoweringly tired. I haven't done Gossie at all, it's too
muddy and slippery. And twice I've felt rather awful for a little
while. It may be psychosomatic, I suppose, it often is. But I've
noted myself just sitting glazedly; too short of energy to do a lot of
things that need doing, and are quite interesting.

I shouldn't be like this at the end of the hols.

Department of Trade and Industry   *Tuesday, 12 January*

I sit wearily in the office. My 'In' tray is high to twice its own depth.
In the mornings, when I am fresh and fast, officials bring me very
little paper. But after five pm and a day of 'meetings' and outside
engagements, the folders flow thick and insistent. I must also finish
the *Spectator* review of Terry Coleman's book.[1] Even so, I am
sticking to my record of never taking boxes home. I will not leave
this desk until the tray is empty; and there is nothing so pleasing as 'I
think I'll lock up now, Minister . . .' and off goes the last one. But
it's never Rose. Why? She could easily stay late if she wanted to.
Perhaps the others prevent her. Most officials are fearful spoilsports.

House of Commons   *Thursday, 14 January*

I lunched in the Members' dining room with G-J and Rhodes
James. RJ relatively amiable; not drunk, though cigaretting might-
ily. Talk was mainly of Willie.[2] Rhodes James claimed already to
have written his obituary, 'not entirely friendly' (I can't imagine

---

[1] *Thatcher's Britain* by Terry Coleman. In accordance with an understanding
between AC and the Cabinet Office, the text was shown to Sir Robin Butler,
who advised against publication.

[2] Lord Whitelaw had suffered a slight stroke attending the carol service in the
Guards Chapel, but was now 'on the mend'.

Robert writing an *entirely* friendly piece about anyone). We swopped anecdotes. Richard[1] joined us for coffee and told the most pleasing. He had approached Willie, late at night, but early in the Parliament and before its full horror was apparent, and asked him what he 'thought of' the Poll Tax.

The great man stopped in his tracks, and glared. His shoulders heaved, went into *rigor*, his face became empurpled and sweat poured down his forehead, cheeks and the end of his nose. He wrestled with some deep impediment of speech; finally burst, spluttering out the single word – 'TROUBLE'. Then he turned on his heel.

Department of Trade and Industry   *Friday, 15 January*

I get on well with the Labour Party. The MPs, that is, not the functionaries who hang about in the corridors, still less those crazy hyped-up 'researchers'. There's that dreadful little tick with curly hair and glasses, four foot six or thereabouts, I've never seen him smile.[2]

Frank Dobson[3] and I swop stories. His are *so* filthy that really they're unusable, even at a rugger club dinner. At the moment we're into 'fuck' eg Question: who said, 'What the fuck was that?' Answer, 'The Mayor of Hiroshima.' Who said, 'Talk about scattered fucking showers'? Answer, Noah, and so on. The fun is to pass notes across the Table during debates. Juvenile. I know who wouldn't like it if he knew – Sir Robert Armstrong.

Last night, while waiting for a division I had a word with Bob Cryer.[4] Speaking as an historian as well as an old mate, I told him Prescott *must* stand.[5] He became very enthused, said Prescott was

---

[1] Richard Ryder, now under-secretary at the Ministry of Agriculture.
[2] Dave Hill, Director of Communications, Labour Party.
[3] Frank Dobson, MP for Holborn and St Pancras since 1979, and shadow Leader of the House.
[4] Bob Cryer, MP for Bradford South since 1987 (Keithley, 1974–83).
[5] The Labour Party had changed the terms of its leadership selection, and it was being considered whether Neil Kinnock should be challenged. John Prescott, MP for Hull East since 1970, was eventually a candidate as Labour leader when Kinnock relinquished the role in 1992.

checking with his Exec Committee, and certainly would. Bob
agreed completely with my analogy with the Tory Party in 1976,
and how we recovered our confidence when Mrs T. gave us a bit
of conviction. The Labour Party is full of 'idealists' (sic), it
depended on ideals. 'That's right,' I said. Stirring.

Department of Trade and Industry   *Tuesday, 19 January*

Little John Moore is in trouble.[1] It's the NHS debate today and the
whole House will turn out, hoping for blood. The poor fellow has
been in bad health (Health Secretary, bad health, etc, etc) and has
been 'on the sick list', ie not around.

At one of the long tables in the tea room people were gloating,
his own colleagues particularly: 'Are you aglow with excitement at
the prospect of actually setting eyes on this legendary figure?' said
Eric Forth.[2] Titters. Someone else, cruelly, 'You may set eyes on
him, but you'll have difficulty hearing him.' The wretched man
has had throat trouble for ages, goes terribly hoarse a couple of
minutes into his speech.

Why is everyone so beastly? John was literally golden. Although
in his forties he has golden kiss-curls like a babyfood ad. He is
athletic, and 'trains'. He did time in the States on some election
trail or other and has an American wife in PR. What-a-team, etc,
etc. Last year, Number 10 were 'letting it be known that' he was
the chosen successor, and his speech (not at all bad really) at
Conference was billed on that basis. I can see that this can arouse
envy and, not that his is scrabbling, *Schadenfreude*. But John has
always been perfectly pleasant to me. Shallow, but amiable. Not
like some of those wankers who are so ambitious they won't even
tell you the time when you ask.

Of course he is mildly of the Right, and has attached himself to
Her. I am told that in Cabinet he echoes her views and then later

---

[1] John Moore, MP for Croydon Central since 1974. Secretary of State for Social
Security since 1986, after spells at Transport and Social Services.
[2] Eric Forth, MP for Mid-Worcestershire since 1983. Parliamentary under-
secretary, Trade and Industry, since 1986.

(or even on the same morning) if she alters her view, echoes that too. This irritates. But if I ask myself why Tristan, and Patten, get so cross about him; why is it said that John Major[1] (outwardly the mildest of men) is reputed to have sworn to 'get' him, I must suppose it is because he is the only possible contender for the leadership of the Party who is outside the 'Blue Chip' club.

That tight little masonic group, so ably managed and convened by Tristan, is determined to monopolise the allocation of higher office, to the exclusion of the Right.

Hounslow Suite, Heathrow   *Friday, 29 January*

I sit here, acid from wine at lunch and weary in my bones and joints. I have been in attendance all day at the French Summit meeting at Lancaster House and then tried, through wet Friday evening traffic, to get to Heathrow in a half hour. I don't think even Joan could have managed it (although I must admit that with her I never actually missed anything). Now I have to wait for nearly two more hours until the next Zurich flight.

I had been looking forward to Davos,[2] and planned that Rose should be 'asked' to accompany me. Predictably, the office thwarted this, although she had coyly agreed. So now I am on my own, flushed and hypochondriacal.

The Summit was interesting, although more for the opportunity that it gave to make personal observations than for any outcome of policy. At the start, The Lady was to greet Mitterand as he came up the steps into the central hall (*not* at the entrance, I was glad to note), and lesser acolytes hung around in the background. I fell into conversation with Douglas. His is a split personality. *A deux* he is delightful; clever, funny, observant, drily cynical. But get him anywhere near 'display mode', particularly if there are officials

---

[1] John Major, Chief Secretary to the Treasury since 1987.
[2] The World Economic Forum, a conference of 'world leaders and opinion formers' convened every year at Davos.

around, and he might as well have a corncob up his arse. Pompous, trite, high-sounding, cautiously guarded.

Douglas said to me how he used to be so excited before these Summits – history in the making, all that – now no longer. I said it was a bad sign. We were getting jaded. Perhaps we ought to get out? I said that I wanted to get out every Monday morning, as I got dressed and shaved. Rather splendidly, he agreed.

Before the Plenary started I had a few words with Michel Noir. As always, attractive, intelligent. A true Gaullist. I agree with him on practically every issue.

Punctually we were seated. Opposite me, [Jacques] Chirac yawned and cigaretted. He is in his prime. Handsome in a fifty-five-ish sort of way, smelling beautiful, but ill-at-ease with *Le President*. Mitterand himself is seventy-one, a pale elderly sage, a BB[1] with balls. And plainly determined to hang on. Winston and Anthony must sometimes have seemed like this, although in Chirac's case the succession is far from assured. But at least he looks fit, while poor Anthony was already sickening in 1952. I did notice, too, that whatever he may think of her, Mitterand's manner with the PM was courteous, and grave. Chirac, on the other hand, lounged and fidgeted and doodled and smirked at his own thoughts.

A faintly absurd 'structural' device had been introduced, at the behest of God knows who, whereby Ministers in Attendance (ie, myself and Noir, Lynda [Chalker] and some little runt from the Sûreté who smelt of garlic and hadn't shaved) should 'present papers' before the summing up.

Naturally, this was a great bore for all concerned. But it did offer scope for The Lady to give one of her little mini-displays of bitchiness and mischief. The order was to be Lynda (as 'Deputy' Foreign Secretary), then the runt from the Sûreté who was going to talk about border control; then Noir, then me. ('I don't think anyone is expecting you to talk for very long, Minister,' ie, the Foreign Office have asked us to keep it snappy.)

---

[1] Bernard Berenson, art historian, connoisseur and sage, who lived in Florence, dying in 1959 aged ninety-four. Always known as BB.

But when the moment came for our contributions, the Prime Minister, who was of course in the Chair, said, 'Minister for Trade.'

Buoyantly I sparkled, noticing high indignation among Lynda's officials. Then came the little Sûreté man, then Michel. All the time Lynda rustled with her notes and made kind of 'ahem' noises. Finally, with every indication of reluctance and distaste, the Prime Minister just said, 'Mrs Chalker.'

How I love her for that kind of reason!

Albany   *Monday, 22 February*

We are just back from a dinner at Number 10 for Cap Weinberger.[1]

Sixty-four guests – but only four Ministers – Howe, Parkinson, Younger[2] and myself. I was high up the table, and this disconcerted a grand lady on my immediate left.

'Why are you here?'

'Because I have been invited.'

'Yes, but why were you invited.'

'That, surely, is a question better addressed to our hostess.'

'Well, I don't see what you are doing here.'

'If you find my presence offensive, then I suggest that you restrict your conversation to the person on your left.'

I turned, ostentatiously, and began to speak to the woman on my right who, fortunately, was 'open'. Nobody pulls rank on me, least of all the dried-up wife of a Permanent Secretary (if that be what she was). We were a mixed bunch. Themes, if one could detect any, were the Falklands, and Anglo-American camaraderie in war. Willie was there, and with him any conversation, however brief, is always a pleasure. I had a word with Charlie Sweeney – now must be the ugliest man in London, bright pink and hairless, though pale eyes still glinting with residual lechery at age seventy-five. I also saw

---

[1] Caspar Weinberger, American Secretary for Defense, 1981–87.
[2] George Younger, MP for Ayr since 1964. Defence secretary since 1986.

Rowse,[1] A.L., shy and benign but with an *appalling* melanoma on his temple.

The Prince of Wales had (apparently) suffered a *mauvais placement*, being put on Cap's right whereas he should, or so the clucksters maintained, have sat at the right hand of the Prime Minister. Lady de Lisle,[2] who is very splendid in many ways but is not, I suspect, a raging fan of the PM, stirred this incipient row primly but firmly.

Charles [Powell], however, was adamant. Tetchily so.

'Of course we checked with his office. I wasn't born yesterday.'

On Monday Charles had asked me to provide some 'possible headings' for the PM's speech of welcome. In fact I wrote the whole thing, from beginning to end, and was delighted that she used most of it. It was the first time that I have heard my own words and phrases from the mouth of another. Cap responded excellently. Started out funny, then moving. I recall the first time I heard him, at a Congressional Committee in Washington in April of 1982, just after the Falklands War began. He was flat, and colourless — though he did let go that most excellent remark, deprecatory and engaging, which I have often myself used since, on inviting questions, 'because then there is a reasonable chance that what I have to say should be of interest to at least one person in the room'.

I was pleased to learn afterwards that he had been touched by what The Lady had said 'and the beautiful language', and had asked for a copy of the text.

Sandling–Charing Cross train   *Wednesday, 24 February*

This morning I was out very early with Tom. A completely blue sky without a single trace of cloud and the grass blades all crisp and

---

[1] A. L. Rowse, Shakespearean scholar and Fellow of All Souls.
[2] Lady de Lisle, second wife of the former Conservative Secretary of State for Air and herself the widow of the 3rd Baron Glanusk.

frosty. We went as far as the lake, which was iced over, but treacherous.

On our return I saw Tom alert and bristling, hackles up, at something in the corner of the 'peppercorn' field where the fence crosses the dyke. Fearing a dead or wounded fox (John often sets a snare at that point, as the fence wire is taut across the water and animals can use the bank to squirm underneath), I walked over with a sinking heart.

It was a badger, still with some life in it. I bellowed at Tom, and he reluctantly followed me, running, back to the house where I telephoned angrily to the farm.

John appeared prompt, but sulky, with one of the Apps boys, and then another. He was carrying a pitchfork with which he tried to pinion the unfortunate creature's neck and head. But the badger was strong still, and dangerous.

'Get some sacks,' I told the boys.

I muffled the badger and he went quiet, knowing I was a friend, while John worked with the wire-cutters.

Once he was released the little Brock squared up to us, bravely and aggressively. Then, when we made no move, bumbled off at a very fair pace toward the old railway line. I hope and believe that he was saved by his rib cage. What is awful is when they worm their way down the noose by exhaling (as foxes, being more intelligent, do) and then tighten it against the lower gut in a final effort to break free.

In spite of my early start this diversion caused me to miss my train, and thus the first of the morning's dreary Meetings with Officials. Good! What are they beside the saving of a beautiful and independent creature of the wild?

Hotel Insulberg, Konstanz   *Saturday, 19 March*

I write this at the conference table – always a good spot for an entry. People think that, assiduously, you are making notes. And the setting is conducive. Universal boredom and a sense of futility make the atmosphere *piano*, sepulchral, almost. This is a *World* (not just EC) Trade Ministers Conference so my next-door neighbour is a little Thai instead of the usual Portuguese mouse. We have been sitting for an hour and a half, and he has smoked seven cigarettes.

Slow and repetitious as are our proceedings in the chamber, they are as nothing to the longeurs of the 'cocktails' and the Reception. I dodged the morning coffee break (far too long) and walked along the Lake front, saying hullo to some feathered friends who quacked and jostled amiably beside the water's edge.

On Thursday evening Bruce [Anderson] told me that he had been in conversation with Wakeham,[1] who had told him, 'She'll have him in the Cabinet if she can.'

And it is true that I am in good favour at the moment. Perhaps because I send her a multitude of little notes and reports, but always through Charles, and I never ask for anything

But my status is precarious, and I fear that I may be heading for an unwelcome passage of arms, because I have now cleared every single hurdle, even the assent of the Secretary of State himself, for my Fur Order. But the Prime Minister watches everything. She has a lot of furriers in Finchley. And she, herself, has I fear very little empathy indeed with the animal kingdom.

Velikiye Tournovo   *Thursday, 14 April*

Today should have been quite agreeable – a motor drive across Bulgaria, some pleasantries on arrival with the Mayor, and a more or less private dinner in a tavern with the rest of the party. But nothing (nothing good, anyway) is as we expect it.

In the early part of the afternoon we drove through acres and acres of rose plantations, not yet in bloom, and they told me that it took three tons of rose petals (Heliogabulus)[2] to make a litre of oil.

---

[1] John Wakeham, now Lord President of the Council, chairman of many cabinet committees and believed to be highly influential within government.
[2] *The Roses of Heliogabulus* by Alma Tadema, a famous Victorian painting depicting the Roman emperor being smothered by, and wallowing in, rose petals.

The interpretrix said that 14 February was St Tristan's day, the patron saint of pruners.

In Britain, I said, you send a card, with a message of endearment, to your loved one, but without signing it. And I reflected on how often I have missed this date, with a particular subject in mind. Why, for example, did I not send one to Rose this year – or last, come to that?

British embassy, Bucharest   *Friday, 15 April*

We changed Jaguars at the Danube bridge and set off through flat, wet country; many horse-drawn vehicles. Just before the frontier a wonderfully ramshackle peasant lorry had rendezvoused with us and the occupants had 'shown' the cane garden furniture which, impetuously, I had ordered in Sofia. I issued a cheque for 270 US dollars – a bargain, if I ever see it again.[1]

On the Danube   *Saturday, 16 April*

This is the river trip to Calstock[2] in spades, with diamonds and oakleaves cluster. Rule of life, learned far too late, most recently at Konstanz is – never 'put in for' boat trips. The tiny, ill-built, thrumming *Riubeni* is conveying us down the Danube canal to the hotel at Sulina at the mouth of the delta. The return journey, tomorrow, will be against the current and slated (sic) to take over eight hours.

A teeny 'sandwich' (cold) has been served, and an 'orange juice' – the thinnest of wartime 'Jacks'[3] orangeade. In an adjoining cabin, the 'lounge', I can hear the Ambassador valiantly holding his own

---

[1] The cane furniture was punctiliously delivered in a Bulgarian lorry to the gates of Saltwood and was installed in the Garden House.

[2] A habitual constituency engagement on the River Tamar which AC used to find particularly irksome.

[3] A tuck shop adjoining the fives courts at Eton.

with the heavily made-up *Romantourist* lady who communicates in bad French.

Yesterday evening, however, was more fun. Dinner at the Athenee-Palace in a lovely 1907 dining room with fine-quality Tiffany glass lights set into the ceiling and a (too modest) Orpen maiden in a blue dress and an oval frame over the fireplace. *Musica* interrupted my desultory conversation, in (on his part, at least) poor French, with Mr Vadura, the State Trade Secretary. The violinist and his band played every tune from the big musical box at Saltwood.

Then some 'local' dancers came bouncing on and performed very merrily in national costume. I 'fixed' the best female, a nicely built blonde. Later, in a 'tableau' of four cloggie-type performers, I spotted that the one in a dog's mask was really a girl – from her slightly smaller size and quicker, neater movements. And sure enough, at the end she threw off the mask and a lovely mane of copper red hair fell out. A good round of applause and Mr Vadura said that he had thought she was a man.

The plump and corrupt 'manager' of the hotel suddenly whipped out a medal and sash, of a *chevalier de fromage* kind, and hung it round my neck. 'Now follow me.' He took me down a narrow spiral staircase directly into the lobby of a *Hullo* nightclub, barking at a couple of (quite good-looking) whores who were sitting on the banquette. HE[1] and the rest of the party were following, I was sorry to see, sheepishly and at a distance.

Live band. From time to time HE would lean over (he was about four places away at our table). 'You don't really need to stay, Minister'; and 'They won't be at all offended if you leave, you know'; and (desperate now) 'We've got a very early start tomorrow morning . . .'

Unusually for me, I had accepted a huge delicious Cuban cigar from the commercial attaché, and wouldn't move until it was finished. But the night was not so comfortable. Very cold indeed and I had to pee twice, once after a nasty dream about Tom being burned in a train.

---

[1] Hugh Arbuthnott, British Ambassador to Romania since 1986.

Aboard the Riubeni   *Sunday, 17 April*

Last night, I lost patience at course 4, a nasty-looking steak, and asked for a jug of boiling water. Somewhere in my night case I had a 'portion' package of delicious Swiss *cacao*, pinched from the hotel in Konstanz for just this emergency, and my plan was to retire immediately, drink it, and have a (relatively) good night. But even this took fifteen minutes to arrive and to my – first pleasure, then annoyance – the task of taking it up to my room, with me, was entrusted to the sweeter of the two little waitresses who, in spite of poor complexion – unmade-up, poor little dear – definitely 'had something'; notably a large bust. But she was, we were, escorted most clumpingly up the wooden staircase by the huge and powerful manager and also by the police spy. So she wouldn't even catch my eye when I thanked her and said goodnight.

Later

The Captain, in spite of having four rings on his sleeve, has made a succession of balls-ups, twice ramming the bank, getting entangled with floating tree-trunks, throwing the little craft into 'hard astern', etc. Revving belchingly, he broke off a lot of willow (destroying, incidentally, our aerial so we are now completely incommunicado). I saved two sprigs in case they could be . transplanted at Saltwood. I will put them straight into the basin in my bedroom at the Embassy, but I fear they will die before I can get them home.[1] I did manage a 'formal' thompson, one ranking for the *extremis* star along with the all time winner – under the trucks at Ascension Island, Wideawake airport. There was no lock on either outer or inner door, and the 'toilet' itself so narrow that, say, Cyril Smith could not have fitted in, much less on, it.

I caught sight of myself in the shaving mirror. Very heavy and jowly I look. I must get out soon, and was cheered by the thought

---

[1] One survived, and is growing on the south bank of the stream flowing through the arboretum at Saltwood.

of the Privy Council list.[1] But of course there's always 'And
yet . . .' This trip illustrates in microcosm. *What* a bore it is having
to meet the local Party Chairman (the same all over the world),
listen to his wooden exposé of the district's 'technical, social and
economic achievements in the co-operative sphere'. Yet how
agreeable to have instant access and treatment.

And so in my life. Lovely to have the time, now I know what to
do with it; sad to discard the trappings.

Department of Trade and Industry   *Wednesday, 27 April*

David Young and I dined together last night at Brooks's. He was
very friendly and confiding. 'You're the only person I can talk
to . . .'

I asked about his little grand-daughter, a few pleasantries, then
moved in.

'David, it's rather earlier in the meal than I had intended, but I
must speak frankly as I have something to say which you may not
find welcome.'

'No, no. Far better speak frankly. I'd much prefer it.'

(I suspect David was thinking that some rebuke might be on the
way. In yesterday's papers he was criticised for not being in the
Lords enough – an obvious plant by Bertie Denham,[2] who docs *not*
find David congenial.)

'Well, the point is approaching when you must start seriously to
turn your mind to the question of whether you should enter the
Commons.'

I could see at once that he was delighted. 'I'm not talking about
the mechanics of it at present. They are not insuperable, if the will
is there.'

We discussed the alternatives. His own 'scenario' had him
moving in September, to take health out of DHSS (the present

---

[1] A recurrent theme of AC's.
[2] Lord Denham, government chief whip, House of Lords, since 1979.

Dept is to be split into two), sort that out, and become Chairman of the Party to win (eh?) the next Election.

His reward – to be Foreign Secretary.

At some point in the *next* Parliament a by-election would be arranged, with the PM's assent. David would then be poised to contest the succession.

I shot this down. Full of flaws. Time-scale too long (at mercy of the unpredictable); uncertainties too prolific – would she consent? Would his 'record' sustain it? Wouldn't it be too obvious that the move was simply in order to pitch at the succession?

I told David that if he was really serious he *had* to have a period in the House of Commons behind him, and experience of one of the great Offices that are open only to Commoners. (Naturally he would like best to be Chancellor.)

David asked me where I would like to 'go' in September. I emulated Lord Halifax, indicated, but did not say, that I was reluctant to move 'sideways'; Trade was the best of the Min of State jobs, and so on. But equally, of course, I had done it long enough. (Foolishly, as I now realise, I did not say that I had to be made a Privy Councillor in June.) I said that I didn't really care, would just as soon go out.

'Oh no. You mustn't do that.' He asked me about Defence.

'I really feel that unless I were made Secretary of State I would find it so frustrating, I couldn't bear it.'

David made various tangential remarks about George Younger[1], his father dying, wouldn't be able to hold his seat in Ayr, and so forth.

I didn't get the point until David said that if I was *in situ* when this happened (as Procurement Minister of State) it would be easier for me to slide upwards.

I tried to backtrack. Earlier, when I had said that I would like Paul's job[2] he had nodded, perhaps *over*fast. But he did say, 'She's got to have you in the Cabinet. She *must*. She's so short of supporters.'

---

[1] George Younger, Secretary of State for Defence.
[2] Paul Channon had been transport secretary since 1987.

Department of Trade and Industry   *Tuesday, 14 June*

We are now poised to put in place my personal *chef d'oeuvre*, the Fur Labelling Order. It has to lie on the table for a month, and then a brief debate in the House, after ten, and if necessary a perfunctory whipped vote on a two-liner. I have devoted enormous energy and time to this measure, and it is a purely personal triumph – over lawyers, Ambassadors, senior civil servants in several Departments including my own; eskimos, furriers, 'small shopkeepers' – they have all been in and alternately (sometimes simultaneously) threatened and cajoled.

But yesterday, sinisterly, Charles rang from Number 10 to say that the PM 'would like a word' on the subject, could I come to her room in the House after Questions?

H'm. Could be bad.

Later – House of Commons
Charles was waiting behind the Chair, to catch me before I went in, a bad sign. He tried to soften me up.

'The Prime Minister really wants to drop the whole thing.'

'Not a chance, I'm afraid.'

'She's very worried about the effect on these local native communities of their livelihood being destroyed.'

'That's all balls.'

'Apparently Carol has just come back from there with heartrending stories.'

'She's just been conned.'

'The Prime Minister would like you first to go out to Canada and see for yourself.'

'Sure, I can do that. But it won't make the slightest difference.'

'No, but the Prime Minister's idea is that this would allow you to come back and say that you had seen for yourself and that you were not going to proceed.'

'Forget it.'

'You know that she herself is visiting Canada shortly?'

Of course! She could probably have resisted the Finchley

furriers. But that blasted High Commissioner in Ottawa was winding her up with predictions of demos, placards, bad atmosphere, 'attention diverted from principal objectives of the visit', I could see it all.

'Let's go in.'

Hamilton[1] was there, on an upright chair. The PM and I sat opposite each other on those yellow damask sofas in the 'L' of the room.

'Alan, how are you?'

I ignored this. 'I'm so sorry that you should be getting all this trouble from the Canadians.'

'Oh it's not really *trouble*. I think there's more to it.'

This was going to be very difficult. She had a letter from Mulroney; from Resource International (I remember being warned about the clout they carried); she was going to address the Canadian Parliament. As the Prime Minister developed her case she, as it were, auto-fed her own indignation. It was a prototypical example of an argument with a woman – no rational sequence, associative, lateral thinking, jumping rails the whole time.

'Why not labelling of battery hens, of veal who never see daylight, of fish which had a hook in their mouth – what about foxes? Do you hunt?'

'Certainly not. Nor do I allow it on my land. And as for veal, I'm a vegetarian.'

'What about your shoes?'

I ignored this the first time. The second time I said, 'I don't think you would want your Ministers to wear plastic shoes.'

CP and Hamilton smiled. She did *not*.

Too far gone in indignation now, she just said something about the feet breathing better in leather.

'It's not you, Alan. It's so unlike you to respond to pressure.'

'I'm not "responding" to pressure. I'm *generating* it. I believe in it.'

Off we went again. Her sheer energy, and the speed with which

---

[1] Archie Hamilton succeeded Michael Alison as PPS to the prime minister in 1987.

she moves around the ring, make her a very difficult opponent.
There was talk of wolves around the house.

'How would you like that?'

'I'd love it.'

Her argument, if such a confused, inconsequential but ardent
gabbling can be dignified by that Aristotelian term, was 'it's-all-
very-well-for-suburban-bourgeoisie-to-inflict-this-legislation-
but-what-about-the-noble-savage?' I was prepared to respond on a
philosophical plane. I said something-something about it being
'the first step'.

This was a mistake. She grittily repeated the phrase to herself
several times, half under her breath, '—the first step?'

'In enlarging man's sense of responsibility towards the animal
kingdom.'

She shifted ground again. Didn't like labelling orders, weren't
we trying to move away from all that?

After four and a half minutes of this I realised I'd lost.

The meeting, scheduled for fifteen minutes, went on for forty-
five.

About three-quarters of the way through I said, 'Well, if that's
what you want, I will obey you.'

Later I said, 'When you go to Canada, don't have anything to
do with that "Humane Trapping Committee". It's a put-up job,
you'll just make a fool of yourself. They'll think they've conned
you.'

She grunted assent.

'I hate quarrelling with you, Alan.'

I snarled, 'I wouldn't do it for anyone else', and went out of the
door.

Later – Department of Trade and Industry

A few minutes ago Charles rang. The PM was anxious to try and
help me 'out' of this. No note had been taken of the meeting. (All
that means, of course, is that the note which *was* taken will not be
circulated.)

'I won't land her in it' (thinking of all those nice sincere young
people in Lynx whom I was letting down).

No no, of course not, it wasn't that, she just wanted to see if she/we could help at all. Charles suggested that the order did still go on up to OD (E)[1] and that he would put up the Attorney and the Foreign Secretary to co-ordinate a very strong expression of legal opinion that would stop it in his tracks.

I like Charles. But *au fond* he is an apparatchik, although one of superlative quality. But my relations with The Lady are damaged – perhaps beyond repair.

Should I preempt? It would be the first time that a Minister will ever have resigned on an issue concerning the welfare of creatures that don't have a vote.

I rang Jane and she was wise and calming, though sad. Said, don't do anything hasty.

Albany   *Wednesday, 15 June*

I rose at four am and made tea. The House has been sitting all night and, I am assured, will 'lose' today's business. A small stroke of luck as I am First for Questions this afternoon. A delicious sense of benefice – an unused day! I think I will go down to Saltwood, take breakfast there, and tackle estate papers.

But the oppression of yesterday's defeat is unresolved. I woke just after two, lay unhappily thrashing until four. Why had I woken so early? What was that waiting to come through the sub-conscious? The brain scans for seconds (it seems longer) then all the weight of those as yet unanswered letters, hundreds of them, of praise and encouragement; the thought that at this very moment animals are being caught in the wild; all the pain and despair on which their exploitation depends, I felt utterly dejected. I felt rage, too, at the PM having so totally swallowed the commercial lobby's case. Who has been feeding her all that stuff?

When the cock blackbird started up, on the dot of four, I put my head out of the window, the better to listen to him. So

---

[1] OD (E): the cabinet committee whose responsibility it would be to consider this topic.

clear and beautiful, as he went through his whole repertoire, he passed to me a lovely message of Nature's strength, her powers of continuity and renewal.

And I drew some small consolation from this.

Nature's timescale is so different from ours.

House of Commons terrace, evening   *Tuesday, 28 June*

It is humid. Warm but with a very light drizzle. I haven't sat out here to make a diary note for many years. The river boats going back and forth, always with some drunks, who jeer; the smells and breezes still, after forty-three years, evocative of 'Rafts'.[1] It is so hateful being stuck in the House during the summer months. (I must have written this a hundred, two hundred, times.)

As I left Saltwood this morning I said to Jane, the days are getting shorter again. One barely notices it at first but I believe myself at this point to start getting older and stiffer and sleepier, like the peacocks loosing their tail feathers. Whereas in the happy months of April and May, as the light lengthens, I am goat-like, and scrawnily boyish.

My Private Office are hopelessly incompetent. I had a bad brief for the ECGD[2] meeting. And they themselves are being timid and useless over the text of the press release. This should by hyping the extra billion which I have finally secured for special 'national interest' cover in defence equipment contracts. But there comes a point when officials suddenly lose their balls, become nervous of the Public Accounts Committee, or the National Audit Office.

However dear John Major very nobly allowed me to appeal directly to him, and overruled his own officials who had forbidden me (through *my* officials) to use the word 'extra'. This would of course have robbed the announcement of any impact at all, thus achieving what the civil servants wanted, as they can't bear

---

[1] The rafts and sheds on the Thames at Windsor used by the Eton rowing teams, or 'wet bobs'.

[2] ECGD: Export Credit Guarantee Department.

Ministers making announcements on any topic unless the ideas originated with them. I often think that in their ideal world the 'Line to Take' is prepared before the policy concept itself. No programme, but *none* is so true to life as *Yes, Minister*.

At eleven o'clock I left the Department for Aldershot, where the MoD has sponsored an arms sales 'exhibition'. I travelled down by car. Beside me on the back seat (I never like this but could hardly say 'sit in front, please', as I had never set eyes on him before) slumped a totally useless senior official who didn't know the name of any weapon, the calibre of any gun, the size or specification of *anything*, it seemed. Said he'd 'only been in the job six months'. Really! Six *hours* should have been enough for him to answer some of my queries.

I did a tour of the stands with the official following at my heels muttering to himself. I made all the running. Weapons are one of our best exports. If I ever get to the MoD I'd be able to do a lot more. But the whole subject is blighted, in policy terms, by input from three separate Departments, DTI, MoD and Foreign Office.

At lunch I sat between Prince Michael of Kent and Frank Cooper,[1] the Prince in his ludicrous high collar and 'stock' like a cravat. He warmed to my talking about the Mille Miglia.[2] Anyone who has driven a DBR 1 in that ordeal can't be wholly without interest.

Frank was fascinating. He told me that at some conference in 1977, when she was still only (just) leader of the Opposition, the PM had turned to him and said, 'Must I do all this international stuff?' 'You can't avoid it,' was his reply, and she pulled a face. Frank says she remains a Little Englander through and through. I'm not so sure. I think she now relishes the role of statesman. Who wouldn't, after all, prefer the motorcade to being shouted at twice a week by little Kinnock. Frank said that during that period she and he had met Reagan and Carter, and she was *astonished* at how stupid they were. 'Can they really dispose of all that power?' etc.

---

[1] Sir Frank Cooper, retired civil servant. Permanent Under-Secretary, Ministry of Defence, 1976–82.

[2] A race over public roads in Italy, restricted since 1958 to 'classic' cars.

Some interesting vignettes about the Falklands. That first Friday evening FC was dining with John Clark and Alistair Frame.[1] The phone rang before they could sit down, and he was called at once to the Prime Minister's room in the Commons. Henry Leach[2] (*not* in uniform, incidentally, that story is a myth) was the only Chief of Staff available.

Leach made a quiet, confident, measured presentation of how he could deploy the fleet. No one, curiously (and in retrospect fortunately) mentioned air cover at that time. Foreign Office officials cowered in a corner, sulky and apprehensive, but quiet. The Army were 'useless, couldn't take it seriously'. The RAF were slow to wake up, then panicked at the idea that the Navy would get all the credit, started moving on flight refuelling, insisted on deploying *their* Harriers for ground attack, etc.

Frank said that at one point there was a school recommending that *all* the Commanders be changed, including Woodward![3]

Department of Trade and Industry   *Tuesday, 19 July*

Tedious day. To the Arab-British Chamber of Commerce exhibition. Like an old cavalry horse, I dozed on the hoof as I went round the stands. The Prince of Wales 'opened' it. He has a strong handshake, like all polo players, but is pretty useless, I judge. Trite, tinky sentiments, prissily delivered. During his speech I dropped off into a mildly erotic dream. I am tired and nonno-ish, and my stubble is going grey – *why?*

Department of Trade and Industry   *Thursday, 21 July*

I was in today before eight. By six I was completely exhausted, but still thought I might look in on Stephen's goodbye party, on the

---

[1] Sir John Clark, chairman of Plessey, and Sir Alistair Frame, chairman of RTZ.

[2] Admiral of the Fleet Sir Henry Leach, Chief of the Naval Staff and First Sea Lord.

[3] Admiral Sir John (Sandy) Woodward was Senior Task Group Commander, South Atlantic, during the Falklands campaign, April–July 1982.

off-chance of setting eyes on any of the girls I fancy. There was a fattish blonde whose name I don't know but she once said, or sang, 'there's someone following me . . .' when I was behind her, and admiring her dimensions, in the lift lobby – but no favourites.

However S of S was present and in ebullient form. We left together and he asked me back to his room. He said he'd had a 'good talk' with The Lady that very afternoon, and recommended me for Defence (at what rank? I didn't have the courage to ask). He said she had 'not reacted badly'. I was elated. David then said that I should try and get to see her in August 'when there is nothing much going on'. I said, 'But one should never argue one's own case. It's always counter-productive.' Oops! He wanted me to argue *his* case (!). He wants to go to Health, zap it before he becomes Chairman.

So I'm none the wiser. I don't know whether he *really* pushed my case, or whether she *really* reacted favourably, or whether he was saying all that in order to get me to boost *him*. Gossip and tittle-tattle in our game is only very rarely pure invention. The skill lies in objective interpretation.

Only two hours earlier I had been feeling appalling. Now, effervescent with glee and anticipation, I shot round to Brooks's and my dice sparkled. I took £500 off Nick Blackwell and we all crossed the road to dine at Boodles. Delicious claret, and Michael Stoop told several good stories – poignant was his recollection of a beautiful Belgian lady, a Madame Charlier, forty-two years old when as a subaltern in Rhine Army, he loved her after the war. Her body, 'and what we used to do' he recalled perfectly. Forty years later, eighty-two and unrecognisable, she hailed him at a restaurant in Brussels. 'She,' I said, 'who was once the helmet-maker's beautiful wife.'[1]

Department of Trade and Industry   *Monday, 25 July*

This morning I was tranquil. Little work pressing, and my office is full of flowers which Jane has sent up from Saltwood and which, queenly old sommelier, I took time and pleasure arranging.

---

[1] The title of a sculpture of a very old woman by Auguste Rodin.

I thought I might get G-J to dine with me at the Beefsteak (in the summer that long table with the bay window at the end is so much more congenial than Pratts. Pratts is more of a winter burrow).

'Yes,' he said. 'And we can talk about the reshuffle.'

Got the point a bit too obviously, I thought, but never mind.

Some twenty minutes later I wandered into the outer office – Rose is looking so gorgeous in her yellow dress that, on one excuse or another, I have put my head round the door about six times already – and there on her desk was the early edition of the *Standard* – RESHUFFLE IN PROGRESS. 20 CHANGES.

I knew of course that I was safe, but I was annoyed at its suddenness and disappointed at being passed over. I sat brooding for a few minutes, and was then interrupted by a summons to go round to the Secretary of State immediately.

David was a *husk*. Hadn't been consulted, hadn't even been warned. Wicks (as always somewhat off-hand) had simply rung to say the 'the name' was Newton.[1] I said that John Nott[2] told me he had absolutely no choice in who his junior Ministers were, and it was very unusual for a Secretary of State to be consulted.

But David was shattered – 'not even the courtesy of . . .', then stopped himself. His hands shook, his blue eyes were watery. He sees the writing on the wall – a drastic diminution of his own influence.

Clutching at straws I said that 'the big one' (ie affecting the Cabinet) could be later. But no, Wicks had squashed that too. Nothing until 1989. Just another year to go through while we all grow older and the young Turks, Patten J., Patten C., Waldegrave,[3] glint and glister.

I tried to extract some comfort from the situation by saying, 'The Nigel thing isn't finished yet . . .'

David agreed. And it is true. But what use will that be? And

---

[1] Tony Newton, minister for health, had been made Chancellor of the Duchy of Lancaster and a minister of state in Trade and Industry.

[2] After his resignation as defence secretary in 1983, John Nott left Parliament and became chairman of the merchant bankers Lazard Brothers.

[3] William Waldegrave, MP for Bristol West since 1979.

who is she talking to? Not Wakeham; not Cecil; not repeat not, DY. Waddington?[1] But that's mechanistic only. Willie? Possibly. He was in London last night.

I drifted over to the House. Francis Maude[2] was already there and we sat at the stationery table in the Aye lobby. Francis was tearful.

'I thought that at least I might have some recognition for all my work in the Financial Services field.'

Francis said that he had a brief meeting with David immediately after me. That he told David to remind Newton that he was only a Minister of State who happened to have a place at the Cabinet table.

DY, apparently, said that he would. But of course he won't, he's too shell-shocked. *Meni Meni Tekel Upharsin.*

Anyway, Newton is quite harmless, not a threat to anybody.

Tristan turned up at the Beefsteak. I thought it more tactful to talk about him – why had he not accepted (sic) a ministerial post? He had to work in Government in order to qualify as Chief Whip in the next Parliament, surely?

Tristan waffled around. I got the impression that he, too, had been somewhat taken by surprise.

He was not optimistic, in the wider sense. Tristan is over-poweringly Europhile, and (as with his opponents in the Party) the subject becomes obsessive, and towers above all others. Great bore. The subject of 'Europe' is almost, though not quite, as bad as Ireland must have been at the turn of the century – and still is for some poor souls, like dear IG. Tristan said that 'confrontation' in Cabinet (what did this mean?) was inevitable 'one way or another'.

But when I ask him what he means he just bites his lip and nods his head, makes elliptic remarks like 'You'll see' and 'Just you wait'. In the end, he said, the Prime Minister will find herself isolated by her three 'heavies' – Howe, Hurd and Lawson – and in a crisis Brittan would go native at once, and add to her troubles.

---

[1] David Waddington, MP for Ribble Valley since 1983. Chief whip.
[2] Francis Maude, currently Minister of State for Europe.

I changed the subject, and urged that Nick Soames be appointed to one of the vacancies at the Whips' Office. Tristan said that Nicholas didn't want it. His life was very complicated at the moment. Great mistake.

After dinner I told Jane and she said no, no, you must get hold of Nick and tell him not to be an ass.

I had to speak to him that evening, which wasn't easy. He was 'with the Prince of Wales'. But the Downing Street switchboard were magnificent, as always, and located him *via* Clarence House at the US Residence in Regent's Park, and got him away from the Ambassador's dining table.

Nick was sweet, effusive – but adamant. I told him that it's very difficult to make progress as a Minister unless (thinking ruefully of myself) you have done a stint as a Whip. He simply must grit his teeth. But he is worried about looking after his baby son. A good fellow.

Albany   *Monday, 12 September*

I have come from dinner with Richard Ryder at Pratts. He's such fun. So intelligent, and has the right views on practically every topic. But he does repeat himself which, in someone his age, is a bad sign. Or at least it is if he doesn't know he's doing it. Yet some of his stories are so stylised that, Homeric, they depend on and are embellished by repetition. I've lost count of the number of times I've been told the story of Julian Amery on the (recent) parliamentary delegation to Rumania asking about Count Dracula and, after some inter-consultation between the guides, being told that 'Count Dracula is being reassessed'.

But of all Richard's stories I think my favourite, and one he tells with great panache, is a Battle of Britain folk epic which delights me however often I hear it. He and Douglas Bader were debating on opposite sides at a classy girls' school. Somehow, Bader got involved in telling of one of the occasions when he was shot down over the Channel:

'. . . And my engine was on fire, I had two of the fuckers on my tail, one fucker was coming up at me from the left, and there were two more fuckers about a hundred feet above me waiting for . . .' (At this the headmistress panicked and interrupted. 'Girls, as of course you all know, there was a type of German aeroplane called the FOKKER.') But Bader: 'I don't know about that. All I can tell you is these chaps were flying Messerschmitts.'

Department of Trade and Industry   *Wednesday, 14 September*

Last night I walked back from the 'Kundan'.[1] The previous evening I had walked from the Department to Albany. There was a mass of starlings in St James's Park, chattering and jostling as they turned in for the night. I always like going past Clive Steps, especially in the evening when there are few people around, and I conjure up images from 1938; the great Foreign Office crises, Halifax and Cadogan walking anxiously in the Park.

As my legs stretched I still had an appetite for more. But how long will this last – five days or so? All too soon one is back in the debilitating routine, slumping on the back seat of the Jaguar even to make the journey from the Department to the House of Commons.

I have a bundle of interesting papers to read this evening. The Lady is going to make a speech at Bruges on the occasion of some Euro-anniversary or other. The Eurocreeps have written for her a really loathsome text, *wallowing* in rejection of our own national identity, which has come up to me for comment in the trade context. They even managed to delete a ritual obeisance to Churchill, his ideals, all that and substituted the name of *Schuman*. Really!

I hardly know where to start in pulling it to pieces, but Charles, too, is having a go. We must win this one.

---

[1] Kundan, the curry restaurant in Horseferry Road.

Saltwood   *Friday, 16 September*

Yesterday morning I felt vaguely, non-specifically ill; but cheered up when Jane arrived and we went over to Lancaster House for a lunch for the Prime Minister of Malta.

The PM made a *point* of seeking me out in the pre-drinks throng before the meal. She thanked me for my help, said she was going to press ahead with the Bruges notes virtually unchanged, in spite of FCO complaints. (I had earlier seen the revised, third version, and was glad to note that it hadn't altered, at all, from the second.) 'You and I agree on this, but Douglas Hurd is completely committed.'

'Bugger Douglas Hurd,' I said. 'He's only the Home Secretary.'

She looked away with that lovely, distant smile she puts on when I 'go too far'.

A pleasing encounter. Fortified, I told a fabulous little blonde waitress, whom I have never seen before at Lancaster House, 'You're incredibly good-looking' as I went into the dining room, and took pleasure from watching to see how long it took for her blush (or flush) to die away.

I sat next to the Maltese High Commissioner, Manduca. A good Anglophile. I hope he's being properly treated. On my right was Carla Powell,[1] and on *her* right sat Rocco Forte.[2] Carla is always so full of life: 'Look at me, what fun to be sitting between two such handsome men, da da da, etc.' But as far as Rocco was concerned she somewhat spoilt the effect by pronouncing 'Rrrocco' repeatedly in an accent that my dear Mama would have categorised as *proprio siciliano*. This had the effect of making Rocco *chétif* and ill-at-ease, as clearly he would prefer to be considered, in this setting at any rate, as an English gentleman.

Carla told me that Charles was *not* leaving immediately, but they were terribly short of money, having to borrow against the

[1] Carla Powell, wife of Charles Powell, private secretary to the prime minister, 1983–91.

[2] Rocco Forte had risen in the eponymous restaurant and hotel chain founded by his father, Lord (Charles) Forte, whom he was to succeed as chairman in 1992.

little house in the *Laghi* which had been left to her by her father.
He didn't want an Embassy, not unless a real cracker (by which I
inferred Paris or Washington), would really rather go straight into
the City. I will try and talk to Hanson, or David Alliance.[1] Some
weeks ago, when I mentioned this problem to Jimmy [Goldsmith],
he said, 'That man is so important he really ought to be paid
£200,000 a year just to stay where he is.' Yes, of course. But
Jimmy is not always reliable, although his judgements are seldom
wrong.

As the lunch broke up I had a quick word with Charles.
Practically every suggestion that the Foreign Office have made[2]
has been rejected. Charles is in a difficult position personally, I can
see that. But he is resisting his own Mandarinate without flinching.

Department of Trade and Industry   *Monday, 19 September*

An incredible autumn morning, still and hazy. At seven or thereabouts, before going to the station, I walked the dogs over the
Seeds.[3] All the fields are yellow with corn stubble, but in the valley
the trees are dark, dark green; in that last cycle before they start to
shed their leaves.

I am filled with gloom at the thought of having to go through it
all again for yet another year. I am often mindful of that passage in
the Moran diaries when Churchill is complaining of certain
degenerative symptoms – 'Why can't you do something about
them?' and Moran tells him, 'You were born with the most
wonderful physical endowment. But now you have spent it,
every last penny.'

I have appointed a new secretary, as Peta is leaving to get
married. Tedious. Her name is Alison Young. She was not Peta's
preferred candidate, but at the interview she showed spirit. I noted
that her hair was wet, for some reason, although it was a fine day.

---

[1] Sir David Alliance, chairman of Coats Patons.
[2] For the text of the Bruges speech.
[3] A 40-acre field at Saltwood home farm.

Saltwood   *Sunday, 2 October*

The place if full of Phillips' employees, doing an inventory. They shuffle about amiably, opening cupboards and chests, peeping and poking. I'm amazed at how ignorant they are. I mean some of them have specialised knowledge, of course, which I can't match on porcelain or silver or 'gems'. But most of them give the impression of learning as they go along. There's that mysterious greenish picture that hangs over the fireplace in the red study; the man from the Getty (I can't remember his name and he's been sacked since coming here) said it was a Bellini; v. unlikely, I feel, but it is important. The 'paintings expert' looked at it for a bit, literally scratching his head, finally said to Jane, 'Did Lord Clark ever meet Bernard Berenson?'[1]

So different from real enthusiasts like Peter Wilson, or Byam Shaw. Something would catch their eye and they would look at it for ages, and really love it. What was it worth? Oh nothing really, two or three hundred pounds, but that didn't matter, the point is they *loved* it.

No one's got into the keep before, and I'm only doing this at the behest of the Revenue. With a bit of luck some of Phillips's definitions will be sufficiently imprecise as to be untraceable.

Another thing that irritates me is that they are all *men*. Why no birds? I know that the atmosphere at Saltwood, creepy passages and little chambers and casement windows, can have a mildly aphro-disiac effect on female visitors. Once I've separated the girl from her group she gets alarmed, which is fun. They breathe faster, talk nineteen to the dozen, keep changing the subject. (I fear that if I'd come from 'an underprivileged background' I'd probably by now have done time for GBH, or assault, or even what Nanny calls *the other*.)

Damn. Bruce is coming down for a chat over lunch.

---

[1] Lord Clark worked under Berenson in Florence for three years after leaving Oxford. They remained close friends and colleagues for the next fifty years.

Sunday evening

We opened a bottle of Palmer '61. Bruce laid down the law on personalities, and *ratings*. My own shares are badly down after that slip on the Channel Tunnel. She was not going to keep Paul on. Bernard had the briefing to hand. Then at the last minute Paul was reprieved. At the time, and since, I felt that that was my last real chance to get into the Cabinet. And at lunch Bruce made things worse by telling me that the next Transport Minister would be Lynda.[1] How does he know? He can't know. And yet I still believe him.

Bruce was dismissive about Tristan: 'not up to it'; and Gow 'can't get a grip on things'. I don't like this. These are my friends, I mean my close friends. Then he made matters worse by saying that he had had a talk with Michael. 'He is formidable. He' – pause – 'is' – pause – 'formidable.'

These lovely autumn days . . . Dear God, please spare me for at least one complete season on my own, enjoying freedom. The Philosopher Prince, adding to the store of human knowledge.

Albany   *Monday, 17 October*

Today the Anglo-Italian Summit, in Maggiore.

I rose early and confident. But Dave *lost the way* in light fog. We had to enter Heathrow by a special security gate on the north side of the perimeter that gave direct access onto the tarmac. Like all the lower classes, he went to pieces quickly and sat rigid at the wheel, slightly leaning forward, squinting into the fog, being overtaken by vans on either side. Too flush-faced to admit that he'd 'done wrong', he would neither turn round, nor even stop to get his bearings.

I was fidgety. I am only too well aware that as a Minister of State I attend these summits only at The Lady's whim. As far as Hurd, Howe, Lawson, *et al* are concerned it's very much on sufferance:

[1] Chalker. In fact it was to be Cecil Parkinson.

'We seem to be waiting for Alan . . .' From time to time I uttered peremptory instructions and we would backtrack through sleepy suburban crescents distant, it seemed, from the airport. Paperboys with orange *Guardian* satchels.

Finally, with only seven minutes to spare, we found ourselves at the familiar Spelthorne entrance. I leaped out and asked for directions. Naturally, it was a gate some distance along the perimeter which I had already suggested. It was apparent that we were only milliseconds ahead of the PM. Frantic policemen holding Uzi's waved us on, on . . . Air Marshals covered in gilt and stripes saluted. Whumpf! I alighted in my seat. Hurd and Younger were opposite in the adjoining foursome bay. Before I could fasten my belt – for The Lady had followed directly on my heels – the engines screamed and we were off. No nonsense about waiting for the tower.

At Malpensa a large, but somewhat scruffy, guard of honour was lined up. Would they play God Save the Queen? Always a source of mischievous pleasure. And yes, they played it. I put on my raybans and walked over to where the helicopters were waiting. Douglas Hurd and I boarded a Bell 212. The Home Secretary, next to me, was nervous and thrummed his fingers. Sadismoidly I drew his attention to an adhesive notice in red just above my window: '*Sling load not to exceed 400 lbs until next* (sic) *overhaul*'. 'It's the word "next" I don't like,' I said. The Home Secretary licked his lips but didn't answer.

On the return flight in the VC 10 the PM invited me to sit at her table with Hurd and Geoffrey Howe. She was fussed about Barlow Clowes.[1] Should we bail out the 'investors'? Yes, I said. They were greedy, but small. It's the *big* greedy ones who should be punished, like that slob Clowes himself. I took the opportunity to warn her about Jaguar[2] being in jeopardy, which she didn't like. But what can we do? We just don't have the industrial or financial firepower any longer. But I was interested and gratified to hear her

---

[1] A financial 'bucket shop' offering very high rates of interest that had just gone bust, stranding hundreds of depositors.

[2] Sir John Egan, managing director of Jaguar Cars, had told AC that Ford of America were buying Jaguar shares systematically and threatening a takeover.

pass a comment showing that she had read *The Audit of War*.[1] She
only drank orange juice.

After a bit Geoffrey Howe started getting restive. No one had
addressed a word to him. He heaved himself past me, saying that he
was going to change into a black tie. 'Good,' I said. 'Then you can
serve us all drinks.' He pretended not to have heard, but when he
came back, 'Two large gin and tonics, please, and Prime Minister,
the maître d'hôtel is here and wants to know what you're going to
have?' She didn't say anything, but grinned engagingly.

Department of Trade and Industry   *Tuesday, 20 December*

Last night I went down to Highgrove.

Late, of course, and the position not helped by Dave getting
into one of his M-way trances and slowly, oh-so-slowly (sic),
slowing down – from 80 to 75 to 70 to 68 to 62 – then I say,
'Why are we going so slowly? The road's completely clear.' And
he lurches forward and attaches himself to the tail (to the *tail*) of
whatever is the next vehicle, preferably a TIR lorry, which he
catches up.

As we covered the A429 from Malmesbury to Tetbury, past the
house where little Sir John Rothenstein[2] took refuge in the early
months of the war, and then the corner where I abandoned the
Ford V8 drophead, as a child terrified of fire when Newy[3] had left
the cigarette lighter stuck in (a good early example of *cigarettes'
dyslexia*) and it was smouldering – I thought, that *was* a long time
ago, fifty years.[4] And now I'm a Minister of State, going to a
private dinner with the Prince of Wales. George VI was on the
throne then, and Charles didn't exist. It was 'the little princesses'.

I was the last to arrive, and the Prince had already 'joined the
other guests' (in spite of the pretended informality we had all been

---

[1] By Correlli Barnett.
[2] Sir John Rothenstein, at that time director of the Tate Gallery.
[3] A governess who looked after AC and his siblings as children.
[4] During the early years of the war the Clarks were living at Upton House,
   Tetbury.

issued with a meticulously timed programme. Guests were advised to arrive between 7.45 and 8 pm. From 8 to 8.15 they would talk quietly among themselves; at 8.15 they were to be joined by the Prince, etc, etc, all the way through the evening).

I looked about. Chintzes, Edwardian furniture of good quality, masses of photographs of 'The Firm', as they somewhat affectedly style themselves. A few big maritime watercolours of a Wyllie-ish kind, and some washier ones that may have been by the Royal hand. No ivories, snuff-boxes, miniatures, objets d'art of any significance. Why not? Royalty have amassed these huge collections, by presentation and acquisitiveness, over the last two hundred years. Where is it all? In vaults, I suppose. Sometimes shown under glass to a dullard public procession. 'The Queen's treasures on view', all that. But this bourgeois unease in only two generations old. Edward VII had a kind of Farouk-like taste, and George V, as I know from my father, had a good knowledge of his drawings, and where they all were.

I had a few words with the Prince. Banal subjects. At one point a pleasing pup materialised, smooth-coated and self-assured, and with a Coster tail[1] and HRH told me that it was a Jack Russell that hadn't been 'docked'.

The purpose of the dinner was to bring together a few favoured 'Captains of Industry', the Secretary of State for Education and Science (Kenneth Baker[2] was in the room, with his Cheshire-cat grin, glinting glossily) and the Minister for Trade, and discuss what could be done to remedy the almost universal inability of British managers effectively to communicate in any language other than English (and not very well even in that).

An important subject. And certainly worth a high-level committee, *provided* it had the power to see its recommendations through. But the trouble that affects all attempts by Royalty to 'inform' themselves is that the other participants are mainly, no, solely interested in scoring goodboy points and ingratiating

---

[1] The name of a dog belonging to Juliet Frossard, one of AC's personal secretaries, whose tail curled round like a whiting.

[2] Kenneth Baker, MP for Mole Valley since 1983 (Acton, 1968–70, St Marylebone, 1970–83). Education secretary since 1986.

themselves with the Royal Chair. Whatever for, one is tempted to ask. They certainly wouldn't bother if they knew how the Honours system actually operates.

Prince Charles has a nice voice, as I have often noted in the past. Distinctive, and every word beautifully clear. But he has a certain unhappy searching style of manner and expression, rather like his father, though less aggressive. At one point during the meal he hit the table, not authoritatively, but petulantly. '*Why* can't something be done? . . . We've got to do something . . .'

I was a long way off. As far, indeed, as I could be. At the opposite end of the table, facing the Prince but heavily covered by a row of cut-glass vases containing (quite prettily arranged) flowers or blooms. Very little drink. Nameless uniformed minions did not refill guests' glasses. Periodically they tried to deflect the Royal Russell and shoo him back through the baize door. But he was equal to this, and weaved his way around under the table. Furtively I fed him titbits.

With the (unbelievably minuscule glasses of) port, the main subject was addressed. Each visitor in turn was invited to make a contribution. In the main, it was auditioning for the All England Local Government Officials' Triteness (Bronze Star) Award. I came late. I tried to sparkle.

'Japan is already the most powerful country in the world. In 1943 she had learned the lesson that military power is a function of industrial power, and vowed to overcome this. Now already she has. Don't be misled by the fact that Japan doesn't make weapons. She could go on to a war footing in six months, produce missiles that would make the US versions look like muzzle-loaders.

'In thirty years' time, although English will be the *lingua franca*, Japan's dominance will mean that English will be no more than the language of the global peasantry. The tongue – *and the calligraphy* – of the Elite will be Japanese.'

The businessmen glowered at me through the cigar smoke. HRH looked uneasy. Only dear Kenneth's smile remained benignly in place.

And the Prince was distant to me when he bade me farewell. But I was glad to see toys and general disorder in the porch.

On the way back Dave (inevitably) 'came over queer' and I had to take the wheel. When I told Cranley [Onslow], he said next time I should simply accelerate away and leave him on the verge.

All I got out of the whole experience was a pleasing demonstration of what happens when you don't dock a Russell puppy's tail.

Department of Trade and Industry   *Wednesday, 25 January*

I long for July. Today I flagged the last week of that month in my engagement diary with a yellow marker, *Enfin la clef des champs*.[1]

I am visiting Plymouth a lot at present. Alison comes with me, and we do the constituency correspondence on the train. She is more efficient than Peta, and more fun to be with. Her eyes are blue-grey.

Saltwood   *Saturday, 4 March*

Tristan has been trying to get hold of me.

He told me that Bruce Anderson had come in the previous evening, slumped down in a chair, and said, 'I think Clark is a sell.' Elaborated.

Earlier – not much earlier – BA had in fact telephoned to me, said he was depressed about my prospects but 'the shares are down, but they are undervalued. A buy at this level.'

Politics. How I adore it.

★ ★ ★

On the early morning of 13 March, AC left for an unofficial visit to the Maghreb. Some of the luggage, including the case containing his notebook, was mislaid and his first entry for the period is subsumed in a letter to Jane dated that evening.

---

[1] Verlaine.

British embassy (the Villa Dar al Ayoun), Tunis

Monday, 13 March

Hello Lovey!

This is the most interesting building, quite grandly laid out –
like a Moorish Gloria, with all the walls tiled (as well as the floors)
and many old-fashioned fixtures-and-fittings. Given to Queen
Victoria the Bey in 1850, it was Alexander's HQ after the German
surrender in 1943 and Macmillan lived, as resident Minister, in the
annexe. I am occupying his actual bedroom.

We had tea on the patio where they spread their maps (a little
round jug like the one we use[1] squinted at me reproachfully). HE a
good man – wrote a thesis praising 'football supporters' for his
Foreign Office promotion exam; now that *is* courage!

He told me, prompted by his wife (who is an 'invalid') the story
of the resident donkey. This creature was tied to a tree, all the year
round, suffering terribly from heat and flies in the summer, for
seventeen years. Towards the end of his life he was so downcast
that the staff didn't even bother to tie him up. He just stood,
cowed and stooping, among the thorns. His plight came to the
attention of two maiden ladies who run the Distressed Arab
Donkey Society (or whatever it's called) and they reproached HE
for setting a bad example. Rightly, in my view. So HE issued
directions for its welfare and instructed his staff to get another
donkey to keep it company. They, corruptly, bought a broken-
down mare actually from *within* the abattoir (and, presumably, kept
the change). The mare, covered with sores and her rib-cage
showing, nonetheless showed some spirit. She bit the guard at the
gate on arrival, lashed out with her hind legs at all and sundry, sank
her teeth into the shoulder of the – presumably startled – elderly
local resident and chased him round the paddock. In the end the
vet had to be called to sedate her (thus, as so often, costing more
than the amount 'saved' on the 'bargain'). However (that was a

---

[1] At one point in his career AC most disreputably pouched or pinched from
government hospitality a tiny white milk jug with a crown on it, and the Clarks
frequently made use of it on their early morning tea tray.

year ago) things settled down. The elderly resident 'picked up'; the
mare put on weight and her sores healed; and now, most pleasingly, is pregnant!

Lots and lots of love

Al

Mamounia Hotel, Marrakesh   *Friday, 17 March*

Arrived here 'for a complete rest', '*se reposer*', entirely at my own (I
judge likely to be considerable) expense. I am curious, yellow, as
Winston was here before the Casablanca Conference; and down
the years other louche figures.

Alas, it is my impression that the hotel is now little different
from any other heavy clip-joint. The assistant manager is pressing
me to come to 'cocktails' this evening, but in truth I feel little
more attracted to this than I am by the prospect of the Western
Area cocktail party when I am changing in my hotel room at
Blackpool.

Later

After a bath I felt better, went down to the Reception. But it all
looked terribly dull, waste of time. I veered off and made for the
dining room.

I'm pretty sure M. Calouri would procure for me, but I haven't
got the nerve to couch (sic) my requirements. And anyway, think
of the *boredom* potentially. They'd be bound to take photographs,
tape, video everything. For all I know, my bedroom has got a two-
way mirror. So embarrassing for the dear PM – 'I'm afraid it, er,
looks as if Alan has been behaving, er, badly . . .'

British embassy, Warsaw   *Monday, 17 July*

I am now on what must be my very last trip as Minister for Trade.
When I get back to London the reshuffle will be in full swing –

perhaps over – and I will be at either the Ministry of Defence or the Foreign Office.

I read in the papers that the Defence Secretary after this weekend is going to be Tom *King* (for God's sake). Any idea that I will do Defence Procurement under that man is OUT. And I will give The Lady my reasons.[1] I'd really rather be back on the estate.

I am tortured by impotence – that utterly negative feeling, a void; zero between the loins. I must look up when I last suffered from it. Also, I am bored blue by the company of businessmen. I have absolutely nothing in common with them. I don't like sitting around with a glass in my hand. I don't understand references to Chelsea FC. I couldn't hit a golf ball to save my life. I like only the heavy movers, people like Arnold[2] or Jimmy [Goldsmith].

I must suspend this entry as it's HE's reception in half an hour and I have neither had a bath nor read the brief.

Masuria   *Wednesday, 19 July*

David Young's message duly arrived, in code (that he 'wanted to meet me on Monday') to say that I was remaining in the Govt. But I have almost decided not to accept anything except S of S Defence. Procurement would be impossible and FCO only acceptable if I was quite clearly Number 2, and *recognised as such*. I will talk it all over with Jane. But it is fun to have the option and to be able to toy, over the weekend at least, with the idea of 'cutting peat'.[3]

Masuria   *Thursday, 20 July*

I woke at four o'clock and the room was quite light. Thinking it was the moon shining, I rose and went on to the balcony to catch

---

[1] But see in fact entry for 24 July, below.
[2] Lord Weinstock, chairman of GEC.
[3] A family phrase for escaping to the Highlands.

the light on the water. But it is already dawn, and the swallows are chirruping excitedly. We are very far north here, deep in the Runic lands. A long, long way from the Judaeo-Christian ethic.

I got dressed and strolled out to the wooden jetty that adjoins the lodge. The forest comes right down to the water's edge, turning immediately into reed-swamp that forms a belt about sixty to a hundred feet deep around the rim of the lake. Here, seventy-five years ago almost to the day, the wretched Russian infantry sought refuge and were cut down, for hour after hour, by the German machine-gun teams, and the waters were stained dark red for a hundred metres out from the shore.

Today we are driving to the *Wolfschanze*.[1] Stauffenberg's bomb exploded, forty-four years ago, just after two o'clock. I hope we get there in time.

House of Commons   *Monday, 24 July*

I have been hanging around all morning. It is foully hot, and I keep the windows open on to Star Court, which makes the room noisy. There are wild rumours. Maddest of all is that Geoffrey Howe is to be sacked. Apparently he has already been twice to Number 10, and emerged without a statement.[2]

So who would be Foreign Secretary?

I see all this from my own aspect. There are only two jobs that I could be offered (or would consider). One, that Chris Patten mentioned when I made an official call on him a couple of weeks ago, is to be 'Mister Europe', keep an eye on the Commission. Tristan has also hinted at this, and David too – 'as a joke'.

But would it actually be Lynda's job? Could I really work with Geoffrey and, more to the point, could he tolerate it? (Although if rumour is correct this won't actually arise.) It would be lovely to

---

[1] Hitler's headquarters at Rastenburg.
[2] Howe, who had been Foreign Secretary since 1983, became Lord President of the Council, Leader of the House of Commons and deputy prime minister. John Major was appointed Foreign Secretary.

try the FO – but I would have to keep my nerve and insist on the continuity of Lynda's title there, and be *Deputy* Foreign Secretary.

I still think Defence is more likely. So many people have said that I am to go there first as M of S in order to be poised to slither upstairs if George [Younger] inherits, or goes somewhere grander. And it would be bound to be Procurement. Partly because I know all the weapons system specs off the top of my head, partly because the Army brass won't have me in AF because of *The Donkeys*.

Other junior Ministers have been drifting in and out of here all morning. Most are fretful. Peter Morrison doesn't know anything. A couple of years ago he was always first with the news.

Later

The phone rang. It was the harsh-voiced telephone operator from Number 10. I don't know any of their names, but there are two with lovely friendly voices and manners, and one, this one, who is like Goneril in *Pinfold*.

'Mr Alan Clark?'

'Yes.'

'Hold the line for the Prime Minister.'

I held on, for an eternity. Then the operator came back, snarled, 'Are you still there?'

'Yes.'

'She [sic] is tied up at the moment. Will you be remaining at this number?'

'Of course.'

Over an hour passed. Nervously I fantasised. Could some miracle be taking place? There was another false start.

Then, finally, it was the Prime Minister.

'Alan, I want you to go to Defence.'

I said nothing.

Her voice flattened in tone. 'As Minister of State.'

'Who is going to be Secretary of State?'

'Well, don't tell anyone, because it hasn't been released yet, but Tom is coming back from Ireland to do it.'

Christ alive! Not only was this an appalling prospect, but it also put paid to my secret scheme/hope of slipping into George's shoes when he moved on.

'I'm sorry, Prime Minister, but I can't work with Tom. I went through all that when I was at DE, I can't do it again. He's too ghastly.'

'I know what you mean, but he is much better now.'

'I just can't do it, I'm afraid.'

'Alan, you've always wanted to go to Defence. I've stood out to get you this job (uh?). You can't let me down by refusing.'

'Oh all right, Prime Minister, thank you very much.'

'Right then, that's settled.'

Oh dear! *What* a feeble resistance. Just a few shots in the air.

It's up to me what I make of this, I suppose. But it will be difficult. In that Department, of all Departments, seniority is everything.

I feel more than a little down. I have always wanted this. But it has not quite come in the form that I would have liked. I see trouble ahead.

And it was all so rushed and terse. Quite different from that lovely private encounter when she made me Minister for Trade.

Garden House   *Saturday, 29 July*

Is it really only five days since the reshuffle? It seems an eternity. I have had tension headache most of the day. There is *so* much to do here – cars, papers and estate. And what should be the very best weekend of the year, the weekend of the *clef* is already warped and occluded by the curtailing, *yet again*, of the holiday summer.

I am having to come to terms with a new set of officials, and they with me. So far I detect two clear divisions. There are polishedly respectful, or rather formally courteous seniors, who probably don't give a toss for a Minister of State '*en passage*'. And an almost openly sceptical Private Office who radiate their unease at my dilettante style. I read Notes for Incoming Ministers in an hour and a half (meekly and subserviently this should have taken me three days or, preferably a weekend).

I had called them in immediately: 'The first thing I want to make clear is that the "Friday box" comes up on Thursday. Right? I'm not having everyone clearing their own desks at three pm on Friday and sending it up here to sod up my weekends.'

'But Minister, what about the weekend box, Minister?'

'There isn't one.'

They shuffled off into the outer office. I have the communicating door open at all times so that I can bellow and this curtails their own conversation.

After a little while Julian[1] came back in. 'What would you like me to do with Friday's material, Minister?'

'I will read it on the train to Plymouth.'

'But what about material that comes in after you've left?'

'I will see it on Monday.'

'But what about urgent material, Minister, what about weekends when you are Duty Minister?'

'I have a portable telephone and there is a land line to the office in Plymouth.'

'But what if it is too highly classified . . . ?'

'That is a problem to which, I do not doubt, a solution will be apparent when it arises.'

They load my In-tray with papers of widely varying importance and density, stacked haphazardly – the oldest, corniest trick in the Civil Service. I insisted on colour-coded folders (it is perfectly incredible that in this vast and brontosaurian Department so simple an aid to efficiency should be unheard of). I rang dear Rose at DTI and she sent round immediately a batch – Blue, letters for signing; Yellow, key information; Orange, useless information; Red, action.

It was apparently impossible to get a paginated notebook in which I could make my *own* notes of meetings (another thing civil

---

[1] Julian Scopes, private secretary. Within a few weeks (see later entries) he and AC had become firm friends and confidants, and cooperated closely in the gestation period of 'Options for Change'.

servants don't like) and ideas. Very difficult even to raise a pencil.
When I asked if Ministers could, ever did, circulate each other
with notes the concept was greeted with startlement, if not
consternation.

I want to send off two notes straight away. One on the importance of retaining the Armilla Patrol;[1] the second on the idiocy
of overriding a planning authority refusal to extend the nuclear
store at Devonport. Both issues show the Admiralty at its worst.
They don't like Armilla because it 'strains resources'. What are
'resources' *for*, for fuck's sake? And they want to extend a dump
for radioactive waste that abuts on an infants' school at Weston
Mill.

I got the little Admiral round. People tried not to tell me his
name, just referred to him as CFS[2] (every one, or thing, here is
denoted by their acronym. All part of a conspiracy to befuddle
incomers.) I told him that nuclear power was essential to the
security of this country in two fields, and two only: warheads, and
maritime propulsion. If we were to retain public support, or at least
assent, for these we must lean over backwards in assuaging their
environmental concerns. What he was proposing to do wasn't just
bad PR, it amounted to wilful sabotage.

He bounced about in his chair crossly. Conveyed he thought I
was half Red spy, had do-gooder academic. Card marked.[3]

At present my game plan is to stay in for six months, until
Christmas, see my way around the Dept, what's happening exactly,
particularly *where the money is going*, and let The Lady have a considered three-quarter-page report for reading over the Chequers
Christmas weekend.

But the first thing to do is get Private Office in on Monday and
sort a few things out. They've picked me off with a series of papers
about weapons, and the attendant procurement 'problems'. But

---

[1] Since the Iraq–Iran conflict at least one destroyer or frigate was permanently on
station at Jebel Ali for emergency response.

[2] Chief of Fleet Support, Admiral (later Sir) Jock Slater.

[3] From the outset of his tenure at the Ministry of Defence AC found that the
Admiralty press office in Plymouth was always ready to brief local reporters
about his failings.

how can I pronounce judgment unless I know the background, the kind of war we are expecting to fight? Or even against who we are expected to fight? I see that everyone's career is predicated on the horrendous Soviet 'threat'. But that's all balls. My problem is that as far as 'top management' is concerned I appear to be both a Red agent *and* the man who's going to wreck their careers.

I think I'll also give them a fright about the gauche and spastic way in which their muttered enquiries and complaints about me are getting straight back, after hours. Rhodes James tells me what his secretary, Polly, reports to him. But Julian is married to Polly's daughter and Polly is the doyenne of the secretaries' room in Deans Yard where everything is repeated. The Westminster hothouse. Doug[1] himself even said to Alison, 'Does he realise how hard he has to work?' which she repeated back to me, at dinner in the Kundan that same evening.

Tom King, meanwhile, is true to the form which I remember so well from DE. Kept me waiting for an hour on Friday afternoon by the phone, then left the building. Much later his office 'stood me down'. Loathsome puffball. Archie Hamilton[2] is something of a *faux bonhomme* and already suspicious of my 'encroachments'. (Just wait until I get started!) Michael Neubert[3] is serious and hardworking but (according to Julian) did not want to be switched across from Armed Forces and be my subordinate instead of the amiable, but somewhat *unversed* Tommy Arran.[4] All rather fun, but draining also.

I must not lose *élan*.

Michael Quinlan[5] is benign. Always hard to tell what he's really thinking. Which is as it should be with Permanent Secretaries. The Chesterfieldian masque should be discarded only at times of acute crisis.

---

[1] Douglas Wiedner, assistant private secretary.

[2] Archibald Hamilton, Minister of State (Armed Forces) since 1988.

[3] Michael Neubert, MP for Romford since 1974. Parliamentary under-secretary newly moved across from Armed Forces to Defence Procurement.

[4] 9th Earl of Arran, parliamentary under-secretary for the armed forces, 1989–92.

[5] Then Permanent Secretary at the Ministry of Defence. Both AC and Tom King had worked as ministers with him at Employment.

Saltwood   *Sunday, 30 July*

Bruce Anderson had asked himself down for a general gossip. I
always said I'd open a bottle of 1916 Latour when I got to MoD so
we split that as an *apéritif*. He's in my good books as he wrote
percipiently about the Government changes, 'Mixing Alan Clark
and Tom King could be the only mistake of the reshuffle.' He said
he was interviewing David Owen first. 'Why don't you bring him
down?' Bruce said he would try. Sure enough, they both turned
up.

In strictly social terms David is oddly *un*sophisticated. Almost ill
at ease, he said he didn't 'know much' about wine. Gently, I *tâtai le
terrain* on the political scene. David said that 'she' had tried really
hard recently, got hold of Debbie[1] at a Number 10 reception and
really turn it one. But he couldn't. How could he switch a third
time? 'Winston did,' I said. How could he disappoint yet another
group of followers? (What he meant, I suspect, was how could he
get re-elected.)

David has this lovely grin – the most engaging grin in politics –
and a good sardonic expression at other times. He commented
freely and without inhibition. But he is a realist, and he *doesn't see
his way*. Ll G, Enoch, now him. Great men, of massive authority
and vision, find themselves disqualified by chance of circumstances
and their own transient misjudgments. It seems to have nothing to
do with quality. But I see no future for him.

While I was out of the room both he and Bruce said to Jane that
I could 'quite easily' now get into the Cabinet.

Eriboll   *Thursday, 17 August*

This morning I bathed, before breakfast, in the loch just opposite
the targets. I don't know what the temperature is; a tiny trace
of Gulf Stream perhaps, but not much. One feels incredible

---
[1] David Owen's wife.

afterwards – like an instant double whisky, but clear-headed. Perhaps a 'line' of coke does this also. Lithe, vigorous, energetic. Anything seems possible.

It was a still, mild day, high cirrus cloud, and I was half minded to attempt the great walk to Loch Stack.[1] But I did not leave enough time, and had to settle for a reconnaissance. I pressed right on beyond the oakwoods at the top of the Stra'beg valley, and started to ascend steeply, past the first of the two big waterfalls there. The second I could only reach by balancing on a succession of huge slippery boulders. Below me the black peat water flowed in that fast and silent manner that denotes great depth. I splashed my face and drank from one of the pools.

Then I left the watercourse and traversed the upper Polla valley – strewn with rowan trees, all carrying their bright orange fruit – and began the assault on the An Lean Charn Ridge. This is very steep, both hands are needed. But there is a profusion of heather, and foliage of stunted holm-oak and silver birch – rather like the opening passages of *Erewhon*. Near the col the treeline stops abruptly, and one must negotiate a series of dried peat watercourses, storm channels I suppose they are, which must be terrifying when in spate, with banks six to eight foot high. On the crest of the ridge there is a track (shown on the Ordnance Survey) for the stalkers' ponies and, indeed, hoof marks could be seen. I contemplated following it, but this would have slowly wound me down to Dionard – one of the bleakest and most remote of all the Highland lochs, a kind of landlocked Coruisk – then to God knows where.

I trailed down the hill on the SW side for a little while while being unable, for some reason, to bring Foinavon into view, then swung back and down to the Polla valley.

By the time I was back at the Land-Rover I had been on the hill for more than seven hours. The walk *is* feasible, but one would have to allow up to ten, and pray for good visibility.

---

[1] From the shore of Loch Eriboll (north Atlantic) to the shore of Loch Stack (running into the Irish Sea), a distance of some twenty-three miles with the ascent of two ridges over two thousand feet, eluded AC until May 1991. He and Jane repeated the expedition in July 1992.

*

Yesterday we went to the Lairg Sale.[1] Poor Michael Wigan had the transporter with all his sheep on board in collision (fatally) with the district nurse in her Metro on a corner of the road between Boroboll and Rogart. The great truck turned over and about 100 lambs perished.

In the meantime little Moncreiffe was strutting about in his new plus fours, as pleased as punch with having sold Ribigill for three million or, rumour has it, thereabouts. I couldn't remember his Christian name (he was at Eton with me, but it was thought 'unhealthy' there to know other boys' Christian names) and when I whispered to James 'What's little Moncreiffe's Christian name?' he very splendidly answered, 'Little.'

Moncreiffe made a short, not very good, pompous speech about '. . . the farm will carry on', 'thankyou for buying my sheep', that kind of balls.

He was listened to quite attentively (most unusual in the Ring at Lairg) because everyone wanted to know who had bought Ribigill. Naturally, he didn't say. All it boiled down to was, 'Well, I've trousered a couple of million, and I'm off.'

Royal Navy Equipment Exhibition, Portsmouth
                                            Tuesday, 26 September

Last night I travelled down to Portsmouth for the Royal Navy Equipment Exhibition.

That evening I hosted a dinner at Admiralty House for the more important foreign delegates. Admiral Jeremy Black[2] received me. Quite impressive (most senior sailors at the present time strike me as hopeless). For some reason – perhaps for that reason he is unpopular with his peers. This may relate to his period in command of *Invincible* during the Falklands. I remember at that time

---

[1] A great annual event in north-west Sutherland combining social and economic activity. It is considered obligatory for all the landowners to attend.

[2] Admiral Sir Jeremy Black, Deputy Chief of the Defence Staff, 1986–89, recently appointed C-in-C, Naval Home Command.

his colleagues were briefing journalists about how bad tempered and obstinate he was. He was not particularly friendly but to my gratification said, 'Didn't you come to the EFA meeting?'[1]

'Yes.'

'I thought it strange that the Minister for Trade should be opposing this project. I thought it would have the support of the DTI.'

Of course we could have blocked the whole project if The Lady hadn't changed her mind halfway through. Whether she was right or wrong I simply don't know at present, although I am inclined to think that the best solution is to maintain design and research teams and keep giving them more and more advanced projects to work on. But defer going into production for as long as one can. The moment something goes into production it is obsolescent and all the in-service problems start crowding in.

Surprise of the evening was the US Admiral Peter Hekman. After a slow start he showed himself to be an original thinker, well read in economics and philosophy. Both agreed that Paul Kennedy demanded a place – to my surprise he had read all Kennedy's learned treatises in historic and foreign affairs. I suggested Keynes's *Economic Consequences of the Peace* but Hekman said although it had had tremendous influence this would be seen as short-lived.

Keynes had formulated the poison but not the antidote.

Saltwood   *Saturday, 30 September*

I have just returned, exhausted but triumphant, from the Chequers CFE Seminar.[2]

Although we left early Dave got in a muddle after leaving the M40, and more time was lost because I, starting nervous, soon

---

[1] When he was minister for trade, it was arranged by Number 10 that AC should attend a special briefing for Treasury ministers at the Ministry of Defence, where the case for the European Fighter Aircraft was to be argued. At the time Mrs Thatcher was doubtful about the wisdom of so large a programme and hoped that AC's technical expertise would be of use in attenuating the RAF case.

[2] The Conventional Forces (Europe) Treaty, under which mutually agreed force reductions were to be tied to a timetable. From having been obstructive the 'new' Soviet regime under glasnost was actually leading the way.

developed hyper-anxiety and forced him to stop twice in order that I could relieve myself. Just in time (were we the last? I expect so) we turned down the back drive and into the roadblock of merciless-looking police sharpshooters.

I stayed quiet for most of the first half – although an awful lot of balls was talked, mainly by the heavyweight military men present, and by Michael Alexander, our Ambassador to NATO, whose higher intelligence has made him see that the writing is on the wall.[1] 'The Threat' (that always slightly ludicrous term) has now become a personal one – to their careers.

After an hour or so the discussion moved on to the kind of equipment that was going to be needed in 'the new scenario'. Lawson, who knows that I will be able to save him money, said, 'Prime Minister, could we hear on this subject from the Minister of State?'

I set out my stall, named and costed a number of programmes which could be eliminated without any risk. This induced *show* intakes of breath from the military men, but I could see Lawson and Lamont[2] beaming with approval. Martin Farndale[3] tried to come back at me, but the PM cut him off and she started on a quite well informed (Charles's hand clearly in evidence) summary of the approach to equipment problems, and the need for 'inter-operability' across NATO.

When the Prime Minister said that 'further work was needed' I jumped in. It was now or never.

'Prime Minister, may I have your instructions to draw up a schedule of our equipment requirements over the next five years, in the light of anticipated progress in the CFE negotiations?'

It simply is not allowed to interrupt the Prime Minister when she is summing up at the conclusion of a discussion. Everyone at the table turned and looked at me. I could see TK, some few place

---

[1] Sir Michael Alexander, diplomat. Former assistant private secretary to Sir Alec Douglas-Home and James Callaghan, and Private Secretary (Overseas Affairs) to Margaret Thatcher, 1979–81. Ambassador, Vienna, 1982–86.

[2] Norman Lamont was at that time Chief Secretary at the Treasury.

[3] General Sir Martin Farndale, outgoing commander-in-chief of the Brtish Army on the Rhine.

away on the other side, jaw dropped open, saucer-eyed. I could guess what *he* was thinking.

'Yes. We must be able to make some savings now. But . . . (going dreamy-voiced – I know this – it is a defensive tack) . . . I want particular attention paid to inter-operability.'

What a coup! The meeting ended, and there was no scope for anyone else to get in.

I was ebullient, foolishly so.

'Well done, Alan,' said Lawson, as we drifted down to lunch, but he said it *sotto voce*.

'Do you realise what this means? This is the Defence Review. I've got a free hand to write it.'

'Yes, if you play your cards right. I wouldn't shout it from the rooftops.'

I came up behind Quinlan. 'How about that, then, Michael? This is the Defence Review. We're off.'

'Well, don't call it that, whatever you do.' He didn't seem too happy.

Once in the car I telephoned to Julian at his home.

'We've made it! Single-handed you and I are going to write the Review.'

He couldn't really believe it. I took him through the whole thing stage by stage.

Julian said, 'Minister, you *must* be identified in the Meetings note, otherwise S of S's office, or the Permanent Secretary, or both, will take the whole thing over and smother it.'

'Don't you worry. Leave it to me.'

I was exultant, convinced it was the ox's hide.[1]

As soon as I got back here I started trying to reach Charles. I *had* to speak to him before he finalises the note, which he will be doing this very weekend. Finally I got him at Number 10.

---

[1] From the legend of the baron who asked his king for 'only so much land as can be encompassed by an ox's hide' and, getting permission, slew the largest ox he could find. He then cut its hide into a long leather lace, within whose circumference the baron constructed a powerful castle which soon dominated the surrounding country, and from which he came to challenge the king himself.

He started friendly. 'I think that went rather well.' (All civil servants use this expression unless there's been a complete disaster.) I explained the problem.

'Oh no, I couldn't do that. It would be most unusual. I can really only name the heads of Departments.'

'If you don't identify me, the whole thing will be stillborn.'

'Oh, surely not. Tom was there. He heard what the Prime Minister said.'

'Come on, Charles, ha bloody ha.'

'Well, I don't really see how I can.'

'Will you please ask the Prime Minister? Will you please tell her of this conversation?'

'If you insist. But I must warn you of my opinion that she will take the same view.'

'Even if she does, I'm no worse off. Please tell her.'

'All right.'

Fingers crossed!

Ministry of Defence   *Wednesday, 4 October*

Yesterday there was still no paper on the 'Conclusions' of the Chequers meeting. Strange. Number 10 are usually so efficient. But I did not dare ring Charles, it would have seemed importunate. There's nothing that I could do now. Every time Julian enquired of S of S's office the answer came that they had not yet been received.

But I was in the cafeteria at lunch, and saw Norman Lamont. He started talking about it. When did he get his copy? Monday. Again I tried Julian, again a blank wall from down the corridor.

In the evening I rang Number 10. Charles was away but his secretary said yes, they had gone over to MoD on Monday. 'Actually, you got the first batch.'

I explained that I hadn't received mine, must be stuck somewhere in the pipeline, could I come over for a copy?

'I don't have any spare copies, they are all restricted circulation.'

But she very sweetly agreed to make a copy of my copy (ie, of the copy I should have had). I was to collect it first thing this morning.

And, sure enough, at the end of the instruction were the magic words, *Minister, Defence Procurement, to take the Lead* (!)

I showed it to Julian. He could barely believe his eyes. Yet Tom's office will not release our copy, which was sent to them by Number 10 for onward transmission. The most we can get from them, late this afternoon, is that S of S 'is considering how best this can be tackled'.

Ministry of Defence   *Thursday, 5 October*

Ministers was cancelled today, which is highly unusual. At ten o'clock word came for me to go along (subject of discussion not disclosed, again unusual).

Tom was standing behind his desk, motioned to me to sit at a small chair facing him. Simon[1] padded out and shut the door.

'I just want to get one thing straight.'

'Uh?'

'I'm in charge.'

'Well, yes.'

'I've talked to her. I've talked to Charles. I'm handling this.'

'Quite.'

'If we're going to work amicably together, which I'm sure we are, we've got to trust each other.'

'Quite.'

'I cannot have you passing notes to the Prime Minister down the chimney.'

'No.'

When I got back to my office they were all peering at me; what for? Contusions?

'Fear God, and stay calm,' I said. 'No man's way leadeth to harm.'

---

[1] Simon Webb, head of Tom King's private office.

They don't know that aphorism. Perhaps sometimes they think that I am going off my head.

Plymouth train   *Friday, 10 November*

My days in the Department are very full at present. Because in addition to my routine ministerial duties I am covertly preparing the secret draft of the Defence Review – of *my* Defence Review, I should say.

Alison and I have really done the whole thing together, on the word processor in my Commons Office. The only 'trace elements' have been the periodic requests for facts and figures which Julian has sent down to various desks within the Dept.

Julian is being wonderful. Helpful, tactful, assiduous; he warns me when he thinks that I am going too far. Though sometimes even he can be made to look slightly pop-eyed and startled. We were working late the other evening and when he brought some papers to my desk I smelt whisky.

'Julian, you've been drinking!'

'Yes, Minister, I have had a small whisky, yes Minister.'

I am a spoilsport really. All Ministers have a huge drink allowance, administered by Private Office, and a vast store of bottles for 'entertaining'. It is common practice for Private Office to help themselves in times of need. I never touch it. But many colleagues are convivial, and do a 'sun's-over-the-yardarm' act most evenings.

I am in despair about the Navy or, rather, the sailors. This is the Service which has to be the centre-piece of my plan – swift, flexible, hard-hitting. Yet the only thing they want is to be the forward ASW screen for the United States Navy in northern waters.

That's all over, I say. Forget it. The Soviet 'threat' no longer exists. Raise your eyes. Have not any of them read Mahan? Or Arthur Marder? I suppose the whole thing started to go to pieces when (effectively) we abolished Dartmouth. The soldiers are little better. The careers structure of the British Army is, and for the last forty years has been anchored on 'Rhine Army'. They simply cannot come to terms with the change that has occurred. They won't even *train* differently – I suppose because to do so would involve admitting that there may, conceivably, be other enemies, other 'theatres'.

On the whole, though, I am getting on well with the civil servants. They are clever, of high calibre, most of them and not irredeemably set in their ways. And I am lucky that the Permanent Secretary immediately answerable to me, Peter Levene,[1] is thoroughly congenial. A quick mind and – so important – a sense of humour.

Ministry of Defence   *Thursday, 21 December*

It's all a bit awkward. I live dangerously.

But the key thing is, I have finished my paper, boldly entitled it 'The 1990 Defence Review', and lodged it with Charles at Number 10. Afterwards, Alison and I went to the Pugin Room, split half a bottle of champagne; then another.

My paper is succinct and radical. And I have followed the two guiding principles in such matters – keep it short, (5 pages and an annexe) and get it in first, ahead of any other(s) that may compete for attention. (One thing I have learned in Whitehall is the need to be first 'on the table' and take pole position against which all else is judged.)

I just – *just* – beat the great 'official' departmental paper which Quinlan has been preparing for months, ever since he had that nasty shock at Chequers.

But Quinlan's is a Motherhood paper. All in all, the possibility cannot be excluded, it seems likely that; existing uncertainties, need to consult closely with Allies at every stage, must be careful not to drop or, as important, *seem* (or is it 'seen'?) to be dropping our guard; real savings a considerable distance in the future, need for absolute secrecy, discussion confined to a very small group.

---

[1] Sir Peter Levene, Chief of Defence Procurement since 1985.

The first meeting, to discuss the Dept's own paper, is scheduled for this evening, at which the Permanent Secretary is to distribute draft 'Headings', and explain how he is proposing to 'draw the threads together'.

Julian rightly and shrewdly said that I must get my paper to Tom, and to Quinlan himself, before (but of course only just before) this meeting is convened. Deftly I altered the first page so that of the four copies they appeared to be getting Numbers One and Three.

Unusually, the meeting started in time (Tom is driving down to Wiltshire tonight, immediately the meeting is over, for the Christmas hols). When I got in everyone was reading, avidly and urgently.

Quinlan had his head bent right over my text, lips moving occasionally – like my father's description of Picasso when first confronted with a portfolio of Moore drawings.

No one bothered about the Dept's paper, indeed it was hardly referred to throughout.

Tom waved mine in the air. 'This is pretty drastic stuff.'

He launched into a rambling dissertation on the unwisdom of reducing our strength in Germany, followed by a (clearly) prepared passage on a 'scenario' that involved starving Poles storming a Red Army food train. Bizarre.

'Could put NATO in a very difficult position.'

But he is not a fool, Tom, in matters such as this; and he was eyeing me closely.

'What we have all got to ensure is that this does not get into the hands of the Prime Minister.'

Silence, except for a grunt from Hamilton, who was looking very bad-tempered.

'She'd get hold of completely the wrong end of the stick.'

I said nothing.

'Not straight away, anyway, Alan? Huh?'

'I find myself in a very difficult position.'

'Why?'

'She knows that I am writing it.'

'How does she know that?'

'Because I am doing it at her request. You recall the note of the Chequers meeting?'

'Well, not until we've cleaned it up a bit. It'd be very bad for morale here if this got out in its present form.'

'I don't think it would for a minute.'

'Oh yes, indeed, I'm afraid it would. At least, we must hold on to it until after Christmas.'

Then, poor Tom, he said – was it plucking, or was it sinister? – in front of four other people it was certainly odd: 'You promised that you would not send her any notes without showing them to me at the same time.'

'I am showing it to you.'

'Well, that's agreed, then. We'll all keep tight hold of this until after Christmas.'

'Yeah.'

I was on ultra-thin ice. I could *just say* that, I pretended, because I hadn't handed it to her, but to Charles.

The breathing space didn't last five minutes. Back in my office I used my direct line to dial Charles direct. Engaged. I redialled half a minute later. Still engaged. Then I heard the phone in the outer office.

Julian came in, white-faced.

It was Simon. He had rung Charles to excuse the delay in submitting the departmental paper, which had been promised *for* Christmas, and said that the 'Min DP has also written something to which we are giving consideration'.

'So am I,' Charles had answered. 'It's on my desk now.'

I could feel myself break into an instant sweat. *So* embarrassing.

'Christ. What do I do?'

Julian was thoughtful.

I just wanted to leap into the car, drive down to Saltwood, hide for a week or so. Time, the great healer.

'I wouldn't do that, Minister. I think that you'll have to go round straight away and apologise.'

'Impossible. Anyway, he will have left by now.'

'Just let me see.' He rang Simon again.

'The Secretary of State is still there. He can see you now.'

Tom was seated at his desk in I'm-in-charge mode. And the chair stood directly in front, ready for a pre-caning homily.

'I'm most frightfully sorry. I just couldn't own up in front of all those people.'

He waved my explanation aside, said something about you should always feel free to let me see everything, it makes it so much easier for both of us.

'Anyhow, I've had a word with Charles, whom I know well. He agrees that the Prime Minister should not see this paper before Christmas – otherwise, ha-ha, she'll be making all our lives a misery over the holiday . . .'

'Very good of you to take this line.'

'No, no. Yes, yes. It's just one of those things. Anyway, have a good holiday. Going skiing?'

I felt a bit of a shit. But how else could I play it? Good old Tom, though. Magnanimus Sextus.

Saltwood   *New Year's Day*

Here come the Nineties! It's impossible to write anything contemplative without sounding demi-E.J. Thribb.

But am I, for a start, going to achieve my life's ambition?
Auguries at the moment – poor.

Total silence from Chequers. Nothing indeed since Charles,
rather gruffly, acknowledged in the Cabinet Room at Number 10,
the personal delivery, by me, of The Paper before Christmas.

My zest for life is stronger than it has ever been. My energy is
excellent; the *width* of my appreciation continues to expand, and
there is no sign of fading intellectual powers. This is going to be
my year. Or . . .

In fairness, I should say that I really love my job (being racked
only by the pains of not being Secretary of State). For the first time
in Government I actually look forward to the end of the holiday,
getting back to my desk, where all the papers are so interesting.
Before Christmas I was dropping with fatigue and nervous tension,
but already I have fully recovered.

First to be decided though, is will I get to the next Chequers
meeting? I had hoped, secretly, for a phone call over Christmas.
But no contact.

I put my all into that Report. Truly it was the apotheosis of my
whole career both as a historian and in public life. But it has turned
out, it seems, an embarrassing non-event. Not to be alluded to.

If I am excluded from the meeting TK will be cock-a-hoop. He
will no longer be fearful of me, as I will have played my big card,
and been ignored. Also I will have lost face with my own Private
Office. All Julian's doubts will be confirmed just as, by sheer intellectual vigour, I was converting him. Sad, because he has been
splendidly loyal over these last difficult weeks.

Have I overreached? Did I gallop too soon and too recklessly?

It's impossibly difficult to set great reforms in train from a middle-ranking position. But I *know* I'm right. Mine is the only way we can keep military clout and not go bust. I couldn't just sit back and duck it in exchange for a comfortable life signing documents and having little exclusives in the HS 125.

This is my last job, isn't it?

Be realistic, Clark. If you're going to make S of S you won't do it just by sitting still and being a goodboy. And we are at one of those critical moments in defence policy that occur only once every fifty years.

Always remember, 'At times of acute crisis in the course of human affairs, a man will emerge. If he does not, it means that the time is not yet ripe' (*Wolf*).[1] A curious inversion of conventional thought. But even if true, not especially comforting.

Saltwood   *Sunday, 14 January*

I've made it! The Chequers meeting (Mark II) is fixed for 27 Jan – to be *utterly* secret, 'The Prime Minister has asked me to emphasise that if any . . .', etc.

I am invited, listed at Number 4, below Hurd, Chancellor and TK. (How maddening for TK. Hee-hee.)

My paper is, it is clear, *the* lead document. How shrewd and good I was to get it in first! The FCO papers are bulkier, came later, and carry the imprimatur of a committee of officials.

Willie Waldegrave, whose task it is to co-ordinate the material, was not friendly when I saw him in the dining room. Reddish with drink, and small-eyed, he said it was 'very petty' not to circulate the Annexes (which contain the financial provisions).

'Not my idea,' I said.

'Anyway, the Treasury have got hold of a copy.'

Too right they have, I thought, I sent them one.

On the day, everything will depend on (a) her mood, and the

---

[1] AC sometimes refers to Hitler by this cognomen, which was used only by his 'Bayreuth' circle, Elizabeth Wagner, etc.

level of counter-distraction (b) my own confidence and sparkle-ability.

Word has spread through the Department, and I am buoyed up by the now open tendency of senior officials to defer to me, quote my views with approval even when (normally unheard of) Tom is present. I retoy with the idea of supplanting him, and promptly.

Of *course* I should be in charge, handling the whole thing at international level also, Washington, Brussels.

My present solution is to move TK to Health, where he could be pinkly affable and repair some of the damage caused by my 'abrasive' namesake. But that could only happen if Clarke has a nervous breakdown – unlikely in one so fat – or – perfectly possible at any time, he must make the Norwich Union wince – something 'happens' to him. One mustn't be uncharitable (why not?) but this after all is the roughest game, at the biggest table.

On Thursday afternoon Soames, who was sitting just behind me, occupied a lot of Agriculture Questions (and I don't doubt a lot of TV footage, so it's as well the audience couldn't hear) telling me about an incredibly powerful new aphrodisiac he had discovered.

I liked the sound of this, and after Prime Minister's Questions I drove him back to his flat and he brought down a 'phial'. It has to be kept in the fridge.

Ministry of Defence   *Wednesday, 17 January*

Tom is frantic. He is harrying and pestering officials all over the building to get 'his', ie, *The Official MoD Position* paper(s), prepared.

He won't let me see it in draft. I doubt if I'll get a sight of it before I walk into the room – if then.

But not only was my paper first in, it was only five pages long. All this stuff they're sending up now is ten, twenty pages per memo. On-the-one-hand, on-the-other-hand balls. No one will bother, and in any case all will be read in the context of my argument.

Julian told me that the Treasury had commented that mine was 'the first decently written paper they had seen for thirty years'.

Ministry of Defence   *Friday, 19 January*

Today I *dominated* the Dept. Repeatedly I sent for Quinlan, Spiers,[1] John Colston.[2] Periodically I talked to Arnold Weinstock. By sheer energy and clarity of thought I put together the deal that saved Ferranti, and its Radar, and thus EFA[3] in time for us to out-face Stoltenberg[4] on Monday when the German delegation come over.

John Colston took notes, and tried to keep TK (*baffledly* at the end of a 'bad line' outside his house in Wiltshire) in touch.

I ran the whole thing at a break-neck pace, and afterwards Donald Spiers said, 'It's a wonderful feeling, to get hard decisions and clear instructions.'

But the sweetest moment of all came at the end of the day, after our third meeting, when Quinlan materialised, Jeeves-like, beside me; 'Fingers crossed, but well done!'

Ministry of Defence   *Friday, 26 January*

Yesterday a great gale swept through London in the afternoon, tearing at roofs and scaffolding. The police, as usual, overreacted and closed off streets and by-ways at random, blocking motorists and shouting at pedestrians through loud-hailers. The whole of Westminster and the West End went into 'gridlock' from tea-time

---

[1] Donald Spiers, Controller Aircraft, and head of Profession, Defence Science and Engineering, Ministry of Defence, since 1989.

[2] John Colston, an assistant secretary at Defence.

[3] The Germans were already voicing their misgivings about the European Fighter Aircraft (EFA) project. At this time their excuse was that Ferranti (stipulated as the radar contractor) were commercially unviable and this put the project at risk. AC encouraged Lord Weinstock to take Ferranti's radar enterprise into GEC, thus totally altering its commercial status.

[4] Gerhard Stoltenberg, German defence minister since 1989.

until about nine pm, with angry and resentful drivers lurching and clutch-slipping up on to the pavement and abandoning their cars.

I cancelled my trip to Plymouth and, seeing Archie Hamilton in the library corridor, fell into conversation.

I am in the ascendant at the moment, with my place at the Chequers summit assured, and drawing much deference from officials. On Wednesday night there was a big dinner at the RAF College at Bracknell. Moray Stewart,[1] very slightly in his cups it must be admitted, said to me, 'Why don't you take the helm?'

Not bad, from a Deputy Secretary. But I must be careful not to have a tumble. And I wanted to find out a little more about the PM's attitude (her real attitude as distinct from her public posture) to German reunification.

Archie Hamilton and I went into the smoking room – to be alone. Strange, the decline of the smoking room, even in my time. In former days there was spirited discussion, conviviality. Friends and colleagues spoke ill or, very occasionally when they hoped it would get repeated, good, of those who were absent. But now it is frequented only by soaks, traditionalists, and Memory-Lane buffers.

I suppose that the implication was that I would try and conform with whatever her own line was – although this has never been my style.

But Archie was interesting. He claimed not to know what she really thought, just said, 'She's against it, ho-ho.' (You'd think that, having worked as her PPS, he'd know a bit more but I never, I suppose, make enough allowance for the actions of people who want to set me back a few pips.)

Archie said that was the mistake John Moore[2] had made. During the high months of his status as her chosen successor he framed the Health Service reforms exactly on the basis of what he thought she wanted. But she kept changing her mind. One minute she wanted

---

[1] Moray Stewart, Deputy Under-Secretary of State, Defence Procurement, since 1988. He would become Second Permanent Under-Secretary, Defence, later in the year.

[2] John Moore had been dropped from the government in 1989, after three years as Social Security Secretary.

to go further, the next she got an attack of the doubts, wanted to
trim a bit. Each time the unfortunate John agreed, made the adjust-
ments, came back for approval. The result was a total hotchpotch
and 'she ended up thinking he was a wanker, and got rid of him'.

Saltwood   *Sunday, 28 January*

I am flat and reactive after Chequers.

Last night on my return I was still on a high . . . Percy Cradock[1]
had made a point of telling me 'how much the Prime Minister
admired your paper', and going into lunch – although we had had
quite an argument during the morning – she had said how good it
was, 'so full of original thought'. But perhaps I overplayed my
hand? Did I trespass too aggressively into the field of Foreign
Affairs?

But surely defence policy can only be considered in the context
of our foreign commitments?

I suppose, on reflection, that I did not make enough allowance
for the fact that every colleague (except the Treasury) and every
official (except Charles and Percy) is hostile to me. The Prime
Minister herself is friendly, but implacable. I argued cogently for
accepting, and exploiting, German reunification while they still
needed our support.

No good. She is determined not to.

'You're wrong,' I said. 'You're just wrong.'

Everyone at the table smirked at each other. Now he's really
torn it; fucking little show-off, etc.

During the coffee-break I cornered her.

'These are just a re-run of the old Appeasement arguments of
1938.'

'Yes,' she said, eyes flashing (she's in incredible form at the
moment), 'and I'm not an appeaser.'

---

[1] Sir Percy Cradock, distinguished diplomat, who had been British ambassador to
Beijing before leading the UK team in negotiations over the future of Hong
Kong in 1983. Adviser to the prime minister on foreign affairs since 1984.

John Major,[1] whom I like more and more, said to me *sotto voce*, 'You're a military strategist. Oughtn't you to be sending your tanks round the flank, rather than attacking head on?'

Saltwood   *Wednesday, 31 January*

In a calm frame of mind I was eating chicken livers on toast when the phone rang. Jane answered. It was Julian.

'Julian at seven pm?'

As always looking on the bright side, she suggested, 'Perhaps TK's had an accident?'

'He hasn't. You have,' could well have been Julian's answer.

A leak about the Chequers meeting is to be in tomorrow's *Times*. It is said that it comes from me.

'We *know* it's him,' according to the S of S's office, passim 'Number 10' – in other words, Charles himself.

Julian was grave. Very, very grave.

'As you remember, Minister, the PM reminded everyone of the need for total secrecy.'

This has to be a frame-up. It just has to be. Because I know to whom I have spoken, and it's no one. Not just no journalist, no one. Except Julian himself and, very obliquely, Peter Levene.

I padded off, sweating profusely in my dressing-gown and having suffered a total regression, to the tower office, and rang Charles at Number 10. He was bland, diplomatic, but said it was 'regrettable'. Too bloody right. This sort of stain hangs with one a long time. And *completely* without reason.

On reflection, though, as I write this, my suspicions are aroused. Apparently it is to be carried in an article by Michael Evans.[2] Now I've never met Michael Evans. I wouldn't know what he looked like if he came into the room, still less am I on terms to 'leak' him something.

---

[1] John Major, briefly Foreign Secretary, 1989, before becoming Chancellor of the Exchequer following the resignation of Nigel Lawson.

[2] Michael Evans, defence correspondent of *The Times*.

But when I said, both to Julian and Charles, 'I'm going to find Michael Evans and have it out with him' they both counselled strongly against.[1]

Ministry of Defence   *Thursday, 1 February*

During the afternoon Peter Levene came in. He is concerned, like me and practically everyone else in the building, at the pace of progress on the Review. Tom muffles everything, sits on it for weeks. Even his Private Office admits that he is driving them mad. Yet in a way I understand. The buck stops with him. He's racking his brain for catches. He knows there will be a lot of opposition from within the Party.

Let's face it, though. His real problem is he doesn't understand what's going on.

Peter was frustrated and (unusually for him) gloomy. Then *he* said to me, 'Why don't you take the helm?'

That's two Dep Secs in less than a week!

'But how?'

Peter had an ingenious solution. To set up a 'Review Controllerate' with him in charge; three Young Turks from the three Services; *reporting to me*. Mouth-watering. If the original September Chequers remit was the ox's hide then this surely (to pursue the analogy of medieval politics) would be a permit for my own

---

[1] On Julian's advice AC raised the matter with the Permanent Secretary. On 8 February came Michael Quinlan's graceful and elliptic response:

'As promised, I caused Hugh Colver to make some enquiries on Tuesday about the piece in *The Times*. He spoke to Bernard Ingham.

'Bernard said he knew nothing about the idea that Evans had "owned up" to a source, and he found it strange. His assumption was that anything Charles Powell believed about sourcing could only be inference from the piece's contents. Hugh took the opportunity of conveying to Bernard, on my instructions, that I was wholly satisfied that the content did not come from you. Bernard (who is often at odds with Charles) has his own suspicions.

'The only way of taking this any further, it seems to me, would be for you to tax Charles Powell directly. I think it has to be for your judgment whether that would be a useful operation.'

chivalric Order. But Tom would see it a mile off. The Review is the only real activity in the Dept at present. If I'm put in charge, effectively I'm running the whole shoot.

There's only one person who can ordain this. We'll have to see. At least it wouldn't be so brazen as the time I asked her to take ODA away from Geoffrey and put it into Trade.[1]

Albany   *Tuesday, 20 February*

I dined at the Cavalry Club with Ian Gow.

He is deeply apprehensive of the future, said that no Government had ever been consistently (over six months) behind in the polls at this level, and at this stage – halfway he said – in the electoral cycle, and gone on to win.

'We aren't halfway, we're three-quarters. The Election would normally be in '91.'

Ian said that all the indicators were bad for this year, and that inflation would still be at 8.5 per cent in November. (He's a terrible old Jeremiah about the inflation rate.)

'Evidently you do not appreciate the significance of the month of November?'

Of course! The leadership election.

Ian elaborated. There is a real risk of a challenge, and this time a serious one. He said that even when Meyer was standing last year he had a hard time persuading many colleagues to vote for the PM – although then most of them were minded to abstain.[2] He had told them that if they really were still discontented, felt that there has been no improvement, 'You will have another chance next year.'

'Are there many?'

'Yes. I am sorry to say there are. Very many.'

---

[1] Recorded in July 1986, but not included in this edition.
[2] Sir Anthony Meyer, MP for Clwyd North West since 1983, had challenged Margaret Thatcher as leader of the Conservative Party. The result: Thatcher, 314; Meyer, 33; abstentions, 24.

I didn't like to ask. Not out of tact but because I didn't want to hear the answer.

Ian said that Heseltine's disclaimer, 'I can think of no circumstances in which I would challenge Margaret Thatcher', is susceptible to any number of let-outs. Acute crisis, Party's fortunes, irresistible pressure, etc, etc.

'It'd be all or bust for him. I don't think he'll dare,' I tried.

Ian replied, but without much conviction, that Heseltine would lose anyway.

I'm not so sure. He might win the contest, but lose the General Election. Then where would we all be?

We are off this afternoon to Scotland. The IEPG conference[1] is booked at Gleneagles. It's a freebie, really, and wives are invited.

But first I must prepare some more notes for the PM on 'Bruges II'.[2] Am I helping her to dig deeper her own political grave?

Later

A note on the subject came over from Charles, marked SECRET, PRIVATE and PERSONAL.

'A good way of drawing attention to something,' I said to Private Office. It enhances my status in the Dept. But it's in total breach of Civil Service convention, there may even be rules of procedure.

If a civil servant at Number 10 wants to get a message to a Minister in another Department the correct way to do so is to communicate with the Private Office of the Secretary of State of that Department – and if it is a junior Minister (itself an unusual enough contingency) then it is for the S of S's office to pass it on down to the head of the office of the junior Minister concerned. Good old Charles.

---

[1] Annual meeting of European Programme Groups (a euphemism for those senior civil servants who had oversight of weapons procurement).

[2] At that time the prime minister was minded to deliver a sequel to her celebrated speech at Bruges the previous year.

Gleneagles   *Wednesday, 21 February*

This morning, before the session, I went for a constitutional with
Peter Levene, and we walked down to the lake, looked at all the
manic golfers milling around the clubhouse. Righteous and crazy-
faced, they glared back.

Peter is restless. His time at MoD is drawing to an end. He is
tempted by Industry, and Arnold Weinstock teases him constantly
with chimeric offers.

But Peter fancies also the possibility of remaining, advancing
indeed, in the public sector. He would like to be Permanent
Secretary at the DTI.

Tricky, I said. The Dept is starved of cash these days and
anyway, haven't they just appointed Gregson?[1]

He toyed also with the idea of becoming (sic) a diplomat.
Really? Yes, what he'd like best is Washington.

I don't often gulp but, privately, I gulped.

'Well, Peter Jay[2] got it,' I said. 'It's one of the posts that does
occasionally go to an outsider.'

I suppose that I am just the same. All vigorous and ambitious
men live by considering that anything is within their capability.

Saltwood   *Sunday, 25 February*

I remain in depression. I might give up drink for Lent. A good start
in Arabia next week, as I always enjoy refusing it from an
Ambassador – they are so loathsomely *arch* when they produce the
whisky bottle, 'I expect you'd welcome some of this, eh? Ho-ho' –
and the orange juice at all those meetings is the best in the world.

I thought I would play on the piano. But when I got to the
music room there was water pouring in and down the east wall.

---

[1] Sir Peter Gregson had moved from Energy (Permanent Under-Secretary) to
Trade and Industry (Permanent Secretary) in 1989.

[2] Peter Jay was economics editor of *The Times* when the prime minister, James
Callaghan (and coincidentally Peter Jay's father-in-law), appointed him British
ambassador to Washington in 1977.

Last year I spent £11,000 replacing the lead just on this one roof. What's the point? The Aubusson can really no longer take any more punishment.

Bugger it, I thought, anyway. It can't stop me playing.

Melodiously I strummed. 'Sentimental Journey'; 'Smoke Gets in Your Eyes'; 'My Guy's Come Back'; 'Stormy Weather'.

Always I think of that Pole who played in the NAAFI at the Army Mountain Warfare Training School at Llanberis, in 1945. For hours on end he played – Chopin, Rachmaninov, Liszt, anything from ENSA naturally – preferring when the hall was empty, and it echoed. Was he thinking of home, and his dead children? Of his horse, shot from under him in the last September battles on the Vistula?

I have done, seen and experienced an awful lot of things. And I like in these tall Gothic rooms, with all these beautiful possessions around me, accumulated by my father and by my grandfather, to nostalgicise.

Why am I still, in the main, so zestful?

I know, but I don't like to say.

In case the gods take it away.

Saltwood   *Saturday, 3 March*

Yesterday went on too long.

I left Paddington by the early train to speak at a Party lunch in Truro. Low key, upper-class candidate, a few bright(ish) sparks. I thought these old Etonians were extinct by now – they certainly are in 'safe' seats – Central Office toad/clones have seen to that. Clearly the Association have reverted to the Piers[1] mould.

In any case it's ridiculous that Truro should not be a Tory seat.

---

[1] Piers Dixon had been MP for Truro, winning the seat in 1970 and again in February 1974, only to lose to the Liberal David Penhaligon in October 1974. Following Penhaligon's death the resulting by-election in 1987 saw Matthew Taylor retain the seat for the Liberals. In the 1987 general election he had a majority over the Conservative candidate of 4,753; in 1992 this increased to 7,570.

All these rentiers, a few landowners, some contented farmers and a lot of holiday-dependent shopkeepers and boarding house landladies.

The Liberal technique is to force people to lower their sights, teeny little provincial problems about bus timetables, and street lighting and the grant for a new community hall. They compensate by giving the electorate uplift with constant plugging of an identity concept – no matter how minuscule – to which they try to attach a confrontational flavour: 'Newton Ferrers Mums outface White-hall' and a really bouncy commonplace little turd (or big turd in the case of Penhaligon) as candidate, and they're in.

So I am rather pessimistic concerning the prospects for this pleasant, diffident young man, even though I firmly, and repetitiously, referred to him as the next Member of Parliament for Truro.

I just caught the train back. A long journey.

The box didn't take long and I fidgeted, did a trawl of the seats for discarded reading material, bought and consumed two Mars bars, which gave me a headache.

I couldn't get home as there was a little dinner at Lyall Street.[1] Just Aspers, Jimmy Goldsmith and Charles Powell. The 'guest' was Conrad Black,[2] the purpose to see to what extent he was amenable to being leant on, in the gentlest manner of course, to steer Max[3] away from plugging Heseltine so much. The answer, it soon became clear, was – not at all.

Black is young, quite attractive looking, very clever and widely read. If I look back over the newspaper tycoons I've known it is only Beaverbrook with whom he compares. Some, like Vere, are just thick, others like Roy Thomson bluff away and you don't know, but they're boring. Cap'n Bob is the most entertaining, I suppose, but you never quite feel he's giving you his full *attention* – and this for reasons, let's say, unrelated to the setting in which the conversation is taking place.

---

[1] 1 Lyall St, town house of John Aspinall.
[2] Conrad Black, Canadian newspaper proprietor, born 1944, who had come to London and bought the *Daily Telegraph* in 1987.
[3] Max Hastings, editor of the *Daily Telegraph* since 1986.

The subject had to be approached delicately. Charles was diplomatic, Jimmy blunt. But Black simply couldn't care. He made a competent, almost dismissive defence. It's my paper, I do what I think right, anyway he (Heseltine) is an interesting chap, we look like we're in a mess, heading for a bigger one, etc.

Black's preference seemed to be for talking about Washington. He's knowledgeable and interesting here too. But as to its principal objective, the dinner was a failure.

Saltwood   *Sunday, 4 March*

A beautiful day of early spring, quite perfect in light, colour, the shadow and tone of stone and lawn and blossom. We have started to mow with the sit-down mowers that roll and stripe. No more rotaries until September when the plantains grow.

I was resigned to settling back 'with the Heritage' when I had a long call from Tristan which electrified me.[1]

We're 28 points behind in the polls, and the leadership is in a panic. The Lady has rocky moments of self doubt. (This has happened before, I told him, Carol used to tell me how dejected she became in 1985 when all the economic indicators were look-ing good but people still wouldn't respond.) The Cabinet are all over the place. Most of them are 'pretty doubtful about' (read *loathe*) her but don't know what to do. G. Howe is behaving 'poorly', *chétif* and unsupportive. The Government have got to find a billion, at once, to buy off the Poll Tax complainants.

'That won't be enough,' I sniggered.

No, wait, he said, I told them 'the only person who can give this to you is Alan Clark'.

John Major, somewhat ruefully, agreed.

Exultant, I waxed on how I could square things in Washington, fix it with our various collaborative partners that we got out of these fearful projects, kick ass in the Army Council. I ended, for the first time, actually *asking*. I said the only thing for it – and to be

---

[1] Tristan Garel-Jones had been deputy chief whip since 1989.

done promptly. Whitsun at the latest – was to make TK leader of the House and me S of S Def.

'Thank you very much,' he said. 'This conversation has been very useful.' Then added the usual disclaimer that there was nothing he could do . . . etc. I feel that I am closer to my ambition than I am ever likely to get again.

Saltwood   *Sunday, 25 March*

Yesterday we lost Mid-Stafford, poor little Heddle's seat, on a swing of 23 per cent.[1] In Plymouth I'd be obliterated. Just as well I'm not standing again.

And yet . . . Jane told me that on the drive down she had been held up by some motor-cycle police for a Jaguar which swept into the Intelligence HQ at Ashford. Suddenly she had a taste of what it was like '*on the outside*'.

I think what saddens me most is the so near and yet so far experience at MoD. I have written the Defence Review. It has, to all intents and purposes, been accepted by Number 10. But no one is getting on with it. It's all being screwed by this absurd 'Options' exercise, which muffles everything.

On Friday I had to circulate a rebuttal of some batty recommendations that we should – effectively – *annexe* East Germany, run exercises there, defend the air space. Simply crazy. A transparent power-play by those in the Dept who are determined to keep the Central Front alive as a magnet/concept for their own careers. But that's all I could do – circulate a paper. It's miles outside the Procurement responsibilities. However taut you stretch the Ox's hide it won't cover straight AF matters, and Hamilton's office (not, to do him justice, Archie himself; or at least he doesn't allow it to show) get angry, make trouble with Julian.

This happens the whole time. It's not just the slow balls-up of

---

[1] John Heddle, MP since 1983, had committed suicide in December 1989. At the 1987 general election he had a majority of 14,000.

the 'Options' project, it's a hundred examples a week of waste, blinkers, vested interest, idleness and failure to put the country before narrow personal, regimental or sectarian considerations. Unless or until I'm Secretary of State I just have to watch them go rolling past, make a private note to chase it if I ever get the chance. Julian, though, is sympathetic, and does what he can.

A long letter today from beloved Tip. He says that the whole of Rhine Army is completely demoralised. There's a 'freeze' on spares, so if vehicles break on exercise they're just towed back to Sennelager and abandoned. The great Panzer workshops that featured in Hitler's exchange with Jodl after the fall of the Remagen bridge are now a scrapyard for broken Land-Rovers. The 'chaps' are good, still, and keen. *They* want to get out into the Empire, sort out the 'trouble spots'. But he says some of the new recruits are almost illiterate. They can't even do sports because these are banned at school as being too competitive.

It's all so depressing. Especially when you think we've had a Tory Government for the last ten years.

House of Commons   *Wednesday, 28 March*

The Lady is under deep pressure now. It just won't go away. As soon as one paper goes quiet another one, or two at a time, start up.

As far as I can make out practically every member of the Cabinet is quietly and unattributably briefing different Editors or members of the Lobby about how awful she is. This makes it easier for people like Peter Jenkins[1] to say that 'she has virtually lost all support in Cabinet'. Malcolm Rifkind[2] is actually quoted today as saying, 'I'll be here after she's gone.'

There is even talk of a coup in July. Heseltine is quite openly

---

[1] Peter Jenkins, political columnist on the *Independent*.
[2] Malcolm Rifkind, MP for Edinburgh Pentlands since 1974. Secretary of State for Scotland since 1986.

spoken about as the heir-presumptive, and preens himself in public.

How has all this been allowed to come about? The Community Charge has got on everyone's nerves of course, and generated the most oppressive volume of correspondence. Persistent deficits in the polls of a nearly insuperable order rattle people. But I am inclined to think that the Party in the House has just got sick of her. She hasn't promoted her 'own' people much. Her 'constituency' in this place depends solely on her proven ability to win General Elections. But now this is in jeopardy she has no real Praetorian Guard to fall back on. There's been a lot of talk about 'one of us', all that, but most of them are still left to moulder at the '92 dinner table. When's the Revolution? In the meantime, all the wets and Blue Chips and general Heathite wankers, who seem ineradicable in this bloody Party, stew around and pine for her to drop dead.

Most critics move, in the open, under (pretty transparent) camouflage. A number of 'heavy' backbenchers of the 'Centre' (ie Left) of the Party have let it be known that her 'Decision-making Circle' should be widened, that they are uneasy about the 'privileged access' enjoyed by 'certain key and unelected advisors'.

This of course is a shot across the bows for Charles and Bernard. But without them she really would be lost, as the Chief Whip, Tim Renton, is Howe's creature; Peter Morrison is of little use as a PPS under these conditions; Gow is neutered and doesn't cut ice any longer and Garel-Jones, who would relish the task of rescuing her as Victor Ludorum in the Whips' Challenge Trophy, is tied up in the Foreign Office, and on overseas visits half the time.

My own position is affected in a number of ways – all unwelcome. My special *access* is less potent because, with the rest of the Cabinet more or less openly plotting their own positions, and jockeying, her disapproval counts for little. We're almost getting to the point where they are no longer afraid of her. And indeed, her sponsorship could actually be damaging. Second, it disturbs my own plans for smooth and easy withdrawal, booking a 'K' at once and a Lords ticket in the next Parliament. Will I even get my PC in May? Finally, I could be faced with the ultimate hideosity of being stuck at MoD during a Heseltine 'reconstruction'. Should I leave immediately, or hang on for certain humiliation forty-eight hours later?

Oh dear. How quickly everything can change.

House of Commons   *Monday, 2 April*

Last night there were riots in Central London – just like 1981. All the anarchist scum, class-war, random drop-outs and trouble-seekers had infiltrated the march and started beating up the police.[1]

There is this strain in most Western countries (except, curiously, the United States) but it is particularly prevalent in Britain, where this rabble have – confirming their middle-class social origins – their own press in the *Grauniad* and the *Independent*. Far from having their capers cut by the revolution in Russia, the removal of a distant but supportive ideological menace, they are flourishing in that very curtailment of discipline and order which the fall of the ancient Soviet autocracy has brought about.

But it is bad. *Civil Disorder.* Could cut either way, but I fear will scare people into wanting a compromise – just as did Saltley Colliery and the three-day week in 1972/3. In the corridors and the tea room people are now talking openly of ditching The Lady to save their skins. This is the first time I've heard it *en clair* since a bad patch (1977?) when we were in opposition. Some of the Lobby, Tony Bevins[2] in particular, hang around outside the Members' post office and fly kites.

There is a wild rumour going round that she may be 'deputised' at the end of July. 'Uh? Deputised?'

'Yes, you know, receive a deputation, the Chief Whip, the '22 Executive, Willie, that kind of thing. Told to throw in the towel.'

Contemptible.

---

[1] An anti-poll-tax demonstration in central London.

[2] Anthony Bevins, political editor of the *Independent*. His father, Reginald, had been an MP, and Postmaster-General, 1959–64.

Ministry of Defence   *Tuesday, 3 April*

For months I have been resisting expenditure (some hundreds of millions) on a completely unnecessary new piece of Army Equipment known by its acronym ACEATM.

It is a 'sideways firing mine' – itself an unlikely, indeed contradictory concept, surely? The idea is that you position one of these incredibly expensive and 'intelligent' devices in the window of a house and when a tank goes past it shoots out at it, 'sideways'.

From the first moment I saw the papers it was clear that this was a complete waste of money, conceived at the height of the Cold War, and now totally unnecessary. Trouble is, I'm not really meant to question 'Operational Requirements'. I'm meant to 'seek' and then, by implication, follow advice on anything about which I have doubts. In the nature of things, the advice comes from the same people who drafted the 'Requirement' in the first place.

Finally, after much deferment, a full-scale 'Meeting' was called.

'You leave them behind, you see, to slow up the enemy's advance.'

'What advance?'

'Well, er, his advance, Minister.'

'What enemy?'

'The Warsaw Pact, Minister.'

'The Warsaw Pact no longer exists. It's disintegrated.'

'In villages, in built-up areas,' shouted somebody else, also in uniform. Why the fuck are all these people in uniform? It's not allowed. Just so as to intimidate me, they think.

'I thought the first rule in deploying armour was to avoid built-up areas?'

'Roads, Minister. Choke-points.'

'What happens if a truck goes past? That would be a waste, wouldn't it. How does it know not to shoot?'

'Well it knows, Minister. It's programmed with all the Warsaw Pact silhouettes.'

'Warsaw Pact?'

'There's a lot of Russian stuff Out of Area now, you know.'

'I do know.'

'It's Next Generation, Minister. A very intelligent sensor.'

'Better programme it to recognise all the French stuff, then.'

'Ha-ha, Minister. Oh, ha-ha.'

What can one do? Nothing. I can block this spastic weapon, and make them cross, and complaining. But about *them* I can do nothing.

I want to fire the whole lot. Instantly. Out, out. No 'District' commands, no golden bowlers, nothing. Out. There are so many good, tough keen young officers who aren't full of shit. How can we bring them on, before they get disillusioned, or conventionalised by the system? If I could, I'd do what Stalin did to Tukhachevsky.[1]

Ministry of Defence   *Thursday, 5 April*

The Lady scowled startledly at me on Tuesday when she came in for Questions. Although she is completely absorbed in her own brief, hyped to the nines for her ordeal against little Kinnock, and pays no attention to her surroundings whatever, her presence beside one on the bench is always a little constraining.

My own last Question was reached, and my performance was not as relaxed and dominating as it should have been. Is my voice losing timbre?

She spat at me again during a somewhat ponderoso question for Nick Soames about Rhodesia. I reminded her about BMATT and our training detachment out there, but she didn't use it.[2] Preprogrammed.

Somehow this little experience brought home to me how utterly unrealistic is any idea that she might make me S of S. How? Why? Lucky even to get PC next month.[3]

---

[1] The purges of the Red Army in 1938/39, when three-quarters of all officers of field rank and above were put to the firing squads.

[2] BMATT: British Military Assistant Training Team. AC's younger son, Andrew, had done a year of duty with the unit attached to the Zimbabwean army.

[3] AC was thinking of the queen's Birthday Honours when the names of new members of the Privy Council would be announced.

Our position continues to worsen. I urge for blood, and still more blood.

The Last Days[1] and the Whips are divided among themselves. Some want blood. Some, covertly, want 'a change'. G-J's own position is equivocal and he probably thinks, may even have been told, that Heseltine would make him Chief. Renton, the existing Chief, doesn't think strategically – or even tactically. He is amiable, social; but never did his groundwork as a junior in 'the office'.

Gow, Ryder, Aitken and I dined at 'Greens' the 'new' restaurant on Locketts' old site, set up under the aegis of Simon Parker Bowles (*relation*, I assume). Confirmed the bad impression when Alison and I tried it out last week. Waiters either *completely* incapable of understanding English – or French, or Italian. Are they Rumanians from an AIDS hostel? – or chinless youths, spacedoutly smiling and chatting to each other in upper-class accents, waiting to get on the waiting list (sic) for Cirencester.

The boys were gloomy. We none of us see our way. Quite difficult to approach The Lady at the moment, as Ian is finding. And what advice do we give her? Shed blood, I said.

When I fell asleep I had a curious dream; gently ascending the hill behind Sandling station, having resigned, and being at peace with the world. Bernard Braine[2] came into it somehow – perhaps because Jonathan had been telling me that he was determined to stay on, in order to block Ted from becoming 'Father of the House'.

Ministry of Defence   *Wednesday, 11 April*

Last night I won £1,000 off John Sterling at backgammon. This always makes me wake up in a good mood. But today, the last of the 'Lent' term, is just too full. I woke at 5-ish, had made tea and

---

[1] *The Last Days of Hitler* by Hugh Trevor-Roper, AC's tutor at Oxford, now Lord Dacre.

[2] Sir Bernard Braine, MP for various Essex constituencies since 1950 and Father of the House since 1983. When he finally retired at the 1992 election, Edward Heath (also elected in 1950) gained the Father of the House soubriquet.

enjoyed Cadogan's memoirs by 7, collected the boxes from the Lodge and read the brief for the DOAE[1] visit by the time the car arrived at 8.15. With luck I will be through in time to catch the 7 pm train to Ashford.

I'm looking forward to five lovely days at Saltwood, and mustn't fritter them. Last weekend we drew up a little daily schedule.

As I went along the Rope Walk this morning I worried about the blackbird. No sign this spring. Sometimes, at first light, I can hear one a very long way away. But surely, even if he/she is dead there should be some offspring here? I suppose the *same one* can't still be alive as it has been causing me pleasure since 1975. But to have none is sad.

There is a thrush in Speaker's Court who sings goodnight so beautifully each evening. When I can, if I'm in my Commons office, I come upstairs and listen.

How could anyone shoot a song-bird?

Saltwood   *Friday, 20 April*

A date which usually marks a period of good fortune, and the transition from spring to early summer. But it is cold and blowy, and there has been a fall of snow on Hampstead Heath. Only at Eriboll is it shirtsleeve hot, with the loch like glass. James rang and said that he had ferried fourteen tups across to their summer quarters on Eilean Chorain.

Yesterday evening Tristan and I repaired to Wiltons, and took a pullman.

I told him (uneasily aware that somewhere the cock would be crowing) that very reluctantly, and with great sadness and not a little apprehension I had come to a certain conclusion. Tristan said that he was glad I had admitted to this. Some weeks ago he had written a paper in his own hand; circulated it to the Chief Whip,

---

[1] DOAE: Defence Operational Analysis Establishment.

Ingham (?!), Andrew Turnbull,[1] John Major and Mark Lennox-Boyd.[2]

Not, I noted, to Charles. No point, he said, CP 'too fanatically committed'.

Each of the recipients had 'tried to push him through her door' (ie to say it in person).

'Well, why don't you?'

Yes, he was going to supper at the Number 10 flat on Sunday – just him and X-B[3] – and told me how he proposed to play it. The Party was 'lazy, sullen, and frightened'. Unless there was a marked improvement by early to mid–October *over* 100 votes would be cast against her at the leadership contest, which was inevitable, in the month following. Tristan's view was that over 100 against would mean that she would have to stand down.

I couldn't help grinning. 'Try telling her that.'

I said that 'Mid October' was balls. The time scale was far shorter. It had to be settled before the Party Conference and that meant, effectively, in *this* parliamentary term – which in turn means before 15 July, because for those last two weeks of the Summer Term we are all in a limbo of rumour, lassitude and low motivation. Proper consideration cannot be given until after the May local election results have been analysed, so that means that the *band* stretches from mid–May until mid–July, no more.

At this exact point in our conversation I spotted Heseltine coming up the steps from the bar! And with Mates! He was shown, not to a nearby, but to the *adjoining* table. This was ludicrous. He and Mates sat down, got up again immediately, were spirited away.

A nearby group of 'businessmen' were oggly. 'Didn't take long to get rid of *him*,' I said, without reverence.

But I bet Michael was thinking, 'They won't treat me like that

---

[1] Andrew Turnbull, principal private secretary to the prime minister since 1988.

[2] Mark Lennox-Boyd, MP for Morecambe since 1979, parliamentary private secretary to the prime minister since 1988.

[3] X-B: AC uses here the abbreviation employed by James Lees-Milne when referring to Mark Lennox-Boyd's father, Alan (later 1st Viscount Boyd of Merton), colonial secretary, 1954–59.

when I'm Prime Minister.' One more score to settle with Clark. A little later I signalled to Albert[1] and said would he please give Mr Heseltine my compliments and apologies for spoiling his evening. I would be very glad if he would allow me to settle his bill.

But whether Albert did so or not, I don't know. If he did, the offer was not accepted.

House of Commons   *Tuesday, 1 May*

I had a conversation with IG in the smoking room. Aitken joined us. What could we do to succour The Lady? Do we even want to? We were stuck with the same inflation rate as when we came into power in 1979. Ten, eleven years of endeavour (or however we call all those deprivations to life and family) and nothing to show for it but the passage of time and the intrusion of age.

We had moved into the chess room for privacy, but it was dinner time, and posses of MPs moved past on their way through to the dining room, and made mocking comments. Atkins, in particular, is cocky and hostile now, as he watches the decline of the Praetorians.

We came to no conclusions, but aggravated each other's dejection. After about a half hour I lied about a dinner engagement and made for the Kundan, but it was closed for a reception. I went to Brooks's, lost £150 and my appetite waned. Returned here and ate a toasted bun, first food since a banana at 1.30.

In the tea room I had a chat with Fallon, a nice cool Whip.[2] I complained to him about all this rotten, irrelevant, unnecessary legislation which clogs our time. Firearms; Football Supporters; War Crimes; *Supermarket Trollies (Local Authority Recovery Powers) Restricted Amendment* . . . etc, *ad nauseam.* Compounded with the abject failure to sort out the rioters at Strangeways prison it was all accumulating evidence of a government in decline. To my

---

[1] Head waiter at Wilton's.

[2] Michael Fallon, MP for Darlington since 1983. Shortly to become parliamentary under-secretary at Education and Science.

considerable pleasure, he was in complete agreement, citing, additionally, the Iraqi supergun. 'We should be making them, and selling them to everyone.'

'Good God,' he said. 'All this stuff about a decline in our manufacturing capability, but they had to come here to get the barrels made, didn't they? We should put it in a Trade Fair.' Splendid fellow.

Of course, in the nineteenth century this is what *would* have happened. And this morning I was on the roof of the old War Office building, looking around at Whitehall. The Admiralty opposite, the Cabinet office, the Treasury, the Foreign Office. How well it was all planned, how *confident*. We ran the Empire, and the world with the same number of civil servants as presently exist in one Department. Instead of spending no more than ten per cent of our Social Security budget on the Royal Navy, the proportion was exactly reversed.

I had wandered through the building, empty for years, but destined to be the nerve-centre of the intelligence services. The PSA[1] have a giant job-creation scheme running here. Dust, bare cabling, little transistor radios blare.

Magnificent rooms; heavy Edwardian panelling; oak plank floors one and a half inches thick; all being torn up to take the giant computers and their wiring. I stood in the central hall, grimy but forbidding still. 'Only Major-Generals and above could use the main door on Whitehall.' (Who thought that one up, I wonder?) I tiptoed into Jack Profumo's private bathroom, still bearing traces of Valerie Hobson's redecoration, and telepathised for him; those moments of anguished realisation, when he must have known the Keeler affair was breaking.

Particularly, too, as I meandered along those gloomy corridors, still untouched, I reflected on past characters, long dead, who had paced excitedly there during those difficult months of the Great War when 'The Big Push' – and then again 'The Big Push' – was being planned. How many hundreds of thousands of Death Warrants were stamped in these rooms?

---

[1] Property Services Agency.

Albany   *Wednesday, 2 May*

I woke too early for *The Times*, even here, where Herbie delivers it
at 6.15, and turned to Chips for solace with my EMT. I became
absorbed by some of the very late entries:

Arturo Lopez-Wilshaw at 18, Rue du Centre, and Neuilly.
Alexis de Rede, 'the Eugene de Rastignac of modern Paris' (who
he?) at the Hotel Lambert. 'Eighteen, semi-gratin and very
grand . . . Footmen and candelabra on the stairs; gold plate . . .
the Palazzo Colonna *en petite*.'

'I was particularly glad to see the Etienne de Beaumonts again.
They are so intelligent, so *fin*, so decadent, so old, so painted and so
civilised.'

This was only forty-five years ago. Now we live in a squalid
scrabble. It's nonsense to say we're better off. We're catastrophically poorer due to (a) death duties and (b) 'levelling up' of
standards and expectations in the lower classes so that it is completely impossible to find, even if one could afford, domestic
servants.

Poor darling Jane drained and cleaned the pool *herself* yesterday.
Of course she felt utterly exhausted. Saltwood slowly disintegrates
round one, sector by sector (presently the Great Library and my
father's study) as poor William – *aet* 70, and *cum* some 370,000
Virginian cigarettes, is terminally ill – gets 'out of reach' and needs
a major blitz, up to two full days, to get it back 'up'.

We're too exhausted, and time is too precious, to 'entertain' –
although we have the perfect setting. Anyway, it's so expensive,
with good claret at £100 – minimum – per bottle.

Albany   *Thursday, 10 May*

Today is the fiftieth anniversary of the German attack in the West.
The day that Valentine Lawford, the 'rather second Empire'
secretary, omitted to tell Halifax that Rab Butler was waiting in
the outer office with a message (that Labour would serve in a

coalition under him). Halifax slipped out of the other door – to go to the dentist (!). By the evening it was too late, and Winston was Prime Minister.

I really don't know, I still can't judge, whether that was a good, or a bad, thing for the Britain that I love and cherish, and whose friendly, stubborn, dignified and sensible people have so often been let down by their rulers.

House of Commons   *Monday, 14 May*

The whole Department is in a state of frustration. What *is* happening to the Review?

'Options for Change' – I ask you!

Spastic title. There shouldn't be any fucking 'options'. It should be – 'It's like this. Now get on with it.' As it is, we're just haemorrhaging away on needless expenditure, and morale is plummeting with the uncertainty.

I have 'leaked' the situation. I chose Andy Marr[1] because he is young and clear-headed, and politically acute. We met, clandestinely, on the terrace, at the far end by the Lords fence. He will run something in the next issue, probably on Monday.

House of Commons   *Tuesday, 15 May*

I am in tremendous form at the moment.

This afternoon I pleased the House at Questions. It is a triumph if you can make *both* sides laugh good-humouredly, as I first discovered, memorably, questioning Merlyn Rees in 1977 [see p. 57].

Dale Campbell-Savours[2] came in with an ill-natured supplementary – 'Will the Minister ensure that his Department . . . does

---

[1] Andrew Marr, parliamentary correspondent of *The Economist*.
[2] Dale Campbell-Savours, MP for Workington since 1979.

not get into bed with any of the companies from which the Member for Petersfield is drawing a retainer . . .'

Mates sat staring straight ahead, face as black as thunder.

Much uproar, 'show' indignation, points of order.

When it settled down I was expected to make a pompous rebuttal; at the very least a reference to the Committee on Members' Interests, every confidence, etc, etc.

But I don't like Mates; the House doesn't like Mates.

I said, 'One thing I have learned, Mr Speaker, is that it is never the slightest use telling people who they shouldn't go to bed with.'

Everyone was delighted – except, of course, Mates.

House of Commons   *Thursday, 31 May*

I am getting a marvellous press.

The Economist article was just right, all the more so because Andy had sought, and quoted, corroboration from senior officials in the Dept.

Last week I had lunch, privately, at the *FT*, and sparkled. A highly complimentary piece followed on the Saturday – 'one of the most atttractive (Hullo!) as well as one of the cleverest of Mrs Thatcher's Ministers'.

'Profiles' everywhere, none of them too embarrassing. I got off the sleeper this morning to find a full leader-page article in the *Mail* by Gordon Greig:[1] 'Could this be the moment when one politician finally gets a grip on the Cold War warriors after 50 years of meekly obeying orders?'

TK is putting a brave face on it. The message from along the corridor is that 'he is keeping his own counsel' (ie, wondering how the hell he can get even).

---

[1] Gordon Greig, long-time political editor of the *Daily Mail*.

Saltwood   *Friday, 8 June*

Yesterday evening I got involved with some kind of 'decision-makers' groupette at the LSE. Brainy people on the up-and-up, with a few heavies to pour cold water.

On my left the scatty (American) boffin in whose honour the meal was being held; on my right, David Sainsbury the (now reluctant) funder of the SDP.[1] Actually, if you didn't know he was so rich you would just think he was a dreary little Jewish accountant.

I made some provocative remarks about 'The Nation State', and Sam Brittan,[2] who has disapproved of me for a very long time, shifted uneasily on his (not unmassive) haunches, and mutter-heckled. Finally he came out with it.

'What *is* "The Nation State"?'

'If you don't *know* what The Nation State is,' I said, 'you're decadent.'

John Moore was also there. Oh so golden and youthful looking. But a husk, a husk. Cut down so young.

Albany   *Monday, 11 June*

We went to the Gilmours' garden party, at Syon.[3]

The weather was fearfully cold and, as we wandered the gardens, elderly dowagers were complaining of 'frostbite'. Mollie Buccleuch, with a stick (who was it in the Thirties who referred to her and Mary Roxburghe as being 'randy as schoolgirls'?)

---

[1] David Sainsbury, deputy chairman of the grocers since 1988, had been a trustee and major contributor to the Social Democratic Party since its inception in 1982.

[2] Sam Brittan, principal economics commentator of the *Financial Times* since 1966 and elder brother of Sir Leon Brittan, a vice-president of the Commission of the European Communities.

[3] Sir Ian Gilmour, 3rd Bt. MP for Chesham since 1974. Married to Lady Caroline Margaret Montagu-Douglas-Scott, younger daughter of the 8th Duke of Buccleuch.

People were keen to talk to me, and admiringly curious. I am still in the backwash of the 'Defence Review' publicity.

Young – *policeman* young – Victor Smart[1] came up, after bobbing round a group, and introduced himself. Light-heartedly I protested about his piece: 'There is now considerable doubt as to whether the two Ministers can continue to exist in the same Department', etc.

Then Adam Raphael[2] came up, all ingratiating: 'We're running a Profile of you in the next paper.' After he'd gone Smart said, '*He* was the one who insisted on the "Two Ministers" bit.'

Willie Whitelaw I also talked to. He was nice, and on the ball and – I was delighted to see – still rheumy-eyed and *repeatedly* calling for his glass to be refilled. He told me I was 'quite right; absolutely right . . . to do what you are doing' at MoD. It had to be done. 'A lot of people will try and block you. But you must press on.'

I was hugely cheered by this. If only Willie were still 'around'.

But Willie was deeply gloomy, in the traditional High Tory way, about electoral prospects. There was a bit of 'does anyone tell her anything?' and 'No good getting mobbed in America, and thinking that's going to work here.'

The fact that Willie no longer has a proper consultative role (in which he was so immensely valuable) is an indictment of our present system of government. He was worked off his feet as Lord President in order, nominally, to 'justify' his position in Cabinet. He chaired a lot of bloody stupid committees that easily could have been steered by any number of different nonentities. In the evenings he had stuffy dinners, on weekends Party functions.

As a result he got a stroke.

Much better to have been four days a week in Penrith, and just coming up for Cabinet, and critical meetings.

We brought Ian and Caroline a tiny present. Their parties are so congenial – pretty girls, children in party clothes excitedly running

---

[1] Victor Smart, political correspondent of the *Observer*.

[2] Adam Raphael, Executive editor of the *Observer* since 1988.

hither and thither, bishops, Whig heavies, clever journalists, *Refusés* – and I never write a bread-and-butter letter.

It was a bottle of '67 Yquem. I stood it on the dining-room table (we had arrived late and our hosts were already mingling). When we said goodbye it had gone. I hope the staff didn't drink it.

Ministry of Defence   *Thursday, 14 June*

I was host at the NATO Defence College lunch at Lancaster House. Made a routine Darling-you-were-Wonderful speech. The Italian General thought (according to David[1]) that I was Secretary of State and TK was 'just another Minister'.

Kenneth Baker[2] is a clever fellow. When I went to see him at Central Office – to clear my slate in 'Party' terms – he was effusive. 'You're doing brilliantly well. A textbook. You have my fullest admiration.'

But to TK he had said, 'You must find it very difficult working with Alan.'

I like this. If you are a serious player, it's no good being 'straight'. You just won't last.

Saltwood   *Sunday, 17 June*

This morning I killed the heron.

He has been raiding the moat, starting in the early hours, then getting bolder and bolder, taking eight or nine fish, carp, nishikoi, exotica, every day.

I had risen very early, before five, with the intention of getting a magpie who has been pillaging all the nests along the beech hedge. But returned empty handed. They are clever birds, and sense one's presence.

---

[1] David Hatcher, APS in AC's private office.
[2] Chairman of the Conservative Party since 1989.

Suddenly Jane spotted the heron from the casement window in my bathroom.

I ran down and took the 4.10 off the slab, cocked the hammer. He was just opposite the steps, took off clumsily and I fired, being sickened to see him fall back in the water, struggle vainly to get up the bank, one wing useless.

I reloaded, went round to the opposite bank. Tom beat me to it and gamely made at him, but the great bird, head feathers bristling and eyes aglare, made a curious high-pitched menacing sound, his great beak jabbing fiercely at the Jack Russell.

'Get Tom out of the way,' I screamed.

I closed the range to about twenty feet and took aim. I did not want to mutilate that beautiful head, so drew a bead on his shoulder.

The execution. For a split second he seemed simply to have absorbed the shot; then very slowly his head arched round and took refuge inside his wing, half under water. He was motionless, dead.

I was already sobbing as I went back up the steps: 'Sodding fish, why should I kill that beautiful creature just for the sodding fish . . .'

I cursed and blubbed up in my bedroom, as I changed into jeans and a T-shirt. I was near a nervous breakdown. Yet if it had been a burglar or a vandal I wouldn't have given a toss. It's human beings that are the vermin.

At breakfast I had a handsome photograph on the front page of *The Observer*. There was a heavy and tendentious piece about 'Service chiefs have lost confidence in Ministers'. Three columns wide, lead item. 'The Deputy is making all the running.'

Too bloody right he is. But will he bring off the *coup royal*?

Glasgow–Inverness train   *Friday, 22 June*

The closing entry for this volume. The second half of the year will overlap with 1991, in a new notebook which, crisply expectant, sits in the drawer of my desk at MoD. What will it record? A continuing ascendancy – for verily I am in the stratosphere at the moment? Stagnation? Or decline? Or perhaps, most romantic of all, the sudden stop. When the lunatic or the assassin do their work or, simply, the gods lose patience.

How I do enjoy my job! And how full of vitality I feel – mind racing, gifts of expression, spoken and written, better than at any time. My self-confidence is complete. I don't even use the folder at Questions any more, just lounge on the Bench and answer off the top of my head.

'For the second day running,' said the BBC *Yesterday in Parliament*, 'the star of the Defence debate was Alan Clark, the laid-back but cerebral Minister of State.'

Two more Profiles, both laudatory, are due out on the weekend.

So where do I go from here? The objective must be now – and I mean now, very shortly, July at the latest – to displace the Secretary of State.

Tom remains affable, but wary. He sees Hugh Colver, the Press Officer *for an hour* every day. (I shouldn't think I've had more than five minutes with a press officer since walking into the building last summer.) Tom's office have 'let it be known' that I am 'getting more publicity than is desirable'. 'Desired' by who, pray?

But what can happen to the Secretary of State? Where can he go? Leader of the House is really the only practical possibility now.

But I don't plot. I sleepwalk. My timings are rarely calculated, more often luck and intuition. I cannot predict what will happen I have no feel for it at all.

Ministry of Defence   *Wednesday, 27 June*

This morning I went out to Greenwich – *what* incredible buildings, better than Versailles, really we ought to be doing something more important with them.

The traffic was heavy, and I had time, on the back seat, to embellish the dreary little text – 'user friendly' – which officials

had given me to utter as an 'introduction' to the morning's proceedings.

I am impatient with the sluggish pace, the caution and deriva-
tiveness of our warship design. There are many clever and original
naval architects, in our ancient tradition, still around – at Vosper, at
Swans, at consultants like Yard. But they are feared and disliked by
the huge overstaffed troglodyte Admiralty settlement at Bath. Why
the fuck isn't *that* place privatised? How can the private sector ever
compete with an organisation so closely linked, in terms of career
advancement, with its own main customer?

So I added in a good bit about changing needs, different
theatres, the need to allow ships the capability to fulfil their new
roles. You get pirates in the straits of Malacca, terrorising and
robbing civilian traffic. A corvette answers a distress call. Then
what? The pirates will have armour piercing 0.5 in Brownings in
rubber boats, Republican Guard stuff. What do you use against
that, an Exocet?

This was received in pretty piggy silence by my audience,
whose 'mix' I couldn't quite, through the footlights, determine.
The Admiral, Kenneth Eaton,[1] who was on the platform with me,
remained expressionless throughout. But as he neither applauded
nor, when others nervously did, laugh, his view was plain enough.

There were high-ranking uniforms scattered about, but the
majority were suits, 'industrialists'.

I stayed on for the first 'real' speaker, a Professor of Industrial
Trends (I must tell John[2] about this new 'chair'), and he made a
few mildly critical remarks about the government, which were
clapped.

I thought if any of those sodding sailors was clapping I'll have
him cashiered. As for 'industrialists', they're almost (but nothing,
no one, not even 'Claimants' Unions' can be) *as* bad as farmers. If
I said to them, 'Look an "exciting" (correct usage at last) new
Initiative: In order to cut down on bureaucratic form-filling red

---

[1] Sir Kenneth Eaton, Controller of the Navy since 1989.

[2] John Sparrow, Warden of All Souls, was a fastidious critic of fashionable trends
in higher education.

tape, etc, I've arranged for you to go next door and my assistant will hand over a cheque on the Bank of England, pre-endorsed. All *you* have to do is fill in the amount' . . . 'Wha'?' . . . 'according to your needs' – they'd still grumble.

To Brooks's, where I had a tryst with Peter Jenkins. He was already there, pouring the tea. He doesn't smile much – at all, you could say. And like many charmless people, he is immune, even when it is being deployed towards him. The only thing he respects is power, or access to power. So I am gratified that he should have invited me. I have come some distance since he used to describe me as a zealot on the far Right, then more recently as a 'loose cannon'.

Now, it's 'the highly intelligent Mr Alan Clark'.

Peter does recognise that I am trying to do something at MoD, that it is logical, but difficult. He warned me that the Party would turn against me, if it has not already started to do so. Yes, I said, but not if I was Secretary of State, because I could explain and persuade. As it is, I am tongue-tied, and the vested interests in the Department leak against me.

One of the anomalies is that 'Defence Correspondents' practically never talk to Politicians. They have no sympathy with or understanding of politics. They get all their briefing, and their leaks, from soldiers.

I explained that I was doing my best. But I had to balance Party, Treasury, the PM's own periodic bouts of cold feet and waverings.

Whether any good will come of this meeting time alone will tell. But a certain mending of fences. Of all the Lobby he has the least gossip, and the least small-talk. Admirable, but no fun.

Albany   *Thursday, 28 June*

Last night we spectated at the Queen Mother's special ninetieth birthday parade from the big window at Admiralty House. Chiefs of Staff and their wives, Hamilton, a few minor Royals and the Prince, tetchy and inattentive. TK was beside the QM on her dais for 'taking the salute'. The concept was pleasing. Instead of a lot of bands and soldiers, there was a little detachment, all puffed up and

spick and span with pride and pleasure, from each of the organisations of which she was Patron.

Actually, you don't really get a very good view from these
windows, especially if you have to be 'polite'. But some participants
I did notice, and was cheered by. The pleasing Jack Russell, who
confidently led one section; and the jolly beige hens – *Orpington
Yellows*, apparently they are called – in their wicker cage. Two fine
bulls in trailers also drew applause – was I the only person to reflect
on their fate, all too soon? The squalor and terror of the stockyard
corridors, the mishandled 'stunning', the mechanical guillotine?

Jane sat in the centre front, with Princess Margaret on her right.
The Princess smoked resolutely throughout, at one point reprim-
anding her nephew who had moved *out* of her line of sight, thus
exposing her to a telephoto lens.

Afterwards we repaired to a huge reception at the RUSI. The
Queen Mother herself was perfectly incredible. In spite of having
stood for at least half the time on the saluting dais, she moved
among the guests for nearly two hours, radiating a deep personal
happiness and concern for all to whom she was introduced.

Somewhat reluctantly TK finally produced us. 'This is Alan
Clark, he must be a neighbour of yours in Scot . . .'

She sliced through the booming and asked me, 'How is the
library at Saltwood?'

We had a nice little chat. She said that Saltwood had one of the
loveliest atmospheres of any place she had ever visited.

TK, out of things, got restive and tried to move her on. She
showed her reluctance.

What a marvellous performance. I could never have managed it,
and I'm thirty years younger.

Albany   *Wednesday, 4 July*

I was reading Cadogan's diaries with EMT. Something made me
look up Oran, and I found that this very day is the anniversary of
our destruction of the French Fleet at Mers-el-Kebir. Winston
Churchill's greatest stroke (not least because it must have been so

hurtful for him). But that action, more than any other, showed that we were going to fight, and fight rough. From then on we were undefeated – Battle of Britain, Sidi Barrani, Tobruk, Benghazi. We could have made peace at the time of the Hess mission and the world would have been completely different.

Spontaneously, I wrote a note to the PM reminding her, and of the Foreign Office memo pleading that it would make 'all the difference' (yeah) to our relations with Vichy if we allowed the French battleships to return to Toulon. Pat[1] dropped it off at Number 10 on our way to the Dept, and I hope she enjoyed it.

Later, when I was in the Commons, I was caught on the stairs to the committee room corridor by Don McIntyre[2] thoughtfully, as is his wont, attentively strained and agonising. He told me that the Chiefs of Staff, who were seeing the Prime Minister next week, were going to 'complain' about me. Exceeding my authority, doing 'damage', who's in charge? etc. This is lowering. Of course she'll resist it. But it may shake her faith, make her think it's impossible to promote me there. And this, presumably is what they want, a pre-emptive strike.

Plymouth train   *Friday, 13 July*

My father's birthday. He would be eighty-seven today, if Nolwen hadn't poisoned him, pottering about and probably something of a nuisance. After all, Uncle Colin, Russell and Alan are all in fine health, and in their nineties.

I am in good spirits. Last night at the seven o'clock vote the talk was all of poor Nicky.[3] I said to Ian Lang,[4] so tiredly drawn and

---

[1] Pat, Ministry of Defence driver.

[2] Donald McIntryre, political correspondent of the *Independent on Sunday*.

[3] Nicholas Ridley was under pressure to resign following an interview in *The Spectator*. Ridley claimed that Dominic Lawson, the editor, had kept the tape running after the interview had ended, and then revealed the full text. Certain forthright remarks by Ridley had caused offence in Germany.

[4] Ian Lang, MP for Galloway since 1979. Minister of State, Scottish Office, since 1987.

handsome, 'There's nothing so improves the mood of the Party as the imminent execution of a senior colleague.'

Robin Maxwell-Hyslop[1] told me that on behalf of the Trade and Industry Committee he had passed a message that I would be their preference as Secretary of State to succeed Nicky (unlikely to swing it, but can't do much harm); and going out through the vote doors Paul Channon[2] fell in beside me. 'Well, I hear you're going to be Secretary of State for Trade and Industry.' Now Paul has very good antennae. Secretly thrilled, I dissimulated.

'Seems obvious to me,' he said. 'Would solve a lot of problems simultaneously.'

Thoroughly delighted with myself I held court in the Lobby. Around me I had John Cole, Colin Brown,[3] a swarthy little fellow from the *FT* and a very short cheeky chappie from one of the comics. George Jones[4] hovered; but as he has a low opinion of me – he only talks to Mates and the Left – didn't approach.

I said that Nick's performance was a welcome return to the old doings of the nineteenth century, when major figures in the Govt could digress giftedly and constructively on the issues of the day, without constantly being hauled over the coals by some wanker in the FCO Press Office.

'But in those days it took three weeks for the papers to get to Berlin,' said John Cole, not without reason.

All evening the tide continued to run. Jane and I were at a dinner at the French Embassy – little tables – and as we drifted into the drawing room for coffee the Chief Secretary[5] made a point of coming over. 'By Monday you could well find yourself Secretary of State for Trade and Industry.'

Jane, bless her, is secretly delighted. *Into the big frame at last!* But we dare not say anything, even to each other. And in this morning's

---

[1] Robin Maxwell-Hyslop, MP for Tiverton since 1960, had been a member of the Trade and Industry Select Committee since 1971.

[2] Paul Channon had returned to the back benches in 1989.

[3] John Cole, political editor of the BBC since 1981; Colin Brown, a political correspondent on the *Independent*.

[4] *Daily Telegraph*.

[5] Norman Lamont.

papers I am tipped as Number One probability by Gordon Greig in the *Mail*, and as a likely contender in *The Independent*.

At intervals I stop writing, and fantasise. The Prince's Return. To occupy that very office to which formerly I was summoned by Norman, by Paul and by David. To get Matthew to run my Office, with Rose as the Diary queen; sort out a few of those officials who 'took against' me and bring forward the loyal ones.

We'll know soon.

Saltwood   *Saturday, 14 July*

This morning I swam very early, before seven, and the view *from the water* was unbelievable because the sun is on the towers:

> And Lo! The Hunter of the East has caught
> The Sultan's turret in a noose of light.[1]

– which happens only for a couple of weeks in high summer, and the tobacco plants are in flower. The rays are too flat, still, to touch the poolside and the Morning Glory flares purple. The whole pool area is wonderfully overgrown this year, and enchanted.

I was pleased to find myself tipped this morning in *The Times*, the *Telegraph* and the *Independent*. How fickle and derivative the press are. In many cases these are the same people who regularly predict my dismissal whenever there is talk of a reshuffle.

I spent most of the morning out of doors, though fretting (for the first time in my career) that the phone might be ringing. Why was I so unsettled this time? Realising subconsciously, I suppose, that the chance was good, but it was the last.

I remember saying to Jane, 'Actually none of this really matters compared with whether James will beget a son.'

I took calls from Wastell, B. Anderson, Sherman (time-wasting) and *W. Evening Herald*.

This last, naturally, wanted to talk at length about the Plympton

---

[1] Edward Fitzgerald, *The Rubaiyat of Omar Khayyam*.

Water Works. Not a word about Ridley or my prospects in Government, although I don't doubt there would have been plenty if I was being criticised, however oblique, remote or irrelevant the source.

(As I write this I am reminded of an exemplary occasion, which I don't think I recorded at the time, when a *Herald* [female] reporter rang me, all of a state, and said, 'You've been black-listed by the Esperanto Society. What have you got to say about that?')

Bruce was his usual slightly dampening self – and nothing from Tristan, a bad sign. Did BA mention Lilley?[1] I think he may have done. He is usually pretty well informed about undercurrents.

By mid-afternoon my private hopes had waned. Then, at tea, the news came through. Nick had resigned, 'and his successor will be announced in about a half hour' – then back to some prat standing outside Number 10.

We sat in silence, rustling stale newsprint, and clinking cups as we poured and repoured.

Some fifteen minutes later the announcement that it was Peter Lilley, 'at forty-six the youngest member of the Cabinet'.

Flatly we sat, reading and grumbling.

Then the phone rang. I made Jane answer, in case it was a reporter or a colleague calling for a concealed gloat. But it was Sally. And I could tell from Jane's sudden squeal of pleasure, and the nature of her questions, that she was giving news of a confirmed pregnancy.[2]

How wonderful! And so magically soon after my remark that very morning! With tears in my eyes, I congratulated her. Everything seemed to fall into place now, all the careful structuring of the Trusts, the interlocking provisions and possessions.

I took out the SS 100 and drove down to St Leonard's, prayed and gave thanks in that same pew where I had sat at my father's funeral, immediately behind Nolwen.

I had forgotten his birthday, but now I realise that it must have been confirmed on that day – and is due in February![3]

---

[1] Peter Lilley, MP for St Albans since 1983. Financial Secretary at the Treasury.

[2] Sadly the child was later miscarried and Sally divorced James the following year.

[3] Both AC's own sons were born in February.

Albany   *Friday, 20 July*

The last day of 'term', effectively. There is some patchy business next week, an Opposition supply day on Tuesday, but nothing to speak of – ending with the Buck House garden party and a reception at Number 10.

This morning I woke very early, and with that special late July tranquillity, before even the buses start in Regent St, and the sky is still pale grey from heat haze. No shadows as yet, and the promise of another very hot day.

There are few things more delicious than anticipation of the imminent long summer holiday – particularly while we still have to taste the piquancy of the 'Junior Reshuffle'.

Last evening we had the 'End-of-Term Dinner'. Not quite a dining club, as we only meet on the Thursday before the Long Recess. There is no actual election process. Membership (and discardment) are osmotic. Ian 'convenes', though Soames and Ryder are each active in organisation. Class is undeniably a factor.

The oval room at White's. Boring food – smoked salmon, roast beef. Who the hell did this, in *July*?

In attendance were Gow, Heathcoat-Amory, Bertie Denham, Jonathan Aitken, Hamilton, Garel-Jones (a 'first' for him!), Alexander Hesketh and Cranborne.[1] Fun to see Robert, and a tribute to IG's discernment as in theory he is out, until 'Harare'[2] dies. But Robert keeps his finger on the pulse, and is knowledgeable.

An uncomfortable atmosphere. We don't like what we see, and we don't like admitting, even to each other, that our beloved leader may be fallible. Not in front of Ian, anyway. But because we don't see our way, substantial political discussion was at a discount. Gossip was stale, and people fell back on dirty stories. Pure dirt, I mean, the Dorm.

---

[1] David Heathcoat-Amory, Parliamentary Under-Secretary, Environment, since 1989; Lord Hesketh, now Minister of State, Trade and Industry. Robert, Viscount Cranborne, heir to the Marquess of Salisbury, had stood down as MP for Dorset South at the 1987 general election.

[2] 6th Marquess of Salisbury.

I had Soames on my left. 'You'll be in the Cabinet by Monday. Oh no. This is what I hear . . .', etc. He is shameless ('Straight to the Lords'[1]).

A propos of the Lords, was Bertie Denham sounding me out when he kept asking 'what I wanted'? Was he trying to lead me into hinting at the Lords as a working Min of S? Perhaps I muffed it by saying I wanted to be S of S for Defence. He looked disappointed. He seemed pretty tight, but the Upper Classes *remember* what they (and you) say when they were tight.

At the end of the meal, significantly and in contrast to earlier years, instead of a *tour-de-table* and monologues on the topics of the day, a colleague's failings, or whatever, each person gave a little 'performance'.

Ian, *very* boringly, gave us 'Albert and the Lion'. Waste of time. Bertie was the bluest, Richard the funniest – still – with the Bader at Roedean story. I did 'Frankie and Johnnie'. Most people know the first few verses, but the punch line is in the last:

> Sheriff came over in the mornin',
> said it was all for the best.
> He said her lover Johnnie
> was nothin' but a doggone pest.

We don't *need* to have an Election for two years, we kept telling each other. Technically true, but balls as well.

I thought there would be more talk of a possible 'challenge' in the autumn but, ominously, there was none. The prospect, though, is implacably in the middle distance. A towering thunderhead of Alto-Cumulus, precursor of change not just in the weather, but in the Climate.

That evening, at Saltwood

This must have been the hottest day of the year. Everything is so full, and overripe, and pale yellow.

I am worried about growing old. After I had been swimming I

---

[1] A phrase in the Clark family signifying a glorious finale.

went to the top of the towers and hung on the bar. I couldn't do
one pull-up. In the summer of 1955, my last at Saltwood before I
went to Rye, the summer of Marye thirty-five years ago (and yet it
seems like six or seven) I could easily do four. And over twenty
swings of ankles above my head.

Saltwood   *Saturday, 21 July*

Eight o'clock in the evening, and still overpoweringly hot. I sit out
by the pool, which is yellowy-green, and touching eighty degrees.

Today I went to the helicopter show at Middle Wallop.
Lunchtime in the VIP tent was a furnace, worse even than the Ifa
in Madrid,[1] or the BAe tent at the LaserFire demo in Dubai.

Interesting discussions. The two units on which I would most
like to spend money freely are the Army Air Corps and (to provide
them with a quota of medium-heavy weapons) the Parachute
Regt.

But the AAC are guarded in their approach to the 'Air Cavalry'
concept. We have a number of good ancient Cavalry regiments
which, because of the shrinkage in armoured deployment on
the 'Central Front', will have to amalgamate or even disappear
altogether. The need to expand the AAC is obvious (or obvious
to me, anyhow). These regts have been already – as they saw it –
traumatised once when they lost their horses and went into tanks.
Would not a reversion to helicopters by symbolic, and welcome?
But the officers here (I've noticed this with the SAS at Hereford
too) like to keep it small and cliquey, where you know everyone,
NCOs and men as well, by their Christian names.

James came and collected me this early morning with a Gazelle.
His co-pilot was a Staff Sgt Pengelley, whom I remember for his
enthusiasm in the AAC mess at Stanley when I visited the Falklands with the Defence Committee in October of 1982. Like all
who have flown in combat conditions he is adamant on the urgent

---

[1] Ifa: a hotel in Madrid where AC was once marooned with his family after their
Mercedes broke down (see p. 17).

need for *fighter* helicopters, to intercept enemy transport and ground attack, and to defend our own.

As we arrived at Wallop James was at the controls, and too insouciant for Pengelley, who got anxious.

'These lose speed very quickly on approach.'

'That's OK.'

'You can get caught by surprise.'

'I have control.'

I was proud of him. Even more so on the return, when he made a beautiful, totally accurate landing opposite the Garden Entrance after taking the neater (but more difficult and funked by many visitors) approach from behind Thorpe's Tower.

When they left James was still at the controls and performed a salute on the east side. Going straight in from the hover he stood the little Gazelle on its tail and went straight into a vertical climbing torque turn directly over the great sycamores.

It was spectacular. But in the midst of Life we are in Death. A tiny malfunction of the gearbox, a hesitation in the tail rotor, and the frail little machine would have crashed – before my very gate – and burned to a cinder. I draw strength from reflections such as this. Because if God wants to plunge in the knife, then He can do so – at any time.

The Garden House   *Sunday, 22 July*

I think this is my first entry from over here. It is very warm and silent, well separated from the cares and pressures of the castle. A true *Pavillon* in which to work or contemplate, and extravagantly accoutred to 'self-catering' status. We have cleaned it up, painted the weather-boarding, spent money, 'got it very nice'. Now the easiest part, and the most fun – furnishing and arranging. Few traces of my parents. Of Colette, none whatever. Save for some missing electric light bulbs, she might never have set foot in the place.

I wonder what its fate will be?

★

This afternoon we went to Bethersden to pick up Jane's Citroën. On the way over we found ourselves drawn to explore the overgrown drive of a concealed manor house.

The façade was dark and had an abandoned air. But the back quarters were a delight. Heavy vegetation had encroached on the yard, and there were saplings everywhere pushing through the brick pave. A half-hearted attempt had been made to cut the very long grass with an Allen which stood, well-maintained looking, but inoperative. Just adjacent was a (still) working oast house.

Formerly there had been HONEY signs fixed to the gate, but not today and Jane needed some persuading to reconnoitre. But our reward was this beautiful friendly home, with low-roofed intercommunicating rooms, comfortable and sheltering. Hens talked inquiringly, and walked in and out of the kitchen. A fine fluffed tawny tabby strolled by assertively with his tail up.

The owner appeared, pleasant, elderly. He could almost have been ex RFC. Most courteously he did produce honey, and passed the time of day.

I felt overcome by a wistful nostalgia for starting again. As Jane said, an utterly perfect place to live as young marrieds, and bring up children.

But you can't put the clock back by two seconds – never mind twenty-five years.

On the return journey I cut across to the old A20, passing the sign for Hothfield where in the nurses' quarters on a summer's evening in 1955 I experienced the most perfect physical sensation, never before or since, with Marye. Jealous and inquisitive colleagues tried and rattled her door, departing in the end to get Matron. She, stout woman, portentously interrogated Marye through the keyhole, but the sweet girl (who looked, now I come to think about it, not unlike a bustier version of Jenny on HRT) kept her superior at bay for some precious minutes while I got dressed and climbed out of the window, to stumble across unlit lawns and rose bushes.

Ministry of Defence   *Monday, 30 July*

I must record a curious phenomenon. If something is happening, or has happened, that affects one adversely, is upsetting – 'bad news' – one feels very tired (over that time) even though one still doesn't know. I remember Jane telling me that she had experienced this on the afternoon we were driving back from Hawtreys and Jason was run over.[1] And this morning I felt dreadful in the Sandling train. It's not just feeling a bit sleepy; it's feeling absolutely shattered, as if one was getting polio, only without the fever.

When I got to the barrier Julian was waiting, looking anxious.

'Minister, I have some very, very bad news.'

For a split second I feared it must be Andrew. But something in his eyes was missing (the look of fear, I suppose, and embarrassment that I might actually *break down*). 'Ian Gow has been killed by a car bomb.'

'How spiteful of them', was all I could say. But I thought particularly of the poor Lady. She wept at the first casualties in the Falklands. I wonder if she did today? Because Ian loved her, actually loved, I mean, in every sense but the physical. And then in the end, as lovers do (particularly that kind), he got on her nerves, and she was off-hand with him. He played his last beseeching card: 'I will have to resign.' 'Go ahead, then.' (I foreshorten the exchange, of course) – and that was it.

We talked briefly by the newsagents, and I cautioned Julian to hold his tongue in the car as I did not want Bob 'horning in' and trying to curdle our blood.

Even a silence would have been 'pregnant', so I outmanoeuvred Bob by talking in matter-of-fact tones throughout the journey about the Options Statement, and kindred subjects.

Once ensconced here, I became thoughtful. My old friend. Ian got me into Government, surmounting much opposition and, even from her, misgiving. Very few people had so clear and cogent

---

[1] A sad episode in family history when a favourite Labrador puppy was killed.

JULY 1990   437

an understanding of how Whitehall, and the Cabinet Office
building worked. Although in recent years Ian had become a little
saddened and, indeed, irritated by the way in which the Court had
changed and Charles Powell had got the whole thing in his grip.
And this, together with his increasing distance from the reality
of office, had led him to indulge in *manneristics.* He practised,
sometimes beyond the bounds of tolerance, the always tricky *jeu* of
self-parody. But Ian remained always witty, clever, industrious,
affectionate and almost *painfully* honourable.

My closest friend, by far, in politics.

He was *insouciant* about death. In the garden of his tiny little
house, south of the river, he would point up at the tower blocks
which loomed to the east.

'The Paddys are up there,' he would say, in good humour, 'with
their telescopes.'

Now they've got her two closest confidants, Airey [Neave] and
Ian. I suppose I should be apprehensive that they might come for
me. But, strangely (because I am in many circumstances cowardly)
I'm not. Just as well, because 'The Police' down here, as in Sussex,
are completely useless, if not actually hostile. It was those same
Sussex police, wasn't it, who 'cleared' the Grand Hotel in Brighton
before the bomb went off?[1] And whose constable didn't like using
dogs, 'in case it upset the miners'?

I've only seen the local police twice in the last ten years. Once
when a spotty constable threatened to arrest me for using 'insulting
language' on the (fat) wife of a parish councillor who had been
stealing firewood; once when, very reluctantly, a red-faced
coming-up-for-retirement constable 'took particulars' from two
youths caught by me red-handed, and detained, while vandalising
and trying to steal valuable stained glass from the south guard-
room. Naturally, they were never prosecuted. And Jane was once
visited by a couple of CID men who wanted to look at some
cannabis plants which hippies had planted far over in the

---

[1] Of course, it was in fact the security services which had responsibility for
checking the hotel. Allowance must be made for the grief and indignation from
which AC was suffering at the time of making this entry.

woodland, and they suggested (because no one must be beastly to or about hippies) that it was 'probably one of your children'.

I fear that the police have abandoned their old class allegiances. Indeed many of them seem to carry monstrous chips, and actually to enjoy harassing soft targets. And where has it got them? Simply widened the circle of those who resent and mistrust the police. Two or three stabbed every day and the assailants usually discharged by the Magistrates.

There *are* good ones, young, tough and dedicated – just as there are in MoD – but it's the devil's job bringing them forward; because of that customary (and very English) repressive conspiracy of the incompetent.

So, I'm not particularly frightened. I just feel 'What is written, is written'. Although I wish my affairs were in better order, and I could have passed on more to Jane. The tax authorities would love it. A sudden death allows them to really sink their teeth in.

A huge fine, for doing one's duty.

Saltwood   *Sunday, 5 August*

It's crazy hot. The shade temperature today in the yard was 95°. In and out of the pool all day long. But, perhaps because of this, we are listless, and out of condition. We can neither afford the time nor the money to go to 'Champneys', and detox. But Jane had a brilliant idea – we'll go there 'in all but name'. As from this evening, no alcohol (naturally); no fats, practically no carbohydrates; no eggs, no nothing. Fruits and astringent. Mineral water. Sluice the kidneys. Torture the body. Lissomly we will emerge, and purified.

Saltwood   *Tuesday, 7 August*

Yesterday I was in MoD all day. The Iraqis are starting to throw their weight around.[1] I wouldn't have believed it possible, not on

---

[1] Iraq had invaded Kuwait on 2 August.

this scale. For nearly two years the FCO section of Cabinet minutes was a long moan about how the Iraqi Army was on its last legs, and the Iranians were going to break through. Now it turns out there are more Soviet tanks there than in Poland, Hungary and Czechoslovakia combined.

The only consolation is that sooner than expected the Clark *Bahrein* yardstick[1] has its credentials confirmed. But there is no credit in being proved right, here or anywhere else (except, occasionally, the Futures market).

I felt ghastly all day long. Persistent headache, stiff joints, 'lassitude', generally out of sorts. Returned by train and cursed and mumbled at all the holiday-makers, so carefree and (some of them) fetching, in their summer frocks.

But at the station Jane admitted that she had been feeling exactly the same. Of course! 'Champneys!'

As fast as we could we prepared, and then stuffed on, an enormous meal; poulet l'estragon with rice and lots of little vegetables cooked in butter and (baby carrots) sugar; fresh home-baked bread and butter (again); six or seven – each – lemon curd tartlets and gobbets of heavy Jersey cream. I drank half a bottle of good Burgundy. We slept like tops and felt incredible this morning.

Saltwood   *Wednesday, 8 August*

We drove over to Ian Gow's funeral service in St Saviours, Eastbourne. An ugly Victorian building selected by Ian – I assume – because of its inordinately *High* practices.

The heat was oppressive and we set off in casual clothes, intending to change *en route*. Some little distance from Pevensey we diverted and found a wooded glade just nearby to the canal,

---

[1] In developing his original 'Options' thesis, AC discarded the traditional NATO requirements and asked instead, 'How effective will it (or they) be in holding the end of the Bahrein Causeway?'

and started to undress. This aroused the disapproval of two people, fat and ugly, who were slumped in deckchairs by the canal bank and who clearly thought we were going to make love. To tell the truth I would have liked that. The proximity of death always makes me feel sexual. But our timing was tight. Guests were enjoined to be in their places at least forty-five minutes before the service started.

I cannot adequately record how ugly those people were. The man squat, paunchy, resentful in his horn rims; the woman *gross*, runkled-up nylon skirt, varicose veins, eating from a paper bag. At intervals each drew on a cigarette. Beside them glistened two luckless baby bream which the man had caught with his line.

Jane had a brilliant idea. That, once impeccably dressed in our funeral weeds, we should reverse back to their site and kill them, leaving the wreath which we were taking over for Ian. And removing instead, a fish, to lay beside the open grave. Lovely and black, that humour. Pure Buñuel.

On and on went the service. The PM read the first lesson beautifully. But there was *too much* jingling, and scattering of incense, and High longueurs. Afterwards (about one and three-quarter hours) we gatecrashed the tea party at the Dog House.[1] Uninvited, and thus not on the police list – whether by intention or accident I know not – we were nonetheless hailed at the door by Peter Hordern and our presence accepted as quite natural.

I spoke with the PM at some length, and to Cecil's evident irritation as he had (literally) cornered her against a hedge in the garden. He kept interrupting and trying to edge between us. She was ultra gung-ho on Saddam Hussein,[2] wanted to send a CVS,[3] etc. But I am a little uneasy. Where will it all end?

Jane Gow had quite consciously and admirably left the – very disagreeable – crater in their yard where the bomb had detonated, and there were flowers strewn around. I went through and stood there alone, in meditation, for a while. Jane told us a macabre little

---

[1] The Gows' house at Hankham.
[2] Saddam Hussein, Iraqi president since 1979.
[3] An 'Invincible'-class aircraft carrier.

tale. After she had returned to the house, following some forty-eight hours of continuous and intensive forensic scrutiny and searches, one of the dogs wandered. When it returned it brought in its mouth a garter of Ian's, blackened by the explosion, though fortunately without any of his body adhering to it, that he had been wearing that morning, retrieved by the wuffler from a nearby paddock or hedge. Further testimony to (let us say) 'overstretch' in the Sussex Constabulary.

Not many members of the Government had bothered to turn up. From the Cabinet only Howe, Brooke, Waddington, Cecil Parkinson. Of junior Ministers just myself, Ryder and, bizarrely, the Bottomleys.[1] She has lost her looks almost as fast as I did when I first went into the House. And her husband is so *odd* that it grates. Even watching him, and that curious little half-giggling smile and 'scamp' haircut, brings out the worst in me.

Saltwood   *Monday, 13 August*

It's very late, and Pat has just left, bearing a secret note for Charles at Number 10.

The day started slowly, and tiresomely.

Officials, who relish – and award themselves points for – getting Ministers back from holidays, preferably on a Monday, had insisted I come up in order to approve a response to something that had come over from Number 10.

TK is in Scotland and they couldn't get hold of him. Grimly certain that he would have surfaced by the time I got to the building (I've been caught like this so many times in the past), I set off.

But no, he was still incommunicado – the moors, come on – and I was in charge. Charles's queries were all perfectly valid,

---

[1] In the 1989 reshuffle Peter Brooke had been made Northern Ireland secretary; David Waddington home secretary; Richard Ryder economic secretary at the Treasury; Peter Bottomley Parliamentary Under-Secretary, Northern Ireland; and Virginia Bottomley Minister of State, Department of Health.

points about Rules of Engagement, Command Structures, relation
to US Command, Air Traffic Control, etc.

Unfortunately Simon is away and those in charge of the office
are simply not in the same class. Their limp, partially illiterate (as all
too easily happens when fusion is attempted of advice from three
separate Desks) response would have irritated Charles and in-
furiated the PM. I sent for the officials.

Robin Hatfield (not bad, but not used to my 'ways') came up
immediately, but there were others whom I found less impressive.
They muddled up the various Tornado designations, ADV, GR5,
etc, and cross-permed them with Harriers.

I spent some time tautening the response, making sure my name
was prominent at the start and at points in the text; made it plain
that TK was on holiday and (unlike the PM who is also on holiday
in Cornwall but *manically* in touch) ungettable. While they were
working it up I had a good meeting with the US chargé, and his
younger, gung-ho aide, who nodded when I was speaking. We
must get uniformity of ROE. It's humiliating, and dangerous, that
the RAF should be subject to a legally binding process of hesitation
when the Americans and the Saudis can shoot on assumed hostile
intent. But officials, and Peter Harding,[1] were cooperative, and
pleased with the result. I dashed for the train, confident that the
note would be shortly over with Charles.

Negligent boy. You *can't* be too careful, or too suspicious,
in this game. I should have made Pat drive me, so as to be on
the phone. But the roads are dreadful with holiday traffic at the
moment and the train faster. In fact, I shouldn't have left the
building at all until the note had gone over. S of S's office, rightly
anticipating his wrath, wouldn't transmit until they had succeeded
in contacting him, in spite of frequent promptings at my behest.

At lunchtime TK finally surfaced, on a very bad line (as I have
already discovered at Eriboll our special high-power secret-agent
type portables are defeated by the Scottish Highlands and don't
work north of Inverness).

He took, or rather snatched, the helm. Anything to stop AC

---

[1] Air Marshal Sir Peter Harding, Chief of the Air Staff.

getting prominence, currying favour. All references to me were deleted and the text watered back down again to conform with Douglas's (ie, FCO wankers' line) preference.

Immediately I sat down in the office here and drafted a commentary note, based on my original text, for circulation within the Dept. But the real point, of course, was to get it over to Number 10, show that there is someone here with balls, and it's AC.

Then, an unpredictable stumbling block. Again showing that one should (in Mr Gulbenkian's invaluable – but too often disregarded – phrase) *never leave the Bridge*. Isn't that what had landed TK in it? Instead of indulging myself down here I should be camped in the bloody place, with a sleeping bag, interfering in all and sundry.

David Hatcher said that he 'couldn't' deliver it to Number 10.

'Why not, for God's sake? It's only across the road.'

Well, it wasn't appropriate. He couldn't be party to communication with CP 'behind the back of' the Sec of State's office. Sodbollocks. Am I always to be thwarted? Surrounded by nincompoops and inadequates?

Shortly afterwards TK's 'agreed' draft, characteristically turgid and evasive, came through Jane fortified me. She said Mrs T *must* see the stronger version. So out I retyped it, on the old Swedish machine in the summer office here, and gave it to Pat who, very loyally and inscrutably, has guaranteed to put it through the door of Number 10 tonight.

She'll have it when she starts – usually five ish – tomorrow

Ministry of Defence   *Tuesday, 14 August*

At twenty past eight this morning the phone rang. It was the Downing Street switchboard. 'Mr Clark? Charles Powell wants a word.'

I assumed that it was about the note, but he brushed that aside, though clearly grateful for it.

'The Prime Minister is anxious that a Minister of State should go out to the Gulf immediately, and the fickle finger of fate seems to be pointing at you.'

I was exultant. 'Bugger the fickle finger. I want to be told that I am the PM's personal choice.'

Ass, Clark. Of course he couldn't possibly say that. Just as at the Chequers seminars, I was being extended over and above my actual rank. Charles was tactful.

'It's probably better to aim (sic) to leave tomorrow.'

I rushed back into the kitchen and hugged Jane; I could feel the adrenalin coursing. Was I to be Resident Minister in the Middle East? Macmillan at the Dar al Ayoun?[1]

I had to have a VC 10, ideally *the* VC 10 which the PM uses. I rang him back. And the press statement had to say that I was the Prime Minister's personal emissary.

Yes, I could have *a* VC 10, but for obvious reasons the wording of the statement would have to be carefully drawn.

'If I'm to have the authority I need it must at least say that I am travelling on her instructions.'

Well, yes, that could probably be included. A 'small pool' of reporters should go along, as well.

I telephoned at once to the Private Office, who were pleased and excited thinking, rightly or wrongly, that it was consequent on yesterday's note about which they are now more than a little shame-faced.

I believed that everything was in hand and, having done a lot of shouting, to staff and to civil servants, I took tranquillising therapy. I polished the top of the tallboy in my bathroom, then tidied and arranged the objects that sit there. When I return, they will greet and smile at me. A last rushed bathe while Jane packed my tropical suits and aertex, then back to the station.

In the meantime, however, a drama had been unfolding. TK, finally contacted on the moors, had taken the idea badly.

'I'm not going to have Charles Powell giving orders to my

---

[1] See AC's letter, 13 March 1989.

Department without going through me . . . What? Hullo? This is a very bad line', etc, etc.

Jane Binstead was in a bit of a jam, unfortunate female.

Finally:

'I order you to stop these arrangements. I myself am going out there very shortly. I will bring the dates of my departure forward. This is something *I* handle, it's my area. Nothing to do with Procurement. I order you . . .'

'Wha—?'

'I ORDER you to stop all arrangements concerning this proposal.' Bellowing.

Jane unhappily came along the corridor and gave an account of her predicament. After she had returned David, quite making up for his attack of nerves last evening, adroitly and stealthily rang Charles at Number 10, who at once contacted the PM in Cornwall.

What was then actually said to TK, I don't know. But he climbed down.

A little later another note came over, this time direct (a 'top' at last!) to my office, reaffirming the PM's intention.

And still later TK phoned me, all bland. 'I was a bit doubtful, but I've thought it over . . . Good luck.'

He went on – inaudibly as well as unintelligibly – to express reservations about the press, and 'Publicity'!

I went over to a meeting at the Foreign Office. Nothing that ever happens anywhere must take place without the Foreign Office claiming (at least) foster-parenthood. Tiny room. Diffident officials. W. Waldegrave chairing. All hunka-munka food. No real info.

By the time I got back to the office TK had again 'thought it over' (that's one of the advantages of Scotland, I said, it's a wonderful place to think) and said 'NO PRESS'.

Uh? But CP had said he/she had wanted reporters to go along. Once again we had to refer back, and once again he was overruled.

One might think all this would impair my relations with Tom. But he's so rubbery that it just bounces off. He's a true professional. Whatever our feelings may have been during a duel, we are always

genial in each other's company. Or am I being too complacent? Is
he harbouring terrible resentments?

Who cares? I am off tomorrow on a wonderful adventure.

VC10 en route   *Wednesday, 15 August*

We are all rather congested in the front portion of a *tanker* VC 10
(storage tanks empty, I trust. I can't believe that we are actually
flying fuel out to this so fuel-rich region). Every seat, and they are
none too comfortable, is taken and 'facilities' are at a level between
'Business' and 'Standard' classes on a civilian flight.

Alas! All our efforts to get the famous 'White' aircraft with its
drawing rooms and beautiful linen were to no avail. But we do
have tables, rather like the Plymouth train, on which I am writing
this note.

Opposite me is VCDS, Vincent,[1] and his two acolytes. He
is a very good man. Clear-headed. I first encountered him at
Chequers, where he impressed. Beside me David, and a rather
congenial man from the FCO, with hooded lids, who is in charge
of subversion and 'dirty tricks'.

On the other side of the bay some pressmen – 'Diplomatic
Correspondents' (ludicrous title), of whom the *Times* chap,
McEwen, seems amiable; and dear Bruce, beaming benignly. I
hope that they don't get disappointed. I have given instructions
that they be plied with drink at all times.

When first charged with this I wanted to be more contemplative, solitary, classicist. There may still come an opportunity,
although the schedule looks ninny-tight. Maddeningly, I couldn't
find my Doughty,[2] and I now feel myself becoming a little rattled.
This could be due to loss of sexuality (or could be causing it).
Travel jitters can sometimes have exactly the opposite effect, and I
need to jump on the nearest WAAF. But in any case all the cabin
staff on this trip are male.

---

[1] Vice-Chief of Defence Staff, General Sir Richard Vincent.
[2] *Arabia Deserta* by C. M. Doughty.

Abu Dhabi   *Saturday, 18 August*

The palace of the Amir is surely the most extravagant building in which I have ever trod. The whiteness of the Carrara marble (I was reminded of Jim Lees-Milne's anecdote of the rich American lady who, noticing a mousey governess's necklace and inquiring of what it was made (malachite) said, 'Yeah? At home we've got a staircase made of that stuff') the richness and depth of the Savonnerie, the newness and cleanness of all the silks and stuffs, the glistering of the gold, is dazzling.

In Europe, or in the East, palaces have grown over the centuries, acquired their contents at the behest of many different tastes and proprietors. But in the Gulf the palaces of the Sheikhs are *instant*. One huge cheque was written, wham, and there you are.

The only flaw, but in this instance it is an intrusive one, is the weak and hesitant proportion of the staircase. I see that it is ornamental only, as everyone uses the lifts, but it is central to the hall, and the scale is wrong. Better suited to the 1929 Florida villa from which, I would guess, it was copied.

They are cool, these buildings, and I am comfortable in any one of my identical Lesley and Roberts blue suits. Much more of a uniform, in every way more appropriate than the pale 'summer' fabrics, already at 11 am rumpled and sweat-stained, of my entourage.

And I am welcome. The Sheikhs are glad to see an English Minister, especially one who smoothly opens the courtesies by saying, 'The Prime Minister has charged me personally with conveying to you, Your Majesty, her very highest expressions of personal regard.'

These old Sheikhs are very wise. And of them all my own preference is, I think, for Sheikh Isa of Bahrain. Such beautiful manners. Such cool and practical judgment. Only very occasionally does he become agitated, shifts in his robes and worry beads appear in his hand.

They have come from the desert, these old men, and their fathers fought with Lawrence, with their rag-tag cavalry and camels, against the Turks. I quite see that their new wealth is so abundant, so vastly prolific that they cannot keep a really close eye. What is wealth for, but to improve the quality of life? If hours every day are to be consumed with checking 'books', complaints, rival claims of scheming accountants, then what's the point?

But one or two tiers down lies a whole stratum of parasites, competing, dealing, cutting each other's throats. Everywhere a pudgy 'Crown Prince', café-au-lait smooth, will sit in on conferences, puzzled and fidgety, sometimes in military uniform. He will be his father's favourite. But lurking, too, and occasionally glimpsed, are the lean and hawk-eyed 'nephews'. Expressions burning with ambition and lust.

When we get down to business, it is soon plain that these 'Ruling Families' are more than a little apprehensive. Iraq, more than any other, is the country of the mob. And was not Baghdad the city where the mob, it seems like yesterday, burst into the Royal Palace and dragged the regent Nuri es Said into the street, cutting out his entrails and pulling him along the gutter, still alive, behind the royal limousine?

So the assistance they hope for is of a specialist kind. Each, in their different way, has asked for a strong detachment, preferably with light armour as well, to protect *them*, personally. Because of course if things really start to disintegrate they couldn't trust even their own bodyguard.

The request is never put so crudely as this. The danger of 'raids' by Iraqi 'Special Forces' is usually the closest they approach to an admission of their real fears. But I understood immediately, and as soon as I did and began to expound on the kind of mix needed they would become excited and pleased.

Free water, of course, open facilities of every kind, special provision for RAF aircrew – and much else. There is no problem with any of these. But it is their own skins that concern them most.

Nor is this a request that should be treated lightly. If the ruling families start to pack up, emigrate to their lodges at Newmarket or Longchamps or, worse, patch up some 'Arab Solution' deal individually with Saddam, as that oily little runt Hussein, the King of Jordan, is openly recommending, then we've had it.

Midnight

We have landed at Riyadh to take on fuel.

Tom has specifically 'barred' me from going to Saudi, claiming it as 'his' area. But the Ambassador, Alan Monro, a very good man indeed, keen and clever, came out to meet me.

The airfield is half blacked out and we walked, he and I, in the heavy night heat – it must still have been over 85°. I could sense, and occasionally hear, junior officials searching for us. Periodically we stopped, tacit co-conspirators, in the deep dark shadow of a C 140 wing, or took cover behind an undercarriage leg. We were joined by Sandy Wilson,[1] another very good man. Both of them told me that the Americans were going to attack, no doubt about it – but when?

There are F 16s here wingtip to wingtip, and more transport aircraft than I have seen since Wideawake on Ascension Island in 1982. Once a military build-up passes a certain stage battle becomes almost inevitable.

It is the railway timetables of 1914, and the Guns of August.

Albany   *Sunday, 19 August*

I got in to Brize at 3.40 this morning, and drove directly to Saltwood, alternating between Red Boxes (three) and all the Sunday papers. After two hours the back of the Jaguar was a giant rat's-nest of mussed-up newsprint, 'supplements', and official folders.

Home at last! And, again, unscathed.

I changed into softies, ate a big scrambled egg breakfast, lots of coffee, bread and honey; and wandered over to the Garden House to look at the new 'summer' furniture which had been delivered while I was away.

After a very long flight I like always to *oxygenate* by taking a really strenuous walk, expelling the toxins of recycled air and 'petit

---

[1] Sandy Wilson: Air Vice-Marshal Sir Andrew Wilson, at that time Commander, British Forces, Arabian Peninsula.

fours'. But something (thank God) made me first ring the Duty
Clerk at Number 10, to check in.

The clerk was crisp, unready to be generous. Sunday was no
different from any other day. Worse, in this particular instance,
because Mrs Thatcher was due to return from her 'holiday' this
evening. He left me in little doubt that she would be expecting my
report at the top of her first box.

'But I haven't even typed it out, my handwriting is illegible,
there's no secretarial staff at MoD . . .'

'The office facilities here are at your disposal' (*not* calling me
'Minister').

Groan! I thought I'd gorge some of the caviar, take the 2.40.
Then realised – providentially, as it turned out – that this would be
too tight, so skipped lunch entirely and just made the 1.40. No
driver, so walked in warm humid rain from Waterloo to the House
where confused and faltering 'Security' men reluctantly emerged
to fumble and mutter with bunches of keys. (The police all seem to
take Sunday off.) It took me about fifteen minutes actually to get
installed in my room. David had kept the folder, and all my 'green'
notes.[1] The whole report had to be written, from scratch, in my
hand. *Then* – but was there time? – transposed into a clear typed
text. I was much interrupted by reporters and radio who jangled
me at the desk.

Round, finally, at 5.35 in the faithful little Porsche, to Number
10. There I dictated solidly, for over two hours to Sally, leading
Garden Girl and brilliant typist and screen operator.

By that time the PM was almost due back from Cornwall. I did
not want to be caught by her in 'half-change', with the Porsche
lending a somewhat frivolous tone to the Downing St car rank, so
accelerated away straight after signing the fair copy – except having
first rather cruelly but deliberately booked a call to TK through the
Downing St switchboard, though not staying to take it. ('What the
hell's Alan doing at Number 10 on a Sunday evening?')

Now it is late, and I have been 'on the go' for nineteen hours, or

---

[1] When writing in his own hand on government papers AC always affected a
green pen.

longer if you include the flight. Tomorrow I am to attend a
meeting at Number 10 at 9.30; just Hurd and TK besides the PM.
The inner, inner group. Anything could happen. But I must thank
God. He could have lifted his protection a hundred times in the
last eight days.

Ministry of Defence   *Monday, 20 August*

My report was 'On the table'. Both The Lady and Charles congratulated me. But Hurd put in the standard courtesy put-down,
'looking forward to reading it'.

Unless a document has been written by a FCO Minister or,
better, filed by one of those useless resident 'diplomats' it is not a
real 'report'.

Tipped off that I was attending by, I would guess, Len Apple-
yard, a former ambassador and now No. Two in the Cabinet
Office, Douglas had insisted that Waldegrave also came along. If
Tom has a Minister of State with him then the Foreign Office
should also field two Ministers. When William appeared there was
a certain amount of agitation of a 'the Prime Minister wants to
keep this to a very small group' kind. And, at intervals during the
meeting, she snarled and spat at him which, in his rather splendid
nonchalant way (Etonian education, of course, because I happen to
know he actually feels quite rattled), he took in his stride.

At lunchtime I was on the news both going into, and emerging
from, Number 10! I do hope Jane saw it at Saltwood.

Ministry of Defence   *Tuesday, 21 August*

I was caught today, had to say 'No, Prime Minister' at the morning's meeting.

The whole thing was a complete set-up. The Foreign Office
control the telegram traffic. There was an important telegram
referring to a new Resolution of the United Nations, governing
our powers of interception on the high seas. Hurd's office kept it

until the very last minute, then sent it over to Simon just as (it transpired) we were on the verge of setting out. Naturally nothing came near me.

Consequently when The Lady said, to me, 'Have you seen it?' and I said, 'No', she will have assumed that it was just idleness on my part. Al not doing his homework properly.

One of the oldest tricks in the Civil Service.

Ministry of Defence   *Thursday, 23 August*

Early this morning Tom sent for me. He was bumbustious. Archie should go to these meetings. Of course quite often there was no need for a Minister of State, but if there should be, then obviously it ought to be Archie.

'Quite.'

Tom then, shamelessly, picked my brains for three-quarters of an hour. He's going through one of his terrifically good-form phases, which usually coincide with his having got the better of me.

As soon as I got back to my room I rang Charles. But he had a lot on his mind. 'It's a bit hard to justify giving the Procurement Minister a higher access rating than the Armed Forces Minister at a meeting of this kind.'

Shafted.

Saltwood   *Wednesday, 29 August*

I have been in a vile mood all day, and beastly to Jane.

This fucking Saddam thing has given the AF side of the Dept a renewed *raison d'être*. A war to fight! Whee-ee. As a result everything has gone on hold, the Consolidated Fund 'tap' is unlocked – buy anything, order anything. All great fun, but I sense that those who are opposed to me and what I am trying to do are in the ascendant.

I am 'back in my kennel'. I have a lot of extra approving to do, of emergency procurement. But I am completely excluded from policy meetings (although TK often picks my brains ahead of them). The irony lies in the fact that this is exactly the kind of conflict which my Chequers paper anticipated – but before we are ready for it.

Saltwood   *Friday, 31 August*

A long day yesterday. I was up at six, took an early train to Cannon St, then drove to Plymouth via Bristol. The picture restorer in Bristol is helping with the huge Duncan [Grant] centrepiece; the enormous canvas of the youth (Present it to the Terrence Higgins Trust, Jane said) and the two only slightly less big ones of the ladies playing their lutes. They are good craftsmen but the whole operation now looks like costing more than £20,000 – good money after bad?

I got to Addison Road about three-quarters of an hour late for my surgery and gaga-ly went into the wrong house via the back door, interrupting a solicitor's conference.

'Can I help you?' said a lady, pretty icily.

'No thanks,' I said. 'Oh well, yes. You could move that white BMW that's stopping me putting my car there.'

At the Conservative offices Roy Williams was in charge as Anne is taking her holiday.

'How are you then, Alan, all right?' He always says that, like that. Quite a few times. Is it paranoia, or do I detect a hint of (non-specific) reproach? How very *black* his hair is, and how yellowish-ill his skin seems through the cigarette smoke.

I went down to the Council Chamber to a specially convened 'Policy' committee.

The meeting was wholly pointless, as far as I could see. Simply an ego trip for the deputy leader while Tom Savery, the titular Tory boss, was away. Mike Lees (how muddlingly ludicrous, infuriating and utterly Plymouthian that the Association Treasurer and active wheel, a very *short* man, should be called Mike *Leaves*, and the chairman of Plymouth's largest private employer, another

very short man, should be called Mike *Lees*) read out the text of an
internal letter which had already been leaked. Neither of the two
committee members, who are also Tory councillors in Sutton,
made any attempt to speak to, or to acknowledge me. They get
cross when I turn up at these sort of events as it interferes with their
dossier of malfeasance.

Their problem is, they don't see how they can quite get rid of
me while I'm still a Minister. Their immediate concern is of course
the local elections next year when, if they are trounced, they will
blame the Government; if they are returned they will delight in
recounting how 'on the doorstep' people are saying we'll vote for
you, but we're not going to vote Conservative in a General
Election.

It was gone six o'clock when I got away. Ravenous, I turned off
the motorway, to stop in the Johnnie Crow lay-by[1] where,
exhausted, we sometimes took a snack during the campaign. As I
wolfed my Marmite sandwiches I thought, Well, I *am* glad not to
be going through all that again.

I know, and they *don't* know. As I think about it I realise I could
have only a year left. Relief at last! But I fear that I will be sad to
leave the 'tawny male paradise'.

The House is being recalled next week, which will be fun. An
occasion. But unlikely, I feel, to compare with 2 April 1982 – the
most electric moment that I have ever experienced in that place; or
it for many years I suspect, perhaps since 8 May 1940. There is
something about the atmosphere, the clarity of purpose, that will
be absent.

Because the whole Gulf affair has sunk back into a kind of
stalemate, with the wily Saddam paying out the hostages like a
salmon line and – God knows how he fixed it – the ghastly
Branson 'standing by' with an airliner for his 'mercy mission'.

---

[1] Johnnie Crow lay-by: so called after a large and benevolent crow which would
perch on driving mirrors and ask for sandwich crusts.

Saltwood   *Saturday, 8 September*

I've done, it seems, what I have managed to bring about in quite a few years since entering politics: just *lose* my summer holiday.

Exceptional circs, of course. But when it happens it's always exceptional circs, of some dimension.

Trouble is, I always fall for the beguiling notion that if you let everyone else go in August you have an easy time while they're away, and are then due a pleasing free period when they all start work.

But it never goes like this, although admittedly I stole a march on TK with the Gulf trip. The departmental diary is filling up – and with things which I miss at my peril. I am tired, with that late August staleness that only the Alps can remedy. Even as I write this, I am determined to get to the Chalet – if only for forty-eight hrs.

The martins have gathered, chattering urgently, and gone. The swallows are diminshing in number – just a few fussed parents and their second broods. It is grey and breezy. Dead hollyhock leaves lie on the surface of the pool, and the water temperature is below 70°. It won't go back through that band until next May.

Ministry of Defence   *Thursday, 13 September*

There were two boxes in the car, lots of interesting stuff. Pat drove me directly to the Dept and I had to go straight in to a meeting which TK had convened to discuss publicity – his favourite subject – for tomorrow's announcement.[1]

It went on for one and three-quarter hours. I was dry and sardonic. A palpable chill of embarrassment spread across the room when Tom said that he would like a huge montage of a tank behind him, a photo blow-up. The soldiers weren't too keen. But 'I suppose you could wear a flak jacket,' I said.

---

[1] Conveying our participation in the Gulf Force.

Laughter, in which, good naturedly, he joined.

I recommended against having an FCO presence. Waldegrave wants to sit on the platform.

'At least make sure he doesn't bring a child.'

Smirks only. Officials aren't meant to laugh (except in Private Office) when one Minister makes a joke about another one.

I am scratchy and ill-tempered. TK consults and asks my advice the *entire* time. On technical questions. And also on strategic and political ones. Before meetings with Generals, before going to Number 10. But in truth, deftly and effectively, he's sidelined me.

If I was really a clever politician I'd lay a trap for him, suddenly and critically give him *bad* advice, watch him get in a twist. But I just can't. It would offend against the Socratic concept.

Saltwood   *Sunday, 21 October*

Bloomsbury evening at Saltwood. We entertained the 'Friends of Charleston'.[1] I don't know what they charged for tickets, but I hope they made money.

I had the brilliant idea of stuffing the Garden House, which has been standing more or less empty since Colette moved out, with all our Bloomsbury 'items'. We hung and distributed everything, thirty-seven in all, plus a good few ceramics, save only the giant Queen Mary Duncans. The whole made a pleasing, and entirely private exhibition.

I made a little speech of welcome, fraudulently and bogusly referring to my father's death 'from a falling tree'. What mischievous impulse made me do this?

Pure Roger Irrelevant. I did just manage to keep a straight face, although William, from the far end of the room, gave me an odd look.

We then processed over to the Great Library, rich and enclosing

---

[1] A charitable body dedicated to the maintenance of the farmhouse where Duncan Grant and Vanessa Bell had their studio, where Keynes wrote *The Economic Consequences of the Peace*, and Lytton Strachey and others were habitués.

as always on such an occasion, for the performance by Eileen
Atkins of Virginia Woolf's essay, 'A Room of One's Own'. How
well she did it! And what a beautiful, moving and dignified text it
is. The audience listened in a rapt silence and at the end I had tears
in my eyes.

Olivier Popham materialised; benign and knowledgeable. I
remember her, just, at Portland Place. Very sleek and dark like a
young seal. She asked to see Graham's pictures, and chided me
gently for selling her portrait which he had painted in 1939, in the
great Death Duties sale.[1] I could hardly say, 'I thought you were
dead.'

Her big, deliberately common-voiced daughter Cressida, who
is famous for 'fabrics', accompanied her. Both showed a true
Bloomsbury mocking spirit when confronted by the great Nurn-
burg 1490 iron safe in the lower hall.

'Is it a Coca-Cola machine? Or a coffee dispenser?'

Saltwood   *Sunday, 4 November*

The papers are all very bad. Tory Party falling apart, the death
blow,[2] that kind of thing. Something in it, I fear, unless we can get
a grip on events. The only person who can restore order in the
parliamentary ranks is Tristan. He can do it short-term (like many
intelligent people T. can only see things very long or very short)
but that's enough. Get us past November.[3]

After breakfast I telephoned Chequers.

'The Prime Minister is speechwriting.'

'Who with?'

'Charles Powell.'

---

[1] Olivier Popham was the mistress of Graham Bell, who was killed in the RAF in
1943.

[2] Sir Geoffrey Howe had resigned from the government the previous Thursday,
and his resignation speech was awaited with some trepidation.

[3] November was the month when under the leadership rules a challenger was
permitted to offer himself. Once the month had passed there would be no
further opportunity until the new parliamentary session.

'When will she be free?'

'There might be a minute before lunch.'

'When's that?'

'One o'clock sharp.'

I was being kept at bay. Unusual. The Number 10 switchboard girls are always helpful. With Chequers I've had this problem before.

'Oh well, please pass her my name, in case she wants to take a call then.'

I was a lovely crisp day of late autumn. I had said I'd join Jane in the garden. Now I was going to be stuck indoors waiting for a call. But I had barely got to the doorway to give her a shout when the phone started ringing.

'Alan . . .'

I tried to cheer her up: 'There's an awful lot of wind about', 'Hold tight and it'll all blow away', 'Geoffrey was past it by now, anyway.'

I said, with suitable preface, that I would never seek to tell her who she should employ or why; but that if she could find something for 'Tim' to do . . .

'Tim who?' (thinking, I suppose, that I wanted her to bring someone called Tim into the Cabinet. Blast, blast. Too oblique. Never works with her.)

'Renton. You really ought to make Tristan your Chief Whip.'

A very long silence. I almost said 'hullo', but didn't.

'Oh but he's enjoying his present job so much . . .'

I don't think she realises what a jam she's in. It's the Bunker syndrome. Everyone round you is clicking their heels. The saluting sentries have highly polished boots and beautifully creased uniforms. But out there at the Front it's all disintegrating. The soldiers are starving in tatters and makeshift bandages. Whole units are mutinous and in flight.

Saltwood   *Sunday, 11 November*

Back from Plymouth with what is, by tradition, the nastiest weekend of the year behind me. The Constituency engagements are dense and unyielding. The surgery is always particularly crowded and irksome. I invariably have a cold, often flu, and the Remembrance ceremonies on the Hoe drag and chill. New, and unwelcome, ecumenical balls caused the service to grate. Some nameless mystic read out words, unintelligible, from an unknown text. Drenching rain.

But at the civilian Memorial a magnificent Grenadier in a bearskin handed me my wreath, and (as I always do) I *hammed* the role, stiffly bowing and clicking.

At last I was free. I climbed into the valiant Little Silver, and drove exhilaratingly fast. A lot of the time I was running up to 120 mph, and the very last home straight on the M20 at a continuous 140. Average speed for the whole journey from the Hoe car park to Saltwood Lodge gates, including fuel stops, contraflow, caravans in Langport, roadwork lights, was 77.8 mph. One of the best ever.

I had not time even to open a newspaper. But now I see that they are all packed with Heseltinia. Plugs of one kind or another. Some, like the *Mail on Sunday* (who had heavy flirtation with David Owen at one point, I seem to recall), have quite openly changed sides. Every editor is uneasy. In the woodwork stir all those who have lived for the day when they could emerge and have a gloat without fear of retribution.

It looks to me as if Michael is going to get forced into a position, whether he likes it or not, when he'll have to stand. He's cunning and single-minded, yes. But he's also a bit, well, *dyslexic*. Galvanised, jerky movements. On the only two occasions when I have had anything to do with him on matters of policy, I recollect him getting into a great state.

When I was at Employment the question arose of whether a second frigate should be built at Cammell Laird, or at Swan Hunter. Michael has this infatuation with Liverpool, Merseyside, and it was all bound up with him showing his mettle to the crowd. He gabbled over the phone, was wild-eyed in the lobbies. Apparently threatened to resign. Why not? Get lost, she should have said, *then* give the contract to Cammells.

The second time was, of course, Westlands. I only spoke to him twice, something to do with Bristow's new fleet, quite marginal really, and found him almost off his head with rage and – to my mind – persecution mania.

Ministry of Defence   *Monday, 12 November*

I lunched today with Charlie Allsopp[1] at Christies. He's unsquashable really. 'Sharp' but engaging. He told me that Ian Woodner[2] had died.

Good old Woodie, the auctioneer's friend. He will have been sad not to have outlasted Armand Hammer who was (a lot) richer and (only a little) older.

He loved drawings, and he bought and bought in the closing years of his life, almost as if to prolong his expectancy. He went to prison for a while, as rich people in America sometimes do but, like Eddie Gilbert, was revered by the convicts, whom he helped in those tiny ways which make uneducated people grateful.

I have two clear memories of him. Bidding, implacably, at the Chatsworth sale in the summer of 1984. Some of the stuff was wonderful, worth every penny. Not all, though.

Once Col brought him down to Saltwood and made me set out a lot of drawings, normally kept in the safe, for his edification. Woodie was silent in the main, and stroked his moustaches. He made a half-hearted show of interest in the Renoir Circus girls; but the only piece that really excited him was the Quail and Lute. In the Catalogue Raisonée[3] I showed him the entry *Locativa Incognita*, and he became agitated.

Not only did Woodie have taste, but he was an accomplished artist in his own right, modelling himself on, and being obsessed by, Odilon Redon. He once threw a huge dinner party at Claridges, taking the entire dining room and, at the end of the meal, he delivered one of the most moving personal testaments of the meaning of art, and draughtmanship, to which I have ever listened.

---

[1] Charles Allsopp, chairman of Christie's since 1986.
[2] Ian Woodner, an art collector with long-standing Clark connections.
[3] Of the work of Giovanni da Udine.

★

On the way out Charlie showed me into the room where the English furniture for the next 'important' sale was accumulating. A *quite* nice cabinet, bow-fronted, was offered up; faded walnut and marquetry.

'Did you know Billy Wallace? It came from his widow.'

Poor Liz! So pretty and bejewelled as a smart-set groupie when we were all at Oxford. She must be in her mid-fifties, and childless. And Billy, too. Whom I remember meeting and half hero-worshipping at Lavington in 1945 when he had an old SS 1 with a blown exhaust, and drove about at night. Two years ago he died from cancer of the mouth. What a lot of people I've seen 'out'. And still I prance.

I came back here, but couldn't concentrate, and strolled over to the House. We are on the verge of great events. Wild rumours are circulating about the leadership 'contest' for which nominations close on Thursday. Today's favourite is that there just won't *be* a contest this year.

'Too close to the Election, old boy. Frozen.'

This has to be balls.

The Whips have totally clammed up. A bad sign. Already they have gone into 'neutral' mode. Secret policemen burning the old files, ready to serve.

The ballot would, should, be on Tuesday of next week. Only eight days to go and I have a dreadful feeling – not all the time, but in waves – that Heseltine will stand, and that he will win. I haven't communicated this to anyone. No one at all. But I wish Ian was alive.

House of Commons   *Tuesday, 13 November*

The Party is virtually out of control. Mutinous. People are not turning up for divisions. Dissidents get bolder and bolder with their little off-the-cuff TV slotettes. Code is abandoned. Discipline is breaking up. Geoffrey will make his resignation speech this afternoon, and apparently the entire text is the work of Elspeth.

Received wisdom is that this will finally tear the whole thing wide open.

But why should it? Who gives a toss for the old dormouse? Yet I suppose on the Berkeleian principle, if everyone thinks something is important, then it is important.

After Ministers this morning I signalled Andrew MacKay[1] to come into my room. He is so shrewd, he really knows the Party as well as any Whip. Why has he twice refused an invitation to join the Office?

We agreed that the situation is serious, very serious. It's the arithmetic that looks so nasty. There is this *bolus* of wankers, mainly in the North, who are fearful of losing their seats, and will try anything. Elizabeth Peacock:[2] 'We can't be any worse off than what (sic) we are.' Add this to Michael's own claque, itself at least fifty because adhering to it is the whole *Salon des Refusés*, plus all those like Charlie Morrison who have always loathed her, and before you know where you are you're dam' close to 150. Then, there is the considerable body of the soft optioneers, the abstentions. 'An honourable protest.' Crap on every side.

What a lot of people don't realise is that if we get a bad result, closeish figures, she will be hamstrung.

One can write Hugo Young, Peter Jenkins, Robin Oakley,[3] all those who've been waiting for this moment, off the top of one's head. Broaden the Government; must think very long and hard about policy; Heseltine must enter the Cabinet; 'effectively Number Two'; the death-knell of Thatcherism – the clichés, leavened by spite, will roll.

At mid-day I had a meeting with Peter Levene. He told me that at the Lord Mayor's banquet last night she was greeted with virtually complete silence. She started punchily, then got flatter and flatter. I've seen her do this in the past. If the punchy bits don't get them going she reverts to text, and only rarely (Conference being one of the exceptions) are any texts any good.

---

[1] Andrew MacKay, MP for Berkshire East since 1983. PPS to Tom King.

[2] Elizabeth Peacock, MP for Batley and Spen since 1983.

[3] Columnists Hugo Young (*Guardian*) and Peter Jenkins (*Independent*); Robin Oakley, political editor, *The Times*.

We are at present in a state where any news, however slight and tenuous, spreads like wildfire if it is damaging. The effect is cumulative, and reinforces doubters, sceptics who need an excuse for transferring loyalties. 'She's virtually lost all support outside, you know . . .'

I change my own mind by the hour. In some ways it would be better for her to go completely than to hang on mutilated, forced to take in a Trojan Horse. But she has not got the nature to make a withdrawal to Colombey, and for that course it is now really too late. We're down to ensuring that Heseltine doesn't win in a stampede. And Douglas, who could play a role here, is deeply reluctant.

Later

I forced my way along the Minister of States' bench, stopping two places short of Jane [Fookes], who always sits, massively, in the camera-hogging spot just behind the PM. The House was very full indeed, with much chattering and giggling from recusants. The loyalists are glum, and apprehensive.

From the moment he rose to his feet Geoffrey got into it. He was personally wounding – to a far greater extent than mere policy differences would justify. Elspeth's hand in every line.

All those Cabinets (seven *hundred* he said) when The Lady had lashed and basted him (there too, it must be admitted, more savagely than could be explained by nuances of attitude. But it was to a smaller audience and did not, I think, start until about three years ago). In his mind he will also have been carrying the brutal briefing on the 'non-existent' role of Deputy Prime Minister, the messing-around over the houses. It all seethed and bubbled in the cauldron.

The Labour benches loved it. Grinning from ear to ear they 'Oooh'd' and 'Aaah'd' dead on cue. At one point he illustrated his sense of betrayal with some cricketing analogy, being 'sent in to bat for Britain . . . only to find that before the game the bats have been broken by the team captain'. Everyone gasped and I looked round to catch Jonathan's eye. He had that special incredulous look he occasionally gets, mouth open.

Geoffrey ended his speech with an ominous, and strange, sentence: 'I have done what I believe to be right for my Party and for my Country.' (They all say that.) 'The time has come for others to consider *their own response* to the tragic conflict of loyalties with which I myself have wrestled for perhaps too long.'

Afterwards a lot of people, semi-traumatised, didn't want to talk about it. The atmosphere was light-headed, almost.

I spoke with Norman Lamont. He very naively ('I can see *you* weren't at Eton,' I said) questioned whether any member of the Government – not Cabinet, *Government* – could vote against her on the first ballot. 'Quite monstrously disloyal,' etc.

Afterwards I thought maybe it was a plant. You can't trust anyone at present.

We were joined by Tebbit. Wildish and gaunt he seemed. He mouthed a bit about a special role he was going to play; he had been in close touch with Peter M., and so on. Interestingly, he said we must *not* go for a compromise candidate. We must fight all the way, to the death.

This appeals to me. Leonidas at Thermopylae. But we don't win. It's the end of me. I came in with her. I go out with her.

House of Commons   *Wednesday, 14 November*

A curious state of limbo. Briefly, and unaccountably, the House has gone quiet. Many are leaving early for their constituencies to take the temperature.

The Lady is said to be 'foundering'; 'holed below the waterline'; 'stabbed'; 'bowled middle stump', and similar far from original metaphors. Much worse than Westland. There are even rumours (in the press, I can find no trace of them in the corridors so it may be a plant by Mates or Hampson[1]) that Cranley Onslow[2] is going to advise her not even to *contest* the election.

Perfectly ridiculous. No one seems to have given a thought to the constitutional implications, still less the international. How can

---

[1] Dr Keith Hampson, MP for Leeds North-West since 1983 (Ripon, 1974–83). PPS to Michael Heseltine, 1979–84. Before becoming an MP he was a personal assistant to Edward Heath in the 1966 and 1970 general elections.

[2] Cranley Onslow, MP for Woking since 1964.

a narrow caucus in a singular political party unseat a Prime Minister just because it calculates that it may improve its election prospects thereby?

Tristan rang from his car. He's driving in from Heathrow, just back from some pointless and diverting voyage when he should be tirelessly cigaretting at the very centre of things here. Counting and calculating and ordering our deployment. Naturally he was *very* against NT's idea of a 'last stand'. He thinks he can fudge up a solution that will keep H out.

'Of course,' I said. 'If it works.'

'It's got to fucking work,' he answered.

Exciting, but unnerving, times.

Saltwood   *Saturday, 17 November*

I have been listless and depressed most of the day, with ill-at-ease tummy. Perhaps I drank too much in Denmark.[1] But it was mainly Schnapps. Poisoned on the aircraft, more likely. The papers are terrible. Only exceptions being the leader of the *Daily Telegraph*, and Paul Johnson.

Everything else is tipping Heseltine. Bandwagon. And the five o'clock news was even worse. Heseltine doing this, doing that; going down (or up) escalators; leaving (or arriving at) his house. And all the time with that uneasy, almost Wilsonian smirk. But among Conservatives *in the country* she still has majority support. Alison, who is sensible, remains a fervent fan. 'What *are* you all doing?'

The Lady herself is away, out of the country. It's absolute madness. There is no Party mileage whatever in being at the Paris summit. It just makes her seem snooty and remote. And who's running the campaign? Who's doing the canvassing? Who's putting the pressure on?

I became more and more dejected, decided to telephone Tristan. He attempted to calm me, said that Peter Morrison was in charge of collating the votes, that he was calmly confident. But

---

[1] AC had been in Copenhagen for an IEPG meeting.

when pressed Tristan shared my scepticism as to whether this was really the true picture.

He launched into some dissertation as to how Douglas (who will be in Paris with the PM, about to go into a Banquet – shades of Potsdam) and John Major (who will – for God's sake – be in *hospital*, having just had four teeth taken out) will speak to each other in that first critical hour between 6 and 7 pm on Tuesday and, it is to be hoped, settle what should happen next.

I don't like the sound of this. It will be Halifax, Churchill and George VI, and they may decide who runs. In which case, *passim* Halifax, Douglas will probably stand aside. We're then left with John Major who, being calm and sensible, is infinitely preferable to that dreadful charlatan, H. But John is virtually unknown, too vulnerable to the subtle charge of 'not yet ready for it'.

He has personal handicaps, not of his own making. The product, indeed of his virtues. He's not at all *flash*, and a lot of colleagues think it's flash that we need at the moment. And he's not classy, which doesn't worry me in the slightest, but worse, he doesn't (like Mrs T.) even *aspire* to be classy.

Pinkish toffs like Ian [Gilmour] and Charlie [Morrison], having suffered, for ten years, submission to their social inferior see in Michael an arriviste, certainly, who can't shoot straight and in Jopling's damning phrase 'bought all his own furniture', but one who at any rate seeks the cachet. While all the nouves in the Party think he (Michael) is the real thing.

'Look,' I said. 'All these arguments are being tossed around on the assumption that we have to go to a second ballot.'

'That's right, Baby.' (A strange affectation of Tristan's, calling me 'Baby'. I don't mind, but I do know from experience that it usually presages some piece of news which I am not going to like.)

An appalling thought struck me. Michael couldn't actually *win* first time round, could he? I put the question convolutedly. 'Do you think it more likely than not that he won't get a majority in the first ballot?'

'Yes.'

'Do you put the odds on this happening at worse than (longish pause) sixty per cent?'

'No.'

This is terrible. He's barely worse than evens.

Did I start gabbling? I don't remember. Tristan cut through it saying if there was any 'uncertainty' (good neutral word for the tapes) a group of us are to meet at Catherine Place after the 10 pm vote that evening.

I remain deeply anxious that The Establishment simply hasn't got the machinery, or the people, in place to operate effectively in that very narrow timescale.

I went down to the Winter Office, and drew up a little table showing the three alternatives. There are only three, none of them other than bad, though in varying degree, for me.

1) The PM survives, but maimed. The wind-down period, perhaps to a Gentleman's Coup in the spring. This is the best one can hope for, and would at least give me time to make some plans. I suppose it is just possible, by a combination of luck and circumstance such as she has enjoyed in the past, for her to make a gargantuan effort of 'projection', dump the Poll Tax, win the war, call a khaki election at once (it'd be nearly four years, after all) and once again be mother of her people. Certainly that is what I would advise. But good though she is, she's not in the shape of 1983, or even 1986, when she routed them over Westland.

2) It's A.N. Other, after a messy second ballot. Either Douglas or John Major would keep me, I'm pretty sure. Fun to watch a new administration getting the feel of things, but I would no longer be on the inner loop.

3) MH wins. Sudden Death. He might even have time to strike me off the PC list. Would anyone else refuse to serve? Cecil, I would think. Micky Forsyth[1] and Eric Forth[2] certainly ought to. Peter Lilley and the rest would just cower until he sacked them.

That's Politics (Baby).

---

[1] Michael Forsyth, MP for Stirling since 1983. Minister of State, Scottish Office, since 1990.

[2] Eric Forth, now parliamentary under-secretary, Employment.

House of Commons   *Monday, 19 November*

The whole House is in ferment. Little groups, conclaves everywhere. Only in the dining room does some convention seem to
have grown up (I presume because no one trusts their dining
companions) that we don't talk 'shop'.

'Made your Christmas plans yet?' All that balls. God, the dining
room is boring these days, even worse than Pratts'. Big, slow
buffers 'measuring their words' oh-so-firmly; or creepy little narks
talking straight out of *Conservative News*.

But in the corridors it is all furtive whispering and glancing over
shoulders. The institutional confidence (seen at its most obvious in
those who have served a prison term, and which I first noticed in
my early days on Warren Street[1]), that special grimacing style of
speech out of the corner of the mouth, eyes focusing in another
direction, is now it seems the only way of communicating.

Most people are interested – not so much in the result, as in
knowing what the result will be in advance, in order to make their
own 'dispositions'. To ingratiate oneself with the new regime – *a*
new regime, I should say, because the outcome is by no means
certain – even as little as a week before it is installed, looks better
than joining the stampede afterwards. This issue, which can be
discussed semi-respectably, is who is most likely to deliver victory
at the General Election? But it is packaging, conceals a great basket
of bitterness, thwarted personal ambition, and vindictive glee. Talk
of country, or loyalty, is dismissed as 'histrionics'.

And there is a strange feeling abroad. Even if The Lady wins –
and here I am writing 'even if', pull yourself together Clark, say
'even after she's won' – there will be no escaping the fact that at
least one hundred and fifty of her parliamentary colleagues will
have rejected her leadership. That's a big chunk. Some people,
particularly those who pose as Party Elders, like Tony Grant,[2] are

---

[1] AC worked as a dealer's runner in Warren Street (at that time the focus of the
trade market in used cars) for several months after coming down from Oxford.

[2] Sir Anthony Grant, MP for Cambridgeshire South-West since 1983 (Harrow
Central, 1964–83).

intimating that it might be 'better' if, faced with so blatant a show of No Confidence, she decided to 'heal' the Party by announcing her intention to stand down at a given date (ie, become a lame duck which the Labour Party could taunt and torment on every occasion, and a busted flush internationally).

And as the savour of a Heseltine victory starts to pervade the crannies and cupboards and committee rooms, so more and more people are 'coming out'. 'Oh, I don't think he'd be so bad, really . . .' 'He's got such a wide *appeal*.' 'My people just love him, I must say . . .' 'I know what you mean, but he'd be so good at dealing with . . .' (fill in particular problem as appropriate).

Most conspicuous in canvassing are Hampson (loonily), Mates (gruffly) and Bill Powell[1] (persuasively). Michael himself is quite shameless in offering all and sundry what they have always wanted. For example, he would probably have got Paul's support anyway, but 'sealed' it with an assurance that Paul would be Speaker in the next House; Soames fell straight away for the 'your talents are long overdue for recognition' line, as did little [Tony] Nelson and Rhodes James ('you've been treated abominably').

Michael stands in the centre of the Members' lobby, virtually challenging people to wish him good luck. He gives snap 'updates' to journalists, and greets suppliants who are brought along for a short audience by his team. The heavier targets he sees in his room. The Cabinet play their cards close to the chest, although Mellor,[2] apparently, speaks to Michael twice a day on the telephone. Some, like Kenneth Clarke, want her out so badly that they don't need even to blink. And I would guess that there are a fair coterie of Ministers of State and Parly Secs like Sainsbury[3] and Trippier[4] who feel uneasy with The Lady and like the idea of a change.

At the top of the ministerial staircase I ran into G-J. He was bubbling with suppressed excitement. I don't think he actually

---

[1] William Powell, MP for Corby since 1983.

[2] David Mellor, Minister of State, Home Office, since 1989.

[3] Tim Sainsbury, MP for Hove since 1973, at that time a parliamentary secretary at the Foreign Office.

[4] David Trippier, MP for Rossendale since 1979. Minister of State, Department of Environment, since 1989.

wants 'Hezzy' as he (spastically) calls him, to win. It would be
disruptive of the Blue Chip long-term plan. But he's high on the
whole thing.

Tristan said, 'Of course every member of the Cabinet will vote
for the Prime Minister in the first round.' Like hell they will.

I said to him, hoping he'd deny it, 'One cannot actually exclude
the possibility that Heseltine will score more votes than her on the
first ballot.'

'No, I'm afraid one can't.'

'Can one, even, be completely sure that he will not get both the
largest total and the necessary margin to win without a second
ballot?'

'No, I'm afraid one can't.'

This was really chilling. Apocalypse. Because time is horrendously tight if we have to organise an alternative candidate. Four
working days and a weekend. But if Michael scoops it in one gulp
then that is the end of everything.

Maddeningly, I had to return to the Department. Meetings, and
an official lunch. Scandinavians.

'I assume that there is no likelihood of Mrs Thatcher being
defeated for the position of Prime Minister?'

'Oh no. None whatever. It's just one of these quaint traditions
we have in the Conservative Party.'

But the encounter made me realise the enormity of what we're
doing – *changing the Prime Minister* – but without any electoral
authority so to do. I thought I'd have a talk to Peter,[1] although he
doesn't encourage it, and I cancelled my early afternoon engagements and went back over to the House.

I listened outside the door. Silence. I knocked softly, then tried
the handle. He was asleep, snoring lightly, in the leather armchair,
with his feet resting on the desk.

Drake playing bowls before the Armada and all that, but I didn't
like it. This was ten minutes past three in the afternoon of the most
critical day of the whole election. I spoke sharply to him. 'Peter.'

He was bleary.

---

[1] Peter Morrison was in charge of Mrs Thatcher's campaign.

'I'm sorry to butt in, but I'm really getting a bit worried about the way things are going.'

'Quite all right, old boy, relax.'

'I'm just hearing bad reactions around the place from people where I wouldn't expect it.'

'Look, do you think I'd be like this if I wasn't entirely confident?'

'What's the arithmetic look like?'

'Tight-ish, but OK.'

'Well, what?'

'I've got Michael on 115. It could be 124, at the worst.'

'Look, Peter, I don't think people are being straight with you.'

'I have my ways of checking.'

'Paul?'

'I know about Paul.'

'The Wintertons?'[1]

'The Wintertons, funnily enough, I've got down as "Don't Know's".'

'What the fuck do you mean, "*Don't Know*"? This isn't a fucking street canvas. It's a two-horse race, and each vote affects the relative score by two, unless it's an abstention.'

'Actually, I think there could be quite a few abstentions.'

'Don't you think we should be out there twisting arms?'

'No point. In fact it could be counter-productive. I've got a theory about this. I think some people may abstain on the first ballot in order to give Margaret a fright, then rally to her on the second.' (Balls, I thought, but didn't say.)

'What about the '92? They're completely rotten. They've got a meeting at six. Are you going?'

'No point. But I think *you* should.'

In deep gloom I walked back down Speaker's corridor. It can't really be as bad as this can it? I mean there is absolutely no oomph in her campaign *whatsoever*. Peter is useless, far worse than I thought. When he was pairing Whip he was unpopular, but at least he was crisp. Now he's sozzled. There isn't a single person

---

[1] Nicholas, and his wife Ann, MP for Congleton since 1983.

working for her who cuts any ice at all. I know it's better to be feared than loved. But these people aren't either. And she's in Paris. '*Où est la masse de manoeuvre? —Aucune.*'

I went into the members' tea room. The long table was crowded with Margaret supporters, all nonentities except for Tebbit who was cheering people up. Much shouting and laughter. Blustering reassurance. Norman was saying how unthinkable it was to consider dismissing a Prime Minister during a critical international conference. 'Like Potsdam in 1945,' I said. No one paid any attention. If they heard they didn't, or affected not to, understand the allusion.

The crowd thinned out a little and when he got up Norman said that he wanted a word. We went into the Aye lobby and sat at that round table in the centre with all the stationery on it.

'Well . . . ?'

'It's filthy,' I said.

'It could be close. Very close.'

I agreed, '*Fucking* close.'

'If it's like that do you think she should stand in the second ballot?'

I simply don't know the answer to this. Governing would be very difficult with half the Party against her. She might have to make 'concessions' to the left. I asked Norman if he thought she would have to bring Heseltine into the Cabinet?

'She'd certainly be under a lot of pressure to do so.'

'Renton.'

'Yeah.'

I said that the key tactic was to get Chris Patten to stand, and draw off the left vote. At least the hard left vote, Charlie Morrison, Bob Hicks,[1] all the wankers. Norman said, 'And Ken Clarke.' I told him no, if you have too many candidates people just get in a muddle and Heseltine walks through them, just as she did in 1975. Norman said that a lot of people now regarded Michael as a *right-*wing candidate anyway.

'Well, we know different.'

---

[1] Robert Hicks, MP for Cornwall South-East since 1983 (Bodmin, 1970–March 1974; October 1974–83).

'Too true.'

Norman said, 'If it's open season, I'm dam' well going to put my name in. The right must have a candidate they can vote for.'

'You'd lose.'

'It's likely I would, but at least we'd know our strength. That could be useful in a changed situation.'

'Look, Norman, we want to put additional names in to reduce *his* total, not ours. I don't think Heseltine has that big a personal vote. It's just an anti-Margaret coalition.'

I could see he was thoughtful. But he didn't want to prolong the conversation, which we were conducting in tones just above a whisper, though still arousing the curious attention of passers-by.

Raising his voice Norman said, 'Well, this time tomorrow everything will be settled,' and gave one of his graveyard cackles.

The '92 meeting was in one of those low-ceilinged rooms on the upper committee room corridor. The mood was tetchy, and apprehensive. There was a kind of fiction running from several (Jill Knight, for example, shockingly), just as Norman had foreseen, that 'Michael' – as defectors call him (supporters of the Prime Minister always refer to him as 'Heseltine'; and this is quite a useful subliminal indicator of how the speaker is going to vote when he or she is being deliberately or defensively opaque) – was 'really' on the right.

The trouble with this club, to which I was elected almost as soon as I arrived here, but with which I have never really felt comfortable, is that it personifies in extreme form two characeristics found in the majority of MPs – stupidity and egomania. It is only the shrewd and subtle guidance of George Gardiner that has prevented them becoming a laughing stock in recent years. But such integrity as they might originally have possessed has been eroded by the inclusion of many from marginal seats. None are quite as awful as Elizabeth Peacock, who spoke squatly and fatly against Margaret – why bother, she won't be here in the next Parliament anyway[1] – but most are concerned solely with saving

---

[1] In fact AC's prediction was shown to be defective. In the 1992 general election she retained her seat by a margin of 1,408.

their own skins. I spoke loyally and, should have been movingly, of our debt of loyalty to the PM. But there was a hint of what's-she-ever-done-for-us from the audience and with some justification, so few ministerial appointments having come out of the '92. I tried to make their flesh creep with what Michael would do, got only a subdued ritual cheer when I said Margaret is undefeated, and never will be defeated either in the Country or in this House of Commons. I'm not particularly popular with that lot. They think I'm 'snooty'. Perhaps my boredom threshold shows. But in the ballot tomorrow I'd say they will divide no better than 60/40.

After dinner I had a word with Norman Lamont. He'd just come back from somewhere-or-other. 'I don't like the smell,' he kept saying. 'There's a bad smell to the whole place.' He's right, of course. It's the smell of decay. It's affecting everything, the badge messengers, the police, the drivers. Something nasty is going to happen.

I write this very late, and I am very tired. Perhaps I'm just needlessly depressed. I'd ring The Lady if I could, but she's at a banquet. She's not even coming back for the ballot. Lovely and haughty.

Albany   *Tuesday, 20 November*

I was at my desk in MoD early, but spent most of the first hour scanning the newspapers. At nine o'clock Carla Powell rang. 'We must do something about poor Bruce.[1] Couldn't you ring Conrad Black, and get him to give Bruce back his job?'

I told her that we were all in limbo. No one, not even Mrs T. herself could today cut any ice at all with anyone.

'Poor Bruce. It's so unfair.'

Yes, yes, I quite agree, it's awful. Everything's awful. It was a little foretaste, the first one, of how diminished, how deprived of influence and access we are all soon to become.

---

[1] Bruce Anderson had been fired by the *Sunday Telegraph* following an alleged breach of confidential information.

Of course I write this very late on the night, in the full know-ledge and shock of what has happened. But I think that even this morning we, those of us who can *feel* these things, were despondent, fatalistic.

I worked for most of the morning and had lunch, a long-standing engagement with Robert Campling.[1] Hard to get further away from politics than that. Alison brought him down to the Strangers' tearoom, and the three of us talked about his ideas for Bratton, about Charleston, and Bloomsbury matters in general.

The afternoon hung interminably. Labour MPs were every-where, ghoulish and heavy-handed with their jokes. Our fellows seemed all to be in hiding.

As is my style at all 'counts' I went up to the committee floor very late. A huge crowd in the corridor. The entire lobby, TV teams from all over the world. (How did they get in, pray – all part of the general breakdown of order and discipline which is licking, like stubble fire, at everything in the Palace these last two days.)

There was, inevitably, a balls-up over the figures. We, the Tory MPs, packed tight and hot and jumpily joking to each other in the committee room, did not (a monstrous error by Cranley Onslow, for which he will pay at the next election[2]) get the figures first. We heard a loud noise, something between a gasp and a cheer, from outside the door, as the journalists digested first the closeness of the result, then the killer element – that there had under the rules to be a second ballot.

Four votes, that was all there was in it. I get so cross when I remember Peter Morrison asleep in his office. For want of a nail a kingdom was lost.

I dined with Jonathan Aitken and Nick Budgen. Bruce was at the table. To my amazement they were all confident. 'She'll wipe the floor with him next time round.' 'The abstainers will all come

---

[1] Robert Campling, a young artist who paints in the Bloomsbury style and whom AC had commissioned to redecorate certain rooms at Bratton.

[2] The error was to give the voting figures to the press first. At the next election for the chairmanship of the 1922 Committee Onslow was defeated by Sir Marcus Fox.

in.' 'You don't understand, Alan, all those people who wanted to give her a fright, they'll support her now she's up against it.'

How can people get things so wrong?

Perhaps there was a lot of this kind of muddled thinking around before the ballot. But that's historic. She's a loser, now. Doomed.

I hardly bothered to argue with them. I suppose my dejection was infectious because, by the coffee, we were all silent. Save Bruce who, although jobless, is going to shut himself away and do a Randolph,[1] an instant book on the leadership campaign.

At the ten o'clock vote Tristan found me in the lobby, pulled me into the window bay by the writing table. 'We're meeting at my house, straight after this.'

'Who's "we"?'

'Oh just a few mates; *Chris* and people. We need to talk through the next steps.'

'How do you mean?'

'Ways of supporting the Prime Minister.'

But he wouldn't accede to any of my suggestions; Aitken, Maude, David Davis[2] or Lilley, in that order. Even Andrew MacKay (not obviously of the right, as were the others) caused Tristan to pull a long face.

'We're all friends. It's a very small gathering, we all know each other and can speak freely . . .'

As soon as I walked into the room it was apparent why no one else from the right had been allowed in. 'Blue-Chips' wall-to-wall. Five Cabinet Ministers. Rifkind, who was the most dominant, and effective; C. Patten, also good but (relatively) taciturn; Newton, and Waldegrave.

Waldegrave was sympathetic, in a relaxed, jokey way. The only person to say what a personal tragedy it was for her, how she was still of a different dimension to all the others. Lamont was there,

---

[1] In 1963 Randolph Churchill wrote *The Fight for the Tory Leadership: A Contemporary Chronicle* (Heinemann), an account of the way in which the Conservative Party selected Lord Home as leader following the resignation of Harold Macmillan.

[2] David Davis, MP for Boothferry since 1987. PPS to Eric Forth, parliamentary under-secretary, DTI.

stood throughout, Mephistophelean in his black tie. He shocked me by saying at the outset that he could conceive of Michael as being quite an 'effective', *tolerable* (sic) Prime Minister.

Patten said, 'Well, he's not mad, is he? I mean after you've had a meal with him you don't get up from the table and think, that fellow was mad, do you?'

There were three Ministers of State in the room, besides myself, Hogg and John Patten. Tim Yeo[1] was there 'representing' Hurd, whose PPS he is, but stayed silent.

Douglas Hogg piped up, 'I think any one of us could serve under him [Michael].' And there was a sort of cautious mumble of assent. What I assume he meant, of course, was, 'I don't think any one in this room is likely to be sacked – so we can all enjoy ourselves.' Mutual preening took place.

I said it wasn't quite as easy as that. What we had to ensure was that the person who replaces her is the one most likely to win the Election.

'All right, then, Al; what do you think?'

Michael was unreliable, I argued. Any electoral capital he brought would soon be expended. What we needed now was a Baldwin, someone to reassure rather than stimulate. I expanded, people were nodding. But when I said Tom King, Chris Patten laughed aloud. And John P., taking his cue, said, 'I presume you're joking.'

Tristan said, 'Come on, Al, you'll have to do better than that.'

Only Douglas Hogg, surprisingly, admitted that he saw the point.

I had one more go. I did *not* say that Tom was Willie's choice as well as mine. That might have generated a class backlash. But I dwelt on his overall departmental experience in Northern Ireland, how good he was on the stump, as I had often seen.

Yet as I was speaking it dawned on me that winning the Election was not uppermost in all their minds. They were, most

---

[1] Tim Yeo, MP for Suffolk South since 1983. He had been PPS to the Foreign Secretary since 1989.

of them, twenty years younger than me, carving out their own career prospects and wanting to identify with the new winner.

Not only was there no one of my generation, there was no one (although Richard, who is a Norfolk Squire, came in very much later) of my background. There was no one, except possibly Tris, who understands and loves the Tory Party for all its faults, knows it as an old whore that has been around for 400 years.

Young Turks. And Young Turks are bad news, unless there is some dilution. They all poke fun at Tom now. But if he became Prime Minister, assumed the authority, he could metamorphose and put them all in irons. The old Postman in Remarque's *All Quiet* . . .

Although I had been expecting Tristan to try and rig it for John Major, the consensus did in fact build up quite rapidly for Douglas. I remained doubtful. He is *too* much of an Establishment candidate.

Of course, this is a crisis for the Establishment, and they have left it horrendously late to organise. But DH looks, speaks, moves, articulates as prototypical Establishment. I'm not sure the Party wants that. It's very risky, unless there is another candidate for the left who will peel off a tranche of Heseltine's total.

It is difficult. If we confine the contest to two candidates, the issues are starker. If there are more than two there will be some cross-transferring, but there remains a danger that Michael's core vote will be strong enough – just as she herself (opposed by the Establishment) was in 1975. Never mind the abstruse calculations according to the 'Rules', the third ballot is a foregone conclusion. Whoever gets the highest total next time, wins.

It was only when I got back here, at ten minutes to one am that it dawned on me: at least five of the people in that room fancied themselves as 'New Generation' candidates, in the nearish future. They want Douglas, but *as a caretaker*. They're not quite ready, themselves. As we were breaking up one – it could have been William – actually said, 'If we put John in, he'll be there for twenty-five years.'

The really sickening thing, though, was the urgent and unanimous abandonment of The Lady. Except for William's little opening tribute, she was never mentioned again.

Albany   *Wednesday, 21 November*

This is going to be – politically – The Longest Day. I woke very early, in spite of having gone to bed at twenty past one, and with a restless energy matched only by that on the February morning in 1986 when I knew that at last I had escaped from the DE and was to be appointed Minister for Trade. Yet today it is the exact reverse. Not only my own prospects, but the whole edifice which we have constructed around The Lady, are in ruins.

It's quite extraordinary. Fifteen years have gone by and yet those very same people – Dykes, Charlie Morrison, Tony Grant, Barney Hayhoe – who have always hated her and the values she stood for, are still around in the lobbies, barely looking any different, grinning all over their faces – 'At last we've got her.'

I can't think of a single anti-Thatcherite who has died or receded throughout that entire period.

By 6.30 my tea was cold and I had read the papers. Still an assumption, in some columns, that Michael will be defeated in the second ballot – but by whom?

Always remember what she did in '75; all that shit about now it's 'really' going to be Willie, or Jim Prior, or you name it. The Party may be just entering on one of its periodic bouts of epilepsy.

I put a call through to Paris. They're one hour ahead, and I wanted to interrupt the pre-breakfast conference. Peter came on the line. I said I must have two minutes with her. Charles would have always put me through. So would Bernard. He gave me the usual run-around. Frightfully tied up just at this minute, try and fit it in before we go down to breakfast . . .

'Go *down* to? Don't you have it in the room?'

'There's a Working Breakfast.'

'With a lot of fucking foreigners, I suppose. I want to talk to her about last night.' I gave him a (selective) résumé of events at Catherine Place.

'I'll try and call you back.'

'When?'

'Well, within half an hour.'

'Peter, you will tell her I rang, won't you?'

'Yes, yes. Yes.'

'Because if you tell her, she will call me. And if she doesn't call me, I'll know it's because you haven't told her.'

High-pitched giggle. 'Don't worry. I'll tell her.' He won't though. Cunt.

Later – Ministry of Defence

No work is being done in Whitehall today, whatsoever. My 'In'-tray is about an inch deep. I don't think a single Minister in the Govt will be at his desk; or if he is, it will be only so as to telephone to a colleague or to a journalist. The civil servants (all of whom, down to Principal level, I suspect, were terrified of The Lady) just cannot believe their eyes.

Yet still she won't return. There is talk of a 'fighting statement' later. But this wastage of time in Paris is sheer lunacy. Harold at Stamford Bridge.

It is the general sense of disintegration now affecting everything, that is so damaging to her. Unless MH is slaughtered in the final ballot – impossibly unlikely – she herself is going to find it highly difficult to reassert her authority, even if eventually she emerges as the victor. Short, that is, of giving them the full coup-loser's treatment – arrest, manacles, beaten up in the interrogation room, shot while trying to escape. Real blood, in other words. Fun, but a bit *Angolan*.

Before walking over to the House I called Andrew MacKay into my room and we had a long talk about Tom. Earlier, we had both lingered after Ministers and sounded him.

Tom likes the idea, preened himself, straightened his jacket; but he is cautious. He would need to be sure of at least thirty votes to even 'put down a marker'. And in any case, convention obliges that no member of the Cabinet puts his name forward while she is still standing. (I hear rumours that that pudgy puff-ball Kenneth Clarke is considering breaching this, but am keeping that in reserve.)

'Look,' I told him. 'If The Lady is doomed, our Number One priority is to find, and install, a leader who will win the next

General Election. And we haven't got long. Who is best suited to
do this?'

I told him that Heseltine would burn out very quickly. His
rhetoric pleased Party Conference, but was less reliable in the
national context. Anyway people are sick of passion, they want
reassurance.

The only two figures who can do this are Tom and John Major.
Douglas is now past it; is thought rightly or wrongly to be a buffer
and a bureaucrat. John is more engaging than Tom in some ways,
with a lovely grin, but seems really too youthful. There is no time
to project him. Even in the House he is barely known, has never
been seen under fire. Tom, on the other hand, does have gravitas.
Also he's good in small groups, canteens and so on.

Andrew was in broad agreement. But:

'Tom won't make a move while she's still in the field.'

'So what do we do?'

'I tell you what I'm doing, if she stands second time round –
voting for Michael.'

I was appalled. Here was this good, intelligent man, tough and
(in so far as it still means anything) right wing . . . More than any
other experience this conversation has made me realise that she
will lose, finally, head-to-head against Heseltine. But if she does
stand again we are in a log-jam; the only people who will join in
the contest are wankers like Clarke who are not worth twenty-five
votes.

Andrew said that he would, very quietly, take soundings for
Tom. The immediate priority is to find a way, tactfully and skilfully,
to talk her out of standing a second time.

Now I must close this entry and walk over to the House.

House of Commons

I was greeted with the news that there had been an announcement.
'I fight, and I fight to win.' God alive!

Tebbit is holding an impromptu press conference in the Members' lobby.

Fifty feet away, down the tea-room corridor that mad ninny
Hampson is dancing around on his tippy-toes calling out to

passers-by, 'Tee-hee, she's standing. We've made it. We can't lose now, etc.'

I came back here, to my room. I kept the door open and an endless succession of visitors trooped in and out. No one seems to have any idea of what we should do. Her 'Campaign' is a shambles now. John Moore (who he?) is running around with bits of paper – 'draft statements' – asking people what they think. He seems to have a temporary HQ in Portillo's room,[1] which is next door to mine. First I heard that Norman Fowler was going to take charge; then John Wakeham. Or was it the other way round? Gamelin's been sacked, Weygand is on the way out; Pétain's in the wings. '*Où est la masse de manoeuvre? –Aucune.*'

Every time I trawl the corridors I run into another batch of chaps who say they're going to switch, or abstain, or when-are-there-going-to-be-some-more-candidates-to-choose-from? The only visitor who has made any real sense is Francis Maude. He claims, forcefully, that John Major has a better chance than we all realise. But John won't make a move while The Lady remains in the field. 'I must get to see her. Can you help?' Apparently Peter stands sentinel, and is outside her door the whole time.

I have closed the door. These random conversations are too discursive. Tomorrow is the last day for nominations. I must clear my head.

1) If she fights head on; she loses.
2) Therefore the opposition vote has got to be diluted by a candidate from the left – preferably Patten, making it triangular. Besides dilution, this has the advantage that it will crack Cabinet 'solidarity' open and others may lose their scruples. Therefore:
3) Try and talk Patten into standing. QED.

Archie Hamilton's just been in. Didn't make any sense. One minute he says she 'could still' win; the next that we've all 'had it'. I'm off now, upstairs.

---

[1] Michael Portillo, a rising star in the Conservative Party, MP for Enfield Southgate since December 1984.

Later – Kundan restaurant
It is very late, and finally I have withdrawn here for a vegetable curry, and to write up the traumatic happenings of this evening.

I made first for Chris's room. On the way I passed her outer door and said to Peter that I must have a minute or so. He looked anxious, almost rattled, which he never does normally. 'I'll do my best. She's seeing every member of the Cabinet in turn . . .'

'Francis wants to see her too.'

'I'm doing my best.'

Chris wasn't in his room. The Secretary of State's corridor was deserted. Hushed, but you could feel the static.

The policeman by the lift said he was 'in with Mr Rifkind'.

I knocked and went in without waiting for an answer. Also in there, loathsomely conspiring, was little Kenneth Clarke. Her three great ill-wishers! Clarke wasn't friendly at all. If he'd said anything to me, I'd have answered 'Fuck you', so just as well.

Chris was quite amiable.

'How many votes she got at the moment?'

'It's a rout. She's down to ninety.'

'*Ninety?*'

'You've got to stand. You can't let Michael corner the left.'

He was diplomatic. A discussion was impossible. God knows what they were talking about, but it stank. Never mind, I have sowed the seed; or watered what was already there.

I went down the stairs and rejoined the group outside her door. After a bit Peter said, 'I can just fit you in now – but only for a split second, mind.'

She looked calm, almost beautiful. 'Ah, Alan . . .'

'You're in a jam.'

'I know that.'

'They're all telling you not to stand, aren't they?'

'I'm going to stand. I have issued a statement.'

'That's wonderful. That's heroic. But the Party will let you down.'

'I am a fighter.'

'Fight, then. Fight right to the end, a third ballot if you need to. But you lose.'

There was quite a little pause.

'It'd be so terrible if Michael won. He would undo everything I have fought for.'

'But what a way to go! Unbeaten in three elections, never rejected by the people. Brought down by nonentities!'

'But Michael . . . as *Prime Minister.*'

'Who the fuck's Michael? No one. Nothing. He won't last six months. I doubt if he'd even win the Election. Your place in history is towering . . .'

Outside, people were doing that maddening trick of opening and shutting the door, at shorter and shorter intervals.

'Alan, it's been so good of you to come in and see me . . .'

Afterwards I felt empty. And cross. I had failed, but I didn't really know what I wanted, except for her still to be Prime Minister, and it wasn't going to work out.

I sat on the bench immediately behind the Speaker's chair, watching the coming and going. After a bit Tristan came and sat beside me. But he had little to say. What is there to say? She's still seeing visitors. Then, along came Edwina.

'Hullo, aren't you Edwina Currie?'[1]

'Now then, Alan, there's no need to be objectionable.'

'If that is who you are, I must congratulate you on the combination of loyalty and restraint that you have shown in going on television to announce your intention to vote against the Prime Minister in the Leadership Election.'

'Alan, I'm perfectly prepared to argue this through with you, if you'll listen.'

'Piss off.'

Which she did.

Tristan said, 'She's not a bad girl really.'

At half past eight I left to come over here. The archway exit from Speaker's Court was blocked by the PM's Jaguar. She had just

---

[1] Edwina Currie, MP for Derbyshire South since 1983.

taken her seat, and as the detective's door slammed the interior light went out and the car slid away. I realised with a shock that this was in all probability her last night as Prime Minister. I came in with her. I go out with her, and a terrible sadness envelops me – of unfinished duties and preoccupations; of dangers and injustices remaining, of the greed, timidity and short-sightedness of so many in public life.

Albany   *Thursday, 22 November*

Very early this morning the phone rang. It was Tristan.

'She's going.'

There will be an official announcement immediately after a short Cabinet, first thing. Then the race will be on. Apparently Douglas *and* John Major are going to stand. I said I thought it was crazy, Heseltine will go through between them. I could sense him shrugging. 'There you go.'

Anyway, would I come over to his room at the Foreign Office and watch it from there?

Afterwards, very *triste* and silent, I walked back to the MoD and sat in on a late (and unnecessary) Ministers' meeting. Tom told us that it had been 'awful'. She started to read a prepared statement to them, then broke down, and the text had to be finished by the Lord Chancellor.

Listless, I drifted over to the House. I had a word with Charles, drafted a couple of valedictory passages for her speech[1] this afternoon, did I don't know how many impromptu TV bites.

Heseltine is meant to be coming to Plymouth tomorrow, for a fundraising dinner. I rang Judith,[2] told her we couldn't possibly allow him to use us as a platform to plug his own candidature. She only half agreed, so I immediately telephoned to the *Western Morning News* and told them that I had 'instructed' that the

---

[1] Not in fact used. Mrs Thatcher told AC that if she had, she would have broken down again.

[2] Judith Roberts, chairman of the Sutton Division.

invitation be withdrawn. (Not unrich, considering I was not the host, and had long ago told everyone that I wanted nothing to do with it.)

I didn't think I could bear it, but curiosity drew me into the Chamber for The Lady's last performance. It would have been too macabre to have sat in my habitual place, next to her PPS, so I watched and listened first from behind the Chair, then from the Bar of the House. She was brilliant. Humorous, self-deprecating, swift and deadly in her argument and in her riposte. Even Dennis Skinner, her oldest adversary was feeding her lines; and at one point Michael Carttiss[1] shouted, 'You could wipe the floor with the lot of 'em.'

Too bloody true. What is to become of her? Acclimatisation will be agony, because she is not of that philosophic turn of mind that would welcome a spell at Colombey. Can she just remain on the back benches? It will be hard. What happens when she starts to be 'missed', and the rose-tinted spectacles are found in everyone's breast pocket?

This evening I had a strange, possibly a significant experience. There is a semi permanent prefab studio on College Green, where endless conclaves of MPs record their comments on the respective vices and virtues of the second-round candidates. Around it are many secondary groupings, each with a shoulder-held video and a very bright light, recording any, yes any, it seems, comment by any, yes, anyone who is going past.

Emerging from this brilliantly lit pool into the darkness at its edge, I was accosted by a familiar figure who, being dazzled, I did not at first recognise.

'Hey, Alan, take a look at this.'

It was Bob Worcester.[2] He showed me a poll, the first to be run, asking how respondents would vote if (names) were leading the Tory Party. One of Michael's great hidden strengths has always been the huge margin which he had over Mrs Thatcher in this very

---

[1] Michael Carttiss, MP for Great Yarmouth since 1983.
[2] Robert Worcester, head of MORI, the opinion polls organisation.

context. To my amazement, I saw that John Major had already drawn level! And in one case was actually ahead, actually preferred – notwithstanding the *continuous* exposure which Michael has had these last two weeks.

'Christ, Bob, these have to be rogue figures.'

Bob took umbrage. 'Look, Alan, we're MORI. We don't have "rogue" figures.'

This could be critically important. If John can break through here, he's won.

Not so many in the Party really want to vote Heseltine, for himself. Some do, and will, just to spite her. But the bulk of Michael's support comes from his so-called Election winning powers. People have guilt about condoning what he did to Her. Once they have a real reason to do so, they'll abandon him.

Tomorrow's papers will tell us more. I am taking an early train to Plymouth to 'sound out' feeling (ie, get cover for the way I cast my vote). But even if I can't get a single person in the town to tell me to vote for John Major, that's what I'm going to do.

In the Ruler of Oman's DC-9   *Wednesday, 28 November*

I am winging my way out to the Gulf.[1] I am *not* a Minister, as Private Office were (unhealthily) eager to explain to me. So there will be no HE to greet me with his Union Jack bedecked Jaguar. I will have no status with dignitaries or administrators (like hell, I thought, just watch me). This is because, with a new PM, all ministerial appointments lapse, revert to his gift, and have to be 'confirmed'.

Immediately in front of me is the bald pate, surrounded tonsure-like by a wreath of wispy white hair, of my old friend the distinguished historian Alistair Horne. He wrote *The Price of Glory*, that brilliant and harrowing study of the battle of Verdun;

---

[1] The *Cercle*, an Atlanticist society of right-wing dignitaries, largely compered by Julian Amery and Herr Franz-Josef Bach, staged one or two conferences a year and this one was travelling to Oman at the invitation of the Ruler.

still, I believe, the best of non-contemporary accounts of the Great War. But after that he went a bit soft, and got heavily involved with Macmillan who I still think would have been better done by Robert Rhodes J.

Now we are all on our way to Muscat, as guests of the Ruler, the whole thing most ably arranged by dear Julian Amery[1], so that one can be confident that it will be smooth, interesting, and subject to much deference. There is a distinguished attendance list, and Jonathan Aitken, who knows absolutely everybody in the world has, amusingly and indiscreetly, guided me through it.

It is pleasing to be at 35,000 feet, carving our route to the warm waters of the Arabian Gulf, while behind in Britain colleagues lick their wounds, or feel stale with anti-climax. Was it only last night that Jane and I watched Cranley, on the TV screen in Needham's office,[2] bellowing the figures, and then very shortly after, Michael conceded?

There was one strange, unscripted episode. Very late in the evening, after I had seen Jane off in the car, I was coming up that back staircase which leads from the transport office and comes out in the Members' lobby. At the last turn in the landing I heard the top door open in a rush and there, quite alone, wild-eyed and head to head stood Heseltine.

'Hullo Michael,' I said.

He made no answer, rushed past. He could say he had 'cut' me. But he was a zombie, shattered.

It was Mates who brought him the numbers. Must it not at that moment have been:

> A Great Hope fell.
> You heard no noise
> The Ruin was Within.[3]

---

[1] Julian Amery served Conservative prime ministers from Churchill to Margaret Thatcher.

[2] Richard Needham (Earl of Kilmorey, but does not use the title), MP for Wiltshire North since 1983 (Chippenham, 1979–83).

[3] Emily Dickinson.

Later – Eighth floor at the Al Bustan
I have a vast suite here. Bedroom, master bedroom, bodyguard's
bedroom. Sitting room, dining room, conference room, ante-
room (for the bodyguard).

With all my traveller's experience, I still think this is the best
hotel in the world, with its incredible hall, like the new Mosque in
Islamabad, and a thousand minions to bring room service at any
time of the day or night.

Andrew[1] appeared, tall and beautiful as ever. He moves among
the delegates with a very faint smile on his face, but his eyes are
always watching. What experience in childhood, what gene,
makes him instinctively so observant, and from which side of the
family does this gene come?

I detached myself from the group and we had supper together.
Andrew told me of his tales, and of the mood among the Military.
Oman is a long way from Iraq, and their traditional apprehension is
of Iranian muscle, their principal irritant is South Yemen. But the
men, many of them, think privately of Saddam as a hero, who is
leading the West a dance.

A certain undercurrent against the 'white-eyes'.

Can it have felt like this in Cawnpore, in 1857?

Al Bustan, Muscat   *Friday, 30 November*

I sit at my balcony. It is not yet 6 am and all is still, save for the soft-
soled attendants who are cleaning, bleaching, arranging the towels,
chairs and surroundings of the vast swimming pool, a hundred feet
below.

Last night our delegation had dinner with the Ruler, Sheikh
Qaboos, at the Barakha Palace. The drive was nearly a mile long,
and every palm tree was floodlit. On either side of the entrance
there were great braziers of smouldering frankincense, and the
odour was all pervading.

---

[1] AC's younger son Andrew, a major in the Life Guards, was serving as second-in-
command of the Sultan's Armoured Force.

Qaboos had put me on his left, with Julian in the place of honour on the Ruler's right hand. He is intelligent, quick, almost feline in his responses, and commands the most perfect English – a mixture of Sandringham and Miss Newman.

In contrast to the other Ruling Families on whom I had called in August, he is not frightened of Saddam. And his contempt for the oily little King of Jordan, who is, was palpable. Qaboos said that Saddam was, at this moment, scared, but that he was a 'slippery fellow' and had a reputation in the bazaars, which he cultivates, for getting out of scrapes.

'He's going to need an awful lot of MiG's to get out of this one,' I said.

But Qaboos was thoughtful. Arab coalitions are fragile creatures, he told me. If it should be thought that Saddam may survive there are many who would like to 'take insurance'.

Qaboos is delightful company. Wholly royal in manner and deportment, but never *remote*. He engages with you. Detached yes, but so different from the Windsors (except the dear QM) who are all of them remote – and obtuse.

At lunch I had sat next to General Schwarzkopf,[1] and formed a high opinion of him. At West Point he was an amateur wrestler, and looks it. But he has a keen brain and an infectious humour. Earlier he had given us a most competent and interesting 'presentation'.

Schwarzkopf was in Vietnam, first as an Adviser, then in command of a battalion, and has no illusions as to the military prowess of Third World countries. He told me his one dread was to find his spearhead still stuck in the 'berms' and wadis of the enemy line at first light after a night attack, and then to be drenched with chemicals. Gas is of little value in the mobile battle, but can be seriously nasty against fixed positions.

Already this morning I have swum. The sea temperature must be about 85°. I walked the length of the beach, barefooted on the volcanic sand, in a state of reflective melancholy, brooding on the sadness of affairs of the heart, and unrequited prospects.

---

[1] General Norman Schwarzkopf, commander of the US forces in the Gulf, who would gain celebrity during the Gulf War.

'Behind a gift, designed to kill.'[1] Whenever I am in the desert I think always of that brilliant, worrying poem and its strange imagery.

My own career is now on a descending parabola. The events of last week have inserted a new generation and, episode by episode, the effects will make themselves felt.

Both Jonathan [Aitken] and Paul [Channon] are teasing me mercilessly, and with not a little secret spite, about how probable it is that ('sadly') I will be left out of John Major's new administration.

'You've lost your protector,' Paul kept saying.

Rude, because it implies that I have no individual merit, just held the job(s) down for seven years because I was a favourite. There are no true friends in politics.

We are all sharks circling, and waiting, for traces of blood to appear in the water.

Now I am going to start work on the script of my lecture. I am lying low this morning, in order to get it polished, although I fear it will not be widely welcomed. This entire outing is a right-wing think (or rather thought) tank, funded by the CIA, which churns Cold War concepts around. I am going to tell them that the Cold War is over and NATO is washed up, unnecessary, a waste of time and money and (as is the 'streetwise' expression) space.

Al Bustan   *Saturday, 1 December*

Last night another huge dinner, given by the distinguished Doctor Omar. Lashings of alcohol – the claret was all '85, and there were some wonderful white Burgundies. Sinuous and scented lovelies shimmered about.

At the end of the meal a belly dancer performed. On and on she went with graceful, but ever more suggestive, rhythms. Her stamina was unbelievable and never once did she repeat herself. From time to time she 'fixed' particular guests in their places, a special treat.

There was a French Admiral sitting next to me, his face

[1] Keith Douglas.

expressionless. I said, it helps one to understand how women can experience ten or eleven orgasms in one night. Myself, three render me *complètement, totalement épuisé*. Ruefully, he agreed.

Albany   *Thursday, 6 December*

There was a rumour running round the Lobby that Tom, who had gone to Brussels to attend some idiotic NATO meeting, had taken ill with 'flu' (covers everything) and come back prone, on a stretcher.

I kept my ears pricked, and at the ten o'clock vote Andrew MacKay *pulled* me from the chamber and recounted that Tom had been 'taken straight to' St Thomas's and operated on immediately for a quite minor 'blockage' (uh?) in his 'back passage'.

'Quite,' I said, and, 'What bad luck', thinking I hope that never happens to me.

I went back to Brooks's, where I was playing in the backgammon tournament, in high spirits. Room here for some fantasising.

When finally I left the Club Bruce Anderson was standing on the pavement with a pretty willowy blonde in a black coat. 'What's happened? What's the matter? What's he got?'

I was in good form and treated it lightly. 'I don't know, I wasn't in the theatre.'

She giggled. Are, suddenly, the stars running?

Albany   *Monday, 10 December*

This evening I gave the Liddell Hart Memorial Lecture at King's. My text was a cleaned up version of the 'NATO today – a bureaucracy in search of a pension' theme, with which I had teased the Cercle at the Muscat seminar.

It went well, and afterwards Laurie Freedman[1] and Frank Cooper (both good judges) were appreciative.

---

[1] Professor Lawrence Freedman, Professor of War Studies, King's College, since 1982.

But for me, it was symbolic. Basil was my tutor in Military History, and in much about life, as well. He was godfather to James, and nurtured me when I was young and obstreperous and made mistakes. But he always had faith in me, told people like Michael Howard[1] who (quite understandably) disapproved, that I would go far.

Many of Basil's aphorisms are essential in politics. 'When questioning the validity of a piece of information ask always who was the original source', and, 'On every occasion that a particular recommendation is made, ask yourself first in what way the author's career may be affected.'

I stood at the rostrum, and I knew that he would be beaming.

It was a close-run thing, though. I had to get *some* cover because what I was saying was very contentious. Shamelessly I 'bounced' dear Peter and an unfortunate junior in 'Policy' who, unable to master – or perhaps to believe – the subversive conclusions that were implied, reluctantly 'passed' it. I was meant to be at King's for tea and small talk at 4.15. Like the Review, it had to be done 'privately', and it was not until 4.30 that Alison took the last sheet out of the printer. We got there, helter skelter at 4.58 to deliver a lecture billed for 5 pm.

Thirty years ago, when I was writing *The Donkeys* at Bratton, I would have thought this evening the very pinnacle of attainment and recognition.

But now, alas, having 'arrived' I know that soon I am about to depart.

Ministry of Defence   *Tuesday, 11 December*

Tom occupied most of Ministers this morning telling everyone how his 'complaint' was very common, happens to practically everyone at some time, and so on.

As we dispersed he indicated that he wanted me to stay behind. The 'pupil's chair' was drawn up facing his desk, and he told Simon to leave – always a bad sign.

---

[1] Sir Michael Howard, former Regius Professor of Modern History at Oxford and a noted military historian.

'How are you?' I drawled.

'I'm perfectly all right. It's you I want to talk about.'

He gave me a heavy basting. 'If you want to criticise Government policy, then you must do it from outside the Government.'

'I wasn't criticising Government policy.'

'Well, that certainly isn't the impression held by the Prime Minister. Or Douglas. Or the Chief Whip.'

Suspected balls, I thought.

'I can't go on defending you, you know. I think you'll have to look on this as your last chance.'

Back here I thought about it. If I am sacked (which I don't think I will be) then it is for saying what I believe, and what is manifestly true. How much consolation is that? Some, I suppose. But there's poor old Keith Speed, sacked for 'speaking out' nearly ten years ago, and still no 'K'.[1]

Ministry of Defence   *Wednesday, 12 December*

Last night I dined with Franko and Perry at Wiltons.[2]

Perry, *vu grand, comme toujours.* He spoke of the sweep of the Thatcherite legend, how we all had a duty to propagate it. Both were plainly getting ready to be 'disillusioned' with the unfortunate John – whom I personally believe to be tougher and more clear-headed than they realise.

I took the whole thing as a bit much coming from Perry who, in his day, has written the most flesh-crawling stuff about the dear Lady not having the 'class' that you need in adversity, deploring the absence of Gentlemen, all that sort of demi-balls. Frank, at least, has shown real affection and loyalty, only pulled her leg from time to time.

There was some talk about who would do *The Book*, how

---

[1] As Parliamentary Under-Secretary (Navy), Keith Speed resigned in protest at the reduction of frigate numbers set out in the 1981 Defence White Paper (Cmnd 8288).

[2] Frank Johnson and Peregrine Worsthorne.

important it was. I must say my spirits fell when they said John O'Sullivan was going to 'ghost' it.

Ghost! Good God! The greatest political story of the century, and they're looking for a 'ghost'.

During the night I thought, why shouldn't I write it? She would trust me, I'm sure, with the papers. As a Privy Councillor I can get access to Cabinet Office records. I am trained as a historian, and she has often said (in public) how much she admires *Barbarossa*.[1]

Early this morning I caught Peter on the ministerial floor, and expounded. He was enthusiastic. Said the present situation was 'a mess', 'too many cooks'. He promised to speak with her, and this time I think he is going to.

Ministry of Defence   *Thursday, 20 December*

Tom is looking strained and lined, still. He cut his leg on the weekend with a sickle and now, being full of every kind of antibiotic, finds it going 'septic', and has to keep it propped up on a chair.

All due to Al, Jane said, who is harrying him while he is run down. An article by Peter McKay, always fresh and amusing, in yesterday's *Evening Standard* – 'Top Dogs, Wrong Collars' – suggested that we should simply change places. Harmful to me, but fun nonetheless.

I was having a chat with David Davis, and he told me an interesting footnote to the leadership affair.

After they received the figures of the second ballot Heseltine's claque – notably Mates, Hampson and Macfarlane – were frantic that he should hang in there, contest the third 'in order to strengthen his position'. H. ignored this, immediately conceding. (Presumably calculating that his total could well go down, and reduce still further his bargaining strength.)

---

[1] *Barbarossa*, AC's third volume of military history, following *The Donkeys* and *The Fall of Crete*.

However, when he met with John Major Heseltine made no attempt whatever to get places for his acolytes, being concerned only for himself, and cut the painter immediately. Later Mates threw a tantrum, and has apparently been promised something (unspecified) 'in the next Government'.

Saltwood   *Friday, 21 December*

The shortest day. Darkness and depression.

Bruce Anderson came to lunch, arriving terribly late. We didn't sit down until 3 pm.

He left me in little doubt that my shares are a listless market. I am the oldest member of the administration. My chances of getting into the Cabinet are nil. There was some (I thought slightly bizarre) talk of my being John's PPS in the next Parliament. I'd have done it straight away, but I won't do anything in the next Parliament unless it's from the Lords.

I have OD'd this last month, on politics. I have a huge backlog – for the first time – of work in the Dept, most of it turgid. But after I had seen Bruce on to a train I felt limp, and sated. Even my PC, to which I am greatly looking forward, is somewhat blighted by having acquired, it seems, the status of the *Medaille militaire* in the Charennes hospital at Verdun.[1] (The Lady's list, out today, contains little of interest or importance, although a K for poor Peter M, and a KCMG for Charles Powell – the latter most signally deserved.) Bruce told me of a comment on Derek Lord, the gay, intelligent, ludicrously self-assured black companion to Michael Brown, who was active in the Gayfrere Street bunker. From a rough Derbyshire farmer, a constituent of Michael's: 'Eee that twat's dad moost've eaten a posh missionary.'

---

[1] Awarded to those dying of their wounds.

Saltwood   *Christmas Day*

Leafing through a bound copy of *The Car* of 1906 I came across a delicious piece of useless information. Byron (no less) once rhymed 'intellectual' – troublesome, admittedly – with 'hen-pecked you all'.

I must contrive an opportunity to use this, 'spontaneously', in the House.

1991

Saltwood   *Friday, 4 January*

Just as obituary pages nearly always cause satisfaction – if not *Schadenfreude* – so do Honours Lists invariably irritate. Like Parliamentary Selection, they seem always to be bestowed on the wrong people.

I have tried very seldom to secure 'recognition' for anyone – although I did get an OBE for Betty.[1] So by now my two particular nominations – Phil Drabble for all he has done to enlarge our knowledge and enjoyment of nature and the countryside and the relations between man and beast; and Alex Moulton, for being a brilliant inventor, who has always risked his own money in putting his ideas into practical effect – are overdue to come up. But no. Who got the 'Industry' K's? A couple who personify all that is wrong with British 'businessmen'. Morton[2] – aggressive, nasty and stupid. And Sheehy[3] – self-indulgent, nasty and stupid. It's a practically infallible rule (though, most fortunately, vitiated in our recent leadership election), that the bad guy always wins. I can barely think of a single 'businessman' who has ever deserved a K except Ian MacLaurin[4] and Colin Chandler.[5]

I was with The Lady today. A strange menage. The tiny little house, lent her by Alistair McAlpine,[6] on College Green, still carries the faintest whiff of Number 10. Sloaneish secretaries bustle about on the ground floor, where telephones ring; handsome,

---

[1] Councillor Mrs Betty Easton, OBE, chairman of the Sutton Division for many years.

[2] Sir Alastair Morton, British chairman of Eurotunnel since 1987.

[3] Sir Patrick Sheehy, chairman, BAT (formerly British American Tobacco) Industries since 1982.

[4] Sir Ian MacLaurin, chairman of Tesco, knighted in 1989.

[5] Sir Colin Chandler, managing director, Vickers plc, since 1990.

[6] Lord McAlpine of West Green (life peer, 1984), honorary treasurer of the Conservative Party, 1975–90.

though slightly effete young men slide in and out of her sitting room, bend over her ear, carrying sheaves of papers.

'I detect a distinct aura of Elba,' I said.

'Elba? Elba?'

'Where Napoleon was exiled before his return.'

'Yes, yes I know *that*, I mean – how interesting.'

We talked for a little about the events of last November, and Peter Morrison sat in, lobbing her the occasional softball. Her sense of betrayal is absolute, overrides everything. Lamont had been scheming; Patten plotted the whole thing; Kenneth Clarke had led the rout from the Cabinet Room. Rifkind was a weasel. Even John Major (who announced yesterday that some benefit was to be uprated, depicted in this morning's press, gleefully, as a 'Reversal of Thatcherite Policies') is by no means cloudfree.

I remembered a remark I had once heard Norman Tebbit address to her in private. 'Prime Minister, it is you who chooses your Cabinet', but said nothing. What was the point?

Gently, I brought the subject round to the book.

'I want *you* to do it, Alan, because you are a believer.'

'It shouldn't be "a believer's" book. It doesn't need to be.'

'How can you say that?'

'The facts speak for themselves. They illustrate the scale of your achievement.'

'But look how it ended. The treachery . . .'

'Margaret, these aren't Memoirs. You don't want to get into that game. This is your *Biography*. Where you came from, how you got there, what you did for the Conservative Party, and for Britain. A major work of political history. It will go into every university library in the World.'

As our conversation developed I could see she was having second thoughts. I told her that I would pay proper attention to the strange and disreputable circumstances of her ousting. That I could see the symmetry between what happened to her, and the way Grantham Council treated Alderman Roberts (being a subject to which she adverted several times).

But the standpoint *had* to be objective. A tract, even a great big thick tract, would be a wasted opportunity.

She didn't much like all this. I changed the subject to that
of money. Michael Sissons[1] had told me that he could envisage a
total take of about eight million (sterling). I said I didn't want any
royalty. I would write it for a fee, but it would take me three
years . . .

'Three *years?*'

'Minimum. This is a major book, six hundred pages. It has got
to be impeccable. I'll have to pay an assistant.'

I have often found that once sums of money under discussion
pass beyond a certain level – no more than a couple of million
usually – reality tends to be discarded, 'quotes' get wilder and
wilder. It's all Monopoly.

Apparently Mark [Thatcher] had been winding her up:
'. . . Could be as much as twenty.'

Who's going to 'handle' it, anyway? There was talk of a hot
lawyer in New York. Mark's favourite was apparently someone
called McCormack, who plugs Sports 'Personalities', where the
sums are enormous.[2]

I'm doubtful about all this. It's tempting, I can see, to allow
yourself to be regarded as a 'property'. But slightly demeaning for
the premier politician of the Western world. Better by far to keep
the whole thing on an astringent, almost academic level. In the
long run the yield will probably be little different.

Feeling the whole thing to be slipping away, I thought I ought
to make one point absolutely clear. 'I am the author, not the
Ghost. It's the Official Biography *by* Alan Clark. Not "as told to",
or anything of that kind.'

I think that tore it. Perhaps just as well. I don't want another
round of 'negotiation' in which she makes some concessions, and is
then taken aback by my request – and I appear 'unreasonable'. But
what she wants, I fear, is *Margaret Thatcher. My Story.*

It's all rather sad, particularly for future generations. Dilks[3] could

---

[1] Michael Sissons, chairman and managing director of the literary agency Peters,
Fraser and Dunlop.

[2] Mark McCormack, chairman of International Management Group.

[3] David Dilks, Professor of International History, University of Leeds, since 1970.
Edited *The Diaries of Alexander Cadogan.*

do it. But he'd take an eternity. Possibly John Charmley.[1] But a 'ghost' hack will spoil the tale. Hard to say of course, as it depends who they choose, but could be even worse than if she tries to write it herself.

Winston did, why shouldn't she? she may be thinking. But consider for example that wonderful passage in Moran when Churchill explains the difference between scansion and resonance in a text. I don't think she would be aware of that, bless her.

Saltwood   *Sunday, 6 January*

First dinner of the year. David Davis and his wife (good strong chap, very much our sense of humour. Did the 'black' route without turning a hair, then retraced his footsteps, hands in pockets – first time *that's* ever been done!). Richard Ryder and Caroline,[2] the Deedes, the Michael Howards. We were eleven and the table and the food were terrific. But the meal somehow lacked *Stimmung*.

Tristan, a last-minute addition, performed sparklingly. But Bill Deedes, though splendid, and still a minter of delicious unfinished sentences is going deaf and 'misses' things. Even so, he remains one of the great ingredients in any grouping. He is wise, politically shrewd, still; and has a vast, archival fund of historic experience. Bill told Jane that he used to play golf with Philip Sassoon[3] before the war and Philip was so impatient that he employed two extra caddies who were sent ahead to see where the balls landed, so that Philip and his partner wouldn't waste time looking for them. (I know nothing about golf, but thought that 'looking for the ball' was one of the secondary ritualised pleasures?)

---

[1] John Charmley, historian, lecturer in English history at the University of East Anglia. Author of *Duff Cooper*, *Chamberlain and the Lost Peace* and *Churchill: The End of Glory*.

[2] Caroline Ryder, MBE, the daughter of a former clerk to the House of Commons, was a secretary to Margaret Thatcher.

[3] Sir Philip Sassoon, 3rd Bt, Unionist MP. Private secretary to Sir Douglas Haig, 1915–18. Under-Secretary for Air in the National Government in the 1930s.

Lady Deedes, whom I called 'Evelyn' but Michael Howard (I don't doubt correctly) addressed as 'Hilary', was a pool of tranquil, though amiable *longueurs*.

When the ladies exited, I started the conversation on the lines of what are we to do about Margaret?

Following my meeting with her on Thursday, and the very bitter feelings of betrayal which she so evidently holds, my feeling is that she, her behaviour, could present the Party with one of its most vexatious problems over the coming months. There was some desultory talk about 'the book' (I gave nothing away. Only Richard knows that she and I are talking). Agreement on the general 'problem' of Mark. We couldn't really get into a good gossip, as Tristan would have done, left to himself.

Bill to some extent inhibits this – the Old School. And Richard was totally, *owlishly* silent. So much so that I thought he must be terribly tired, half asleep (he had been shooting in Norfolk all day). But on the few occasions that he uttered, monosyllabically, it was slicingly to correct errors of fact made by the participants. As a personality he is deeply pleasing – intelligent and '*aimable*' in the French sense.

DD also impressed. The concept of having clever, tough, *congenial* people in the Whips' Office is relatively new. In former times they were just fieldsport enthusiasts whose last and only fulfilment-period had been bullying (and in some cases buggering) Lower Boys at Eton. Now it is recognised as a nursery for junior Ministers. (I remember Nigel,[1] when I reproached him for going there, saying that the experience was essential – how Parlt works, how 'Business' is arranged, if one is to do a ministerial job properly.) As for myself, although I like to boast of having been blackballed – 'both to have been proposed, and to have been blackballed is equally complimentary' – I am sad not to have done a stint there.

At present we are all a little constrained. I first noticed this at the End of Term dinner last July.[2] The polls are implacable. The date of

---

[1] Nigel Lawson had been an opposition whip, 1976–77.
[2] See 20 July 1990.

the Election approaches. I think we will win, but I can't tell how. And behind everything lurks this tedious, unnecessary but debilitating 'question' of Europe. We are all (except for dear Tristan) true Tories. But we cannot give expression to our true feelings.

Ministry of Defence   *Monday, 7 January*

I have been 'on call' all day, ie, can't leave the building, because TK 'may' want to see me urgently.

The UN deadline[1] expires in a week's time and the place hums. But it has been conveyed to me, *via* the Private Office network, that I am not to take any part in the TV coverage of the war. The Press Office have been instructed to refuse all 'bids', and I am to refer those that are made to me personally. Where? Back to the Press Office. Catch 22. 'Must make sure we all speak with the same tongue.' But of course it's not that at all. They recognise that I am more glamorous, and have a quicker mind, than the other Ministers, who mustn't be 'outshone'. It's like a trendy Local Authority banning competitive sports.

Ah! Peter has just come in; it's coming up to 7 pm and S of S office have rung to say I can 'stand down'. I assume that he was intending to huff-locute this instruction to me personally, then either lost his nerve or got involved with some other topic.

I have been whiling away the time reading through a bundle of congratulatory letters.[2] Those from officials please me most, and of them Charles wrote much the nicest. A document to be treasured. But do officials write in much the same way to every Minister who gets a PC? Perhaps. With very slight variations.

It is an important, but highly specialised form of recognition. The *Herald* came on, but couldn't understand it at all. 'Does this mean you'll be able to do more for Plymouth?'

---

[1] The ultimatum requiring Saddam Hussein to withdraw his forces from Kuwait.
[2] On the announcement of AC being appointed a Privy Councillor.

Plymouth train   *Friday, 11 January*

I have already finished the box. Very little for me these days. The whole Dept is concentrating on the war and, at all costs, Archie and TK have to keep me away from that.

Ministry of Defence   *Tuesday, 22 January*

TK is bumbustious this morning. His press conferences are being carried live in the US! Heaven help us.

Ministerial meetings are a complete waste of time now. Jokes and small talk. They were all in good form, though keeping straight faces, this morning.

There had been a heavy headline in the *Sunday Express*: REVENGE IS SWEET AT THE MoD.

A biggish picture of me, entitled – *Disliked*: Alan Clark. If I'd been in stronger form I might have enjoyed it. 'Deeply disliked by both Civil Servants and Ministers . . .', went on to talk of one of the most prestigious posts in the Government in coming weeks, 'the front men will be King and Hamilton. Clark will be kept entirely [sic] out of the limelight.'

Buttocks. The whole piece is long, and prominent. I know how the press works. This isn't just a sliver of overheard gossip. It has to be a specific plant from the Press Office, with the tacit concurrence of Tom or Archie. Quite unnecessary, as I had already agreed to this arrangement. No one at all mentioned it at Ministers, which is a clear (though gauche) indicator of a guilty conscience.

Ministry of Defence   *Wednesday, 23 January*

We're five days into the [Gulf] air war, but I am unhappy about the strategy. Attacking missile sites is always wasteful, has very little tactical effect and occurs mainly in response (as most obviously now) to political demands.

We lost another Tornado last night. That's now *five*. I can't help noticing that traditions (ancient and revered) of Bomber Command are reasserting themselves. From the Tabuk mission last night, out of ten sorties six either aborted for technical reasons, or 'jettisoned ordnance while manoeuvring to avoid (sic) SAMs', or took targets of opportunity. (Uh? At night?)

The sad thing is that it's always the brave ones, the true grit, who press on regardless (the contravening tradition) and get killed. Of the Italian flight of six *five* turned back and only one brave boy went ahead. They got him. It's the difference between James and Andrew. But I want James to survive, don't I?

MGO[1] has been here for an hour and a half. There's a potential ammunition crisis in some calibres.

We talked about the Battle Plan. It's good news, at least, that we have been moved out now to the 'left hook', on the desert flank. But I was apprehensive that our Sappers, 'because they are so good', were going to have to lead the breaching operation. There shouldn't *be* a breaching operation at all. We should go to the Euphrates, Basra if necessary, and draw the Republican Guard out in the open to attack us. Alam Halfa.[2] Not bother to go near Kuwait until it just falls off the tree.

Saltwood   *Saturday, 26 January*

It's a Saturday, but I've got a splitting tension headache.

I was doing a regional broadcast from Bristol on Thursday night, fairly routine stuff, when the commentator suddenly asked how well our NATO allies were helping.

Just as one can sometimes be less on one's guard abroad, or in a foreign studio (foolishly and recklessly ignoring the fact that news can be flash-faxed to Whitehall before one has even got out of the

---

[1] Master-General of the Ordnance. Sir John Stibbon, the senior general under AC.
[2] The classic 'drawing on' armoured battle fought by Montgomery before Alamein.

door) so one can easily think that regional radio is a bit *hick* – particularly in the W. Country.

Hick! They had a teeny television camera concealed in the sound room and gleefully sold the whole interview as a TV performance (which of course I have been 'banned' from doing). I was cross, and feckless. I made some rude remarks, 'more concerned with heading for their cellars', totally unreliable in a real crisis, etc.

Afterwards, as always, a certain remorse. There was a lull. Was it all a strange dream?

But after a day's lull it has exploded, first in the *FT*, quite small, then everywhere.

I am under siege, refusing all requests for comment or interviews. Could still go either way. It had to be said. People *in the street* are very supportive.

Ministry of Defence   *Monday, 28 January*

I loathe being in London on Sunday evenings, and last night I had to come up so as to be in time this morning for another of these useless ministerial conferences, scheduled for 8.30, never start until after 9.

The flat is bleak and shabby, and takes a couple of hours to heat up. There is dust and grime, and crumbs in – not on, *in* – the carpet. The great damask curtains, that originally hung between the Partridge pagodas at Upper Terrace, are torn and fragile, so that the soft white felt lining bulges through the fabric. I hear of 'Sets' no different from mine changing hands for seven, eight hundred thousand. But B5 is squalid – almost, the straitened quarters of an Edwardian bachelor on his uppers.

The 'Conference' follows its usual pattern. Beforehand, at about 8 am, one is shown, with much flaring of feathers, a folder marked SECRET, an 'Operational Sitrep' consisting mainly of items little different, it seems, from those to be found on page 2 of that morning's *Daily Telegraph*. Then (always late, although TK has only to walk across the street from Admiralty HO) we sit round for a monologue. On and on goes the droning, round and round come the (same) subjects. As we dispersed this morning Tom indicated that he wanted me to stay behind.

'Well, you're not exactly flavour of the month, again.'

'Oh really?'

'John isn't at all pleased.'

'Oh dear.'

'You go and do this just at the moment Douglas is trying to get Kohl to stump up some cash towards our costs in the war.'

'I'd have thought it might help. Shame them.'

'The fact that you can say something like that, shows, *if I may say so, that you're really not quite au fait with things*. It's all a bit tricky.'

Actually, the old thing wasn't unamiable. He knows I'm not a threat to him any more and he can draw mild satisfaction from my digging deeper into my own hole.

I'm dreadfully tired. I hardly slept last night and the adrenalin that would pump if I had any role whatever in this place at present just isn't flowing. I'm indifferent about resignation – were it not for the fact that I want to put certain *concepts* in place before I go. And particularly to order the new tank. There's a lot of pressure building up there – in the wrong direction.

CSA[1] came in to see me. A routine call, but our conversation took flights of fancy. He is a nice man, and clever also. Furthermore, he always searches for the best solution *for Britain*; none of your fucking 'in the interests of reaching an acceptable compromise' balls.

The need for an intermediate nuclear weapon. The danger implicit in the American development of G-PALS[2] (a good litmus test of the Nationalist, this. I see it as most unwelcome that the US should have implied power of veto over our ballistic systems, still further concentration of power in the Washington dung-heap). The advisability of getting back into the (satellite) launch business. (*I* had to suggest using the old Polaris rockets, constructing a makeshift

---

[1] Professor Ronald Oxburgh, Chief Scientific Adviser, Ministry of Defence, since 1988.

[2] The US-developed anti-ballistic missile system, Global Protection Against Limited Strike.

base area at Ascension.) We agreed on the need for extending the range of EFA. Adapting Tomahawk to SSN 20 tubes. The total untrustworthiness of the French, in any co-operative context whatever. All in all, the US our only reliable friends – and even there the limits may start to encroach as the Pentagon-Congressional Committee axis loses weight.

All rather depressing, and the only effect to make me wish, or re-wish, that I was Secretary of State.

A little later came a message via Private Office that Quinlan had been 'very impressed' with my contributions at the Steering Group meetings. Butter. I expect he wants to restrain me from being too radical. You never know with Clark. He's underemployed at the moment. He may be writing some tiresome paper.

To cap it all, I believe myself to be 'fighting' flu. In my experience, 'fighting' flu is like 'fighting' cancer. You always lose.

And I have run out of fizzy Redoxon.

Albany, 11.40 pm

Just got in from the House. At the ten o'clock vote I was 'lionised'. Colleagues from all sides coming up and saying how they agreed, endless 'well-done's' from people I hardly knew. The press has been kind, and I hear that even *Time* magazine is going to run a favourable para.

My cup runneth over; with a typical performance by that creep Hugh Dykes who told the TV cameras I should be sacked at once.

Albany   *Wednesday, 30 January*

Today I visited Shorts in Belfast. Interesting weapons, the 'Streak' family. Very much the next generation, light, accurate, crazy-fast. And conforming with my long-held view, which I expressed in the Sopwith Memorial Lecture last year, that missiles should be *multi-elemental*. One close-range type should be adaptable to sea, infantry and helicopter use. It's always the Navy who resist this, isn't it? They love to spend millions and millions on 'systems' that only sailors can use.

Northern Ireland is unbelievably nasty. Grey, damp, cold. Big puddles just lying; blackthorn hedges; low standard of life. I saw one pretty girl, in a crowd that had been evacuated from a building on account of a '200 lb bomb scare'. They were all standing, patient but dejected, on the pavement. White police tape everywhere. On her own, she was jumping about excitedly, *very* nice legs.

But the general atmosphere is bleak; overlaid with the oppression of terror; deep and perpetual feuds, suspicion and callousness.

I am confirmed in my opinion that it is hopeless here. All we can do is arm the Orangemen – to the teeth – and get out. This would give also the not slight advantage that, at a stroke, Infantry 'overstretch' is eliminated.

Constituency Office, Plymouth   *Friday, 1 February*

I got off the sleeper this morning and picked my way along deserted streets to the Duke of Cornwall, which opens for breakfast ahead of the other hotels in the City. 'Picked' I say, because it was *black ice*, and I was carrying a heavy box and an overnight bag and wearing *tutti* town slippers. If one had been on form, showing off and laughing, the gradient outside Sainsburys was schussable.

I ate my international traveller's breakfast – a double cornflakes and natural yoghourt – which I have consumed all around the world from Sydney to Bogota to Anchorage, often the only swallowable food offered all day, and read the local paper. It must be over a year since I called here, and I doubt if I will ever do so again, as I have no intention of getting into that sleeper train any more if I can possibly avoid it.

The place is redolent of memories, particularly of the early days. The downstairs 'Conveniences' were always unpleasant, wiped rather than cleaned, and smelling of beer and ablutions. But I could find, still intact and unchanged, now nearly twenty years and no one has yet thought to put a hook on the back of the door for your coat, the little private thompson loo on the first floor, and used it well.

Now all I have left, at the very most, is a year. I am trying to
steel myself to the great transition. What are my objectives?
Limited, I suppose, by comparison. Full and proper attention to
my papers and to the Heritage. A dilettante man of letters? A (old
Etonian) Guru? A more attentive husband? Freedom to travel at
will, and EARLY NIGHTS. The deferral of old age, I suppose.
But this is in itself rather wet and feeble, and invites Nemesis.

The sheer scale of the enforced change, the fact that I will be
excluded from the Commons, from the beloved, magical electric
aura of the Chamber, and by my own hand, has yet to sink in.
Although periodically, as now, I try and face it. But I would not
wish to grow old in the House. Rumpled. Dandruff. The young
ones pushing past.

Will I get a peerage? Claimants always say they want it for their
wife, but I would so like to present it to Jane while she is still
young and pretty. Sometimes I have been foul to her. Why?
Hormones, I suppose.

But they'll do their best to stop me. I have lots of enemies at
middle rank, perhaps even in the Cabinet Office – although not, I
hope, Robin [Butler] whom personally I like (although it is easy to
make the mistake of thinking that those one likes reciprocate the
feeling). I doubt if I have a single friend in the whole Foreign
Office, not a male one anyway.

Then there are the two heavies. Hurd has always been against
me, told The Lady not to make me Minister for Trade – which she
very splendidly repeated to me on the evening of my appointment.
Arsehole. He's looking more and more like Aldridge Prior.[1]

And of course Michael. Michael *knows* – just as when one has
had some frightful bout of food-poisoning one always by instinct
knows which particular dish caused it – he knows that it was me
who tipped the scales in the two days immediately after the coup,
by winding up the Constituency Associations. And my podgy
namesake.[2] He's always been suspicious of me, and actually *sued*

---

[1] Aldridge Prior – the Hopeless Liar, a character in a strip in *Viz*.
[2] Kenneth Clarke, the health minister.

the manufacturers of Trivial Pursuit because they had muddled us up.

None of these people can face the idea of me in the Lords because instead of treating it as a Garden of Remembrance I might actually say something. *Unpredictable.*

Only dear Richard [Ryder], who is intelligent and sweet, would be my advocate, though not, I fear, as resolutely as Ian did in finally persuading The Lady to 'try' me in Government some eight years gone by. And Chris (Patten), I don't think would mind. I hope not, at least, as he is a good guy.

If they could, my enemies would block a 'K' as well, although this is more difficult unless the subject has actually been corrupt (practically the only failing, I suppose, that I never have had).

Perhaps better to compose myself always to being 'Mister'. Like John Wilkes.

House of Commons   *Tuesday, 5 February*

Today I was inducted into the Privy Council. A rehearsal of the ceremony had been fixed twenty minutes before at the PC office in Whitehall. I changed – in the dark little lobby outside the bathroom which I share with the Chief of the General Staff – into my new navy suit, which still carries O'Brien's[1] 'delivery' creases and which I don only very sparingly. I thought my shoes looked scruffy. No one in the outer office (why not? Julian always had a pack) had any shoe polish. So I had to go via the Commons. I bickered briefly with Alison, got my fingers black-streaked with the Kiwi. Had to go into the drivers' loo and continuously scrub under the (boiling) tap. All water, everywhere, in the House of Commons is *always* screeching hot, especially in July. I was now late.

Just as we drew up outside the Cabinet Office the carphone rang. Private Office. Where was I? etc, etc. All right, all right, I'm

---

[1] Mr O'Brien, head cutter of Lesley and Roberts in Savile Row.

at the door. I could feel my bladder contracting and remembered I'd forgotten to pee. Blast.

A discreet attendant in spectacles was waiting for me. He conducted me into the presence of the Privy Council Secretary, a dear old thing not unlike Farky[1] at Kings in 1943. He and, more particularly, *his* secretary sized me up at once as being 'difficult', ie, not sufficiently overawed and softspoken. 'We've just got time, I think,' he quavered.

'*Just*,' snarl/sneered the assistant secretary.

They 'took me through' the ceremony. Quite long drawn-out and, because of its repetitious quality, easy (as I was to discover) to skip a stage.

'I think we'd better go to the Palace now.'

'I'll follow you.'

'I'm afraid we may get separated. I've got a special ivory pass that lets me through Horse Guards Arch.'

'So've I.'

Taken aback somewhat he told me a put-down story about when he was a Dep Sec at the Home Office he had tried very hard to limit the issue of the ivory passes. I retaliated with the tale of the occasion when Andrew refused to let Geoffrey Howe through. Deuce.

At Buck House I was indeed the last to arrive (I should nervously and respectfully, have been the first). MacGregor,[2] the Lord President, Bertie Denham, Paddy Mayhew,[3] Nick Scott, Wakeham. We hung about in the hall through which one processes on Garden Party days. Small, very small, talk.

We were joined by two Palace functionaries – handsome, nicely dressed, middle-aged; both of them with that shallow courtesy, smooth complexion and careful coiffure of the Establishment homosexual.

Tactlessly, I interrupted a lot of cant about cold-weather allowances for the aged – poor people, what a good idea, etc, etc

---

[1] Warden of the college, 1929–43. AC was taken over to visit him by John Sparrow from Eton in 1943.

[2] John MacGregor, education secretary since 1989.

[3] Patrick Mayhew, Attorney General since 1987.

– with a crack about the opening that very day at the QE II Centre of a World Conference on Global Warming.

Conversation petered out.

Then, jarringly, a 'household' electric bell rang and little MacGregor sloped off for a preliminary audience. About eight minutes later it rang again. The Councillors trooped in, me last. Stop at the door. Bow. Approach the Monarch, bow again. Take the Hand, *ultra* lightly. Walk backwards or rather crabwise, into the line-up.

A smallish room, much Savonnerie, indifferent pictures. The Queen sat at, or rather adjacent to, a *secretaire* copiously encrustulated with boule. A vase of blueish flowers, conventionally arranged. Moyses Stevens.

The business of the Council was announced. First item 'to receive into the Council', etc (they gave me my courtesy title). I stepped forward, knelt awkwardly on the stool (bloody difficult), held up the Testament in my right hand and the dear old boy read out the oath. 'I do,' I said, firmly. I rose, advanced about ten feet diagonally to *another* stool, bowed, knelt, took the Monarch's hand and 'brushed it with my lips', rose, bowed, back into line.

A pause ensued. Why? I made to go forward, down the line, shake hands with the Lord President as forewarned and instructed. No. Blast, fuck, etc. There was *another* oath. The old Clerk, secretly delighted, rolled his eyes in mock resignation and signalled me to raise, again, the Testament in my right hand. He then read out a very long passage the substance of which, as far as I could make out, was that I undertook to maintain total secrecy even, particularly indeed, about colleagues concerning whom I might hear unsatisfactory things. (The more I think about this the odder it seems.)

This time, when I said 'I do' I looked directly at the Queen. I bet many don't. But I was glad to see that she was looking directly at me. I then did the handshaking act, Lord President, Attorney General, the rest, and returned to my place at the end of the line. At which the Queen got up from her chair and moved over, *regally*, to initiate a painfully, grotesquely, banal conversation, loosely devoted to the various other Orders in Council that were on the business list. Inevitably, these were all concerned with Euro-legislation. Most of

them, today, seemed to be concerned with lifts, or *ascenseurs*. Some
light banter was attempted, notably by Paddy Mayhew. Splendid
fellow, totally unsquashable. And when there were a couple of
hesitant jokes about continental lifts 'that don't have sides' I nearly
told one about the Ganymede lift at St Thomas's that goes round and
round and can invert the passengers. But I was just too far down the
line to guarantee getting it across.

This last phase was somewhat drawn out. Not for the first time I
wondered about the Queen. Is she really rather dull and stupid? Or
is she thinking, 'How do people as dull and stupid as this ever get
to be Ministers?' Or is, for her, the whole thing so stale and *déjà vu*
after forty years that she'd really rather be going round the stables at
Highclere, patting racehorses on the nose? I suppose it might feel
different if she had real power. And yet she *does* have the power.
It's all there in the Constitution, all she has to do is renounce the
Civil List for her ill-favoured siblings, pay taxes on her private
wealth, and get on with it.

I drove back to the House, and had a boring, overcooked lunch
in the Members' dining room.

*AC here included some lines from the Second World War poet Keith
Douglas:*

> And all my endeavours are unlucky explorers
> come back, abandoning the expedition;
> the specimens, the lilies of ambition
> still spring in their climate, still unpicked;
> to find them, as the great collectors before me.

White Office   *Tuesday, 12 February*

Still regrettably obsessive. After Ministers TK 'held me back'; he's
nervous of me, still needs to pick my brain – in this case just before
going to Washington. But *won't* let me 'in on' anything, TV,
Radio (Archie is on every day) or even meetings with PUS and

Mottram, CDS, Vincent,[1] etc, etc, because I will show him up in front of them.

Lunched with Dilks at Brooks's. He was quite interesting about Mrs T's 'Memoirs', said they could easily be ghosted – but it was critically important that the 'ghost' should have access to all her papers. It was something that ought to be spoken now with Robin Butler, certainly ahead of the next General Election.[2]

Saltwood   *Sunday, 17 February*

Talk of an Election in May–June. Less than three months to go, it would seem or could be. And at that my life really will turn. A major crossroads – but I refuse to accept that thereafter it's all downhill to the grave. I just will not. ACHAB.

Ministry of Defence   *Thursday, 21 February*

The Lady has now decided *against* my doing her biography – going for the big mechanistic technique of researchers and capable hacks. She's got no sense of art or scholarship at all, really. And has always been unreliable, loses her nerve and goes conventional.

Ministry of Defence   *Thursday, 28 February*

The Gulf War is over. Too soon, I think. Bush[3] has ordered a ceasefire. Now a long and messy interlude with Saddam stalling and dodging and quite likely to start shooting again. The Foreign Office has no idea what it wants. Never seems to have given any

---

[1] Permanent under-secretary at Defence, Sir Michael Quinlan since 1988; Richard Mottram, deputy under-secretary since 1989; Chief of the Defence Staff, Marshal of the RAF Sir David Craig since 1988; Field Marshal Sir Richard Vincent, Vice-CDS since 1987, was about to succeed as CDS.

[2] Sir Robin Butler had been Secretary of the Cabinet since 1988.

[3] George Bush, US president since 1989.

thought to the post-war pattern, the western military presence, commitments – OBJECTIVES. I could write a scintillating paper on this, but I'm exhausted and my morale is at zero. Last night Mrs Thatcher (as she must now be called)[1] chided me for being asleep on the bench when Tom was making his statement.

There is now talk of a General Election in June. Just time to claim, massively, some allowances out of 91–92! Interviewed by Melanie Phillips[2] last evening and she asked me about the adrenalin of power, how it keeps one going through this hellish existence; I said, 'But look what happens when people retire or get flung out – they shrivel up and get cancer immediately.'

Ministry of Defence   *Monday, 4 March*

Darling Jane is looking a wee bit strained. She knows something is up, and is quiet a lot of the time. But she doesn't question me at all – just makes the occasional scathing reference. I do want to make her happy – she's such a *good* person.[3]

I *very* much wish an early Election. I popped over and spoke to Richard Ryder this morning. He was in agony from a recently (18 hours) ricked back – playing tennis. But benign and delightful as always, said wait until 20 April – but of course it doesn't matter giving late notice to the constituency.[4] Registered my bid for a

---

[1] Margaret Thatcher, usually referred to by AC as The Lady, although no longer prime minister, was still MP for Finchley; she was not created a life peer until 1992.

[2] Melanie Phillips, journalist with an influential column on the *Guardian* before moving to the *Observer*.

[3] AC had become infatuated with his secretary, Alison Young. The full account appears in *Alan Clark: The Biography*. The infatuation was to cause considerable tension with Jane, and at one point he even contemplated leaving her and 'starting again'.

[4] AC was subject to conflicting advice. Over lunch, three days before, Tony Fanshawe (formerly Anthony Royle, MP for Richmond, 1959–83, and now a life peer) told AC not to 'antagonise people' by leaving his 'standing down' announcement until too late.

'working peerage' with a smile, but indicated approval. Also nodded sagely when I said what a fool and how objectionable, was TK.

Winter office, am   *Tuesday, 19 March*

In a state of abject depression – cross-streaked with apprehension so that my hands and forearms shake and feel watery. Poor old Archie H came into my office yesterday afternoon and stayed for $\frac{3}{4}$ hour whingeing on about end-of-an-era, all over, etc, etc. The pretext was on being 'boxed-in' on Options,[1] Treasury squeeze all that and I made some tangential slagging off of TK, his indecisiveness, inability to make any judgement save that of short-term political 'impact', 'how will it go in the house', etc. We are back to the old Conservative Government days, Eden at best. I said at least we broke the unions in the last decade, you won't hear much from *them* in the future. He agreed, but was still doleful. There's the general feeling that the baddies are getting away with it again – most apparent as Jane said at the weekend with all that fuss about the 'Birmingham Six',[2] yet one more excuse to slag off the police, wretched fellows. Jury wouldn't even convict an IRA gunrunner with their Kalshnikovs in the car and hands smelling of Semtex!

Saltwood   *Saturday, 23 March*

Bruce Anderson rang,[3] and we gossiped around a bit. He is of the *agnostic* school concerning JM's private life.[4] But admitted that

---

[1] The Ministry of Defence was, like other government departments, looking at the future, in this case the role of the British armed forces into the twenty-first century. AC concentrated on equipment.

[2] The 'Birmingham Six': six men who spent sixteen years in prison after being wrongfully convicted of the 1974 Birmingham pub bombings.

[3] Currently with the *Sunday Express*.

[4] The press had been full of concern at John Major's state of health. He had been PM for little more than 100 days, and was suffering from intermittent ear and throat infections. His wife Norma was quoted as saying, 'He's awfully tired and not getting enough sleep.'

Norma had told him 'John's not nearly as much fun now; doesn't
seem to have the energy . . . always into the boxes, etc'. Bruce said
that Richard [Ryder] now 'pro' me, and there was some talk they
might both come down for dinner and the night at Easter. But he
said my enemies were rampant. Charles P[owell] had told him,
'Under no other Prime Minister would Alan have been either
given office or promoted; and under any other Prime Minister he
would long since have been sacked.'

Sunday's papers show the Party in considerable disarray – now
likely to be aggravated by the six-point deficit shown in MORI.
Although actually, it would be slightly more tolerable to be out
under Labour than under a *new wave* Tory administration.

Saltwood   *31 March, Easter Sunday*

The special moisture in the spring air – if not the foggy inland –
with the sun lightly obscured, but a luminous promise. We went to
Communion this morning. I enjoy it now because of the opening
prayer, whose significance (as with so much until now) I never
before appreciated. '. . . to whom all hearts are open, all desires
known, and from whom no secrets are hid . . .'

Albany   *Tuesday, 30 April*

An awful night, little more than three hours' fragmented sleep.
This morning Valerie rang, claimed to be coming over in May – so
what?

Only good thing. Jane is better. Quite cured you could say. I try
and tell myself that this is what is really important. But (more than)
half of me says no it isn't – what counts is the incredible joie de
vivre, the physical and mental delight of being in love and in the
company of your adored. God alive! This confusion has been
going on for nearly five months. At least I do the stairs in MoD,
now weigh 11.6 and Gossie last Sunday evening in an incredible
2'28". All for what?

HE's residence, Qatar[1]   *Sunday, 12 May*

Out to Shaafa today and then to see Tip who was magnificent, handsome, clear-headed and hugely popular with his brother officers. In great heat (43°) was shown round the 'sheds'. Impressive installations, promising recruits, grotty equipment (CVRT[2] and Chieftains and M60s). Our helicopter, a shabby Bell Huey, wouldn't start and we switched to another, even shabbier one. Our pilot – slightly James-like, young, blond. On the return journey he said we'd make a detour on the Jebel Akhdar. At the time I thought this sounded a bit dodgy, said nothing. Drank some camel's milk (quite delicious) in the mess, felt pretty good. But in fact he lined up a gorge with 3000 ft sides – less than 40–80 ft wide in places, climbed up to over 9000 ft looking at little villages, mud hut settlements etc. One of the most obviously dangerous things I have done for ages, and not enough lateral margin for side draughts or gusts ('whoops!' he said at one point). After it was all over, and were all in the HS125, I, and the others, felt a real *high*. The beginning, it seemed, of 'feeling better'.

Eriboll: the great walk   *Saturday, 25 May*

Today I completed the great walk that has been on my mind almost since seeing it on the map some six or seven years ago. A wonderful taste of the remote glens, and now whets the appetite for some of the crueller and steeper corries.[3]

Saltwood   *Sunday, 9 June*

I am still miserable. I have been all year (with the exception of the long three weeks which I was recovering ground in end March

---

[1] For his official visit to the Gulf, AC flew on an HS125 via RAF Akrotiri (Cyprus), and moved on to Oman before reaching Qatar.
[2] Combat Vehicle Reconnaissance Track.
[3] Elsewhere, AC summed up the great walk: 'as good as a "medical".'

early April). I just can't go on like this. I am being beastly to Jane; one had another awful night yesterday after I collapsed on hearing that Andrew had been sent a letter saying 'I am crying as I write this.' But really this incident, it's my way, I suppose, of venting my own despair. For once in my life I'm going to stick to the plan. *Nothing*, I'll try not even to see her until Thursday evening, and just see if she turns up from the train.

Finally getting to the arboretum I made a balls of pruning the rowan tree,[1] didn't really get much done although Jane was incredible, staking and planting.

Saltwood   *Saturday, 15 June*

A bad day. We had really been looking forward to a 'free' weekend, particularly the open Saturday. But James is here having run away from Sally. *Désoeuvré* as always, standing around or going out to get cigarettes. So what the hell's going to happen here? I think they're irreconcilable – or is it irreconsilable? The idea is that he's going to Eriboll for a trial separation. But he can't live there alone indefinitely, and anyway half admits that he's drinking too much. And what does he do to occupy himself? So there we go – *worrying about James*, just as my parents, or mother particularly, worried about Col on and off all his life.

Then another setback. I don't think those bloody hormones are making the slightest difference. No night or morning erection – an initially, mildly heightened sexuality, I suppose. But this morning at breakfast Jane suddenly said – I think when I was trying to fluff her, on my knees – 'Having your skin-cancer tests?' (Having slyly seen, but not commented on, the bill for the path lab in the bathroom at Albany.) I had to explain what it is for – unhappily cancer, but I needed, also, a path lab for my nose spot. Started whingeing, then went off to do the henhouses.

Jane and I finally had a short walk, snapping at each other. I said, 'this is going to be a very bad year, I know somehow that it is . . .'

---

[1] AC believed in the magical properties of the rowan.

'I wish you wouldn't keep on saying that, I really dislike it.'

So health, sex, money, politics (Labour now settled at 10 points ahead and *Mail on Sunday* openly plugging Heseltine again) all bad – and with a long run ahead.

Saltwood   *Sunday, 7 July*

A lovely fine day, really hot – so much so that I bathed (three times) in *last year's* black water (at 72°!) and felt wonderful. As we brought Saltwood to life, and looked at all the lovely vistas and possibilities (in Garden House too) I thought there is so much to do here. I must get a book, a couple of Saltwood ledgers and write them up, so that the boys have something to refer to – contents, vistas, possibilities. They or my grandchildren would be interested.

King's Cross train   *Sunday, 14 July*

Last night we went to *The Magic Flute* at Glyndebourne. Frightful naff, pretentious audience, longueurs etc – but in fact it was rather fun. David (Young)[1] had invited us, and he's always fun to meet and talk to – though still with that slight hesitance, deference almost, that was his undoing in the upper reaches of the Party. He asked me (depressing) about my plans, implying I would not be in the next Government. But as Jane and I agreed this morning at EMT *at present* the Home Secretary[2] (also there) went out of his way to chat; the Employment Secretary[3] made a point of asking for a drink and a private meeting; 'Sir' Geoffrey Leigh[4] was gravely courteous and I 'stung' him for an iced coffee and a Dundee cake. All this will evaporate when we become penniless hermits.

---

[1] David Young, now executive chairman, Cable & Wireless.

[2] Kenneth Baker had been home secretary since 1990.

[3] Michael Howard, employment secretary since 1990.

[4] Sir Geoffrey Leigh, property magnate with strong arts interests; founded the Margaret Thatcher Centre, Somerville College, Oxford.

Is everyone now enjoying it? One good moment at supper
when Lita [Young] squawked when Jane told her how old I was.

Bratton   *Saturday, 20 July*

A nice free day here, until the 'frolic' (ugh) this evening. The place
slowly coming round to shape up; the empathy and 'studio' giving
it a new dimension and Campling's unfinished work making the
link.

Then there is the restoring of the place. *Massive* expenditure
(Jane has now very sensibly acceded to a total overhaul of Albany).
The cars are unsaleable – except, possibly, the SS, my 'folly'
(although I like it very much) and the R-type Continental. But
if I'd kept the 8-litre money on deposit I could have bought
the Napier for nothing (ie inclusive of profit of 225) we'd all be
millionaires.

More uncertain is the career prospect. There could well be a
'standing start' reshuffle now, or in September. Albany just done
up in time to entertain, but, as Jane said, 'no one will want to
know us!'

Ministry of Defence   *Tuesday, 23 July*

I parked the Porsche in the members' garage and walked along
the cloisters and through the tunnel. A badge messenger acknowledged me deferentially. Not for the first time I reflected that all
this will be over next year. This is my very last *chef des champs*
summer. And I have *no* idea where or what I will be in July 1992.

Saltwood   *Saturday, 10 August*

I don't really know what happened to last week. Not really very
happy. This morning I said I was more unhappy than at any time
since I could remember – Jane, too, she's terribly standoffish and

cries at intervals. She is confronting me with things that I've done in the past which have been 'out' many times before and were 'kissed and made up' since, but still I'm basted. We had dreadful row coming back from Bratton. A journey which I drove continuously in the Discovery using m-way the whole way and with my foot absolutely flat down 95–100 in pretty thick traffic, under four hours, but small thanks I got etc etc. I've promised (a) not to whinge (b) not to swear (c) not to 'drive fast'. It's all part of the castrating syndrome.

There is a certain type of woman of which Jane is one and Valerie (to take an obvious and most emphatic example) is not who would rather have their man a eunuch than have him 'chasing around'.

Zermatt   *Saturday, 24 August*

Yet again the Zermatt magic has worked. Blissful in the chalet,[1] fine, dry, clear weather. Pleasant routine of late breakfast, picnic, expeditions. We're still too exhausted to read, or write or think. Sexual powers completely returned, back almost to the sixties and later seventies. Jane 3 times in last four days, each one more pleasing than the last.

Saturday, 14 September

Arrived at Cromlix,[2] very sleepy, but relaxed and philosophic.

It took exactly 8 hours (including an hour stop south of Stoke at the Welcome Break) to do the 522 miles from Saltwood to Gleneagles, a total average of 65mph and cruising of 75mph. We left at 6 am.

---

[1] Seven years later AC contemplated retiring to Châlet Caroline – 'a beach hut as Jane quite properly calls it'.
[2] Cromlix House, a favourite hotel of the Clarks, near Stirling, Perthshire.

Blackpool train   *Wednesday, 9 October*

And so to the very last conference. One's written this before of
course, but this time it's got to be the last one. I've got, at most, six
months left in the House of Commons. I whinged a bit to Jane in
the train on the way up, and she quite rightly said 'you could do
another four years going down to Plymouth, stuck in the House of
Commons, what, who, etc, are your . . .' True. But my chance of
actually going to the Lords is 3–1 *at best*. Every diarist (except
possibly Jim Lees-Milne[1]) toys reflectively with this idea. None of
them made it. I've been sort of promised it by Chief Whip,
Tristan, Tony R. etc. But doesn't really amount to anything.

We had quite a nice room at the back of the hotel, changed, ran
Alison through the ladies' cocktail party – providing her with some
good 'contacts'.[2]

We listened to Heseltine's 'come-back'. Quite accomplished,
though as always symbolic and vulgar. We steadfastly sat throughout the 'ovation'. Yet today (Friday) the camera showed him
during John Major's speech looking spaced out, almost gaga.
What was he thinking? This is the speech, the occasion, which I
so narrowly missed, perhaps for ever? Or had he just had a little
too much wine with journalists at lunch, before coming on the
platform? John M is so lucid, and decent, and genuine. What a
lucky escape we had.

Plymouth train   *Thursday, 17 October*

I 'opened' on the second day of the Defence debate. I had been
headache-light preparing the speech all morning. But by sylphless
cutting (of Civil Service balls, on-the-record stuff) and adlibbing
on Julian Amery, regiments and Labour problems, a put down of

---

[1] Whereas three of AC's favourite diarists, Sir Henry ('Chips') Channon, Leo
Amery and Sir Harold Nicolson, were MPs, much of the career of James Lees-
Milne centred around the National Trust (*Ancestral Voices* and *Prophesying Peace*).

[2] Alison was seriously considering going into politics, did in fact speak in a debate.

'Captain Browne'[1] much acclaim – whips, Godfrey Barker the next day.[2] This may well be the last speech I ever make in the House of Commons.

Yesterday I dined with Bruce Anderson at Greens. There is no longer any balls of my getting into the Cabinet – even the H of L project has diminished; a certain amount of 'you'll miss the House of Commons . . .' Well I don't think I *will* much. As I trod the Pugin patterned carpets yesterday, popping up to the Members Tearoom to get some fruit cake to bring down to the cafeteria, I thought 'really I've had quite enough of this . . .' Stale and fetid, etc. I know I can't go back, and I may regret it. The real problem is: I'm still active; bags of energy, keen mind, good health and appetite (now with an 's'), sleeping, stamina. It will be depressing feeling this atrophy – reading Ann Fleming letters, she (and practically everyone else) seems continually to be ill – terminally ill in the sense that they were degenerative conditions that left you older and weaker and nearer the grave even when 'cured'. Only Nico Henderson[3] has emerged unscathed from the *Galere*, still preening and striding.

VC10 to Akrotiri   *Wednesday, 6 November*

For the first time am on an abroad journey in a state of pleasurable exploration. The VIP VC10, lots of space, food, service, crew of five in the cockpit, as far as I can make out. First stop Akrotiri, then on to Dubai for the air show, then to Diego Garcia (nature notes), then Malaysia. The kind of trip that would have had me out in

---

[1] John Browne, MP for Winchester since 1979, had previously risen to the rank of captain in the Grenadier Guards.

[2] In the *Daily Telegraph*, Godfrey Barker wrote that AC 'gave a lesson in how to cope with trouble from all sides. After a speech which was vivid, thoughtful, historical, witty and ad rem, Mr Clark complained that he was "amazed at the docility with which the Labour party has received my remarks . . . a caricature of what happens to a party when it has absolutely no policy, just a great gulp of crocodile tears" over any changes that had to be made. And to attempted trouble behind him from Mr John Browne. "I can't give way to everyone" '.

[3] Sir Nicholas Henderson, former ambassador, had been seriously ill.

boils ten years ago, but now is an adventure, a comfortable
adventure.

All this year I have been neglectful of my papers, have been
unable – it seems – even to find time to concentrate my thoughts,
think strategically (as the PM would need to do, now, I suspect,
over his successor). I will be sad and depressed to be out of office. I
ought to be S of S, but only a miracle can bring that about, and
'that's enough miracles' – Ed.

Diego Garcia[1]   *Sunday, 10 November*

This morning I was determined to bathe *privately*. Much of the
charm of this place is spoiled by the constant surveillance of
officials (the Commission is about as bad as Peter Watkins[2] who is
adhesive in his silent quality), yesterday at the old plantation
manager's home, a Somerset Maugham setup on East Island, I
realised what Royalty must feel like. But this morning I rose slyly
and stealthily, let myself out – yes, there was the Commissioner
moving across the grass quadrangle. He said something to the very
pretty (dark, lovely bones, ultra discreet/shy) WRAC whom I
noted, and scored by calling, 'Doreen'.

I was aware of the fact that the Commissioner wanted to follow
me, or call out, but couldn't quite. I walked in light, delicious
humid rain to the edge of the beach. Low tide, lovely pale green
ripples slapping the sand. The water was delicious, like silk. To
Ascension and the Al Bustan I have now added Diego Garcia. My
morale uncertain now, though not as bad as when I bathed at the
Al Bustan in May. On my return I saw a little polished crab claw
on the sand and pouched it. I don't know what power it will have,
but it will be a reminder of a curious voyage when pain is still
around, uncertainty is everywhere and the terrible incurable
infatuation has one in its grasp afresh.

---

[1] British Indian Ocean Territory and a military base with access only to military or
civilian contractors, and the occasional visiting British minister.
[2] Peter Watkins, head of AC's private office at the Ministry of Defence.

Saltwood   *Sunday evening, 15 December*

I was cheered by a letter from Charlie Allsopp saying the Gainsborough was 3–400,[1] which eases my mind about the pending
arrival of the C-type.[2]

Poor Jane has had a 'blip' from Tom Bates[3] this time, sending
something along to be analysed: 'my secretary will be in touch in a
week's time . . .' – what bad luck!

I feel myself continuing to lose standing and attention in
politics. Work in the Department has wound right down I seem
to spend much of my time shopping for, or tidying B5 in its new
'naff' form. This is going to be 'very successful'. It had to be done,
and the boys will be pleased, although I don't want them using my
bed. But ironic that it should be complete, and a place for people
to come back for drinks – or even eat – at the very moment when I
am about to retire and don't need it.

This morning at EMT Jane and I discussed her anxieties and
finality of 'standing down'. I *dread*, of course, telling Alison. A
certain cowardliness, too, in telling the [constituency] Association.
But we both agreed that you have to go out while they are still
calling for more and anyway (my own dread) I might *lose* worst
of both worlds.

Will I then get very 'slow' and change my appearance? We'll
see. Christmas first, and Andrew's young lady, and most important
of all, the result of Jane's test.

Never seem to have done any shopping this year.

Saltwood   *Boxing Day, 26 December*

I'm very depressed – not from hangover, as had drunk little,
though Christmas lunch was always lovely and I consumed (sic)
three glasses of Stolichnaya with the caviar, then more Roodeburg

---

[1] Gainsborough's *Going to Market*.

[2] AC paid £360,000; it arrived in time for Christmas.

[3] Tom Bates, a private consultant in Kent. AC had also seen him.

than Andrew with the turkey and pudding. (His young lady, Sarah, was a success.)

I must pull myself together . . . I will 'hold the line' at the Department – might even get in a couple more jolly trips. Then it's cutting peat in the Highlands and the fallow period of editing the diaries[1] and inventorising the contents and dispositions.

I wonder how long I've got? I have this nasty feeling that things are going to go so badly this year that I will be 'on the way out' next Christmas. My hair is white in certain back lighting. When I'm 65, sadly, I will actually look 65. Shopping for Jane on Christmas Eve I 'happened on' a ski shop in Folkestone's main street, thought to buy her an anorak and also found myself buying a ski suit for myself. It made me feel ten years younger. Oh if only I could really regenerate!

---

[1] Rather than memoirs, AC had now decided to see whether he might emulate Chips Channon, Harold Nicolson et al. and publish extracts from the diaries he kept while an MP and minister.

1992

Saltwood   *Monday, 6 January*

I've been 'lying up' here since Dai Davies[1] on Thursday. An
expensive affair since I had it 'in theatre' in order that the path lab
could pronounce it 'clear' (sic) on the (nose) spot – which they duly
did. I don't know how long any disfigurement will last. Sometimes,
these last days, I've got frissons of impending ill health and demise.

Thursday, 20 February

Yesterday I had a great 'triumph' on my last occasion at the despatch
box, pleasing the House and teasing the Labour Party. I had forced
Jane to come up, and sit in the Gallery. 'A "last" is always important,' I told her, 'and you can compare it with the Lords.'

Ministry of Defence   *Wednesday, 26 February*

Left out the traumas of the 'Final decision'. The 'statement'. The
deceptions and hesitations. Got a *very* good press. A nice piece in
the *Mail* followed up by a 'commission' to write four articles
during the election.[2] Fun! I sent a reproachful *handshüd* to Simon
Jenkins[3] and he responded with a glowing leader in today's *Times*
trailing oh so subtly the idea that I might 'continue my ministerial
career in the Lords . . .'

---

[1] Dai Davies, London-based consultant, who removed AC's 'nose place'.

[2] Gordon Greig, the *Mail*'s political editor, wrote that AC, 'who has amused and
shocked his party over the years, leaves it just three weeks to find a replacement
candidate'. 'Personal reasons' for his departure were mentioned by the Sutton
agent, to which AC riposted: 'I never said that. "Personal reasons" usually means
there has been a scandal, and I can assure you there is nothing of that. It's just
time to go.'

[3] Simon Jenkins, editor of *The Times* since 1990.

Lord Clark's study, Saltwood   *Wednesday, 18 March*

Immensely serene. I must record that I am settling down very
calmly to a pleasant detached existence with so much to hand in
the way of diversions and accoutrements.

Just talked to Alison who is going down to Henry Bellingham[1]
for the 'campaign'. Gosh, I'm glad to be out of it![2] It's delicious
speculating, with just the right amount of access through the *Daily
Mail*. But the polls this morning are bad, *very* bad, each showing
5% Labour lead. I don't particularly mind, even a touch of
schadenfreude if it weren't for my lost peerage, even my lost 'K'.
Although, intriguingly (sic) the lunch yesterday with Alastair
Campbell[3] opened, just by a chink, the possibility of a semi-
alignment with Kinnock – 'the other side'. Whew!

Friday, 27 March

Last night we dined at the French embassy. My last Ministerial.
Beatty's old house in Regent's Park, a pleasing dwelling with,
unusually, Nash getting the proportions just right. Jane looked
pretty in her turquoises, and slimline black dress, well holding
her own over the French ladies. On the way back Pat drove
sepulchrally. Earlier he had agitatedly told me the MoD was
investigating his 'prudent' overtime claims.

Paddington train   *Wednesday, 8 April*

Well, now the era has ended. I am in the Paddington train; warm,
comfortable, porridge breakfast; so evocative of jolly journeys with
sexual tension high, and delight at being in the loved one's company. I will never be able to afford this again. £38 one-way from
Exeter, and that with an OAP reduction card. Briefly back to

---

[1] Henry Bellingham, MP for North West Norfolk since 1983.
[2] The general election had been called for 9 April.
[3] Alastair Campbell, political editor of the *Daily Mirror* since 1989.

MoD for farewell calls. Then load up carpet and clock and sundries and leave Whitehall – for ever, as it now looks.

Garden House   *general election, polling day, Thursday, 9 April*

Lovely and fine. Yesterday very weary and creaky (both Jane and I have got the 'Office Virus' – an exceptionally tenacious head cold). I got out of the car, last journey with Pat, having sadly and foot-draggingly left the MoD after 'farewell calls' from Moray Stewart[1] and Quinlan, and Saltwood was benign. The first day of spring.

Last night an early one. But before going up I saw the 9 pm news – the gap has closed to 1%. Tristan rang this morning – always a good sign – and said we could just shave it. So today is one of total limbo like – though not as disagreeable – awaiting the result of *tests*.

General election result
Conservatives: 336; Labour: 271; Liberal Democrats: 20; Others: 24.
In Plymouth Sutton, AC's successor as the Conservative candidate had a majority of 11,950.

Friday, 10 April

Up all last night, bed at 3.40, and then up at 6.10 to 'catch up'. A 'private' car to TV Centre with George Younger[2] and Nicky Ridley, gossip with (inter alia) John Cole and Barbara Maxwell[3] and several times nearly dropped off in the Porsche on the return journey. Much pain on the screens – Kinnock and Glenys; Patten and Lavender.[4]

---

[1] Moray Stewart, Second Permanent Under-Secretary of State, MoD, since 1990.
[2] George Younger had retired from the Commons at the general election after representing Ayr since 1964. He had been defence secretary (1986–89); a hereditary peer (4th Viscount Younger), he was made a life peer in 1992.
[3] Barbara Maxwell, producer of *Question Time* from 1979–1990.
[4] Neil Kinnock, Labour leader since 1983, had now lost two elections. Chris Patten, chairman of the Conservative Party, had lost his Bath seat (which he had represented since 1979) to the Liberal Democrats: majority of 2,009.

Sunday, 12 April

The days are lengthening rapidly now. It's 8 pm and quite light. Jane is still planting trees down in the 'new woodland' along the iron fence. I am very flat and *désoeuvré*, brought on by contemplating the year – the whole year in which there is nothing, but *nothing*, to tie the structure to. I make various noises about when we go away to Scotland, to M. Goisot, to Zermatt etc etc. The whole thing curiously in vacuo. I always wanted time, even a day, three hours was priceless. Now it is limited only by my death or infirmity.

Another boring thing. Income will be much lower. No facilities. I will miss particularly the Library at the House. I thought I'd save the £30–50 a week in petty cash from 'going to London' but there are so many other new demands. Even, as Jane said, having to buy your own *New Statesman*. There was a good few hours today of weak fantasy. TK was sacked (along with Baker, Waddington; Waldegrave lucky to survive).[1] And this made me hope briefly that Hamilton would also be chopped, and for the sake of continuity, they'd keep me on – but from the Lords – my original scheme: I even went so far as to visualise the Black Turbo B from P. & A. Wood[2] for Pat; the Minister's room with red leathers and the computer; Alison back as my PA while she also doubles at another job at Westminster. A reunion dinner at Wilton's; in the Smoking Room – for the first time really since 1974. Wouldn't it be luvverly . . .[3] As it is I suppose I will have to subliminate into asceticism, restoring order and the journals.

---

[1] Kenneth Baker, home secretary; Lord Waddington, Leader of the House of Lords, life peer 1990; William Waldegrave, who had been health secretary, became Chancellor of the Duchy of Lancaster.
[2] P. & A. Wood, Rolls-Royce and Bentley specialists favoured by AC.
[3] AC's own footnote is in the form of musical notes (*My Fair Lady*).

Sandling train (!)   *Tuesday, 28 April*

Withdrawal symptoms only flare periodically, but a lot of suppression is going on. So in subconscious it festers. I dream of reviving Commons privileges, tearoom, reference library and so on which I wake and realise are closed to me for ever. In the daytime I have to close my mind to the full extent of my depression. I am 'put out' by my friends ignoring me. Especially wounded by Richard. I did think that he was a friend, and I a confidant of his. I am filled too with distaste and resentment at all the new Conservative MPs and some of the new Ministerial choices. But there's no point in dodging it, when you're out you're out. The people who are *in* simply don't have time to waste on someone who, however 'amusing', is not au fait with the daily round of gossip, of 'men and events'. I suppose, if I were to get my peerage promptly I could still 'catch up', swoop into the tearoom, mob around. But notification for the Dissolution Honours has passed, and so – almost – has that for the Birthday. I guess it will be like the PC and take at least two years longer than postulated (sic).

As for life at Saltwood – well it is pleasing, more so in some ways than I had anticipated. Delicious food (too much indeed, I'm putting on weight, am 11.7+ and at intervals get it at 12 even when dry).

Saltwood   *Saturday, 9 May*

I have been wrestling with the lawn in the Inner Bailey. We bought a new ATCO and it cuts crazily well so that even a half stripe needs its large plastic basket emptying. But the lawn remains obstinate – resistant to striping and with ridged 'bare marks'. The garden is relentless in its demands on time. Not only is the lawn like the Forth Bridge, it needs restarting as soon as you finish, but there is scything of nettles and use of the tractor in the arboretum and the wood, and a few 'artist's touches' in the Garden House.

I have a mountain of paper. The far end of the Green Room

seems to have about four running white boxes in it, while the Summer Office has simply been evacuated, like the old battlefields of the Somme, and about 300 separate filing items lie around.

The cars – far too many of them – have overflowed the accommodation, they need drastic culling, but I seem not even to have time to write up a favoured culling scheme. Jane has a good amount of spare cash, and I want to work out an investment scheme for her – but that, too, needs time and care. Perhaps even more importantly, I cannot get *in* to the diaries, although many (namely Michael Sissons and George Weidenfeld) are pressing me for them.[1] Never mind, today is foul; wet and gusty, and I may get some preliminary order. I am taking a year's sabbatical – slightly under – and hope that this will leave me next summer 'off' before the die is finally cast at the July or September reshaping of the Government. It is a huge waste of my talents that I am not in. Partly self-inflicted, I admit. At least I jumped, *really* jumped I mean, off the deck, before people even got round to thinking about it.

Tristan rang yesterday. He was reassuring, but non-committal. Said he would try and have a word with Richard soon; with the PM in the summer when he stayed with the G-Js in Spain. Agreed that there was plenty for me to *do*, but I needed a 'perch'.

Garden House   *Wednesday, 20 May*

The whole place burgeoning beautifully, and the last thing I want to do is go to London and on to Oxford to make a speech at the Union. Started filling the pool yesterday and I had a pm splosh in two feet of water. The wall-chart is totally blocked out, it seems, for June; worse than the DTI already. So we're back to 'observe' Parliamentary recesses. Altnaharra for sale for £7m. Can Marcus [Kimball] really have got in that deep? It was an idyll for me, even

---

[1] George Weidenfeld had published one previous book of AC's (*Aces High*), but also AC's favourite diarist, Chips Channon.

at Eton when he talked about this, and his blue Chevrolet. I wrote
him a (guarded) letter of commiseration.

Saltwood   *Sunday, 14 June*

It's ridiculous, really. I sit here, on a hot Sunday, cloudless but
hazy, and round me the Bailey is, *passim* Bruce Anderson (now
never heard from), 'one of the loveliest places in the world'. The
cistus are out along the border, and many of the roses. The
honeysuckle by the pool, and a particularly fine 'French' geranium
fills the 'plinth'.

My 'sabbatical' has really got nothing to show for it, except,
perhaps, the beginnings of a familiarity with the word processor.
What has really depressed me is the list of 'working' peers. I mean
Hayhoe! How ghastly and mediocre – the archetypal safe Tory
politician – can you get? Stewart,[1] little Stewart and dear old Bill
Clark (which will cause problems if I ever get there) and they were
all knights, so my exclusion from the 'K' list doesn't mean
anything.

Saltwood   *Tuesday, 23 June*

We went up to London for Enoch's 80th birthday. A ragbag of a
dinner, ill assorted – wives and husbands sitting (as I had predicted
to Jane) together, and so on. There were some eminent people –
George Thomas, Robin Day, Mrs T etc and a lot of strays. This
mix never works very well, although I was glad to have a word
with Portillo.[2] Jane was in a good cache of politicians, said little
Budgen was very chippy, 'I've only got two friends . . .' he said
maudlinly at one point. 'I'm not surprised,' she said.

---

[1] Bernard Stewart (who took the title Lord Stewartby), MP for N. Herts, 1983–92
    (Hitchin, 1974–83).
[2] Michael Portillo, Chief Secretary to the Treasury since 1992.

Speeches were *de profundis* in seniority terms – old Salisbury,[1] George Thomas, Enoch, combined ages 243.

Monday, 29 June

Private Office came down yesterday evening and gave me a tree. Very sweet of them. Perhaps gifts should have been 'exchanged'? Carol told Jane that it was an endless 3-line whip and Jonathan[2] was never allowed away. 'AC couldn't stand it.' But as I sit here, in oppressive heat, too-hot–Henry condition, almost the only thing I can do is 'amend' the dictionary on the word processor. But I wish, in spite of it all, I was in the Commons, stirring all this 'M' stuff,[3] using the underground car park. Oh dear. I'm very low at present.

Tuesday, 30 June

Yesterday, after writing that entry, I trained up in the great heat to London (2 hours – dozing off and waking with a start – only Marden and Headcorn). I had Indian tea, having gone through the usual cycle (vide) of total dejection, rising towards paradise, then being disappointed. I set off for Chris Patten's Durbar Court farewell party[4] parking my car – actually Andrew's Audi – in that side street beside DE. I walked to FCO, Clive Steps, passing St

---

[1] The 6th Marquess of Salisbury had been president of the Monday Club, which, as Simon Heffer, Powell's biographer, has pointed out, was in the 1960s 'self-appointed Praetorian Guard of Powell and the Powellite interest'.

[2] Jonathan Aitken had succeeded AC at Defence as Minister for Defence Procurement.

[3] What became known as Maastricht began as an idea of Jacques Delors, president of the European Commission since 1989, for an International Governmental Conference on European political and monetary union. It was swiftly to act as a lightning rod, polarising the pro-Europeans and the Eurosceptics. The key issues became the ERM – exchange rate mechanism – and EMU – European Monetary Union. The conference led to a Treaty, which had to be ratified by each EU member.

[4] Patten was leaving UK politics to become the last governor of Hong Kong.

Stephens Tavern where officials hang out. *Very* hot, dreamlike almost. I was in a suit, still a perfect Minister, but ethereal. Orphée. I could do nothing, give no instructions, penetrate no sancta. The Party was the following day, a lone custodian informed me. And I walked back – like a masque – and set course for Saltwood.

Garden House   *Monday, 13 July*

A grey day. A time for planning. We really should operate to a timetable. Things that must have black lines set aside for them (not necessarily every day) are:

(a) house work in Garden House – cleaning kitchen, hanging pictures, plugs on lights etc.
(b) word processor – already 7.30–8.30, provided this is working after KK. 7.45–8.45?
(c) Filing in summer office – *at least* one hour per day
(d) Cleaning cars   ⎫
                              ⎬ possibly alternate
(e) Scything and forking   ⎭
(f) SUNDAY FREE

                                                        Thursday, 16 July

I gave the 'RAF' lecture at the RUSI yesterday. Quality good audience – but I suffered from not having a typed-up text. Afterwards I ducked out of a dinner at the House. I just did not want to go into the Strangers Dining Room until I'm a Peer. People ask me if I miss it. 'Yes, dreadfully,' I say.

Garden House   *Wednesday, 22 July*

So little to actually *show* for the last 12 days. I am low, and *serene* – almost Lenin Stadium with a feeling of total emptiness at the groin,

as if I was a man of eighty. Page[1] yesterday, and casually he said
he'd send my blood for the Prostate Cancer Test as well as a
testosterone count. I said surely if I had it I'd know? He said oh no,
80 per cent of postmortems show 80% of people over 80 (that's
enough 80s! – Ed) or more do have it. 'It can be dealt with quite
effectively.' But I know how I'd deal with – by chemical castra-
tion. There are worse things, I suppose, like going blind. But it's
bad luck on little Jane, after this lovely year – for which eternal
thanks. Would it have to be 'allied' with chemotherapy so that all
my hair falls out? The effect has been to devastate me utterly –
combined of course with the fact that it's now nearly six weeks
since the last injection. And so much to do. The diaries, the
inventory, the files, the 'dispositions'. I've been aware that my
looks and general stamina (I seldom want to do weights and press-
ups) are much less than last summer. What a long 'Indian' summer
that was!

Garden House   *Sunday, 26 July*

I feel the biggest mistake I ever made was to 'walk away' from the
Commons.

Garden House   *Tuesday, 28 July*

When I got to Albany, there was Page's letter marked on the front:
Personal, Medical and Confidential – an invitation to snoop if ever
there was one! 'No trace whatever' of PreCan, testosterone right
down, everything else ok – he sent me print out – except for
cholesterol, about which I could not care. Can now revert to
thinking demi-clearly about the summer and autumn. I must
organise a proper car cull.

---

[1] Dr Nick Page, who had taken over from the Clarks' long-time doctor, Dr
Rowntree.

Monday, 31 August

David Owen has got the Euro-rep at Yugoslav Peace Conference job. So he's back in the stream.[1] Julian Critchley writes in the *Observer*[2] that I was the kind of MP (person in – sic – politics) who had style. I am pleased by this. But I don't see my role. I am OUT not IN and I notice the difference more and more.

B5 Albany   *Thursday, 17 September*

A very bad night. I woke at 1.20 – rather less than an hour after putting the light out, with complete insomnia. Could have made tea (*did*, in fact, after padding down to a night porter and collecting some milk) and driven the Little Silver anywhere.

I dined with Jonathan, Ryder was there, Tristan came in later (I'm glad to say, because he wasn't as much fun as the other two, showed his limitations). Jonathan told me that Conrad Black had told Moore to pay *anything* to ensure that he collared the diaries, and Richard said that Jonathan Holborrow[3] was a great fan of mine (seemed surprise, *why?*). But I felt *out* particularly when they started talking about the new MPs, and their disorderly behaviour, 'the hunger for the soundbite', as I put it.

Shore Cottage   *Sunday, 20 September*

Yesterday evening I spoke to Max Hastings.[4] We talked about the Government turmoil and how *bad* they all were (including the

---

[1] David Owen had been appointed European Union co-chairman, International Conference on Former Yugoslavia.

[2] Commenting on a *Sunday Telegraph* interview with AC in which he touched on many wide-ranging matters.

[3] Two newly appointed editors: Charles Moore of the *Sunday Telegraph*; Jonathan Holborrow of the *Mail on Sunday*.

[4] Max Hastings, journalist and military historian, editor of the *Daily Telegraph* since 1986.

PM).[1] Max said he had threatened Norman Lamont[2] with implacable liability if he didn't resign. Max had lunch with Ken Clarke[3] (it's really too awful that the choice of alternatives should be Michael Heseltine – still – and Ken Clarke) who had ruefully said that, in Thursday's emergency debate, the Government couldn't admit that it had neither an Economic nor a Foreign policy.

I drove very slowly back down Eriboll Street in the (nasty) Range Rover in the dark and realised, almost with panic, just what I had thrown away by 'standing down'. I suppose I should have continued to trust in God, that He would give one the opportunity for the sword in the lake. Essentially it was selfish, opting for a quiet and comfortable life, sidestepping humiliation. God has given us self-determination, too, and of course if we are determined we can reject his gift.

Garden House   *Wednesday, 30 September*

Adrian Lithgow down this morning to 'help' one with a second draft of a 'conference' article for the *Mail on Sunday*. Neat, saturnine, 'slight' and cigaretting. An easy way of earning £2k, you could say. I don't know how it will look, but I remain restless and discomforted at being *out* of the House. Pat Kavanagh has failed to improve on the *Mail on Sunday*'s offer of £200k for the serial rights.[4]

---

[1] The twin causes of the turmoil were the Maastricht Treaty, which had caused twenty-two Conservative MPs to vote against the government, and Britain's membership of the European exchange rate mechanism (ERM). Sterling had crashed, and on 16 September, swiftly dubbed 'Black Wednesday', interest rates were raised temporarily to 15 per cent and British membership of the ERM was suspended. In short, the government's economic policy was on the ropes.

[2] Norman Lamont, Chancellor of the Exchequer since 1990. At this point he did not resign.

[3] Kenneth Clarke, Home secretary since the general election and a rising star in Conservative circles, even though AC would immortalise him as a 'pudgy puffball' when *Diaries* came to be published.

[4] For the 'Diaries of a Junior Minister', as they were provisionally titled; Patricia Kavanagh, director, Peters, Fraser & Dunlop, AC's literary agents. Following the 'viva' of the hardback contenders to publish his diaries AC chose Weidenfeld & Nicolson.

But half paid now and half on publication so let that sort a few things out (but not, I fear the Turbo R Cont). Then next week, agreeably, all those hardback contenders of £150k are going to make 'presentations' to ingratiate themselves.

Garden House   *Monday, 12 October*

Poor Eva is now in terminal decline. I had to carry her off the bed and down the second flight front stairs today. I could never have done that in the great days of the 'room fighting'. For the first time she is herself really low, and hangs her head as in the last minutes in the bullring. Thank God for the long break in Scotland, where we have a lovely picture of her, beautiful in the heather.

The Old Bailey   *Wednesday, 4 November*

Testifying in the 'Matrix Churchill' trial.[1] Day wasted, though I get £70 for an ITN interview at lunchtime on 'John Major leadership' (Maastricht vote today, but the dignitaries have sold the pass – George Gardiner, Rhodes Boyson etc – presumably because they realise there's no one to take his place).[2]

Yesterday I met VH [Valerie Harkess] for a drink, not looking bad, really. Well-preserved. V good 'bust', and *very* restrainedly dressed. She said I would have been leader, 'got the leadership' if I'd still been in. It didn't need saying. I said 'it was the most catastrophically bad decision'. We walked up Piccadilly and parted outside the Park Lane Hotel, past two clubs where – in bedrooms, in the Ladies, etc we'd coupled. I said to her (which is true) 'I have

---

[1] During his period as minister of trade (1986–89) AC had a meeting with machine-tool exporters who as a result thought that the British government would turn a blind eye if they declared that exports to Iraq had general engineering rather than specifically military applications. The trial of the Matrix Churchill directors accused of selling weapons to Iraq, what became known as the 'arms-to-Iraq' affair, had begun on 12 October.

[2] Sir George Gardiner, a council member of the Conservative Way Forward group, was seen by the party hierarchy as a key rebel where Europe was concerned; Sir Rhodes Boyson, MP for Brent North since February 1974.

never felt the same degree of sheer physical desire as I did with you with any other human being.' She was pleased. She said I'd never given her any (sic) money. '£10,000', I said. 'Do you think I'm worth £10,000?' 'Well,' I paused, 'if you *can* quantify it, I'd say you were . . . "worth" £450,000.'

Garden House   *Tuesday, 8 December*

And what about testifying to Scott?[1] Last night Detective Inspector Lawrence phoned, asked for an appointment 'after Christmas' (brain washing to wreck in the holiday) for a meeting 'with my solicitor' and a 'statement'.

'I have nothing to say,' I said. Well could I put him in touch with my solicitor . . . etc.

'I don't see why I even need to pay a solicitor.' He was puzzled.

'Come and arrest me.'

'It's not an arrestable offence.'

My only choice is to 'clear my name' with Scott.

Garden House   *Friday, 11 December*

We buried dear 'E' today. She looked lovely, literally asleep with all the tension gone out of her body; and we put in 'Squeaky', an American bone, and some other mementoes and Jane's headscarf.

---

[1] The Matrix Churchill trial had folded on 10 November, following AC's answer to Geoffrey Robertson, defence counsel, who had remarked that a statement attributed to AC – 'that the Iraqis will be using the current order for general engineering purposes' – could not be correct 'to your knowledge'.

AC: Well, it's our old friend being economical, isn't it?

GR: With the truth?

AC: With the *actualité*. There was nothing misleading or dishonest to make a formal or introductory comment that the Iraqis would be using the current orders for general engineering purposes. All I didn't say was 'and for making munitions'.

Sir Richard Scott, a Lord Justice of Appeal since 1991, had been appointed to chair an inquiry.

Last night she was so collapsed and intermittently crying in pain, even when I picked her up she couldn't stand. That morning, Jane said, she had gone out into the yard, the Bailey, just looked around – for the last time – and turned back.

Garden House   *Saturday, 12 December*

I had a tiny stroll with Jane. She said what an annus horribilis it had been for everyone. Only want to escape. Saltwood is such a mess, so distressing, absolutely nothing 'to hand'. I would like to be minimalist. A south sea island, a Club Med hut, some decent books and a 2CV. Perhaps, after the 'publication' [of the diaries] I can escape, totally?

I am lucky, surely, still to have my health and energy. 'No warnings'. But how long have I still this dispensation?

Garden House   *Monday, 14 December*

I have just finished transposing the entry for 20 September 1984.[1] Should have been much less cliquey, widened my circle of friends, never let my boredom threshold show. I should have entertained, in cycle, members of the 92, little dinners. Pressed on. I didn't realise, until too late, the prestige I commanded. I thought that they would think I wanted something. I should really have had a dinner every fortnight.

Now, in this dead and dingy and aimless parliament everyone would be talking about me.

I SHOULD NEVER HAVE LEFT THE HOUSE OF COMMONS.

---

[1] In which AC describes a letter from Julian Amery ('you stick out like a red poppy in the hayfield of mediocrities surrounding you . . .') after surviving the reshuffle (*Diaries*).

Garden House   *Sunday, 3 January*

Never[1] have I contemplated the end of the holiday with such gloom, and headhung pressure. I am under *such* pressure with these *Diaries*, and my eyes are going red-rimmed. Piccolo row yesterday after my (very well-written) piece in *The Times* on 'Winston'.[2] No more writing now, until the end of the *Diaries* (whatever I write people will always look for the ooh! 'controversial' bit).

Garden House   *Saturday, 20 February*

I have come over here to write and to pray, for my 'game plan'. Could God give me just this one more chance? Since my last entry Judith Chaplin has died suddenly at Newbury (a very bad seat).[3] It would have to be ACHAB – as never before or since.

Is the sword still there, though now at the bottom of the lake?

Thursday, 25 February

I am in limbo. Ten days to complete delivery of *Diaries*.[4]

But everything is overshadowed, made slightly *unreal* by

---

[1] AC's own footnote: 'not for a long while anyway; since European Bill Committee'.

[2] Inspired by John Charmley's about-to-be-published biography, *Churchill: The End of Glory*, 'the most important "revisionist" text to be published since the war', said *The Times* on its front page. AC's thesis, which would even be called 'ludicrous' in the pell-mell that followed, was that Churchill, by refusing to make peace with Hitler in 1940/41, betrayed the Commonwealth, lost the Far Eastern empire and shattered the British social order.

[3] To call it a 'very bad seat' seems on the face of it surprising as Judith Chaplin, former political secretary to John Major, became MP for Newbury in 1992 with a majority of 11,057. But it marked a crucial electoral test for the government following sterling's ejection from the ERM the previous September.

[4] As they had finally been titled.

Jane/Bates, need for slides and tests. I can't believe it. But hope the ju-ju hasn't gone wrong somehow. I feel slightly depersonalised, almost demob happy by all this.

Would almost have forgotten about politics, were it not for a call from Jonathan Holborrow and a full political fix. Apparently Richard R[yder] is going to be eased out to be Minister of Agriculture, and David D is to be chief [whip].[1] Which will be good. But where do I fit in?

Garden House   *Sunday, 28 February*

A series of little extra pieces fall into place. On Friday evening Dobbie[2] rang me and asked if I would do a piece backing Paul Keating's attitude to the Royals.[3] 'Look, if I'm going to fight the Newbury by-election, the last thing I want is an anti-Royal article.' 'Cor, Alan, you're having me on . . .' etc. This just covered me, as it turned out, because the very next morning, in *The Times* leader 'Newbury die' I was named twice!

So this morning good friendly coverage in Black Dog (top),[4] and v reasonable in *Sunday Express*, thanks to dear Bruce who is coming down for lunch, and wants to be my campaign manager.[5] Perhaps more importantly and *complimentarily*, my verdict on JM in Graham Turner's *Sunday Telegraph* piece 'I have a high opinion of him . . .'

It all has a strange, magical quality. Almost as if I, and other forces, was willing it. Could I really bring it off? A year's sabbatical to assuage Jane, get the *Diaries* done. And then back to the second serious phase. And the lights of AC1800 in the garage, and the big

---

[1] Turned out not to be so.

[2] Peter Dobbie, long-time *Mail on Sunday* political writer.

[3] Paul Keating, prime minister of Australia since 1991, had, typically, been making some provocative remarks about the queen.

[4] *Mail on Sunday* political diary.

[5] Bruce Anderson had suggested AC to Richard Ryder as the candidate who would do least badly. Norman Fowler, apparently, thought it a crazy idea.

party in the Jubilee Room, 'to celebrate the result of the Newbury by-election'.

Garden House   *Thursday, 4 March*

Still the accumulation of events. Yesterday Jane's 'tests' proved *negative*, and thus a fresh boost as the overshadowing lifts. Then Matrix, DPP 'cleared' me, good TV coverage – 'vindicates' etc.[1] Spoke to Gill Shephard[2] – she very indiscreet, said, 'You must put in' and (without telling Jane) I now intend to 'take things one stage further' today. Then, after a Ch 3 [lunchtime ITN] news, phone rang and, rather quiet and sorry for himself, Richard!! It's all so impeccable, the timing. Polling just before the book comes out; and also the lawyers suggested excisions [to the *Diaries*] made it much easier to sanitise without upsetting the publishers.

Saturday, 13 March

What I will never know is whether in fact I had any chance of being 'seen' at Newbury or not *before* little Sarah Sands' interview in the *Standard* yesterday.[3]

I suppose it was a mistake – led astray by a pretty girl, as usual.

Terrible row with Jane followed. All I wanted to do was step into a hole.

Trouble is this was really my last 'window'. Because once the book is out – with its crazy indiscretions and element of romping – I will no longer be taken seriously.

I am *not* released. A bit apprehensive of bad publicity. Heard

---

[1] AC had feared he might be charged in connection with the Matrix Churchill case.

[2] Gillian Shephard, MP for South West Norfolk since 1987, employment secretary.

[3] Sarah Sands, feature writer on the *London Evening Standard*, had interviewed AC at Saltwood, where he was indiscreet about the forthcoming *Diaries*, about affairs and much else.

from *Daily Express* (typically) that 'down to 18' and not on list. Very flat and depressed. I slept after tea on the floor of the Green Room. I am tired and aimless. I must also try and restore the body a bit more. I have been drinking too regularly, taking very little exercise. I am creaky and fatigued ('ravaged' in appearance – Sarah Sands).

Sunday, 28 March

Walking down to the Long Garage this evening I felt something on my nose, right-hand side. Asked Jane, she said it was a 'little melanoma'. That's how the last nodel began, a little black dot. But in the mirror it's more of a line. Strange and depressing.

Garden House   *Friday, 2 April*

First of the galleys – to 1985 – arrived today.

I'm not so sure about the book. Is it really very *slight* indeed? I am nervous and apprehensive. I have been going through a phase of hypochondria about my melanoma and my right shoulder. It is certainly a worrying shape, a configuration rather, but not large. But my real problem is that there is this huge void – between policies and frivolities.

Garden House   *Tuesday, 27 April*

Walked from Sandling [station], darling Jane had made a balls-up of the arrival times and gone to Folkestone. London had been blocked solid. And now I return to find Jane is being bullied by Bates again and he's taken *twelve* slides. Uncertainty, complete, prevails.

Saltwood   *Sunday, 9 May*

A week, much filled, but little achieved.

The flat surfaces in the Green Room are choked and towering; 'key' letters like RREC Alpine and LPF[1] are still unattended to; the yard and workshops are a shambles and the lawn is never quite fully under control.

Jane was forced by Bates to undergo an operation – a 'lumpectomy'. We were in silent abjection (I will always remember, though not as vividly as if had marked the end of an era, answering his phone call to say it was a bit 'suspicious' after I had (demi-randily) my first after-lunch rest for ages, a Bank Monday – which had to be bad). But it turned out, on Friday, to be 'all right'. He splendidly rang me at supper. So I feel free to restart again, so soon after making or implying all those promises in St Leonard's where I had repaired after reading the interview which made me feel so sad and proud of her. But her being away is appalling. The pups[2] are a delight, but needlessly demanding: the weather is foul, with a high wind blowing all the time. I get up at 5.30, but still have only just got the kitchen in order, pups fed and walked by 7.

That was a lucky break at Newbury![3]

Garden House   *Wednesday, 26 May*

I feel very tired. The 'pressure' of all those interviews, publicity, serialisation, never anticipation of *disappointing* sales[4] plus need to

---

[1] L. P. Fassbender, the Clarks' accountant.

[2] Two Rottweilers, sisters, to whom the Clarks gave names with German association: Hannah (Jane's, after Hannah Reich, Hitler's test pilot) and Lëhni (AC's, after Hitler's favourite film director, Leni Riefenstahl).

[3] AC was indeed fortunate: the Conservatives were mauled at the by-election held on 6 May, with the Liberal Democrat candidate, Old Etonian David Rendel, overturning the Tories' general election 11,000 majority to achieve a LD victory by over 12,000 votes. As for the referendum/anti-Maastricht candidates, together they polled fewer than 700 votes.

[4] *Diaries* would be published following serialisation in the *Mail on Sunday*.

really do quite a lot of paperwork before leaving. I pine for Eriboll, the long May light, where James is enjoying wonderful weather and no one can badger me.

Garden House   *Sunday, 13 June*

The last Sunday here for some while.

When I am back the days will be shortening, and the peacock feathers will be all over the grass. I am relatively tranquil. The 'worst' seems to be over on the *Diaries*, thanks to Michael Cockerell's film[1] and Jane's attractive performance (relegating me to 'best supporting actor').

B5, Albany   *Tuesday, 15 June*

I woke too early for *The Times*, and read Chips. So interesting on Nazi Germany,[2] his trip there in 1936 (the best year for everything from Miro to the $4\frac{1}{4}$ Bentley). Chips will be remembered for his diary, and so will I. But I have one already over Chips – I'm still alive! – so ACHAB.

Saltwood   *Wednesday, 21 July*

Yesterday we went to the [Buckingham Palace] Garden Party, calling first at Andrew's dear little house in Farnell Mews. He was grave, though beautifully handsome.

I had interviews with two high cards at once. First Mrs Thatcher, rather unmade up, blonde hair not usual etc. Denis looking ghastly,

---

[1] Michael Cockerell, a BBC political journalist, had produced a much-admired television profile of AC, called *Love Tory*.

[2] 'Hitler was coming and he looked exactly like his caricature – brown uniform, but not grim look . . . I was more excited than when I met Mussolini in 1926 in Perugia, and more stimulated, I am sorry to say, than when I was blessed by the Pope in 1920' – *Chips*, 6 August 1936.

thin, grey, though cigaretting massively. As always, she doesn't actually engage in conversation, but states propositions and concepts. But no ill-will there, in spite of all the innuendo and interpretation in the hype. Then bumped into (literally) Geoffrey Howe in the cake queue, and mobbed him. He came and sat with us, talked about Scott, and the Commons. As I said to Jane the mafia band of politicians in the same party is such that we really can't bear grudges, it's not worth it.

Garden House   *Friday, 30 July*

The opening of a new volume, in which events are likely to be lower-key – a gradually declining trajectory.

Last night I slept from 10.40 to 7.10 without waking at all – 8½ hours. I had been incredibly tired yesterday after Soames's end of term, when we stayed up drinking until 1.30. Soames looked ill, sweated a lot and at one point very splendidly *took his temperature* (it was 98, having been 102 earlier in the day). He's had his gall bladder removed and I remember from my tonsil operation that one does suffer afterwards from violent fluctuations in fever and depression. The boys were genuinely friendly, and tired; but I sensed, as I wrote afterwards to Richard, the 'gossamer curtain' between those in power and those who are OUT. Jonathan, so thoughtful and wise, asked me what I would say if Faust offered me a miraculous translation straight back into the Commons – Government or back benches as you wish – at the price of surrendering the *Diaries*. Initially, I suppose, one says 'no'. But always there is the heavenly recollection of the sword, now on the floor of the lake's bottom.

This morning we went to Ashford market, the Hobbs Parker sale of agricultural oddments. The 'Poet' (I can't recall his name at the moment) appeared and talked knowledgeably. He is a habitué of such functions. He told me that the Channel Tunnel people had acquired the site – why? With what powers? To build a supermarket and the auction was going to be moved to a 'green field site'.

Shore Cottage   *Tuesday, 17 August*

Was it only yesterday that I welched on the Los Angeles trip?

Said to Jane I was going because I was 'bored'. I wish I was there, talking to one and all, spotting new self-styled experts in the 'movement' and filling my reservoirs. Then, on return, I could savour the low pace and the cleanliness of the Highland tempo. I am still more restless than I thought, I suppose. Or is it the consciousness of the days left reducing all the time in number? So that one which goes by without anything to fill it is a waste? Unless of course it is occupied by *rehabilitation and recovery*.

B5, Albany   *Tuesday, 21 September*

I have been walking about London, somewhat *désoeuvré*. Tomorrow a snoop on 'Scott'.[1] Poor JM under screeching pressure – in Tokyo, of all places – and in Brooks's, extempore, I drafted a note to send him.[2]

Saltwood   *Sunday, 24 October*

I had sat down to write a passage, a couple of days ago, in the Garden House, but was interrupted by the urge to write a note to Richard Ryder (following my lunch with Willie Whitelaw at Mrs T's Foyle[3]). I asked him to set up a Defence Commission with me

---

[1] AC's only comment afterwards was that he 'quite liked Presiley Baxendale', counsel to the inquiry.

[2] Major was leading a party of senior UK businessmen to Japan, but before he left Britain there had been leadership speculation, possible stalking horses for a contest in November. Norman Lamont, now the ex-Chancellor of the Exchequer, writing on the first anniversary of Black Wednesday, had criticised the prime minister; and on the flight to Tokyo, Major had been indiscreet to the press party on his attitude to the Eurosceptics. AC eventually sent his note to Major, 'trying both to cheer him up and ingratiate myself'.

[3] Foyle's, the booksellers, had as their guest of honour at a lunch Margaret Thatcher, whose memoirs, *The Downing Street Years*, were published the previous week.

as Chairman. Naturally he didn't reply ('Alan goes mad every so often and wants to get back in, last time it was a week before the Matrix trial'). It was strange that lunch. Sweepings really. Is that really all she could manage in terms of distinction, being between the Indian and the Hungarian ambassadors?

But I still want to be a *player*. Thing is – on *Question Time* I had a heavy time. Peter Mandelson[1] said, 'you're still so young.' Peter Sissons [chairman] talked sensibly and confidentially to me about broad trends and JM's PR men, and so on.

I can't quite settle down. Although the lure of de-escalation is delicious I am under heavy financial pressure. Can't see prospect of fresh earnings ('new money'). I am going to have to cull both cars and pictures.

Saltwood   *Friday, 29 October*

When I got home I pottered in the Long Garage, realised I didn't actually want to sell *anything*. Earnings won't cover everything owing – anywhere near – so will have to do it from Art. Why not? The cars are a collection – bit of 'Applied' rather than 'Fine' – Art. It is the full moon, Halloween tomorrow. Unusual combination.

Of course, £350 for the Mask[2] would do very nicely thank you, but I'm glad I resisted that. It must work spells for me, because I saved it, will have to make other sacrifices.

Saltwood   *Sunday morning, 31 October*

Woke, and shrank instantaneously with thought of pressures – financial and paper. But we went for the 'w' and the trees were so beautiful, a perfectly still morning of late autumn so early that no one was about, and vistas and colours that you get only once every

---

[1] Peter Mandelson, MP for Hartlepool since 1992. Previously the Labour party's Director of Communications.
[2] See entry for 9 May 1985.

three or four years. I was worried about the bark on the great oak —
it must be done next month. But the walk — the dry leaves were so
lovely and calming, that we both felt better.

When we got in, Jane said, 'we've got everything, and yet we
don't enjoy it.' So true, so very, very true. But she said it in good
humour.

Garden House   *Thursday, 11 November*

A lovely fine still day. At the eleventh hour, of the eleventh day, of
the eleventh month we walked, almost by chance, to Lord C's gate
and were seated there when the Western Front fell silent.

Garden House   *Monday, 29 November*

A very cold, clear day. Our undulant 'virus' is still around, and Jane
coughed continuously for the latter half of the night. Last night,
watched the second half of *To Play the King*. Ian Richardson so
good[1] . . . the scenes in the Commons made me wistful and
nostalgic. 'You can never go back,' Jane said.

This coming year I had planned on, virtually, a sabbatical. I
don't know if I would just get fossilised. But such a relief to move
away from deadlines and 'engagements'. But in the familiar phrase,
'I can't afford it.' It's not just the pressure of tax demands, but it is
simply grossly irresponsible to pass up £300,000+.[2]

Saltwood   *Tuesday, 30 November*

I went over after tea to shut the drive gates of Garden House, and
on the way back I looked at the dark outline of the Mains, the

---

[1] Ian Richardson had earlier played in *House of Cards*, also by Michael Dobbs and
also with a Westminster background.
[2] AC had been offered this sum for the book and newspaper serial rights to a
second volume of *Diaries*.

Santé wall. My open prison. I am not ready to stand back yet. But I
am nervous of *using up time* – even when, eg, 'polishing' the Buick
– because I dread that suddenly, I may 'go'.

Shore Cottage   *Wednesday, 22 December*

Christmas marks the end, and the beginning of 'our' year, and
already since getting here I have been 'unwound' and contemplative.

A pleasing journey, with just the right amount of 'challenge'. I
ended up in the ditch just out of Altnaharra pine woods on the
Tongue road. How? Most odd. I took my eyes off for one second,
laughing and joking with Jane and next thing I know we were
bouncing about on the verge, snow going in all directions. Jane
screaming.

A kindly fisherman (*most* providentially) soon put in an appearance in a Japanese 4WD and pulled me out backwards (with,
thank God, a very slight gradient) and I was none the worse except
for a broken or bent o/s wheel trim. We still managed, just, to get
to Eriboll before the light faded.

Boxing Day

Very cold, all the roads have frozen hard, in to its ridges and the
puddles are solid translucent grey. We went beachcombing from
Whales Corner and, unbelievably, bathed in the glass-like loch, in
the low sun (we have bathed from there before in the summer).

I have now been here five days and each day have taken two
hours on the hill – in one form or another – and then one fine
evening meal, an early night and 10 hours' sleep.

Something cautions me away from *Diaries II – Towering Inferno
II* etc. Also I'm not quite ready to get locked into the Great Work[1]
preferring to pick, still, and read round it (greatly enjoying

---

[1] What would become *The Tories: Conservatives and the Nation State, 1922–77.*

Beaverbrook by A. J. P. Taylor at present). So my considered favourite, at present, is to take up Jonathan Holborrow's offer and try and make something of it.[1]

Shore Cottage   *Thursday, 30 December*

One of my great preoccupations remains to put off old age. It has started to show – very slightly – in my hands. The cross vein remains in place, and several pale death spots are appearing. My neck is sometimes really quite embarrassingly thick – even between the video of the Alpine and the start of the books-of-the-year interview with Jack and Jill.[2]

Shore Cottage   *New Year's Eve*

Sadly I realise I will never (unless God is exceptionally kind) live to see my grandchildren marry. Will I ever have any? We have this slightly unnatural existence at the moment, Jane and I. The boys grown-up and (in theory) settled, but no Grandparental duties.

---

[1] A weekly political column in the *Mail on Sunday*.

[2] AC means John McCarthy – held hostage in Beirut – and Jill Morrell. Their joint memoir was called *Some Other Rainbow*. The three of them appeared together on the Sky book programme.

Shore Cottage – New Year's Day

A day spent with chores and various, before heading south on a
great drive tomorrow. There is always so much to do at Eriboll.
Some things have been left undone for six, seven years. And the
Maid of Morwen still lies on her side, her entrails slowly rotting.

Just as the light faded I walked with Jamie, to Birkett Foster.[1]
He is much, much better. And sensible. He might get married this
year, to Julie. Laughed when I said, 'breed, anyway'. He was
realistic about the onset of old age, concurred with my analogy of
the hourglass triangle.

Saltwood   *Friday, 28 January*

I am depressed at being excluded. You only really know what's
going on if you are inside the Commons. Although I suppose as a
peer I would have access. I miss it dreadfully. When I was there
living on physical reserves, I spent these, all but, but accumulated a
huge intellectual bank. This is slipping through my fingers fast and
in a year's time I will be left with nothing. If 'Scott' clears me, and
if JM survives I suppose there is a faint chance of New Year '95.
But after that I'd have to wait for the next Conservative government even for the offer of a 'K' – at the age of 76.

Saltwood   *Sunday, 30 January*

The wretched JM is under appalling pressure still. Right across the
front page of the *Sunday Times* a terrible photo of him at the Leeds

---

[1] AC owned a small seascape by the Victorian painter Myles Birkett Foster, with
rocks like those at Eriboll.

dinner, hands clasped behind his head held over the plate.[1] Could have been doing a Bush in Japan. And the usual row – extended now to include total non-starters like Redwood[2] – of leadership contestants.

Saltwood   Thursday, 3 February

And now Pin[3] has got cancer. Of the prostate. Perfectly ghastly. How long have I got? It's hard to know what is right   straight into the hands of surgeons or hold out – and when it comes just GO. Force yourself over the edge on the Creaggan. I fear the latter is probably right – but would one have the courage? It would be like turning the gas on, or pipe from the exhaust; it's no good changing your mind when you get drowsy. Then it's too late.

Saltwood   Friday, 4 February

I suppose I will be remembered for the Diaries (still at No 2 in the Evening Standard).

Jimmy Goldsmith's, Cuixmala, Mexico   Wednesday, 16 February

In the swimming pool pavilion, with its straw roof, by Jimmy's pool, itself drained and refilled with salt water every day. Everything is oversize, mattresses, deckchairs, urns, parasols. Lovely chevron clay tiling on the pool floor. The staircase down is pure

---

[1] John Major was speaking to the Leeds Chamber of Commerce. Whatever the photograph appeared to show, Major was particularly relaxed that evening. Anthony Seldon, in his study of the Major government, wrote, 'The audience appreciated his spontaneity and his wit, and he spoke well . . . at one point later in the evening he doubled up and was photographed head in hands, an image to be endlessly recycled in the press thereafter as evidence of a man at the end of his tether.'

[2] John Redwood, MP for Wokingham since 1987; Welsh secretary since 1993.

[3] Colin Clark, AC's younger brother.

Alma-Tadema, out of Port Lympne, with many a coign of vantage and beautiful pots of blooms so bright and vulgar that, as Jane says, you need acrylic to do them justice and the delicate box of water-colours is inadequate. The whole level of sumptuocity is magnificent – separate 'villas' for the guests cunningly sited within the flower and jungle hillside of the condominium. Makes Jeffrey Archer's 'apartment' look like a journalistic bolthole.[1]

Garden House   *Tuesday, 15 March*

All my 'friends' have abandoned me. Only dear Soames was on the answering machine this morning, and still keeps in touch. Jonathan [Aitken] is having me at his dinner for Richard Nixon on Thursday, but is correct on other topics.[2] Richard – silent; the PM – silent; 'Tristan' quite openly trying to shift the Scott blame on to me as the 'direction of the Inquiry's finding starts to emerge', and winding up toadies like Bruce Anderson to say as much.

Politically, I'm now really a non-person. And at least half of me wants to go North – for good. 'Care and maintenance only.'

Dear Tip is determined to leave the Army, which formerly he loved so much. Got down by the new tendency – the book-keeping and being wankily career conscious, sneaking a 'late luncheon', going 'classless' etc. He's no idea what he's going to do . . . 'travel'. Won't get a pension or a golden handshake. But his face is a little crumpled, and unhappy. Today Malcolm Rifkind is going round – with David Hart (strange ménage).[3] They are looking at it[4] to see about selling it off, to Jews, to make into offices. Andrew, partly because he is marginalised and out of favour, is deputed to

---

[1] Jeffrey Archer, author, former MP (Louth) and deputy chairman of the Conservative Party, had a high-level flat with panoramic views across the Thames to Westminster.

[2] Jonathan Aitken had published a well-received biography of former US president Nixon.

[3] Malcolm Rifkind had been defence secretary since 1992. David Hart had been an *éminence grise* among special advisers, originally to Margaret Thatcher, now to John Major and soon to Michael Portillo.

[4] The headquarters of the Household Cavalry.

show them the men's bedrooms. Don't despair, I said, that's all politicians are interested in.

I asked, what about the horses? How can you move out of those lovely stables? Ah no, a 'report' is being prepared at the moment (by a *sailor*) on possible 'options' for reducing the cavalry strength – or even getting rid of it altogether.

This, as so many other things at present; the toadying to Delors, the impossibility of getting offences against the person punished, the politic and contemptible appeasement of Ireland. With each fresh atrocity they get up and bleat about '. . . will not alter our determination to . . .' (now 'search for peace'; formerly 'crush terrorism').

It is an extraordinary interlude, the Thatcher decade. Now we are back with Mr Wilson, or worse. The moment will come when I have to say this (so to that extent I am fortunate still to have the column in which to say it) – but not just quite yet.

Having been loyal through thick and thin, all the scapegoating etc, what will finally cause me to turn is that they are leading the Party into a barren defile where it is going to be *annihilated*.

Saltwood   *Tuesday, 29 March*

Jane has gone on a 'massive' shopping round – Glass Co, Geerings, possibly Canterbury map shop. It's really rather pleasant and relaxing being left in the empty house.

I would like to get out and play out-of-doors. But here I am two years out of retirement and chained to the paper, and the desk, more than ever. (Just reread an interview with Robin Day who has said on the difference between capital and income – 'with high capital you are a free man; with high earnings you are a slave'.) And tomorrow the Coutts team are coming down – like tea for the IMF.

Garden House   *Thursday, 31 March*

I am low, and feel that things are slipping away from me.

A re-run of November '90, but without, of course, the platform or perch.

The week's papers have been blazing – Major finished, end is nigh, not a friend left, sooner he goes the better. Sterling crisis – you name it.

Jonathan H talked for an hour on Tuesday. He'd had lunch with Jeremy[1] who gave him 'the whole thing is over' spiel; then that afternoon JM did poorly in the Commons and Marlow bagged a headline with his you-must-go declamation. Dobbie got more and more apocalyptic – finally calling at 9-ish pm.

I booked a meeting with Richard – 'the Chief Whip will come and have tea at Albany at 3.30 pm.'

Later in the evening Soames phoned – part II – and said it was a shambles, Baker was taking people on one side and saying 'JM was dead in the water' etc. I asked him if he wanted to be chairman of the Party and he said yes. Why anyone wants that job beats me, but anything can happen . . . if I could afford it myself I'd grab it.

But (later) when I put this to Richard he said 'Nick who?' 'Oh, give him a director-general to pay the wages,' I said, and got the only real chuckle of the afternoon. RR was reasonably communicative. Admitted that the only real danger would be a Cabinet welching; a 'difficult' meeting at which one or more people expressed reservations.

Quite.

Richard was amiable, almost Gow-voiced in his insistence on a 'dinner' soon after Easter. But of what clout does he actually dispose? At one point I said, 'You must find something for me to do.' Did he even acknowledge? I will return to this next time.

But this morning I have been trying desperately to keep Jonathan Holborrow from 'plunging in'. Apparently M. Heseltine

---

[1] Jeremy Hanley (MP for Richmond & Barnes since 1983), currently armed forces minister, but in the summer cabinet reshuffle would succeed Norman Fowler as chairman of the Conservative Party.

was imploring Dobbie last night to take his side – 'on his knees'. Perhaps mistakenly, I said to Jonathan, *you* see him; make your own mind up. You're in the strongest position of the Sundays, not in anyone's 'camp', not concerned with personalities.

They put the whole thing in place immediately. So that while I was talking to M Howard (he, too, took my call immediately!) – also very splendidly said, 'tape the interview and run that.' It may have been a miscalculation; Jonathan H could be overcome as he is still, in one sense, politically *naif*. At present I've got calls in to Bob Worcester (the polls are crucial in this) and David Davis. Tristan is no longer friendly, and I see no point in showing my hand.

My handwriting is terribly disturbed.

Garden House   *Easter Monday, 4 April*

Today, I think for the first time, I actually found myself accepting the reality of defeat.

The old analogy – with the Reich in 1943–5 – is less valid than Vichy France in 1940. I have now to go through a Pétainist period. Really quite hard to see what will extricate me. No one rings any more – except people who want to pick my brains on the cheap, or also want to put me on their programme and lift its status – for £35.

Anyway I am going to get everything in order – and then I will be free. I can walk out – but without going to 'another woman' (although, of course, it will be suspected that I have). Where do I go to? I would really prefer Scotland, but I suppose it has to be Bratton, as that's the only place, absurdly enough, that belongs to me. I might start in Zermatt, in fact.

During the night there were *five* interruptions: Tom (urinated twice on the white carpet); then Lëhni urinated in my bathroom, went out re-Thompsoned; then Tom had to go out Thompsoned; then Hannah met me on the stairs, took her down – she Thompsoned. Finally Tom hyper-ventilated, looked into the Yard briefly, settled for the Green Room.

Jane, I may say, made absolutely no effort whatever to cope

with any of these episodes except the first when she ably removed most of the stain using rubber gloves and Jif.

So this morning I am utterly exhausted. Had to come straight over here after EMT to type some letters. Now I'm back here, very depressed, nothing on the machine, and will spend 40 minutes or so 'Windolening' the plate glass before shuffling back across to the Mains.

Garden House   *Tuesday, 5 April*

I was over in the Great Hall study with Jane, looking for some of my father's articles which I need for 'Michael Delon' (sounds quite scholarly in his approach). I came across some tiny pocket engagement books of my grandfather,[1] *very* sparingly entered: 'out', 'shooting', 'Inverary', 'Mrs MacArthur to lunch'. Some are clearly future engagements, clear (if the word can be considered applicable) records.

In August of 1914, the week of the great seismic tilt, when the earth plates buckled, they were sailing off the west coast of Scotland – 'Oban', 'Poolewe'. About the 14th, they took the train to Euston, spent the night in their London house (visited v rarely) in Berkeley Square (come to think of it, all the satinwood stuff must have been bought for this, from Malletts – just round the corner) the next day took the train to Sudbourne.[2] Stayed there (shooting) all through the Battle of the Marne. What a style! Three large and expensive houses (plus the lodge at Poolewe and the villa at Cap Ferrat), the yacht, hordes and hordes of domestics.

My own structure still shadows it – but with no support whatever. Like the Royal Navy in the 1970s, compared with the Grand Fleet.

---

[1] Kenneth McKenzie Clark, who inherited wealth and enjoyed it to the full.
[2] The Clark estate in Suffolk.

Garden House   *Sunday, 10 April*

This is, as it were, the birthday-boy entry – next week is 'a horrible' and I won't be back here Thursday morning.

Recently I have been thinking about an escape plan. It goes like this:

Put Saltwood on 'care and maintenance' ('it is already on care and maintenance', Jane says).

Reduce the contents virtually to modern museum level – bare, clear walls – except for the Red Library and the dining room (in mothballs for 'crash' meeting). Garden House ticking over warmly for a visit when necessary.

Look for a low 18th-century stone house with nicely proportioned rooms in Perthshire – 200 acres for wintering the Eriboll flock, a good chunk of hill and a nice black-spate salmon river for Jane to fish in. Plenty of outbuildings. I even fantasise about getting Bill Holdings to put up one of his sheds there. That way we would be near enough to James and Julie, especially as they are now talking of 'winklers'. It would mean selling Seend for Tip.

I've always said I'll never move, and probably won't. Lord Astor sold up Hever, went to Scotland and died of cancer very soon afterwards. It would mark the transition into an old man I suppose from (*passim* today's *Sunday Times*) 'much-missed in the corridors of power'. A final abandonment of the sword and helmet. Even as I write that I realise I can't do it. But pleasant to fantasise.

Saltwood   *Wednesday, 20 April*

Fearfully beleaguered by pressures – which have 'got to me' that I feel extremely tired and don't see any sunlit uplands. I sit at the table in the Green Room – absurdly laden, now, with the various trays. Behind me several Pisa towers of sundry newsprint, car sale catalogues, important incoming letters interleaved (I don't doubt) and every kind of unexpected document I've beside my chair and on the bookcase.

Yesterday evening, after [dog] training (which did not go well; I was distracted by a pretty young woman with a nervous Alsatian), I walked down the valley in fading light, which I used to when I was living here and before going away to Rye. I thought: I suppose to a detached observer at least, my life in terms of potential, is over. But instead of pleasing open days I have in front of me a Matto Grosso of paperwork and filing which I must try and get in order before I depart.

Nixon had a stroke today. 81. He can understand, but he can't talk. The worst of all, because so soon they start talking about you in the room, *audio oblique*. The days are lovely now, longer daylight than in August. It would be so lovely to be meandering about outside, like one used to at Seend. Will one ever be free of *will we ever*?

Tomorrow up by train to see [Charles] Jerdein at 3 pm about selling the Mask (his *client* is raising his bid), which I can't really do.

Sunday, 15 May

I just dare not accept Jerdein's offer for the Mask: $100, plus £265. Would solve all debts. But if I keep it, it will go on generating its protection, I believe.

Ritz dining room, Paris[1]   *Sunday, 29 May*

Just drank a delicious glass of orange juice. A very good hotel (except no tutti slippers in the bathroom). Staff – unusually for French – courteous and obliging and I had a lovely room on the 6th floor with double windows and balconies looking out over the roofs.

Oy! What cramped and nifty writing . . . A bit apprehensive, I suppose, though basically dutch, at the Harkess 'story' which has broken – manically – in the *News of the World* and been, gleefully, I

---

[1] AC was in Paris for Jimmy Goldsmith's 'L'autre Europe' party.

don't doubt, picked up by the *Sunday Express*. Jane is gamely meeting me at Manston and I may have to ride from Sandling to Saltwood in the boot of the Big Red.[1] It's really too boring. I don't enjoy this kind of 'publicity' at all and it has been running on and off now for a year really. I suppose it may sell some more books, but expect Orion won't be able to provide demand, just use the 'subject' to clear their stocks.

Saltwood   *Tuesday, 14 June*

This is my first *contemplatif* for over two weeks. I was under some pressure – all those journalists and questions [over Harkess]: '. . . are you going to answer the charges (sic)?' actually assume one's guilt. I couldn't even fill out the Green Diary day-by-day.

I suppose the tide actually turned on 'the' Wednesday. Tristan rang that evening (welchly late, as I said to Jane, but an indication that we had made 'if not port then the lee of the shore').

If there were turning points I would say, Richard Littlejohn aside, *The Times* leader,[2] the *Daily Mirror* dope on Joei and finally the Judy Finnegan show which showed them – thanks to Judy and her husband – *in a poor light*, culminating in a vote when the score was 72–28.

I may even have 'come out ahead' having sold at least another 20,000 paperbacks and, ludicrously, been approached to go into a 'National' Police advertisement scheme (I'm still doubtful about this) with an appearance fee of £25,000 plus (!).

In my present form all really I want to do, though, is to stand back and become a guru-sage.

---

[1] AC arrived in the Goldsmith private jet at Manston. Jane had forced her way through journalists outside the Saltwood gates, saying she was just going off to do some shopping. She returned, with AC in the capacious boot of Big Red, drove straight to the Long Garage; AC did not emerge until they were safely inside.

[2] 'With his *Diaries*, he has written himself into the life of our times with a panache and candour that ranks him next to Boswell or Pepys' (*The Times*, 10 June 1994).

Wednesday, 22 June

The seat by the moat after EMT. Mid-summer, the anniversary of Barbarossa. This time, fifty-three years ago the whole Eastern Front was ablaze and the YAKs were smouldering carcases, wing-tip to wing-tip, on the Soviet airfields. But only three years later it was the collapse of Army Group Centre (always one of the strangest failures of nerve of the magnificent German army) and the 'rush' into Poland.

Things have taken a turn for the better for us. So far this week I have been a 'triumph' (*passim* Paul Channon) on *Frost*;[1] then a call from Cdr Aylard[2] saying how interesting the Prince of Wales had found my piece in the *Mail on Sunday*. Selina Scott wants to include me in her next series with Clinton, Murdoch, Pavarotti etc – 'from a woman's point of view'.

We went up to Jimmy's great party. Lovely fun. Everyone was there. And Princess Diana turned up 'for the coffee', looking incredible as always. Isobel Goldsmith sat on my left wearing the most beautiful necklace. 'Do you deal with the Nortons?' I asked. Of course she did. It had come from Nicholas.[3] Opposite me, on Conrad Black's right, sat Jane Wrightsman[4] gone from being blonde to being gypsy black; with tiny birdlike movements of vain, elderly women who are trying to conceal their age.

My 'approval' rating remains high ('four times that of the PM,' as Charles Moore giggled) and people as varied as William Shawcross (who he?) and the doorman – who was a Serb, wonderful people – came up to 'shake my hand'.

Jane drove me back in the Big Red and I lollingly dozed. Slept like a top. Strangely, I don't think I have been happier, or more fulfilled since Seend. And I thank God.

---

[1] Sir David Frost's Sunday morning 'sofa' show, as AC called it, was required viewing for polticians. Frost had come a long way since satire shows of the 1960s.

[2] Commander Richard Aylard, private secretary to the Prince of Wales since 1991.

[3] Nicholas Norton of S. J. Phillips, jewellers in Bond Street.

[4] Jane Wrightsman, widow of Charles Wrightsman, American oil billionaire.

Sunday, 26 June

A lovely hot still day and we rose early and sat breakfasting by the pool, then afterwards in the long chairs by the fig tree reading the Sundays. Publicity – I get it. Absurd really. Only cloud is little Page who came in when I was having an injection, said I should have a check-up. Wouldn't have minded so much if it hadn't been Col's doctor who said, 'Your brother should have a PSA test.'[1] So this hangs over me. But I am much calmer now, and seem none the worse (dare I say it, slightly better for the whole experience).

Great Hall study, Saltwood   *Sunday, 10 July*

Last night we went over to Sissinghurst, arriving early for dinner and walked round the gardens. Lovely, and no public, and very redolent of Harold and Vita and 'Miss Niggeman'.[2] 'Cleaned up' as NT properties always are, but one could still imagine the old boy driving back from Tunbridge Wells station (old Austin taxi, of course) and thinking about the countryside during the Battle of Britain and then, much later, shuffling out of his study in the tower, and collapsing. 'Is this where he collapsed?' I rehearsed in the car going over, and Jane had a *fou rire*. At dinner I was lionised. Marvellous to be compared to Byron, Shelley and Pepys in one's lifetime – and by such good judges. Stephen Spender and Elizabeth Longford[3] quite effusive, Natasha Spender, whom I remember as being dark and voluptuous and rather frightening still very attractive, at 70+, with short blonde-dyed hair and lovely eye ditches.

I sat next to Rebecca Nicolson[4] and she and some ambassador[5]

---

[1] Protein Sequence Analysis for early detection of prostate cancer.

[2] Kent home of Nigel Nicolson, author, former Conservative MP, son of Harold Nicolson and his wife Vita Sackville-West, who restored the house and its gardens, now in the hands of the National Trust; Elvira Niggeman, Harold Nicolson's secretary, 1938–65.

[3] Sir Stephen Spender, poet; Lady Longford, biographer.

[4] AC 'tried to get off' with Rebecca Nicolson. She was flattered, but refused.

[5] Michael Pakenham, British ambassador to Luxembourg; son of Elizabeth Longford.

gave me a bit of 'when are you going to take the helm?' treatment.
All v gratifying, but frustrating also. Phone and fax silent all day.

Next week the result of the 'test'. Will I be 'cleared'?

Talking of which, little Archer[1] again in trouble over 'insider
trading'. Every week a new scandal.

Saltwood   *Wednesday, 13 July*

We have had two days of very great heat – 86° and more in
London. On the Monday we drove (in the Jaguar, as Big Red has
gone away for part exchange[2]) to Highgrove. HRH very magnetic
– greatly to my surprise. I took a liking to Paul McCartney, saw a
few other notables (little Gummer[3] notably unfriendly). A slightly
bizarre grouping.

Highgrove is terribly nice, really organic. But the place was
incomplete, without a woman.

Saltwood   *Saturday, 16 July*

As I walked back from the Garden House, having finished my *Mail
on S* 'column', I saw the mother hen and the little black baby
bantams under the beech hedge and went over to talk to them. On
the other side of the moat one of the moorhens was busying itself. I
was deliciously at ease, not having drunk anything at midday, felt
marvellous. In the late afternoon drove with Jane in the KGV car
to collect some of her framed pictures from the Evegate Art Shop
and then on to get petrol at Tesco. Tea with black bread and
pepper salami (only a croissant so far today) and then I wandered
up to the top of the house to open the tower playroom door for
the swifts. I found an old, very old Bartholomew cloth-backed
Ordnance Survey map of Sutherland (Tongue and Cape Wrath,

---

[1] Archer had been accused over Anglia TV, of which his wife was a director.

[2] AC was exchanging his present Bentley for a new one, identical in colour, also
called Big Red.

[3] John Selwyn Gummer, environment secretary since 1993.

sheet 26) possibly even Victorian as it showed the Creaggan as fully
driveable, two ferries across the Loch, one going to 'Port Eriboll'.
Then I hung on the bar without ill-effect. On the way down
through the upper floors I fantasised about ways of 'doing them up'
and realised what lovely things there still are here. A day of real
contentment and tranquillity, unchronicled for a very long time,
and thanks be to God.

Thursday, 13 October

My very last Party Conference – short of a miracle. It must be all of
20 years – could have been '69 or '70 when I went to Blackpool
nervous about being, as it were, *visually probed*, been keen (how
little I knew then) to find and suck up to chairmen. Now most of
the cheeky-chappies, 5' 8" high and with 'waisted' jackets and
exact templates/candidates of the kind that were all over the place
then, and saying the same things. CCO standard issue.

I comment[1] shrewdly and drawlingly at the start and end of
sessions. But glimpsing myself in the monitor at the end of the
day's session with Huw (Edwards, I think?) I thought how old I
looked. Earlier in the day the sweet little make-up blonde was
getting friendlier and friendlier, expressed sympathy at the idea of
'going for a walk on the beach'. But when I asked her, she said,
'You mean take off our shoes and walk barefoot in the sand?'

'Yes, yes.'

'I don't get a lunch hour.'

Was she mocking? She didn't turn up all afternoon.

I walked along the beach alone . . .

Portillo and Heseltine 'clashed'. Portillo got the better ovation.
The first time anyone has beaten MH for years (except, of course,
and by rote, the PM).

MH, also, looked old at times. Almost 'Mr Chips' in his half-
moons. And last night as I worked the conference hall it was so clear
that people were unhappy, and longing for a lead. They cheered

---

[1] The BBC had employed AC for interpretation and summing up.

Hanley,[1] but only a kind of knee-jerk – because basically he was *low*.
You can get laughs, and 'affection' that way, but it's not leadership.
(I must say, though, that I did get a pang when Malcolm Rifkind,
introducing his front bench, pointed out that the entire previous
line-up – Aitken, Hanley and Cranborne – had all gone into
Cabinet.)

On the way back I was waylaid by the *News of the World* gang
and had an open-air negotiating session with Piers Morgan. Quite
engaging (high flown, aet. 29). Offered him a clear run for
£25,000 – including my costs. Very generous.[2]

Shore Cottage   *Tuesday, 20 December*

Arrived in the afternoon, very wet lying, but light beautiful and
Julie had got the croft in shipshape order. James had made a really
beautiful strong bench for me and sweetly had stuck a red ribbon
on it – my Christmas present.

Shore Cottage   *Saturday, 24 December*

It is a truism that any holiday only lasts three – or possibly four –
days before some jarring episode or reminder changes the atmosphere and arrests the process of unwinding.

At EMT Jane and I were sitting this morning, still utterly
comatose and uncoordinated. She was dressed, and after a bit
decided to take the dogs, starting ahead of me while I Thompsoned and dressed. Quietly, ruminating on the loo with *Three Years
of War in E Africa* (first time this hol)[3] I thought I heard shouting,

---

[1] John Major had made Jeremy Hanley party chairman in his summer reshuffle,
believing that Hanley, with his easy manner, might do for the Conservatives in
the mid-1990s what Cecil Parkinson had done for the party early in Margaret
Thatcher's time as prime minister.

[2] Following the *News of the World*'s serialisation of the Harkess's story, AC was
threatening legal action; Piers Morgan, *News of the World* editor.

[3] By Captain Angus Buchanan; another Eriboll favourite.

rather Saltwood-like. Thought no more of it, then unmistakably Jane SCREAMING hysterically. Rushed out naked, barefoot in wellingtons with only a Jaeger dressing gown on. The dogs had attacked a sheep, forcing it in and out of the stream. Poor darling, she was white and gasping; hit Hannah fiercely with my stalking stick. This made me deeply gloomy – can we never let the dogs off the lead – much less free range – again? It's hard enough to get her to come to Eriboll, still less to stay here for any length of time . . .

Shore Cottage   *Monday (Boxing Day)*

We went to midnight carol service in Tongue. As always, ahead of a 'function' felt comatose and reluctant. But it was pleasing. All the good tunes, and perfectly sensible message of reassurance about the resurrection, a good audience (including some in crew cuts and bomber jackets) and not one mention, from start to finish, of the Third World or the need to 'combat' racism or homelessness or poverty or any of that crap.

Now it is hailing and with a cold wind and I sit at my delightful study window and at the Seend gratis desk and ponder.

Saltwood   *Thursday, 29 December*

Back here and in a high state of nervous readiness (quite the reverse of nervous randiness). We 'did' the post (nothing from John Major or the PoW), caught up with a few cards and I sent off £5800-odd worth of cheques.

More and more I incline to the view that in art it is the representation of light that ranks above all else. 'Form' is a poor second, cubism all that. Cézanne is colour, that and light – just a mess, really, of splodgings vaguely evocative of sans illumination. Monet, Heade, Church, the 'luminists'. And what about the distant horizon in, eg, the little Rousseau of the Becs[1] before

---

[1] A picture owned by the Clarks.

'cleaning' away, for ever, the pale lemon dividing streak between sea and sky.

One has only to write these all down to see that it is not simply a matter of going back refreshed and tackling things with vigour. The whole day, like the flat surfaces indoors, is impossibly congested. 'Discipline,' Jane says. Yes, that would help. But the sheer scale of the task may force, in the end, 'its own modification'.

1995 – so hard we must strive. (Followed, perhaps, by 1996 picking up sticks.)

Saltwood   *New Year's Eve*

More and more I am convinced that the most precious commodity in the world is TIME (was it not the clip of my father comparing himself to the White Rabbit perpetually looking at his watch that moved me to tears in Michael Cockerell's film?).

Today I just squandered it. Only managed three letters – one of them completely unnecessary and will make bad feeling, on Jeffrey Archer's personal number plate to the *Guardian*,[1] and still not typed up the new setup for BB. Was in a vile mood, no food except a digestive biscuit and two cups of Darjeeling at 7.30. Rotten post, and the Honours list.

It really is too much, Hosker (Treasury solicitor who 'allowed' – sic – certain documents for the Matrix trial – admitted it to Scott) got a knighthood.[2] Also Rocco F[orte]. The line-up of the 'businessmen' looked even lower, scruffier and more venal than the politicians. I have simply been bypassed. And once 'bypassed' it is virtually impossible to get 'streamed' again. Why? Scott the

---

[1] The *Guardian* diary ran a competition when Archer crashed his car. The number plate was blanked out in the photograph and readers were asked for suggestions. AC produced a cutting, from the *Glasgow Herald*, with the original number plate clearly visible. He also disclosed a second Archer number plate, a 'low-digit Exeter registration . . . at present (one assumes) on a retention certificate'. The *Guardian* diarist made AC runner-up.

[2] Gerald Hosker, solicitor to the Department of Trade and Industry (hence his involvement over the Matrix Churchill matter), 1987–92, then Procurator General, Treasury Solicitor and Queen's Proctor.

excuse, of course, but when I am 'cleared' (a nice Christmas card from C Muttukumaru[1] cheered me up) it will be too late. The excuse will be my 'private life' – even though that was known to the Cabinet Secretary and the PM before I was appointed to the Government.

The photos of Christmas at Eriboll are dreadfully revealing of me. Red-faced, thick necked, something almost of Evelyn Waugh ('all right then, Grandad?' Jane said). Something of Tom King and Marcus Kimball – who was portrayed stoutly *Jorrocks* in the saddle in *The Times* yesterday. He's hung up his riding gear, poor Marcus, for ever. One thing after another closing in on him.[2]

So it has been a very frustrating day. And this pen, which seemed so nice, is actually foul and making my already disturbed writing disagreeably – as opposed to codedly – illegible.

---

[1] Christopher Muttukumaru, lawyer and Secretary, Scott Enquiry.
[2] Marcus Kimball had been joint master, at varying times, of the Fitzwilliam and Cottesmore Hounds.

Albany   *Tuesday, 10 January*

Dined with Richard Ryder at the Berkeley. He told me Churchill wanted Tommy Dugdale to succeed Margesson as Chief Whip,[1] but was 'talked out of it' – who by? It's a colossal task, to complete Big Book in the two years left. Today I signed the first of the cheques for Big Red (looking identical – what's the point?) and then funked ringing Hoare's to tell them. I went back with Richard for the 10 pm vote so that his driver (Janet) could take me home. A strange, sad evocation as we passed all those cars double-parked on a wet night, for the first 3-liner of the New Year. First time I have seen them like that for over two years, must be nearer three. I feel older and sadder, and somewhat more convinced of the impossibility of return.

Saltwood   *Wednesday, 25 January*

I think I have only a very short time left to live. I am desperately worried about finishing Big Book, which could/will be so good. A possible 'researcher', Graham Stewart, came down this morning.[2] I took to him almost at once; good mind, sympathetic attitude, we think alike on the main subject. Oh so lucidly and giftedly I took the entire drive from Sellindge to Albany expounding, got quite hoarse. But made a convert I suspect.

---

[1] Captain David Margesson, very much Neville Chamberlain's man; Churchill did not trust him. Dugdale had been Stanley Baldwin's PPS.

[2] AC was looking for a researcher to help him on *The Tories*. Graham Stewart, who studied modern history at St Andrews University before going up to St John's College, Cambridge, was at work on his first book, eventually published as *Burying Caesar: Churchill, Chamberlain and the Battle for the Tory Party*.

Saltwood kitchen   *Saturday, 11 February*

How delicious is 'the quiet hour'. There are few more agreeable (intellectual) conditions than a pot of Indian tea, a nice pen (earlier I was fussed because I could only find a biro) and a blank page. I find it impossible to do this if first I sometimes glance at a newspaper, so it is critical to start before the papers can have arrived (and that is why the entries are so much smoother, and better written, in Scotland).

Tuesday, 14 February

Back from a long day (though the journey was smooth) to Coventry to Jill Phipps's funeral.[1] I had hoped for a pilgrimage, a Mecca, a mullah's funeral. But although the Cathedral was respectfully full, it was nothing like at capacity. The Sutherland altarpiece is incredible, magnificent, and one of the most impressive works of art I have ever seen. The size of Saltwood towers inner façade, perhaps even a bit under. The lady priest (deaconess?) was lovely, attractive and with a lovely clear voice, looked not unlike Presiley Baxendale. The service, with some nice blessings, none too awful in even the new English – and then an address, quite an ordeal for him, I suppose, by 'Justin' thingummy. (Jill, who clearly was attractive, was hop-picking in Kent four years ago!)

Sunday, 19 February

On Friday the little yellow cockatiel died. Poisoned by that sprouting seed-corn which I had brought in from the silage dump by the level crossing and put in their cage. She was so bonny and curious and alive. I felt awful. The grey one is going to die tonight, I know. He is just a few days behind her, being more cautious and

---

[1] Jill Phipps, thirty-one, had died after being run over by a cattle truck used to export veal calves to the Continent.

discreet. I talked to him, softly. Told him that he was going to the rainforests where there would be sunlight and warm and shoots and leaves and roots that would keep him well and happy. I am, to my surprise, even sadder about him – because it was he who found us; was frightened by the dogs and then returned, of his own accord, to the yard. Had a miserable time in a tiny cage, then came into his own in the big cage, spread his wings so beautifully at breakfast time and particularly enjoyed the apple stump with its many perches.

My tongue is sore on one side and I am tired and low.

Saltwood   *Wednesday, 22 February*

Henrietta Royle rang. Lately I have – I just don't know why – been thinking about Chelsea as being the ideal constituency.[1] Albany resident, garden parties at Saltwood, safest seat in the country, etc. She told me that they had booked the meeting for Chelsea HQ and were advertising it in the Chelsea newsletter! Suddenly I thought – could this be a sign? I know Chelsea are considering their vacancy, how far have they got? I don't want to know. All I do know is that – for all my fatigue and listlessness at intervals when surrounded (as now) by paper I am still driven. I just feel that something may happen. After speaking to Henrietta I popped over to the Great Hall and said a prayer at the long table where I composed my speech for the Sutton selection twenty-three years ago.

Senator Dole, I'm glad to see, is the leading character for the Presidential Election in two years' time and he is already 71.[2]

---

[1] Following boundary revisions Chelsea (MP – Nicholas Scott) and Kensington (MP – Dudley Fishburn) were merging to become Kensington and Chelsea. As it was a safe Conservative seat by any standards, the selection of its new candidate guaranteed a seat in the Commons at the next general election.

[2] Senator Robert Dole, Republican senator (Kansas) since 1968, had just become Leader of the United States Senate, as well as a contender for the Republican presidential nomination.

Saltwood   *EMT, Friday, 10 March*

Last night dined with Andrew Roberts[1]. Expensive flat in Cadogan
Gardens, quite nicely fitted out with lovely library shelves. The
Hamiltons (Neil)[2] – he a little pinched and nervous; she very bossy
and almost Miss Newman disapproving. That evening a somewhat
unguarded interview by Rory Knight-Bruce in the *Standard* in
which they said they were 'dining with Alan and Jane Clark'
(demi-boring for Andrew and Camilla) and Christine H then
went on to say, 'I do wish Jane Clark would do a bit more to
stick up for herself.' Andrew's neat little fiancée [Camilla] is Welsh
(it turns out) and her mother also. Attractive, both of them.
Conversation didn't quite mesh, somehow, at dinner. Disparate,
and too many guffaws. But I had a pleasing pic with Andrew in the
library afterwards. Much journalistic gossip. Not many people
seem to get more than £100 a year. A. A. Gill was mentioned.
Apparently I am being considered as literary editor of the *Sunday
Times*. Would I like this? Yes, for a five-year contract I suppose.
But Big Book must not suffer any longer.

The night before I had been to Eton. Distorted, at least in its
approaches, by traffic. And seeming much smaller, everything closer
together. The Provost, Acland,[3] was his usual diplomatic self, benign,
but reserved. The boys polite and effete. 'Thank you for being so
entertaining' said one of the wives. I was tired, and couldn't drink.
Just adequate, I hope. The names preceding me in the book were
Aitken and Jeffrey Archer! Earlier I had done a teeny home movie on
'Eton during the war', masterminded by a boy/beak team. And was
disconcerted at how thin were my memory and recollections.

---

[1] An historian whose first book, *The Holy Fox* (a life of Lord Halifax) had been
highly praised.
[2] Neil Hamilton, MP for Tatton since 1983, a junior trade minister, 1992–94, and
his wife Christine. Hamilton had issued a writ against the *Guardian*, which in
October 1994 had alleged that he (and a second Tory junior minister, Tim
Smith) had taken money to ask questions on behalf of a lobbying company.
[3] Sir Antony Acland, diplomat (head of the Diplomatic Service, 1982–86;
ambassador to Washington, 1986–91), before becoming provost of Eton in
1991.

Saltwood   *Sunday, 12 March*

Tip and Sarah went off, having bought some tropical finches at the
garden centre. Next week Sarah is going to Thailand and Oman
on her own. She is a character. They are a modern couple. While
James and Julie, really, are old-fashioned. Much more like Jane and
me.

Saltwood   *Tuesday, 21 March*

Occupied myself with an exchange of correspondence with Max
Hastings over Scott (useful to have heard from him that the Prime
Minister was trying to persuade people to accept me as a 'burnt
offering').

This morning a row with Jane at breakfast as the tablecloth had
been laid over crumbs. The one thing I can't bear are 'previous'
crumbs on a table when you sit down to a meal, even in Zermatt
this upsets me.

Albany   *Tuesday, 28 March*

Drove up in the Old Ministerial, very flat and quiet.

Walked along Whitehall, noting the new smart gates outside the
MoD, past the 'new' building entrance, an official car was coming
out of New Palace Yard.

At St Stephen's entrance I 'shot' the queue and a policeman
called out, then recognised me and was amiable. The pretty
policewoman ditto, and asked me to take my cap off. I walked
up, past the benches noting that the tiles have degenerated even
more, like the hall at Chenonceau; the first time I was in that
corridor, I suppose, was with Malcolm McCorquodale[1] – thought

---

[1] Malcolm McCorquodale (1901–1971), created baron 1955, later chairman of
McCorquodale & Co., printers, a National Conservative MP pre-war and MP
for Epsom, 1947–55.

it all so boring. It was agony. I wanted to tinkle, thought how easy it would be to dodge left into the one at the end of the Members' cloakroom – MEMBERS ONLY. Standing in the Central Lobby I watched MPs scuttling across to meet 'delegates' whom they had kept waiting – 'so sorry', 'hul-lo' etc etc. Before I turned into the gate I had briefly fantasised about slyly going in that way after winning the by-election. I was half in a dream, half awake.

Met up with Frank Pakenham, lunched with him and Fr. Seed.[1] I don't wholly dismiss all that, and will read Newman over Good Friday.

Garden House   Tuesday, 11 April

Yesterday I was frantic with frustration and pressure and then, on top of it all (sic) I was phoned to ask if I would do a leader-page piece.

'How much?' – 'Pound a word.'

I laughed. 'Not nearly enough.'

'How much do you want?' – 'Two.'

'Done.'

So all afternoon I was locked into the little white computer room. Not sure I got the tone quite right, and eleven phone calls of different kinds including a lady doing an article on mid-life crisis ('I've been enjoying one for the last 40 years,' I said). So I was an hour late filing, and walked out of here leaving the French windows open all night.

All based on my brief crack on the *Today* programme. *Today* is like *Breakfast with Frost* – everyone listens to it. I said that whether a government of celibates and train-spotters would be any different from what we've got . . . I didn't know.

In the meantime Jonathan Aitken went demi bonkers and

---

[1] Frank Pakenham, former Labour minister, in his ninetieth year, who succeeded his brother as 7th Earl of Longford in 1961. Father Michael Seed, Roman Catholic priest, credited with a number of high-profile conversions to the Catholic faith.

staged a press conference in Central Office.[1] Certain fatal (*Hello*-type) cliché 'the fight back starts here . . .' etc.

On the 'early evening news' I saw that Senator Dole had got the Republican nomination – at the age of 71. This cheered me up immensely. A classic example of ACHAB. All (sic) I need is, somehow, to get back into the Commons. The Lords I'm no longer really bothered about.

Easter Monday, 17 April

How I long for solitude and tranquillity! This must be one of the most pressured Easters ever – and yet I am 67 and 'retired'.

We did the whole lawn yesterday. Tomorrow night I set off for Eriboll with sundries in the Discovery (sit-down mower, enamel sign, iron chandeliers for the chapel, etc) on probably the last Motorail journey ever.[2]

Monday, 24 April

How am I ever going to get out of this?

I can buy 'space' I suppose, by letting the Degas[3] go. But as I said to Jane late afternoon it's really Saltwood – the whole ethos of the great curtained room almost unchanged into which I can wander, and reflect, go back 20–30–40 years and play the piano. I have never left the Music Room without feeling stronger. And

---

[1] Jonathan Aitken was yet another Conservative involved in 'sleaze' allegations. He was suing the *Guardian* for defamation over their allegation of improper commercial relationships while Minister for Defence Procurement. His statement included a phrase which would enter modern dictionaries of quotations: 'If it falls to me to start a fight to cut out the cancer of bent and twisted journalism in our country with the simple sword of truth and the trusty shield of British fair play, so be it. I am ready for the fight. The fight against falsehood and those who peddle it. My fight begins today.'

[2] The Motorail service from London to Inverness was being withdrawn.

[3] *Femme s'épongeant le dos.*

I remember the pain of selling the bronze (so fortunately re-captured).[1]

EMT, Tuesday, 25 April

I am most heavy-hearted at losing the Degas. Go up and look at her often, at different times of the day – and last evening sat there, on the facing sofa for quite a while talking to Jane. Jane is 'definitely uneasy' about it. But is it not the practical solution? We can't really 'freeze' everything – Mask, Zurbaran, Moores[2] (cars, 'C' and Big Red etc etc). That would be so unbalanced. And to make up the cash from lesser items would involve 'stripping' (which both boys have objected to and warned against) to a far greater degree. But now, just as I notice and remember the hip of the dancer only in Crowe's office, I notice so many extra colours in the whole picture, that reddish around the basin; shadow on towel?

Sunday, 30 April

Yesterday it was pressure, pressure. Finishing the 'piece' (not a very successful one on Ashdown) and clearing up for the Americans (coming today) and 'Little' and – 'Littler' – his partner.[3] They'd hardly been in the place five minutes before I wanted to say to Jane 'these guys are just a couple of bull-shitters'. 'Little' probed me about the Degas, which I had originally mentioned no more than in passing as the reason for trying to sell the 'Coptic stuff'.[4] He said he could get his 'big client' straight on to the case, wouldn't hesitate. Lyingly said I had been guaranteed £800, wouldn't, couldn't deal under 1.5. They prowled about, 'Littler' peering at

---

[1] The dancer bronze (also by Degas) was sold and then bought back.
[2] Kenneth Clark and Henry Moore were friends, and the Clarks had a number of Moore's works.
[3] Two London dealers.
[4] Framed tapestry fragments.

everything – Burne-Jones Angel, 'torchères' in the Great Hall
(known fakes) up a ladder to look at the Alexander the Great
tapestry etc. Afterwards there was a long courtesy recital of
travellers tales ('3-card trick', as Jane pleasingly called them), half
Jewish, half just straight Mews.

Saffria, 'Charles Cates' (who he?), Lord Wimborne, of getting . . . 'my big client' Saffria again (who strangely put 'Little's'
back up by walking into the showroom and saying to 'Littler', 'I
like you, we can work together'). 'I can think of worse things he
might have said,' I suggested and Jane giggled, but they didn't.
This went on for too long and was too circular. A cursory look at
the carpets, clearly they didn't want them. 'A rug like this, Alan,
would be 70–90–100 if it was in good condition.' 'Surely in this
condition it would be 35 then?' I wanted to say, but didn't. Off
they drove. Later the phone started ringing. We had been working
all afternoon in the Great Hall and were exhaustedly lying low in
the Green Room, left it to the machine. Hung up a few times then
finally 'Little' soft-spoken with a message to ring a number (which
I had already checked out on 1471). His 'client' – I can't believe
this – is ready to buy the picture unseen. But was it in the book?
Jane and I had a long, but unsuccessful time, rooting about in the
library and various sources of books including the package I
removed from the Garden House. Never mind, an 'Art Critic'
called Sylvester (never heard of him)[1] was coming down *today* at 2
pm – naturally coinciding with the US visit – to look at it. Nothing
will come of this, because he will spot the two worm holes, and all
rich people bother about is 'condition'. But all quite fun.

Saltwood   *EMT, Friday, 5 May*

I walked to the Beefsteak, sat next to little Hague.[2] Cagey, like
all people who have a great future ahead of them . . . Mark

---

[1] The art interests of AC and David Sylvester obviously didn't coincide. Sylvester's expertise included Moore, Magritte, Bacon, Spencer and Giacometti.
[2] William Hague, MP for Richmond, Yorks, since February 1989; social security
and disabled people minister since 1994.

Lennox-Boyd came round at the end of the meal and said that 'Alison Young' was working for him.

I sit here, on a lovely fine still May morning; but I funk ringing Henrietta Royle and asking if Chelsea has yet 'chosen'.

The carpetsellers, after much phoned bull-shitting put in a pointless demand – for the Christie's guarantee – the 'client' obviously thrashing around for a way out. I said piss off and Christie's, a week later, are collecting it. But at least we are through the psychological hurdle of selling it and Jane has made that incredible, inspired copy.[1] I will now attempt to force the pace and continue with cash-raising: Broomhayes, R Cont, SS100, possibly Zurbaran for $1m with Feigin.[2]

Garden House   *Monday, 8 May*

Frightfully tired and glazed. Almost last engagement this evening – colossal longueurs at the Savoy for the AT&T book award. That £5000 fee, which looked so tempting has actually worked out at about £20 per hour – less than a 'daily' in a posh bit of Hampstead what with reading 150 books, four judges' meetings, general hassle and a 5-hour award ceremony.[3]

Thursday, 1 June

Ted Heath spoke in the Bosnia debate last night. His voice now rich (I said). Jane: 'no, it's gone.' Voice timbre is so indicative. My own is at its peak; will decline, I suppose in my seventies. Seventy-five is when it goes off, the last thing really except for sight.

---

[1] Jane Clark, an accomplished painter, had never previously worked in pastels. She measured the picture, studied what she thought it might have been painted on, selected the nearest (some brown laundry paper), and set to work. Looking back, she says she was inspired. Her reproduction has fooled experts. She did, though, refuse to replicate Degas's signature. AC marvelled at what Jane had done: 'her brilliant, spooky translation' (27 May 1995); 'Jane's miraculous substitution' (19 September 1995).

[2] An American art dealer and friend, Richard Feigin.

[3] The £25,000 award went to Mark Hudson for *Coming Back Brockens*.

MFS, Great Hall   *Wednesday, 7 June*

On 27 May (less than two weeks ago) I said that I needed a sign.
Three days later, or so, Nick Scott 'crushed' a pushchair when
reversing his car after a 'party' in his constituency, then shambled
off 'to a friend's house', but was pursued, breathalysed positive, and
arrested.[1]

Well, of course, for some reason (I forget its origins), perhaps
the Henrietta Royle initiative, the agent's own invitation to speak
next Monday at their 'garden party', I have had my eye on Chelsea
for these last months.

Took a cab, to Chelsea, ostensibly (sic) to talk to the agent
about arrangements for Monday. On the way the cabman – who
had shown no sign of recognition – chatted.

Self: 'Fucking King's Road always blocked; half these fucking
people ought to be at work' etc.

He got going on the Tory Party: 'John Major all right, but what
he wants is a bit of panache (pronounced 'panarsh'). No style, too
apologetic' etc etc.

'Well,' I said, 'who do you fancy?'

'Do you really want me to tell you?'

'Yes.'

'I'm a bit embarrassed . . .'

'Oh, really? Go on.'

'You.'

It was a real sign. He was serious and I was serious.

I spoke to Tip on the phone this morning.[2] He was serious,
said huge numbers wanted me, 'scaffolders etc, as well as upper
classes'.[3]

---

[1] Nicholas Scott's career in government had culminated in seven years as Minister
of State at DHSS (latterly Social Services). The episode AC refers to led to a
series of cliff-hanging reselection and selection processes in Chelsea over the next
eighteen months.

[2] Andrew and Sarah Clark were living in the constituency.

[3] Elsewhere AC recorded a constituency bigwig asking, 'Where is the Well-
ington?' AC mused, 'Something in his manner made me think he wanted me to
say, "it's me"; or he wanted to say, "why don't you do it?" I didn't answer.'

MFS, GL   *Saturday, 24 June*

How I love Saltwood – for all its pressures and 'claims'. After EMT
I went into the front part to wind the clocks. It is peaceful there
and still quite timeless. I wonder how long the boys will maintain
it, and felt a pang (I am getting these more often lately) at not being
able to see my grandchildren.

Here I am using, in my father's old study, the far side of the
Great Library, the only remotely clear flat surface in the entire
complex, and the great Adam long-case clock ticks readily (one per
second) as the jackdaws chatter busily and unbeknownst outside
the windows.

Really my diary is my only true solace.

I am wrecked, *wrecked* by my impotence at the turn of events.

John Major has offered himself for re-election,[1] and the television shows the blue door (another blue door this time in Cowley
Street) of his headquarters, people scuttling in and out. But somehow, transposed 1939 to an old 1918 shot.

Yesterday I went to Gordon Greig's funeral. Sensibly choosing
Big Red at the last moment so that I was 'on the phone'. Jane rang
to say Douglas Hurd had resigned![2]

MFS GH   *Tuesday, 27 June*

I swam a couple of lengths in the pool now only one week full but
67°. At such a time, and in this season, the pool at Saltwood is 'one
of the loveliest places in the whole world'.

---

[1] John Major resigned the leadership of the Conservative Party, immediately
offering himself for re-election. This was his offensive against what he called 'a
small minority in our Party' who opposed him, undermining the government
and damaging the Conservative Party. 'I am not prepared to see the Party I care
for laid out on the rack like this any longer.' John Redwood immediately
resigned from the government and announced that he would also be a candidate.

[2] Douglas Hurd, foreign secretary since 1989, had told John Major some time
before of his intention to retire at the next reshuffle; he had turned sixty-five in
March.

The previous night I had dined with Gill Shephard at Wilton's. To my surprise she had accepted at three hours notice on a phone call from Saltwood. I was worried about the whole party going into meltdown. I can't believe that Heseltine would get it by default – but to be sure of that there must be someone from the centre-right to come through. And, as I have often said (including to her) I think Gill is that person. She is keen, did some – but not too much – personal boosting. Expressed her irritation with the chaps' atmosphere at Major's headquarters and when I raised the question of who might inherit his organisation if it went to a second round said she thought it could be Ian Lang.[1] She is a tiny bit too short. Has lots in reserve and I think would be good against Blair in an election.

Saltwood Tower office   *Sunday, 2 July*

A great psychological cloud lifted by letting the Degas go at 515 so can now (a) keep Big Red, which Jane really likes, and (b) set about Trusts.

Shore Cottage   *Wednesday, 23 August*

On Sunday we had left Saltwood at 3.30 am – bathing before, on Jane's initiative, and I had *(for the first time)* a wonderful and perhaps never-to-be-repeated experience – swimming on my back, frog-legged, and looking up at the stars.

Slept again for eleven hours; woke with slight sinus headache, still v feeble.

I suppose if one did this for 2½ weeks – no alcohol and 'rest' alternated with writing and physical – one should show results. 'Feeling' better though comes before improvement in appearance. It takes longer – three months rather than three weeks – to reduce sacs of fluid and build up muscle tone. I should be encouraged by

---

[1] Ian Lang, Scottish secretary since 1990.

Tom, who is now 115 and his back legs cause him to stumble quite a bit – he fell into the burn yesterday after failing to recover from rolling in something – then he goes up and down the banks sorting out the burrows and led the way along the shoreline to the 'Great Burrows' before turning and separating from me to return to the croft. This morning he did a most wonderful prancing leap over a broken rung in the footbridge. As so often in the first days here I simply let my mind stray, I don't look at the papers, we have no radio and I don't rootle in my briefcase. It is all I can do to send postcards.

Saltwood   *Wednesday, 27 September*

What should have been a delicious *désoeuvré* day, free of obligation, and with choice, soon evaporated. On came that tricky little prick Sebastian Shakespeare.[1]

'Always a pleasure to talk to you.'

'You may not think so this time . . .'

Asked me about putting in for Chelsea; I referred him to the agent. 'People are saying you wrote your CV on House of Commons notepaper' (Gaaah!) I explain I'd paid to print it myself. But what a lesson in how everyone is just waiting to fault-find. Whispering he mentioned something about the 'Matrix Churchill scandal'. Silly little runt.

Saltwood kitchen   *Friday, 29 September*

Still very unsettled. My jaws ache (both sides) and I have split a back molar on the right due to avoiding (funking) Bertie Arbeid[2] for the last three weeks. Naturally he's away until next week.

Quite a friendly piece in today's *Independent*: '. . . allowed his name to go forward.' That's more like it – just the phrase. So far

---

[1] Sebastian Shakespeare, editor of Londoner's Diary in the *Evening Standard*.

[2] The Clark's dentist.

I'm managing to keep this out of Jane's notice, as it's still 50:50 that nothing at all will come of it. Alastair Stewart[1] wants me on Sky TV – but I'm not so sure that's wise at the moment.

What is really irritating – but totally 'serves-you-right, Alan' – is that – muddled and fatigued – I refused Carla [Powell]'s dinner for Jimmy [Goldsmith] last night; all she could say is that Redwood and Jonathan A were going to be there. I didn't specially want to see Redwood who I think slightly loopy.

But now it turns out to have been a really interesting conclave. Conrad Black, David Frost, Alexander Hesketh, John Patten, Evelyn de Rothschild[2] and many others (including Jonathan A). I could have made a real contribution. Then today, pm Jonathan H[olborrow] rang softspoken. Stewart Steven[3] has resigned from the *Standard* and Max [Hastings] (of all people) has taken over. Key question, therefore, who is going to get the *Telegraph*? Jonathan wanted me to approach Conrad. I couldn't, left a message, but hasn't called back. If I'd been at the dinner last night it would have been so much easier. Why did I duck it?[4]

Saltwood   *Saturday, 30 September*

Very heavy-hearted now that I know I'm (barring a *total* miracle) finished. I think all my 'public speaking', TV, column, phoning, lunching and dining with colleagues – Portillo, Gill Shephard, M Howard, the rest – has been in the context of assuming/hoping/fantasising that somwhere somehow I would be offered the choice of a constituency and a return.

Up through the members' cloakroom, the big staircase (or the little front one by the loo) along the corridor, past the big octagonal writing table in a bay window and into the Members'

---

[1] Alastair Stewart, newscaster and TV presenter previously with ITN.

[2] Evelyn de Rothschild, chairman, N. M. Rothschild & Sons Ltd.

[3] Stewart Steven, editor of the *Evening Standard* since 1992, *Mail on Sunday*, 1982–92.

[4] Charles Moore (*Sunday Telegraph*) succeeded Hastings; Dominic Lawson, editor of *The Spectator* since 1990, succeeded Moore.

Lobby – through the door that only Members can use, so that as
they swish open any waiting journalist will know that only an MP
can be coming through. Then a glance at the telephone message
board perhaps a 'badge-messenger' (handsome in their white ties
and tailcoats) will spot me and shout 'Mr Clark' and bring a letter
from the message board on the other side. Perhaps look into the
Chamber, see what's up, how full it is; stand 'at the bar' for a
minute or two. Then down the tearoom corridor looking in there,
or on into the library; drift up past colleagues busy at the various
desks – Nick Budgen, Enoch always in his traditional place (last
time I was there) and on to the No-Smoking and the Silence room
(where if people talk too loudly you can call out 'ORDER') and
slump in a chair there to read the *Spectator*, or something more
esoteric.

Yes, all that still mesmerises me and for three years I used to
dream about it, half certain that I would return. But now that
Chelsea (which, somehow, so much seemed pre-ordained – the
speaking invite, Nick's accident, the audience reaction etc) won't
even see me, I realise that, in fact, it is hopeless.

Saltwood   *Tuesday, 3 October*

Went over to Garden House. My phone had twelve messages on it
– goodness knows when it was last cleared. Among them a perky-
sounding Barbara Lord. With thudding heart I returned the call
(perhaps mistakenly starting by saying '. . . I assume it's bad'). But
no, she was just apologising for the piece in the *Standard*. We had an
amiable conversation getting down to twenty before Conference –
interviews afterwards. I felt wonderful – lifted. But now as I write
this I fear it means that 'notices' will go out before Conference and
so if I'm not in the twenty I will be thoroughly out of sorts (again). I
went to the Great Hall (by chance as I left the light on there) and sat
at the long table. God told me to ask for serenity and balance. If I
didn't make it – well, decks are clear. Because contemplating being
back in, delightful though it is, consider the implication of enchain-
ment until old age or death. In spite of everything I said, I will

become a buffer – or quasi-buffer – in harness. Easier to commute to Saltwood, of course. And I know how to 'swing the lead'. But I would be turning my back on will-we-ever?

MFS GH   *Thursday, 5 October*

I was all day at P. & A. Wood having the new steering wheel fitted to 'Big Red'. What a luxury! Raises it to the level, almost, of 'the ultimate driving experience'.

This evening I pottered over here because the Executive is sitting in Chelsea deliberating the twenty. Am I, actually, a 'front runner' – *passim The Independent* – or is the whole thing ridiculous? I prayed at the long table. And drew some strength from the fact that it may not have been a bad idea to 'stand down'in '92. Because in the last three years I have become a FP – my status may work in my favour; may not. But it helps me to become philosophical. If I lose at Chelsea then I will become a sage.

Monday, 16 October

Yesterday, another bullish signal. I rang the Kensington-Chelsea paper to find out about back issues, giving my name. 'Oh, uh, Alan Clark? . . . You're going to be the next MP for Kensington and Chelsea.' This from the News Editor herself! Greatly boosted I started putting my speech into shape, and running it through the tape recorder. A useful trial – as seemed far too slow at first. I can't decide whether to use the jokey opening or not. But there is no doubt that the Scott extract works.

Sunday, 22 October

After return from the selection committee.

A curious experience – seemed to go well; almost too well? Barbara Lord said to me, on the way out, 'you were marvellous.'

But then went on to say, 'I think . . . [hesitation] what will tell against you is your age . . . If they do decide to replace Nick it will be with someone much younger . . .' I was bland and understanding, though hiding it. 'But . . . who can tell?' she added. Did she mean *on the night*, or 'today'? The nice fat girl who gave me a map of the constituency said the calls would go out 'about 5.30' which is what it is now.

I ought to welcome release. Three and a half years later. But I am really tense (this morning in Albany mirror I had 'stress stripes') which means the let-down will be dreadful. So many signs were good, all the way through.[1] *Waiting for the phone.* One of the great ordeals of modern politics.

Great Hall, Saltwood   *Monday, 23 October*

I suppose that I knew last night by 7 o'clock that it was over – for certain by 8 pm when I went sadly through to the kitchen. Nothing this morning save some probing gloats from the *Standard* and the *Independent*.

Only consolation is that Franko is back as Editor of the *Spectator.*[2]

Saturday, 4 November

An interesting lunch with Phil Hall.[3] Pleasant, but *naïf*. Needs me on the paper to advise and consult about politics, write leaders at intervals . . . Rupert[4] himself is putting the pressure on. Jane is totally opposed (but I have fixed her reward). Alastair said 'grab it'.

---

[1] In a brief diary note on 19 August following 'a trail in Black Dog (*Mail on Sunday*)' about the Kensington and Chelsea selection process, AC remarked, 'all the angst, tension and (probably in the end) humiliation'.

[2] Frank Johnson succeeded Dominic Lawson, who had been editor of *The Spectator* since 1990, with Lawson becoming editor of the *Sunday Telegraph*, where Johnson had been deputy editor.

[3] Phil Hall, newly appointed editor of the *News of the World*.

[4] Rupert Murdoch, the owner of the *News of the World* through his company News International.

Jonathan Holborrow I am dining with on Tuesday. I hope he doesn't offer a lot more money (Phil has already gone to 125) as I think I am better 'standing back' from that anyway. But he won't be pleased.

Wednesday, 8 November

Dined (modest dinner) with Jonathan Holborrow at Wilton's. He is keen for me to stay at M o S, is 'reorganising the paper round you, Alan . . .' Has said he will be faxing his 'offer' today. We got on well; my only slip-up, when setting out the 'generous' terms which Rupert (alias Phil H) was offering, was when J said, 'He's not offering you a seat on the main board . . . ?' 'Oh, no, I wouldn't want that.' Perhaps that was what J was going to work up to?

It is a difficult decision. Associated are (marginally) more congenial to work with − but I don't see how they can match Phil's 125 (+25).

EMT   *Friday, 10 November*

Last night was the Chelsea selection. Am I strong enough to recognise that this has to mean the '. . . end of that particular road' − *passim* Ted Heath at the Party Conference?

Saltwood   *Saturday, 16 December*

Jane is happily whistling and singing in the hall doing Christmas greenery. She really loves Christmas; and I am such an old Scrooge and wet blanket. Twice in the last two days to Canterbury, and everyone so busily bustling and rich. Coats' are going down which always puts me out of sorts.

The vein across my hand (particularly left hand) is permanently bluely raised − as I used when a child to notice in people of '60' (ie old people). My face has become so crumpled and jowly that it is irreparably downgraded. Still more muscle tone lost.

Saltwood   *Sunday, 17 December*

Helped Jane erect the (lovely and big) tree on an empty stomach. I had felt awful on waking – stiff, tired, de-energised – and was in the 'siren suit' over my pyjamas. Then I drove off in the green Continental to post some last-minute cards and collect a *N o W*. Tom had escaped (through a gap in the 'Roman' wall, involving a long glissade the other side – how's that for activity at age 17, '119 human'?). Walked over to the farm, collected him from Ann.

Darling Jane was decorating the tree. The lights were fixed and I – 'watchman', most ceremoniously – lit them. Lovely. But the whole thing so *hollow* somehow. How many are we going to be? Four; five with Julie's mother. Later we looked through the window and it looked so lovely 'Why aren't there children scampering about?' I asked sadly. I will never live to see my grandchildren marry. And what worries me is that I will now be old; shaky and selfish, when they have difficult passages between the ages of 9 and 18. Sex, drugs, shocks and bikes. Later we watched that (excellent) film on the Labour Party. Poor Kinnock – too much himself. Fatal in politics. Lessons, most of them melancholy, for the Tory Party in its present condition.

Saltwood   *Saturday, 23 December*

One pleasing thing has happened. The Yeats 'Rose in a Basin' has actually come back here (cum expenditure of some £21,000 in legal and sundry expenses).[1] I never really thought that would happen. Now, of course, I look at it more closely just as I did those Yeatses in the room at the National Gallery in Dublin (incredible, so strong). Interesting, and satis because yah-hoo to 'McCann' (the thief) and his solicitors Stephens Innocent (sic).

---

[1] The picture, by Jack Yeats, had been stolen from AC's stepmother, and turned up in Ireland.

1996

It is only a week since I started on the Winstons.[1] But the tendrils had been moving below the surface for so long . . . (no, a poor analogy; I should say the material was all tinder-dry in my brain so the fire spread at colossal speed). And have done sixteen pages plus, in spite of being up in London on Thursday.

Big Red up and down. What a magnificent vehicle it is. Virtually no fatigue factor. Every mile a pleasure, and comfortable-in-the-knowledge-that . . . but cars are going to have to be sold. It's very sad, but at least 300-worth needed really.

I have one more year of this high earnings – from which no savings will be makeable, all directed to debt and taxes.

I must try and get Zermatt sorted out this year, too – and that requires a substantial sum (preferably in US $) on deposit and a kind of treuhand [trust].

James reported that Andrew – who has already claimed Broom-hayes much to the indignation of the other couple – is complaining about my affairs in disorder. What happens when Daddy dies? . . . etc. (This must be the first time the young adults are starting to worry along the same lines as I used to.)

I was planning really to devote myself to the Winston this year. A long haul. Fired by progress I talked to Ion about length. We agreed at 450pp. That's 40 pages a month (allowing for holidays and wastage) or 10 per week. At this rate I'm ok, just. But plainly it is unsustainable. The timing is going to be perfect – for Tory conference 1997. But I'm sure others will be doing the same thing. 'Spoiler' operations.

Last night I had a talk with Tony Benn.[2] He was the only person

---

[1] One of AC's many names for what would become *The Tories*.

[2] Tony Benn, devoted MP for Chesterfield since March 1984 (Bristol SE, November 1950–60; August 1963–83), a radical, a parliamentarian, a diarist and a minister in the Wilson and Callaghan Labour governments (including Postmaster-General, Industry and Energy).

even half-right on the subject of North Sea oil. And how fascinating he is to talk to! His mind so quick and versatile – but the
loony prejudice (and this of course the motivation that keeps him
active) never far below the surface. 'We want an Asia economy so
as to be like Singapore – with its penal code' etc.

Politics still consumes and fascinates me. But I am conscious of
being a little slower (at last). Somehow I can't always remember a
name.

Kundan   *Thursday, 11 January*

Up in London – goodness knows I did not want to leave the Mains
this morning. On a (virtually) empty stomach spent 2½ hours with
mustard keen Mark Fulbrooks of Parliamentary Services, preparing
my CV.[1] And my gosh he knows his onions.

And although I thought for the first time, I am too old for this,
I've lost it. I don't want to get on a constituency interview list. The
last time I have really experienced this sensation, all at once
anyway.

But after Jon Snow – Channel 4 News (watching The Lady's
'domestic' speech) then being door-stepped by the little untidy-
haired but lively BBC *Breakfast News* interviewer *I smelt powder and
flint*. The special exultation, a version of which I felt after the first
friendly/apologetic call from Barbara Lord at Chelsea. I am good
on TV. So important. Who knows?

Saltwood   *Friday, 12 January*

Got back this morning, picking up a thin and unappetising-looking
mail. Opened a letter stating something-something Sevenoaks Conservative Association. Almost before I got to the end of the paragraph
I skimmed ahead, as it were, simultaneously to an invitation to 'put

---

[1] AC had been advised that a professionally massaged CV would help in his quest
for a parliamentary seat.

my name forward' (!!!). And from a vice-president association treasurer for five years: 'I write in my personal capacity, but feel I am confident I have the support of many of my colleagues.'

So in a state of total euphoria. Second, really, only to Chelsea from the point of view of convenience.

A new roll has started. How lovely life is, and thanks be to God.

Saltwood   *Wednesday, 31 January*

After cup of tea at Albany went round to No 10. JM came to fetch me from the little reading room – so boyish and jokey. Really immensely attractive and in good form. He has had a magnificent weekend[1] and is buoyed up by it. 'I'm beginning to think you might make it,' I said. Delighted, he agreed.

Saltwood   *Friday, 9 February*

Nothing like the peace of mind after 'filing'. I have now really got into the hang of the *N o W* column. Although this evening, just as I was talking to Bob Warren[2] – very surprising cultivated 'suit' – he said a huge bomb had gone off in Canary Wharf.[3] And now the IRA has declared an end to the ceasefire. (So I have to rewrite something for it.)

Do I really want to 'put in a bid' (*passim* the Italian newsagent at Sevenoaks) for the various seats, Guildford, Arundel? It really is going backwards – and Simon Hoggart's interesting article – on the barrenness of the chamber was off-putting and sad. No more F. E. Smith and Baldwin.

---

[1] The PM had given an upbeat interview to the *Sunday Telegraph* that weekend, which concluded, 'I like elections, and clearly we are within fifteen months of an election, so I am beginning to sniff the wind and feeling much happier about it.' AC had an audience with the prime minister to mark the start of his column in the *News of the World*.

[2] Bob Warren, of the *News of the World*.

[3] The IRA ended eighteen months' ceasefire by trying to destroy the new symbol of a resurgent Docklands; two people were killed.

EMT   *Thursday, 15 February*

Two punches landed yesterday. Clydesdale suddenly wanted their
money back – 45 – all of it, at once. And Coutts wrote to say o/d is
just over 60 (how *can* it be? I nearly always keep rough tallies in my
head and thought it was about 35–40 at most). Rattled by Scott
build-up[1] (some stupid Scotch wanker rang last night about the
Al Habobi missile 'when you were defence minister'. 'When was
that?' 'In 1986.' 'I didn't go to MoD until 1989.' Curiously rang
off at once).

Later
Strange how one can feel better – more confident, ready for
adversity and exploitation (should read 'opportunity', but exploitation sounds better, no double '-ty') after three cups of EMT.
Caffeine is a stimulant, alcohol a depressant, isn't it?

Le Bourget   *Friday, 16 February*

In the (chocolate and cream painted) 757.[2] Not very imaginatively
fitted out. Rather Arab with the seating arranged in grouplets – no
private snuggery, but the loos are sumptuous. A taxi-driver had, or
so he claimed, waited for three hours, took me to Le Bourget. Still
cost £20. Now a long flight in prospect.

Jimmy is being charming to me. Speaks brilliantly on USA (high
opinion of Pat Buchanan,[3] naturally) and French campaign of
Michel Noir[4] now finally in total trouble – 'a write-off'.

---

[1] Sir Richard Scott's report was due to be published that day.
[2] The private jet owned by James Goldsmith. AC joined a house party put
together by Goldsmith for a few days at Cuixmala, his estate in Mexico.
[3] Pat Buchanan, right-wing Republican, aiming to get his party's nomination for
the next US presidential election.
[4] Michel Noir, former mayor of Lyon, who had been supported by Goldsmith in
his attempt to become French president.

Cuixmala   *Saturday, 17 February*

4.0 pm English time. It is 9.10 am here? I'm muddled. But slept
well and had a delicious Cuixmala breakfast.

I just so wish Janey was here. There is cloud, patchy, and the sea
is less angry. A breeze, humid and gentle refreshes. I contemplate
the rough, almost Cornish, coastline of the eastern Pacific sea-
board; with reddish rock outcrops sparsely covered in vegetation
and breakers foamily dousing them.

I am already feeling better. Although still worried-ish about sexual
mechanism, problems building up in UK (are papers bothering
Jane?[1]) and certain sign of age – particularly random memory failure.

We talked about Aspers (has got leukaemia, but 'under control'.
Had a dreadful abscess in his mouth necessitating a double operation
as 'they left some tools in' – eh? Uh?). Politics: Jimmy told me, most
relevantly to the work I am reading up at present on the two '74
elections, that Heath had sent him out to Brussels to inquire of
Christopher Soames what he wanted as price of desisting – apparently
he was in cahoots with Peter Carrington – from furthering their plot
to deseat Ted (illustrating, but I must look this up in Campbell's
biography,[2] Ted's obsession with 'heavyweights' – just like JM's
notorious phrase 'we've had a very good Cabinet' – and ignoring the
electorate, in this case the parliamentary party). Soames said he would
lay off if he got the Foreign Office in the next government. But there
wasn't going to be (this was between the two elections) 'a next
government'. Presumably he was talking about the 'Cabinet of
distinguished people of good will outside party politics'. When I
pointed this out to Jimmy he said – old Mexican political adage – 'in
politics assurances only bind those who receive them'.[3]

---

[1] There was a huge row over the government's handling of the Scott report, but
AC was exonerated.

[2] John Campbell, *Edward Heath: A Biography*, 1992.

[3] AC researched this account further. It was not quite as Goldsmith related in
Cuixmala. In 1974, Jimmy, whose father had been a Tory MP, was already rich
and, wishing to make 'rapid ascent within the Conservative Party', he joined, on
an unpaid basis, the Conservative Research Department, where he came to
Heath's notice. Heath used him as his emissary to Soames.

In the night I was gloomy. I thought, what, at all, has been achieved in the two years since we were last here? A high profile, but even that seems to be going off a bit. How right I was not to do or say anything pre- or post-Scott.

Bernard [a French guest] said – when Jimmy was trying to explain the 'scandal' – 'I hope you made a lot of *monnaie* . . .'

Jimmy, like me, sometimes looks like my father in his stooping movements and expression. Last night he escorted us to the villino, and I was worried by how old and shuffly he looked.

At breakfast he said he kept no papers – none. Because anyone in the USA can sue you, and hard disks are impossible to wipe.

Cuixmala   *Wednesday, 21 February*

Happy to be going back. I have missed BLJ so many times. Not specially worried about the flight – only it is always disagreeable suddenly waking from a catnap and realising one is over the Pole. Also I don't like all those people in the back of the plane spewing germs into the system.

I am returning (barring major and specific crises) to press attacks,[1] financial pressures, correspondence (even five days) backlog. Funny about James, Andrew, why no grandchildren? Humiliation at Sevenoaks. Days just being frittered, however good one's intentions may be. Breakdown of discipline. And until one masters discipline nothing will ever happen.

Jimmy meanwhile is recovered from his brief malaise (he is congenitally manic). He bubbled with enthusiasm. I note that he does sometimes forget the place in mid sentence, almost Hiram-like.[2] On Monday, just before lunch and down by the pool he suddenly said, 'What's the time?' 'Five to one.' 'I must go and have an insulin injection.' He walked round to the car park, went up in one of the FWDs; I'm lucky not to be *on* anything.

---

[1] The aftermath of the Scott report.
[2] Hiram Winterbotham, a mentor of AC who taught him to drive. A specialist in Georgian domestic architecture, he was a friend of Kenneth Clark and responsible for AC becoming a governor of St Thomas's Hospital in 1969.

EMT   *Tuesday, 27 February*

Jane said she is still stressed, couldn't get to her studio. I pointed
out that at least the Webbs[1] were now installed and the dogs had
taken to them. She said it was because I wasn't working on Big
Book. Quite right. I did eleven letters yesterday, all ullage, and easy
for any competent secretary. Another sixty to do.

Later

I am in strange, if not 'poor' shape. I walked the Giorgione,[2] half
draped in a suit bag, half wrapped in bubble-plastic, to Emily Black
at Sotheby's. She is very pretty, with grey eyes. Unimpressed, 'too
badly damaged', N. Italian, 'Putto with apples.' 'Really not worth
very much at all.'

'It's a matter of complete indifference to me what valuation you
put on it,' I smiled.

'£4–600.'

When I told her, she (actually claiming to know Jaynie Anderson[3]) held her ground. 'How do you know?' etc.

Next I went to Christie's. Here it looked better propped up on a
chair. Unfortunately the atmosphere was slightly rarefied by the
receptionist recognising me and calling me 'Lord Clark'. So when
Ben whatisname looked at it he realised 'there is something important here'. Thrashed about, though getting that it was a fresco
transferred to canvas, and declared it at £2000. I tried to get Charlie
H[4] down to look at it, but he was tied up in a mega-deal.

---

[1] Lynn Webb, who became housekeeper at Saltwood, and her husband Ken.

[2] *Cupid in the Guise of an Angel*, a fresco fragment acquired by Kenneth Clark from
the Ruskin picture collection in 1931. He identified it as by the Renaissance
artist Giorgione, from the Fondaco dei Tedeschi, the German customs house in
Venice. AC had even attempted some restoration on it in 1972 and, as a result,
his father observed in a letter, 'a certain amount of it has come away. But there is
still enough to be of considerable interest'.

[3] Jaynie Anderson, art historian, who was writing the *catalogue raisonnée* on
Giorgione (not published until 1997).

[4] Charles Allsopp, chairman of Christie's since 1986, had become the 6th Lord
Hindlip in 1993.

I came back to Albany. Drank five cups of tea, etc, Danish pastry and fell (deeply) asleep. Woke up not knowing where I was, hyper-chesty and with a pulse-rate of 82. Found a thermometer, but only 97°. Strange. I cancelled any thought of going to Pratt's.

EMT   *Wednesday, 6 March*

When I wake I groan with the sheer – self-inflicted – pain of how I am expending my time.

Yesterday I went over to Sevenoaks. The agent Ann Barrow dark, pale, unmade-up, in black, was pleasant, mildly cynical sense of humour, seen-it-all.

There were two members of the selection committee there fussing about with papers. Each, outwardly amiable (-ish), plainly were working their own schemes. She took me through the set questions. All matters of policy – concerning which, of course, I am completely ignorant. Also a good, not very encouraging and hard to memorise rundown of the wards. After a bit I just felt terribly tired and hopeless. Thoughtfully I drove back to Saltwood (after contemplating going straight on up to Smith Square to collect the briefings).

I rang the Research Department of CCO. A pleasant-voiced, but coolish young secretary would make no promises. I faxed a set of headings. I will drive up (in the Discovery of course) this morning to get to CCO at 11, then down to Sevenoaks to talk to the chief reporter of the *Chronicle*. This individual, like all provincial journalists, totally clueless about politics, very hack – asked what I was 'doing' now and then, 'I hope you don't mind my asking this – how old are you?'

As I said 67 it kind of came through to me how ludicrous this whole thing is. And yet Bob Dole (now doing well), Ross Perot[1] and the 'entire Chinese Cabinet'.

---

[1] Ross Perot, wealthy Texan businessman (born 1930) who ran as an Independent in the US presidential elections, 1992 and 1996.

EMT   *Wednesday, 13 March*

A 'full' day yesterday, but not wholly satisfying. Up to London by train (incredibly cold, knife-like, wind) and walked along the Strand – very much against the tide of pinched bustling office workers – to the Temple to hear Richard Scott on Matrix Churchill.[1] He is a splendid man – cool, clear-headed and witty. He was interesting – it was by and for lawyers – on case law. Lambasted discreetly Tristan Garel-Jones[2] and the whole deception of the 'response' document in the House of Commons Library.

(On the way back I glanced at the doorway of the chambers where I crammed successfully for the Bar Finals in 1955, a good discipline.)

MFS GH   *Sunday, 17 March*

I went up, somewhat against my inclination, but at Jane's prompting ('V-sign them') to Frostie. For some reason the camera stayed on me practically the whole time so when I wasn't speaking I could seem to be wanting-to-sit-on-my-tinkle-face and fidgeting. Also a weenie bit more mature now. Some shots good, some not so good.

John Redwood was there. More authoritative than formerly, less ready to smirk deferentially. Said JM's only skill was staying in office.[3] I wonder what he feels? There is a lot of talk now about a 'long' parliament, or a small Labour majority. I'm not so sure. I still think it could be very, very bad. (And of course finally, if I don't get back – which now seems virtually impossible – would prefer

---

[1] After his report was published, Scott gave a number of talks to lawyers and at universities.

[2] Scott called the evidence of Tristan Garel-Jones, who had been a Foreign Office minister at the time, 'risible'.

[3] John Redwood has stood against John Major the previous July in the leadership contest.

this. All those second-rate Tories just threshing around getting nowhere.)

On the walk we released a woodcock, which had got stuck between the two fence lines – always satisfying. But earlier I had been caused heartache by 'Cross Bencher' [*Sunday Express*] relating to the Sevenoaks shortlist – Stephen (ghastly), Fallon, Johnson[1] and thought of that note: 'You were in the frame until quite [sic] late'.

I suppose I really ought to concentrate on the BB. But it is the lure of the sword that agonises me. Will anything happen?

MFS GH   *Saturday, 13 April*

Already Birthday Boy; the year one-third gone and this notebook coming up to half distance. Rather more melancholy than on previous birthdays. But oppressed, too, with the need for BB to do its stuff.

I have a perfect vantage point *in the wilderness* – but with just this horrid dissatisfaction – I have no seat.

I bought myself a birthday present (self-indulgently). A huge royalty cheque came in, £78,000,[2] abolishing at a stroke the Coutts overdraft. Almost within 12 hours I spent 40 on Core's 3-litre.

I would like to write a where-do-we-go-from-here piece. Must be over further to the 'right' – you cannot have two competing centre parties. But never forget that Mrs T, who was, suffered endless criticisms and ridicule for telling us where we ought to be going up to '79. To leave the EC and simply to anticipate its natural – and inevitable – implosion.

This ought to go in *The Times* – but can't (I will offer it to them,

---

[1] Michael Stephen, MP for Shoreham since 1992; Michael Fallon, MP for Darlington, 1983–92, who was ultimately selected as Sevenoaks candidate and won the seat in the 1997 election; Boris Johnson, *Daily Telegraph* journalist (whose route to the House turned out to be at Henley, where he succeeded Michael Heseltine in 2001).

[2] In particular, sales of the paperback edition of *Diaries*, but also the ongoing success of two of AC's campaign histories, *The Donkeys* and *Barbarossa*.

though) because all they do is put Libby Purves, Bernard Levin in the prime place.

Albany, EMT   *Tuesday, 16 April*

Once again a lovely open evening – and it is 'to London', the night at Albany. Dined with David D (he has taken the place of Richard R as my principal *fix*). He said 'something-something your seat'; 'we did want to talk about . . .' I am dismissive and he didn't press the point.

He made some good remarks: 'MPs are different these days, socially and economically. They are a levee. And what happens when a levee is put under pressure? It runs.'

'Twentieth-century politics is the medieval warfare. The leaders are in the front line and the standard is what is important for rallying. The standard must be high, and it must be visible.'

And 'in' politics the natural (Darwinian) selection process for the larvae is quite different than that for the survival and advancement of the adult/leader . . .

These are real aphorisms.

MFS GH   *Sunday, 21 April*

To record a lovely day. These last two or three I have been low – concerned that I may have cancer of the colon ('any change in bowel habits should be investigated immediately'). And since Mrs Frowd[1] – most sinisterly – had asked one about indigestion, and the 'colon' it seemed to deteriorate – so that I was convinced that I was not evacuating properly.

However the sun shone and the air was lovely, still and clean.

I rose very early and looked at some texts for Big Book over EMT. Later I said to Jane ¾ of my stress derives from not properly

---

[1] Mrs Cindy Frowd, Hythe reflexologist.

addressing Big Book; I can feel the level easing off as I get near it. So much twist (or 'spin' as it is called) to put on this subject.

After breakfast we loaded the Discovery with stuff for the dump. Had our boilies early and only collected the papers on our way out. Dabbled our toes in the water at Hythe beach (Jane rightly pointing out a film of dilute sewage which lay on the surface). I finished cutting the Bailey and we had a pasta and salad, followed by mangoes and Belgian chocolates, which the young had given us.

No time for a zizz, but did a formal 'w' along the woodland (a fox by the stream bank now sojourns the day at the edge of his earth by the bottom tree).

EMT   *Friday, 26 April*

The Party yet again in trauma. If you have no sense of direction ('no compass' in the current code) you don't know where you are going. This makes you vulnerable to attacks of panic and, particularly, mutual recrimination.

Of course it all makes me regret so sadly not being in the House. Not just for the gossip; but because I believe that I *could*, just possibly (certainly I could now with the acquired experience of knowing what to do), have been urged to take the helm myself. Anyway for the fourth, or is it the fifth, time in this Parliament the Party is in turmoil – this time over Jimmy.[1]

It starts with the feeling that seats are threatened – threatened more than is usual that is – then a feeling spreads – why not? There is talk of major figures (*passim* Redwood and Lamont) insisting on a referendum now, declaring a splinter Conservative Party and forcing an early election with all the Goldsmith money and campaigning zeal getting behind them. It could be valhalla of course.

---

[1] Sir James Goldsmith had announced the formation, and funding, of a Referendum Party, which would put up candidates against Tory MPs who were pro-Europe.

But if between now and the local election results, JG gets serious, plans a campaign and this means saying what he will do in power, there could be a creditable freshness for the second stage. This means getting in professional campaign managers, a chief of staff, and an analyst (all, I know, uncongenial to Jimmy who likes to be a solitary buccaneer).

EMT   *Friday, 3 May*

The local election results. Has the tide turned? Or is it perhaps '*on the turn*'? A 2–3 point recovery, no more.[1]

I suppose for both selfish and nostalgic reasons I would welcome utter defeat. I don't want to see all those colleagues who no longer court my attentions preening themselves.

Quietly back to 'where we came in' – a Labour government and a long period in which to foster nostalgia and in which my book (oh the book, how good it will be – and how difficult it is to 'put it together') will be a guiding light. But the vox-pop session for Basildon made me uneasy. No one offered a reason for voting Labour – only about voting against Tory. I feel in my bones that there might be enough of a rally to produce an 'almost-hung' parliament. And what wheeling and dealing this would give rise to!

Lovely in a way, like pining in love, this sadness that I can induce about here, going down the wide corridor from the members' staircase to the Lobby, past the bay window where Clay Freud[2] used to sit and work out his bets before diving into an adjacent telephone booth to ring his bookie.

---

[1] With only 27 per cent of the vote, the Conservatives lost 567 seats, but Central Offices's worst estimates approached 700. This allowed the party spokesman to say that the results were less bad than in the 1991 local election, which was followed a year later by a Conservative general election victory. Would the same happen in 1997?

[2] Clement ('Clay') Freud, journalist and droll broadcaster; MP (Liberal) for Ely, July 1973–83; Cambridgeshire NE, 1983–87.

Bank Monday, 6 May

Very low today. I should have gone to Duxford[1] for the anniversary rally of the Spitfires. But slept in, intermittently, 30 minutes at a time, and was/would clearly be late leaving. Wanted to hear the Merlins,[2] see Alex Henshaw and get him if possible to sign the Mew Gull para in Jane's [*All the World's Aircraft*]; tell him how I saw him win the King's Cup air race at Lympne when he dived under the little blue Pobjoy monoplane.[3] I felt a tremendous pull to this, and hated myself and my intentions for shirking it. Totally frittered the day. Mainly spent helping Tip wash and clean S16 (which responded beautifully, I must say).

I just hope the Zurbaran which I am taking up tomorrow can be placed. Really one needs £1 million in the Trust to yield income, relying on remaining contents to 'protect against inflation'. I absolutely refuse to sell, but perhaps the grandchildren will thank me.

B5   *Wednesday, 8 May*

At the flat phone ringing – would I take a call from the Chief Whip? Paraphrasing Chips I said – 'I can never resist a Chief Whip', Alastair [Goodlad] – worried about David D. 'He's going to chuck it in . . .' (?) Had seen the PM on Thursday, was going to talk again to him that afternoon. What had he been like at the weekend, etc?[4] That's my third call from a political notable in 24 hours.

Somehow I got the feeling that the tide had turned. I got back, ate scrambled eggs and finished polishing S16.

---

[1] Former Second World War RAF station in Cambridgeshire, now an outpost of the Imperial War Museum.

[2] The Merlin, the Rolls-Royce engine that powered the Spitfire and many other aircraft of the period.

[3] In 1938, when AC was ten years old, Alex Henshaw, a distinguished air racer of the 1930s, was piloting a Percival Mew Gull monoplane.

[4] Now an FO minister, David Davis was said to be disenchanted by the government's handling of the EC's ban on British beef following the outbreak of 'mad cow' disease, and by not being promoted in cabinet.

Shore Cottage, Eriboll   *Monday, 20 May*

On Saturday we went to look at the great Arnaboll Forest project.
Could be incredible. Already the game are back in copious (*passim*
Jane) quantities. Strange and unknown vitality in plant life, secret
and long dormant mosses and lichens. From a rocky outcrop James
showed us the contoured lines of the plantings that leave plenty of
glade and open areas for the wildlife to congregate. As far as the eye
could see, some seven or eight miles on and over to Cashel Dhu.
In ten years' time it will be noticeable. I hope to come as a buffer,
in my plus fours, with a stalking stick and stompily survey it, but
even James will be dead in seventy years, when it comes to full
fruition.

On the way back we looked at some of the foundations, some
of them even pre-Christian of the original Arnaboll settlement. At
the graveyard the children's headstones were in the main still
standing. But some vandal had – most recently as a fresh apple-
core was nearby – levered out the lead lettering, scratching the
marble with his knife, of little Jane Mackay who had died aged 5½
in 1867 and had such a pretty gothic stone. Loathsome scrounger. I
hope some ill fortune befalls him.

Shore Cottage   *Tuesday, 21 May*

Our last day. Bright sunlight, bit windy. And there are two
swallows back in the long shed – though none, yet, in the
boathouse. I am hating the prospects of getting back. Almost as
bad as leaving Portmeirion for school in 1942. Speaking engagements, Clara,[1] mail, police proceedings (unspecified); always the
relentless pressure of the Mains, at the centre of whole vortices of
claims.

---

[1] Clara Glynn, director of a TV series based on *The Tories*.

Saltwood   *Sunday, 26 May*

Jane's birthday, and she has been absolutely sweet all day since we
had EMT upstairs and talked about things – children, car-culling,[1]
possessions generally.

I did my ten letters, and we then attacked the 'slab' – dispersing the
dust of 13 years – since, I would think, last public openings as a tiny
packet of 'Cadet' cigarettes stuffed with butts smoked down to the
filter was found in the old shell-case that holds the walking sticks.

But for much of the day I have been uneasy, almost to the point of
AF. *The Sunday Times* was loathsome – page 3, and huge colour
mock poster plus – needless to say pictures of Valerie and Joei, various
actors – 'Clark gets cold feet' etc. Thank God, and due largely to Jane,
I'm out of that. Phew! But of course 'damaging' like being summoned 'Minister faces jail sentence' just in time to wreck Reigate.[2]

MFS GH   *Monday, 3 June*

Still apprehensive, Jane this morning said, 'I'm frightened for you.'
But the likelihood of imprisonment (slight, surely?) for obstruction
('they always go mad on anything to do with bombs', she rightly
said) is not what is rattling me, but the strange silence on the
Harkess book front.[3] Just behave with dignity, like Charles I.

---

[1] 'Yet again we return to the car cull,' writes AC opposite this entry, and then lists,
with his estimated prices in £ (thousands): 4½ litre Bentley (100); SS 100 (110);
New Bing (40); XK140 (15); Loco (45); Big Red (120); B'Bang (18); plus in US
$ Buick (45).

[2] AC was having second thoughts about a dramatisation of the *Diaries*; his court
appearance was imminent; Reigate Conservatives were looking for a successor
to George Gardiner, Eurosceptic rebel.

[3] AC's court appearance, for driving through a police cordon in Piccadilly, took
place at Bow Street; AC pleaded guilty, apologised, and was fined £650 plus
£50 costs. But next morning headlines and photographs concentrated on the
fact that he gave a homeless man (also due in court that day on a begging charge)
£5 towards his fine rather than allow him to face a jail sentence. Meanwhile a
Harkess memoir had been announced to the press in South Africa, Valerie
Harkess's domicile. In fact nothing more was heard of it.

MFS GH   *Friday, 7 June*

A lasting feeling of complete disengagement.

A hot, hot June evening and because the shadows are so long and the light so persistent with all the full green foliage and wild flowers we could be in north Italy.

We went over today to Bromley – the 'Kentish Gadabouts' all over 70, it seemed. And I talked for 40 minutes without notes. Asked, of course, if I want to return to Parliament and gave a reasoned reply. Jane came, fluffed them impeccably and looked sweet in the white silk dress and pearls.

On our return I took a call from Mike White[1]. We chatted. It wasn't either Redwood or Portillo. The AN Other should be me. I know that. History knows that. Apart from anything else I 'so good on television' *passim* Clara.

But for this to work only the very last combination of fortune will do. Reigate *and the by-election*? I went into the Great Hall and prayed, aloud.

Dear God
    You have given me so much. A lovely family, wonderful possessions, this incredible place, and now, even, the promise of a grandchild.
    So I don't like to ask you for things. Because if you give then you can take away. Which is demanding of one really, I suppose. But I want to go back to the House of Commons, because I want to save my Party. And only you can so order this. Because of course you can do anything.
    I funked Sevenoaks, which you offered me. Have I learned from that? Whatever happens, I need you to save me from myself.
    It is lovely to communicate. Please stay with me.

---

[1] Michael White, political editor of the *Guardian*.

Saltwood, EMT   *Thursday, 27 June*

It is 7.10 am and I have just read a little Chips to get in the mood to write.

Little Tom came in a second ago. He wagged his tail at me so pleasantly, and I let him out at once where he quickly did a giant tinkle. Alas, and for the first time, real old age seems to be troubling him. He is (rightly) cautious about 'ball-play' and uneasy beside the pool.

He stumbles when he walks (how he still goes up, and even more dangerously, down stairs I just don't know) and didn't quite get on net with 'Keegan' and the ball at the England–Germany semi-final last night. I couldn't bear to put him down so hope he passes away suddenly.

Albany   *Wednesday, 3 July*

Up today for Jimmy's Press Gallery lunch.

Greatly to my delight I was 'lionised' – might never have been away. George Jones said, '. . . and I see Alan Clark there,' or something of the kind; 'Thank you, George, and thank you for singling me out . . .' Hugh Pym spirited me away to some 'clips' on MPs' pay, the Somme, and the Referendum Party.[1] Julian Brazier[2] talked to me about the great homes row at MoD. Yesterday, after the sad news from N. Dorset,[3] I was even more determined to return. And at David Frost's party on Thursday dear Gill Shephard was specially encouraging.

---

[1] Two political correspondents, George Jones (*Daily Telegraph*) and Hugh Pym (ITN).

[2] Julian Brazier, MP for Canterbury since 1987.

[3] North Dorset, yet another possible seat in which AC showed an interest, chose Robert Walter, who had contested the Labour stronghold of Bedwelty in south Wales, 1979.

GH   *Saturday, 3 August*

One thing I must note – both welcome and unwelcome. I am
almost an alcoholic. I 'have' to have my half (a generous half,
often) bottle of wine, usually Burgundy red or white, in the
evening. If I don't get it by about 7 pm I feel irritable and (similar
to) hungry.

But, when I don't drink I feel much better waking-up in the
morning (we never go to lights/bed before 11 pm now it seems).
And, particularly, if I don't drink at lunch I feel much better at tea-
time and in the evenings. Today, for example although we had late
salami-cheese lunch by the pool and it is a Saturday, I still would
not slurp. Nor do I intend to drink tonight, although I would love,
if I think about it, to drain a glass of the Marquise's Chasagne
Montrachet. Champneys in August? It is only the second day. But
not only do I feel better, but I feel more sexual. And my prostatic
symptoms have completely disappeared. Strange.

GH   *Saturday, 10 August*

The cockatiels escaped. Jane brilliantly – how? – recaptured the
little grey. But the yellow (maiden) is flighty – literally – and calls at
intervals from different points around the Mains; venturing this
afternoon bravely to the giant sycamore over the Long Garage.

Saltwood, EMT   *Friday, 13 September*

Short of miracles, this is the last charge. I went over there [Tun-
bridge Wells] on a recce on Wednesday. Recognised almost
immediately by a charming man who accosted me and said how
glad he was that I am to be 'the next MP'. The agent, Steve Owen,
not just grumpy and rebarbatief, but slob-like; with shoulder-
length hair and a beer belly. A dreadful ward official in his late
sixties – the kind of organisation that illustrates the tenacity of the

human body when exposed to carcinogenic factors – and common-voicedly talking to the agent. Ignored me; then at the end said, 'Hello, young man.' 'Hello,' I simpered.

Archie Norman[1] is the favourite. 'I hope he trips himself up,' indiscreetly said the agent. Mrs (sic) Fookes[2] is the dark horse, according to my contact, Kenneth Miller. I'm not so sure about him, either, now. He talks almost loonily – 'I seethed for an hour' when people said I was being interviewed for 'entertainment'; and is very keen on telling me people's objections.

The whole thing is too ridiculous. I am telling myself to fight a seat that is worse than Plymouth in 1992. Once this is out of the way then I really can revert. I think the odds against me must be in double figures. But it is possible – if I am inspired. Will K-C inspiration come?

By 'The Boy' [statue by pool]   *Saturday, 14 September*

A simply beautiful, still September morning. I drove over to Bob Worcester to get the (very expensive, £7+) MORI printout for Tunbridge Wells. He briefed me – on the inevitable Tory defeat. Even T-W, 42 last night is now down to 40! He has this theory that the Lib-Dems will actually benefit as a stop-over from switching Tories. I'm not so sure. Could be that all these SE seats split 40–30–30 for us.

But I still don't see how we can do anything but deteriorate. At present our majority is ONE. Are we actually going to *win* seats?

I am leaving my *revision* dangerously late. I know nothing about Education, Hospitals, etc. *But this is it, Alan . . . !*

---

[1] Archie Norman, chief executive of the Asda Group since 1991, who had political ambitions.
[2] In boundary changes Janet Fookes's seat – she had been the constituency neighbour of AC as MP for Plymouth Drake since 1974 (Merton and Morden, 1970–74) – was disappearing.

Saltwood   *Friday, 20 September*

V convincingly Archie Norman 'walked' Tunbridge Wells. Same
age as I was when chosen at Plymouth Sutton – a generation ahead
I ought now to be calm and free – 'relaxed'.

EMT   *Tuesday, 8 October*

Drove early to Gatwick and at Geneva Airport lashed out at Caviar
House, bought a medium-sized tin of Beluga, bottle of Fondant
and sundries. Delicious picnic in Geneva train and took the
supplement old-style coach on the Glacier Express (restored and
not very comfortable – should have had period prints). The châlet
at first seemed a little shabby and dated, but soon we are happily
ensconced. Gamely we walked up to Ried – raising heartbeat to
140+ and fibrillations – and to a high tea and early night. The next
day a lovely Zermatt meander in the morning, up to the Winkelmatten Chapel where I said a real prayer of thanks and back via the
watch shops.

   The day after our return we drove in Big Red to Broomhayes
and found Andrew and Sarah had really settled in happily. After tea
across the fields to the church and over the wall by the gravedigger's hut and found the Marley shed still with its windows
intact, but besieged and entangled by brambles of wire rope.

Saltwood, EMT   *Thursday, 10 October*

Back late last night, having driven the Little Silver *without glasses*
from Bournemouth in 2¾ hours on 3 gallons of petrol (it seems).
Slept like a top.

   Conference, as always, left no time for anything. Lionised, still,
but selectively. Middle-rank colleagues (except, interestingly those
on the Right, like Townend,[1] Gardiner etc) are suspicious, don't

---

[1] John Townend, MP for Bridlington since 1979.

want intercourse. Old mates – Ancram,[1] Goodlad ('love thy neighbour' was his elliptical parting shot) just as if I'd been speaking to them yesterday. Nellies, some of them up-market, are always friendly, and I am universally recognised by policemen. Some tough young 'graduates' (the best). Most of my time I seemed to spend in the company of ladies, Clara, of course, Jackie Ashley,[2] Sue Tinson[3] started me off on Tuesday evening. She saying 'you must see Major, he loves you . . . etc' (shades of 'she'll have him in the Cabinet if she can'). Then at the dinner I sat between two fat ladies – both amiable and intelligent. Although I had thought it would be low-key, a second XI and was wary of Gary Streeter[4] and his hostile wife. Actually, fortified by a late, giant gin and tonic with Sue Tinson and some champagne and red wine I deftly whizzed over and sat next to and mobbed/flirted most indiscreetly with Rebekah Wade[5] (!) who I was interested to see was a flame-haired lovely (and must in 1993 have been even more luscious).

To some extent my whole performance was bogus. I have no standing. Am I famous, or infamous? Sarah Baxter, looking very attractive, wanted me to be 'interviewed' for the *Sunday Times*.

MFS GH   *Sunday, 13 October*

I was pleased by Sarah Baxter's article – 'busy reinventing himself', a perfect formula. On the way back from Aldeburgh we detoured to Sudbourne. The great house demolished, but wonderful stablings, and outbuildings still, although the glass canopies for resting the cars and carriages are gone, like the huge greenhouses – although the

---

[1] Michael Ancram, minister, Northern Ireland Office since 1994, MP for Devizes since 1992 (Berwick & East Lothian, February–September 1974, Edinburgh South, 1979–87).

[2] Jackie Ashley, *New Statesman* political writer, married to Andrew Marr, the daughter of former Labour MP Lord (Jack) Ashley.

[3] Sue Tinson, DBE, associate editor, ITN, since 1989, its link with Number Ten.

[4] Gary Streeter, AC's successor at Plymouth Sutton, a whip since 1995; his wife Janet.

[5] Rebekah Wade, deputy editor of the *News of the World* since 1989.

walled garden perimeter is still intact. What a huge property! All the
cottage ornée are untouched – almost vulgar, but my goodness they
were well built. We wandered about. It is sad not knowing more
about inventories and schedules and how many staff there were and
so forth. The whole garden now a wilderness and the lake grown
over.

When we returned I got out the albums – everything so spick
and span. But a vast undertaking. My grandfather went there quite
a lot; taking trout in May, pheasants in October and November. In
between to Scotland – on the yacht. Yet Sudbourne could never
really have been kept on – which Shielbridge [at Ardnamurchan]
could. Though both estates so vast that without perpetual super-
vision you were going to get ripped off. When we got back to
Saltwood I wondered if, in ninety years time, my grandson would
still be here and to what extent the estate/property would have
been forced to yield.

Saturday, 19 October

A curious 'turn-up' on – as so often can happen – several different
fronts at once. On 16 October at 6.31 little baby Albert McKenzie
was born. 'King George VII' I call him mindful of the signature
'Bertie' in the Port Lympne visitors' book (though even as I write I
realise that this would have been Lord Bertie – a courtier of some
kind – as it also contains the signature in a round, juvenile hand –
'Albert').

We went to see him the next day at the very pleasing and brand
new Chelsea-Kensington Hospital.

I felt sad, curiously so, when I looked at the tiny baby. 'A page
turns,' I said, only half-jokingly, 'on to a new chapter of anxiety
and heartache . . .' Curiously I found that birth gives one a sharper
sense of one's own mortality than death. How seminal was that
film *2001*![1] What a strange sensation and experience, to open one's

---

[1] Subtitled 'A Space Odyssey', and directed by Stanley Kubrick, 1968.

eyes for the *very first time* ('He's nought', Jane said) in one's life, and take in the surroundings of a maternity ward.

I did privately notice that Nick Scott had barely improved his position by being 'found' collapsing face-down in a side-street in Bournemouth, and saw he had been summoned to his Executive Council on 4 November. Last night Soames rang, claimed to have been told that people in Chelsea who had voted for him once now going to vote for me. 'But don't do *anything*, Alan. Promise me you will say *NOTHING*' etc.

Largely fantasy of course, but fun. I mustn't think about it. But no doubt I am on a roll at the moment.

Garden House   *Sunday, 3 November*

Just took time off from BB to record how immensely happy I am. I must thank God, and do something for him — but I don't know how or what.

Albert is sweet and healthy; Andrew and Sarah are 'excellent parents'.

All is as well as can be expected at Saltwood.

Jane has 'passed' with Tom Bates just as I did a couple of weeks ago.

We may go to Venice on 23 November — think of that!

BB is potentially terrific. I am devoting more and more hours on it, and recovering confidence (and shape). A difficult passage, the Churchill–Eden government to Suez has turned out very readable.

And Nick Scott comes up (*again*) for de-selection tomorrow.

Garden House   *Sunday, 17 November*

Really resigned to the fact that even if there's now a vacancy I probably won't even be *seen* (re) by Chelsea. Also (perhaps because of this) it is all much more through-a-glass-darkly now. That last draft of nostalgia. Now it seems remote, being desirable. A new miracle needed.

This is reflected in my standing. Many fewer approaches now. No Christmas party invitations. I wrote to JM suggesting a supper with myself and Simon Jenkins and Sue Tinson – no answer. Soames' own voice print kind of gives it away.

I must just concentrate on BB. But last night, v 'frail' and jumpy (I am lividly jarred when Jane bangs saucepan lids in the kitchen), I came over here to do a couple of pages on Ted. For some reason the machine went shifty and I kept getting 'You may not leave Winword' in a large oval white box after doing 'exit windows – ok'. In the end, livid, I switched it off and lost a whole evening's work. Ha!

Tower office   *Monday, 2 December*

Nick Scott is clearly going to win his public meeting tonight (his *third* in tenure) – but in any case, no one remembers me any more. I've suddenly become, and look, 'too old'.

Saltwood   *Tuesday, 3 December*

Back from Julian Amery's memorial service at St Margaret's.

Little Winston's address quite good – don't know who wrote it – and reminded one of how long and rich Julian's life had been – though never with complete fulfilment. Mrs T let him down; just as she did today by not attending. And last night Nick Soames said, quite true, that he was weak at the base – though wonderful on his feet as a back-bencher.

St Margaret's was less than two-thirds full. Jonathan [Aitken] very splendidly intercepted us and conducted us to the centre aisle.

As Jane said in the car everyone seemed a good deal older (has it all happened in the last two years?), and she meant people like Richard Shepherd[1] and Mark Lennox-Boyd – but they/we are from a generation after Julian, he was our father. His death marks

---

[1] Richard (Rick) Shepherd, MP for Aldridge-Brownhills since 1979.

the passing, finally, of an era. We, too, have been shunted up a tier, and are now obsolete.

I must record I have personally had some setbacks. Blood in the urethra, attack of 'distorted vision', heavy eyestrain (glaucoma). No longer race up stairs, some strange AF attacks in middle of night, pulse rate 140 plus. Appearance rather cross and alarmed or apprehensive, with hair white and receding. Sexuality declined almost out of sight. Even so – lucky to be around, to have so much, sweet Jane and the little baby grandson.

Saltwood   *EMT, Tuesday, 10 December*

I am depressed. I am worried simultaneously about my health, my book (BB) and the state of the party/politics. My entire morale seems to have suffered, and it is only on the great Beechborough walk (slightly over two hours) that I feel better and freer (I can't remember when I last did Gossie – was it a true 'last'?)

On Sunday, having got a lot of logs in and pleasingly exhausted, I phoned the PM, after his broadcast. He was pleased and friendly, though seemed a little unhappy. What is happening to the Party? They are now a medieval army in the reign of King Stephen – pre Ironside – each one concerned to preserve their individual estates (constituencies) fragmenting into even smaller Margravates around dignitaries who may, or may not, be in a position to distribute favours and booty. Discipline has completely broken down, and they loot the countryside as they march and counter march. It is the warlord syndrome. Harold and Stamford Bridge; Afghanistan, Mozambique. Am I half pre-empting disappointment at being rejected by Chelsea? Do I want to be back at the House – right back – in opposition and in smaller numbers, I would judge, than in even October 1974–79?

Saltwood   *EMT, Saturday, 21 December*

Decks clear for Christmas! (Whatever that means.)

I am still somewhat blighted by my head (eye) ache. I have sat here at the kitchen table for nearly 40 minutes pressing my temples with fingers and trying – very occasionally succeeding – to defocus. Yesterday I forced myself to do one page of 'Heath II' (BB) at the white computer. A brain tumour would be moving faster than this, surely?

K-C remains a mirage. I get little bursts of enthusiasm, but have suffered too many disappointments (I mean I really did think I was a shoe-in for Sevenoaks). But at Max Hastings' party (he had raging flu and a high temperature) I spoke with David Heathcoat-Amory. Always an interesting, clever man. He said the whole course of history both of the Party and the country would be decided in conclave after the Election by who backed whom for the leadership.

MFS Garden House   *Monday, 30 December*

I must set out a résumé – both 'where am I', and what has been.

Jane excelled (even) herself over Christmas; the whole house so beautifully, and tastefully decorated. Greenery everywhere, quite pagan, a calling out almost. But this time, first occasion for thirty years or more there was a *pram in the hall*! Nanny's great grey, which pushes and rides like a silver ghost, was wheeled down from the Rabies Room and, somewhat, admittedly under HE's-Reception conditions I Autosolvol'd the wheels and the dumb-irons, Simonizing the 'coach-built' body. Little Albert was lovely, changing each day. We all went to Canterbury for the carol service and he was a little starfish in his blue ski-suit, and quite placid. I carried him (v heavy) a little way in the aisle when we left – to approving glances. But how much of him, or of any brothers or sisters (or cousins) will I live to see? I am multi-hypochondriacal at present – after a sign of prolonged gestation.

I must admit that the likelihood of my going back to the House, even being interviewed for Chelsea does seem quite remote. It no longer seems realistic. A colossal effort of inspiration would be required although there are of course reserves which I can draw on if they will allow me to.

Paradoxically, if I were back in the House there would be more free time. I suspect because life is more orderly and compartmentalised, and much is done for you. I have been my own secretary now for nearly five years – and it shows.

If I could just get BB (and the TV show) out of the way this year perhaps in '98 we can choose.

1997 – could go back to Heaven.

1998 – a lot less/more on his plate.

So I simply don't know. I don't know if my health will hold up, or the book get finished, or I am finally excluded from public life. Or if by some strange and miraculous concatenation I return as a big player.

Garden House   *New Year's Eve*

The handwriting recently has been abominable. Is this poor vision, or 'nerves'? I went down to Hythe P.O. (long queue) to record the letter and CVs to K&C.

1997

Garden House   *Sunday, 5 January*

A little calmer, which is surprising, because the entire morning was spent 'doing' the top of the tallboy in my bathroom. But fortunately I 'forced the pace' and went through to the end – ie polish and rearrange the tortoise-shell objects, so that tiny sector is now 'clear'. But, as I said to Jane, Walcheron Island. Consumed the entire Canadian Corps from Sept '44 to March '45 and when it was over, and the Scheldt clear, so what? My eyes are better today. Last night I wrote a my-patience-is-exhausted letter to Goodlad. Eleven lists since I stood down, and no recognition of any kind.

Saltwood   *Sunday, 12 January*

Lovely and enclosed by snow/fog. The M-way is silent, and one is reminded how peaceful, magical Saltwood could be transferred to a position in, say, Herefordshire, or the Welsh marches.

David D down – talk at breakfast, then dinner. A clever boy, but like Major a little chippy still. Neither he nor Michael Howard says anything of the 'you're needed' type, and Soames hasn't rung for weeks. A quiet recognition that my time has passed. Well, that's all right if what is written is written – though I am still haunted by the fact that it is *my fault*.

EMT   *Thursday, 16 January*

On Monday, sitting quietly at the 'white' screen in Garden House, at 8 pm I felt so overcome by depression, sense of waste of being out *due to my own idiocies and weak character*. I love the history, the participation, the minutiae. But at the back lurks, too, the sword.

And yet the *machine*, the pigginess of the Party, will not allow me ever to be seen.

The hour has come, and passed, when the call should have come through.

So I prayed – properly, but shortly. Thought little more of it. Patrick Hennessy for the *Standard* on the answering machine – presumably for a gloat. I was out-of-sorts. Doing paperwork with Jane in the Tower Office (she is so good at that, quadruples over rate). Then on came Barbara Lord. I was to be interviewed – I gave her the works; she very sweetly said she preferred me. I have got quite a good vote ('which surprised her' – compliment?) set out rules of secrecy. A huge wash of adrenalin *surged* through me. I went straight to Beechborough. What *is* written?

The next day she rang again – purposely to apologise for the leaking (as they had the whole list it couldn't have been me), but significantly said that Trish Sill Johnston[1] wanted to talk to me, tell me of a few local points. Now this (I thought) was significant. An overture from the Nick camp as well . . . ! For the first time it seemed to be realistic. Sitting on the Green Room floor I got flu symptoms alternating with AF. Could it really be feasible? Jane, as always, was brilliant, though drily unimpressed. I had a baddish night, semi near the surface most of the time. Up in the Big Red this morning to lunch with Dean [Godson]. Intense, indefatigable, something of a young Isaiah (Berlin) about him. I thought he was a teensy bit guarded – but we have agreed to dine on Saturday and he will 'tell me the questions' (shades of Graham Butland). I've got to come up on Saturday morning, that's quite clear, to 'walk the Borough', get to know local issues etc. And so there we are – the last offensive, April 1918, on the Ardennes.

EMT   *Monday, 20 January*

I must record the developments in this big eerily, crazy, half-tragic, almost incredible and possibly calamitous final charge. I had a *nuit*

---

[1] Patricia (Trish) Sill Johnston, secretary to Nicholas Scott.

cassée on Saturday night. Went to bed with the speech unformed; a reasonable end paragraph, an opening formed on my long adrenalin-dispersing trek that afternoon but no third link passage about the majority party and social events. These sort of formed into shape in a two-hour half-sleepy period from about 4 am. But it was still far from solid. And untimed. Soft-spoken I 'rehearsed' after losing the place. Then parked, beautifully timed, on the corner of Flood Street. Ushered more or less straight in. Atmosphere very pleasant. Andrew Dalton[1] hyper-smooth. They did, I must say, 'put me at ease'. Speech just got past; a couple of good passages. The first question from 'Big' Barry Phelps:[2]

'Mr Clark, last time you appeared before this committee and I asked you a question you delivered a prepared answer that had no relation to it whatever. This time would you like to give the answer first, or second?'

'Well, Barry, the committee should know that with your customary sensitivity to the feelings of others you have always told my younger son and daughter-in-law who are constituents of yours, that there was no point in my putting in for the candidacy as I didn't have a chance and I was just wasting everyone's time . . .'

Great applause and laughter (in which he chiefly joined). Got me off to a good start. After that, not too difficult, could be statesman – giving my 'single-currency' answer.

Interrupted at this point: I was going to write about all those people on the committee who had rung last night 'taking out insurance' as I said; but Lynn spotted the fact that I sounded 'coldy'. I am snuffly, runny nose, eye-ache and pulse 84 (it only goes to 72–76 if just 'agitated'). Spoke to Barbara Lord and she said that every single person on the committee had voted for me! But what's the use? – flu for the final – I cannot believe it – McEnroe.

---

[1] Andrew Dalton, chairman of Kensington and Chelsea Conservative Association.
[2] Barry Phelps, local councillor.

EMT   *Tuesday, 21 January*

Today the most tiresome bit. The 'Executive'. But 150 (!) of them
so had to include a number who are opposed, and a mike necessary, which I hate and am unused (*Brideshead*) to.[1]
   When I woke I thought so fondly of darling little Jane. I am
putting her through this ordeal. She is so loyal. Doesn't, of course,
want me to get through. And she is right, but I am driven by the
sword. My stars are incredible. Everything seems to be falling into
place. Is it to be 'all my life seemed but a preparation for this
hour . . .'? Or back here, having 'lost' 10 days which I can ill-
afford, to be an academic?

EMT, Albany   *Tuesday, 28 January*

The Executive, as I had anticipated, the most difficult audience.
Preceded by a 'cocktail' party (the glass of white wine most
welcome) at which Jane was lovely and made 'a conquest' of the
intially un-twinkly battleaxe who had been allocated as our
'minder'.
   But I underperformed. I was carried away by my supporters.
So although I came out top it was not done by conviction, but
by allegiance. Even the voice print of Andrew Dalton's message
carried the faintest nuance of uncertainty when, having slept
exhausted but fitfully, I staggered down in the morning with Tom
to switch it on.
   So now we are committed. The last great offensive. In the
afternoon of Thursday the reconnaissance. The Kensington Town
Hall so red and soulless. The hall, and the gallery. At 6.40 pm we
parked Big Red in some nameless, expensive street and made our
way to the doors where a mass of hateful paparazzi and brutal
reporters with mikes mobbed us.
   'Why do you think K&C will choose you?' 'Aren't you even

---

[1] AC adds his own note: 'Marquess's son unused to wine'.

worse than Sir Nicholas Scott?' 'What do you think your chances?' etc.

'Well they can't be worse than 3 to 1,' I said bleakly. The press (literally) was frightening and hostile. I got separated from Jane – literally manhandled by Central Office officials through the doors to where a huge crowd of disapproving members were queuing for ballot papers. Most of them avoided my eye. We were all confined to an underground 'green room', windowless, tableless with four bottles of mineral water (three of them fizzy, so liable to induce a burp when answering questions).

The other candidates all had something. Trish Morris – nice-looking, long copper-curled hair, vivacious, had wowed conference earlier on the ERM.[1] Daniel Moylan outrageously camp, but a former president of the Union and with a high-profile record in local government; and Martin Howe, 'the Eurosceptic QC' with a pretty wife and a portentous manner. I was last. I found a make-up room with a flat-surface in front of a mirror and rehearsed, timing three lines through – being interrupted only once by a tiny, tubby Asian man who came in to urinate – what was he doing in the Ladies anyway? I was demi-transcendent, the space-craft was on course – collision, burn out, or triumph. Jane quite rightly came and fetched me out, knowing that I would be unsettling myself. Daniel had returned – frightfully funny and quacky about Elspeth Rhys Williams' intervention – and the atmosphere lightened. We all started to talk among ourselves, agreeing, naturally, how awful they all were. Daniel smoked eleven Camels. Longer and longer we waited. What on earth had happened? Then suddenly, Andrew Dalton re-appeared – I think he was actually doing what my mother called *priest*, dry hand-washing. 'Well, the contest is over . . .' making across to me, '. . . and Alan has won. Alan has won.'

I was incredibly happy. But also got a hint of 'all my life has been but a preparation for this hour . . .' Now almost at once, it seemed generally preeordained. (It turned out that they had been

---

[1] Exchange rate mechanism, which at the time was rarely out of the headlines when the European single currency issue was being discussed.

counting all three ballots without telling us.) We went up the stairs to a loud cheer. I made a few anodyne remarks of gratitude; then congratulations, including lovely ones from Sarah and Tip – and out to a battalion of flash bulbs and that most incredible sense of euphoria. Finally we were hauled away, followed Barbara to Jeanie Craig's house (all I wanted, desperately, was a pint of beer. I couldn't/didn't drink the champagne). Took calls, immediately, from David Davis in the car – *he* saw the point! – and then home at 2.30 am.

Albany   *Monday, 10 February*

Almost a fairy tale come true. This morning William Rees-Mogg in *The Times* – across four columns – 'Who will be the next Conservative leader? I suppose Alan Clark is too much to hope for.'

B5   *Thursday, 13 February (Jane's birthday)*

I am looking ghastly in the glass. Scrawny, jowls all too easily hanging. In the night I woke at 3.40. I had sweated (nothing new about this) and my faint, disparate, oculo-related headache 'came in'. I worry about my health and when it will perceptibly disintegrate. The headaches are related to inability to defocus/relax.

MFS GH   *Saturday, 8 March*

I am serene and contented. This afternoon the christening of tiny Albert. In the kitchen last night, horrified by the 'alternative' form, printed on a cling-film-coated card which 'Reg'[1] had handed the young, I went upstairs and fetched the little white parchment-bound prayerbook, inscribed by my father for Jane at the time of

---

[1] The Reverend Canon Reg Humphriss, rector of Saltwood.

our wedding, and read to them the true form of service. I don't know what Andrew did, but most pleasingly Reg intoned the age-old phrases while the little prince was humped and jigged by me, fretting just a little, on and off, but easily distracted by the stained glass. Afterwards we posed, the three males in line, beside my father's gravestone.

Thursday, 13 March

I had lunch in the 'Churchill' room [at the Commons] with Jonathan Aitken and Alastair Goodlad. It is glorious being back in the Commons. Everywhere I went I was hailed by staff; no one questioned my right of access (I put my luggage in a locker in the dining-room corridor). Dawn Primarolo[1] held a door open for me – or was it Tessa Jowell[2]?

Saltwood, EMT   *Sunday, 16 March*

Last night at 3 am precisely poor T.O. had, or rather started, a very long fit. He convulsed into walking movements, though lying down, defecated. I thought he was going to die – but he's so tough. We carried him outside, legs completely paralysed it seems, his ear cocked, but he slowly picked up. Back indoors he walked round and round incessantly, would not settle. We went back to bed and after two hours' sleep I went down – he was still pacing up the corridor through the top Green Room door, then back and round. He must have walked to Ashford. This morning he is still muddled, but drank his saucer, went out as is routine. He's 18 years old.

---

[1] Dawn Primarolo, MP (Labour) for Bristol South since 1987.
[2] Tessa Jowell, MP for Dulwich and West Norwood since 1992.

Summer Office   *Tuesday, 18 March*

We are on the verge of annihilation it seems. Polls this morning
show Labour 26 points ahead and the *Sun* has turned.

I haven't had a normal pulse for ten days.

Sandling train   *Thursday, 20 March*

David Davis interesting – cool as always. Suggested that they
would probably prefer Tom King as 22 chairman. Key thing is to
get Major to make a statement immediately that he will ask 22
chairman to convene an election before the summer recess –
doubting that we could extend it to November. JM himself may
anyway not stand; but would have time to test the water and
recover.

MFS GL   *Saturday, 5 April*

More apprehensive and ill-at-ease than I should be. Was it only
yesterday the the *Evening Standard* came out showing that I had a
6-point advantage over the Party average in London(!). I am really
chuffed. The hottest currency in politics. Then (in all probability)
blew it by telling stupid little Michelle Stephens, who was trying to
set up an 'open' debate between me and Robert Atkinson[1] – fired
by his 'triumph' with the pensioners he thinks he can parade local
issues around which is, of course, all a 'local' paper wants. Were
they interested in my 6 points? – not at all. Foolishly, in explaining
it, I lost my temper and said the 'Royal Borough is bloody lucky to
have me as a candidate.' What a headline! Fool, Clark, fool, etc.

---

[1] Robert Atkinson, Labour candidate at Kensington and Chelsea.

B5   *Sunday, 6 April*

The Candidates Conference in that very low-ceilinged room with its strange overhead pipes, like the ward-room of an escort carrier. Some pleasant young boys, friendly and fresh-faced, who were going to be cut to pieces by the *jagdstaffel*; some old warhorses (everyone looking quite a bit older, I must say) and some sharp and indeed Semitic-looking template figures who presumably had taken the best seats. .

Mrs T spoke fantastically. Turned to the man on my right – 'she could still win the election', and her charisma, vitality and blue-flashing eyes, still could. John M was competent, better than adequate. I was filled with gloom at my manifest inability to answer questions on any topic. Came back here and wrestled with my Election Address text. Completed it about 7.30, very much 'in my own write', but on the phone Jane liked it.

Tuesday, 15 April

Almost completely soft-spoken and AF because Carol Midgley, of *The Times*, said 'Max Clifford keeps telling us of something really big – but he won't tell us what it is.'

Albany, EMT   *Tuesday, 29 April*

The news is dreadful. 'The Tory Party gives up' – headline in *Independent* (Anthony Bevins, naturally, he's not a reporter at all, but a Labour Party activist). The gap is intractable, widening indeed. Can this really be the case? Yesterday we decided to watch Major's last, and only, 'soapbox' performance on (ironically) College Green. A 'papered house' and only got to hear of it because CCO rang Barbara and asked for 20 activists to be bussed round and applaud. As we walked to and from the site, the streets of Whitehall seemed curiously empty. A sense – though not to the same degree – of the atmosphere in the Palace of Westminster just before The Lady fell. Not so far distant T34s were again at the fortification on the Oder. I was calm. 'I have arrangements for my family to travel to the Argentine.' Even though as I composed this I was conscious of lapsing into 'parody' as Peter Bradshaw (whose last entry, after a miss the previous week, was very funny).[1]

Poor Major looked exhausted, his voice flat – and Jane said Norma looked absolutely shattered.

EMT   *Thursday, 1 May*

I walked in very fragile sunlight to the paper seller in Piccadilly Circus underground and bought the whole lot. Robert Cranborne with whom I had a very interesting talk in his delightful comfy house at Swan Walk last evening, Robert was grave, but admirable in his sense of scholarship. First we must brush Redwood out of the way. Then keep Major in long enough for Heseltine's faults (of which we are all aware) to become apparent. Much depends on timing, and how to manoeuvre. In particular, the 'structure' of the 22 committee and its executive and chair.

It was apparent as the first results came in that, as the polls predicted, Labour had a landslide victory. Labour: 417 seats; Conservatives: 165 seats; Liberals: 46 seats; others: 28 seats. At Kensington and Chelsea, AC had 19,887 votes; Robert Atkinson (Labour) 10,368; Woodthorpe Browne (Liberal Democrat) 5,668; others just over 1,000. AC's majority 9,519.

Saltwood, pm   *Friday, 2 May*

Down here after two hours' sleep and looking like death. Saltwood is beautiful; a completely still day and the greens yellowy-

---

[1] Peter Bradshaw, author of *Not the Alan Clark Diary* in the *Evening Standard*, over which AC would later sue for 'passing off'.

springlike. Doves, jackdaws and swallows go about their business in the Bailey. I am so exhausted I cannot bear to look at a press cutting or a newspaper or even talk to David D, or whoever. Already Jane is quite rightly making me 'take calls'. People in London appear to be more shell-shocked than 'in the constituencies'. Archie Hamilton was far the most compos. Asked me straight out if I wanted the 22; some stuff about Butterfill[1] had beaten him for vice and Townend[2] was going to go for it, but yes he did want it for himself. Geoffrey Johnson Smith is the Whips' candidate.[3] Alastair Goodlad was so taciturn as almost (no, delete) to be unfriendly. Perhaps because of my 'anti-European' stance. Actually he was rather unpleasant.

Monday, 5 May

Most of yesterday seems to have been spent on the phone. The candidates are a mouldy lot. Portillo, probably the strongest, out.[4] Ken [Clarke], supposedly the most genial and experienced – won't get past the hard right. Little Hague – my aphorism about 'the guys' a golf ball' has already got currency, I'm glad to say. Redwood is fluent in today's *Times* – but I don't like him. Lilley is cerebral – should be the leader, but hasn't got the oomph – white rabbit in the teapot at the Mad Hatter's tea party.[5] Michael [Howard] presents me with a problem. I ought to support him, but I'm hesitating.

---

[1] John Butterfill, MP for Bournemouth West since 1983. He served as vice-chairman of the 1922 Committee until 2001.

[2] John Townend, MP for East Yorks since 1997.

[3] Sir Geoffrey Johnson Smith, MP for Wealden since 1983 (East Grinstead, February 1965–83; Holborn and St Pancras, 1959–64).

[4] Michael Portillo had lost Enfield Southgate, which he had represented since December 1984.

[5] Peter Lilley, newly elected as MP for Hitchin and Harpenden. Trade and then social security secretary in John Major's cabinet.

EMT   *Thursday, 8 May*

Yesterday I was up in the Commons. The whole thing should have been too delicious for words – but I was haunted by apprehension, and also a curious sense of hostility from colleagues, even Tebbit, whereas staff, and Labour MPs – Skinner (walking back from Church House, 'I thought the idea was to take power, not to give it away'), Mark Fisher,[1] Tony Benn – brilliant speech at the swearing-in.

Saltwood garden   *Friday, 16 May*

Woke at 4 am this morning in a panic that I wouldn't get anyone to sponsor me for the 22 chair. Got up, wrote composite letter to Peter Brooke who was cool and abrupt to me in the 'Aye' lobby last night – leading to the fantasy nightmare that Peter Lloyd[2] had said, 'I gather you've put up Alan for the 22?' 'What?' etc etc. Also doubled up in seeking sponsorship from Francis Maude, David Heathcoat-Amory. *The Times* arrived, and I saw I was at 2% – same as Dorrell[3] and only one point behind Lilley (!) – but drawing support equally from Labour and Con – so wrote also to Gill Shephard.

Urgent message from Soames. I knew what it would be about. 'You can't do this. You're mad. You'll be slaughtered' etc.

My line, I'm sticking to, 'don't want to split the vote' ('for the things I think need to be done'). We'll see how it is taken. My star was heavily in the ascendant. A lovely piece by Don McIntyre today in the *Independent* and yesterday in the tunnel Peter Oborne[4] was ruefully laudatory – said 'a great recalculation might have to be made'. Something though tells me I wouldn't have got it. Might

---

[1] Mark Fisher, MP for Stoke-on-Trent Central since 1983.
[2] Sir Peter Lloyd, MP for Fareham since 1979.
[3] Stephen Dorrell, MP for Loughborough since 1979, Health Secretary since 1995.
[4] Peter Oborne, political columnist with the *Sunday Express*.

next year *if* (and even that is not certain) I get on the Executive.
Memories soon heal over in the House – provided I perform. But I
must get my speech for Tuesday spruced up.

H of C library   *Wednesday, 21 May*

This absurd and embarrassing 'leadership contest' rambles on. In
fact, as I was saying to young intense Bernard Jenkin[1] in the aye
lobby this morning, they may have 'thrown their hats in the ring',
but the election campaign can't formally open until the nomination papers are filed with the (as yet unconstituted) 22 committee.
The Left has now decided to make a showing for Ken, then switch
en bloc to Hague (Dorrell is an irrelevance). Soames, a baleful
though pleasing *éminence énorme* was going to vote for Ken, 'one's
got to make sure he gets a good initial vote' – on Monday; then
switch, 'it's got to be Hague'. Garel-Jones is running the Hague
campaign. Let's hope he doesn't get a peerage.

Garden House   *Tuesday, 27 May*

Went over to Lympne. Michael (H) alert, and full of life-force,
although he knows he's 'up against it'. Also there, particularly
thoughtful, was Norman Lamont, and Rosemary. Norman was
grave, but mock-statesman. Told how at 5.45 on election day he
had set out for a last leaflet drop (an admission of pressure, and bad
auguries, if ever there was one). Some slob of a councillor had
refused to get up, but said 'would they drop in his leaflets as
well . . . ?' Then at 9 am a champagne breakfast for 40 people,
paid for personally by NL. Hung-over all day, and through to the
humiliation of the count. What ordeals everyone suffered![2]

---

[1] Bernard Jenkin, newly elected MP for Essex North since the election (Colchester North, 1992–97); his father, Lord (Patrick) Jenkin, had been an MP
(Wanstead and Woodford, 1964–87) and minister in the Heath and Thatcher
governments.

[2] Norman Lamont had lost his Harrogate seat to the Lib Dems, majority 6,236.

Refuge is taken in the assumption that Labour will hang themselves and people will say, 'this business of Government not as easy
as being claimed . . .' Possibly. But will they then turn to the
Tories? I think not. If only because they want not to admit so soon
that they were wrong/conned? What part do I play? I'm guilt-free.

Friday, 30 May

The meeting of the [K&C] Executive at 1a was intensely depressing and I drove back, after 2 hours, very slowly and sadly. One of
them harangued the meeting about not having 'right-wing policies' in an American accent ('a Jewish accent', Barbara said);
another that we should wait for 'the Governor of Hong Kong'.[1]
When they voted it was: KC 35; Hague 28; Lilley 14; Dorrell 2;
Redwood 1. Poor Michael got zero! But an overwhelming vote
for the Left. How lucky I am, to get selected there! Or at least what
additional proof this offers of divine intervention.

I spoke to Michael (he rang me at 9 am) this morning. Explained
I couldn't now 'come out' in the Sundays. He took it very well.

I don't actually know which candidate, *for me*, will be best. I had
driven in the C-type and put £200 on Ken Clarke (now only evens).

GH   *Saturday, 31 May*

I am excruciatingly, unhealthily fatigued. Missed lunch entirely,
but had a cream-scone tea – a private opening. At one point dear
sweet Jane told me that she had been intermittently bleeding poor
darling, and ought to see Ursell. Poor little pet. If she actually fell
ill, my life would be effectively over. I would be a total recluse and
try all the time to talk to her. I would close down Saltwood, I think
– 'care and maintenance' – and live here half the time. But for long
periods 'Ansoning' at Shore.

---

[1] Chris Patten was in his final weeks as governor of Hong Kong before its return
to China. He was fifty-three, and his future was much speculated upon.

Friday, 6 June

My confidence had earlier been raised by a meeting of the '92'.
The good ones – Duncan Smith,[1] Shephard etc – interrogatingly
having an audition of candidates. Clarke, cleaned up in appearance,
but not especially friendly; Hague, shifty little bureaucrat (voice
jarring, like Wilson); Howard white as a sheet, but still impressive.
Dorrell has now dropped out, but is dutch in the tearoom (*also*
white as a sheet, and looking ghastly). At one point in the
'discussion' I bellowing dominated the room. Half-serious Iain
Duncan Smith said come round here, give us a talk, take some
questions, 'throw your hat in the ring'.

Oh! But what bliss this all is. The sheer ecstasy of having walked
out of a dream, and found it to be real . . .

EMT   *Monday, 9 June*

Today Bill Cash[2] having a *petit comité* for a hard right grouping after
the ballot. And I will give my spiel. By sheer force of personality I
am in fact the epicentre of the 'Right'. And with two delicious
corollaries (i) I am completely independent (of constituency pressure), (ii) whatever the solution – except possibly a Michael
Howard victory – it will be explainable.

Barbican seat   *Sunday, 15 June*

The 'leadership' contest continues. Both Lilley and Howard
welched on Redwood most odiously. I shall be voting for Redwood in the 2nd ballot in order to maximise the recognisable

---

[1] Iain Duncan Smith, MP for Chingford and Woodford Green since 1997
(Chingford, 1992–97).
[2] William Cash, MP for Stone since the election (Stafford, 1984–97), founder and
chairman of the European Foundation.

numbers of the Right; then for Clarke in the final on the basis that he is the weaker; least likely to last the term, easiest to attack.

1 Parliament Street   *Thursday, 19 June*

Sat in the smoking room drinking (iced ginger beer in my case; scotch and g. ale in his) with David D. Shaun Woodward[1] hovered. Pure bliss. Was I really lounging in the smoking room, talking of politics from the inside track?

Earlier in the afternoon, while walking along the pavement outside New Palace Yard, a voice behind me said, 'That's a very smart car of yours which slid past me this morning.'

'I love it,' I said.

'But every police force in the country must have the number?'

Thinking he was 'trying to be nice' I said, 'I never thought I'd find myself saying this: but I wish you were in the running . . .'

MH [Michael Heseltine] replied by going into a long thing about 'I never could understand, you were taking the wrong briefs, we could have worked together' etc etc. I reminded him of the message I sent through Peter Levene from MoD.[2] He tried to push it aside.

When I told David D he made an interesting reply, 'you're opium now, he had to have some. He's aching with withdrawal. No, worse, you were a still smoking stub on the pavement which he picked up for a last drag.'

The delicious irony of it all. Now I'm going over to hear the count.[3]

---

[1] Shaun Woodward, MP for Witney since 1997.

[2] Lord Levene had a long association with Michael Heseltine, being his personal adviser at Defence, Environment and the Board of Trade, 1992. He had also been Chief of Defence Procurement, MoD, during AC's time as a minister there.

[3] In the final ballot of Tory MPs, William Hague had a 22 majority over Kenneth Clarke.

EMT (Albany)   *Thursday, 10 July*

A year ago if you had said to me, etc etc. Last night I was elected (by a very good vote, as Patrick McLoughlin[1] said) to the 22 Executive. Most notable that there is real attendance at 22 elections; not like those somewhat spare grouplets that contest the Party committees.

Felt immediately an elevation of status. David D, who always keeps a lot of himself to himself, but was loyal in my wilderness years, had a chat in the smoking room afterwards. 'Get a group of the new "good" ones down to Saltwood,' he advised me, an end-of-term picnic.

Strange, his 'sponsorship'. What is going on at the back of his mind? Could it be the same sort of thing that lies in mine?

Saltwood   *Sunday, 13 July*

My father's birthday. He would be 94, just – I think – older than Bernard Berenson was when he died. Now the Great Reaper moves without disguise among my own generation. There is poor Jimmy [Goldsmith], in agony for the last 30 days at (Burgundy) where his new 'Indian' doctor is curing him (yeah) by 'withdrawing' painkilling drugs. French doctors are good at keeping you going right up until the end, Pompidou, Mitterand, by ruthless use of steroids and others. Then, finally, the body collapses. After all it was only 1 May that Jimmy was chanting in triumph at the odious Mellor (who now, or so we are told, is to go 'straight to the Lords'[2]).

---

[1] Patrick McLoughlin, MP for West Derbyshire since May 1986; a whip.
[2] Although David Mellor had lost his Putney seat at the general election after twenty years as an MP, AC was unnecessarily pessimistic: he was not elevated to the Lords.

EMT   *Friday, 25 July*

Yesterday we went to the end-of-term party at Buck House. One
had been 'placed' (I suspect by a resentful Lord Chamberlain) on
the duds day. Not a single member of the governing classes up at
the top corner of the tea-tent, where, naturally, one gathers; just as
the domestics separate themselves at a grand wedding and congregate around the great circular tree seat by the lavatories. I drank
four of the delicious iced coffees. The iced coffee at Buck House is
the most delicious in the world.

Saturday, 2 August

Blair created 57 new peers today. The Upper House is being turned
into a sort of Senate (by appointment) and JM gave a peerage to
Tristan!

EMT, Saltwood   *Saturday, 9 August*

In the night (4.30) 'wind-Thompsoned' – thought 'change in
bowel movement' (now a year old). The evening before coming
back over for supper I had 'field of vision' restriction (plus 'jagged'
not intense halo) lasted about 18 minutes. I went on working
through it. In the afternoon I got relaxed voice ('easily tired' – Dr
Thomas Stuttaford[1], first sign of throat cancer) driving back from
Allington.[2] And during the night I had to tinkle at 4.10, 5.30 and
6.30 – copiously. The only frightening symptom is return of the
glaucoma. My eyes are taking such a beating at present from the
'white screen'.

---

[1] Thomas Stuttaford, Medical Correspondant, *The Times*.
[2] Allington, like Saltwood also originally restored by Lady Conway; now the
home of Bob Worcester and his wife.

EMT   *Saturday, 16 August*

Yesterday afternoon for 3½ hours Clara and Nick[1] and I sat in the
hall of the Garden House and agreed the 'mods' necessary to
programme four, the Thatcher–Major section. So the TV will 'go
out' on 14 September for 4 weeks. I think it is rather good and
glossy, though quintessentially superficial, because that is the
medium.

As for my state – I am unfit, saggy, scrawny, bags under my
eyes. I am using up my margin fast between being 70 and looking
70. (Yet I still can't visualise myself as 70.)

Shore   *Friday, 29 August*

Our last 'real' day here. I am deeply apprehensive. So often in my
life I have felt this mixture of gloom and foreboding before return.
As always I think to myself – why can't one 'see the seasons round'
or at least dig in for a meaningful session? Surely next year BB will
be 'behind me'.

In the night I had some kind of muddled dream that James and
Julie's child was going to be a little girl. Poor little darling, a rich,
brainy, beautiful blonde, but what awaits her? James would be
secretly disappointed, I know. He would be such a wonderful
father for a little male-bairn.

Shore   *Sunday, 31 August*

We went to the island, although the breeze was getting up. Lovely,
although my mind was on the return. Jane found a cowrie, and we
looked at the site of the island house. As we were pulling the
dinghy ashore Julie arrived at the boathouse in the Range Rover.

'Have you heard the news?'

---

[1] Nick Kent, producer, and Clara Glynn, director, of *Alan Clark's History of the
Tories*, as the TV series was now titled.

'I don't want news. Just don't tell me.'

'Diana and Dodi have been killed in a car crash pursued by paparazzi.' So soon after my article![1]

We felt a great rage. Nothing will change, except that a lovely icon has been destroyed. Most fortuitously it was the Eriboll service that afternoon – in the Gaelic – and Donny[2] adapted beautifully. (Unlike, I was horrified to note that evening, the service at Craithie.[3])

EMT   *Friday, 5 September*

We are off this morning to park the car in the Commons, camp in the office at 1 Parliament Street for the cortège tomorrow. In the evening, a service at St Mary Abbots, with the Mayor, dignitaries. Rather fun, in its way. And pleasing to note the discomfiture of the 'the Royals' as they struggle to cope with this great outpouring of love for someone they were trying (and succeeded) to destroy – from jealousy and incomprehension. Also, can't get away from the here-I-am syndrome. It could scarcely be more convenient/ privileged, than to park in both senses on the very corner of Parliament Square.

EMT   *Sunday, 7 September*

Back yesterday for Diana's funeral. Very slowly and sadly one drove along in Big Red – twice yellow 'high' bikes trailed their coat at me, but I had no will to respond, and 'proceeded' at, mainly 58–65 mph (this using, by comparison, practically no fuel at all).

The day before we had been to the service at Kensington Church, a nice formal duty. And heard at the outset while waiting

---

[1] AC had written an article in *The Spectator* headed 'Death by Press Gang' in which he criticized press harassment.

[2] The Reverend Donny McSween.

[3] The church for Balmoral, where the queen and many of her family were on holiday.

in the pews, the Queen's broadcast – clipped, formal, utterly without warmth and affection. Then we walked in Kensington High Street and along to the memorial – an exciting atmosphere of happening, of unity of purpose. A crowd entirely friendly, each recognising one another in this common purpose.

A quiet curry at the Kundan – we neither of us wanted to read – and then strolled back through the crowds mainly now with candles, and little make-shift shelters. We slept, not badly, in the office; Jane on the tried and proven camp bed used at Netherton Grove and even on the Le Mans 24 hours, in the fifties. I on the armchair and snoof. A rattling on the door at 5.20, and I called out 'we're in here' thinking it to be the waste-paper lady. But the voice which answered was (surely?) Trish's. I put on my trousers and staggered out blearily in the Cuixmala T-shirt. There was Trish, immaculate in a white trouser suit. I reeled off to the gents to sluice my face and she bossily moved in, rustled papers and without so much a by-your-leave to Jane, turned on the television! This, and Stewart's [Cill-Johnson] presence – triumphantly with his walking stick – in the most comfortable chair did somewhat cramp the atmosphere in the room. But the combination of cortège, TV, crowds, and the service itself was overpowering. My only wish is that I could, for the service, have been transposed to Hyde Park, watched there on the enormous screen, and applauded with the crowd at Charles Spencer's brave utterances.[1]

Saltwood pavilion   *Saturday, 27 September*

This morning the news (leaked) that Hague was going to dispense with hereditary peerages (ie adoped Blair's 'reforms'). For me this is the last straw – already. Coming on top of message to Gay Pride, Notting Hill carnival (aren't there any worthwhile causes he could send a message to?) It's got him marked. Give him a good bit more

---

[1] In an interview with the *Guardian* (15 July 2002) Spencer said: 'Alan Clark wrote me . . . and said I agree with every word you said but just watch now. The press and the royal family are two of the most powerful institutions in the country and they will make sure your name is dragged through the dirt.'

rope, though. We have the advantage that whatever he does he
can't pick up any points this year.

Pavilion   *Sunday, 28 September*

I think the Party has had it. Our grip was ephemeral while Labour,
even in the low, low times post-1983, had its hard core of TU and
urban support. Now the hard core remains – 'it has nowhere else
to go' – but the whole sticky-crap consumerist ad-speak culture
has seduced our centre.

Saturday, 4 October

Today our 'last' bathe at Hythe beach.

Each afternoon we have been going down there; Jane always
'mock' reluctantly, but with her bathing dress under. It is quite
delicious, the water now clean and the great long arc of the shingle
like the Chesil Bank – or even Biarritz.

Now I am somewhat debilitated, but still happy and well, and
my shape not unrecognisable, and I thank God.

Garden House   *Wednesday, 15 October*

The moving sideways from the sword in the lake. It was almost
within my grasp before Blackpool. Oh! That silly, show off (as
always) aside.[1]

---

[1] At the party conference AC had said in an audible comment (apropos the
continuing Northern Ireland stalemate): 'The only solution is to kill 600 people
in one night. Let the UN and Bill Clinton and everyone else make a scene – and
it is over for 20 years.'

EMT   *Thursday, 16 October*

Jane slept badly (how many good nights does she get per year? Three maybe). Poor little soul, she carried all the problems of my (ir)responsibility. She never goes to the studio now, simply sits reading newsprint. This ought to be redundant now with the agency; but actually she finds quite interesting general things. On 19 September we had a fraught discussion about her going to her mother – and we must find time for that.[1]

EMT   *Sunday, 26 October*

Yet another beautiful late autumn day. I thought, said to Jane, 'Will we ever?' now widened to 'will we ever relaxedly be able to say to each other – "what shall we do today?"'

Jane was in happy form and we set about, at 7 pm, a magnificent repast: started with fresh orange juice instead of gin and tonic; ½ bottle of Bourgogne '93; chicken liver pâté and toast, slice of red pepper tart; two helpings delicious venison from Eriboll and red cabbage, Anna Koumar[2] carrots, mashed potatoes, horseradish. Then fresh apple puree, double cream and meringues. We staggered up to bed, didn't stir for over ten hours.

Thank you, God, quite literally, for my good luck.

EMT   *Monday, 10 November*

Yesterday we went to the memorial service and I laid the wreath at St Mary Abbots. We are WW1-minded at present. Jane has done her beautiful Passchendaele series, so upsetting. What a remarkable artist she is.

---

[1] Mrs Beuttler had lived in Spain for many years.
[2] The Clarks' cook.

MFS Saltwood   *Saturday, 15 November*

A wonderful feeling of tranquillity as the volume ends surpassing, I believe, any other.

Yesterday we walked across wind-blown pavements and over the River Tay to Inverness Cathedral where we knelt in church (what a cold building) for the birth of baby Angus (George McKenzie). The consummation of that wonderful moment (on par with Andrew Dalton in the basement of Kensington TH) when 'Boy' was on the answering machine at the flat – just read out his names. James was ebullient last night as we waited in the (far from unsympathetic) lounge of the Station Hotel at Inverness. And then I enjoyed what must almost be the recognitory apotheosis of my political career – a complimentary ticket for the Scottish TUC cealídh on Friday night.

Saltwood, EMT   *Monday, 8 December*

Early on Friday morning, before it was fully light, I walked from Albany to the House, carrying three pieces of luggage, but dressed in softies. I passed by Clive Steps – always a mixture of evocations, from Chips: 'The Chief Whip's car is waiting . . .' to the feeling of absolute exclusion at the seat tryst (April 1992) and 'best-attended memorial service since Aircraftsman Shaw' as I said to Chris Patten when he staged his great party in the Durbar Court. And this time I really revelled, wallowed in the pleasures of my condition. Here I was, having voluntarily selected the wilderness and then (been) returned to a position of huge strength. The previous night, at Norland ward, people had again been saying how awful Hague was and why didn't I . . . ? etc etc. Now I am going to enter the sleepy House of Commons which I love so much to collect my Little Silver and whizz down (more likely creep down as it's bad light and I'm low on fuel) to Saltwood for scrambled eggs. So, except for my eyes, and approaching old age, and guilt/withdrawal symptoms about BB, I would be extraordinarily happy. Absence of sexual activity I barely notice. I welcome it almost; and prostatic symptoms totally dormant. Have abated, indeed, virtually since Tom Bates a year ago.

But the future, the future of the sword is opaque. The Conservative Party is utterly shattered. Our total in the opinion polls is 22% and the Liberals at 17%. On Wednesday the 22 Committee met for 1½ hours to talk about 'the Party reforms' and when they came out into the corridor there was not a single journalist waiting. We have become irrelevant. And quite soon after our return from the Christmas recess, I predict, the Liberals will be at 22 and we will be at 17%. Part of the problem, I have no doubt whatever, is the hopeless, exhausted and repetitious quality of our 'Shadow' front bench. Dorrell, Lilley, Mawhinney, Howard, Redwood, I can't think of the others, the Electorate has already said 'No thanks' in the biggest possible way. They owe their place, in any case, not to merit, but to a series of deals patched up and traded off during the whole ludicrous 'Leadership' contest. At present, I do not see the way forward. Soames rang last night, talked for hours. Said we must rebuild around 'householders, farmers, small businesses'. I must read a lot of that new stuff from the residual Left. But will this actually be enough to fuel a party resurgence? Careful thought on the holidays required.

Wednesday, 10 December

Up early, and waistcoat for an interesting day.

I plan to stir the 22 Exec on our supporting the government to reject a Liberal amendment on Single Mothers. 'I was not sent here by my constituents to go through the same lobby as Blair, Prescott and Harman.'

Still apprehensive about my eyes and panicked last evening that they might seize up before or during my reading at the Sloane Street church carol service. But it passed off ok – after last-minute scramble to get a King James text. Earlier, in a very busy day, I had spoken to the (mature) students; and won their approval and spontaneous chat and answers. One (long face, long hair, still attractive and classy) said 'do you want to be Prime Minister?' 'Of course,' I answered, and she was delighted.

The night before (Monday) I went to the Privy Council dinner – Royal Gallery, and overflow in the Robing Chamber presided by Prince of Wales and including – God alive, how did he get one? – Atkins, R.[1] Copious and excellent wines.

The Queen is transformed, no longer the wicked stepmother with her frumpish and ill-natured features that have been permanently in place since Mrs T rescued the 1992 election. As I said at the time, the whole Royal Family delighted at the elimination of Diana, and now has settled back comfortably into their favourite role – preservation of their own perks and privileges at the expense, whenever necessary, of other individuals and institutions. The Empire, the Church, the Law, the hereditary principle, the Lords, even a yacht, and now there are faithful servants who are being dismissed in droves as they modernise Sandringham and Balmoral.

MFS GH   *Friday, 12 December*

I seem to remember this is always a baddish time.

My eyes are really causing me concern – thirteen months since the opthalmicist in Hythe told me to go to hospital. I now have had a slight frontal headache and inability to 'defocus' for over 24 hours. And was advised yesterday to make an appointment (via Nick Page) with 'Spender'(?)[2] in Harley Street. Don't mind glaucoma so much – unless it stops me getting a driving licence – but am terrified of cancer of the optic nerve. 'Very rare,' Nick said, 'only in infancy and the elderly.' But that day I have read of poor old Walter Matthau (aet. 77) 'going blind' for this reason.

Then, 'on top of it all he was diagnosed as HIV positive'; ie the INLA man[3] is over here with the intention (according to sources)

---

[1] Robert Atkins, made a Privy Councillor 1995.

[2] Actually David Spalton, Harley Street eye specialist.

[3] A representative of the Irish National Liberation Army.

of levelling scores. Can only take it demi-seriously, but . . . *Plus*
Denton Hall[1] all next week; I worried that my witnesses will fold.
Plus how *do* we get to Eriboll, with a 3-line whip on Monday?

MFSH   *Sunday, 14 December*

On the Green Room table we found this card . . .

> *6 August 1996*
> What <u>are</u> you
> doing – London today
> when you have no time
> to spare or so you tell me.
> Well I've gone too –
> don't know when I'll be
> back – to feed dogs, water
> things, iron things, tidy things
> cook things, find things –
> the 'things' wives do –
> we have so much and yet we
> don't have time for each other.
> Well make it, or lose it you
> selfish genius. It's been
> one moan all these past
> weeks. If it is my fault say so.[2]

I suppose at that time I was ghastly to live with. I was consumed by
the search, not for the sword, but at least the path, through rocks and
undergrowths, to arrive at the lake. Yesterday evening I said, 'I could
step down now, I suppose, because I proved, to everyone, that I
could come back and get adopted for the safest seat in Britain.' I still
half believe that my moment may come. I cannot predict its shape.

---

[1] AC had decided to sue the *Evening Standard* for its *Not the Alan Clark Diaries*
column. His solicitors were called Denton Wilde Sapte.
[2] AC had stapled Jane's actual message into the diary.

House Library   *Monday, 15 December*

Very tired and low. I haven't eaten anything except two digestives and a small slice of camembert 'in the conference room at Denton Hall'. And yet I am not hungry. I am apprehensive about my eyes, which ache dully and resist 'defocusing'. Print vision poor. I barely think about the 'INLA man', though will lock the back door tonight. I listened to 'proceedings' all day in Court and was wearied by their repetitious quality and treadmill feel. The Judge – 'Lightman' was beady, but I sensed hostile (perhaps having heard on the grapevine that I am 'anti-Semitic').[1]

Thursday, 18 December

Sitting in Albany kitchen – still in dressing-gown at 11.05; and the delightful, and unusual pleasure of the two clocks striking simultaneously 'across' each other. Very Edwardian, or early twenties. I am hugely calmer and more contented – although of course anxiety in new form will always flow into the vacuum created by the extinction of a real one, and I am apprehensive. The trial has not gone badly and the judge seemed sympathetic, although Prescott[2] was odious at every stage. If I lose, of course, I will be open season. But my real consolation, fresh boost, is Spalton. Stuttery, amiable and bespectacled (naturally) oculist. He tested me, I told him all my symptoms [here AC draws on the page the edge of a spot]. He was unphased. Said the optic nerve ok etc. And I really haven't had a headache of any kind since . . . ! Defocusing, and periodic lights and 'flooders' of no consequence. This is such a relief; I clap my hands in prayer of thanks a lot of the time and when I wake up at night.

Just in time. As I need to think long and hard about the next

---

[1] AC was oversensitive. Mr Justice Lightman, QC 1980, had been an admired High Court judge since 1994.
[2] Peter Prescott, Counsel for the *Evening Standard*. QC, co-author of *The Modern Law of Copyright*.

three months. The real damage and threat to Parliament. The cogent conspiracy between Blair and Hague. We are actually going along with what Blair is doing.

Shore Cottage, 8 pm   *Wednesday, 24 December*

An anxious Christmas Eve. Not since Andrew had bad asthma at Zermatt in 1965 and Gentinetta wanted to put him on steroids. I slept like a top – uninterrupted from 9.10 to 6.10. Janey not so well, complained of a 'sore tummy', and said she felt sick(-ish). I didn't put too much to this until, at EMT, she said she didn't even want to finish her ½ cup (we were in the kitchen; it must have been about 7.30). She was leaning against the wall, just by the window, suddenly said 'God' or something like that and her legs buckled, she went down with a terrible crack (like my father's description of my mother having her stroke at Albany in 1973). I rushed over to her, called out, begged her to move a hand or an eyelid, could she hear me? etc. I kept telling her I loved her. Her head, utterly limp, was at a curious angle when she first fell, and I wondered if Nanny had looked like that when Jane found her at Garden House. After an age, she came round. She hadn't even felt my putting a pillow under her head, or moving all the dogs into the wheelhouse etc. Then she 'came to'. 'What happened?' I wanted to move her to the sofa. She said she felt sick again. Would she like me to help her to the loo? I picked her up, was holding on to her elbow and her knees buckled totally. She collapsed with a terrible unconscious groaning. She vomited, but not properly. Some of it must have caught in the windpipe and she made dreadful draining coughs. I really thought she was going to die. She recovered a little. Still couldn't remember anything. I settled her, drove up to the Lodge and Julie rang Dr Belbin who said he would come straight over to examine her in the kitchen; then the ambulance and the paramedics. Now she's in Raigmore [hospital] and (naturally) the floor sister is guarded. She is 'tired' and all wired up to a heart machine etc. X-rays. Blood tests. Would I be able to take her away tomorrow? Unlikely.

Poor, sweet, sweet Janey who was game and pleasant even in this tearful adversity.

I took the dogs along the shoreline; back over the top. I thought of how catastrophic if she died. I had to see it in personal terms. I would withdraw utterly. 'In mourning.' Instantly become a recluse (and a pretty scrawny one. All I have eaten today is bread and butter!)

But even so. Things are cyclical. The hubris (partially intended) of that card. The extraordinary good fortune that has blessed us this year. There had to be a downturn. I'm off up to the Lodge for dinner.

Shore Cottage   *Sunday, 28 December*[1]

Immensely contented and at ease.

We have been sleeping 9½–10½ hours per night. Jane is not yet 'quite right', and Tom is ill-at-ease, now definitely in his closing months and wanders around the house making little wheezy noises. How unhappy is he? Head of the house until the end. Nineteen years old next month (Feb).

I am reading simultaneously Rhodes James's *Lord Randolph Churchill* and WSC on the same subject. Hugely enjoyable to read of:

'The announcement in *The Times* this morning immediately and sensationally terminated the Christmas calm in political circles. Holiday plans were abruptly cancelled . . .' etc.[2]

and the calm in the knowledge that I can myself now go back, wreathed in fantasy yes, but *potent*, and push through the doors marked 'Members Only'. Who (save me) a year ago would have conceived of this as in any way feasible, still less likely?

---

[1] AC has written above this entry: 'Poor handwriting for being written on knee in wheelhouse as Jane's artist's materials over table.'

[2] This is how Robert Rhodes James, in only his first book, wrote of Lord Randolph's resignation. Winston Churchill's life of his father was published in two volumes.

EMT   *Wednesday, 7 January*

Chris Patten (Phil Patten I call him, a 'wishee-washee', the
Chinese laundryman, as *Private Eye* do) has surfaced increasingly
and everyone is saying how he has a huge political career ahead of
him. (What about D. Owen, by the way?[1]) I don't know what I
have to do to be taken seriously. Win the *E. Standard* case, for a
start. I am too busy now even to open Romeike.[2] Everyone is out
to get me. Radio silence from Denton Hall.

EMT   *Monday, 12 January*

Still most unfit. Much of my listlessness explained, perhaps, by the
fact that the scene, the Commons etc, really is changing. Politics
has become different. I am old now, also. In my last decade before
a true sage. I don't want to die, but if I do, let it be on the
Creaggan Road and my last sight being of little Jane's face.

EMT, Saltwood   *Friday, 30 January*

Yesterday the unpleasant experience of being sacked (over lunch)
by Phil Hall[3] – who seemed, as his words ended, to change from an
enthusiastic *naïf* into a ruthless and beady 'senior executive' in
steel-rimmed spectacles. Went back to B5 feeling immensely tired.

---

[1] The fortunes of the Social Democratic Party, of which David Owen had been
leader since 1988, were in steep decline.

[2] Romeike & Curtice – a cuttings service to which AC subscribed.

[3] A week later, though, AC noted: 'Am cheered by the fact that my departure
from the *N of W* coincided with their disclosure that a fellow Conservative MP's
daughter was "a hooker".' He added: 'So cruel and irrelevant an attack on a
colleague would make it impossible for me to write for the paper anyway.'

Couldn't, just had the sense not to, go to bed and zizz, as Tip came round with some pheasants. Lovely and giggly as always. Went of on his little bzzip scooter – in which I fear he does the most horrifying dangerous things. He crisply cornered out of Albany courtyard.[1]

House Library   *Thursday, 5 February*

House totally empty on our side except for Anthony Steen.[2] Libs everywhere; many 'New' Labour members who had ousted our own people in May. I had quickly to bodge together some remarks about organic farming, Scottish communities, 'affordable' housing etc etc. It is really too depressing. There is our great Party, its historic roots dependent on rural dwellers and walkers in the countryside – and we don't even turn up, still less illuminate the Debate.

Later Soames performed massively, and statesmanlikely on the Middle East peace process. His father would have been delighted.

House Library   *Wednesday, 18 February*

I went to Enoch's [Powell] funeral. A beautiful, perfectly chosen service. Not one word out of place – which is hardly surprising as he wrote it all himself bar (sic) John Biffen's address which was even better. In the congregation outside Ronnie (I had a mental block, as always, on his name until someone came up to us – 'Ronnie') Grierson[3] he said 'have you written yours yet?' or perhaps it was 'I assume you've written yours?'. 'I'm not 70,' I answered, hearing that EP had written his in 1983 when he was, in fact, just 70.

---

[1] AC makes no mention of the verdict in the *Evening Standard* case, where the judge found for him.

[2] Anthony Steen, MP for Totnes since 1997 (South Hams, 1983–97).

[3] Sir Ronald Grierson, vice-chairman, GEC, 1968–91.

1 Parliament Street   *Friday, 27 February*

On Wednesday of last week we [22] had a meeting with little
Hague. (Still terrified of me, I was glad to note; caught his throat and
swallowed when he had to say 'Alan Clark'.) Pretty disparate. Some,
but not total, brown-nosing. Hague in his usual stuff about our
being 'arrogant and out-of-touch', said the polls were 'just turning
now'. I said my bit, that I was 'arrogant and out-of-touch' and
proud of it, and still got large audiences – cited Kent University,
overflow room etc.[1]

The following day Norman (Archie) was in the tearoom and
talking a lot of rot about Euro-MP selection and how we would
now be putting the 'good' ones at the top of the list. 'What *is* a
good Euro-MP?' I asked. He scowled, blackly.

EMT, kitchen   *Thursday, 5 March*

Came back last night having 'not eaten all week'. *Delicious* 2-egger,
demi-braised venison and rhubarb and clotted with remaining ½
bottle of Palmer '88.

Exeter station   *Monday, 9 March*

Been down to Bratton, leaving Saltwood at 5.35 in the Porsche,
which I dropped at Carrs for its big service; borrow a Golf again (v
nice – and no problems at all).

The whole place very scruffy indeed. Only the 'studio' is pleasing with Campling's door,[2] and the giant (and, as it now turns out,
not invaluable) Duncans for the Queen Mary.[3]

---

[1] Three weeks earlier AC had noted, 'Hague is slowly emerging from his "right
wing" carapace (as I predicted to the '92, within a week of getting back, that he
would – "Hague is *of the Left*").'
[2] Robert Campling's painted door is now on one of the Saltwood tower office
walls.
[3] Duncan Grant, Bloomsbury artist, had, on the recommendation of Kenneth
Clark, received a commission to paint huge pictures for the *Queen Mary* liner in
the 1930s. They were rejected. Jane and AC bought them in the 1970s.

It's strange, for ages I was sad and calm and nostalgic about
Bratton. Now I see that we never really got it right, should have
planted dense shrubs etc. It was monstrous of my father to keep us
so short of money that I had to sell the fields – 'the cream of
Bratton' for £500. I did write (most of) *Barbarossa* there, and I
recall walking up the 'dump' road, looking over 'Bennett's' gate
and feeling immensely content. Not much later came 'Jollyboy'
and 'more run' in the white pushchair.[1] Also pining for Tilfy and
the magic afternoon with the girl from Bray Shop. But I only
developed into real living at Seend – Anna Koumar and the banks
of sweet peas in the 'secret garden', which we 'dedicate to the
church'. So it seems perfectly natural and proper that Seend
survives (and the garden and workshop too) and is now 'dedicated'
to the Amazings.[2]

In the second drawer down of the 'Rye' desk I found a lot of
old diaries, of the early 60s. Somewhat mannered writing. Written,
indeed, more 'for publication' than subsequently. There are a few
lines worth saving. But in the main it is a time-warp, and of a time
when we were pushed for cash, and made-do-and-mend. Even
when I was 'local MP' I never really got it *up*, although a lot of
'2nd house' allowance money went on it, to hold my position in
my last Parliament.

EMT   *Monday, 23 March*

My 70th birthday approaches. Hard to believe, in some ways,
when I sit at the table in the tearoom. What do colleagues think?
There is a man of 70? But I am creaky in my joints. Erection is a
total loss. My arms are weak now (and look it).

I have arrived in Parliament at the very point when it is being
'marginalised'. Neither leader wants to have more to do with it
than is possible. Blair because it's a nuisance, interferes with news

---

[1] 'Jollyboy', yet another name for the Clarks' elder son James, who so enjoyed
being pushed at speed in his pushchair that he invariably asked for more.
[2] 'The Amazings' – Andrew and his wife Sarah, who had a habit of using the word
'amazing' to describe everything.

'management' by the exploitation of 'focus groups'.[1] Hague because it raises issues about majority support – particularly of the 22
Executive.

Harrogate   *Sunday, 29 March*

On Friday evening we set off for Harrogate Central Council. V
jolly as we had the eight centre-seats on the train. Jane and I had
bought pleasingly at Fortnums and I went of and got a 'bottle' (of
Australian Chardonnay). How lovely and friendly and uninhibited
K&C are compared to any other constituency I have ever visited. I
had hoped to be lionised a bit more than I was.

Hague's performance, though illuminated by some good lines
and showing stamina (he went on for over an hour), was strangely
flawed and insubstantial. He had clearly watched my programmes,
the way he went into *history*, and talked about 'one nation' (which
shows (a) why he is so scared of me, and (b) how/why he never
talked to me about it or anything else).

Theresa May[2] is the upcoming bête noire as I spotted some
months ago. Yet she is the No 1 conventional plug at the moment.
Even John Bercow[3] in whose Buckingham constituency I spoke
on Thursday, was fulsome (though not as fulsome as he was about
me in his vote of thanks). A strange and long drive that was, in his
F reg Ford Sierra leap-frogging along the M-way. When we
arrived an unmistakable smell of burning brake-pad which I had
thought, hoped, might be coming from HGVs adjoining us in
traffic jams. And on the way back John's view of high-beam was
bizarre. So much so that some big lorries were reduced to putting
on their reversing lights.

---

[1] Elsewhere AC wrote: 'There must be few things so tediously misleading as the
"focus group", a lot of total strangers sitting round in a room trying either to
show off or recycle the fashionable clichés of the moment. Yet they are
dominating the "forming of policy".'

[2] Theresa May, MP for Maidenhead since 1997.

[3] John Bercow, MP for Buckingham since 1997.

EMT   *Friday, 17 April*

The photos of me with the babies (Albert and Archibald) show an old, maddish man, scrawny and streaked, aet. 73 – first time I have ever looked *more* than my age. I wake at 6 am with ringing in my ears. I dread getting a stroke, like my mama.

Garden House   *Saturday, 2 May*

On the way back from the post I saw an amiable, though rumpled figure hammering in 'Garden Open Today' signs. It turned out to be Harland, whom I have not ever consciously met. 'Last year nobody came,' he said. I took Jane up there at teatime. Absolutely lovely. The age of the rhododendrons and azaleas – some going back to 1820. A lovely boggy valley of a garden with endless glades and dells and sudden *aperçus* and vistas. That's why it is called 'The Garden House' (hitherto I always thought because of his fruit farm).

The house itself, long and low, must have been sensational in its heyday (could have been 1911, or 1922). Now needed a lick of paint all round – but sympathetic. The little summerhouse where we had an excellent scone tea (though served in paper cups) was cottage *ornée* 1860 or earlier and presumably attached to an earlier building which was pulled, or burned, down. The green tennis court was spongy and ill-maintained, indeed the whole place bore signs of one-man maintenance, with the marks of tractor tyres on the fairway. But the more magical for that very reason. There appeared to be four generations around. Old Harland (aet. 95, or so he looked) had parchment skin and needed to be helped. Liquidity is clearly a problem, as with so many valuable (as this so clearly is) properties. I felt nostalgic there, and at tea thought of the tennis parties, and their personal desires and tensions.

Why is it that good manners and the domination of the world's oceans by the Royal Navy did coincide? Now both have vanished. I'm sure there is a linkage.

House Library   *Wednesday, 13 May*

I must write about something which I have long avoided. Dear, game, lion-hearted little T.O. is now in his last stage. He can't even 'seahorse' again, even when he tries he stumbles suddenly and falls on his chin, so now only walks about bandy-legged and his spine a little twisted. He sleeps a great deal, sometimes he bleeds from his scrotum. Often he is very 'bad' and bumps into things. But still he will eat, and he is not incontinent and only two or three days ago caught his 'markie' at night-night with that same old satisfactory clunk of the jaws. He is 19½ years old. It's fifteen years since we had him on our election address in Plymouth, and an item in the *Western Morning News*. Watching his decline is depressing; not just for its depiction of a game little soul slowly being dragged down, but also for its implications for me, at 70. And my suspicion that recovery will be more difficult, as decline steepens over the next five years. And then old age will supervene.

Saltwood, tearoom terrace   *Friday, 12 June*

First entry this year from a favoured spot. Brian has started to scythe the sycamore slope and we are near to the longest day (by which, I hope and trust, BB will be delivered and I will be quietly awaiting my first tranche of £50). I am calm.

Parliament Street office   *Thursday, 18 June*

In that slightly rattled, dry-mouthed condition one gets into following a 'gaffe'.[1] I don't in the least regret speaking out on behalf of the 'fans'. Part, as Charles Moore said, of my *weltanschauung*. But usual correspondence of cor-there-he-goes-again type. And

---

[1] On BBC's *Today* AC had praised the 'martial spirit' of English football fans in Marseilles involved in fighting French riot police. 'Football matches are now the modern equivalents of medieval tournaments.'

Conservative Central Office – predictably – got in the act 'condemning' me.

Great Hall   *Saturday, 20 June*

Poor Aspers is dying. What will happen to the animals? Do they
know their protector is in travail?

I got the better of everybody over the football-supporters
'gaffe'. Central office are briefing against me, as always. 'Tough
on dinosaurs; and tough on the causes of dinosaurs.' Hague is ill,
with flu.

Saltwood, EMT   *Monday, 22 June*

Big Book is finished. At 8.50 pm last night I put the very last
sentence onto the computer.

Sunday, 19 July

A lovely hot day, almost the first of this summer. I am sitting out
by the tearoom (not in use this year). I drank the delicious new
Riesling and could be at a café table beside a *place* in Normandy,
'putting the world to rights'. If I was also sexual I would be
completely happy. With this one exception, my good fortune is
so TOTAL that it makes me apprehensive – both as to possible
reverse, and also regarding my debt to 'put something back in'.

Bratton   *Thursday, 23 July*

Yesterday I was absolutely depressed. The sad, final news that Tom
– missing since 8 pm yesterday – had been found dead or drowned
at the Towers end of the moat; its many sad reminders of – in slow
motion – my own steady decline. Then an inconclusive (as nearly

always) meeting of the 22 Executive followed by 'the Leader's address'. Hague really awful. Trite, insecure, verbal disconnection. Worse, I think, even than Ted. Certainly Major was incomparably better. What is to happen to the Tory Party?

Last week DD, who is proprietorial for me, suggested I give a lecture on the constitution in our history, preferably at Conference with Robert Blake[1] somewhere around. Just right, if it weren't for the fact that if BB 'flunks', which clearly is going to, my reputation (always partially spurious) as a 'historian' goes with it.

Now this afternoon, after getting up at 5 am we are at Bratton for the last time.[2] It is smiling, and I sit in the front garden after a lovely tea. I have practically no pangs (though disappointed at the price of £180,000). It took us 5½ hours to drive here from Saltwood. The West Country is inaccessible in the summer months, and much here has changed. It is peaceful, on a sunny July afternoon, because there is no background noise, no 'M-way roar'. But the house looks dreadful from outside now, paint peeling off all the windows, and a generally neglected air.

Bratton remained intermittently while I was Plymouth MP kept going by periodic grants from our 'second-house allowance'. But now we haven't visited (much less lived) here for seven years. 'More Run' has surfaced – my *Rosebud*. The furnishings will be dispersed around the family.

Outside Long Garage, Saltwood   *Saturday, 1 August*

Yesterday was our wedding anniversary. Forty years. Janey still looks incredible; I have deteriorated since last summer. In the early morning I am so stiff and weak that I almost fall over (as, presumably, like my father – and grandfather – I will at some point in the next decade). I am hypochondriac about my jaw – is it rotting slowly under Bertie's great carapace? What does one do when the

---

[1] Robert Blake, historian of the Conservative Party who taught AC at Oxford.
[2] In a note three days later AC recalls how he and Jane were 'absolutely knackered' after the double drive – Saltwood/Bratton/Bratton (Broomhayes)/Saltwood.

teeth go? Like the king elephant in *Babar*, it is the end. No more photocalls either.

BB is going to cause me damage. I will not be the Party's historian and (as I had intended) its sage; still less its Maxime Weygand.[1]

Wednesday, 12 August

Although we have been sitting by the pool (the last 4–5 days have been incredibly hot) saying that we wished we need not move, now suddenly the pull of Scotland is felt. So tomorrow, up the A1 with the customary 5.50 am 'through the gates'. For the first time ever, though, without T.O. on his 'jump seat' – although his hairs are, as Jane would say, copious on the seats and carpets.

Shore, Wheelhouse   Tuesday, 18 August

Last night I slept – without interruption of any kind, barely even 'surfacing' – from 10 pm until 7.10 am. Opened my eyes, said a few words, then slept again until 8.20. After lunch I slept in the deckchair in the wheelhouse until woken by Hannah for the 'w'. Each time we are in Eriboll I sleep like this ('too much') for the first week. I remember Peter Morrison when I asked him what he 'did' at Islay just answered – 'sleep'. That is what Scotland is for.

At tea in the wheelhouse I looked across and thought – 'if two years ago I had been told that I would be sitting here, and beside me a beautiful little baby boy in a high chair being fed by Julie with chunks of fruit salad, I would have thought, "there is nothing more I can ask for . . ."' Two roots of the generation tree now started in the soil. But continuity is now as much in God's hands as in mine.

---

[1] Maxime Weygand, who was recalled in June 1940 to take on the crumbling French army.

Shore Cottage   *Saturday, 29 August*

The recall of Parliament.[1] Yes, it is a chore, cuts into other 'options' for departure day. But just think of it! What would I in 1992, 3, 4, 5 or 6 have given to be recalled from Eriboll to an emergency sitting of the House of Commons! And at the same time to be leaving behind James and Julie and the tiny baby Angus! How can I even for half of one minute start to whinge or question my unbelievable good fortune?

EMT, Saltwood   *Saturday, 5 September*

Demi-serene. I performed in the emergency session. I stumbled – why? Slightly alarming in retrospect – calling Madame *Deputy*-Speaker, then my honourable *members*, but got professionally into my stride. 'I am fortified . . . ('all too true', chuckled that bearded nameless who bothers me from the other side; v unfair as I hadn't drunk anything all day, but no one would believe it) . . . by fact that deputy leader of the Liberal party has just withdrawn his name from a motion signed by his own chief whip' (this thanks to injunction from Mackay[2] and Michael Howard).

It was a most classic example of the House of Commons coming alight while the two front benches sat mute, looking at the floor. A quite brilliant speech by Richard Shepherd, almost on the verge of a breakdown, inspired people to argue.[3]

---

[1] Parliament was reconvened to pass emergency anti-terrorist legislation in the wake of the Omagh bombing by the 'Real' IRA.

[2] Andrew Mackay, MP for Bracknell since 1997; deputy chief whip, 1996–97. Opposition spokesman on Northern Ireland since 1997.

[3] Richard Shepherd had been the *Spectator* Backbencher of the Year in 1987 and *Spectator* Parliamentarian of the Year in 1995.

Ashford train   *Wednesday, 9 September*

The time seems to be galloping past now we are back. This year the September second half of holiday is blighted by the launch of BB. I feel lethargic and passed over; and just lately I am reading a lot about Chris Patten (his book is just out) and his impending 'return' to politics.[1] I can get sad if I think of being finally 'out'. But am I to die in harness? When I am over at the Garden House I think of my retirement there. And when I walk through the rooms at Saltwood now I can half feel my own death. Almost an Orphée-like revisitation.

And yet the 'practicalities' oppress. Three days ago we thought that we might clear one piece, delivered from Bratton, from the Hall, and decided to move a small chest of drawers up to Andrew's room . . . Like everything at Saltwood tampering with the mud and wattle dam released first a dribble, then a jet, then a cascade. The chest seemed better in the bathroom. And that in my bathroom beside Jane's (summer) bed. Thus 'releasing' the ludicrous wooden washstand, which has been her bedside table for the last 25 years into the passage. This involved a total reorganising and cleaning of the original (Rye) chest in my bathroom, polishing the Herman box, the glass desk-top, rearranging the photos etc.

One minor point of interest in the back lid flap of the inlaid writing case we found a letter beautifully written in copperplate complaining about his 'posting' to Ireland, the 'brigands', the delays to the stage [coach] and so on. 'While writing this I have a sword at my side and a pistol, cocked and loaded, on the table before me.' For 150 years or more this has been the 'norm'. How then, about the Peace Process?

Thursday, 17 September

I wrote an article defending Bill Clinton and – unbelievably – on being asked for a quote Hague's office said, 'Mr Clark periodically

---

[1] Titled *East and West*, it proved a bestseller. But would Patten return as a saviour of the Conservative Party? Shrewdly, he did not rise to the bait.

makes a spectacle of himself, but most people know his views are not those of the Conservative Party'.

Sunday evening, 20 September

All depends, really, on the Book and how it is received. Robert Blake reviewing it for the *Sunday Times* – this could be critical.[1]

Zermatt   *Tuesday, 29 September*

This is the time to come here. And now that the silver birch and the larch are so grand their leaves filter and dapple the sunlight.

Last night I had difficulty getting to sleep. I tinkled five, finally six times quite copiously. In the morning Jane found blood on my pidgy bottoms. How? Why? Unsettling. I am absolutely desexualated. A nullity. Up until only two years ago I would always wake with a sleepy erection at 5.30. Seven years ago we started again out here. Absolutely delicious, never been sexually happier with Jane.

Saltwood   *Thursday, 15 October*

Conference – AC1800 parked 'modestly' bang outside the very Blackpool-like (we were of course in Bournemouth) 'Trouville' Hotel. Then Eastbourne for the 'bonding'. I turned up in a 3-piece (sic) suit with a pink shirt – tight collar, accidentally chose a size 15 instead of 15½ – and OE tie. Surrounded by reporters as I got out of the cab. 'It's a statement,' I told them.[2]

Later
'Do you want to be Mayor?' Jane asked.[3]

---

[1] Lord Blake, who had himself written an earlier history of the Conservative Party, was good tempered.

[2] A Central Office spokesman had said: 'we don't want people turning up in suits'.

[3] The Labour government had decided London should have an elected mayor. Candidates were beginning to jostle along party lines.

I just don't know. Or rather I do know and the answer is, by a narrow margin, 'yes'. But what I do not want is a campaign for the mayoralty. Yes, the ideal scenario remains, as Moira Stuart[1] put it, 'become Mayor, then after two years strike for the Leadership of the Tory Party.' And certainly the odds on this are no higher than, two years ago, they must have been for a 67-year-old animal rights activist with a lurid private life and a record for colossal indiscretion, plus falling foul of the Police, HM Customs, and the Scott Inquiry to get selected for the safest Tory seat in the country.

Or the Speaker, conceivably?

I did say to Jane – here we are discussing these marvellous possibilities and here I am with three lovely little grandsons and a safe seat – surely some catastrophe is due to strike? I try and avoid hubris, but do, of course 'show off' (*épater*). Not quite the same thing, but invites Nemesis none the less.

House Library   *Tuesday, 20 October*

Last night the first meeting of the Sybil club. The unlikely duet of Bill Cash and Shaun Woodward have invited twelve 'interesting' colleagues (ten MPs, two peers) to meet on a monthly basis and talk things through.[2] No factional lines. Ruffley (clockwise), Simon Burns (an unexpected figure – but pleasant), Bercow, Cash, Tapsell, Q. Davies, Gowrie, Woodward, self etc.[3] Robert Blake talked, or rather read in very poor light at a slow pace a quite nicely composed text – the plot of the novel, its lessons etc.

---

[1] Moira Stuart, BBC newscaster, in conversation with AC at a literary lunch in Kensington Town Hall.

[2] Political dining club named after Disraeli's landmark novel *Sybil: or the Two Nations*. AC sometimes misspells it 'Sibyl' (after the hostess Sibyl Colefax?). The Woodward–Cash 'Sybil' met at Woodward's Queen Anne's Gate home. Like Bill Cash, Woodward was wealthy, but politically they were on opposite sides of the Conservative Party. One black-ball excluded.

[3] David Ruffley (Bury St Edmunds since 1997); Simon Burns (Chelmsford West since 1997; Chelmsford, 1987–97); Quentin Davies (Grantham and Stamford since 1997; Stamford and Spalding, 1987–97); Lord Gowrie (chairman of the Arts Council since 1994).

All of the contributions were worth listening to. An enormous amount of drink was consumed. Quite suddenly at the end of the meal after port and Sauternes a selection of new, and delicious, clarets were proffered. I smoked, most rarely, a Havana cigar. We 'broke up' at 12.55 and completely stupefied I left the Porsche in the street asking Shaun's butler to feed the meter from 8.30 am.

In spite of walking back at a fine pace and reading at some length from my own published *Diaries* I woke up quite quickly – bitter vomit in the upper throat. Should have got rid of it at once, but this would have meant losing a lot of quite good food as well. Dropped back off, woke again – cold. Tinkled and immediately and strongly came over Norwegian Embassy. Only just got back to bed; a bit worried about cerebral haemorrhage. This symptom is now definitely linked to (far) too much drink.

House Library   *Wednesday, 21 October*

I walked this morning across Star Court, wet and exhausted, and was reminded of that strong, upsetting, and never wholly eradicable relationship – my last, indeed my entire, two years at MoD. A long time now; next year it will be ten years. I get a kind of satisfaction now, looking back at passages when I felt bitterly unhappy, but now think – 'well, I got through that . . .'

Saltwood, in bed, Summer Bedroom   *Monday, 2 November*

Third day of a cold. Saturday night was dreadful, 100.5° at 3.30, I lay diagonally restive – 'simply on the floor at Mother Teresa's, nothing to be done' etc. Hannah occupied most of the space. Jane carrying forward the analogy saw her as a cow, also ushered in to lie among the sick and dying. To complete the image, there was no water.

Had a 'Lem-sip' last night so slept round from 11 to 7 am.

EMT   *Tuesday, 10 November*

A very long 'cold', now in its twelfth day and still bright green, chestily and my voice tenuous in the extreme which worries me.

After the Remembrance Service on Sunday I spoke to little Dr Jonathan Munday our new Mayor of the Royal Borough.

'Feeling ghastly for ten days, eh?' Vomiting, diarrhoea? No. Shortness of breath, chest pains? No aches in the joints? No. Waterworks, digestion? OK.

Hm. I trailed the idea of getting throat cancer from 'straining' the voice. He spluttered. Spoke reassuringly about the vocal cords.

We drove back in Big Red. But I am far from right.

Tower office, Saltwood   *Saturday, 28 November*

This week I put 100,000 Coats into the Eriboll Trust. All too easily they might have been (in the mid eighties/early nineties, when I was jobbing in them at 200-ish) the balancing element against the *Times* dollar portfolio. It is less than fifteen years since I identified the asset objective as 'a million Swiss francs, a million dollars, and a million Coats'. Now they are 25½p! So on a negative basis I suppose that is 'phew!'. 'Shows what can happen' etc and just as well, as Bratton clearly isn't going to sell and we will be down £180,000.[1]

I just took a few moments off to go through and be told that it was pheasant this evening. So opened a bottle of Lynch '62 (the best claret of all time, *I* think) from the case which Jane found among a full case of Yquem '67 and Margaux '61 in Peggy's pantry, under the Great Library of all places.

---

[1] Although the buyer had, as AC notes elsewhere, 'welched' on the deal, we 'very clever to have pouched deposit'.

Tuesday, 1 December

Have done a couple of medias today; the (potentially hateful) Lease-hold Reform Lobby; then 3.15 Pinochet[1] on 'Westminster Live'. Last night I heckled – demi – Hague on the 'Forward Look' Committee on the Lords and PR which has got me on to *Today* on Wednesday. Most people in the room (even, eg, Ainsworth[2]) agreed with me.

As I walked back this morning from Millbank I passed under the windows of the office of my old friend EDG from which sometimes he used to hail me. It was fun in those days popping in there every Tuesday before lunch for white wine. But I was far more frustrated then than I am now. My constituency was in a mess, intense dislike and unease. My political prospects nil. My private life uncertain, as my finances.

Now I am happy and fortunate. Last night sat at my desk, rang Jane, didn't know what to do. Aimless Beefsteak or House dining room? Chose House, ran into Ancram, dined with him and joined by Goodlad who was a little uneasy about being nominated Commissioner. A bad press and Patten has announced that *he* would like it. 'You'll get it,' I told him.[3] Later he said that 'once your radar shuts down even a bit (we were talking about Tom King being deaf) you're finished. You're out.'

Goodlad told me that my radar was always at 360° fucking even when I was out of Parliament.

Leaving the dining room I was taken in by little Duncan.[4] Beautiful, but a weenily bit tiddly, and we sat in the Savoy Room to be joined by Ainsworth and then – TED [Heath]. Mellow and pleasing and a white dinner jacket. His eyes are still alive, very.

Quite like old times.

---

[1] Britain was refusing extradition demands from Spain over General Augusto Pinochet, former Chilean dictator, who was living under house arrest in a house in Surrey.

[2] Peter Ainsworth, MP for Surrey East since 1992; opposition deputy chief whip, 1997–98.

[3] AC was wrong: Patten became a member of the European Commission in 1999.

[4] Alan Duncan, MP for Rutland and Melton since 1992; PPS to health minister, 1993–94.

Ashford train   *Friday, 4 December*

A couple of days ago I was depressed and flaccid. I came across some 'poor' reviews of my book – which has unquestionably proved a 'disappointment' (and, in its reception, to me).

Then, at the Wednesday PMQs, Hague walked me into an ambush which (as it turned out) he had set up for himself. He started asking Blair about 'a deal' to include hereditaries in the reformed House of Lords. No one – either side – had the slightest idea what he/they were talking about. Soon it became apparent from Blair's responses that Hague himself didn't either. Robert Cranborne[1] had done a private deal to save the Cecils' skin and give the hereditaries a toehold in the 'new' House (because of course there never will be a 'stage 2'; there never is). At first sight it was monstrous. The corridors were buzzing and little Liam Fox[2] caught up with David D and me in the Library corridor as soon as we left the tearoom and said it was 'the greatest act of betrayal in the history of the Tory Party'. There was uncertainty, bewilderment and resentment abroad. Most colleagues were low. Another filthy setback (although there was little blaming of Hague's handling).

At the Executive there was much complaint. Everyone agreed it was a miserable affair and the *balance of resentment* seemed to be against Robert. Suddenly there was an agitated tapping at the door. Lidington[3] burst in, white as a sheet and wild-eyed. 'William has just sacked Cranborne and wants to come and address the full Committee in 20 minutes' time.'

Hague himself was 'grimfaced'. Quite clear, but how his voice does *grate*! He's quite like Harold Wilson minus only the bogus and infuriating penchant to suck on a pipe. Wilson, though, would never have got into this jam. The next morning I was woken (one had 13 votes the previous night after 10 pm) by *Today* programme

---

[1] Robert Cranborne, Leader of the Opposition in the Lords since 1997.
[2] Dr Liam Fox, MP for Woodspring since 1992; opposition spokesman on constitutional affairs.
[3] David Lidington, MP for Aylesbury and Hague's PPS since 1992.

and croakily and (when I saw the transcript) incoherently said we were in a 'double-sided mess'. All day, clips and bites. I judged it right to be 'loyal'. But the fact of Hague *afterwards* accepting the 100 exceptions does seem to show that in fact he's all over the place. And in Sunday's (today) morning papers he had briefed that he intends to reform the Upper House 'root and branch'.

As Jane remarked, 'one's instinct is to support Robert; but from the Party point-of-view I suppose that one must stay with Hague – for the time being at least.'

Gratifyingly, Alastair C[ampbell] came on the phone for 35 minutes on Friday night (twice offered me a peerage, incidentally). In the end we were cut off. I assume that the Downing Street switchboard were changing the tape. So when it immediately re-rang I said, 'Are you at No 10?' It was Soames! He gulped and moaned. A little later I phoned Cranborne. Hannah answered, coolish. 'Robert will ring you back, maybe tomorrow.' R came to the phone at once. Spoke for another half hour. Two sides to this tale. Funny about the 'epicene young men' who forced their way into the Peers meeting *with* Hague (quite discourteous and improper). Told of how when he said, 'I can resign now; or later, or you can sack me', Peter Carrington stepped forward, venerably, 'As someone who, so to speak, has experience of resignation, hah-hah, could I suggest . . .'

'NO.' Hague pushed him aside. 'Yah sacked.' It is an indescribable mess. I wrote roughly the same piece for the *Mail* (rejected); then for the *Mail on Sunday* (rejected), each time being paid for. There is the usual talk of the succession. Ken [Clarke] crazily in the wings; Maude hovering. Neither is realistic.

But 'the front *is* collapsing' – as I predicted.

At least it is a lovely winter's day, and crisp underfoot. We are log-splitting and stacking. I have my Mains, and my old-timers. I am content. (My 'ulcerly leg' is healing itself.) The little boys, Albert, Archie, were here yesterday en route for Broomhayes and divine.

But there is just this void. I can only barely see the lake. Over Christmas I must think very carefully.

House Library   *Tuesday, 8 December*

Last night Lëhni suddenly got *full-blown* ear flapping (as in 'full blown' AIDS). On and on she paw jabbed it, yelping and whimpering all the while. We rose, blundered about; Jane found Miss Bett's Powder – stored in a Colman's Mustard tin.[1] Later she paw-licked oh-so-jarringly. 'An *early* *night* always involves an interruption.' Old and true saying.

But why, incidentally, won't Jane pray? Too frightened of it working, I suspect.

                                                             Saturday, 19 December

Bratton sold at auction yesterday. Jane was crossing the bridge, just by the Bratton 'box' implant when a message – quite calm and jolly – reached her. So that chapter is now closed. I was apprehensive that the room (the Red Lion at Okehampton) would be empty. But it was sold to a man from North Lew who hadn't even been inside (saw it that morning) for £167,000. Almost forty years ago that I went there in the blue Olds '88' on a bank holiday Monday in order to exchange contracts – yes, in Okehampton. Estate of Leroy Fielding for £2,500.

Saltwood Tower office   *Boxing Day*

The Amazings left this morning, squeezing most deftly all their belongings plus two 'show' baby box trees, plus all manner of presents and groceries into their 4-door Golf sedan – with the two little boys confidently strapped into their 'space-tracker' safety seats.

When first they arrived my heart did sink a little – 'how the hell are we going to get through this?' – three nights etc, and I am

---

[1] 'Thornit', a patent medicine from Miss P. Bett, Thornham, Norfolk.

getting worried about little Albert, the princeling, who seemed peaky and chesty and easy to tears. In fact it was fine, and Albert 'recovered' amazingly (sic) and ran about and climbed things while Archibald was benignly *Winston* at all times. Now a delicious sense of relaxation – a couple of non-dies (tomorrow and Bank Holiday) then a week 'off'.

Boxing Monday, 28 December

Soames rang last night. We talked and I felt better because together we have time-warped. Could have been Oliver Lyttelton[1] and Julian [Amery]. Lovely to do this from inside. But the Tory party has in fact changed out of recognition. We're not 'new Tories', we are the remains of a beaten, scattered rabble which has in large part discarded its weapons. What we need is a revived guerrilla army that will start a long march and live on the captured equipment of its enemies.

---

[1] Oliver Lyttelton, later Viscount Chandos, served in Churchill's war cabinet.

EMT   *Tuesday, 5 January*

Last night my usual one-hour conversation with DD, burgundy
balloon in the hand. The Labour Party are being buffeted. Whelan
has gone – but under odd circumstances. To Alastair [Campbell]
earlier I had said, 'praise him, don't fire him.' That's three quite
important ships sunk in a week[1] – all while Blair himself is on
holiday still.

What can one make of all this? We can't claim credit for it;
there's no credit around, anyway. We mustn't gloat, and I prefer
the line that it diminishes the whole of Public Life and is to be
deplored. It is/should be cowardly Labour while we (should) seem
to be political and crisp. Some hope! The Party can only think in
terms of wankers like Willetts[2] coming forward with ideas for
clipping the benefit and education policies 'at the margin'. I am not
applying enough thought to what I should be myself doing.

EMT   *Thursday, 7 January*

A *nuit cassée*. Awake from 11.45 till past 3 on and off. After I came
back from tinkling second time (2.30-ish) Jane said, 'are you ok?'
'Not really,' I said. I felt illish and sub-prostatic. I sweat hugely at
night. During the day I am feeling incredibly tired. Yesterday we
went out to the Garden House and while Jane and Eddie were
wrestling (from time-to-time literally) with a tap in the kitchen I

---

[1] Peter Mandelson, MP for Hartlepool since 1992, and New Labour's 'master of
spin', had been forced to resign as trade and industry secretary following
revelation of a loan (to purchase a house) made to him by Geoffrey Robinson,
who had also had to resign his position as Paymaster General. Charlie Whelan,
press secretary to Gordon Brown, the Chancellor of the Exchequer, was blamed
for leaking documents relating to the loan.

[2] David Willetts, MP for Havant since 1992, opposition front-bench spokesman
on education and employment since 1998.

sat at the desk feeling utterly exhausted. I read parts of Graham's book on Churchill – very good, almost excellent.[1] Made me feel sad for my own. Jane, when I said I felt illish, said again, and rightly, you're trying to do too much. One coined:

1997 – 'A ticket back to heaven.'
1998 – 'You may be too late.'
1999 – 'All he does is whine.'

Sandling train   *Monday, 11 January*

Was in excited form; hair wash, looking 'beautiful', clean shirt, pressed suit, etc. 'First day back at school.' Then Big Red totally flat battery.

I do hope this isn't the year of setbacks, when (at last) I still not get to feel, but to show my age.

House Library   *Wednesday am, 13 January*

A lovely crisp day, I cursed and muttered as I dressed – could have taken another two hours in bed (slept without waking from 11.5 to 7, but none the better for it). An extraordinary free run in the Porsche, got from Albany to Norman Shaw lights [at Parliament Square] in under three minutes (!). Yesterday I felt dreadful. Doom-panicked in the morning and rang Nick Page – back from holiday, so when I see him tomorrow he will be (his first appointment) bronzed and youthful.

But when I got back here how lovely and enclosing the Palace is! I took a piece of cake, cheese and a pot of tea and settled behind the screen (Janet Fookes' position) in the tea room and started to reread Routledge for the extra work the *Observer* want.[2] Last night

---

[1] Graham Stewart's *Burying Caesar: Churchill, Chamberlain and the Battle for the Tory Party*. Stewart, AC's researcher on *The Tories*, had been given the use of the Garden House at weekends.

[2] In the light of Peter Mandelson's resignation, AC had been asked to revise his review of *Mandy: The Unauthorised Biography* by Paul Routledge. He called it 'that most tedious of all literary phenomena, the virtual biography'.

I saw Mandelson in the corridor. He was white and shiny and distrait. Had lost weight. Ah, politics!

Saltwood *Saturday, 16 January*

In limbo. But after Nick Page's consultation I slept eight hours for the first time since Scotland.

Bratton money in and earnings building, no o/d (except Barclays), calm about cars, still getting media attention, looking forward to *Observer* tomorrow. If PSA okay must really devote myself to a strategic plan, then talking to Anji Hunter[1] and Alastair. DV. Before the consultation I whispered to God that if it can be done this will be the *year of dedication*. If it fails then spectator, or buffer.

I do like life, and am eternally grateful even if it stops tomorrow – or today.

House Library *Monday, 18 January*

Jane out to Tom Bates and was told she needed a mammogram. Poor darling! This made her low, but very sweet and quiet.

I drove up oh-so-unassertively in the Porsche. Went straight (in softies) to Parliament Street and cleared/signed complete folder. 'Withdrawn' but – therapeutically – in bare feet. The task done, and preparing to go across to the House, I suddenly realised that I felt terribly homesick. I miss Janey at these times, and am sad that effectively we only get one holiday a year – a long period when we can plan things and go on the wing. And only two days, if we are lucky, out of each week. Which means that each year out of 365 we only have 130-ish to each other. So how many days have we got left – a thousand? Perhaps far fewer. I hardly dare write the PSA, for myself.

---

[1] Anji Hunter, the prime minister's personal assistant.

Under 3 – irrepressible
Under 4 – confident
4.2–6 – worst of all – DECISIONS
Over 6 – so what? Just plot what happens; but played, of course, into gloom and apprehension

And yet must always remember these last two fabulous years – it's now exactly two years.

House Library   *Tuesday, 19 January*

(Still) no letters so had to ring Nick P using the little door-phone in the Library corridor and, briefly, thinking that I might faint if the news was really bad. In fact it was ludicrous: nought-point-five. My health *in the clear*; the sheer, total delight of daffodils and birdsong and lengthening days; the relaxed enjoyment of planning jaunts and trips and going 'on the wing'.

But there is the obverse. I have now got a clear two years to make my mark. Perhaps practically too late starting, although BB was useful to have 'behind' me. A heavier handicap is all this ludicrous boxed paper that eats into one at Saltwood when I should be philosophising on my screen. Just at present I am totally exultant, and dreamy. Must somehow get away to pray at the weekend, and Beechborough, too.

Saltwood   *Saturday, 23 January*

A slightly petty piece in *The Times* by Matthew Parris[1] attacking me for my 'love' of animals. This is the third time he has been unpleasant about me since I came back. Triggered, I suppose, by my – much acclaimed – Mandelson review. Essentially, all Parris is interested in is homosexual politics; the emancipation of

[1] Parliamentary sketch writer for *The Times*, previously Conservative MP for West Derbyshire, 1979–86.

homosexuals. Hey, just a minute, I thought they were emancipated? No, no, I mean really emancipated; so that unpleasant, overt
heteros like Alan Clark are seen in a minority, and a slightly
disgusting one to be racially discriminated against. Anyhow, I
doubt it will have done me any harm. But this year I must attack.
Opening say, 'This can't go on.' I attribute no blame, I do not seek
to personalise the problem, but the Party is in mortal danger. If we
went into a general election now could lose another eighteen seats.
And that, actually, would be the end of the Conservative Party.

House Library   *Wednesday, 27 January*

I am wretched – why – its' so unfair.

Still going upper-respiratory (*again*) on Thursday as I got home.
Held it off during the weekend, but deteriorated on Monday with
Willie's eye – so postponed 'Blakeway'.[1] Slept poorly that night –
though not as poorly as last night – and weeping so profusely on
Tuesday morning that walked, 9-ish, to Spalton. Diverted, at some
distance in time to F [oculist] in Wimpole Street. He amiable, if
anything preferable to Sp., almost too laid back. Gave me chlorophormical drops which I got from a nearby Pakistani chemist. I
seem to have deteriorated during that day. Voice went at the
Courtfield and Earls Court AGM. People are *definitely* less friendly
now. 'Where's the bright, ebullient Alan Clark?' asked John Major
at dinner. I announced my 'flu' and was pleased to note that both
he and Tom King moved away to more distantly laid places.

Slept intermittently, woke feeling cold (but not shivery) almost
replay of that last affliction. Made a little 'Ceylon' tea, inhaled from
Vick and boiling water in the eggtimer saucepan. This morning
temp 99.8°, pulse 89+, gobbets of green. No voice at all (it had
gone speaking to Jane the previous evening). Left eye now also
inevitably Willie so popped chlorophormical into that one, also.

---

[1] Blakeway, an independent TV production company.

Tower office   *Saturday am, 30 January*

Expectations disappointed . . . Matthew Parris brilliant, but highly unsettling piece the previous day.[1] I've let a whole year go past.[2] BB, which should have given me status, hasn't really.

In the meantime the Party is in total dumps. People are simply losing interest – period. The climate, and the scenery, is shifting. For some reason I don't have the energy really to tackle this. Most colleagues (like most constituents) 'don't want to know'.

House Library   *Tuesday pm, 2 February*

Last night we went to the Christie's dinner for the Monet Exhibition. All the paintings beautiful, dazzling you could say and all cleaned (save the beautiful fog-bound view of the Palace of Westminster and the seagulls) to the same sanitation standard. The two of the Contarini Palazzo in Venice, some of the water-lilies, particularly those with the willow branches reflecting, were incredible.

Today a wonderful Parliamentary occasion, the House of Lords debate[3] with speeches from Ted, John Major, Robert Marshall-Andrews[4] and Rick Shepherd. Ted spoke, personified gravitas. Good voice still, carried well, miles ahead of Enoch who started in his seventies to go 'piping'. Yes, I should have spoken too, but had no time to collect my theme, nor energy to sustain it.

---

[1] *The Times*, 28 January, headed 'It's time to panic: I don't know what the Tories are about. And neither, it seems, do they'.

[2] A few days before, AC had asked, 'And when am I going to get started?' Mike White (*Guardian* political editor) said, 'Look at Ann Widdecombe. She just kicked the door in . . .' As a further alternative AC confided to his diary (10 January 1999), 'My game plan, if I don't break out in some way in the next 18 months, is to get Alastair to fix my being Speaker in the next House.'

[3] To debate the government bill to reform the Lords, bringing to an end the hereditary peerage's right to sit in the House.

[4] Robert Marshall-Andrews, a QC, Labour MP for Medway since 1997.

Tuesday, 9 February

I am always quiet and melancholic–reflective after Shaun's dinners. Oh-so-gloomy on waking. What is the point? The Conservative Party is a husk, its place has been taken. I am old now, and my enthusiasm wanes easily.

Before going in Tapsell had shouted: 'I want Alan Clark to lead the Conservative Party' and on the way out Willie [Rees-Mogg] said; 'You could be a kind of Reagan, really,' and I reminded him of his favourite article after I was selected.

Drove back (risk-takingly[1]) in the Little Silver. I had Positano steps coming down the B staircase [Albany], just controlled it, then halted and spat at the 4 St James's Street Island and realised I had to go to Brooks's and essay a vomit.

I am not myself the morning after Shaun's dinners.

Saltwood   *Friday, 12 February*

Memorial service today for Alan Hardy.[2] Saltwood Church absolutely overflowing. Afterwards, walking in the woodland, Jane asked what I wanted 'in' my own memorial service. The first time the subject has come up. Originally I said (post *Diaries*) I just want to disappear, like *Zapata*.[3]

I suppose if I am in Parliament still I will have to have one at St Margaret's, W[estminster]. Must have a choir, I said, to sing the hymns and 'God be in my head . . . and at my departing' (probably at end). Also the hymn 'Guide me, O thou great Redeemer' and 'He leadeth me' (psalm 23 sung as a hymn). All prayers and lessons in the Old Form. Lesson: *Genesis* – 'In the Beginning . . .' New

---

[1] At some later date AC added an alternative in green ink: 'oh-so-ill-advisedly'.

[2] Alan Hardy, local landowner with exceptional collection of rhododendrons and azaleas.

[3] Zapata, the early twentieth-century Mexican revolutionary, was shot dead, but his ghost was said to return. AC at one point in the early 1970s affected a Zapata-like moustache.

Testament: 'the star on the edge of Galilee'. Reading: the Hous-
man lament from Enoch's, with an introduction by me to be read
by James. Who shall do the address? Then it all disperses.

EMT, B5   *Tuesday, 16 February*

I read Chips a little. Exactly 61 years ago Anthony Eden resigned
and Chips, to his huge delight, was made PPS to Rab. He was 41
and for him it was, I suppose, the equivalent of being Minister for
Trade.[1] Whitehall in those days being smaller, and the Magic
Circle far, far tighter. This was the moment when Chamberlain
made his bad decision − to go for the 'friendship' of Italy. He
should have seen things globally, but (comparably to John Major)
he simply did not have the confidence to set up a great carve-up
conference plus backing it with selective rearmament.

Tower office, Saltwood   *Saturday, 27 February*

Yesterday I was nearly killed − nearly killed myself, rather −
accelerating hard on a greasy road in Big Red in (as it were)
Bilsington. The great vehicle slewed and skidded. I found myself
going head-on at a truck sixty feet away, lifted off, thank God did
not panic or brake, skidded past. The whole incident over in 3−4
seconds. It would have been a pure accident. Dead. But a 'mystery'. Dead straight road, head on crash, etc. Spared. Like being
spared to go back to H of C. But am I anyway now doing enough?

---

[1] Chips on 2 March 1938: 'Of course I cannot believe it, I, Chips, at the Foreign
Office.' Rab Butler had been made Under-Secretary of State for Foreign Affairs,
with Lord Halifax as the new foreign secretary. AC was appointed minister for
trade in 1986.

House Library   *Wednesday, 3 March*

Yesterday I had my AGM in Chelsea Old Town Hall. A straight victory. Virtually no opposition. I am dominant.

At the 'President's Party' afterwards people congratulated me. One man said he 'nearly' (sic) said 'why don't you take the helm?' (as it were). I drank a glass of delicious iced white wine in the kitchen and was effusive. Janey drove me back to the House to vote, then to Albany. A hint of 'that's that, then'.

EMT   *Friday, 5 March*

Last night on *Question Time*,[1] which I have been trying to avoid for months, in Maidstone. Probably went as well as could be expected. Asked about sex on TV I said 'They're only actors. It's simulated sex, isn't it . . . Myself I prefer the real thing.' A charming, civilised black man said how sex should be pinnacle and when I responded and deplored the yob culture, said how footballers and pop stars were 'role models'. Dimbleby got agitated and said 'Role models etc . . . Do you consider yourself a political role model?' 'That's for others to judge,' I said – and the entire audience clapped delightedly!

I was buoyed up by my 'triumph'. I haven't seen the tape yet, and may have been *too oggly*.

Last night, after lights, I hopped out of bed again and prayed – just pure thanks, for the fact that now I am an MP again, and for the safest seat in the country. While last time I was on to him I was wilful and pluckingly defiant.

I had a long talk with Dimbleby at dinner. Usual beef about BBC management. He would like to have been Director-General, now says he is too old (!). But a pleasant man really.

---

[1] Presented by David Dimbleby since 1994.

Saturday, 6 March

We spent most of the day in Papa's study in the Library block, Jane painting the wall, I 'sorting' books and Liberoning the leather surface of the great desk.

As (per) usual, all I want to do is stay down here. Just a few lightning forays. The weekend gone by so fast and at present I am very tired in the mornings and sleep on after Jane has got out of bed.

EMT   *Monday, 8 March*

Lovely fine morning, and fall in atmospheric temperature so that you can see your breath, which hangs in the air. I thought of little T.O. and gloomily half worried that I am getting more like him. Sometimes just standing, unable to remember what I am going to do. One of the dogs' towels is white with black blobs on it, and when it lies on the floor by the Aga it could, out of the corner of the eye, be Tom.

Tower office   *Thursday, 11 March*

Today I screeched with pain and frustration at being unable to find the insurance certificate for Big Red, so can't tax it. Everywhere I rummaged I found *needy paperwork*. Had meant to come down last night but was – as usual between 5 and 7 pm Connex'd[1] at Charing Cross; unhappy travellers ('customers') on the concourse; in-audible, but bellowing high speech-rate announcements; unhappy and unrecognisable trains appearing one-at-a-time at unfamiliar platforms.

Why do I do all these speaking engagements (still)? Plus endless

---

[1] Connex South East won the franchise to run train services out of Charing Cross including the Dover line. It quickly gained a reputation for unreliability, perhaps no worse than its British Rail Network South-East predecessor.

sundry appearances and journalism. Partly for the money, yes; the odd monkey and grand accumulate at almost the rate they were doing in '92–3. Partly also to 'keep my name forward'. In the tearoom queue yesterday afternoon I said to Gerald Kaufman, 'Thank you for your article bolstering my leadership bid, which will be irresistible once the Conservative Party is down to a dozen seats (there being only seven which we hold by a majority of more than 50%).' He turned and looked at me very seriously. 'Alan, I honestly believe that a successful leadership by you would be the only way left for the Conservative party to survive '

Barbara [Lord], when I raised the question of re-selection, shall I write a letter, etc etc, said, 'Oh no, I don't think there is any feeling like that. There may have been when you were selected, but not now.'

Tower office, Saltwood   *Sunday, 4 April*

It is Easter Sunday. I have changed my 'work station', first from Garden House, then to the dining room here, now to the original Summer Office.

My eyes are giving me a bit of trouble – blurry, intermittent inability to defocus leading to periodic headache. I have an anti-pathy to the crabbed scrawl in the blue Banner notebook. And mindful of the pre-booked (I already have one of the contracts, but not signed it) £450,000 for 'The Early Years',[1] think that with posterity in mind I can now type a bit. The 'Mouse' makes it so much easier to tune and correct as you go along, apart from anything else. Chips wrote in longhand. (Or did he? Robert [Rhodes James] in his introduction does not confirm this. I will telephone to Robert this evening; have been looking for an excuse for some time. He will like to be asked his opinion on Kosovo, but I must also ask him *how he is*, as there is news in the

---

[1] AC had agreed to make a selection of his early diaries, as a 'prequel', and had pre-sold the serial rights to *The Times*.

tearoom that he has had a 'successful' (yeah) operation on his colon.)[1]

Of course a pre-printed is less secretive. If only because it can be read by any nosy parker who finds it. And if it is in a hiding place it will be read – even 'pirated' – still more avidly. It might be possible to get a ring binder with a lock on it; even to have one made, I will ask at Smythsons.

But one of the reasons I am typing is that a full-scale *résumé* of postion-and-prospects is overdue and can be properly set out.

I am hugely depressed about Kosovo. Those loathsome, verminous gypsies; and the poor brave Serbs. The whole crisis is media-driven. Editors have no idea of, or respect for, the truth. They are concerned simply with *scooping* their rivals, and/or pre-empting counter-scoops. But an orthodoxy of public indignation is built up, stoked up, you could say, and the politicians have to respond. Each editorial conference is concerned with how still further to raise the 'temperature'; each political session with how best to be seen as 'seizing the initiative'. I have spoken in the Commons debate, written in the *Observer*, been several times on television – but no one is interested. I doubt that I shall get another invitation.

Now a huge change of mood infects society and politics. It has extended out of touchy-feely, Diana-caring into a *correctness* that has become an orthodoxy. So that 'human rights' can override all considerations of national sovereignty, even of UN Articles and the authority which depends on them. The 'democratic right of protest' now extends its immunities from prosecution or even restraint to demonstrations here in London, and other cities whose governments are not in any degree to blame for the 'plight' of the demonstrators.

---

[1] Since his retirement as an MP in 1992 Rhodes James had returned to writing and was currently at work on a sequel to his study of the later Churchill (to be called *A Study in Triumph*), but became ill with what was later diagnosed as cancer in 1998.

Saltwood   *Wednesday, 7 April*

Skip day. We have been out of doors most of the time loading junk, total detritus accumulated over God knows how long into a skip.

My health not yet right. I feel terribly sleepy, almost Shore-like at 7 am. Jane gets up and goes down. I follow about 25 minutes later. An exact reversal of the 'quiet hour' routine which prevailed for so long. About half an hour into loading the skip I began to feel really tired again and useless. It wore off, then Ann Felce arrived to talk me into lowering her rent. Subtly fault-finding as usual. She said that I should high-pressure hose down all the garden seats. Fucking cheek. None of her business.

She muttered something about her horse, Northern Starlight, running at Ascot this afternoon. I thought I'd put something on it, partly so she wouldn't be able to gloat if it went well, and popped down to the bookies, gave them a couple of new red boys, plus two purps on Skip'n Time which Lynn had ably spotted on the card later in the afternoon.[1]

B5, EMT   *Wednesday, 14 April*

I am 71, and listening to the Albany blackbird doing his repertoire. Outside it is cloudless, but cold.

House Library   *Wednesday, 21 April*

The great Margaret Thatcher anniversary dinner at the Hilton. 'Why have you come here?' asked a reporter. 'To hear Ted heckle,' I answered.

But at my table I was demi-lionised by David Young, Basil Feldman and particularly and interestingly, Phil Harris.[2] Lita Young

---

[1] Northern Starlight came in second, but Skip 'n Time romped home first at 6 to 4.
[2] Lord (Philip) Harris, carpet entrepreneur and contributor of considerable funds to the Conservative Party.

gave me some good lines – she is firm and bouncy, like a *diva*. Then who should come over, but Michael Ashcroft! Talked about setting up the lunch. 'Alan, these are all women you are suggesting,' he said.[1] Earlier Victoria Borwick had embraced me, also raising her leg tango style. Several men, youngish, had sought me out and expressed admiration. A move-on from the sort of function I used to go to as a nervous aspiring candidate in Monday Club days – or even later as an obscure MP. But main personnel hardly changed.

Saltwood   *Saturday, 24 April*

Jane left for Spain today. I drove her to Gatwick, and now I am *en garçon*, with fish cakes in the fridge which I never really seem to be very good at cooking, they break up in the pan.

On the Thursday I had been most terribly depressed by a quite brilliant op-ed piece in *The Times* by John Laughland, whom I had never before heard of, but I rang Andrew Roberts who said he was very good and emboldened I took his number and entered into a brief conversation on the telephone. Laughland illustrated by ruthless logic the inner meaning of NATO's persecution of the Serbs.[2]

Garden House   *Sunday, 25 April*

Little Hague continues to make a complete hash of things. Why is it that journalists cannot work out a bum steer and one with intelligence? There is talk of a reshuffle and whose face is prominent? Why Theresa May, of course.[3] This is because there is

---

[1] Michael Ashcroft, controversial Conservative Party treasurer; AC had earlier sent a list, noting that Ashcroft 'wants lunch, which is good of him considering how rude I was in my reply to one of his demi-reproachful money-raising letters'.

[2] 'The war is being fought to destroy the very principles which constitute the West. This is not moral, it is megalomaniac' – *The Times* heading to Laughland's piece.

[3] Theresa May, the MP for Maidenhead was 'spectacularly promoted', said the *Daily Telegraph*, to education and employment spokesman, 'a phenomenal promotion that has surprised many, for while she is clearly competent she has done little that obviously merits so swift an ascent'.

nothing they like more than an internal row which translates into 'left' (good) versus 'right' (bad).

Whoof! The Sandling train! Monday, 26 April

I have had a dreadful two days. A paltry supper of four tiny fishcakes, and lights at 10.50. Woken by *paws on board* – TWICE. Walked alone (dogs bolshie and puzzled), and very nice and fulfilling it was. I noticed a thread of dead grass on the 'family' camellia, went to pull it away and to my great delight saw a beautiful new nest! No eggs yet, so hope that 'everything turns out all right'. Made some scrambled eggs (quite incredibly, my only culinary attainment over the entire period, as it turned out) and Douwe Egbert instant coffee. Sunday papers all garbage. My hernia seemed to be pointing uncomfortably, but I decided to clean off and black the hinge iron on the Great Library door, wanting something to show Janey when she returns.

Tuesday, 27 April

Keith Simpson[1], yesterday in the tearoom said to me '. . . and Alan what do you make of all this?' . . . (the ludicrous Hague, Lilley row).[2]

'I find it profoundly depressing.'

'But you don't really, do you, Alan? This kind of confusion and reverse should be giving you pleasure. As, I suspect, it is to not a few of our colleagues.'

I sometimes get irritated with Keith. He is mischievous, in general and often towards me personally (*passim* his spastic 'mock' letter of invitation to the Garden Party). But I enjoy his company.

---

[1] Keith Simpson, MP for Mid-Norfolk since 1997. Shared military history interests with AC.

[2] Peter Lilley, in his role as Conservative deputy leader, had been accused by William Hague of speaking out of turn in ruling out big private-funding solutions for health and education.

And he was after all the first to spot the personal analogy between me and Maxime Weygand. Recalled at the age of seventy-something to take command of the shattered French Armies – but with the private remit of keeping them intact so as to maintain 'order'; to defeat, that is to say the battalions of 'workers', who had taken advantage of the political situation in both 1848 and 1870. DD encourages this and sometimes refers to it. Anything is possible, that I do know.

Delightedly, I fell back into this fantasy. 'Yes, I think of the atmosphere in the C-in-C's dining room (not 'mess') in Damascus. On, say, the 27 May 1940.'

Because this was not a simple colonial outpost. Surrounding them are the names – Saone, Krak des Chevaliers, Chastel Rouge, of the great crusader fortresses, so redolent of French chivalry and military prowess. And also, occasionally or so they had been conditioned to believe, of English perfidy and cowardice. In the presence of great art – in the case of the crusader castles the absolute apotheosis of medieval architecture both ecclesiastical and military – one is entitled to feel contempt for the *little worms*, their mediocrity and plodding quest for everything that is banal.

1 Parliament Street   *Thursday, 29 April*

A day of considerable turmoil. Dreadful (for Hague) headlines; MORI figures still further collapsed.[1] At about 11-ish were told that there would be a meeting of the Executive on Tuesday (as soon as we return from Whit recess) and Hague would address us. The Lobby was in considerable turmoil, and I spoke to several – though not all – journalists. By 6 pm, though, he had 'bottled out' and the meeting was cancelled. Order, counter-order, disorder. I left and drove to Gatwick airport where, at 10.15 pm, I picked up Janey, sweet and refreshed from a week at Benalmadena.

---

[1] 'Hague fights to save his political life'; MORI showed 56 per cent for Labour, 25 per cent for the Tories; Hague's personal rating dropped from −26 to −31, meaning that twice as many disapproved of his leadership than approved.

Sunday, 2 May

Really hot sun, and the comfortable knowledge that tomorrow it is not 'Dave-at-eight', but a free day.

But, a potential setback this morning. Around lunchtime I was busy at Bill Holding's[1] shed when I started to feel *odd*. Almost like dropping off (before 'lights') when different reasons and evocations move across the consciousness. I had been contemplating a glass of Puligny Montrachet, but thought first to go down to the Long Garage. But by the time I got there I was feeling peculiar. Headache by side of skull, v livid. Half 'Hungarian embassy', almost sickish. Sat on the seat by the VW axle and started a sub-panic sweat. I worried about a possible stroke. Just about pulled out of it. But had no appetite for a salad of prosciutto-melone, which Jane concocted. Felt, and continue to feel, incredibly sleepy, almost as if v late last night (which we weren't) and/or jet-lag. May be linked with o/d-ing of sunlight which is affecting my blood count. I daren't (although Jane urges me to) put up my feet and drop off for fear of how I may find myself when I awake. Boring, and rather frightening also.

Great Library (study)   *Thursday, 6 May*

A very sad blow. TC died (was killed) at Lëhni's hand. He/she had popped out on my return, had a drink and a good meal from his dish. I had a pleasing double poached egg (having come down on the 3 pm – excellent – train). We decided to stroll down and look at the workings, and putting my shoes on at the asthma rail I suddenly heard Jane shouting – knew at once what it was. Lëhni had clamped him *on the nest*.

We are absolutely shattered. We stood together looking at him on his tablecloth on the kitchen table. So warm and plump, he seemed. I hate the sudden invasion of death – 'in the midst of life we are in death', and was unhappily reminded of the vulnerability

---

[1] Bill Holding's, the Saltwood garden shed, not only for tools, but also sometimes the Mehari and other cars.

of the sweet young. Happily, as soon as we got back from our short and melancholy stroll, the phone rang and I said that may be the young; and it was Boy – very compos and lovable.

Saltwood, EMT   *Friday, 7 May*

We buried TC today at noon, in the *Pavillon*.

He was laid in the little portable hamper, with a host of personal 'belongings' selected from his diverse and conscientious 'nest' assembled over so long and with such Herculean effort. That special silk scarf (which he used to keep purloining even after it was 'reclaimed') also his/her tiny, miraculous eggs; her 'tin'; a biro, a clothes-peg, a silver spoon and the little horse-brass of Jane's which she had carried (although heavy) all the way along the passage from the back stairs windowsill. 'Money-for-the-journey', an 1868 Victorian sovereign which had for several years been lost on the floor of the Winter Office and which I knew his magic would lead me to immediately, and I put my hand straight on it, beneath the desk. Brilliantly, Jane made me snip off with the kitchen scissors a $\frac{3}{4}$ length of the grey marker ribbon from the orange PDF day diary, which he would always try and remove at EMT, and this was about his person.

It was a sad, a very sad, little ceremony. Last night in bed a sad couplet from the childhood nursery rhyme kept going through my head:

'All the birds of the air fell a sighing and a sobbing . . .
– as they learned of the death of poor cock Robin.'

I feel now as if I may be about to die, possibly quite soon, 'nearing the end of my life.' A huge sadness, as if I am/may be looking at so many things for the last time. Somehow I am going to be cheated of my chance to get hold of the Tory Party, and this realisation, coming on top of the accumulated stress, will do me in.

Tea, and we decided to go for a walk, along the front. Almost empty, mild, and tried to take in lungfuls. Some nostalgia for the great days. We returned along the shingle, and could almost have plunged in the sea, which felt inviting. A clinical regime, as in 'Depressed Prince Enters Clinic'. Then a nice bath, and into pidgys. Trying to calm down and de-stress.

There has been (on our TV screen) little Hague, in his 'Bruce Willis' haircut (whatever that is) and his dreadful flat northern voice. I find it just awful, skin-curdling, that the Party – our great Party – formerly led by Disraeli, Balfour, Churchill, Macmillan, Thatcher (even) could be in the hands of this dreadful little man who has absolutely no sense whatever of history, or pageantry or *noblesse oblige*. The whole enterprise to be conducted on the basis of a Management Consultancy exam tick-box, and the 'findings' of a 'focus group'. 'Is not the 1922 Committee a valid "focus group"?' as Eric Forth, justifiably, complained.

Saltwood   *Saturday, 8 May*

The date (although not, of course, the *day*) of the Norway Debate in 1940.

I woke this morning so depressed. The pile of *germane* – or is it mundane? – tasks. Terry [Lambert] wants a copy of the Trust Deed. Where are the Wills? I am fairly certain that I will be dead, or at least *hors-de-combat* in 6–8 months. Weight now 11.4lbs (+).

Saltwood   *Sunday, 9 May*

This afternoon I made a point of climbing over the battered iron railing fence to the 'lake' (in reality a freshwater reservoir). A strange and romantic mystery pervades this location, with the overgrown reeds and water lilies, the occasional wild moorhen. Something, perhaps, of Leslie Hartley, *The Go-Between*.[1] But, less happily, I found out only a couple of months or so ago that the main house had been a convalescent hospital for the Canadian Division in the Great War. Eighty-four years ago, give a week or so, fell the anniversary of the very first use of poison gas in the attack (on the Canadians) in the Ypres salient on 28 April 1915 when those poor brave soldiers stood on the parapet to raise their

---

[1] 'A *Go-Between* trysting place in a hot hot July', as AC described it in November 1995.

heads above the cloud and continue firing. Their only mask was a handkerchief soaked in bicarbonate of soda. How many of them must have been hospitalised afterward to Beechborough, with their lungs terribly damaged.

Saltwood   *Monday, 10 May*

I am really 'poorly'. I wake utterly demoralised and so low that I want only to drop back asleep. I don't want to do anything in particular, no zest. Not even a delicious anticipation at going up to the House to see what 'unfolds'.

On the walk with the dogs I no longer brighten at the thought of coffee and a fried egg and bacon.

Later, House Library
Driving up this morning in Big Red I felt incredibly sleepy and de-energised and zest-free. Had hardly got the other side of Ashford, and was doing 75-ish, unassertively and being overtaken – almost as if in a big old American. I thought to myself, I actually *am* having a nervous breakdown.

I think what was wrenching at my heart was a little conversation I had last night on the telephone with James at Eriboll. I suppose at one point I may have said '. . . got to go now; I'm in a rush.'

Very very sweetly, not at all cross, he said, 'Almost from my earliest childhood, when I wanted to talk to you, I can remember you saying, "I haven't got time just now." But now you are still saying it to me. You still very, very often say it. But I am your son and heir. There is so much I need to talk about. It is to the others that you should say this . . .'

I really love 'Boy'. He has got a lot of greatness in him. I told him that we had now decided to come up over Whitsun, he and I would have a really good 'w', and look at the plantings together. But he wanted to talk *then*.

How awful it will be if I were to die (or still worse he) without our ever really having *taken time together*.

My hernia has cleared. And my 'inner lippen' is not noticeable.

But I do seem to have jawline aches. It may be just because I clench, or grind, my teeth, including the giant 'bridge', in frustration when, notionally, sleeping.

What am I meant to be doing now – 'with myself'?

I did get into the Kosovo statement, and forced Robin Cook to exculpate the RAF from the destruction of the Chinese Embassy in Belgrade. Then up to the 'Forward Look' Committee in room 21, right up on the top floor. Hague jarringly ghastly, as always. I could feel no tremors of inside track, even.

House Library   *Tuesday, 11 May*

Stirrings this morning. In the tearoom I suddenly realised that I was enjoying *looking at* that waitress, what's her name? (who I have long in the abstract – in her striped blouse she is *exactly* like the cutie in a 'Careless Talk Costs Lives' poster of the 1940s – fancied) and I still get testicular writhings, tho' mild. Perhaps another next week before Whitsun in the Highlands.

Wednesday, 12 May

I am seated in the doorkeeper's chair by the chamber entrance, having come in early in order to write a place-card. There is an account in *Chips* of Winston Churchill sitting in one or other of these chairs (when actually Leader of the Opposition) before a late-night Division and making jokes with, and waving at, passers-by, while puffing at his cigar.[1] All sounds a bit gaga to me.

---

[1] 'Winston smilingly made his way towards one of the Porter's chairs and asked for snuff, which the attendant handed him in a silver box. Then, surprisingly, Winston looked at the chair (which he must have known for 40 years) as if he had never seen it before in his life, got into it, and sat there for fully five minutes, bowing and beaming at other Members who looked at him through the little window. A boyish prank. How endearing he is, sometimes. A few minutes later, however, he was making what was to be one of his very greatest speeches . . . to a crowded and anxious house . . .' *Chips*, 28 September 1949.

I still feel awful. Too many times have I made this comment, in the last seven months. I suppose it all (the destruction of my immune system) goes back to October, while suffering from the onset of that strange upper-respiratory virus that shattered, and reshattered us both over many weeks and did, I believe, inflict great damage. Long for relief – and the melancholia of having passed away pre the sword, on the reeds at the water's edge, would be almost welcome.

Pavillon   *Friday, 21 May*

Talked this morning to 'Dr Thomas Stuttaford' (no, actually, I did) whom Jane brilliantly spotted as writing [in *The Times*] on depression. He v splendid, quick and almost reassuring. Said I could be dosed (there is a school of doctors who think in these terms) remedially with Serotonin. 'Replenishes' (sic) the brain. I don't hugely like the sound of this.

Max[1] is around, flies down benignly; a very different kind of presence. I give him didgys from the EMT tin.

Pavillon   *Saturday, 22 May*

I am relaxed here – quite therapeutic – and let the mind run over the sad death of my old friend and in today's obituaries.[2]

Felt awful this morning. A *nuit-demi-cassée*, Guderian on the Meuse in 1940 (exactly this time in May). Woke with an awful headache. Artery muscles in the skull just above the collar-line. Then suddenly *caught unawares* while dressing and retch-vomited tea and biscuits into the wooden loo. Still only 11.3 (+) on the weighing machine. Went down to Cindy Frowd, who was far from reassuring. Said I still had a retentive virus (possibly on chest). But that my *liver* is right up the creek, which may explain loss of appetite and indifference to wine. A bore and sinister.

---

[1] One of Saltwood's jackdaws.
[2] Robert Rhodes James had died on Thursday, 20 May.

Jane said 'Go to Bed' (in the Summer Bedroom). But I was afraid of doing that; too much of an admission; so came over here and put my feet up wrapped in the 2-tone brown cashmere rug. Mrs F had told me that we must go abroad for two and a half (!) months. No. Not Scotland. *Abroad*. Would that we could. Well, it would be lovely, and probably therapeutic, to go to the châlet. I wouldn't mind going via Colombey, either. But if we do go to Shore sitting in the wheelhouse, or walking the Creaggan should be pleasing. Although the Highland melancholy is never far away. We'll see.

But I am not 'right'. No, not by any means. I feel so tired and listless.

As I became drowsy I found (as one can) a formula. Michael Heseltine! Doctors' orders, etc; of course – Al and Heseltine! In no time I dropped off into a perfectly acceptable zizz.

Later, that evening

We then went over to Garden House to collect a plant. We then did the 'w', woodland as always. It can make me sad, will I be doing this next year? etc.

Back at my desk I decided to phone Mrs Frowd: 'If I had liver cancer would you have picked it up?'

'I didn't pick up cancer anywhere . . . You are still carrying a virus around.' (Hey, just a minute, I thought I was suffering from deep depression?) She wants to see me as soon as we are back, clearly expecting an 'improvement'. But I am not looking forward to the trip as much as I would be normally. No point in going to Gleneagles, and the treat of eating in the conservatory, and their excellent *carte de vins* – if you can't *consume*. Must try not to be too much of a wet blanket for Janey.

Pavillon   *Sunday, 23 May*

I sit here (ironic how often I seem to find myself getting like my father, with cashmere rug, writing pad/text on the knee) and am feeling awful and apprehensive, having woken with a headache,

then uncontrollably retch-vomit on the 'w', just at Lynn's Bank.
Now wonder that I may be getting jaundice.

Summer Bedroom, 12.30 pm
It is early afternoon, in May, and I am frightened. Jane, perfectly
sensibly made me come up here – the full sickroom, pad on, teddy
[hot-water bottle] warmly dutiful.

I feel very weak, I doze intermittently, and can't 'keep anything
down', not even half a tumbler of water. I feel as if I am dying, as
indeed I have for several months. There doesn't seem to be any
escape from it – except to 'pass away'.

I am fussed about the impending (tomorrow) flower show. Billy
Wallace's famous intelligence of sitting next to the QM and feeling
sick . . . Am I going to have to dash from the tent – that special,
unmistakable and stooping dash into a giant handkerchief?

I will, I suppose, tell the boys. I would like to have them with
me when I die, as I have always said, like the squire in *Tom Jones*.
Just to hold all their hands and tell them – what?

I see, incidentally, that it is exactly three weeks to the day that I
had my little turn in Bill Holding's shed and walked down to the
Long Garage wondering if 'anything' was going to happen.

Summer Bedroom   *Tuesday, 25 May*

I am still in the Summer Bedroom. It is a fine Tuesday in May.
I am behaving exceedingly like (because, I fear, I am) someone
'with' cancer in the '20s or '30s. Yesterday started better; we drove
to Barton Court for the Chelsea Flower Show. I took a taxi to
Nick Page. Then I walked round to Dr Muncie, who is attractive.
She ran the ultra-sonic scanner over my abdomen. Images linked
to a screen nearby. At the conclusion she claimed to have noticed
that 'everything was all right'. This cheered me massively and I
made a triumphant entry to Simon Hornby's lunch tent.[1] Shook

---

[1] Simon Hornby, president of both the Royal Horticultural Society and the
Chelsea Society since 1994. A former chairman of WH Smith, he had also
twice been a Conservative parliamentary candidate.

little Nick Brown[1] by the hand, then flirted with the red-haired married lady on my right. Disconcertingly, though, a glass of Sancerre had only an adverse effect.

It is very, very busy as the Royals have to be greeted at 4.50 and said goodbye to at 7.15. I was typing at my desk on Monday morning just longing for an excuse (for Jane, possibly), an instruction to abandon it. If anyone at that time had said 'you are going to have to sit next to the Queen at tea' I would have protested quite literally that it would have 'made me ill'.

Jane – darling sweet Jane, she does so much – drove all the way home. Ate a small amount of curry and naan.

Later
Janey was sitting on the bed. 'Are you going to blub?' She nodded. 'Come over here.' The poor sweetheart, her lovely grey eyes were full of tears. This is my real sadness. I just can't bear to be away from her – for so long.

Summer Bedroom   *Wednesday, 26 May*

I forgot Jane's birthday – how could I? Only remembered when Sarah rang this morning. Last night quite soon I was woken by her pretty face against mine, she was distinctly wet with tears. I am so sleepy I suppose I just dropped back off; but was soon rewoken by her touching my cheek, and hair and face. Jackie Kennedy and Jack in the Dallas infirmary. Poor little love. 'I don't want to lose you,' she kept saying. I am so exhausted I couldn't respond properly. What made her wake up to do this? For us both this is a deeply unhappy time.

We went up (1.27 train) to the 'mayor-making'. Then to House, taking tea except I risked a slice of apple strudel. I went up to the 22 Exec, felt illish when I repicked Jane up at the Family Room, but just got to KTH, where cherry black attendant thanked

---

[1] Nick Brown, MP, minister of agriculture since 1998; (Labour) for Newcastle-upon-Tyne East and Wallsend since 1997 (Newcastle East, 1983–97).

us for our Christmas cards. Improvised my way through both the ceremony and the reception. We cut the dinner, then drove back in Big Red. I had most recklessly eaten a canapé. It had the miraculous effect of making me hungry! So on getting back I had a tiny Jane-2-egger cooked in oil. Slept pretty well.

Now with some trepidation am going to speak to Nick Page and hope he doesn't say anything unsettling.

'There is no evidence of any liver, kidney, pancreas or heart disease; and the second blood tests are all normal.

'This tends to confirm the clinical impression that there is no disease here and I suspect it may be the psychological factor that lies behind all this . . .'

This *has* calmed me, and made me feel hungry. I'd like a yoghurt and cereal.

Pavillon   *Thursday, 27 May*

Today Lynn made a brilliantly perceptive suggestion. Jane was shopping, but 'Bill the gardener' had sort of made a balls-up of the Atco. The clutch had started to slip again and he had taken off some of the shields. Wanted to take off clutch, but 'could only be done by bending it.' Certainly not, I said. I cannot bear employees who abuse machinery – as they all love to do, and it irritates me every time I hear the Mehari going.

'Nothing for it,' Lynn said. 'You'll have to retire and take a job as a gardener.'

What bliss! But how totally illustrative of the sort of dilemma which, probably more than anything, is 'stressing me out'.

Summer Bedroom   *Friday, 28 May*

I am suffering from *apprehension*, triggered by an initial attack of panic (brought on by what?). Last night, eg, couldn't raise Eriboll though left several messages and got this awful child-in-the-dark panic – of which I had had an attack earlier on at Garden House when Jane suddenly disappeared and wouldn't respond to my coo-ees.

Now I am really low. Everything seems so ephemeral.

By the evening AC had deteriorated. Feeling awful, headaches and wanting to be sick. Jane recalled sitting up in bed in the middle of the night saying 'I think you've got a brain tumour. I'm going to call a doctor.' That morning he was examined by Chandrakumar (the Clarks' local GP), who said he wanted him to have a brain scan. Despite AC's protests, Jane drove him to the William Harvey Hospital at Ashford. By the time they arrived he was so dehydrated he could no longer stand and had to be admitted in a wheelchair. The scan revealed a massive tumour and despite it being the Whit weekend it was arranged for him to be taken to King's College Hospital, London, by ambulance – Jane recalls someone apologising that it was not 'as comfortable as one of your Bentleys'.

Jane drove up to see him on Sunday. No longer dehydrated, he was in typical AC form, ordering everyone about. The surgeon, Nick Thomas, had arranged for AC to undergo surgery the following day. AC takes up the story:

King's College, SE5   *Whit Monday, 31 May (pre-op)*

Just woken and (a bad sign) thought I was in France. Actually in King's College, SE5 – quite nice private room.

Jollier last night; boosted by talking to both boys, doctors and Jane. Watching TV. Fell asleep instantly 11 pm. But head filling with putative engagements for today . . .

Woken, panicking, by drip alarm. V sleepy. In came nurse and changed reservoir.

Slept totally till 6-ish. Then started looking at clock. Could easily have depressed you (no!). Is this a function of the tumour itself? Heaven knows what it will be like when coming 'round' (sic) from the anaesthetic.

Yet last night the Registrar was charming, said I was the only person who could rival Blair's combination of charisma and authority.

Saltwood, Summer Bedroom   *Friday, 4 June*

Green ink! Originally reserved for holidays (Z or E).

I am back from (in a sense) the dead. I nearly – sic, etc – died last week. My physique (Nick Thomas, surgeon, very splendidly said to Jane, 'biologically, he's young') has taken a real battering. Last night Janey, quite brilliantly drove me back in the Discovery in the dark to get here at 2-ish. (For five hours she had devotedly sat in my room at King's College while we both watched the three blood-transfusion sacs drain down.)

Yow! Did I creep – first real slip-change down into old age/ infirmity with the walking stick – through the Garden Entrance, up the front stairs, line of route in reverse etc. And the previous two days in hospital I could hardly straighten the legs out without setting the heartbeat knocking, the blood coursing.

But today, physically, I am doing more and more. It's the mental work, any kind of analysis which is what I am really trying to avoid. It particularly does/did affect the brain. But quickly leads me into unwelcome little naps with observationalist dreams involving my father, which make me a little frightened.

This morning I woke, thought myself to be a little short of psyche. In spite of reassurance from Nick and Chadrakumar I know it could quite well be George VI valet.[1] Certainly the best (least 'controversial') way to go. Pin just been on the answer-phone. 'I shall be so cross if you go ahead of him,' Jane said.

Yesterday went out, really needed the stick, to Tom[2] and back. Turned at the garden entrance and went to the well. Then on to the sun-dial in the rose garden.

In the evening a personal handwritten letter from Blair. 'Come back and give me a hard time.' Utterly delighted and moved.

Baddish night. Awoke and apprehensive from about 1.30 round past 3.15.

---

[1] George VI was found dead by his valet in the morning at Sandringham; he had died peacefully in the night.

[2] The grave in the bailey of Tom, the Clarks' Jack Russell.

Jane, though, snuggled up and was quite incredibly lovey and reassuring.

8 am Tuesday, 8 June

Nick came down yesterday pm and took out the clips. Forty in number. First 'reasonable' night. (Unexpected, strangely, after being told, indirectly, that you've 'got' cancer.) 2.50 am–3.10 am not so bad. This morning quite hungry and ready for action. Even went down, and 'did' the padlock. This is the first morning that I haven't felt absolutely ghastly. James may be here tomorrow, which I'm looking forward to. I am over-active. I leap from my bed the whole time and am quite ready to 'take over' the Countax, eg from 'big' Bill.

A nice round. Did Roman Tower, then Welsh, then round the half moon and Jane drove me back from Towers in Discovery. Then went to have first bath in the Cork [bathroom]. I have lost weight, a stone, and look like a thin old man. I recalled a lovely high spot of physicality and natural delight when Jane and I bathed naked at the slipway round Eriboll shore towards the sheep fence and a seal came up and said hello and we waved at him.

Thursday, 10 June

First 'good' night. Lovely talking to James about Eriboll, Burrs,[1] lots of things. Jane still incredibly pretty and fresh-faced.

Whether or not I will be spared gradually to consolidate my position as a Renaissance Count is still to be seen.

At 8 pm drove and turned XK140!

---

[1] Burrs, shop and property at Tongue.

Friday, 11 June

'Not quite right' (?mark, eyes, throat, toes etc etc) – frightened of falling asleep – strange dream pattern. But found that achieving is the most therapeutic. Did the gate and just came back now from winding and setting the stairs clocks.

It's just me and Janey after today (which is looming with cars, mowers, etc). Her wonderful remark – 'now' (ie post-King's) 'it's all bonus'.

Later
I just list what God has given me today (lunchtime):

1. A long talk with Andrew.
2. A general feeling of being energetic 'on the case'.
3. The will and impulse to go down and phone DD.
4. A strange feeling of fulfilment (much reduced glazed 'napping').

Later
Eyes a bit out of focus. Dread 'consultation' looming next week on 'Radio Therapy'. Nasty decisions.

Monday, 14 June

V good night.
  The Amazings, including Albert, arrive. If it wasn't for eye trouble (defocusing v difficult) I'd be *in the lead* at still not quite two weeks. God is being marvellous to me.

Monday, 21 June

Chandrakumar arrived to take some blood. Checked on haemo-globin (what's the point?) accompanied by a *nurse*.
  He let fall the dreaded word oncologist about Coulthard (or

whatever he's called)[1] and his radiotherapy. Actually this depressed me dreadfully and today I feel weak in the arms, tired, and at intervals cold.

Now I am listless and my morale low. I feel somehow as if I am already undergoing radio therapy. The VCC visit and even the XKs[2] on 18 July hang over me, because I so love the blank time with Janey.

I must go to Eriboll and see Angus and the Birkett Foster rocks before a decline sets in. That week, just for a few days on the sleeper seems the best bet for a little 'pic'. I somehow can't realistically envisage myself, certainly not at yesterday's peak form, being there for long in August. I am sad today, the first, almost, since the operation three weeks ago.

Wednesday, 23 June

Another stage to make, I fear, a reversal of both fortune and direction. I have been getting steadily better each day, since the operation and since (especially) my sortie to Saltwood. Last night I was incredible, and even this morning 'normal'. But from today I will be in a morale-based decline. The oncologist appeared at 12.30 and I did *not* take to him. Quite clear (as I have all along both suspected and know) that radiotherapy is both disagreeable and useless. 'No cure, so don't expect one' etc. The word cancer was freely mentioned a lot.

Friday, 25 June

A good night. I always sleep well after Cindy Frowd has been.

Yesterday evening I mowed the *wanderweg*.[3] Had spoken to

---

[1] AC thought he was related to the racing driver David Coulthard. In fact the oncologist spelt his name Stewart Coltart.

[2] The Veteran Car Club and the XK Jaguar-owners' club, which had arranged days out for members at Saltwood.

[3] The mown grass path from outside the towers.

Nick who said 'ok' to go to Scotland and he would write the prescription for boost steroids which John the chemist has very gamely agreed to provide. Am I up to the journey? Tinkling and Thompson, Macrae & Dick[1] on arrival etc.

MFS GH   *Sunday, 27 June*

I must record a wonderful day (against all expectations).

I rose early, moved things, fussed. When the [VCC] visitors and their rather boring brass-age cars were assembled I mingled, spoke to them, felt pretty amazing. Jane was pleased with the way everything went. Saltwood 'putting on a show'. Then I slept, went on the 'w'. But I still feel as if I am 'getting better'. Quite remarkable. If I didn't have radiotherapy and Chandrakumar's silent blood tests hanging over me I would be over-confident. Came over here after tea and said a prayer of thanks. It's lovely this kind of demo that God can do anything.

Brian Moore came in his red Ghost with 'Alpine' tourer. I remember how fast the car was the first straight out of Vienna and told him so.

Later I reminded Jane how lovely and romantic was our meeting at the Monaco landing stage in Venice, then going on to Trieste, making love in the hotel room before dinner; and then the rest of the magical [Alpine] rally.

I have this divine serenity at present. I do hope it lasts.

Eriboll Wheelhouse   *Thursday, 1 July*

It's incredible. At 8 pm I sit in the wheelhouse. Troubled only by a full colon (blocked, presumably, by a(nother) tumour). But what an achievement to be here! Came up on the day train yesterday from King's Cross. A lovely journey with attentive staff.

---

[1] Land Rover dealers at Inverness. The Clarks always bought their Land Rovers there.

Derek Presley[1] met us with the latest Discovery – very pleasing indeed. Jane drove and stopped at 9.15 pm at the new curry restaurant in Bonar Bridge. Amiably they produced a beautifully packed and labelled take-away and as we drove along to Lairg we ate one of the most delicious meals I have ever consumed. It was dusk and drizzling when we arrived, but still I walked in my raincoat alone and with the big stalking stick to the boathouse. On the shoreline I thanked God for getting us here 30 days after Room 17. Then a cup of Ovaltine and slept like a log, as did Jane.

Today I have done a lot. Incredibly walked around the walled garden, going to Birkett-Foster, sawing some logs. Almost like old Eriboll crofting days.

Wheelhouse, Eriboll   *Saturday, 3 July*

The Eriboll magic. I felt very tired on and off, but the pluses are unavoidable.

How I wish that I could stay up here and just cure myself by God helping me to regenerate (as he has done so brilliantly up until now). But tomorrow we return, for me to be slowly and systematically destroyed. But how wonderful to have come up here, and tasted its strengths and touched all the beacons.

Monday, 5 July

We got back last night after Jane had driven heroically from Eriboll–Inverness (Scotch mist started on the Moine) and London, H of C car park, to Saltwood.

Later

I am homesick for Eriboll. The sweet oystercatchers all came in a flock, full strength, to say goodbye to us yesterday morning at 6 am, when we were loading the Discovery. I see always the

---

[1] Derek Presley, managing director of Macrae & Dick.

beautiful view of the shoreline from boat house beach and hear the slap of the wavelets. That is heaven for me. But today I seem to be an awful long way from it; and it's very inaccessible. There I would gladly lie down and die. But the gulls and the hoodies [crows] would take out my eyes, which would be upsetting for Jane.

Later still
I bathed today, one length. The first this year. Thank you, God.

MFS GH   *Tuesday, 6 July*

I'm very tired. But today I went to Canterbury for 'planning' – ie fitting the mask.[1] All quite encouraging.

Then I did a lot of mowing, also swam two lengths – just like the old times with Lëhni waiting aggressively on the steps.

My blood test, haemoglobin etc totally ok (as Chandrakumar was forced to admit).

Garden House   *Wednesday, 7 July*

I am in my father's study. I have eye-headache coupled with some dizziness. No great appetite.

I virtually finished the Bailey with the repaired Atco. A delicious machine, but fills its green box in 1½ stripes. Felt very tired, but swam one length. I remain depressed and apprehensive. Just like May, I fear.

I think about when I may 'take my leave'. Once I get to Eriboll to the boat house, I am so close to heaven. But to get there is so difficult. Whereas here, with all those lovely things around me, it could always be '*Suddenly at Saltwood*'.

The Catholics are coming. 'Guild of the Divine Sacrament' on Saturday. I hope I'm up to it.

---

[1] A clear plastic face mask used when undergoing radiotherapy of the head.

Pavillon   *Thursday, 8 July*

This, so far, is my very lowest day. I am so de-energised, almost like May, and have an unpleasant, eye-related frontal headache.

Before lunch I was standing in the Great Library with Jane and Lynn. A month ago I used to go over there on my own just for the fun of arranging books. This time I had to sit down, couldn't do anything.

I dread the inference that there must be another tumour lurking in there. X-rayed today in Canterbury. But then what? All I want to do at present is 'rest'. My eyes complain if I do any kind of paperwork, like, eg, even writing this note.

Progress has come to a halt.

Friday, 9 July

How does it end with cancer of the brain? Mark Boxer and Jock Bruce-Gardyne.[1] Do you lose your faculties, vision, speech, balance? I wish I could conceive of an escape route. It is just so difficult to get to Eriboll. And anyway I must, I suppose, give the treatment a chance. I fear, though, that now I am degenerating into an invalid . . .

MFS, Great Hall   *Saturday, 10 July*

The Guild of the Blessed Sacrament have just left. A wonderful hot afternoon and by 4 pm the Inner Bailey had the appearance of a garden party.

Last night Jane gave me a little reflexology on my thumb to ease the head pain; and amazingly it worked – I dropped off almost at once.

---

[1] Mark Boxer, cartoonist ('Marc'), journalist, editor of *The Tatler*, died 1988; Jock Bruce-Gardyne, journalist and politician (Conservative, South Angus, 1964– October 1974; Knutsford, March 1979–83), died 1990.

Father Michael came up trumps. He produced the Marchmain case out of *Brideshead*, gave me sacrament for the sick, oil, holy bread etc.[1] For a few minutes I felt cured. But it soon reverted. No appetite, or energy, headache. At periods I am back to May – which is particularly lowering.

Monday, 12 July

Continued to deteriorate during the day. Sweet Janey cried, heart-rendingly, after 'lights'. 'I don't want to lose you . . .' The laughing, the chatting, the strength. I went down and rang Nick Thomas who (as always) returned the call immediately. He was unwelcomingly grave. Authorised 2mg of D/M[2] per day. But spoke of 'new' cyst. Could be removed surgically. I am so depressed. The stagehands are now fiddling about with the curtain(s). I took a D/M, and slept pretty well; though immediately on waking unease and pain starts to come through the eyes. I remain very, very exhausted and sleepy. I don't see how this can end now, except with my dying. I do not look forward to the gravediggers clumping about. God, please help to keep Janey's morale up.

Summer Bedroom   *Tuesday, 13 July*

I sat on the bed here, feeling feeble (just had a bath because I, and the pidgys, have become poofy).
     It turned into rather a sad little morning.
     Jane and I had an argument about the size of the D/M dose (not

---

[1] AC often quotes from Evelyn Waugh's *Brideshead Revisited*. If he saw life imitating art one wonders whether he knew that Waugh's novel art was imitating life? As Waugh explains in his diary (13 October 1943) he drew inspiration from the death of his friend Hubert Duggan, and the priest saying: 'Look all I shall do is just to put oil on his forehead and say a prayer. Look the oil is in this little box. It is nothing to be frightened off.'

[2] AC's shorthand for Dexamethadone, one of the drugs he was prescribed.

easy to calculate owing to the confusion of the milligrams and micrograms). Lynn was in the kitchen and Jane ran out crying. I swallowed all eight, told Lynn to find her in the greenhouse and tell her I had done so. I read a piece in *The Times* about a new cure, but with a poor prognosis.

No sign of Jane. So I left a note and went out to walk in the – her – woodland; lower path and twice I missed my footing and fell. I was quite frightened. Only God can give me strength now. I don't really want to die now, or here. Back to the old conundrum. How do I get to Eriboll and the oystercatchers? I suspect that Jane will thwart this. She does not want me to die in the north, probably for administrative reasons.

So I am low. The D/M has banished the headache, but the eyes can still induce nausea and dizziness. What is my *raison d'être*? If there is ever going to be an *être*?

Bonjour Tristesse; comment tu vas – ou vas tu?

Back in Summer Bedroom   *Thursday, 15 July*

am. Eyes really ache. So no appetite at all. How do I emerge from this? Dreading the XKs.

Wrote Jane a letter for our wedding anniversary [31 July] and gave it to Lynn.

We went to Canterbury. Not much encouragement. After the skimpiest lunch I had ever consumed, tried a nap, but disagreeable, blighted by a non-obsessional dream sequence. On waking up – where am I? What's going on? What's next?

Saturday, 17 July

Feeling simply dreadful. Is this how Death approaches? This morning I could eat no breakfast to speak of. The smell of bread frying made me nauseous, as I was going out of the kitchen, Jane snapped 'why?' at me. I tried to explain, but was, I recognise, soft-spoken in the extreme.

'Your problem is', Jane said, 'that you want to die; but are frightened of dying.' Too true. Is is the journey that scares me.

The Amazings are coming in this afternoon to help with the XK rally. Poor Jane is so exhausted. Can one wonder? She does so much. (Jane has just brought me a glass of cool sorrel tea.)

Garden entrance, terrace   *Sunday, 18 July*

The XKs parked all over the place. Andrew extremely competent in coping. The blue, the white and the grey cars all 'won' awards. (So there!) I said to James on the phone. Fitting, somehow, that my impending departure should be attended by this huge retinue of XKs. 'You must think positively,' was all he could say. Useless advice, although well meant.

Tuesday, 20 July

Yesterday in mid-afternoon I felt so ill I wrote Jane a note.

Darling
I think I'm going . . .
    The divide between giving up life and *being sick* is a narrow one.
    You must not forget how much I love you, and regret having caused all this 'aggro'. Talk to Fr Michael. He knows.
    Also get a message to the oystercatchers. And to Tom, also.
    I will always be *for you*.

                                                         A x x x x

When I was writing the note Jane was crossing the bridge, and heard me calling . . . we are very psychic, and she particularly.

Saltwood Summer Bedroom   *Monday, 26 July*

A lot of hustling and bustling with different doctors. My treatment
starts tomorrow and in some apprehension I look at the tube of
Biafine Emulsion[1] which is meant to protect the skin from burns
and (can it?) disfigurement. Last night felt ghastly. At one point it
could have been 'Suddenly at Saltwood'.

Green Room   *Tuesday, 27 July*

Jane drove me back today from the first day of treatment at Kent
and Canterbury Hospital. My vision has gone and I am most
worried about it; now see double images, particularly vehicles
coming towards me, which quite underlines Nick Thomas's early
caveat.[2]

I am very very in despair. Where do I turn? Something told me,
again and again, 'don't come back from Eriboll.'

A little later I rang Broomhayes and spoke to Lilian. As I said
later to Jane I do love the way they have all settled in, after a
fashion, on to the Seend scene. One of Seend's premier families.
After all, the little boys can't be much less aged than when we were
there in the sixties and we were making waves at (say Ned
Whiting's) and forging memories. A lovely, friendly, beautiful
place in Wiltshire.

Blast, as I wrote this I am finding it more and more difficult to
focus, and to alter focus.

Green Room, Saltwood   *Wednesday, 28 July*

Oh dear, I am down! Actually I do not think that I have ever been
worse.

---

[1] Nick Beuttler, AC's brother-in-law, sent the cream, available over the counter
in France.
[2] AC had been told not to drive for three months after his operation.

At present there is a huge vacuum around my life. What am I actually waiting for (that is of course itself exceedingly carcinogenic)? No more comradeship drinking, shared and competing ambitions, gossip, taste.

These are all the things I love in (and about) life. Perhaps that is why at present I am getting so many nostalgic evocations – the N7,[1] the café at Kalpetran,[2] even, Jane remembered, the great expedition down to Zinal when she and (I think) both boys met me in the Porsche.

At some point, as the news gets worse, I find myself resolving to take a bolt. Head for the highlands and put my body at God's mercy.

Saltwood Summer Bedroom   *Thursday, 29 July*

Talked with Boy on topic of Zermatt. Did I imagine it or when he rang off I thought the word Treuhand was mentioned? Suddenly realised this might be the answer to everything. Stuff (sell) a lot of the Sotheby's inventory, which I have got 'forward' into the AG!! Slept more calmly after a nice vol-au-vent supper. Must talk to Janey today, or asap.

AC's wedding anniversary letter, to be opened on 31 July, but written on Thursday, 15 July

Just back from a visit to Kent & Canterbury, not a very good day . . .

Hello, my sweet Janey!
    I am reminded that only 41 years ago I was somewhat apprehensively sharing digs with Celly and Caryl in Victoria Road Westminster – a short distance from Grey-Coat Gardens.

---

[1] The old route to the south of France.
[2] A halt on the way up to Zermatt.

At that time I was already bonded, and would soon formally be *pledged*, to the sweetest, kindest, most percipiently intelligent human-being I would ever encounter. What a union that would prove to be!

Those lovely 'fair-heads', of every generation! And all the sympathy and knowledge for *plants* and *animals* that has radiated out from you and transformed the whole ambience of the family seat. (Am I getting a bit illegible? If so, damn, and apologies.)

For every minute of the day you have worked for me, us and the family. Worked *too hard* (Henry). A hundred times I ask myself how I could have been so cruel to you. Fool Clark, fool. *Nasty* fool, also! What's the use of my saying you are, will always remain, the only true love of my life? If you should ever need me, I will, I hope, be possibly at certain known localities in the grounds (of each property, even Zermatt).

Love, love, love from

A xxx

Saltwood   *Sunday, 1 August*

Fact is, I've got brain cancer. And it is fairly disagreeable.

My body realises that there is no hope. I mean what is the next stage? The next (local) demon with which to wrestle?

My wrist shakes – why? Shades of little T.O. I could not eat, even put into my mouth, any of the delicacies prepared at lunch time today. Or even the 'accompanying medication' which hourly makes Jane very depressed.

I am afflicted by a kind of despair, also.

The Amazings coming in tomorrow. What can I say to them?

The house is like an oven now, excepting the rooms on the north side.

JANE

Although AC did not know it as he wrote, his entry on 1 August would be a true 'last', as he would say, the final entry in a journal that he first began writing almost forty-five years before. His eyes troubled him; he stopped reading and writing and often found the glare even from a clouded sky too much to bear and asked for the curtains to be kept closed. He may have lost his own will to record his decline, but Jane now took up her pen. In a spiral-bound A4, green, soft-covered notebook she recorded the events of each day. What follows are extracts:

Day 5 of radiotherapy   *Monday, 2 August*

Al got dressed and so wobbly – came downstairs on his bottom, me placing his feet on each step. He is really bad.

Day 8 of radiotherapy   *Thursday, 5 August*

Took ¾ of an hour for the pill saga and 1 minute piece of toast to be completed. I long for a meal that I don't have to get up every few minutes for some whim. I long for Al to take the pills without having to yet again explain what each one is for (more than twice, it's 4 or 5 times).

Day 9 of radiotherapy   *Friday, 6 August*

Had got from Rabies Room wheelchair of Bonny mama. Tyres pumped up well and Lynn gave it a good wash. It is jolly good.

In and upstairs via chair – had to walk from Huega tiles as chair would not go through gap. Upstairs on hands and knees.

Bed 10-ish – tired, but no early start tomorrow.[1]

---

[1] The radiotherapy department at Kent & Canterbury Hospital did not operate over weekends.

Rest day   *Saturday, 7 August*

Rained in the night hard, but cleared up and now fine. Woke at normal times, but Al slept well – and only tinkled once at 5.30-ish. Lovely lie-in. Didn't move until 8, swam and made EMT, gave Al his sick pill – he didn't have a biscuit – but did drink a cup of tea. In bed all day dozing on and off. He ate *so* little – 3 teaspoons of spud, a scrape of cheese – then a curtain rest, tea v poor – I had walked dogs etc and went up with tea to find him on the floor in the passage by the banisters. Got him up and back to bed – he has bruised quite badly and small abrasions on his elbow/arm R. It seems to have had the effect of completely unhinging his mind. He mumble rambled – did not really notice anything. Seemed far away – on about a PhD and being on water. Quite frightening and he was so good in am.

Supper 1 banana whisked in milk (½ cup), he had two spoonfuls v reluctantly and then pushed it away saying it was going all round his head. Told him he was a b fool and of course it wasn't. Couldn't, so he drank some more, almost ¾ of it, which was good.

Rest day 2   *Sunday, 8 August*

Bad night. He woke for a tinkle at 1-ish, but could not get back to sleep, so nor did I – at 4-ish or bit before he decided he had a headache so I had to fetch dry biscuit so he had something in his stomach before pills.

Raining – swam, made tea and porridge for Al, which he did eat. Al in bed all day – peed not in pot so changed pyjamas. Have got wheelchair upstairs to take him to loo.

Just been upstairs. He just lies there making bizarre zany muddled sentences or mostly just saying nothing, but lying looking miserable. I find myself so demoralised now being in the room, so deeply depressed by it all.

Decided to run a bath and give him a wash and hair wash too. Back in chair and left him in it by window (curtains closed as

bright sunlight), made tea, and only into bed after tea – just left
him. He has been sick. Damn, damn. Not a lot, says it is the
vitamin pill so *they're* out.
  Cut his toenails and filed rough skin. He looks so much better.
Wish he would read a little or take an interest in things.

Day 10 of radiotherapy – only 10 to go   *Monday, 9 August*

So rushed didn't even do hens today – oh dear, oh dear.
  Mrs Frowd came 4 – was pleased with Al's progress.
  Over to GH to collect other chair – back with Eddie pushing it
– he stayed for tea.
  Came in from the Pavillon about 8. I had a breakdown as first
couldn't negotiate the small rise by yard door, then hit a lot of
things in outer lobby, and ended by kicking everything to right
and left hurling boxes of papers, chairs etc. Shouting at poor dog
(Lëhni) whose paws were slightly in the way. Broke down in tears
in Cork bathroom with Al on loo.
  It's 9.40, I still haven't had a proper meal and am desperately
tired. Al would not eat *anything* tonight just lying there hiccuping,
retching.
  This whole thing is a ghastly nightmare. I do not know how it
will end.

Day 11 or radiotherapy   *Tuesday, 10 August*

At 20 to 12 woken by movement, but Al still lying down – then
the noise of a pee. I can't believe it. He is peeing in the bed, just
peeing. I confess I freak out somewhat – it's through the sheet,
underblanket and saved from mattress by electric blanket and New
Zealand wool underblanket – pyjamas naturally sopping. I take
them off him and hurl them out of the window; all the while he
tells me he hasn't peed. Change entire bedding, put sheet into
machine, feel sick. Poor darling Al. Both take long time to fall
asleep. Up 6.45 – swam, did hens, breakfast, porridge, tea, coffee

for A which he didn't drink today and ate not all porridge. Into car in good time, but oh dear I had left it switched on. Battery *totally* flat. All change into dear S16[1] and into K&C. Saw Stewart Coltart afterwards and he gave me the shattering news that it was pointless to go on with R – unkind to Al and the family. He shouldn't be like he is after 11 doses, bladder going, no balance, lack of appetite etc. Very bad sign. I was in tears – Al had gone out of the room for a blood test. In my heart I *knew* it wasn't right although trying to look positive. We went to find Al, me with tears pouring down my face past all those people waiting – Al didn't really seem to have taken it in – has he? I don't know – although I was in tears he made no sign of compassion which isn't him at all.

Into Pavillon as usual and in to Lynn for a good cry.

It's strange I feel numbed by this news – waves of tears when I sat in Pavillon for tea – he didn't notice at all. Earlier I had come back from hens and walk to find he had an accident with water bottle so had to change every stitch of clothing. Dressing him quite difficult as he is limp, but if you say move this way or that he can't seem to work out how to.

I love God, but this is such a cruel way to demolish such a brilliant brain – I dread to think what lies in store.

Talked to Andrew, Sarah, James and Julie. They are equally shattered. Amazings will be here Thursday and James as well. How long we have got only God knows – but miracles sometimes happen. It is the eclipse tomorrow. For us it was going to be a turning point – but now the beginning of the end.

Eclipse today, 11.20 for us   *Wednesday, 11 August*

Sister Angela Rourke (Irish?) district nurse came 11.30 to 'assess' Al and offer me advice and what have you. Got v cold during eclipse and quite dark – v cloudy, could just see a crescent of sun. Light amazing as it came out so beautiful and bright – '. . . and let there be light.'

---

[1] An old Volkswagen Golf, used as a runabout.

*

9.15 Rang Mummy – she poor darling is v ill too. I should be *there* as well as here.

Crisper and finer day   *Thursday, 12 August*

Spots are worse now.

I didn't bathe, thought I saw worm in pool. Threw in remaining chlorine tablets. Have a headache and feel sickish. No breakfast for Al. Helen Blake from hospice team came, stayed for *hours*, Sister Rourke also came. They discussed anti-sickness pills etc, etc and saw Al. Thought the spots needed something. Dr Mohr coming later to see them. Andrew, Sarah and boys turned up, Cindy Frowd turned up. It was awful – *so* many people – meaning well I know, but I'm not so sure they don't make you worse – *counsellors* – not for me. I need them for making Al's life unpainful, painfree and for access to commodes, sheets, waterproof etc.

Tup brilliantly mowed Bailey and dealt with battery problem – it was totally flat, wouldn't take a jumpstart at all. He also shaved Al and helped move him from Cork to bed, while I ate lunch. Came with me to find depot to collect mattress etc etc. Would *never* have found it if he hadn't come with me.

Very fine and windy after wet night   *Saturday, 14 August*

Al has not spent a penny now since 3 pm yesterday. I do hope James will come before it is too late. I am tearful. Al has just drunk a ¾ cup of tea! More muddled today. Have asked him if he wants to say anything – he likes the idea, but fears it would be too melancholy – his journals through my pen.

Asked Al what he thinks when he looks out of the window.

AC: a path through a jungle really and I suppose the . . . I am being consulted about it.

JC: Carry on, turn back?

AC: you can sort of divert.

James arrived as I was putting him back to bed just in time as he is now difficult to move. My back is going – I get on the bed and pull him on and up if alone.

If this is a game of snakes and ladders we have met the biggest snake – a veritable pit of them.

Still, crisp and sunny   *Sunday, 15 August*

8.30 I must get up. We are lying side by side. Al completely silent and looking so vulnerable and young. Not an old person at all. Tup saw him, said how much he had lost weight from Thursday's visit. It's lovely having everyone about, but feel I am more with them and *cooking* than with Al. We had a Sunday lunch of roast venison, Yorkshire pudding, spinach, beans and spuds. V good for me as I ate well! I took my tea up and lay in the bed with him for 2 hours talking and weeping. It is so hard, he does not really respond as if a river was between us, and he can't/won't hear and can't/won't respond. But I know he hears as when I queried God's role in this he stopped me and said I mustn't blame God. I don't, but why does God think *I* need proof of his powers – what is he trying to say to me, to us both?

Monday, 16 August

Al turned as I put the [EMT] tray down and said, 'Is that all the ships?' I affirmed it was.

Al seems to be slipping away from us. No breakfast (or EMT) – only sips of water.

Dr Chandrakumar and Gail (District Nurse) came 12.20. Dr C briefly saw Al and the rash, and agreed it was caused by drugs – why don't they say *medication*? He then took me and Gail into the Red Study – I called in James and Andrew and he told us it would not be very long now. It is inevitable and so like a dream gone badly wrong – a nightmare of depression. I still keep hoping for someone to say it's all ok.

It is 3.35. I foolishly asked Al to say something I could remember

– something nice about his BLJ. He stared silently away – and when I walked out called me back saying he thought the question 'was about level playing fields on the battlements'. But still no words of endearment – I long for some sign, but he is not really here so I must be content with a squeezed hand and not grumble.

He was so dear as I struggled to get him on to the bed and comfy saying I was angelic. I told him I couldn't let anyone else sit in the room and nurse him and he was so pleased and reassured. Being really ill, if you are a proud and private person, is so cruel it is only your loved ones you want around you at this moment.

Cool heavy rain, but sky blue, too   *Wednesday, 18 August*

Dr Chandrakumar came 12.30-ish – I like him. He does not go for the make-him-eat-drink-and-force-his-bowels-open stuff. Is really quite spiritual in that way – agrees the most important thing is to make sure there is no pain, which, thank goodness, is the situation now. Was v kindly worried about how I was coping and agreed to be my doctor and will put me on the NHS. Talked about what to do when he dies – I did not know and had asked him. I have to notify him if possible – no objection to him staying here and undertakers were always on 24-hours call. It's all essential information and I am calmer for knowing everything.

Earlier Stewart Coltart had come – he is nice too and did not rush us, but gave his time. He took a look at the rash and said it was Epanutin – his wife was a dermatologist and he telephoned her and she confirmed this – so at last we do have a culprit – ok to stop it tonight as still in blood for a bit so perhaps by the weekend it will start clearing. He does not complain of it, but it looks v uncomfortable, and is really everywhere, but face, hands and feet.

Crisp, windy, but fine   *Thursday, 19 August*

Gail, the quiet District Nurse came – do hope we can continue with her – and was very pleased with Al. Said to Lynn how different from Monday he was.

New anti-fit pill is a lovely violet colour!

Rang Mummy whose legs are still v bad – she goes tomorrow to have stitches out.

Crisp and fine today   *Friday, 20 August*

Poor dogs not walked as James did not want to be left to get Al on to commode. He is quite different from Andrew who is a genuine carer. J just like Al would be.

Watched while we had tea the boys and little boys and others playing on the lawn. It was fine and sunny and I cried tears for a future that Al was not to share. It is like a terrible dream and you wake and it's real and oh how I long for it not to be so. Al is not aware of my crying whereas tears would have upset him before – that too is hard – we are already apart yet still both alive and close. Strange.

Crisp and v fine, heavy dew   *Saturday, 21 August*

A quite good night after tinkling at 10 and then asking again at 11, but it was a blank. We cuddled instead, but he was not really here – a strange faraway look on his face. He had left me and I must realise this will happen more and more. He has always been my other half, but the branch is nearly off and the scar will take time to heal over. It is strange to see and feel him and yet know he is fading away from me.

My mind is a complete and utter blank as to what happened on Saturday. I'm going mad, not Al.

Overcast day   *Sunday, 22 August*

Awake on and off but all seems well. Finally fall asleep as usual after 6 and woken by Al throwing the duvet back and wanting to 'dump'. Half asleep I shot round and helped him on to the

commode, but too late and I got it all down left leg of my pyjamas
and I later realised it was a little on floor so he trod that in and all
over front of commode legs tinkly etc and his pyjamas too. A
disaster for first thing and *most* tiring.

James came and popped him into the bed as I was going to wash
him – but before that he suddenly announced he wanted to dump
again so off we got and more produced. Tup came and we got him
back into bed and comfy.

Breakfast reduced one to tears of frustration – he had wanted
porridge, but when it came he refused to taste it. Toast and honey
minute little mouthfuls – 1st one spat out – and gagging ensued.
Coffee ½ a cup ok. Went and made Weetabix + warm Complan
milk, ¼ only but after 3 egg spoons Al was gagging and trying to
retch, so hardly anything.

11.45 now and I am lying on the bed while Al sleeps 'Venice
train'. He was dear though and said he was sorry about all this. I
said I found it so hard that he no longer seemed to notice if I wept
and I wished he would weep with me – are we in this together or
not, I said – if you can't cry with me who can you cry with? He
said he didn't want to give in and only to God could he cry, and he
would look back on this and he would remind me of our conversation. Yesterday – I might have thought it possible – this
morning I feel there isn't any hope. Everyone says it will be up
and down, but oh it's so terribly cruel – when you are up you
think all will be well, this nightmare will end, we have a future to
share.

It is a horrible, horrible, horrible thing to watch someone you
love and who has such an incredible brain slipping into Kafka
rambling and yet suddenly lucidly ticking one off for not reading
something properly.

12.10 It is the silence I find so depressing. He just stares ahead.
Does he hear? I think so but he can't answer. We talked about how
I would miss politics. What fun this last year or so had been since
getting back into H of C, fun for me for once as I could share some
of it.

Supper was lovely fried squid – done by Julie in a jolly good batter. Al asleep – but did not stir when I kissed him. His dear face as I look at him sideways is falling in – oh dear God what a foul and miserable thing you have sent us all on such a beloved husband and father – everything has a reason, but I do not know what this is.

Crisp and fine again   *Monday, 23 August*

8.30 Al still asleep. Made coffee and grapenuts for myself and a piece of toast. Al said, 'You have been crying – so have I.' He seems quite different again, more on the ball and not so muddled. Another cruel quirk of this awful cancer – another 'up' to give us hope before a steeper decline again to despair? He had coffee and noticed today I had put sugar in it! Liked the idea of grapenuts and had 3 spoonfuls (teaspoons) and then two small pieces of brown toast and marmalade – and more coffee (nearly 1 cup of coffee). Drank nearly ½ Redoxon. I stayed with him – carpet swept the room and polished about, talked – he said he felt a weakening of his grip, but I tested it and it is as strong as ever – found him the wrist-strengthener which he used while talking. Quite good form, some wires crossed.

Grey and overcast and light rain fell today   *Tuesday, 24 August*

He seemed good this morning – fell asleep late am and slept over lunch, which is now the norm. I took up soup and yoghurt, but not wanted. Sat for a bit, but left a note and went downstairs to do some bills – red reminder from the telephone as had not done them. Heard a noise and went up to find Al half out of bed having had an accident – changed pyjamas, sheets etc and got him back into bed. James came to help. He is now so heavy and dead-limbed it is awkward to move him – his face is now so thin you can see the 'plate' where the operation was, and his ribs, backbone and hip bones plus legs are too depressing. He is bones with skin and v little flesh. We talked, but he is quite muddled now – will try the lavender anti-fit, but not the anti-sickness one.

Late now after 11.30 and Al thirsty – suspicious even of water so offer to get him a piece of melon – downstairs to find J.J. still up. Back upstairs and Al takes one look/smell of melon and starts to choke retch – frantic trying to get upright. I rushed for James who held him upright. He sat on the edge of the bed lucid compared to earlier and not keeling over. Drank some water and took Epilium – while we talked to him. Julie came through and he lay down and we sat with him and talked.

Wednesday, 25 August

Michael Howard telephoned. I rang him and told him all not well. He was shattered by news.

Thursday, 26 August

Quite a good night for both of us. Al said good morning to me on coming round, but otherwise just stares out of the window or ahead – looking so dreadfully sad.

He has now lost so much weight he looks like a PoW. Slept on and off, is low today – Helen (hospice nurse) came. He was monstrous and grimaced crazily when I tried to lift him and then flatly refused to speak to her at all.

Had tea with him and we chatted. I asked if he'd like Reg or Michael,[1] but he did not answer and when he did much later on being re-asked said no.

Up with Complan for supper. *Very* little – he became quite fussed and asked about it. Was it poisoned, as they were trying to poison him? Andrew with me and we tried to reassure him, but this accounts for the fact he will not eat or drink.

---

[1] Reg Humphriss and Michael Seed.

Fine, cloudy, cooler (windy now)   *Friday, 27 August*

Dr C and Gail came and we have organised everything for a drip should he need one – Gail returned with an enormous tin and bags of medicines, which I have locked away. Al woke and peed, but I was not there and although we were in the kitchen it is obvious that isn't any good. I or someone should be *in the room* from now on as he is not aware of anything today and does not know he has peed or remember to call out. It is a dreadful down day. He does not even speak much, but when I kiss him and tell him I am here he half smiles, which is lovely.

Made tea and upstairs Al asleep. Woken and I went round and he asked for a kiss so he could remember my taste. We talked about it all. If it was for a reason what was it? He said he knew what I was doing for him and thanked me. Stayed until 7-ish – half asleep holding each other's hands.

Heavy dew, but v fine and dry, few clouds   *Saturday, 28 August*

Bromley [jackdaw] appeared at the window for food. 'You tried to spike him,' Al said. 'No,' I said, 'I've just given him a biscuit.'

Up to church with Julie – had a good cry. Felt better for it. James came back with a paddling pool and choc ices. Al actually ate a bit.

Did Al's nails and massaged his feet, creamed his arms and hands. He spat out the fish and peas. Is in a non-speaking mood, which is irritating to say the least.

Out now to do poor dogs who have had no walk or supper and it's 7.35 – I only walk around the top woodland and upper terrace. Back, gave them supper and met James who had taken up lovely picture of swimming pool to Al. J said he was very lucid and loving so I should go up and be with him. Told him I had been there all afternoon and he was just pretty non-speakers to one and I was bloody fed up with him.

He was not loving and friendly so I left him and came down

after changing for lovely dinner of squid. Bed 5 to 10. Al asleep, covered him up and kissed him goodnight – (no response).

Heavy dew, v fine early autumn   *Sunday, 29 August*

5 *to* 5 I leapt out of bed and ½ asleep got bottle ready etc, but he had in fact peed lightly – so changed pyjamas and pad. He did not say a word, just glared. I am going to find this phase *very* difficult and depressing.

It's now 12.30. He doesn't seem good at all – not a good colour and stays mainly asleep. He was dear, though, and kissed me and said I was his BLJ and thanked me when I sorted him out after Thompson.

The children and young have been sitting outside in the sun with paddling pool in use and general jolly chatter/tears etc. It's another world out there, inside here my world is crumbling and yes, I am frightened.

James sat with him for 45 mins, came down and was quite rude when we said supper – he said he was going out for a fag. I then said don't worry I'm going up to bed and went out to get dogs. Dear J came out too and totally broke down in tears: 'I'm nearly 40 and I'm crying. I love him so much.' We both agreed it was absolutely vile to watch someone you love so much being destroyed by such an awful thing. He had his fag and we went in, both calmer.

Dry, overcast, warm   *Bank Holiday Monday, 30 August*

A lovely walk which restored me round the moat with the dogs and then with J J and A to see the combining. Bob kind and stopped the machine for Angus, but it is really so huge he was overcome. Bed late, too late.

Written at EMT, 7.40   *Tuesday, 31 August*

A fairly ghastly night. I am so overtired by everything and things rather came to a head by a call for peeing at 12.40 and then nothing done at all. I fell back into my side of the bed at 1.05 and then another call 10 mins later (or rather not a call, but a throwing off of the bedclothes). Held the pee bottle until gone 2, but had a row with God and tried to tell Al how tired I was by all this and that I would have to get nurse in if this carried on. You always think you can cope, but you can't.

Tiny pee done, but he was a dear and whispered he knew how much I was doing and he was sorry. We talked and I lay with my head on his dear bony chest while he tried to stroke my hair. Oh dear, darling Al. Oh God how I will miss you. I dread the future without my soulmate. I dread being really alone without his wisdom, strength, fun and companionship. For 41 years we have been together, through ups and downs. Can I live without him? For the children's sake I must remain strong – the 'Dowager Empress' he said I would be. I must not let him down.

Al asleep – breathing v shallow today. Like dear Tom, you look closely to see if it is so.

Helen came, said to reduce his Dexa by 1 so only on 2 pills a day. She came up and saw him as Andrew said he was awake having peed again. I stayed and changed him. Tup saw Helen out and J J and Tup had a chat to her. She is worried about *me*. So is Dr C who said I should have 24-hour nursing for him now. I simply wouldn't, not while he is still aware of what's happening and although sometimes he looks through me and glares he will suddenly smile and say 'I know what you're doing and you are incredible' – or tonight he said he loved the gentle look I gave him. How could I just let a stranger take over? It is my job and I will go on.

Seems cooler, but still dry, high cloud, heavy dew again

Wednesday, 1 September

It's now September, the whole summer has gone by in a surreal way. I look out at the changing season from afar lost in this high-intensity 'drama', which is taking place in the Summer Bedroom. Cannot get him out of bed any more, now too risky.

All the family off this am to Dymchurch, girls by car, boys in the little train. Went on the beach on the way home. They are back now, said beach was lovely. Angus bathed so is now wrapped in James's T-shirt.

Dry, fine day, no wind, heavy dew   *Thursday, 2 September*

Woke before 6 to strange noises, put out my hand, but no response at all. I panicked. He was 'drowning' in his phlegm. Tried to put another pillow under his shoulders – not wildly successful. By 6.15 I thought it was the end. Terrible noises and looking v v bad. I rushed down with dogs to see if Tup and Boy there – no sign. Back up, caught Tup going down so asked him to fetch James, who rushed out of room to 'go for a pee' the minute he came in. Poor James, he is only making it harder for himself.

Al still open-mouthed, open-eyed, twitched lower jaw – a very minor fit possibly as it later (1 hour) turned into a shaking of shoulders, arms and hands, so I unpicked my hand from his very firm grip and took a little pill out to pop under his tongue, quite difficult and it was still under his tongue when much later Tup and I moved him to my bed to change and wash him and put a fresh sheet on the bed.

No sign of Reg on telephone, so Tup drove up, but he is obviously away. Tup brilliantly thought of Norman so I went and rang. Patsy, his wife, answered and said he was doing a service, but could come up at 10. She would go and find him. She rang back and dear Norman was coming straight up. He is *so* nice, a truly good, holy man. Both boys came in and we said prayers and he was anointed with oil. Felt so much better for it, and in a way I was glad fate had decreed it was Norman. Although I like Reg, we have known Norman longer and he has been a good man to know. Feel *so* much better that someone came in time; I would have felt guilty before God if I had failed to have him blessed. Waves of calmness are there now.

11.45 Realised he had had *no* medication and so Andrew rang Helen (hospice). Gail will come to put in syringe driver. When??

In fact the syringe driver was put in after 7. Dr C came 6.30-ish and saw Al – confirmed he was in a coma and unconscious and we discussed S-D. James said a fit would be very distressing and so when we realised the S-D would not do anything, but peacefully end him we all agreed.

Dr C came back and Heather the twilight nurse, whose own mother had died of cancer, came to put it in. I could not stay for this as it somehow seemed to be wrong to violate the body. Andrew stayed. Everyone being really kind. Al had been in a coma, but could squeeze your hand until about lunchtime – his breathing so rasping through the mouth, eyes open, but not aware. Oh dear God what a waste, what a waste! It is this I mind so much, not just the fact I shall be losing my soulmate of 41 years, my lover, my friend, my companion, my dearest husband – oh *how* I shall miss him! What an empty horizon stretches ahead, so frightening I cannot think of it, so am blocking it out.

It is now 20 to 10. I am lying on the bed beside him, his breathing fast and noisy, his chest tight and violent in the breathing. I hold his hand, but no response, his eyes now closed. How long can his body hold on to life? I talk to him of what I will do, the office, the woodland walk, the brambles on the cistus bank as well as the woodland. Keeping the paperwork in order, the bank statements in order, my life in order, a Lady Dunn minus Beaverbrook. We were always such a good team and now I shall be leaderless. Still the faith he always had in me will be my inspiration. I must not let him down. The Dowager Empress shall reign.

Now v hot and sunny   *Friday, 3 September*

Sat on bed or lay on it beside Al most of the afternoon. Flies bothersome. I am paranoid about them settling on Al. Do they sense he will shortly be dead? Finally went for a walk round the garden while Andrew sat with him. Several scares, but tonight (10.20) he sleeps ok, head slightly on one side. Eyes sometimes open and still clutching the crystal.

Sarah and Julie both come in and boys a lot. James (and Tup) really worried about *men* bothering me − how *dear* of them. I simply do not see it at all.

Rang Col tonight − Celly out and Fr Michael out too.

Hot and sunny   *Saturday, 4 September*

Not an impossible night, difficult for me to sleep, but Al seemed to be sleeping quite peacefully − one or two hiccups, but then restarted. Talked at 4 to him, was sure he knows. Then at 10 to 6 Hannah got on the bed, plus Lëhni. I put Al's hand out so they could smell him and he opens his eyes and I *know* he senses they are there − a lovely moment.

Later back from a bathe and making EMT I tell him I'm back and have bathed and I love him etc and he squeezes my hand (I have cleaned him up, he had 'dumped' a little and peed − so now he is lying comfortably). Oh such magic moments, but cruel too as you suddenly think perhaps it's stopped and all will be well.

Washed hair. Celly rang, was very sweet and sympathetic. Nick rang worried about me. We both agreed Ma seemed perkier.

Stayed in the room all day on and off. Lunch came up, lovely cauliflower cheese. Father Michael telephoned, is coming down this afternoon. I went and rested with Al − fell asleep so Fr M had to wait − it was ok. Everyone gave him tea and talked. Then he, Fr M, came upstairs. Tup came too. We said prayers and Fr M anointed him with oil (been here before I thought). Downstairs and Fr M and I to Red Study where he talked and he told me Al *was* a Catholic. He had made him one on 10 July when he was with him. He had written down notes of that day. Sarah brought us tea. I was gasping for a cup, then I went back upstairs, Tup had very kindly stayed with Al. I must say I could have shaken Al. I felt quite hurt he had not told me he was made Catholic on 10 July – he only said he had blessing for sick and communion secretly. Why when we can't talk about it do I only know – for a short minute I actually hate him for holding something as major as this back. I had thought we shared all these things. How could he exclude me of all people? In a way it's quite good as I can now distance myself much more.

Tip came in surprised to see me sitting on *my* side of the bed, no 'in the crack' by Daddy. Showed him the letter Fr Michael had written for me. I was cheered up by the fact he didn't think Fr Michael *had* given Daddy last rites. I thought it poor compared to Norman Woods's which was v moving. This was very much a Catholic priest saying something for someone *not* a Catholic. Swing back. I do *not* think he was fully received.[1]

We talked about burying Daddy. I said he'd always wanted a shroud, not a coffin. James has not managed to hire a Kubota [mechanical digger]

Al died at 11.45   *Sunday, 5 September*

Slept fitfully and woke with a jolt at 3.20 (Al's time) as Al was breathing differently now, shorter, tighter rasping breaths – with sighs every so often. Lay awake beside him. He is incredibly hot, 'muck sweat', but his arms are very cold and body temp ok. V hot hands and face.

---

[1] Jane's journal, Wednesday, 8 September: 'A fax from Fr Michael. Long and rambling, sticking to his tale of Al's conversion, but tonight while cleaning my teeth I spotted Al's Day Diary which reminded me I had his journal in my drawer – how silly of me, I could look and see what happened. As we suspected – only the sacrament of the sick. Do you not feel Al would have written up at length such a major thing as being received into the RC church? Of course he would. He didn't, because he wasn't.'

Jolted, no jarred by 2Boy and dogs at 6.45 so let them out and came back to bed. Tup up getting EMT for himself. Down a bit later for EMT and a bowl of cereal. No change from Al upstairs since then although shot down to have a word with Sue. Washing machine flooding the floor downstairs – wish to goodness J had left it alone. It's much worse than just being temperamental with spinning.

Upstairs all morning. Janice [nurse] came 11-ish to change the syringe driver. Al's breathing still bad – and I noticed when I changed his pads that blotches were appearing under his skin on his legs and knees, reddish purple, and on the soles of his feet. Janice says this is the body's way of shutting down. Lynn came up – looking very well after her break in Brittany – and saw Al.

While we were there, she was just leaving, Al's breathing changed and I said we must get the boys in. Luckily, really luckily they were both outside in the courtyard and came running up. Within 5 or 6 minutes Al had died. Silence, then gasp and a little breathing. More gasps and pulse now weaker. He just looked so peaceful and you really felt his soul and spirit had left on their journey, a wonderful calm feeling entered the room. We all stroked him and talked and kissed him. It was such a lovely ending. Then we all hugged each other. The end of an era. Rang SEDOC and a doctor came up. Rang everyone, Ma, Nick, Celly, Col etc etc.

Reg coming up at 3.30 – was very nice and calming. Quite happy to bury Daddy and will ask Norman to help. Rang the gravedigger who can do it and will come tomorrow, at one o'clock. Dr C came and checked Daddy, and was very kind and concerned about me.

Walked dogs. Was sure I felt Al above going towards Roman tower. Talked at length to Celly. Michael Howard telephoned. Was terribly upset by news. V kind.

A big stumbling block. We have to have Shepway's [local council] permission to bury Daddy in the grounds. I am quite shattered. Fear they will say no. It has all gone so well. I do pray that we can bury Al as a family without pressure and where we wanted to, *when* we want. Delay will inevitably mean he will have to leave to go somewhere cooler. To bed after a bit of a sibling outburst over the fact Norman and Reg cannot go ahead without Shepway's ok. Julie very kindly came in and had a chat.

Monday, 6 September

So-so night, only jarred by worrying about possible problems with Shepway. No worries about Al beside me. In fact it was lovely as I could talk to him still. Much nicer than an empty space, which will come tonight, perhaps?

Up 6.20 writing this and the first of may LISTS! Downstairs breakfast. Did I have any? No, don't think so, too tense. Reg telephoned at 9-ish with Shepway's number, a Sandra Francis. She was so sympathetic and I cried, but wonderfully it is all under control and she doesn't see any problems at all. Oh *what* a weight lifted off my shoulders. I feel so calm. Had got myself in a terrible state if the answer had been 'no, not possible'.

Immediately wheels set in motion. James doing base for shroud (wood base). Andrew organised to collect death certificate and have it registered. Sarah has gone back to Broomhayes with little 'fair-heads'. Gail came and took syringe away. Julie and I bought flowers at farm shop in Sellindge. Back and then Reg and Michael Marsh and his son arrived to dig grave. MM and son *really* nice couple. Reg very calming and we discussed placing of chairs and bier. Grave was dug in record time and looks very pleasing. Walked dogs and fed hens on return. Saw Graham who is coming, and Eddie, who is still terribly distressed. Picked bay and wild clematis and a few white sweet peas. Did some flowers for the Red Library – organised curtains for table after tea.

Andrew dressed Daddy, who, I must say, had made our room a tiny bit high and window had to be shut because of flies. We have prepared him in his Cuixmala t-shirt, white silk shirt, his favourite battered cords and his suede shoes, his blue neckerchief. He looked very nice. Tup had re-shaved him as well and sprayed him with Roger & Gallet. Downstairs with Tup – he seems to have got heavier somehow. Have all helped to wrap him in his shroud, beautifully done by Julie and Sarah, and he has taken with him a lot of softies: pricklepins, heart stone, Creaggan early heather, seaweed, markies for dogs, digestives, fruit cake, H of C miniature, Zermatt rock, 2 Swiss francs, his armband, his racing vintage goggles, his H of C pass and a travel warrant, 1 handkey.

Supper omelette in kitchen. James insisted on lasagne.

Bed very late 11.30, but feel so much better.

Tuesday, 7 September

Today is Al's funeral – the first overcast morning which was lovely. It rained the day he died and now a dull day. Up quite early and bathed and made EMT, took it and a bowl of cereal back upstairs to bed. Got up at 8 and downstairs, made some cake as nothing to offer people, then organised everyone and saw Al out of the house on to the Mehari and round on to the table in the Knight's Hall. A white damask tablecloth of Great Granpa's with Albany gold curtain over and then the shroud on its wooden base. Did the flowers, 2 large bowls. The white urns inside the blue pots – full of chrysanths, lilies, bay, rosemary, old man's beard and Russian vine and hops. We put our individual posies on Al – peace lilies from Hannah and Lëhni, mixed little bunches from all of us. Very pretty it looked.

Dashed up to wash hair and change at 5 to 11. Felt very shaky, but hope I looked ok for Al, black plain linen dress, black stockings, black shoes, hair clean and loose. Only jewellery my diamond cross Al had given me, and my sapphire rings.

Celly and Col had arrived, and Sue[1] joined me when I was doing the flowers – dear Sue she was so shattered. Lynn, Peggy, Eddie and Graham, and Canon Norman Woods[2] and Reg Humphriss, resplendent in flowing robes. Julie looked lovely, and so did Sarah and both boys very dashing. I was so proud of them. It was the nicest funeral I have been to, intimate and personal and I do

---

[1] Sue Line, AC's former secretary.
[2] The Rev. Canon Norman Woods, Vicar of St Leonard's Church, Hythe.

hope Al would have been pleased with me. Sue dear and kept saying how proud he would have been of you. The first part of the service over we went across the lawn to the grave. Reg blessed the grave and consecrated it and after a short prayer we lowered Al into it and I threw or rather shovelled 2 spades of earth on to him, the first one rather splendidly landing on his tinkey. All then to the Red Library for sandwiches, gossip and coffee/tea. Both Reg and Norman were so complimentary about it and said it was one of the nicest funerals they had done.

When everyone had gone Sue and all of us retired to the kitchen to thrash out the press releases. Kept to what Al had wanted – 'Suddenly at Saltwood on 5 September. He wanted it to be known he had gone to join Tom and the other dogs.' Good and zany. Informed the Queen first as he was a PC, then Press Association. Phones frantic after that and camera crews at the gate.

Just talked and watched TV and listened to radio. The coverage is absolutely fantastic. On and on it went.

At 9 bizarrely the new Discovery turned up and so James and I went up to the layby by the M-way and swapped our old one for the smartest vehicle ever owned by me.[1] Back and into bed very tired, but so pleased it all went so well.

---

[1] Bizarre is no exaggeration. Ordered earlier in the summer from Macrae & Dick, it had been brought south from Scotland on a car transporter, but the driver's tachograph reading forced him to stop near the Dartford tunnel. The only solution was to go and collect it. But with press cameras still massed outside the castle gates, Jane realised that to drive out past them in her old Discovery on the day of her husband's funeral only to return an hour later in a spanking brand-new machine was to invite trouble. Headlines of 'the merry widow' variety might be the least of it. So Jane and James waited until early evening, when, with deadlines passing, the press began to drift away. By the time they returned with the new Discovery the castle gates were deserted. Phew!

ACKNOWLEDGEMENTS

My first thanks are to Jane Clark, who for more than ten years now has done all in her power to further the literary estate of her late husband. She has never been less than hospitable, encouraging and helpful. I am enormously grateful. My appreciation, too, to the Clark family, sons James and Andrew and also Alan's twin siblings, Colette (Celly) and, before his death, Colin (Col).

Outside the family two names in particular: Michael Sissons, Alan's long-time literary agent; and Graham Stewart, who first became associated with Alan as the researcher on *The Tories*.

At Orion for this particular volume, Susan Lamb and Gail Paten.

A full list of those who have helped can be found in the separate volumes of AC's diaries as well as his other books.

I salute them all.

IT
January 2010

INDEX

NOTE: Titles and ranks are generally those held at the latest mention in the text.